Harnessing Social Media as a Knowledge Management Tool

Ritesh Chugh
Central Queensland University, Australia

A volume in the Advances in Knowledge Acquisition, Transfer, and Management (AKATM) Book Series

Information Science REFERENCE
An Imprint of IGI Global

Published in the United States of America by
Information Science Reference (an imprint of IGI Global)
701 E. Chocolate Avenue
Hershey PA, USA 17033
Tel: 717-533-8845
Fax: 717-533-8661
E-mail: cust@igi-global.com
Web site: http://www.igi-global.com

Library of Congress Cataloging-in-Publication Data

Names: Chugh, Ritesh, 1975- editor.
Title: Harnessing social media as a knowledge management tool / Ritesh Chugh, editor.
Description: Hershey, PA : Information Science Reference, [2017] | Includes bibliographical references and index.
Identifiers: LCCN 2016012753| ISBN 9781522504955 (hardcover) | ISBN 9781522504962 (ebook)
Subjects: LCSH: Knowledge management. | Social media. | Information technology--Management.
Classification: LCC HD30.2 .H3719 2017 | DDC 658.4/038--dc23 LC record available at https://lccn.loc.gov/2016012753

This book is published in the IGI Global book series Advances in Knowledge Acquisition, Transfer, and Management (AKATM) (ISSN: 2326-7607; eISSN: 2326-7615)

British Cataloguing in Publication Data
A Cataloguing in Publication record for this book is available from the British Library.

Advances in Knowledge Acquisition, Transfer, and Management (AKATM) Book Series

Murray E. Jennex
San Diego State University, USA

ISSN: 2326-7607
EISSN: 2326-7615

MISSION

Organizations and businesses continue to utilize knowledge management practices in order to streamline processes and procedures. The emergence of web technologies has provided new methods of information usage and knowledge sharing.

The **Advances in Knowledge Acquisition, Transfer, and Management (AKATM) Book Series** brings together research on emerging technologies and their effect on information systems as well as the knowledge society.**AKATM** will provide researchers, students, practitioners, and industry leaders with research highlights surrounding the knowledge management discipline, including technology support issues and knowledge representation.

COVERAGE

- Cognitive Theories
- Cultural Impacts
- Information and Communication Systems
- Knowledge acquisition and transfer processes
- Knowledge management strategy
- Knowledge Sharing
- Organizational learning
- Organizational Memory
- Small and Medium Enterprises
- Virtual Communities

IGI Global is currently accepting manuscripts for publication within this series. To submit a proposal for a volume in this series, please contact our Acquisition Editors at Acquisitions@igi-global.com or visit: http://www.igi-global.com/publish/.

The Advances in Knowledge Acquisition, Transfer, and Management (AKATM) Book Series (ISSN 2326-7607) is published by IGI Global, 701 E. Chocolate Avenue, Hershey, PA 17033-1240, USA, www.igi-global.com. This series is composed of titles available for purchase individually; each title is edited to be contextually exclusive from any other title within the series. For pricing and ordering information please visit http://www.igi-global.com/book-series/advances-knowledge-acquisition-transfer-management/37159. Postmaster: Send all address changes to above address.

Titles in this Series

For a list of additional titles in this series, please visit: www.igi-global.com

Organizational Knowledge Facilitation through Communities of Practice in Emerging Markets
Sheryl Buckley (University of South Africa, South Africa) Grzegorz Majewski (University of the West of Scotland, UK) and Apostolos Giannakopoulos (University of South Africa, South Africa)
Business Science Reference • copyright 2016 • 326pp • H/C (ISBN: 9781522500131) • US $175.00 (our price)

Mixed Methods Research for Improved Scientific Study
Mette L. Baran (Cardinal Stritch University, USA) and Janice E. Jones (Cardinal Stritch University, USA)
Information Science Reference • copyright 2016 • 335pp • H/C (ISBN: 9781522500070) • US $195.00 (our price)

Handbook of Research on Innovations in Information Retrieval, Analysis, and Management
Jorge Tiago Martins (The University of Sheffield, UK) and Andreea Molnar (University of Portsmouth, UK)
Information Science Reference • copyright 2016 • 580pp • H/C (ISBN: 9781466688339) • US $325.00 (our price)

Societal Benefits of Freely Accessible Technologies and Knowledge Resources
Oswaldo Terán (Universidad de los Andes, Venezuela) and Jose Aguilar (Universidad de los Andes, Venezuela)
Information Science Reference • copyright 2015 • 361pp • H/C (ISBN: 9781466683365) • US $175.00 (our price)

Contemporary Issues Surrounding Ethical Research Methods and Practice
Chi B. Anyansi-Archibong (North Carolina A&T State University, USA)
Information Science Reference • copyright 2015 • 376pp • H/C (ISBN: 9781466685628) • US $205.00 (our price)

Organizational Knowledge Dynamics Managing Knowledge Creation, Acquisition, Sharing, and Transformation
Constantin Bratianu (Bucharest University of Economic Studies, Romania)
Information Science Reference • copyright 2015 • 349pp • H/C (ISBN: 9781466683181) • US $210.00 (our price)

Strategic Data-Based Wisdom in the Big Data Era
John Girard (Middle Georgia State College, USA) Deanna Klein (Minot State University, USA) and Kristi Berg (Minot State University, USA)
Information Science Reference • copyright 2015 • 311pp • H/C (ISBN: 9781466681224) • US $205.00 (our price)

Handbook of Research on Maximizing Cognitive Learning through Knowledge Visualization
Anna Ursyn (University of Northern Colorado, USA)
Information Science Reference • copyright 2015 • 572pp • H/C (ISBN: 9781466681422) • US $325.00 (our price)

IGI GLOBAL
DISSEMINATOR OF KNOWLEDGE
www.igi-global.com

701 E. Chocolate Ave., Hershey, PA 17033
Order online at www.igi-global.com or call 717-533-8845 x100
To place a standing order for titles released in this series, contact: cust@igi-global.com
Mon-Fri 8:00 am - 5:00 pm (est) or fax 24 hours a day 717-533-8661

Syed Afzal Moshadi Shah, *COMSATS Insititue of Information Technology, Pakistan*
Ariel Tikotsky, *Bar Ilan University, Israel*
Kristian Stoffregen Tørning, *Danish School of Media and Journalism, Denmark*
Mark Underwood, *Krypton Brothers LLC, USA*
Huy Vu, *Victoria University, Australia*
Oya Zincir, *Istanbul University, Turkey*

Table of Contents

Detailed Table of Contents

accessing the internet and social media applications to find and disseminate factual information regarding medical tourism facilitators, destinations, super-speciality hospitals, specialist doctors and nurses, quality and accreditation, accommodation facility, cost, waiting period for surgery and sharing their positive and negative experiences to inform potential medical tourists. Healthcare providers and medical tourists acquire information, create, collaborate, communicate and disseminate healthcare and medical tourism related information through the Word-of-Social-Media (WoSM) tools such as FaceBook, Flickr, Twitter, Blogs, Forums, YouTube patient testimonials, Google Plus, LinkedIn, Photo and video sharing, Alexa and mobile applications. Therefore social media has a great potential as an information source and a knowledge dissemination tool for tourism industry to network and create clusters locally and globally, to exploit new innovative technologies for interaction and collaboration between the healthcare providers as well as the medical tourists. The main contribution of this chapter is to explore and discuss the role and use of social media applications for knowledge dissemination by hospitals and the medical tourists in the global business of medical tourism in India.

The role of Knowledge Sharing (KS) in an academic environment, with the framework of KS has been explored in this chapter. The role played by social media (SM) as a technology for KS has been discussed. The different aspects of human attitude towards sharing have been expressed with the role of library professionals, in order to support the research activity of the students within the knowledge management cycle. Few examples like the use of blogs, Facebook, and YouTube in different types of institutions /organizations and the value, purpose and challenges are highlighted. The use of social networking tools by cataloguers as a necessity for current awareness information is also emphasized. It is found that the use of social media in education, health, and other domains is mostly used to enhance reaching out to users. The advantages of KS with the need for sharing of knowledge to enhance the role by the administrators in universities and by the professionals are provided. Further research in the field of SM by specific disciplines can be carried out.

This chapter has examined ways of facilitating knowledge sharing for the benefit of students of international relations and conflict studies in Nigerian universities. It is evident that tertiary institutions' students of the 21st Century cannot study now without the use of social media which serves as a platform for information sharing and knowledge production. It is a medium through which knowledge is transferred to users by think tanks and organisations across the world. Given that not only students benefit, people from all walks of life are not also left out as social networks record large number of users daily. This explains how social media serves as data bank for scholars and why students now need to continuously search to find related materials on social media. Using qualitative data the author used observation method in the classroom setting in the University of Ibadan and Wellspring University, Benin City, Nigeria. It should be stated that the type of digital device used by students can as well determine their level of access to the social media in Nigeria. Observations show that social media is very relevant for students especially in the study and teaching of international relations and conflict studies given the number of global courses

develop a model of how social media characteristics impact cybersecurity knowledge transfer using technology threat avoidance theory. In developing the conceptual model we seek to answer the following questions. How do users discover cybersecurity knowledge on social media platforms? What are the platform and interaction characteristics that enable them to find cybersecurity knowledge and share this knowledge with others? In doing so we consider the impact of the threat and protection context on cybersecurity knowledge transfer which is different from knowledge transfer in the other contexts.

Section 4
Challenges of Social Media for Managing Knowledge

Intranets are almost as old as the concept of a web site. More than twenty-five years ago the text Business Data Communications closed with a discussion of intranets. Underlying technology improvements in intranets have been incremental; intranets were never seen as killer developments. Yet the popularity of Online Social Networks (OSNs) has led to increased interest in the part OSNs play – or could play – in using intranets to foster knowledge management. This chapter reviews research into how social graphs for an enterprise, team or other collaboration group interacts with the ways intranets have been used to display, collect, curate and disseminate information over the knowledge life cycle. Future roles that OSN-aware intranets could play in emerging technologies, such as process mining, elicitation methods, domain-specific intelligent agents, big data, and just-in-time learning are examined.

Social media technologies have been embraced by individuals and organizations on such a massive scale in the last decade that knowledge sharing and application has molded into a totally new paradigm. It has not only changed the social discourse of communication but also affected the knowledge management strategies of organizations. This raises quite a number of fundamental challenges out of which three are being dealt in this chapter. The first challenge is whether knowledge management has fully embraced social media as a channel of mass reach the way it did in case of other means of mass communication. The second one is the question of speed and extent of knowledge sharing in social media. The third challenge is whether social media strategy can provide a high advantage to smaller and newer companies in comparison to older but larger organizations. It is apparent that the commercial aspect of social media is easy for a tête-à-tête but difficult to articulate and design the right strategy because it needs a lot of refinements owing to inherent complexities in the process.

Preface

In order to survive and sustain, organisations need to find ways of managing both tacit and explicit knowledge. The emergence of social media has made it possible to better manage knowledge in organisations (Pawlowski & Pirkkalainen, 2012). Social media enables organisations to connect both internally and externally, and its widespread popularity provides many opportunities for managing knowledge. Hence, harnessing social media as a knowledge management tool has become vital. As we witness a global surge in the usage of social media (Chugh, 2012), it is important that organisations tap into this resource and leverage it for managing knowledge and not solely as a means of day-to-day communication with customers. Social media can potentially make the management of knowledge a less cumbersome facet (Razmerita, Kirchner & Nabeth, 2014) of routine operations. As social media continues to evolve, it brings new opportunities for knowledge management and it is important to tap into this resource.

Knowledge management is a discipline focused on management of information and intellectual capital that is considered to be a valuable resource by all organizations, irrespective of size and type, because of the reliance of their organizational processes on sound information. Organizations have always taken a keen interest in retaining and (re)using knowledge as it is a critical asset for them. There is an emerging consensus that managing knowledge effectively provides a source of competitive advantage. Hence, the importance of knowledge management in improving business processes and creating sustainable competitive advantage cannot be underemphasized. However, the tools and strategies for the creation, collection, storage and dissemination of knowledge have changed significantly over the last decade with the emergence of social media.

Social media is the use of collaborative online applications and technologies for the creation, sharing and application of information by facilitating a social environment amongst users. Social media encompasses a variety of tools such as blogs, discussion forums, chat rooms, social networking websites, video sharing websites, photo sharing websites, wikis/collaborative websites, social bookmarking websites and virtual worlds to list a few. These tools provide both interactivity and collaborative opportunities alongside various other functionality analogous to other knowledge management platforms. A study by Levy (2013) found that the higher the level of knowledge management, the higher the level of social media implementation for knowledge management requirements and importantly, social media implementation in organizations conforms to formal knowledge management activities. Social media can be used for collecting, storing and disseminating knowledge to the right people at the right time in the right place and in the right format and can be seen as an enabler of efficient knowledge management processes. As a result, social media has been embraced by individuals and organizations globally and its role in knowledge management is vital.

The emergence of social media has made it easy to connect with people (internally and externally) in organisations, provide speed, spontaneity and global reach (Asur & Huberman, 2010). Utilising social media for managing knowledge can essentially be seen as an innovative approach in various organisational processes. In fact, social media is a good fit for all knowledge management processes – it can be used to generate new ideas, collect and collate information, communicate and share (both top-down and bottom-up) knowledge, provide collaborative and socialisation opportunities locally and globally, build and store organisational memory, disseminate knowledge and convert tacit to explicit knowledge. Social media can also be seen as a facilitator of social networks, which are considered to be fundamental for the exchange of tacit knowledge. As a matter of fact, the various social media tools can be used to support the four knowledge conversion modes (Socialization, Externalization, Combination and Internalization) identified by Nonaka (1994).

It is evident that a number of challenges (technological, process and people) will confront organisations in the introduction and implementation of social media (Murphy & Salomone, 2013). In the twenty-first century, social media has pervaded almost everyone's personal lives and organisations globally are no exception to it. Social media supports the personal and collective dimensions of knowledge, while integrating a social collaborative facet (Razmerita, Kirchner & Nabeth, 2014). What beckons organisations is evaluating how to use social media to manage organisational knowledge. Nevertheless, the rapidly growing phenomena of social media can be used in a variety of organisational contexts to leverage and support knowledge management processes.

This book was motivated by the desire that people have to manage knowledge. The ubiquity of social media got me thinking about the role it can play in knowledge management at large and the various phases of the knowledge management cycle in specific. Social media appears to be the right fit for knowledge management cycle phases - knowledge acquisition, organisation, storage, retrieval and dissemination. There are innumerable tools currently available that either focus on onc of thcsc specific knowledge management phases or others that can largely serve multiple knowledge management phases. However, the adoption of social media for managing personal and organisational knowledge comes with its own challenges. These challenges stem from technology adoption avoidance, plain ignorance and/or a cultural dilemma. Nevertheless, these challenges are not insurmountable especially in today's widely interconnected global environment. It was evident to me that a book that explores social media issues around knowledge management and outlines application of social media for managing knowledge was required. Hence, this all-inclusive book! This book presents theoretical and research-based practices related to the usage of social media for knowledge management.

OBJECTIVE OF THE BOOK

A current holistic understanding of social media in knowledge management is needed by practitioners and researchers alike. This book aims to fill that gap and offers a variety of perspectives through useful and current information in this field. This book provides a concise and holistic understanding of the issues and challenges that can be encountered when exploiting social media for managing knowledge. Some chapters highlight the usage of social media for knowledge sharing and provide illustrations of its usage in various settings whilst others provide practical guidelines and frameworks that can be adopted to make implementation efforts of social media for successfully managing knowledge globally.

I hope this book will be a very pragmatic resource for information system managers, business managers, administrators, academics, researchers and students who need to understand the multiple applications of social media in knowledge management from both a theoretical and practical perspective, in order to harness the true potential of this rapidly growing phenomenon i.e. social media.

ORGANIZATION OF THE BOOK

The book provides a holistic insight into multiple perspectives of the role of social media in knowledge management. It explores the usage of social media in knowledge management from an organizational and/or individualistic viewpoint, looking at the opportunities and challenges that are encountered in using and implementing social media. The book has chapters related to people, processes, practices, technology, and the environment, which enable the identification, creation, sharing, storage, application and (re)use of knowledge through the use of social media. The book will have both theoretical and practical implications for policy makers who wish to embed social media to help manage organizational knowledge. The book is organized into four sections containing fifteen chapters. Section one contains four chapters relating to usage of social media for knowledge sharing in different domains/settings. Section two comprises of five chapters that focus on the application of social media as an aid for knowledge management activities. Section three encompasses three chapters that outline frameworks relevant to knowledge management and social media. Finally, section four includes three chapters that concentrate on some challenges of social media for managing knowledge. A chapter-by-chapter brief description follows:

Chapter 1 reports the results of a Hungarian exploratory survey that explored the usage of social media technologies through an investigation of the willingness of employees to participate in knowledge sharing. It also explores whether there are generational differences relating to knowledge sharing behaviours. The results have shown that organizations prefer not to allow the usage of social media; but where the employees are supported to reach these tools, high proportion of them utilize these technologies.

Chapter 2 explores and discusses the role and use of social media applications for knowledge dissemination by hospitals and the medical tourists in the global business of medical tourism in India. The chapter outlines that social media tools, also called Word-of-Social-Media (WoSM), are increasingly being adopted and used by private super-speciality hospitals in the business of medical tourism in India to communicate and disseminate healthcare related information to its patients, medical professionals and other businesses connected with medical tourism. The chapter also calls out to the medical tourism industry to develop a Medical-Tourism Trip-Advisor (MTTA) platform to inform potential and current medical tourists regarding all aspects of medical travel from booking an airline ticket to the choice of destination, hospital, surgeon, accommodation, tourism and sightseeing to prepare them for their medical surgery and journey overseas.

Chapter 3 descriptively investigates the role of knowledge sharing in distinct environments through the use of social media. This chapter is predominantly centred on a review of the existing literature and could be seen as a very rudimentary outline highlighting the need of social media for knowledge sharing in libraries. It outlines the value of social media for educational designers and also provides simplistic guidelines for social media usage in libraries.

Chapter 4 examines ways of facilitating knowledge sharing for the benefit of students of international relations and conflict studies in Nigerian universities. This chapter argues that social media is designed to facilitate interpersonal and intergroup relations. It presents an analysis to indicate that social media provides opportunities for learning experiences, with new information generated daily, knowledge sharing in an educational context would aid violence research, and also make teaching and learning easier.

Chapter 5 explores the use of crowd-sourcing as an effective tool for promoting universal primary education. It shows the ecosystem model needed to design a social knowledge management platform. The chapter then proposes a social knowledge management platform that captures and disseminates formal and non-formal knowledge and wisdom of the elderly to educate underprivileged youth online by mobilising a group of experienced senior citizens and quality teaching learning materials.

Chapter 6 provides a theoretical framework for profiling knowledge workers' mainstream social media usage and investigating knowledge workers' mainstream social media usage for personal knowledge management purposes. For this chapter, data has been collected from 325 knowledge workers in Turkey who work in various private sector organisations. The results indicate that knowledge workers mostly use social media for the purpose of identifying experts and least use these platforms for the purpose of participating in online discussions in order to create new knowledge.

Chapter 7 illustrates the role of social media in managing and disseminating organizational knowledge via a case study of a local government's response to a natural disaster. It offers a qualitative evaluation of real-time unfolding of discourse throughout a storm in the town of Grancesso (US), following a rhetorical approach to crisis communication that stresses message development and its presentation. The chapter recommends that building social media communication structures during non-crisis periods could provide a stronger knowledge communication infrastructure for crisis management.

Chapter 8 describes the principles of wiki-based organizational knowledge management solutions and provides detailed descriptions of successful implementations in four global organizations where each wiki serves a different knowledge management-related purpose. The chapter reviews methodological, technical, cultural and implementation aspects of these wikis. Good practices and key success factors for wiki adoption are discussed, which can help organizations to harness the power of a corporate wiki.

Chapter 9 scrutinises existing literature from the Journal of Political Marketing and performs a thematic content analyses of 320 articles to explore the impact of adaptation and use of social media by political actors and organizations on the knowledge production and generation of political marketing. It offers a conceptual context to understand modes of knowledge production and generation and its application in the field study of political marketing.

Chapter 10 presents an exploratory framework to analyze the implications of the use of various types of social media based knowledge management tools on the firm's knowledge collection and sharing strategies. Through the use of intelligence gathered by case studies and expert interviews in India, this chapter illustrates how the usage of social media has enabled smaller firms to quickly build their knowledge bases and increase the pace of their growth. The chapter recommends that social media based knowledge management intervention has to match the firm's requirement based on its knowledge management strategy.

Chapter 11 discusses the 'SECI–SM Framework', which has been proposed in an earlier work by the authors. The distinctive features of SECI-SM model is discussed in the light of previous researches. The framework offers an extended form of knowledge sharing activities highlighted through the renowned SECI model. The model does not undermine the importance of conventional knowledge management efforts rather adds a new dimension of social media to it.

Chapter 12 explores the relationships between social media building blocks and knowledge transfer in the context of cybersecurity using technology threat avoidance theory. Based on the exploration a parsimonious model of social media properties, threat avoidance and knowledge transfer has been developed. The model integrates threat avoidance and knowledge theories to identify how cybersecurity knowledge transfer takes place over social media platforms.

Chapter 13 reviews research into how social graphs for an enterprise, team or other collaboration group interacts with the ways intranets have been used to display, collect, curate and disseminate information over the knowledge life cycle. The role of intranets in the knowledge management life cycle has been outlined. The roles that online social networks -aware intranets could play in emerging technologies are examined and pragmatic steps that can be taken for intranet success have been outlined in this chapter.

Chapter 14 raises three challenges of managing knowledge via social media. Firstly, it explores whether knowledge management practices have fully embraced social media. Secondly, it delves in to the issue of whether knowledge management strategy can cope with the rapid speed of social media adoption. Finally, it leads through a journey of social media adoption and usage for brand building, electronic commerce and briefly explores whether social media can provide a higher advantage to smaller and newer companies in comparison to older but larger organizations.

Chapter 15 provides an introduction and background to Big Data and the technologies used for Big Data solutions, so that data from social media can be harnessed. An overview of the analytical approaches used in Big Data is also outlined in this chapter. The impact that Big Data solutions have on the technology and data architectures are highlighted. A data management framework has been outlined that identifies many areas within an organization's data and knowledge management capabilities that could be impacted by Big Data.

As this journey comes to an end, I hope the readers will find some value in the contributions made by the authors from ten countries representing a broad cross section of university researchers and industry practitioners as they provide a global perspective to this topic. In summary, the book will also open up further avenues and opportunities for future research into the area of social media in knowledge management in a diverse range of cross-disciplinary settings. What works in one setting may fail in another, hence the need for constant experimentation is urged. Moreover, technology in the form of social media itself may not be sufficient to facilitate all knowledge management efforts in organisations. A mixture of technology and other conventional knowledge management mechanisms should be considered. Overall, the book is designed to be a 'one-stop shop' for global information about harnessing social media for managing knowledge. Armed with specific usage practices, applications, frameworks and challenges, readers can make informed choices about the adoption of social media to manage knowledge.

To knowledge management via social media and beyond!

Ritesh Chugh
Central Queensland University, Australia

REFERENCES

Asur, S., & Huberman, B. A. (2010). Predicting the future with social media. In *IEEE/WIC/ACM International Conference on Web Intelligence and Intelligent Agent Technology (WI-IAT)* (pp. 492-499). IEEE.

Chugh, R. (2012). Social networking for businesses: Is it a boon or bane? In M. M. Cruz-Cunha, G. D. Putnik, N. Lopes, P. Gonçalves, & E. Miranda (Eds.), *Handbook of research on business social networking: Organizational, managerial, and technological dimensions* (pp. 603–618). Hershey, PA: IGI Global. doi:10.4018/978-1-61350-168-9.ch032

Levy, M. (2013). Stairways to heaven: Implementing social media in organizations. *Journal of Knowledge Management, 17*(5), 741–754. doi:10.1108/JKM-02-2013-0051

Murphy, G., & Salomone, S. (2013). Using social media to facilitate knowledge transfer in complex engineering environments: A primer for educators. *European Journal of Engineering Education, 38*(1), 70–84. doi:10.1080/03043797.2012.742871

Nonaka, I. (1994). A dynamic theory of organizational knowledge creation. *Organization Science, 5*(1), 14–37. doi:10.1287/orsc.5.1.14

Pawlowski, J. M., & Pirkkalainen, H. (2012). Global social knowledge management: The future of knowledge management across borders? In *Proceedings of European Conference on Knowledge Management*. Academic Press.

Razmerita, L., Kirchner, K., & Nabeth, T. (2014). Social media in organizations: Leveraging personal and collective knowledge processes. *Journal of Organizational Computing and Electronic Commerce, 24*(1), 74–93. doi:10.1080/10919392.2014.866504

Acknowledgment

I tick off another item from my wish-list! It has been a year-long eventful journey with the authors, the reviewers, the editorial staff and the editorial advisory board. I am sincerely grateful to everyone involved with this book for their time and effort as without their input the book would not have been possible.

In particular, my heartfelt gratitude and appreciation goes to the chapters' author/s who contributed their time and expertise to this book.

I would like to thank my parents and my wife, Harita, for constantly supporting my endeavours and in particular my children Aryan & Ria for understanding that I was occasionally stealing some family time away from them.

I also acknowledge that knowledge is power and social media can help to collect, store, disseminate and apply knowledge.

Ritesh Chugh
Central Queensland University, Australia

Section 1

Usage of Social Media for Knowledge Sharing in Different Domains/Settings

Chapter 1
Leveraging Knowledge Sharing over Social Media Tools

Nora Obermayer
University of Pannonia, Hungary

Lajos Szabó
Corvinus University of Budapest, Hungary

Zoltán Gaál
University of Pannonia, Hungary

Anikó Csepregi
University of Pannonia, Hungary

ABSTRACT

Knowledge management and social media have become trendy expressions in the business life. Knowledge is seen as the most important strategic asset and knowledge workers play a central role in value creation. Organizations have an urgent need to pay attention to effective knowledge sharing, thus, it is important to understand what encourages individuals to share their knowledge. Social media tools, like Facebook have become mainstream, modified personal relationships and generated new possibilities to facilitate collaboration. An exploratory survey investigates how social media tools are being used for knowledge sharing and examines the characteristics of the different generations. The results have shown that organizations prefer not to allow the usage of social media; but where the employees are supported to reach these tools, high proportion of them utilize these technologies. This chapter introduces these results and provides recommendations on how to foster employee motivation to use social media for work purposes in knowledge sharing.

INTRODUCTION

Researchers regard knowledge as the key ingredient in gaining long-term competitive advantage because knowledge is the main inimitable resource (Barney, 1986; Grant, 1996; Murray & Peyrefitte, 2007). In organizations knowledge and information are the most important factors of value (Prahalad & Hamel, 1990), moreover intellectual capital (IC) or intangible asset including human capital, research and development, structural capital and relational section (Edvinsson & Malone, 1997; Stewart, 1997; Sveiby, 1997) is perceived as a principal to the achievement of competitive advantage (Barney, 1986; Spender, 1996). Having knowledge supports to cope with daily works and it can also set up individuals to deal with new situations and utilize it when needed. The exchange of knowledge among employees is

DOI: 10.4018/978-1-5225-0495-5.ch001

a vital part of knowledge management, organizations are faced with the challenge of how to get people to share their knowledge. Knowledge transfer theory is concerned with the dissemination of individual knowledge through organizations (Nonaka & Von Krogh, 2009). Knowledge workers may recognize the importance of knowledge management for their business life, but it can happen that their willingness to share knowledge depends on their demographic characteristics such as their age (belonging to a certain generation). When organizations understand the determinants of knowledge sharing, effective technologies can be implemented to improve competitiveness.

The most significant technological development in the last twenty years has been the Internet, which enables everyone to collaborate and share information, knowledge, document, photo, etc. with anyone in the world. Individuals are able to make use of social media tools in order to increase profusion of their networks, accumulate information. Social media tools have taken the world in a storm, it has become a mainstream, modified personal relationships, allowed individuals to contribute to number of cases and constitute new possibilities to facilitate collaboration. The advantage of implementing social media is enormous. Knowledge workers may be reserved to make use of social media because they may not appreciate the power of social media or be concerned about security of reliability. In addition, many organisations do not support their employees using social media because they may be concerned about the risks of a potential misuse.

THEORETICAL BACKGROUND

This section starts with a general introduction into the theory of knowledge management, knowledge sharing and knowledge sharing behaviour. The next paragraph is about social media technologies and the connection between social media and knowledge sharing. The last part of this section is about generations and linkage to knowledge sharing.

Knowledge Management and Knowledge Sharing

Knowledge, knowledge management and knowledge sharing have become popular topics nowadays. In knowledge economy knowledge has also become a strategically important resource and the performance driver for organizations (Yesil & Dereli, 2013). Either located in the minds of the individuals (tacit knowledge) (Polányi, 1966) or embedded in organizational routines and norms, codified in technological devices (explicit knowledge) (Nonaka & Takeuchi, 1995) knowledge enables the development of new competences as well (Choo, 1998). Knowledge management is not a monolithic, but a dynamic and continuous organizational phenomenon (Alavi & Leidner, 1999). In this era characterized by fast change and uncertainty, it is widely accepted that intellectual resources are key organizational assets (Wenger, 2000) and successful organizations are those that consistently create new knowledge, disseminate it throughout the organization, and embody it in technologies, products, and services (Gottschalk, 2007). From the generic knowledge management processes being the acquisition, generation and creation, codification, storing, sharing, transfer and utilization of knowledge certain authors stress the importance of mainly knowledge creation and sharing processes (Davenport & Prusak, 1998). Knowledge sharing thus represents a key knowledge management process in organizations and can also be considered fundamental for generating new ideas and developing new business opportunities (Lin, 2007). According to Mueller (2012, p. 436) at least two people, groups, or organizations are involved in knowledge sharing "the sender, who is willing and able to share knowledge, and the receiver, who is willing and able to combine this new knowledge with his or her existing knowledge and use it".

Knowledge Sharing Behaviour

Based on the approach of Ryu et al. (2003), Lin and Lee (2004), and Bock et al. (2005) knowledge sharing behaviour is considered as "the degree to which organizational members actually share knowledge with others" (Yang a& Chen 2007, p. 101). It is viewed by Yu et al. (2010, p. 33) that "in virtual communities, knowledge sharing behaviour cannot be forced but can only be encouraged and facilitated". Furthermore, they have also revealed that the enjoyment of helping and the usefulness/ relevancy foster knowledge sharing behaviour. Focusing on an Intranet environment Masrek et al. (2011) discovered that both the length of service and the Internet experience are significant predictor of knowledge sharing behaviour. In virtual environment knowledge sharing behaviour appears as a behaviour to disseminate one member's acquired knowledge with the usage of computer mediated communication tools to other members.

Since an individual cannot possess all knowledge and knowledge cannot be hoarded like gold, people should recognize that the old paradigm 'knowledge is power' is less and less relevant. One of the ways of motivating individuals to share knowledge is to introduce how knowledge sharing can support them in executing their jobs more effectively and in helping them in their personal development and achieving their personal goals (Obermayer-Kovács & Csepregi, 2007).

Davenport and Prusak (1998) categorized the potential motivation behind knowledge sharing behaviour as either pure altruism, reciprocity, or reputation.

- **Altruism:** Refers to behaviour that costs an individual and benefit the other person. People donate something to other people without thinking of any returns when showing altruistic behaviour.
- **Reciprocity:** Refers to either a positive or negative response for the actions which one should treat others as one would like others to treat oneself. People share information or knowledge might expect future benefits from their present actions.
- **Reputation:** Refers to a degree of recognition and increased by information sharing among other users. People who share more knowledge receive a higher reputation.

Research works (Davenport & Prusak, 1998; Susanty & Wood, 2011) have also proved that intrinsic and extrinsic motivators influence knowledge sharing attitude. It is stated also that intrinsic motivation plays a greater role than extrinsic motivation in case of willingness to share.

- **Loss of Knowledge Power:** The perception of power and unique value lost due to knowledge contributed (Gray, 2001). Knowledge management literature reports the loss of knowledge power as a barrier to knowledge sharing. People may keep themselves out of a knowledge exchange if they feel they can benefit more by hoarding their knowledge rather than by sharing it (Davenport & Prusak, 1998).
- **Organizational Reward:** The importance of economic incentives (e.g. bonuses, security, and career advancement) provided for individuals (Hall, 2001). Numerous studies argued that a reward system can be a key factor for the success of knowledge sharing in organizations. Bartol and Locke (2000) argued that the system of contribution knowledge to databases is the most willing to reward contingent on knowledge sharing behaviours because of opportunities for the reward allocator to

measure the knowledge sharing behaviours. Kugel and Schostek (2004) found monetary rewards seemed to have an immediate effect on motivation on knowledge sharing.

In the survey of "Organizational knowledge sharing in Hungary 2013/2014" only the first three factors (altruism, reciprocity and reputation) were investigated. In a large-scale online survey – "Knowledge sharing and emotional intelligence in Hungary 2014/2015" has been developed (Obermayer-Kovács et al., 2015), where the researchers expand the analysis with loss of knowledge power and organizational reward factors. This chapter does not contain the results of the mentioned survey as that focuses on knowledge sharing and emotional intelligence.

Social Media Technologies

Social media has a number of definitions, such as "collaborative online applications and technologies which enable and encourage participation, conversation, openness, creation and socialization amongst a community of users" (Bowley, 2009:15), web-based tools and practices enabling participation and collaboration based on individuals' activities. Surowiecki (2005) defined that social media is to make use of the "wisdom of the crowd". Group of people are better at problem solving, fostering decision making than individuals alone. It can also be considered as a tool that facilitates intra- and inter-organizational activities including collaborative product development, learning and creativity (Peppler & Solomou, 2011), corporate dialog implementation (Bonson & Flores, 2011), and knowledge sharing community creation (Yates & Paquette, 2011).

It enables the sharing, storage and synthesis of knowledge from various sources to create new meta-knowledge. It is also possible to participate in a collective knowledge generation processes through experience sharing, criticizing various theories and findings within communities of practices (Sigala & Chalkiti, 2015).

The term "Web 2.0" was generated by O'Reilly (2005). It refers to technologies that allow individuals to interactively participate with information and with other individuals, and to build networks based on mutual personal or professional interest. Web 2.0 facilitates social networking therefore is also referred to as the social media. These technologies - blogs, video sharing, presentation sharing, social networking service, instant messaging service and groupware - foster a more socially connected platform (Anderson, 2007). Vuori (2011) characterises social media by considering the extent to which they support communication, collaboration, connecting, completing and combining (5C).

1. **Communication:** Social media provides new tools to share, store and publish contents, discuss and express opinions and influence:
    a. **Blogs (e.g. Blogger) and Microblogs (e.g. Twitter):** Managed by one or many specified authors, who publishes entries (posts), that are dated and shown in reverse chronological order.
    b. **Video Sharing (e.g. YouTube):** A site, which allows users to upload, view, and share videos, and it makes use of Adobe Flash Video to display a variety of individual or corporate media video.
    c. **Presentation Sharing (e.g. SlideShare):** A web-based slide hosting service. Users can upload presentations privately or publicly.
    d. **Instant Messaging Service (e.g. Skype):** An online conference tool, which can promote the instant communication and knowledge sharing between the community members.

2. **Collaboration:** Social media enables collective content creation and edition without location and time constraints:
    a. **Wikis (e.g. Wikipedia):** A website that enables the easy creation and editing of interlinking Web pages.
    b. **Groupware/Shared Workspaces (e.g. GoogleDocs):** Supports collaborative creation of knowledge. It can be used for sharing the documents without sending them via e-mails, but only sharing the link of the document.
    c. **Communities of Practices (e.g. MeetUp):** Online portals that facilitate group meetings in various localities around the world.
3. **Connecting:** Social media offers new ways of networking with other people, socialising oneself into the community:
    a. **Social Networking Services (e.g. Facebook, LinkedIn):** Enables for a community to create a profile (and topic groups) with the aim to share information/knowledge to the followers (partners, potential customers) of their community page.
4. **Completing:** Social media tools are used to complete content by describing, adding or filtering information, tagging contents, and showing a connection between contents:
    a. **Visual Bookmarking Tool (e.g. Pinterest):** The process of adding keywords (tags) to pieces of different types of media (photos, videos, documents, links). Tagging is used in the bookmarking when users tag the content which can be later found by the categorization of the content.
    b. **News Aggregator (e.g. Digg):** A website that collects, collates, and organizes syndicated web content, creating a customized site where all desired content is centralized.
5. **Combining:** Social media tools are developed for mixing and matching contents. Combination of pre-existing web services that allow a certain user within a platform to use another application, in a specific window, without the need to get out of the initial website.
    a. **Mash-Ups (e.g. Google Maps):** An application that uses and combines data from one or more sources to create new services.

Social media tools create a dynamic, complex information infrastructure that enables, faster, and more widespread sharing of information, reduce the cost of social exchanges - social interaction is much easier; and the variety of platforms provides increased flexibility in how people can communicate (Hemsley & Mason, 2013).

Social media seem a perfect way for knowledge sharing, because social activities contribute to the sharing process and collaboration. It is the success of social media that they encourage social interaction but also exploit it. People can change the contents of others, they can use (action) and respond to it (reflection). The interaction not only leads to new knowledge; it can also ensure that ties with others strengthen or weaken. Several research has been conducted about using social media and Web 2.0 in the workplace for sharing knowledge, next subsection will summarize some of them.

Social Media and Knowledge Sharing

Earlier research has suggested that social media can enable knowledge sharing within the organization by helping employees locate expertise and relevant content (Brzozowski, 2009) since it provides access to new people and expertise (Steinfield et al. 2009) and can increase awareness and contact among virtual employees (DiMicco & Millen, 2007).

A theoretical investigation was conducted by Panahi et al. (2012) who illustrated their findings in a conceptual framework in respect of social media abilities supporting the requirements of tacit knowledge sharing. These abilities include the support of a better place for social interaction, the establishment of opportunities for experience sharing, the building of a domain of informal relationships, the support of facilities to observe, listen, and imitate best practices, and the establishment of a mutual swift trust among participants. Another research investigating Danish company employees' motivation and the factors that affect their knowledge sharing through social media in their working environment discovered that management support, knowledge sharing culture, recognition and rewards, and knowledge management resources as organizational factors, while motivation and perceived usefulness as individual factors have strong effect on knowledge sharing (Nielsen & Razmerita, 2014).

Sigala and Chalkiti (2015) defined a three-layer framework to measure social media's exploitation for knowledge management. On the first level the use of technological tools to search, store, categorize and link information are present. The second level represents the usage of technological tools to achieve the identification and participation in social networks in order to develop and maintain interpersonal relations that can in turn facilitate knowledge management processes as sharing, discussion and negotiation with others. Finally, the third level aims to support knowledge creation processes through synthesis and discussion. Each level also requires certain capabilities to effectively perform on the given level.

Social media have become popular not only among teenagers but also among older adults and effects their how they manage knowledge (Ma & Chan, 2014; Dumbrell & Steele, 2014), thus the next part presents a review of different generations.

Generations

The term "generation" signifies the group of individuals, most of whom are within a similar age group, born in the same time of history and culture, having similar ideas, problems and attitudes (Weingarten, 2009). A person's age may not always be indicative of their generational characteristics, but as a common group, they are likely to have similarities. A generation at a certain period tends to be exposed to approximately similar generic life experiences depending on cultural background. Society is changing constantly which is likely to affect the values and experiences of different generations.

In the Hungarian research, based on some previous researchers' work (Reeves & Oh 2007; Weingarten, 2009; Grail Research, 2011), the authors use the following dates and definitions:

- **Veterans (Born between 1922 and 1945):** Respect for authority, loyalty, hard work and sacrifice for the common good. Their motto is "live to work versus work to live".
- **Baby Boomers (Born between 1946 and 1964):** Grew up with sense that security was taken care of – this left room for exploration and protest. They place high value on youth, personal gratification, health and material wealth. They are generally optimistic, value hope and peace, and believe their generation changed the world.
- **Generation X (Born between 1965 and 1980):** Desires balance in their lives, diversity viewed as norm, motivated by money, self-reliant, value free time and having fun. Their motto is "work to live, not live to work". They assume gender equality in the workplace. This is the first generation that embraces the personal computer and Internet.

- **Generation Y (Born between 1981 and 2000):** The most globally oriented generation. They combine work ethic of Baby Boomers with the can-do attitude of Veterans and the technological savvy of Generation X. They are interested in health, exercise and body adornment.
- **Generation Z (Born from 2000 to Present):** Having grown up in a digital world where technology was ever present. They are more socially responsible, due to greater access to a large online information pool and always communicate through various social networking channels.

A variety of researchers have identified a serious new set of workplace issues related to interactions between distinct generations working together and often coming into conflict as their paths cross. Individuals with different values, ideas, ways of getting things done and ways of communicating in the workplace have always existed. At work, generational differences can affect recruiting, building teams, dealing with change, motivating, managing or increasing productivity.

Social Media and Generations

The three generations (Baby boomers, Generation X and Generation Y) make up today's workplace demographics for the first time in recent history and at the extremes, their working styles and understanding of each other are different. This is clearly evident in workplace adoption of social media. To effectively create a social media strategy that will be adopted by the employees, organizations must consider the unique perspectives and needs of the entire workforce. Baby boomers consider about business as most effectively conducted in face-to-face meetings or at least over the phone. Face-to-face interactions build better rapport and stronger relationships and they have just started experimenting with Facebook and Twitter. Members of Generation X prefer to do business over e-mail, they find it more effective. Face-to-face meetings are needed occasionally but in reality, things can be done via e-mail. They do not have a problem adjusting to Facebook and the other social media sites, but they do not have to use it. Generation Y like to send just a quick text. It is all about efficiency and speed. They think Facebook, Twitter, blogs, etc., are great ways to foster collaboration and innovation in their organization. They do not need to see their peers to build a strong relationship with them.

The combination of new technology and mobile devices with the changing needs of employees presents a significant challenge for organizations. The ability to access information and applications from a laptop, phones from around the world has created an expectation of immediacy for today's workforce. The information is easily accessible, but the question can be whether organizations are prepared to deal with data security and privacy issues if a device is lost. Many innovative and fast-growing companies put the emphasis on collaboration. Finding the right expert to repair a piece of equipment, reusing an existing piece of market research, convening a geographically dispersed "team", etc. all are faster and less expensive with social media tools. Many advanced companies use internal, secure versions of instant messaging, YouTube, Twitter, and virtual classrooms to collaborate (KPMG, 2012).

That is why the authors decided to explore the ways in which social media technologies are being used as knowledge sharing tools among the Hungarian organizations. Next section explains the research framework and discusses the research. The paper ends with practical implications and recommendations, future research directions and conclusion.

ORGANIZATIONAL KNOWLEDGE SHARING IN HUNGARY

Research Framework

The methodology undertaken in the survey was an exploratory research study examining the nature of knowledge sharing activities among Hungarian organizations. The authors were involved in the development and implementation of the "Organizational knowledge sharing in Hungary 2013/2014" questionnaire survey (KPMG Academy, 2014), which was executed with the collaboration of the KPMG Academy, Budapest. The main objective of the research was to determine the ways in which social media technologies are being used as knowledge sharing tools.

Data Collection

Based on the literature review and a previous study (KPMG-BME Academy, 2006), a large-scale online survey - "Organizational knowledge sharing in Hungary 2013/2014" - was developed (KPMG Academy, 2014), which was carried out in LimeSurvey, a web application. In the short introduction to the survey, it was stressed that the answers would be anonymous, and only used for the purpose of the study. Respondents could leave their e-mail address in order to be informed about the results later. More than 1500 individuals received an e-mail requesting 15 minutes of their time to fill in the questionnaire about knowledge sharing and social media tools. The message contained a link to the LimeSurvey. The survey instrument consisting of four demographic questions and forty-three questions related to knowledge management, divided into three main areas: knowledge management (strategy, initiatives), knowledge sharing (technologies, practices) and leadership practice (this chapter does not discuss this topic). The potential respondents were from KPMG Academy partnership database, networks of University of Pannonia and the researchers' social relations. The participation in the study was voluntary. In the course of the survey, answers from 299 organizations were included in the database. The completed questionnaires were exported from LimeSurvey to Excel files and analysed using SPSS.

Participants

The participating organizations all operate in Hungary; they are private-owned Hungarian companies, subsidiaries of multinational companies, and other organizations in the field of public administration, but the exact statistical composition is unknown, as the questionnaire did not have questions about industry sectors' classification. Based on the number of employees, 55% are large companies, 24% are medium-sized enterprises, 10% are small businesses and 11% are micro businesses. Somewhat more than half of the organizations (54%) are domestic subsidiaries of foreign companies, and 46% are Hungarian-owned companies. 27% of the respondents are top managers, 42% are middle level managers and 31% are white collar workers. The participants belong to three generations; 22% from Baby Boomers, 60% from Generation X and 18% from Generation Y (KPMG Academy, 2014).

Data Analysis

The survey responses demonstrate that Hungarian businesses are beginning to grasp the importance of knowledge and knowledge management but still have a long way to go to fully embrace knowledge management practices (KPMG Academy, 2014).

Knowledge Management Strategy and Initiatives

Organizations in Hungary are just starting to implement knowledge management strategies. Overall, still only 37% of respondent organizations have developed a comprehensive strategy in the form of a written document (it is exactly the same percentage like in the previous survey in 2006); however, 81% states knowledge as a strategic asset (which is 4% higher than in 2006) (KPMG-BME Academy, 2006). It can be seen that there is huge gap between theory and reality (Figure 1).

However, significant growth can be detected with respect to knowledge sharing programs, initiatives or projects exist in the respondents' organizations (from 46% to 69%). Elaborating knowledge management strategy is still not a typical activity, but it does not mean that organizations are not trying to support the dissemination of knowledge. Almost half of the participated large companies (45%) have developed a formal knowledge management strategy development while this rate is only 29% for the micro, small and medium-sized enterprises. Making a comparison between foreign-owned organizations with Hungarian organizations, 47% of the former have developed a formal strategy whilst only 27% of the latter have.

Knowledge Sharing Technologies and Practices

The study examined numerous tools of knowledge sharing, several of which did not even exist, or were not widespread in 2005-2006 at the time of the previous research (KPMG-BME Academy, 2006). However, there were three of them, which can be measured. In each case there is a strong growth in the use of these tools (demonstrated in Figure 2).

Figure 1. Knowledge management strategies and initiatives
KPMG Academy, 2014.

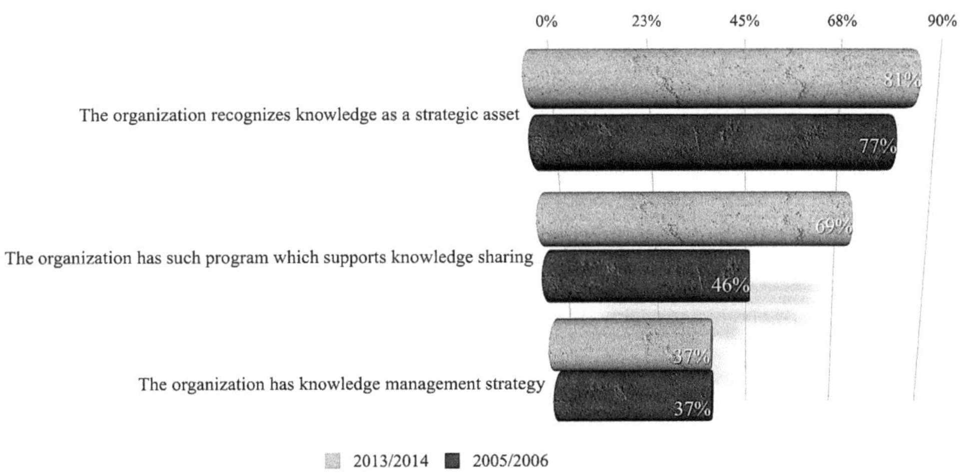

Figure 2. Knowledge sharing technologies/practices in both surveys
KPMG-BME Academy, 2006; KPMG Academy, 2014.

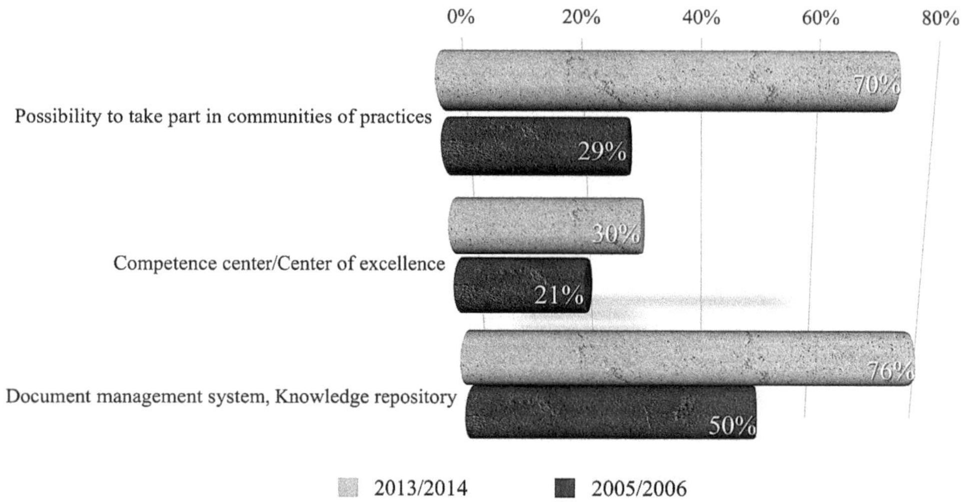

In the examined period participation in communities of practices has more than doubled (from 29% to 70%), and a growing proportion of respondents has turned to competence center or center of excellence for knowledge (21% to 30%). The usage of document management systems and knowledge repository measurably increased (from 50% to 76%).

Internal Knowledge Sharing Technologies and Practices

The following section provides the results of the survey focusing on the existence and the usage of internal technologies and practices. In this context internal means all in-house technologies which can be self-developed or available essentially pre-packaged through an Intranet. The results of the survey indicate (shown in Table 1.) which internal knowledge sharing tools are available to be used by employees for information and/or knowledge sharing internally and which are selected by the employees from the available ones for knowledge sharing purposes during work. The most popular practice for knowledge sharing is internal training, and three-quarters of the participated organizations have a document management system and knowledge repository and have the possibility to take part in the life of communities of practices. Half of the organizations provide support for instant messaging service, but with respect to the other technologies, less than 50% of organizations were made usage possible to employees. However, where the employees are allowed to use any of these tools, a high proportion (in every case more than 50%) of the people utilize them for knowledge sharing during work.

External Knowledge Sharing Technologies and Practices

As regards the general accessibility of external knowledge sharing technologies/practices (Figure 3) many organizations demonstrate considerable aversion (KPMG-Academy, 2014).

There are only two external knowledge sharing tools, which can be found at more than half of the organizations, the participation in communities of practices and social networking service, but only third (or less) of the organizations allow the usage of instant messaging services, blogs, video sharing, groupware or presentation sharing. For example, the usage of groupware is very important from the point

Table 1. Existence and usage of internal knowledge sharing technologies/practices

Tool	Meaning	Existence	Usage*
Internal training	A method of preparing an employee to perform a task.	89%	94%
Document management system and knowledge repository	Providing a comprehensive solution for managing capture, index, storage, retrieve of any information.	76%	89%
Participation in the life of a communities of practices	Groups of people who are formed to share and create skills, knowledge, and expertise among employees.	70%	79%
Internal instant messaging service	Facilitating near real-time text based communication between two or more participants.	56%	83%
Presentation sharing	Offering the ability to publish any kind of organizational presentations to a specific audience or the entire world.	46%	80%
Groupware	Enabling group collaboration over a network, providing flexible communication structures.	44%	59%
Internal social networking services	Providing the network's members access to information and knowledge.	35%	78%
Internal blogs	Offering individuals/groups to capture and publish information about specific topics.	33%	63%
Knowledge map	Presenting what knowledge resides where (people) and for demonstrating the patterns of knowledge flow (distribution).	31%	68%
Competence center/ center of excellence	Consultants with specific areas of knowledge and experience.	30%	68%
Internal video sharing	Offering the ability to publish video content to a specific audience or the entire world.	19%	71%

*Clearly the percentages represent percentages relating to the organizations that provide the various knowledge sharing technologies/ practices and therefore provide the possibility that employees make use of them.

Figure 3. Existence of external knowledge sharing technologies/practices

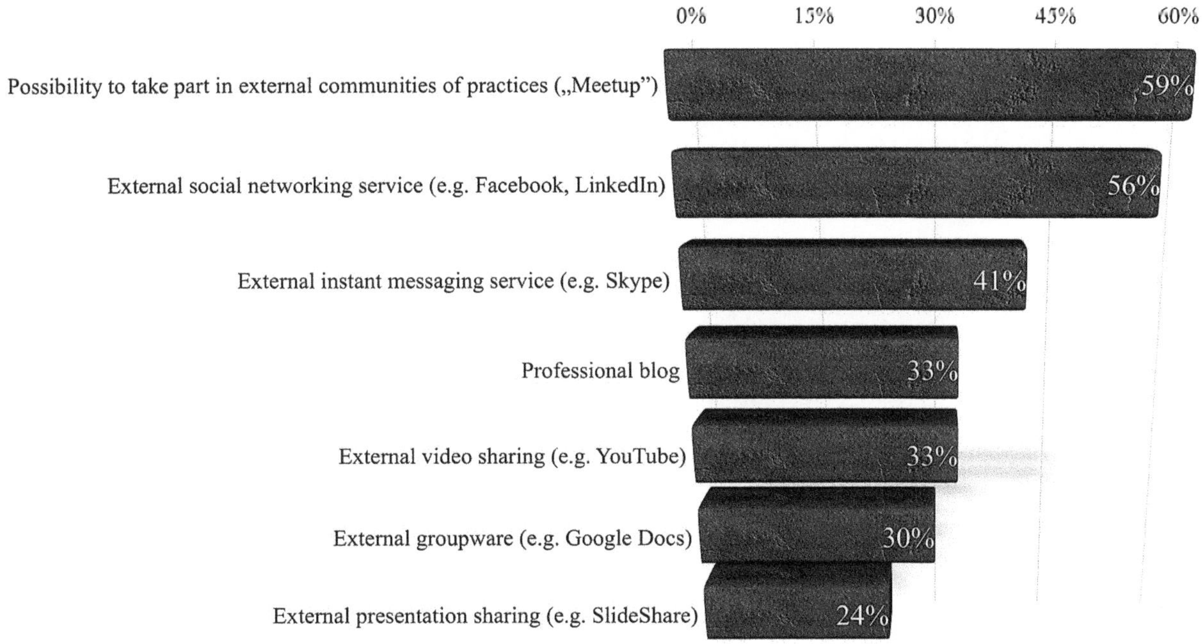

of view of organizations, as it implies that workers are willing and able to work together and to share their knowledge. However, implementation of groupware systems have numerous failures. Janson et al (2008) highlight that the success of groupware implementation hinges on the success that the organizations develop a culture where collaboration and sharing are the norm. Without that, there is no incentive to use the systems to their full potential.

The research investigated which technologies are used for knowledge sharing during work or for professional development at the participating organizations (Figure 4).

It was an interesting result that the organizations where the employees are allowed to use these tools, a high proportion (concerning six tools out of seven, more than 70%) of the people utilize them. Although interest in social media is increasing, organizations do not tend to allow their employees to use social media technologies. This may be because they are concerned about the risks and consequences of a potential misuse. On the other hand knowledge workers and managers may not appreciate the value of using these tools because of a lack of motivation to share knowledge or they may not be aware of the advantages of using these tools for work purposes.

Knowledge Sharing Behaviour (Motivator Factors)

Authors were interested in to what extent the participants agree with the following statements concerning the factors relating to motivation for knowledge sharing. For each category a specific statement is identified which were scored on a 5-point Likert scale ranging from 1 (strongly disagree) to 5 (strongly agree) (KPMG Academy, 2014):

- **Reciprocity:** Willing to share knowledge with the colleagues in order to get useful knowledge from them in the future.

*Figure 4. Usage of external knowledge sharing technologies/practices**

**Clearly the percentages represent percentages relating to the organizations that provide the various knowledge sharing technologies/practices and therefore provide the possibility that employees make use of them.*

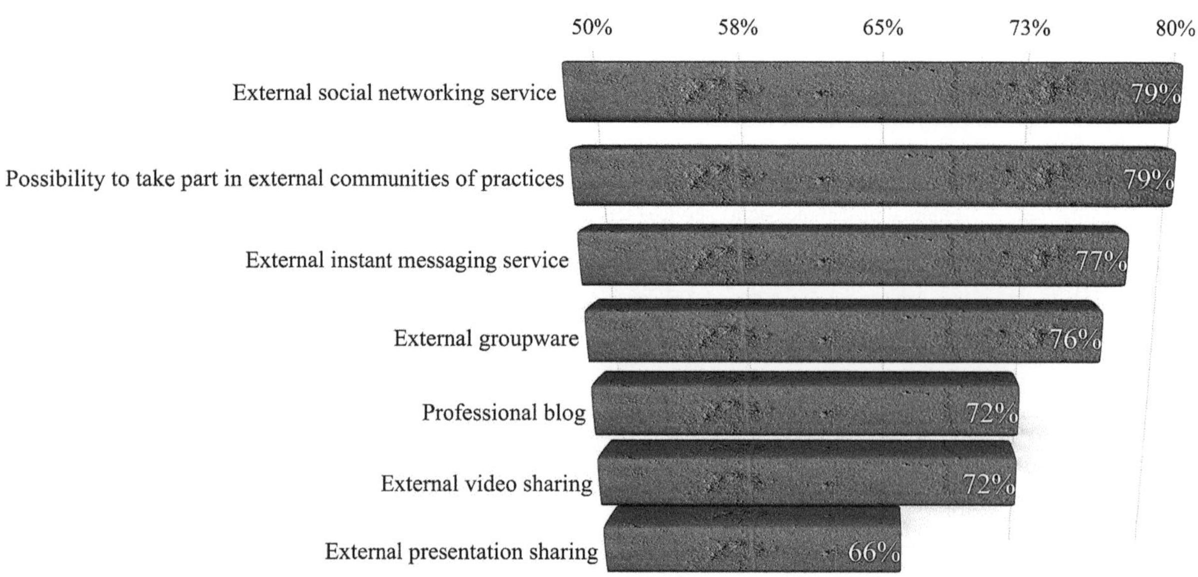

- **Reputation:** Willing to share my knowledge with my colleagues in order to be known as a knowledgeable person with valuable expertise.
- **Altruism:** I am willing to share my knowledge with my colleagues in order to help them.

Fully 95% of respondents claim that they share their knowledge with others because they want to help them. 66% consider that others have knowledge that they may need at a later date. In the sample only half (51%) agree with the statement that they share their knowledge, to be known as a knowledgeable person with valuable expertise. Thus the most powerful motivators, as identified by the survey, are altruism and reciprocity (Figure 5.).

These results run counter to the experience of the study group. In other research knowledge sharing is enforced by mandatory tools. This is followed by the next step when people share the result of their successful activity with others, as they are proud of it. Then when members of the community share information with each other on a reciprocal basis. Only few people reach the level of altruism. It can be concluded, that the practical experience and the self-assessment questionnaire results do not match (KPMG Academy, 2014).

Individuals' knowledge sharing behaviours in the workplace are divergent and highly dependent on their willingness to share knowledge. As a result, it is of critical importance to understand how to foster employees' knowledge sharing. A new research will examine the relationship between emotional intelligence traits (Petrides, 2009) and knowledge sharing. The aim of the research will be to define which emotional intelligence factors (well-being, emotionality, self-control and sociability) influence knowledge sharing. Researchers will use a more sophisticated measurement, for each category of knowledge sharing behaviour (altruism, reciprocity, reputation, loss of knowledge power, organizational reward) 5 component statements will be involved which will be scored on a 7-point Likert scale ranging from 1 (strongly disagree) to 7 (strongly agree) (Obermayer-Kovács & Komlósi, 2014).

Personal Characteristic Correlations

Although individuals might recognize the importance of knowledge management practices for the success of their daily business lives, it might be presumed that the degree of the willingness to share knowledge likely depends on their personal demographic features. The exploratory study examined the correlation between social media technologies - used for knowledge sharing during work – and the personal characteristics of respondents, such as their age and their work position. One typical hypothesis about the

Figure 5. Knowledge sharing motivators

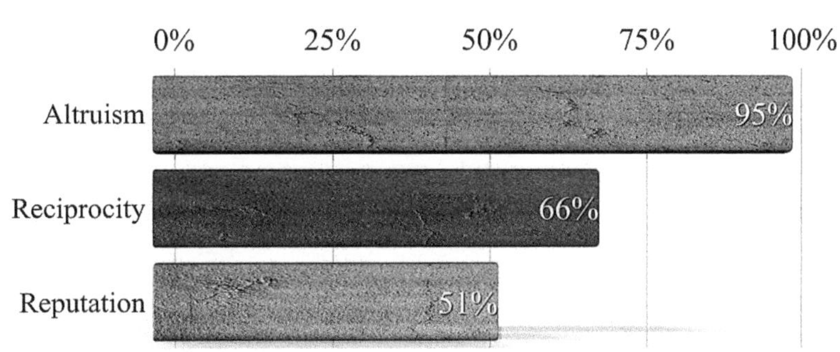

affinity of individuals with respect to knowledge management and social media technologies is that the younger generations are likely to have a greater affinity for using them.

Methodology

Using dataset SPSS, the authors investigated descriptive statistics, including Pearson's chi-squared test and contingency tables. A contingency table (also referred to as cross tabulation or cross tab) is a type of table in a matrix format that displays the (multivariate) frequency distribution of the variables. Pearson's chi-squared test is used to test the independence of variables. The chi-square test is a useful tool to determine whether it is worth interpreting a contingency table. A significant result of this test means that the cells of a contingency table should be interpreted. A non-significant test means that no effects were discovered and chance could explain the observed differences in the cells. In this case, an interpretation of the cell frequencies is not useful. Contingency tables are constructed by listing all the levels of one variable as rows in a table and the levels of the other variables as columns, then finding the joint or cell frequency for each cell. The cell frequencies are then summed across both rows and columns.

RESULTS

The study examined the relationship between individual characteristics and usage of internal/external social media technologies (Gaál et al., 2014).

Internal Social Networking Service

Regarding internal social networking service there is a relationship with both individual characteristics. As the age of the individual increases, the willingness to use this tool for knowledge sharing during work increases: 25% of Generation Y, 41% of Generation X, 55% of Baby Boomers.

Authors investigate the willingness to use internal social networking classified by position, only 26% of white collar workers, while nearly half (47%) of managers (middle level and top management) utilize the internal social networking service. The higher one's position is the greater the need for such a tool, which facilitates to establish collaboration with colleagues working in other departments or in other countries at an international organization. Younger people choose open systems and they use applications that provide free access anytime and anywhere and they do not use the term Intranet at all.

Internal Instant Messaging Service

The survey data demonstrates that the usage of internal instant messaging service is used by 58% of top management a little bit more than one third of the middle level managers and white collar workers (38%). For international organizations, at top management level there are numerous negotiations that take place across national borders, and these tools provide a more cost-effective solution supporting such negotiations.

Presentation Sharing Technology

Utilization of presentation sharing technologies are the following: 60% of Baby Boomers, 39% of Generation X, and only 35% of Generation Y. What could be the reason for this result? How many people make presentations nowadays at all? For example, the TED talks are typically held without any presentation, some photos may be used as an illustration. Or just think about using Prezi, which is an auto-sharing application.

External Social Networking Service

With respect to external social media technologies only one significant relationship was encountered. Regarding the external social networking service (e.g. Facebook, LinkedIn), the higher the position of the individual in the organization, the more frequently they make use of external social networking for work- related purposes. Thus, 68% of top management, 59% of middle level managers and only almost the half (49%) of white collar workers use this tool for knowledge sharing during work. However, it is important to make a distinction between Facebook and LinkedIn. With respect to Facebook, usage would be greater among those in lower positions. However, in the case of LinkedIn it might be expected higher usage among higher positions because it is generally known that the executive head hunting companies often gather information from that site. The result is a demonstration of the fact that individuals at lower levels of the organization (members of Gen Y) are more likely to make use of external social networking for friendship and personal communication rather than work related activities.

PRACTICAL IMPLICATIONS AND RECOMMENDATIONS

Many organizations that use social media struggle how to successfully integrate it into their daily business routines. The challenge can be found within the creation, execution, and enforcement of social media policies. Organizations do not establish policies to govern social media usage or can find their policy difficult to enforce due to lack of employee engagement and training on that topic. Organizations begin to realize the true value to be gained by social media adoption, consideration of workforce risk is essential for avoidance of loss of employee goodwill, information breaches, and reputational damage. Many social media policies are negatively oriented and have the directions for what not to do. It is better to impact employees of a positive social media policy with a positive orientation. Organizations are challenged with fully adopting social media and capitalizing on all of its benefits. Now they have the ability to utilize knowledge from external audiences around the globe that they could never reach before. Additional benefits include the ability to enhance the public image, improve interactions with customers, and promote employee engagement. But it is not without internal and external risk (KPMG, 2012):

- **Internal Risks:**
  - Employees deliberately leak privileged information that belongs to the organization.
  - The creation of public record related to internal employment issues.
  - Ownership issues regarding public forums/networks where employees might engage with customers to discuss business issues.

  - Introduction of sensitive personal information into the workplace (politics, religion, sexual orientation, lifestyle issues).
- **External Risks:**
  - The potential for viral growth of negative sentiment either in response to organization communications or simply a market discussion on products or services.
  - Inappropriate commentary on organization financial performance.
  - Misrepresentation of organization's position on public issues.
  - Damage to company's reputation or desired brand image.
  - Data privacy breach related to lost personal identifiable information.

The research was designed to find out more about the relation between social media tools and knowledge sharing within organizations. It can be stated that in the Hungarian organizations social media has not been widely achieved as most of the organizations do not allow their employees to utilize the benefits of the social media tools and do not support the development of social networks through these technologies. There are several social media tools that can be used by the communities with the aim to share knowledge with the wider audience and within the organization.

Bellow comes a selection of the possible knowledge sharing tools (those which the Hungarian research investigated) that could be used by the communities with the aim to share knowledge with the wider audience and within the community:

- **Facebook:** Communities can create the page to the Facebook with the aim to share information/knowledge to the followers of their community page. Page can be created by focusing only on own community or on wider audience. By focusing on the community's internal communication, the specific information is shared only with the members. By focusing on the wider audience, the page is accessible for all the members and shared information is informative, commercial, focusing on latest news, achievements and so on. Facebook can become as part of the community webpage. Facebook's strength is that most of the people are using it; they don't have to register to another system, but as a weakness, community members may want to separate the personal and professional life and not to use the same account as part of the professional community.
- **LinkedIn:** The community members can use LinkedIn for creating their individual profile page (create their expanded CVs) with the aim to share their professional knowledge addition to personal information. Communities should take advantage of such individual pages for aggregating the community knowledge. It can be a perfect tool for finding information and experts.
- **Meetup:** People are contacting with others generally with the professional aim. Strengths are that most people are members in these services, so they are very quick to set up, but weaknesses can be that the services are not open and tend to be closed towards outside tools and contents. Therefore, the community is dependent on the services offered by the provider, and other services can usually not be integrated easily.
- **Skype:** Facilitate near real-time text based communication and knowledge sharing between two or more participants over a network. Organizations can use it for quick questions and clarifications, for coordinating and scheduling tasks or social meetings. Moreover, it has additional features like the immediate receipt of acknowledgment or reply, group chatting, conference services (including voice and video) or conversation logging and file transfer. It is also possible to save a conversation for later reference. There can be numerous negotiations take place across national borders,

and this tool means a more cost-effective solution. Strength is the possibility to communicate as often as needed and therefor to build the sense of community. The meetings can be in general later re-listened by those members who did not have a chance to participate. The weakness is that this is rather related with the personal barriers than tool – people may be passive participants of the meeting.

- **GoogleDocs:** Community members who have access to the GoogleDocs have a chance to modify the materials. Text documents, spreadsheets, forms and presentations can be created, edited, stored and shared. The tools are useful when a team with Internet access wants to collaborate on the creation and maintenance of files and easily share them with others online. Strength of the tool is the possibility to save the documents in the shared server, documents are modified in the shared space and therefore the information is updated. In general, many people do have the Google account as well, meaning that they do not have to register to the new space.
- **Weblogs:** Where there is access to the Internet, blogs provide an easy way to communicate knowledge. Blogs have the power to help organizations foster relationships with colleagues, partners, stakeholders, etc. They are focusing on partners, employees or everyone with the aim to share information or knowledge. In an organization setting blogs can be used for multiple purposes: promoting products to customers, informing shareholders. Strength can be that weblogs are one of the easiest and quickest ways to reach the wider audience. Entries in the weblogs are usually open to the comments and therefore interesting discussions may occur. Weakness is that dynamically updated weblog of the community presumes quite lot of time and therefore persons should be named who are responsible for writing blogposts.
- **YouTube:** Using video to share knowledge brings a visual aspect that can quickly convey ideas that may take much longer in text. Organizations can use it for demonstration of something (procedure) or to capture of a live event to share widely out on the web to those who could not be there.
- **SlideShare:** The website can be used for businesses to share PowerPoint slides among employees more easily. SlideShare also provides users the ability to rate, comment on, and share the uploaded content. Slideshows can easily be embedded on websites, blogs and shared on social media networks like Facebook, Twitter and LinkedIn. The social sharing allows people to view the slides directly on social media making it a viral content-sharing platform.

Regarding the generational differences, employees from Generation Y may have no issues being asked to use a certain social media tool, a baby boomer may feel overwhelmed and frustrated by such a request and alike prefer face-to-face meetings or phone calls. Generation X and Y do not need face-to-face meetings and would prefer to pick up the phone to send a text versus make a call. Relationship building for this group often occurs through simply "pinging" their social media networks. Implementation of a policy centred on social media can prove to be challenging with a diverse workforce. Age is often not only the basis for the issue; it's more the acceptance, readiness, and adaption to change. In fact, research has shown that the fastest-growing demographic for Facebook and other social media tools is those member of Baby boomers. They are able to quickly learn and use new devices. However, introducing a new piece of technology to this population should be different than introducing it to those who have grown up with technology from their early years.

As adoption of social media tools readily grows, for both internal and external communications, it becomes important to clearly define and articulate a social media policy. While Baby boomers may be more resistant to initially using social media and accepting social media policy, Generation X and Y will almost positively grow frustrated if an organization does not use social media or fails to properly manage or recognize its use. Contrary to popular belief, social media has shown to increase productivity and employee engagement if controlled appropriately. It can also foster innovation through collaboration. As a result, more than half of the organizations using social media technology have achieved best-inclass performance (KPMG, 2012).

For organizations that wish to enhance knowledge sharing it is becoming essential that they integrate social media tools into their daily business routines. Employees must be given easy access to such tools and be provide with appropriate training. Researchers would observe that there are numerous opportunities to use social media tools in a manner meaningful to organizations:

- **Communication between Employees Can Be Encouraged to Support Problem Solving:** If organization needs an expert for a specific task, a post can be placed on a blog and likely receive a response from another employee or search on LinkedIn to find a person, who can help.
- **Convert Personal Knowledge to Organisational Knowledge:** If the senior employees record videos about their work and share it with the new employees, the organization can use these videos instead of expensive training programs to explain the details.
- **Discuss Professional Problems:** With a group of people who are active practitioners in a particular area, professional communities (communities of practices – CoP) can be useful because they are neutral and can provide a way to share best practices, ask questions of and provide support for each other outside the organization.
- **Reduce Time and Money Through Integrated System:** Using a "new" technology, the calendar, but not because of the calendar function, but organizing and sharing events, meetings, making appointment in a shorter time (instead of phone calls or sending lots of e-mails).

In general, it is recommended that management support the introduction of social media technologies, establish the terms and conditions of their usage, communicate the benefits and provide the necessary training for their effective use. Moreover, organizations should develop a reward system to provide additional motivation to employees to use social media tools for knowledge sharing.

FUTURE RESEARCH DIRECTIONS

The research could be expanded, as it would be interesting to make a comparison between knowledge sharing practices and usage of social media tools in other countries. The authors are already working on extending their work in this manner.

CONCLUSION

Amazingly rapid expansion of the content sharing technologies has led to many of these technologies becoming an integral part of many people's daily routine. People can easily collaborate and work with their colleagues at the other side of the world with the support of professional, fast instant messaging services in an effective way.

Communities of practices' "Meetup" video can be accessed almost immediately after the event on a video sharing site. Organizations have to clearly identify what information and knowledge is to be kept confidential and what is to be shared and made available to others. Such practices as crowd-sourcing and open innovation practices have demonstrated the value of sharing information and knowledge that has previously been considered to be confidential.

In future, it can be expected that both the internal and external usage of social media tools will increase as social media emerges a new perspective. Enormous information and knowledge can be shared using powerful tools to a world in which the social factors play an essential role. In the new accelerated world, numerous technologies have been developed to support social capital connections (social networking services like Facebook, LinkedIn) and to communicate in a more effective way (instant messaging services like Skype, Viber).

This chapter introduces a Hungarian exploratory survey that explored the usage of social media technologies through an investigation of the willingness of employees to participate in knowledge sharing. In addition, it has explored whether there are generational differences relating to knowledge sharing behaviours. The sample was gathered in Hungary, so authors made statements only for the Hungarian organizations. However, this permitted an in-depth study, and the scope of the survey with 299 respondents was larger than similar previous research studies. The results have shown that Hungarian organizations prefer not to allow the usage of external social media; but where the employees are supported to reach these tools, high proportion of the people utilize them. Most of the findings were unexpected and are not consistent with stereotypes about the generations. It was hypothesized that younger generations have a greater willingness to use social media technologies. Based on the findings it can be stated that the members of Generation Y (younger generation) or employees with lower level position are less likely to use social media technologies in the workplace. Authors would postulate that this is because social media tools are more common among young people but they use them for private purposes, while using these tools for work (mainly for knowledge sharing or professional development) is more typical for Generation X and Baby Boomers (elder generations).

In 1993 Drucker predicted how Knowledge Economy will need to progress in order to obtain competitive advantage. He stated that "the productivity of knowledge is going to be the determining factor in the competitive position in a company, an industry, an entire country. No country, industry or company has any 'natural' advantage or disadvantage. The only advantage it can possess is the ability to exploit universally available knowledge. The only thing that increasingly will matter in national as in international economics is management's performance in making knowledge productive" (Drucker, 1993. pp. 193). It seems that he predicted the rise of the online, open source, social media tools that can become widely available and prevalent in modern business life. The willingness to use these technologies by Generation Y (and later for Generation Z) will not be enough. These new generations must be encouraged to make use of these technologies for work as well as for non-work related activities.

REFERENCES

Alavi, M., & Leidner, D. E. (1999). Knowledge Management Systems: Issues, Challenges, and Benefits. *Communications of the Association for Information Systems*, *1*(7), 1–37.

Anderson, P. (2007). What is Web 2.0? Ideas, technologies and implications for education. *JISC Technology & Standards Watch,* 1-64.

Barney, J. (1986). Organizational culture: Can it be a source of sustained competitive advantage? *Academy of Management Review*, *11*(3), 656–665. doi:10.5465/AMR.1986.4306261

Bartol, K. M., & Locke, E. A. (2000). Incentives and motivation. In S. Rynes & B. Gerhardt (Eds.), *Compensation in organizations: Progress and prospects*. San Francisco: Lexington Press.

Bock, G. W., Zmud, R. W., Kim, Y. G., & Lee, J. N. (2005). Behavioral Intention Formation in Knowledge Sharing: Examining the Roles of Extrinsic Motivators, Social-Psychological Forces, and Organizational Climate. *Management Information Systems Quarterly*, *29*(1), 87–111.

Bonson, E., & Flores, F. (2011). Social media and corporate dialogue: The response of the global financial institutions. *Online Information Review*, *35*(1), 34–49. doi:10.1108/14684521111113579

Bowley, R. C. (2009). *A comparative case study: Examining the organizational use of social networking sites*. Hamilton: The University of Waikato.

Brzozowski, M. J. (2009). WaterCooler: Exploring an organization through enterprise social media. In *Proceedings of the ACM 2009 International Conference on Supporting Group Work* (pp. 219–228). New York: ACM Press. doi:10.1145/1531674.1531706

Choo, C. (1998). *The Knowing Organization: How Organizations Use Information for Construct Meaning, Create Knowledge and Make Decision*. New York: Oxford Press.

Davenport, T. H., & Prusak, L. (1998). *Working Knowledge: How Organizations Manage What They Know*. Boston: Harvard Business School Press.

DiMicco, J. M., & Millen, D. R. (2007). Identity management: Multiple presentations of self in Facebook. In *Proceedings of the ACM 2007 International Conference on Supporting Group Work* (pp. 383–386.). New York: ACM Press. doi:10.1145/1316624.1316682

Drucker, P. (1993). *Post-capitalist Society*. Oxford, UK: Butterworth-Heinemann.

Dumbrell, D., & Steele, R. (2014). Social Media Technologies for Achieving Knowledge Management Amongst Older Adult Communities. *Procedia: Social and Behavioral Sciences*, *147*, 229–236. doi:10.1016/j.sbspro.2014.07.165

Edvinsson, L., & Malone, M. S. (1997). *Intellectual Capital*. London: Piatkus.

Gaál, Z., Szabó, L., & Obermayer-Kovács, N. (2014). Personal knowledge sharing: Web 2.0 role through the lens of Generations. In *Proceedings of European Conference on Knowledge Management* (pp. 362-370). Santarem, School of Management and Technology Press.

Gottschalk, P. (2007). *CIO and corporate strategic management: changing role of CIO to CEO*. Hershey, PA: Idea Group Publication. doi:10.4018/978-1-59904-423-1

Grail Research. (2011). *Consumers of Tomorrow Insights and Observations About Generation Z*. Retrieved January 09, 2013, from http://www.grailresearch.com/pdf/ContenPodsPdf/Consumers_of_Tomorrow_Insights_and_ Observations_About_Generation_Z.pdf

Grant, R.M. (1996). Toward a knowledge-based theory of the firm. *Strategic Management Journal, 17*, 109-122.

Gray, P. H. (2001). The Impact of Knowledge Repositories on Power and Control in the Workplace. *Information Technology & People*, *14*(4), 368–384. doi:10.1108/09593840110411167

Hall, H. (2001). Input-friendliness: Motivating Knowledge Sharing Across Intranets. *Journal of Information Science*, *27*(2), 139–146. doi:10.1177/016555150102700303

Hemsley, J., & Mason, R. M. (2013). Knowledge and knowledge management in the social media age. *Journal of Organizational Computing and Electronic Commerce*, *23*(1-2), 138–167. doi:10.1080/10919392.2013.748614

KPMG. (2012). *Human resources and social media*. KPMG International Research report. MCGraphics.

KPMG Academy. (2014).*Organizational Knowledge Sharing in Hungary 2013/2014. KPMG Academy – University of Pannonia Research Report*. Budapest: KPMG.

KPMG-BME Academy. (2006).*Knowledge Management in Hungary 2005/2006. KPMG-BME Academy – University of Pannonia Research Report*. Budapest: KBA Oktatási Kft.

Kugel, J., & Schostek, C. (2004). *Rewards for knowledge sharing*. Retrieved June 12, 2007, from http://www.gurteen.com/gurteen/gurteen.nsf/id/rewards-k-sharing

Lin, H. F. (2007). Effects of Extrinsic and Intrinsic Motivation On Employee Knowledge Sharing Intentions. *Journal of Information Science*, *33*(2), 135–149. doi:10.1177/0165551506068174

Lin, H. F., & Lee, G. G. (2004). Perceptions of Senior Managers Toward Knowledge-sharing Behavior. *Management Decision*, *42*(1), 108–125. doi:10.1108/00251740410510181

Ma, W. W., & Chan, A. (2014). Knowledge sharing and social media: Altruism, perceived online attachment motivation, and perceived online relationship commitment. *Computers in Human Behavior*, *39*, 51–58. doi:10.1016/j.chb.2014.06.015

Masrek, M. N., Rahim, H. A., Johare, R., & Rambli, Y. R. (2011). Intranet Supported Knowledge Sharing Behavior. *Journal of Organizational Knowledge Management*, *2011*, 1–11. doi:10.5171/2011.802263

Mueller, J. (2012). Knowledge sharing between project teams and its cultural antecedents. *Journal of Knowledge Management*, *16*(3), 435–447. doi:10.1108/13673271211238751

Murray, S., & Peyrefitte, J. (2007). Knowledge type and communication media choice in the knowledge transfer process. *Journal of Managerial Issues*, *19*(1), 111–133.

Nielsen, P., & Razmerita, L. (2014). Motivation and Knowledge Sharing through Social Media within Danish Organizations. In *Creating Value for All Through IT* (pp. 197–213). Springer Berlin Heidelberg. doi:10.1007/978-3-662-43459-8_13

Nonaka, I., & Takeuchi, H. (1995). *The Knowledge-creating Company*. New York: Oxford University Press.

Nonaka, I., & Von Krogh, G. (2009). Tacit Knowledge and Knowledge Conversion: Controversy and Advancement in Organizational Knowledge Creation Theory. *Organization Science*, *20*(3), 635–652. doi:10.1287/orsc.1080.0412

O'Reilly, T. (2005). *What is Web 2.0? Design patterns and business models for the next generation of software*. Retrieved June 7, 2014, from http://www.oreilly.com/pub/a/web2/archive/what-is-web-20.html

Obermayer-Kovács, N., & Csepregi, A. (2007): Perspectives of Knowledge Management – Investigations at Hungarian Organizations. In *Proceedings of Business Scienes Symposium for Young Researchers, Feast of Hungarian Science 2007* (pp. 27-36). Budapest: Budapesti Műszaki Főiskola.

Obermayer-Kovács, N., & Komlósi, E. (2014). What emotional intelligent traits enable managers to Share knowledge for work-related quality of life? In *Proceedings of Makelearn 2014: Human Capital without Borders International Conference* (pp. 325-333). Portorož: International School for Social and Business Studies.

Obermayer-Kovács, N., Komlósi, E., Szenteleki, C., & Tóth, E. V. (2015). Exploring Emotional Intelligence Trait Enablers for Knowledge Sharing: An Empirical Study. *International Journal of Synergy and Research*, *4*(1), 7–23. doi:10.17951/ijsr.2015.4.1.7

Panahi, S., Watson, J., & Partridge, H. (2012). Social Media and Tacit Knowledge Sharing: Developing a Conceptual Model. In *Proceedings of World Academy of Science, Engineering and Technology, World Academy of Science, Engineering and Technology* (pp. 1095–1102). Paris, France: WASET.

Peppler, K. A., & Solomou, M. (2011). Building creativity: Collaborative learning and creativity in social media environments. *On the Horizon.*, *19*(1), 13–23. doi:10.1108/10748121111107672

Petrides, K. V. (2009). *Technical Manual for the Trait Emotional Intelligence Questionnaires (TEIQue)*. London: Psychometric Laboratory.

Polányi, M. (1966). *The Tacit Dimension*. London: Routledge & Kegan Paul.

Prahalad, C. K., & Hamel, G. (1990). The core competence of the corporation. *Harvard Business Review*, (May-June): 79–91.

Reeves, T. C., & Oh, E. J. (2007). Generation differences and educational technology research. In *Handbook of research on educational communications and technology* (pp. 295–303). Mahwah, NJ: Routledge.

Ryu, S., Ho, S. H., & Han, I. (2003). Knowledge Sharing Behavior of Physicians in Hospitals. *Expert Systems with Applications*, *25*(1), 113–122. doi:10.1016/S0957-4174(03)00011-3

Sigala, M., & Chalkiti, K. (2015). Knowledge management, social media and employee creativity. *International Journal of Hospitality Management*, *45*, 44–58. doi:10.1016/j.ijhm.2014.11.003

Spender, J. C. (1996). Making knowledge the basis of a dynamic theory of the firm. *Strategic Management Journal*, *17*(S2), 45–62. doi:10.1002/smj.4250171106

Steinfield, C., DiMicco, J. M., Ellison, N. B., & Lampe, C. (2009). Bowling online: social networking and social capital within the organization. In *Proceedings of the Fourth International Conference on Communities and Technologies* (pp. 245–254). New York, NY: ACM Press. doi:10.1145/1556460.1556496

Stewart, T. A. (1997). *Intellectual Capital: The New Wealth of Nations*. New York: Doubleday Dell Publishing Group. Inc.

Surowiecki, J. (Ed.). (2005). *The Wisdom of the Crowds*. New York: Anchor Books.

Susanty, A. I., & Wood, P. C. (2011). The Motivation to Share Knowledge of the Employees in the Telecommunication Service Providers in Indonesia. *International Proceedings of Economics Development & Research*, *5*(2), 2–159.

Sveiby, K. E. (1997). *The New Organizational Wealth: Managing and Measuring Knowledge Based Assets*. San Francisco: Berrett-Koehler Pub. Inc.

Vuori, V. (2011). *Social Media Changing the Competitive Intelligence Process: Elicitation of Employees' Competitive Knowledge*. Academic Dissertation. Retrieved June 7, 2014, from http://dspace.cc.tut.fi/dpub/bitstream/handle/123456789/20724/vuori.pdf

Weingarten, R. M. (2009). Four generations, one workplace: A gen x-y staff nurse's view of team building in the emergency department. *Journal of Emergency Nursing: JEN*, *35*(1), 27–30. doi:10.1016/j.jen.2008.02.017 PMID:19203677

Wenger, E. (2000). Communities of practice and social learning systems. *Organization*, *7*(2), 225–246. doi:10.1177/135050840072002

Yang, C., & Chen, L. C. (2007). Can Organizational Knowledge Capabilities Affect Knowledge Sharing Behavior? *Journal of Information Science*, *33*(1), 95–109. doi:10.1177/0165551506068135

Yates, D., & Paquette, S. (2011). Emergency knowledge management and social media technologies: A case study of the 2010 Haitian earthquake. *International Journal of Information Management*, *31*(1), 6–13. doi:10.1016/j.ijinfomgt.2010.10.001

Yesil, S., & Dereli, S. F. (2013). An empirical investigation of organisational justice, knowledge sharing and innovation capability. *SciVerse Science Direct.*, *75*, 199–208.

Yu, T. K., Lu, L. C., & Liu, T. F. (2010). Exploring factors that influence knowledge sharing behavior via weblogs. *Computers in Human Behavior*, *26*(1), 32–41. doi:10.1016/j.chb.2009.08.002

KEY TERMS AND DEFINITIONS

Collaboration: Enables individuals to work together in order to achieve a defined and common business purpose.

Generations: The theory that people born within an approximately 20-year time period share a common set of characteristics based on the historical experiences, economic and social conditions, technological advances, and other societal changes they have in common.

Knowledge: The whole of information, experiences, routines, practices etc. that can be connected with people, can be found in the mind of a person or group or in electronic or paper documents and can be broadened during sharing that occurs between the knowledge giver(s) and the knowledge receiver(s).

Knowledge Management: Describes the processes of acquiring, developing, sharing, exploiting and protecting organizational knowledge to improve organizations' competitiveness.

Knowledge Sharing: A process by which knowledge is converted into a form that other individuals can understand and can collaborate to develop new ideas.

Knowledge Sharing Behaviour: By which an individual voluntarily provides other people with access to his/her knowledge.

Social Media Tools: Collaborative technologies which encourage collaboration, participation and build networks based on personal and professional interest.

Chapter 2
The Role of Social Media for Knowledge Dissemination in Medical Tourism:
A Case of India

Anita Medhekar
Central Queensland University, Australia

ABSTRACT

The use of social media for information dissemination for education, environmental movement, natural disasters, emergency, election campaign, grass root movements, non-profit organisations, public health communication, and marketing for health promotion, e-governance, and political revolutions is well known. The economic significance of the health and medical tourism sector in the global healthcare business should not be underestimated. Internet is playing a leading role as a platform for the dissemination of medical tourism business information. In this century, more and more actual and potential tourists are accessing the internet and social media applications to find and disseminate factual information regarding medical tourism facilitators, destinations, super-speciality hospitals, specialist doctors and nurses, quality and accreditation, accommodation facility, cost, waiting period for surgery and sharing their positive and negative experiences to inform potential medical tourists. Healthcare providers and medical tourists acquire information, create, collaborate, communicate and disseminate healthcare and medical tourism related information through the Word-of-Social-Media (WoSM) tools such as FaceBook, Flickr, Twitter, Blogs, Forums, YouTube patient testimonials, Google Plus, LinkedIn, Photo and video sharing, Alexa and mobile applications. Therefore social media has a great potential as an information source and a knowledge dissemination tool for tourism industry to network and create clusters locally and globally, to exploit new innovative technologies for interaction and collaboration between the healthcare providers as well as the medical tourists. The main contribution of this chapter is to explore and discuss the role and use of social media applications for knowledge dissemination by hospitals and the medical tourists in the global business of medical tourism in India.

DOI: 10.4018/978-1-5225-0495-5.ch002

INTRODUCTION

The current and potential impact of networking through social media tools on the global healthcare industry is significant. Travelling abroad for medical treatment, popularly also known as medical tourism is a growing phenomenon. High healthcare domestic cost, long waiting period for surgery, uninsured or under-insured and non-availability of treatment due to regulation, in developed countries are the key factors driving medical travel/ tourism overseas. Potential medical tourists as patients are gathering information from various sources before they make a decision to travel abroad for medical treatment and surgery. With the adoption and growth of internet, Health 2.0 and e-Health is specially playing a key role in the dissemination of medical travel information through its various social media tools, where healthcare providers and medical tourists as patients develop and create User-Generated-Content (UGC) information communities with similar interest on the internet. The main contribution of this chapter is to explore and discuss the role of social media for knowledge dissemination in the growing global business of medical tourism in general and in context of Indian hospitals in particular. There is an increasing need for online medical tourism and health related information, which demonstrates the use of social media tools to create, communicate and inform the medical tourists.

The use of social media for information dissemination for public education, environmental movement (Vance, Howe, & Dellavale, 2009), natural disasters, emergency knowledge management and information systems (Yates & Paquette, 2010; Turoff, VandeWalle, & Hiltz, 2010; Jaeger, Schneidermann, Fleischmann, Preece, Qu, & Wu, 2007), election campaign, grass root movements (Palen, Hiltz, & Liu, 2007), non-profit organisations (Waters, Burnett, Lamm, & Lucas, 2009), public health communication, promotion and behavioural change (Korda & Itani, 2013; Thackeray, Neiger, Smith, & VanWagenen, 2012), social marketing for health promotion (Thackeray, Neiger, Hanson & Mckenzie, 2008), sharing the wisdom and knowledge of the elderly with the youth in India (Bandyopadhyay, Shaw, Banergee, & Nag, 2013), crisis messages communicated via social media by the businesses, for example; recall of food or faulty cars, e-governance (Freberg, 2012), and for political revolutions (Wulf, Misaki, Atam, Randall & Rohde, 2013) is well known. The economic significance of the health and medical tourism sector in the global healthcare business should not be underestimated. Global medical tourism market is growing at the rate of 25% per year (Howard, 2015), and internet is playing a leading role as a platform for the dissemination of medical tourism business information (Lunt, Hardey, & Mannion, 2010; Speier, 2011; Medhekar & Newby, 2012). Potential medical tourists' as patients also carry out internet searches for information which will guide them to make decision to travel abroad for medical surgery (Runnels & Carrera, 2012).

Medical tourism is a provision of 'cost effective' private medical care in collaboration with the tourism industry and private corporate hospitals (Brotman, 2010) like Apollo and Fortis group in India. It involves international trade or cross-border travel for global healthcare goods and services (Smith, Chanda, & Tangcharoensathien, 2009; Matoo & Rathindran, 2006) whether for diagnostic treatment, complex surgery, surrogacy, cosmetic surgery or for alternative therapies such as Ayurveda, Homeopathy, Naturopathy and Yoga. It needs partnership between the two service sectors of the economy namely; tourism and medicine (Bookman & Bookman, 2007; Medhekar & Ali, 2012). More and more actual and potential tourists are accessing the internet and social media tools to find, produce and disseminate factual information (Pan, MacLaurin, & Crotts, 2007) regarding medical tourism facilitators, destinations, super-speciality hospitals, specialist doctors and nurses, quality and accreditation, accommodation facility, cost, waiting period for surgery and sharing their positive and negative experiences to inform potential medical tourists and provide valuable feedback.

This chapter is structured as follows. The introductory section of the chapter provides introduction to the growing business of global medical tourism industry in general followed by the background to the global business of medical tourism in India in particular, in context of role of social media in knowledge dissemination and management by Indian hospitals. Section two provides the literature review on knowledge management, social media and medical tourism. Section three discusses the role of social media for knowledge dissemination in medical tourism business in case of India. Section four provides some discussion. The final section covers conclusion and future research directions to advance the knowledge in the field of social media and travelling interstate or abroad for medical treatment and surgery.

BACKGROUND

Thus, social media has a great potential as an information source and a knowledge dissemination tool for tourism industry to network, and create clusters locally and globally, in order to exploit new technologies for interaction and collaboration (Sigala, Christou, & Gretzel, 2012; Sigala, 2010; Chalkiti & Sigala, 2008; Bramwell & Sharman, 1999) between the providers as well as the tourists in the way they search, read and trust the information source. Social networking helps to communicate, collect and share information by creating e-healthcare clusters in online healthcare spaces and improve healthcare industry and the patient's knowledge, by leveraging collaboration through feedback and interaction in the medical tourism sector (Keckley, 2010). Social media when applied to the global business of medical tourism helps to overcome the communication barriers, and more so distance-barriers between medical tourists, facilitators and specialists' surgeons and hospitals, before a patient embarks on a journey abroad for healthcare and disseminating pre and post-surgery medical tourism experience to the world.

Further, with rising health and insurance cost and long waiting periods for surgery in home country, pushes the patients to make a decision to travel overseas for medical surgery to a developing country such as India, Thailand or Malaysia (Bookman & Bookman 2007; Horowitz & Rosensweig 2007; MacReady, 2007; Bies & Zacharia, 2007; Hopkins, Labonte, Runnels, & Packer 2010; Lunt, et al., 2010; Connell, 2013). Central Government of India was one of the first countries to recognise the economic benefits from medical tourism (GOI, 2003; Asian Medical Tourism Analysis, 2009), and used the internet to promote and disseminate information about medical tourism. Foreign medical tourists usually search and gather healthcare information online, before they make an informed decision to travel aboard for medical treatment and surgery (Medhekar & Newby, 2013). Therefore, medical tourism related online information is essential for healthcare and this health related knowledge needs to be managed properly by all the stake holders from the demand and the supply side in the medical tourism industry.

According to Davenport (1994), knowledge management is the process of capturing, distributing, and effectively using knowledge. Duhon (1998) defines, "Knowledge management is a discipline that promotes an integrated approach to identifying, capturing, evaluating, retrieving, and sharing all of an enterprise's information assets…these assets may include data base, documents, policies, procedures, and previously un-captured expertise and experiences in individual workers" (p. 9). There are increasing numbers of private hospitals involved in treating foreign patients in India and aboard, which are using internet as a platform to provide all the information about their healthcare facility, super-speciality, and cost comparison, to promote their business globally, besides adopting various innovative social media tools for connecting with the patients as well as healthcare professionals.

The application of social media tools by the tourism business and tourists is well known. However, it can also be applied to the global business of medical tourism which includes creation, collection, evaluation, storage, organisation, sharing and dissemination of healthcare information. The key users would be medical tourism healthcare service providers/hospitals, medical professionals (general practitioners, nurses, surgeons), medical tourism facilitators, including actual and potential medical tourists on various internet platforms of social media tools- Facebook, TripAdvisor, Twitter, LinkedIn, Blog, Pinterest, Discussion Forums, Chatroom, YouTube video and photo sharing websites. Social media is recognised as a critical tool to provide interactive and collaborative opportunities to effectively use, apply, and disseminate information.

The use of the above mentioned web tools which are technologies and are mostly 'user generated content' (UGC), will inform, educate and empower (Vance et al., 2009) from the supply side and the demand side the potential medical tourists by producing, creating, searching, consuming relevant and reliable knowledge and disseminating of information, regarding medical tourism, patient safety, destination, super-speciality hospital, medical specialist surgeons and success rate of surgeries, before they make an informed decision to travel for medical treatment as well as help to enhance the global business of medical tourism.

Even though social media is used by the medical tourism healthcare service providers and the medical tourists, findings from literature review uncovered a gap in the academic literature when it comes to the role and use of social media for knowledge dissemination in global business of medical tourism, where world is becoming our hospital. This will be the main contribution to the field based on the case of Indian hospitals. The purpose of this chapter is to study and explore:

1. The role and use of social media tools by medical tourism service providers/hospitals to promote, and medical tourists to help them make a decision to travel for medical treatment.
2. Which social media applications are used for knowledge dissemination regarding travelling abroad for medical treatment between medical tourists and the medical tourism service providers by exploring the hospital websites?

Global healthcare providers in the business of medical tourism are redefining their business model to suit the special needs of foreign medical tourists as patients. The online social media tools will help on one hand to create and produce information regarding medical travel, patient safety, destination and hospital quality and surgery experience by the actual medical tourists, to be consumed by the potential medical tourist in the future, on the other hand, it will enhance the business of medical tourism by building destination and brand awareness, for example 'Apollo Group of Hospitals' in India and abroad. The main objective is to share and exchange medical tourism related health information as soon as possible by using various social media tools by medical tourists and healthcare providers.

Social media for knowledge dissemination, when applied to medical tourism healthcare service providers and the medical tourists, helps to identify, create, produce and share healthcare related information by various social media applications. The aim here from the medical tourism provider's perspective is not just to promote its business in a competitive global healthcare environment and gain competitive advantage (Laszlo & Laszlo, 2002) but also help the actual medical tourists to produce, disseminate and share their User-Generated-Content (UGC) information regarding medical tourism experience and knowledge using social media tools. Various social media tools help to not only create knowledge, comment around a particular theme like medical travel, but also form e-health communities on the internet which manage the knowledge which has been created (Schang, Li, Wu, & Hou, 2011), and share positive and negative experiences with the potential medical tourists. According to Miller and Derse (2002), *e-health sites and private practitioners now offer, without face-to-face contact, treatments that have long been considered the practice of medicine: access to prescription drugs, a single consultation with a physician who remains anonymous, and ongoing treatment of an identified patient by an identified physician (p.162).*

In the 21st century since the growth of global medical tourism market, medical professionals and key stake holders from the supply side of the healthcare industry, and from the demand side the actual and potential medical tourists as patients, are increasingly using social media tools to create knowledge, exchange and find health information, seek social support with patients having similar health issues and thus network globally to share their healthcare experiences about travelling abroad for medical treatment (see Table 1).

The main motivation to use the social media tools by health care professionals and patients is to find health information, communicate and collaborate with other medical professionals (Van de belt, Engelen, Berben, & Schoonhoven, 2012; Cline & Haynes, 2011; Hawn, 2009; Eysenbach, 2008) and patients look for information on the internet online forums for healthcare self-management (Hawn, 2009; Tanis, 2008; Sillence, Briggs, & Fishwick, 2007) including information about medical treatment and surgery. Healthcare providers aim to improve quality in healthcare delivery (Kaplan & Haenlein, 2010; Chou, Hunt, Burke, Moser, & Hesse, 2009; Van de belt et al., 2012), to improve communication and relationships between healthcare professionals and patients, to improve communication between actual and potential medical tourists (Bosslet, Torke, Hickman, Terry, & Helft, 2011; Wald & Dube, 2007) besides connectivity, with allied healthcare services, collaborate with medical schools, accrediting bodies, insurance agencies efficiency and seek business opportunities for growth.

LITERATURE REVIEW

Knowledge Management

Effective and efficient management of information which is transformed into knowledge is essential for the survival of any industry (health, education, travel or tourism) or an economy in a competitive glo-

Table 1. Knowledge management in medical tourism

	Knowledge Management in Medical Tourism from Demand and Supply Side
Step 1	Knowledge creation
Step 2	Knowledge documentation
Step 3	Knowledge sharing/dissemination via social media tools
Step 4	Knowledge evaluation
Step 5	Knowledge application / medical travel decision
Step 6	Knowledge update (dynamic process)

Source: Developed for this paper

balised world, whether in the public or private sector. According to OECD (1996) a strongest economy knows how to create, disseminate, manage and apply knowledge in economies which is linked to innovation. Reliable and credible information is essential to make informed decisions in a business setting. According to Bennett and Gabriel (1999) knowledge management is concerned with the capture, storage, dissemination and use of knowledge.

Knowledge management for this paper will be defined as availability of health and medical tourism related information on the various social media tools such as LinkedIn, Flickr, YouTube, Blogs, Twitter, and FaceBook on hospital websites. Sometimes little information will be available on the hospital and medical tourism facilitator's website and other times, there will be information overload; which could be unreliable and conflicting and thus may necessitate increased information shifting and processing capabilities by a potential medical tourist with which to make informed decisions. Knowledge management systems via social media tools that will be useful for the medical tourism healthcare service providers as well as potential medical tourists must be factual, to be reliable in a complex global medical tourism healthcare industry, which is different from just tourism.

There are four phases of processing knowledge management which are interrelated as explained by McAdam and Reid (2000):

1. Knowledge construction,
2. Knowledge embodiment,
3. Knowledge dissemination, and
4. Application of knowledge.

All four can be applied in context of medical tourism. Individuals from the demand and the supply side have come together, either physically or virtually since the birth of internet websites to exchange goods, services and ideas. These can be tangible or intangible and thus individuals create, organise and disseminate knowledge via social media tools which is valuable to the medical tourists as well as healthcare service providers. Thus in context of global healthcare industry of medical tourism, knowledge first has to be constructed by the stake holders involved from the demand and the supply side and then embodied within the hospital/ healthcare organisations culture, practices, processes and patient safety culture. In the next step knowledge should be effectively disseminated amongst all the key stakeholders within the medical tourism healthcare organisation to provide two way knowledge transfer as suggested by Schlegelmilch and Chini (2003) that is actual medical tourist provide patient feedback to the healthcare organisation and the potential medical tourists, with the aim to apply the knowledge to improve transparency, healthcare and medical tourism policy, processes, practice, culture, and patient safety for effective and efficient delivery of world class quality of healthcare.

The knowledge based theory of the firm which involves basic knowledge transfers that create value inside and outside an organisation, as developed by Sveiby (2001) can also be applied in the context of medical tourism as explained in the discussion section. There are four channels by which knowledge can be transferred:

1. Knowledge transfers from external structure to individuals,
2. Knowledge transfers within the external structure,
3. Knowledge transfers from external to internal structure, and
4. Knowledge transfers from internal to external structure.

Therefore, internet is used as a platform where actual medical tourists develop and create health and medical related content and from online communities of common interest based on medical travel, particular health issue such as surrogacy or organ transplant in India, to disseminate such useful information and share their experiences with actual and potential (domestic or foreign) medical tourists. It is clearly noted by Hardey (1999) that, *using the internet is an inherently interactive process that involves users in a continual process of decision making* (p. 825). It is such a dynamic and an interactive internet platform of knowledge creation and dissemination, which is beneficial to the medical tourists and the healthcare providers and professionals.

According to Schang, Li Wu, and Hou (2011):

… the users draw from and contribute to knowledge data base simultaneously…and harness collective intelligence that enriches user experience, provides a unique and hard-to-replicate source of information (p.178).

Users can exchange valuable information by asking questions, sharing their experiences and thoughts, via social media tools. Global consumers of knowledge can identify the discipline specific information by knowing where this information is stored and managed by the internet to access and also contribute to that knowledge in real time and create further knowledge. These social media tools are used by hospitals involved in the business of medical tourism, along with the travel and hospitality industry.

Social Media and Knowledge Dissemination

Social media is different from internet. Social media tools, which the researcher calls in this paper Word-of-Social-Media (WoSM), are instruments to manage the content of the conversations on various forums in an online environment. For example: Facebook, TripAdvisor, Twitter, LinkedIn, Blog, Pinterest, Discussion Forums, Chatroom, Flickr, YouTube video and photo sharing websites. It is thus recognised as a critical tool to provide interactive and collaborative opportunities to effectively use, apply, create and disseminate User-Generated-Content (UGC) information. Knowledge on various topics is managed, shared and used on social media by bringing together various stakeholders with common interests (Yates & Paquatte, 2011) and build public relationships (Briones, Kuch, Liu, & Jin, 2011). In a healthcare setting social media tools such as YouTube and Facebook was first used in Europe and USA (Street, 2003). Adaptation of broadband internet and Web 2.0 can also enhance dissemination and implementation of health information which is research-based practices by clinicians and practitioners (Bernhardt, Mays, & Kreuter, 2011).

It is usually an interactive communication where information is shared and is consumer/patient centric, between the e-medical tourists and medical tourism e-healthcare service providers. Alternately terms like Medicine 2.0, Health 2.0 and e-Health technologies (Van de belt, et al., 2012; Chretien, Azar, & Kind, 2011; Hawn, 2009; Eysenbach, 2008) are also used to improve interaction, communication and collaboration between healthcare professionals and patients. Social media tools help in many ways:

1. To create and share health care related information (Kaplan & Haenlein, 2010; Vance et al., 2009),
2. Provide online social support (Bacigalupe, 2011) between patients,
3. Increased connection between individuals through direct participation (Chou et al., 2009) and
4. Participation and collaboration between key stake holders (Change Foundation, 2011).

Social media is emerging as an important medium through which information about medical travel/tourism is disseminated by the healthcare providers in general and more so by the actual medical tourist in particular. Korda and Itani (2013) have conducted an environmental scan about the types of social media used for health promotion. They found from the literature that healthcare related information has a positive behaviour change in health outcomes. They found that nearly 57% of generation X (born between 1961 and 1981) and 56% of generation Y (born between 1981 and 2001) searched for health related information; and in 2010, nearly 80% of the adults searched for health information using the internet search engines.

Social media is defined by Kaplan & Haenlein (2010) as *a group of Internet-based applications that allow the creation and exchange of user generated content* (p. 59). Further, Kaplan and Haenlein (2010 have classified broadly six (6) different types of social media namely:

1. **Collaborative Projects:** Such as Wikipedia, where the user can add, delete or change text based content and social book marking, where web bookmarks are stored and shared.
2. **Blogs:** Personal webpage managed by one person and allows comments by others.
3. **Content Communities:** Users create their personal profile page and share media content such as; text and photos on *Flickr,* videos on *YouTube, and* power point presentations on *Slide Share.*
4. **Social Networking Sites like Facebook and Myspace:** The users create personal information profile and invite colleagues and friends to have access to their profiles, photos, video, blogs, audio files and send e-mails and instant messages once accepted.
5. **Virtual Game Worlds:** The virtual social media where three dimensional environment is created where the users interact with each other in the form of '*Avatars'. They are of two types, virtual games worlds like X-Box and Sony Play-Station which required the users to follow the rules of the game.*
6. **Virtual Social Worlds:** The inhabitants live their virtual life as real life and behave freely without any rules and interact in a three dimensional virtual environment. Second life applications are the examples of virtual world where the user can do all the things in real life, and speak with Avatars, enjoy virtual stars, sea, sand, surgery and sunshine and create once content and sell virtually- like in e-commerce, virtual product, and hospital and destination tour.

Medical tourists and healthcare providers/hospitals can use all or few of the social media tools to seek information and to share their experience of treatment aboard, with friends and strangers, so that a medical tourist can make an informed decision to travel for medical treatment. Further hospitals and the medical tourism facilitators use the internet to communicate between healthcare professionals, advertise and promote their business and brand to attract potential foreign medical tourists (Gahlinger, 2008; Woodman, 2008). Motives underlying the use of social media tools (Twitter, Facebook, LinkedIn and YouTube) by patients and health care professionals, barriers and expectations in a healthcare setting were empirically studied by Antheunis, Tates, and Nieboer (2013). Their results showed that patients (59.9%) used Twitter for exchanging advice and increasing knowledge and (52.3%) used FaceBook for social support and advice. Further, medical professionals (70.7%) used LinkedIn and Twitter (51.2%) for communication with colleagues and for marketing reasons. Many studies have shown the adoption and use of social media tools to disseminate information in different industries (Bordie, Hamel, & Altman, 2003; Eyrich, Padman, & Sweetser, 2008).

Since the 21st century there is an increasing use of these tools in the healthcare sector, in context of health promotion programs, health communication, and health education, which are UGC associated with Web 2.0, discussion boards, blogs, videos, forwarded e-mails and wikis, as mentioned by Thackeray, Neiger, Hanson, & McKenzie, (2008), are *more powerful then agency-based advertising* (p.340), to positively influence the decision, choices and behaviours of family, friends and unknown strangers by networking on social media which is interactive. When people are faced with any health problem, they immediately search for health remedies on the internet, if they have access. Study by Pew Research Centre (2009), found that in 2008 internet related public health information was created and posted on blogs and discussion forums by 37% of adults, and 41% of adults read online health information posted by others on blogs. In addition, 13% of adults listened to health and medical issues on podcast and 29% used social networking sites for managing their health besides 12% shared or received health updates on twitter in two way communication.

Fisher and Clayton (2012) conducted a survey to study the use of social media (e-mails, texting twitter, YouTube, Mobile Apps, LinkedIn, Forums, X-box) by patients and nearly 83% of 111 patients used some type of social media for communication, and 41.6% would consider using it because of healthcare. Nearly 56% of the participants mentioned that they wanted the healthcare provider to communicate via social media for appointment, reminders, reporting diagnostic tests results, health information, prescription notice and reminders on discussion forums. Also younger patients used it more than the older >65 years patients. According to Deloitte (2010) 67% of surveyed physician and 65% of nurses were interested in using the applications of social media for professional networking. In USA nearly 700 hospitals have a social media presence to enhance communication and market their healthcare services to patients, health professionals, physicians, nurses, allied health care professionals, clinicians, researchers, government regulators and accrediting bodies. Thus, medical tourists are mainly seeking information about destination, hospital, specialist surgeon, accreditation, quality, pre and post-surgery care, cost, waiting time for surgery, patient safety and security through internet based online social media tools and also engaging key stake holders from the supply side in the business of medical tourism.

Medical Tourism

Since ancient times in India, people have been travelling for pilgrimage and alternative therapies to the Himalayas and Ashrams for meditation, yoga, herbal medicine and Ayurvedic treatment (Medhekar, 2014). Likewise, during the Roman Empire as well people travelled across border for spa and other herbal remedies (Weiermair & Mathies, 2004). Hence medical tourism where people travel abroad for medical treatment is a sub-set of health tourism and it is not a new phenomenon. It is a growing global healthcare business since the start of the 21st century where people are seeking complex medical treatment and surgeries such as cardiac surgeries, cosmetic surgery, dental, organ transplant, reproductive/ surrogacy and hip replacements. It is also an outsourcing of medical surgery abroad (Bies & Zacharia, 2007), and migration of patients to developing countries due to cost savings (Yeoh, Othman, & Ahmad, 2013). The key pull and push factors to travel abroad for medical treatment to developing countries like India, Thailand or Mexico is affordable cost of treatment, less waiting time for surgery, privacy and confidentiality, comparable or better quality of pre and post-surgical care, uninsured or under insured and treatment not available due to ethical and regulatory reasons (Keckely, 2008; Woodman, 2008; Medhekar, 2014; Medhekar, Wong, & Hall, 2014).

Medical tourism is about medical patients, who are travelling interstate or aboard for medical treatment. Bookman and Bookman (2007) have defined it as *international travel with the aim of improving one's health* (p.1). It is concerned with global international trade in healthcare services (Matoo & Rathindran, 2006; Connell, 2006), where people travel to an exotic destination for complex surgery and may also engage in some tourism activities. Medical tourism is also known as cosmetic tourism (Nassab, Hamnett, Nelson, Kaur, Greensell, Dhital, & Juma, 2010), reproductive tourism (Smith, Behrmann, Martin, & Williams-Jones, 2010), suicide tourism (Huxtable, 2009), stem-cell tourism (Kiatpongsan & Sipp, 2009), dental tourism (Turner, 2008; Barrowman, Grubor, & Chandu, 2010) and organ transplant tourism (Delmonicao, 2009) based on the type of treatment and surgery.

These healthcare related services are also advertised in a global health services market place to gain competitive advantage (Turner, 2010) in order to attract patients from around the world and give them a choice of destination and hospital, based on cost, waiting time, travel safety and quality of healthcare service delivery of medical treatment and surgery. Medical tourism also known as travel for healthcare, is defined as *the act of traveling abroad to obtain medical care* (Keckley, 2008, p. 4). Since the beginning of the 21st century this phenomenon is continuously growing exponentially (Bookman & Bookman, 2007; Keckley, 2008) and now the trend has been reversed where patients from developed country in large numbers are travelling to a developing country (MacReady, 2007; Horowitz, Rosensweig, & Jones, 2007; Medhekar & Ali, 2012), such as India for medical treatment and surgery mainly due to long queue, under insured or not insured, high cost, non-availability of medical treatment and increased disposable income in their home countries (Woodman, 2008; Crooks, Kingsbury, Snyder, & Johnston, 2010; Medhekar, 2014; Connell, 2013). These foreign medical tourists are seeking various types of treatments and complex surgeries using state-of-the-art medical equipment, and technology used by highly experienced and specialised medical professionals for example; dental, cosmetic, orthopaedic-hip and knee replacements, organ transplant, reproductive, cancer, cardiac eye surgery and stem-cell therapy.

Researchers have explored and researched medical tourism from different perspectives for example: economics, international trade, law and regulation, ethical, reproductive, cosmetic, social issues, poverty and inequality in healthcare provision, and quality and patient safety in healthcare. Studies based on content analysis have looked at the content of websites from the tourism provider's perspective for examples: web-based internet marketing by five star hotels and tour facilitators (Wan, 2002), destination image representation on website (Choi, Lehto, & Morrison, 2007), website information about international hotels, government and tourism organisations (Benckendorff & Black, 2000), and the website design and internet site marketing practices of luxury hotels and travel agents in Turkey (Baloglu & Pekcan, 2006; Roney & Ozturan, 2006).

Further, literature also shows studies related to use of internet and social media tools for sharing health related information and communication used by patients, nurses and medical professionals, which can be easily searched on Google (Bacigalupe, 2011; Briones et al., 2011; Van de belt, et al., 2012; Henry, Molnar, & Henry, 2012; Antheunis et al., 2013). It not only improves efficiency and effectiveness in delivery of quality healthcare but also improves relationship between the healthcare providers and medical tourists as patients. There are few research papers related to medical tourism and the use of internet (Lunt et al., 2010; Cormany & Baloglu, 2011; Mason & Wright, 2011; Medhekar & Newby, 2013) describing as to how medical tourists search for various sources of information, use internet and WoSM tools to contribute to patient testimonials and blogs to disseminate medical travel related experience and information on the internet.

The famous guide to medical travel such as ‘Patients beyond Borders’ by Woodman (2008), similarly the ‘Beauty from Afar: Guide to affordable and quality of cosmetic care’ by Shult & Corey (2006) and Industry Report on medical tourism by RNCOS (2010) have also used various medical travel website to write the guide and provide information to the potential medical tourists. Cormany and Baloglu (2011), study concluded that the information regarding healthcare services provided by the medical travel facilitators from the supply side, on their website to potential medical tourists, varied between continents and countries, which may influence the destination choice made by the medical tourist. However, WoSM helps to dessiminate information from the consumer or demand side which is more credible based on their medical travel experience. Mason and Wright (2011) studied the 66 medical tourism website content and found that the websites usually pormote the benefits more, then the risk of travelling abroad for medical treatment. It is usually the expereicnes of actual medical tourists which gives a balanced view of medical travel through the WoSM applications.

In 2009, India was second only to Thailand in medical treatment (IMT, 2009). India specialises in providing high end of medical treatment in super speciality hospitals to international patients (Crooks Turner, Snyder, Johnston, & Kingsbury 2011). The government of India has also played a key role in promoting medical and wellness tourism through its support for medical tourism by infrastructure investment, introducing M-Visa and M-Ex escort visa, advertising campaign, land subsidies for building hospitals, depreciation and import of medical equipment and international trade shows (Medhekar, 2014).

With the growth of international trade in travelling abroad for medical treatment many private hospitals are engaged in treating foreign patients in India, for example Apollo, Fortis and Wockhardt Group. Hospitals and medical patients are using the internet and various social media tools such as YouTube- audio, video patient testimonials, LinkedIn, Blogs and discussion forums to promote their business in a competitive global healthcare industry to promote and disseminate information regarding their super-medical facilities, quality of health care, treatment and specialist medical surgery (Crooks, et al., 2010). Thus from the literature it can be concluded that there is a need for knowledge management in medical tourism via adoption of various social media tools by the hospitals. Next section provides a case exploring the adoption of various social media tools by the branded Indian hospitals.

ROLE OF SOCIAL MEDIA FOR KNOWLEDGE DISSEMINATION IN MEDICAL TOURISM

Social media for knowledge dissemination can have significant impact on medical tourism industry:

1. Social media tools will change the global healthcare firm’s organisational culture, which is involved in treating domestic and foreign patients in the business of medical tourism. They will be under pressure to not only improve efficiency and effectiveness in terms of patient safety and quality in healthcare provision, but also disseminate information and promotion of global healthcare business via WoSM tools.
2. It is essential to establish a section of social media, by the healthcare provider and also from patient/medical tourist perspective, to have open and transparent discussion in order to share information with the healthcare organisation/hospital between medical and nonmedical professionals, to develop trust and thus collate, organise and make available the data related to various issues related to patient safety, surgical errors, quality, good practise) that arises in treating patients internally and

also the actual medical tourists by WoSM platforms such as; YouTube, blogs, and testimonials to share information and improve the delivery of healthcare services. Further, this will also improve patient-physician-partnership, relationship and build trust.

3. It will improve accountability and quality of information from the healthcare provider's perspective (supply side). This will help the potential medical tourist/patient (demand side) to make informed choice and decision before they travel abroad for medical treatment. As the global medical tourists are becoming increasingly informed and knowledgeable and demand information related to various concerns of travelling for medical treatment. The medical tourism healthcare providers all over the world need to become more credible, transparent and accountable regarding the claims they make about quality, cost, waiting time for surgery, state-of-the-art medical technology, accreditation, patient safety and security and ethical issues on their websites.
4. Knowledge dissemination will help to deliver quality and affordable health care service to its patients, by responding to foreign patient's feedback and concerns before they travel abroad, for treatment, that is pre and post travel surgery care.
5. Medical tourism hospitals will become more transparent and democratic by having an inclusive approach to take suggestions and feedback to improve healthcare service delivery. It is essential to thus involve all key stake holders concerned from the demand side (medical tourists and accompanying family) and the supply side (hospitals, government, accrediting bodies, allied healthcare, pharmaceuticals, pathology services, hospitality and accommodation industry, health and safety, security, travel industry, ethical and regulatory bodies related to healthcare).
6. Hospitals are using social media for the promotion of their medical tourism business. Social media helps the medical tourists to express their experiences, needs, likes and dislikes related to a particular medical tourism destination, medical facility or a specialist surgeon. It also helps the medical tourists to connect online in a virtual social setting and give and receive feedback knowledge and support emotionally that they need from fellow patients before or after the surgery.
7. Word-of-Social-Media helps the potential medical tourists to get this reliable information from the actual medical tourist's experience, immediate feedback, to make choices and decisions regarding travelling abroad for medical treatment. In the next section, this chapter explores social media and medical tourism in case of Indian hospitals.

Case of Indian Hospitals

Medical tourism is a partnership between the two sectors: medicine and tourism, where patients travel abroad for medical treatment, and also between two people: patient and physician. Increasingly tourism industry in general and health and medical tourism hospitals in particular, are using social multimedia tools for mass global collaboration between the medical tourists, healthcare providers and medical tourism facilitators on the internet to create and share medical tourism related content, health information, accreditation information, experiences, photos, YouTube, videos and audios as seen from Tables 2,4, and 5. Social media is very social, communicative, interactive, and helping to network and disseminate information and knowledge to the medical tourist. It helps to find information, read, create/produce, share experiences and disseminate knowledge regarding travel destinations, health and medical tourism related to cost of surgery, quality, accreditation, super-specialities and information regarding healthcare professionals, including the availability of all other services related to health /medical tourism that hospitals provide on their internet sites, as seen from Table 3.

Table 2. Web-based applications

Social Media Tools	Definitions
Medical Tourism TripAdvisor	Travel Web sites enable everyone to share and seek medical travel information and experience. Clients may want to share advice about hospital, doctor, super speciality, accommodation, restaurants, or choice of destination, airline flights and prices of surgery.
Twitter	Twitter sites for sharing latest news and photos regarding health and medical travel.
Blog	Blog Web sites are social networks built around the telling of medical tourism real life experiences.
Discussion Forums	People with common interests discuss and share information on a particular specialist topic like surrogacy (communities of interest).
Chatroom	Chat Web sites establish Web-based communication among medical tourist/patients on health and medical tourism.
YouTube video	U Tube video allows users to receive internet videos regarding the hospitals and destination including their treatment.
Photo sharing and Patient testimonials	Photo Sharing Web sites provide online photo services allowing users (healthcare provider as well as from the medical tourists as patient) to upload, manage and share photos about medical facility, services, medical travel and provide patient testimonials.
Mobile- Apps	Smart / i-Phone Mobile Applications for health and medical tourism.
FaceBook	Where people post and share their current status, news and photos.
Google+	Internet search engine with additional applications.
Hospital websites Google	Hospital home page on internet Google search platform • http://www.apollohospitals.com/ • http://www.wockhardthospitals.com/ • http://www.asianheartinstitute.org/ • http://www.fortishealthcare.com/ • http://www.jehangirhospital.com/ • http://www.rubyhall.com/ • http://www.narayanahealth.org/ • http://www.sanchetiinstituteresearchrehabilitation.com/ • http://www.maxhealthcare.in/index.php/about-us

Source: Developed for this paper.

Various social multi-media tools in context of popular branded medical tourism hospitals in India are examined for this paper. Hospitals create, manage and distribute the content of the hospitals and medical tourism facilitators. Further, discussions on various forums in an online environment such as-TripAdvisor, Twitter, Blog, Discussion forum, Chatroom, patient testimonials, U-Tube video and photo sharing website of the hospitals and medical tourism facilitators involved in the business of medical tourism are explored. All these internet tools help the medical tourist as consumers of global healthcare to make informed decisions and choices using the content on the social media sites established by the hospitals for communication. Further, the global medical tourism healthcare providers also need to adopt and develop their e-business models from the supply side and use the social media tools to develop, promote, create, manage and diffuse all their healthcare service information, as well as collect feedback from the medical tourists.

Method

For this study, the source of data collection was from the home page websites of nine famous private hospitals in India (See Table 2 for links) few of which have branches all over India like Apollo (one

Table 3. Hospital branches in India

Hospital Branches	Branch Location of Medical Tourism Hospitals-India
1- Apollo=31	India: Ahmedabad, Bangaluru, Chennai, Delhi, Hyderabad, Kakinanda, Kolkata, Aragonda, Bacheli, Bellary, Goa Bhubaneshwar, Lavasa, Karur, Ludhiana, Madurai, Mysore, Nashik, Pune, Nellore, Ranchi, Ranipet, Indore, Trichy, Vishakhapatnam & Tirivannamalai **Overseas:** Bangladesh-1
2- Narayana Health=19	North India: Jaipur West India: Palanpur, Ahmedabad, Mahuva, Dharwar & Bellary South India: Shimoga, Kolar, Mysore, Kuppam, Bangalore, Davangere & Hyderabad. East India: Guwahati, Berhampore, Kolkata, Durgapur, Raipur & Jamshedpur
3-Wockhardt=9	South Mumbai, North Mumbai, New Mumbai, Nashik, Goa, Nagpur Heart, Nagpur Super Speciality & Surat,
4-Fortis=30	North India: Delhi-6, Faridabad-1, Noida-1, Gurgaon-1, Kangra-1, Ludhiana-1, Amritsar-1, Mohali-1, Jaipur-1 & Dehradun-1. South India: Bangalore-6, Chennai-1 East India: Kolkata-3 West India: Raipur-1, kalyan-1, Mumbai-2, Vashi-1.
5-Asian Heart-1	Mumbai-1
6-RubyHall- 2	Pune-2 Ruby Hall Pune & Ruby Hall Wanorie Clinic
7-Jehangir-1	Pune-1, Partner with Apollo Group
8-Sancheti-1	Pune-1, Aundh Pune
9-MAX Health -11	North India: Max-Super-Speciality: Saket, Patparganj, Shalimar Bagh, Mohali, Batinda & Dehradun Max-Hospital: Noida, Gurgaon & Pitamputa Max-Multi-Speciality: Greater Noida & Panchsheel Park

Source: Developed for this paper current until 2nd of July 2015.

overseas branch in Bangladesh). These hospitals were found from the research reports (RANCOS, 2010), Google search engine, as well as from authors personal visits to these hospitals. Apollo, Forties, Wockhardt, Narayana Health (NH) and Max-Health (MH) have many branches all over India. Other four hospitals such as Asian Heart Institute in Mumbai, Sancheti, Ruby Hall, and Jahangir in Pune have one main branch in one location. These hospitals are involved in treating not only local but also international patients as medical tourist. Hospital home page websites were studied to find out the various social media tools used to disseminate information to the actual and potential medical tourists. Hospitals are using internet and WoSM tools to receive feedback and provide quick source of healthcare information regarding its facility and super-speciality to the medical tourist, medical tourism facilitators and all other businesses involved in medical tourism.

Once the hospitals were identified, which were involved in medical tourism, the social research method of content analysis (Creswell, 2013) of the hospital home page website was used, and the author personally studied and explored the hospital home page websites and other social media links, together with the print format, to extract relevant information and data for this research. Usually, global medical tourists first search the hospital websites and the various social media tools supported by the internet for medical tourism and health related information. The home pages of hospital websites provide a variety of information for the patients, medical professionals, medical tourists/international patients and careers. For example: select a city for the location of the hospital branch, medical service facilities, super-specialities, find a doctor, make an enquiry, accreditation information, online payments and chat, news and media, health information, plan your visit, seminars and workshops and medical research related information.

Table 4. Information on medical tourism hospital Internet home page

Hospitals in India	Apollo	NH	Wock-hardt	Fortis	Asian Heart	Ruby Hall	Jeha-ngir	San-cheti	Max Health
1. Location and Branches	**30+1**	**19**	**9**	**30**	**1**	**2**	**1**	**1**	**11**
2. Vision/Mission	Y	Y	Y	Y	Y	Y	Y	Y	Y
Multi-Speciality	Y	Y	Y	Y	Y	Y	Y	Y	Y
Top Ten Procedures	Y	Y	Y	Y	Y	Y	Y	Y	Y
Healthcare Facilities	Y	Y	Y	Y	Y	Y	Y	Y	Y
NABH/ ISO/NABL Accredit	--	--	--	--	Y	Y	Y	Y	Y
NABH and JCI Accredit	Y	Y	Y	Y	Y	--	--	--	--
3. Find a Doctor	Y	Y	Y	Y	Y	Y	Y	Y	Y
Online Appointment	Y	Y	Y	Y	Y	Y	Y	Y	Y
Online Feedback	Y	Y	Y	Y	Y	Y	Y	--	Y
Online Payment	Y	Y	Y	Y	Y	Y	Y	--	Y
4. Patient Care Guide	Y	Y	Y	Y	Y	Y	Y	Y	Y
Health Information	Y	Y	Y	Y	Y	Y	Y	Y	Y
Get Home Care	--	--	--	--	--	--	--	--	Y
Help Line and FAQ	Y	Y	Y	Y	Y	Y	Y	Y	Y
5. International Patient Special Services	Y	Y	Y	Y	Y	Y	Y	Y	Y
6. Careers	Y	Y	Y	Y	Y	Y	Y	Y	Y
Education-Research	Y	Y	Y	Y	Y	Y	Y	Y	Y
Insurance and Partners	Y	Y	Y	Y	Y	Y	Y	Y	Y
7. Help Line and FAQ	Y	Y	Y	Y	Y	Y	Y	Y	Y
Social media icons	Y	Y	--	Y	Y	Y	Y	--	Y
News and Media	Y	Y	Y	Y	Y	Y	Y	Y	Y
Online health record	Y	Y	Y	Y	--	--	--	--	--
Air Ambulance	--	--	--	--	--	--	--	--	Y
LiveCare help line	Y	--	--	--	--	--	--	--	--

Source: Developed for this paper.
Y-Yes, -- No.

Content was analysed to identify key themes, concepts, images of accreditation, pictures, and YouTube videos, patient blogs and social media icons. For this study medical tourism hospital websites were searched for website content and in particular use of social media tools by the hospitals. The key components of content analysis as seen from Table 4 were:

1. Location and branches of medical tourism hospitals under the study.
2. General information regarding the healthcare provider;
3. Online Patient communication with the healthcare provider;
4. patient healthcare information;

Table 5. Social media applications used by Indian medical tourism hospitals

Hospital	Apollo	NH	WockHt	Fortis	AH	RH	JAH	SCT	Max
Website	Y	Y	Y	Y	Y	Y	Y	Y	Y
Virtual tour- Visit	Y	Y	Y	Y	Y	Y	Y	Y	Y
Live chat	Y	Y	Y	Y	--	--	--	--	--
LinkedIn	Y	Y	Y	Y	Y	Y	Y	Y	Y
YouTube Testimonials	Y	Y	Y	Y	Y	Y	Y	Y	Y
YouTube Health Information	Y	Y	Y	Y	Y	Y	Y	Y	Y
On-Twitter	Y	Y	Y	Y	Y	-	Y	Y	Y
Photo Sharing	Y	Y	Y	Y	Y	Y	Y	--	Y
Video Sharing	Y	Y	Y	Y	Y	Y	Y	--	--
Blogs	Y	Y	Y	Y	Y	Y	Y	--	Y
Discussion Forum	Y	Y	Y	Y	Y	--	--	--	--
Healthcare Mobile App	Y	Y	Y	Y	--	Y	Y	--	--
Face Book	Y	Y	Y	Y	Y	Y	Y	Y	Y
Cloud e-Health Centre	-	Y	Y	Y	--	--	--	--	--
Wikipedia	Y	Y	Y	Y	Y	Y	Y	Y	Y
Phone & E-mail	Y	Y	Y	Y	Y	Y	Y	Y	Y
Flickr	Y	Y	Y	Y	--	--	--	--	--
Video Patient Testimonials	Y	Y	Y	Y	Y	--	Y	Y	Y
WEBINAR- Hospital Channel	--	--	--	Y	--	--	--	--	--
Google Plus	Y	Y	Y	Y	Y	Y	Y	--	--
T-tumblr.	--	--	--	Y	--	--	--	--	--
Alexa	Y	--	--	--	--	--	--	--	--
Slide-Share	Y	--	--	--	--	--	--	--	--
Pinterest	--	--	--	--	--	--	--	--	Y
Live Bookmark	--	--	--	Y	--	--	--	--	--

Source: Developed for this paper.
Y-Yes, -- No.

5. International patient information;
6. information for healthcare professionals, and;
7. Social media tools and helpline.

Various social media applications used by the medical tourism hospitals under study, to communicate with the domestic and international patients including the medical facilitators and professionals are listed in Table 5.

All Indian hospitals involved in treating foreign patients could have been chosen, but due to the limitation of the time the author decided to choose 5 famous hospitals with multi-super-speciality with many branches all over India and the other 4 hospitals with one single branch located in the city of Pune were chosen (see Table 3). From the hospital websites various branches and their locations were identified.

Table below shows that Apollo Group has 30 branches in all major capital cities of India and 25 other hospitals which are affiliated to Apollo in some super-specialty; for example, Jehangir Hospital in Pune. This is followed by Fortis Group (30) branches, Narayana Health (19) branches, Wockhardt (9) branches and MAX Health has (11) branches in all of the major cities of India. Besides four (4) hospitals at a single location one (1) in Mumbai –Asian Heart Institute and three (3) in Pune Ruby Hall, Jehangir and Sancheti Orthopaedic were also chosen as they were also involved in treating local and foreign patients and used the WoSM tools to promote their business and disseminate information. From the websites it was analysed that Apollo, Fortis, Narayana Health, MAX-health, Wockhardt group are major global players in medical tourism business, having branches all over India as seen from Table 3. On the google map-website, one can find the exact location map and the address for various hospital branches at different locations and their super specialties.

The home pages and links of Nine (9) medical hospital websites also helped to determine the various types of information posted by the medical tourism hospitals which helps the domestic and global medical tourists as customers, including medical tourism facilitators, to gather all the information required regarding the healthcare facility. As seen from Table 4, hospitals on their home page provide all the information to the patient, domestic or international. For example, Apollo provides all the information that patients seeks on its internet website, before they make a decision for medical treatment in their hospital. One additional feature is 'Apollo Prism': Your Personal Health Record, provided for the patients by Apollo. 'Apollo Prism' receives and stores patient data in a secure environment so that the patient can access and download their diagnostic test results online. Further, it also helps the patient to stay on wellness-program to manage conditions like diabetes. Apollo Group of hopsitals has recently in 2015, launched a Live-Care help line. Ruby Hall clinic in Pune has one of the largest cardiac and cancer speciality centre and was awarded the Best Medical Tourism facility in India, along with Apollo. MAX Health is unique in having an Air Ambulance Service, amongst all hospitals.

As seen from Table 4, the home pages of the nine (9) hospitals provide detail information and much more regarding location of healthcare facility and its branches in India; the super-speciality of medical procedures provided and promoted; accreditation, various social media application icons, live chats, find a doctor, appointments, feedback and payments; healthcare information and patient care information to the medical tourists; information for international patients, regarding taking an appointment, super-speciality, Visa arrangement, accommodation, cost, surgery waiting time and other healthcare service facilities, travel and sightseeing, to all the patients, before they make a decision to choose a destination and the hospital for medical treatment.

From Table 5 we can examine the various social media tools adopted by the medical tourism hospitals. Home page of a hospital usually has the social media tool icons (**Y** in bold are visible WoSM 'Follow Us' icons on the home page) to show the various ways the patient and professionals can communicate; for example: live talk with Apollo Hospital consultant (window pops up on the right hand corner of the home page), social media 'Follow-Us Menu' icons pictures such as of Facebook, Twitter, Alexa, YouTube, LinkedIn, Slide-share, Alexa, Blogs and, Google plus. The hospitals which do not have a 'Follow-Us Menu' on their home page (Ruby Hall, Sancheti, Wockhardt) then it can be searched by Google search engine to find out if the hospital has for example LinkedIn or a Facebook account to communicate.

Cloud enabled e-Health centres to help patients in remote and rural areas of India has been launched by Narayana Health in partnership with Hewlett Packard in 2014 to deliver quality, affordable healthcare services, which will be have real time disease surveillance (Express News Service, 2014). Apollo Group, Jehangir, Asian Heart, Fortis Group, Narayana Health had the following 'Follow Us Menu' on the margin of the home page: Facebook, Twitter, Blogs, LinkedIn, Google Plus, and YouTube. Apollo had a few extra such as Alexa and Slide Share and Fortis had t-tumbler. There is evidence that WoSM is increasingly being adopted and used by private super-specialty hospitals in the business of medical tourism in India to communicate and disseminate healthcare related information to its patients, medical professionals and other businesses connected with medical tourism.

The power of WoSM tools are not just for social networking, but more significant to disseminate information, provide feedback and create added value which is far beyond we can imagine in the global business of medical tourism, as seen from Table 6, which enhances global healthcare communication as quickly as possible, and provide benefits to the industry as discussed below.

As evident from Table 6 that the hospitals involved in medical tourism, benefit from the use of social media tools via their hospital platform which is username and password protected, to disseminate information and to communicate with their potential and actual patients, as well as with their colleagues:

1. A WoSM application/tools helps the medical tourists to communicate with other actual medical tourists about their overall medical tourism experience, destination, medical treatment and surgery.
2. Provides feedback from the medical tourists to the medical tourism healthcare provider, so that they can improve and provide efficient healthcare services to foreign patients.
3. Actual medical tourists help to disseminate very critical information after information related to health, cost, quality, patient safety, to the potential global medical tourists and wider global patients, before they can make a decision to travel aboard for medical treatment.
4. It helps the healthcare provider to communicate and engage with their actual and potential medical tourists as medical patient/ consumers of their healthcare services by Facebook and Twitter and thus increase communication with the patients, and provide support for medication, patient education, safety, link with patient online support group, promote hospital brand loyalty and make patient and physician relationship more effective and efficient to obtain desired positive patient outcome.
5. Helps the providers to continuously improve the quality, efficiency, effectiveness, exposure of its healthcare service and add value.
6. Finally, hospitals can create and establish global international brand name awareness for healthcare provision in medical tourism, like Apollo group, Fortis group, and Wockhardt group.

Brand awareness can be achieved by having updated websites with accreditation logos, online engagement with patients, blogs, patient testimonials, video sharing, discussion forums, YouTube videos,

Table 6. Types of communication/interaction/feedback

	Types of Communication/ Interaction/Feedback from Demand and Supply Side in Medical Tourism
Step 1	Medical Tourist (MT) to MT
Step 2	Actual MT to Potential MT& vice-versa
Step 3	MT to physician/surgeon & vice-versa
Step 4	MT to Hospital/clinic/medical tour facilitator & vice-versa
Step 5	MT to global public
Step 6	MT to global medical tourism healthcare providers

Source: Developed for this paper.

photos and virtual tour of the hospitals facilities. In case of India, the nine famous hospitals with multiple branches in this study were selected as providers of medical tourism healthcare services to foreign patients. This study will help to build a larger understanding of the role and adoption of social media by medical tourism businesses from the supply side, which not only helps to improve quality, efficiency but also help the potential medical tourists to make informed decisions and choice regarding destination, hospital, specialist surgeons and provide feedback about medical treatment and surgery in India.

DISCUSSION

The aim of this chapter was to explore the role, use and benefits of social media tools by branded Indian hospitals treating medical tourists. WoSM improves communication between the healthcare providers, health professionals and domestic or foreign medical tourists' as patients. Health information exchange via social media tools continues to increase in recent years since the innovation in ITC, broadband internet access and growth in global trade in healthcare services abroad or medical tourism. Tourists search various sources of information, including the internet about the destination, accommodation, tourism sites and local culture and plan their travel (Benckendorff & Black, 2000; Wan, 2002; Hyde, 2006; Lee, 2007; Patterson, 2007; Oorni, 2004; Kah, Vogy, & Mackay, 2008). Similarly medical tourists also search for information related to hospital, specialists, medical cost, wait time, patient safety, privacy and accreditation, on the internet before they make a decision to travel aboard for medical treatment (Medhekar & Newby, 2013). It also helps to provide healthcare information to the global potential medical tourists quickly as possible and prepare them for a positive medical tourism experience as well as possible medical travel risk. Medical tourists can take online appointments and consult with live chats with the surgeon miles away. Medical tourism industry needs to develop a *Medical-Tourism Trip-Advisor (MTTA)* platform to inform potential and actual medical tourists regarding all aspects of medical travel from booking an airline ticket to the choice of destination, hospital, surgeon, accommodation, tourism and sightseeing to prepare them for their medical surgery and journey abroad.

The knowledge based theory of the firm developed by Sveiby (2001) that create value inside and outside an organisation, can be applied to firms in the business of medical tourism industry:

1. **Knowledge Transfers from External Structure to Individuals:** Healthcare organisations learn from feedback provided by actual medical tourists who are external to the hospital and other external stake holders who are their customers regarding the quality, cost, patient safety, security, accreditation, waiting time for surgery and other related concerns relating to healthcare service delivery on social media sites. This feedback will help to improve healthcare service delivery, and attract more medical tourists to their hospital.
2. **Knowledge Transfers within the External Structure:** The actual medical tourists as global consumers of healthcare tell each other via social media platforms regarding the healthcare organisation, hospital, specialist surgeons and their overall healthcare/medical tourism experience abroad. This feedback also helps the potential medical tourists to make an informed choice.
3. **Knowledge Transfers from External to Internal Structure Helps:** The healthcare organisation to obtain feedback from the external customers that is medical tourists and take action to improve their brand image, healthcare service delivery to global patients, in order to make their business competitive and sustainable.

4. **Knowledge Transfers from Internal to External Structure:** The opposite of point three above. In this case the healthcare organisations overall systems, processes, tools and healthcare products improve the competences of key stake holders from the demand and the supply side which creates value to effectively service the healthcare customer through, help desk, online website for Q&A and appointment, product tracing, e-business, patient forums, testimonials, and other multimedia tools by creating and transferring knowledge.

Hospitals involved in the business of medical tourism should decide which of the different type of social media platforms should be used that is cost effective; reach the potential medical tourists globally in a timely manner, to achieve positive outcomes from the supply side, and also patient outcomes from the demand side:

1. Healthcare providers should choose carefully the various social media applications on their home page, for WoSM online engagement, participation, collaboration, and sharing information with the medical tourists from the healthcare supplier side. It is important to realise that the message has to be effectively communicated to potential and actual medical tourists as patient/customer around the globe, who are the target population, whether in a developed or a developing country. Similarly, medical tourists may use social media such as Blogs, Facebook, Myspace, Photo Sharing, LinkedIn, YouTube and Discussion Boards to communicate with other medical tourists and provide feedback to the healthcare provider and use various WoSM for feedback, providing content or virtual testimonials about their medical travel and surgery experience.
2. It is essential for doctors or consultants online, to be active participants. They should post current information regarding the availability of super speciality of treatment, accreditation, quality, patient safety, security and thus develop relationships with the actual and the potential medical tourists by answering their queries in a timely manner and taking action on feedback provided to prevent medical errors. All the queries by the patients on social media sites, through various WoSM applications should be attended to as soon as possible, if the hospital's aim is to attract medical tourists.
3. Hospital and the medical tourists, both should be polite, professional, truthful when engaging on the social media sites when making comments or providing honest and credible information with constructive feedback. This helps to build relationship and trust between the patient and the physician.
4. The message and information from the healthcare providers and actual medical tourists' experiences and testimonials have to be credible and true and not confusing, ambiguous and contradictory across different social media sites and others like TV and print media.
5. In case of the hospital just 2-3 people should be given administrative rights to FaceBook, uploading YouTube testimonials and virtual tour of the hospital infrastructure and medical facilities. Also it is essential for hospital employees and medical tourists to identify, and not be anonymous, when they post a comment or ask a question on social media.
6. Social media thus helps to effectively communicate, share and disseminate medical treatment and surgery abroad related information quickly as possible between medical tourists (domestic or foreign) as patients and between patients and medical tourism healthcare providers who need to provide medical tourist's centred healthcare information. Further, hospitals can target expatriate community, business travellers, actual medical tourists and Indian diaspora going home for holidays, tourists.

CONCLUSION

This study concludes that internet and various social media technologies have changed and introduced not just e-Tourism but also e-Medical Tourism/e-Health Tourism which has broaden the horizon of global health and medical tourism market through knowledge dissemination. Hospitals, allied healthcare services, medical tourism facilitators, and pharmaceuticals companies including accrediting bodies and tourism businesses which are involved in medical tourism should invest in social media tools to enhance their brand identity. This will helps to communicate and provide immediate feedback or interact live with the medical tourists and specialist surgeon/physician, regarding the medical travel potential risks, benefits and also about the choice of destination, surgeon, and the super-speciality hospital for surgery. Content analysis of the websites of nine hospitals, and five of them with many branches all over India, has helped to find out the extent of adaptation and use of various social media tools by medical tourism hospitals and patients to communicate, interact and market different types of information from the supply side to the medical tourists. It is essential that all the hospitals should have the social media icon on the home page as 'Follow-Us-On' FaceBook, Twitter, LinkedIn, YouTube, Blogs, Mobile-Apps and Google plus, essentially for quickly communicating information regarding travelling abroad for medical treatment.

Social media applications are now on mobile and can be used any time anywhere on i-Phone, which is portable by the medical tourists, where CGC, is playing an important role for knowledge dissemination of medical tourist experience. It not only empowers patients to make informed decisions by accessing health and medical tourism related information but also share their medical tourism experience with the world. On one hand, medical tourism market is gradually moving from being medical patient/tourist centric, to being driven by medical tourist from the demand side, where medical tourists are creating, sharing, disseminating and managing medical tourism knowledge, experiences and information through social media websites (Table 5), as potential medical tourists tend to trust more actual medical tourists experience on the WoSM, rather than the medical tourism facilitator and healthcare supplier, who are always posting positive statements regarding their healthcare service. On the other hand, hospitals from the supply side are providing all information related to hospital quality, accreditation, cost, specialist surgeons and state-of-the-art medical technology, to promote their healthcare facility, super-speciality and specialist surgeons to the global healthcare medical tourist (Table 4). It is also essential that medical professionals engage on medical tourism social media in a professional and credible manner. They must have a code of conduct and ethical guidelines to keep the patient privacy and confidentiality and maintain professional boundaries between medical tourists and the physician.

More and more different types of information related to travelling abroad for medical treatment is shared by the actual medical tourists as consumers and healthcare professionals by WoSM, in a two way communication process in real time. The only challenge faced by medical tourist is to sieve, manage and process the healthcare knowledge given the dramatic increase in medical tourism related information online. If correct and credible information is provided via the social media tools at the right time, only then will the potential benefits of social media, regarding the best and safe choice of destination within a country, hospital and specialist by the potential medical tourists will be enhanced to get the best possible healthcare outcomes and values for money.

Given the time limitation for this study, only nine famous hospital websites in India were explored. Further, more quantitative and qualitative empirical research is warranted in the global health and the medical tourism industry to explore the extent of the use and adoption of different social media tools which helps to disseminate medical tourism health information and health promotion. It is important also to examine and find out if the quality of information disseminated on the social media sites such as YouTube, Face book, Discussion Forum and Twitter by the medical tourists and the medical tourism healthcare provider is true, authentic and credible.

Does this information on the social media sites help the medical patient to make informed choice regarding destination, hospital and make cost comparisons seeking medical treatment abroad? Does it encourage forming relationships, exchange information, encourage communicate between the medical tourists as patients, physicians and medical professionals? Which WoSM application is most effective in having a positive healthcare outcome for the patient as well as the hospital? Quantitative survey can be conducted to explore how the generated knowledge in the ecosystem is managed and used by the end-user and how can it be authenticated.

In conclusion, the use of social media for knowledge dissemination from the medical tourism supply side can maximise the full business potential of global healthcare and should be used appropriately and wisely following the code of conduct and ethical guidelines for engaging on social media with medical tourist. From the demand side, information on the social media can indirectly or directly have a negative influence where it prevents people from travelling abroad or a positive influence, which will empower and change individual behaviour and motivate people to make an informed decision to travel abroad for medical treatment. Use of WoSM applications by global healthcare providers improves medical tourists'/patient communication with each other, and with the healthcare provider, by building trustful relationship, which results in improving efficiency, competitiveness of the medical tourism industry and positive healthcare outcomes for the global E-medical-patient as consumer of E-medical-tourism abroad.

REFERENCES

AMTA. (2009). *Asian Medical Tourism Association (AMTA) Growing Medical Tourism Industry in Asia*. Retrieved March 3, 2010, from http://www.1888pressrelease.com/asian-medical-tourism-association-amta

Antheunis, M. L., Tates, K., & Nieboer, T. E. (2013). Patients' and health professionals' use of social media in health care: Motives, barriers and expectations. *Patient Education and Counseling*, *92*(3), 426–431. doi:10.1016/j.pec.2013.06.020 PMID:23899831

Bacigalupe, G. (2011). Is there a role for social technologies for collaborative healthcare? *Families, Systems & Health*, *29*(1), 1–14. doi:10.1037/a0022093 PMID:21417520

Baloglu, S., & Pekcan, Y. A. (2006). The website design and internet site marketing practices of upscale and luxury hotels in Turkey. *Tourism Management*, *27*(1), 171–176. doi:10.1016/j.tourman.2004.07.003

Bandyopadhyay, S., Shaw, V., Banergee, A., & Nag, D. (2013). Social Knowledge Management: Use of Social Media for Disseminating Informal Wisdom of Elderly to the Youth. *International Journal of Knowledge. Innovation and Entrepreneurship*, *1*(1-2), 107–115.

Barrowman, R. A., Grubor, D., & Chandu, A. (2010). Dental Implant Tourism. *Australian Dental Journal*, *55*(4), 441–445. doi:10.1111/j.1834-7819.2010.01267.x PMID:21133945

Benckendorff, P. J., & Black, N. L. (2000). Destination marketing on the internet. A case study of Australian regional tourism authorities. *The Journal of Tourism Studies*, *11*(1), 11–21.

Bennett, R., & Gabriel, H. (1999). Organisational factors & knowledge management within large marketing departments: An empirical study. *Journal of Knowledge Management*, *3*(3), 212–225. doi:10.1108/13673279910288707

Bernhardt. J. M., Mays D., & Kreuter, M. W. (2011). Dissemination 2.0: Closing the gap between knowledge and practice with new media and marketing. *Journal of Health Communication*, *16*(Sup1), 32-44.

Bies, W., & Zacharia, L. (2007). Medical tourism: Outsourcing surgery. *Mathematical and Computer Modelling*, *46*(7-8), 1144–1159. doi:10.1016/j.mcm.2007.03.027

Bookman, M. Z., & Bookman, K. R. (2007). *Medical Tourism in Developing Countries*. New York: Palgrave Macmillan. doi:10.1057/9780230605657

Bosslet, G. T., Torke, A. M., Hickman, S. E., Terry, C. L., & Helft, P. R. (2011). The patient-doctor relationship and online social networks: Results of a national survey. *Journal of General Internal Medicine*, *26*(10), 1168–1174. doi:10.1007/s11606-011-1761-2 PMID:21706268

Bramwell, B., & Sharman, A. (1999). Collaboration in the local tourism policy making. *Annals of Tourism Research*, *26*(2), 392–415. doi:10.1016/S0160-7383(98)00105-4

Briones, R. L., Kuch, B., Liu, B. F., & Jin, Y. (2011). Keeping up with the digital age: How the American Red Cross uses social media to build relationships. *Public Relations Review*, *37*(1), 37–43. doi:10.1016/j.pubrev.2010.12.006

Brodie, M., Hamel, E., & Altman, D. (2003). Health news and the American public,1996-2002. *Journal of Health Politics, Policy and Law*, *28*(5), 927–950. doi:10.1215/03616878-28-5-927 PMID:14604217

Brotman, B. A. (2010). Medical Tourism Private Hospitals: Focus India. *Journal of Health Care Finance*, *37*(1), 45–50. PMID:20973373

Chalkiti, K., & Sigala, M. (2008). Information sharing and knowledge creation in online forum: The case of Greek Online Forum "Dialougoi". *Current Issues in Tourism*, *11*(5), 381–406. doi:10.1080/13683500802316006

Change Foundation. (2011). *Using social media to improve healthcare quality*. Retrieved, May 12, 2012, from https://www.changefoundation.ca/docs/socialmediatoolkit.pdf

Choi, S., Lehto, X. Y., & Morrison, A. M. (2007). Destination image representation on the web: Content analysis of Macau travel related websites. *Tourism Management*, *28*(1), 118–129. doi:10.1016/j.tourman.2006.03.002

Chou, W. S., Hunt, Y. M., Burke, B. D., Moser, R. P., & Hesse, B. W. (2009). Social media use in the United States: Implications for health communications. *Journal of Medical Internet Research*, *11*(4), e48. doi:10.2196/jmir.1249 PMID:19945947

Chretien, K. C., Azar, J., & Kind, T. (2011). Physicians on Twitter. *Journal of the American Medical Association*, *305*(6), 566–568. doi:10.1001/jama.2011.68 PMID:21304081

Cline, R. J. W., & Haynes, K. M. (2011). Consumer health information seeking on the internet: The state of the art. *Health Education Research*, *16*(6), 671–692. doi:10.1093/her/16.6.671 PMID:11780707

Connell, J. (2006). Medical Tourism: Sea, Sun, Sand and ... Surgery. *Tourism Management*, *26*(6), 1093–1100. doi:10.1016/j.tourman.2005.11.005

Connell, J. (2013). Contemporary medical tourism: Conceptialisation, culture and commodification. *Tourism Management*, *34*, 1–13. doi:10.1016/j.tourman.2012.05.009

Cormany, D., & Baloglu, S. (2011). Medical travel facilitator websites: An exploratory study of web page contents and services offered to the prospective medical tourist. *Tourism Management*, *32*(4), 709–716. doi:10.1016/j.tourman.2010.02.008

Creswell, J. W. (2013). Qualitative Inquiry and Research Design: Choosing Among Five Approaches (3rd ed.). Sage Publications.

Crooks, V. A., Kingsbury, P., Snyder, J., & Johnston, R. (2010). What is known about patients experience of medical tourism? A scoping review. *BMC Health Services Research*, *10*(1), 266. doi:10.1186/1472-6963-10-266 PMID:20825667

Crooks, V. A., Turner, L., Snyder, J., Johnston, R., & Kingsbury, P. (2011). Promoting medical tourism in India: Messages, images, and the marketing of international patient travel. *Social Science & Medicine*, *72*(5), 726–732. doi:10.1016/j.socscimed.2010.12.022 PMID:21310519

Davenport, T. H. (1994). Saving IT's Soul: Human Centred Information Management. *Harvard Business Review*, *72*(2), 119-131.

Delmonicao, F. L. (2009). The implications of Istanbul Declaration on organ trafficking and transplant tourism. *Current Opinion in Organ Transplantation*, *14*(2), 116–119. doi:10.1097/MOT.0b013e32832917c9 PMID:19300258

Deloitte. (2010). *Social Networks in Health Care: communication, collaboration and insights*. Delight Centre for Health Solutions.

Duhon, B. (1998). It's All in our Heads. *Inform*, *12*(8), 8-13.

Express News Service. (2014). Retrieved July 2, 2015, from http://computer.financialexpress.com/news/hp-narayana-health-to-expand-cloud-enabled-ehealth-centres-in-india/1222/

Eyrich, N., Padman, M. L., & Sweetser, K. D. (2008). PR practitioners' use of social media tools and communication technology. *Public Relations Review*, *34*(4), 412–414. doi:10.1016/j.pubrev.2008.09.010

Eysenbach, G. (2008). Medicine 2.0. Social networking, collaboration, participation, apomediation, and openness. *Journal of Medical Internet Research*, *10*(3), e22. doi:10.2196/jmir.1030 PMID:18725354

Fisher, J., & Clayton, M. (2012). Who gives a Tweet: Assessing patients' interest in the use of social media for healthcare? *Worldviews on Evidence-Based Nursing*, 100-108.

Freberg, K. (2012). Intentions to comply with crisis messages communicated via social media. *Public Relations Review*, *38*(3), 416–421. doi:10.1016/j.pubrev.2012.01.008

Gahlinger, P. (2008). *The medical tourism travel guide*. North Branch, MN: Sunrise River Press.

Government of India (GOI). (2003). *Government of India (GOI) 2003 Health Sector in India.* New Delhi: Budget Papers.

Hardey, M. (1999). Doctor in the house: The internet as a source of lay health knowledge and the challenges to expertise. *Sociology of Health & Illness*, *2*(6), 820–835. doi:10.1111/1467-9566.00185

Hawn, C. (2009). Take two aspirins and tweet me in the morning: How Twitter, Facebook and other social media are reshaping healthcare. *Health Affairs*, *28*(2), 361–368. doi:10.1377/hlthaff.28.2.361 PMID:19275991

Henry, R. K., Molnar, A., & Henry, J. C. (2012). A survey of UD Dental Practices' use of Social Media. *The Journal of Contemporary Dental Practice*, *13*(2), 137–141. doi:10.5005/jp-journals-10024-1109 PMID:22665737

Hopkins, L., Labonte, R., Runnels, V., & Packer, C. (2010). Medical tourism today: What is the state of existing knowledge*? Journal of Public Health Policy*, *31*(2), 185–198. doi:10.1057/jphp.2010.10 PMID:20535101

Horowitz, M. D., & Rosensweig, J. A. (2007). Medical Tourism-Health Care in the Global Economy. *Physician Executive*, *33*(6), 24–31. PMID:18092615

Horowitz, M. D., Rosensweig, J. A., & Jones, C. A. (2007). Medical tourism: Globalization of the healthcare marketplace. *Medscape General Medicine*, *9*(4), 33. PMID:18311383

Howard, R. (2015). An exploration of the motivation and impact of medical tourism. *Medical Markets and Media*. Retrieved March 20, 2015, from http://www.mmm-online.com/the-patient-abroad-an-exploration-of-the-motivations-and-impact-of-medical-tourism/article/404476/

Huxtable, R. (2009). The Suicide tourist trap:compromise across boundaries. *Journal of Bioethical Inquiry*, *6*(3), 327–336. doi:10.1007/s11673-009-9170-5

Hyde, K. (2006). Contemporary information search strategies of destination-naive international vacationers. *Journal of Travel & Tourism*, *21*(2/3), 63–76.

Indian Medical Tourism (IMT). (2009). *India ranks 2nd in medical tourism.* Retrieved August 15, 2009, from http://www.medicaltourism.org/consortium.jsp?sect=consortiumdetail&id=6

Jaeger, P. T., Schneiderman, B., Fleischmann, K. R., Preece, J., Qu, Y., & Wu, P. F. (2007). Community response grids: E-government, social networks, and effective emergency management. *Telecommunications Policy*, *31*(10-11), 592–604. doi:10.1016/j.telpol.2007.07.008

Kah, J. A., Vogt, C., & MacKay, K. (2008). Online travel information search and purchasing by internet use experiences. *Information Technology & Tourism*, *10*(3), 227–243. doi:10.3727/109830508787157353

Kaplan, A., & Haenlein, M. (2010). Users of the world, unite! The challenges and opportunities of social media. *Business Horizons*, *53*(1), 59–68. doi:10.1016/j.bushor.2009.09.003

Keckley, P. H. (2008). *Medical Tourism: consumers in search of value.* Washington, DC: Deloitte Center for Health Solutions.

Kiatpongsan, S., & Sipp, D. (2009). Monitoring and regulating offshore stem cell clinics. *Science*, *323*(5921), 1564–1565. doi:10.1126/science.1168451 PMID:19299604

Korda, H., & Itani, Z. (2013). Harnessing social media for health pormotion and behaviour change. *Health Promotion Practice*, *14*(1), 15–23. doi:10.1177/1524839911405850 PMID:21558472

Laszlo, K. C., & Laszlo, A. (2002). Evolving knowledge for development: The role of knowledge management in a changing world. *Journal of Knowledge Management*, *6*(4), 400–412. doi:10.1108/13673270210440893

Lee, J., Soutar, G., & Daly, T. (2007). Tourists' search for different types of information: A cross-national study. *Information Technology & Tourism*, *9*(3), 165–176. doi:10.3727/109830507782167006

Lunt, N., Hardey, M., & Mannion, R. (2010). Nip, Tuck and Click: Medical Tourism and the Emergence of Web-Based Health Information. *The Open Medical Informatics Journal,* (4), 1-11.

MacReady, N. (2007). Developing Countries Court Medical Tourists. *Lancet*, *369*(9576), 1849–1850. doi:10.1016/S0140-6736(07)60833-2 PMID:17549816

Mason, A., & Wright, K. B. (2011). Framing Medical tourism: An Examination of appeal, rock, Convalescence, Accreditation, and Interactivity in Medical Tourism Web Sites. *Journal of Health Communication*, *16*(2), 163–177. doi:10.1080/10810730.2010.535105 PMID:21161812

Matoo, A., & Rathindran, R. (2006). How Health Insurance Inhibits Trade in Health Care. *Health Affairs*, *25*(2), 358–368. doi:10.1377/hlthaff.25.2.358 PMID:16522578

McAdam, R., & Reid, R. (2000). A comparison of public and private sector perceptions and use of knowledge management. *Journal of European Industrial Training*, *24*(6), 317–329. doi:10.1108/03090590010346424

Medhekar, A. (2014). Government Policy Initiatives for Developing Sustainable Medical Tourism Industry. *GSTF- Journal on Business Review, 3*(3), 95-105.

Medhekar, A., & Ali, M. M. (2012). A Cross-Border Trade in Healthcare services: Bangladesh to India. *The Business and Management Review, London*, *2*(1), 1–13.

Medhekar, A., & Newby, L. (2012). Information Search for Medical Treatment Abroad. *Journal of Applied Global Research*, *5*(3), 53–72.

Medhekar, A., Wong, H. Y., & Hall, J. (2014). Innovation in Medical Tourism Services Marketing: A case of India. In A. Goyal (Ed.), *Innovations in Services Marketing and Management: Strategies for Emerging Economies* (pp. 49–66). Penn, USA: IGI Global Publishing.

Miller, T. E., & Derse, A. R. (2002). Between strangers: The practice of medicine online. *Health Affairs*, *21*(4), 68–179. doi:10.1377/hlthaff.21.4.168 PMID:12117127

Nassab, R., Hamnett, N., Nelson, K., Kaur, S., Greensell, B., Dhital, S., & Juma, A. (2010). Cosmetic Tourism: Public Opinion and Analysis of Information and Content Available on the internet. *Aesthetic Surgery Journal*, *30*(3), 465–469. doi:10.1177/1090820X10374104 PMID:20601579

OECD. (1996). *The Knowledge-based Economy*. Paris: OECD.

Oorni, A. (2004). Consumer objectives and the amount of search in electronic travel and tourism markets. *Journal of Travel & Tourism Marketing*, *17*(2/3), 3–14. doi:10.1300/J073v17n02_01

Palen, L., Hiltz, S. R., & Liu, S. (2007). Online forums supporting grassroots participation in emergency prepardness and response. *Communications of the ACM*, *50*(3), 54–58. doi:10.1145/1226736.1226766

Pan, B., MacLaurin, T., & Crotts, J. C. (2007). Travel Blogs and the Implications for Destination Marketing. *Journal of Travel Research*, *46*(1), 35–45. doi:10.1177/0047287507302378

Patterson, I. (2007). Information sources used by older adults for decision making about tourist and travel destinations. *International Journal of Consumer Studies*, *31*(5), 528–533. doi:10.1111/j.1470-6431.2007.00609.x

Pew Research Center. (2009). *The social life of health information.* Retrieved April 30, 2015, from http://www.pewinternet.org/Reports/2009/8-The-Social-Life-of-Health-Information/

RNCOS. (2010). Booming Medical Tourism in India. Industry Report. New Delhi: RNCOS.

Roney, S. A., & Ozturan, M. (2006). A content analysis of the web sites of Turkish travel agencies. *Anatolia*, *17*(1), 43–54. doi:10.1080/13032917.2006.9687026

Runnels, V., & Carrera, P. M. (2012). Why do patients engage in medical tourism? *Maturitas*, *73*(4), 300–304. doi:10.1016/j.maturitas.2012.08.011 PMID:23007007

Schang, S. C., Li, E. Y., Wu, Y. L., & Hou, O. C. (2011). Understanding Web 2.0 service models: A knowledge-creating perspective. *Information & Management*, *48*(4-5), 178–184. doi:10.1016/j.im.2011.01.005

Schlegelmilch, B. B., & Chini, T. C. (2003). Knowledge transfer between marketing functions in Multinational companies: A conceptual model. *International Business Review*, *12*(2), 215–232. doi:10.1016/S0969-5931(02)00097-5

Shult, J., & Corey, J. J. (2006). *Beauty from afar: A medical tourist's guide to affordable and quality cosmetic care outside the U.S. Stewart* (1st ed.). New York: Tabori & Chang Publisher.

Sigala, M. (2010). Measuring customer value in online collaborative trip planning processes. *Marketing Intelligence & Planning*, *28*(4), 418–443. doi:10.1108/02634501011053559

Sigala, M., Christou, E., & Gretzel, U. (2012). Social Media in Travel, Tourism and Hospitality: Theory, Practice and Cases. Ashgate Publications.

Sillence, E., Briggs, P. H., & Fyshwick, L. (2007). Going online for health advice: Change in usage and trust practices over the last five years. *Interacting with Computers*, *19*(3), 397–403. doi:10.1016/j.intcom.2006.10.002

Smith, E., Behrmann, J., Martin, J., & Williams-Jones, B. (2010). Reproductive tourism in Argentina: Clinic accreditation and its implications for consumers, health professionals and policy makers. *Developing World Bioethics*, *10*(2), 59–69. doi:10.1111/j.1471-8847.2009.00256.x PMID:19508291

Smith, R. D., Chanda, R., & Tangcharoensathien, V. (2009). Trade in Health-related services. *Lancet*, *373*(9663), 593–601. doi:10.1016/S0140-6736(08)61778-X PMID:19167053

Speier, A. R. (2011). Brokers, consumers and the Internet: How North American consumers navigate their infertility journeys. *Reproductive Biomedicine Online*, *23*(5), 592–599. doi:10.1016/j.rbmo.2011.07.005 PMID:21955489

Street, R. L. Jr. (2003). Medicated consumer provided communication in cancer care: The empowering potential of new technologies. *Patient Education and Counseling*, *50*(1), 99–104. doi:10.1016/S0738-3991(03)00089-2 PMID:12767594

Sveiby, K. E. (2001). A Knowledge-based theory of the firm to guide in strategy formulation. *Journal of Intellectual Capital*, *2*(4), 344–358. doi:10.1108/14691930110409651

Tanis, M. (2008). Health-related On-Line Forums: What's the Big Attraction? *Journal of Health Communication*, *13*(7), 698–714. doi:10.1080/10810730802415316 PMID:18958781

Thackeray, R., Neiger, B. L., Hanson, C. L., & Mckenzie, J. F. (2008). Enhancing Promotional Strategies within Social Marketing Programs: Use of Web 2.0 Social Media. *Health Promotion Practice*, *9*(4), 338-343.

Thackeray, R., Neiger, B. L., Smith, A. K., & Van Wagenen, S. B. (2012). Adoption and use of social media among public health departments. *BMC Public Health*, *12*(1), 242. doi:10.1186/1471-2458-12-242 PMID:22449137

Turner, L. (2008). Cross-border dental care: 'dental tourism' and patient mobility. *British Dental Journal, 553-554*. doi:10.1038/sj.bdj.2008.403 PMID:18500297

Turner, L. (2010). Medical tourism and the global market place in health services: US patients, international hospitals and the search for affordable healthcare. *International Journal of Health Services*, *40*(3), 443–467. doi:10.2190/HS.40.3.d PMID:20799670

Turoff, M., Van de Walle, B., & Hiltz, S. R. (2010). Emergency response information systems. In B. Van de Walle, M. Turoff, & S. R. Hiltz (Eds.), *Information systems for emergency management*. Armonk, NY: M.E. Sharpe.

Van de belt, T. H., Engelen, L. G., Berben, S. A., & Schoonhoven, L. (2012). Definition of health 2.0 and medicine 2.0: a systematic review. *Journal of Medical Internet Research, 12*, e18.

Vance, K., Howe, W., & Dellavale, R. P. (2009). Social internet sites as a source of public health information. *Dermatologic Clinics*, *27*(2), 133–136. doi:10.1016/j.det.2008.11.010 PMID:19254656

Wald, H. S., Dube, C. E., & Anthony, D. C. (2007). Untangling the web: The impact of internet use on healthcare and the physician-patient relationship. *Patient Education and Counseling*, *68*(3), 218–224. doi:10.1016/j.pec.2007.05.016 PMID:17920226

Wan, C. S. (2002). The web sites of international tourist hotels and tour wholesalers in Taiwan. *Tourism Management*, *23*(2), 155–160. doi:10.1016/S0261-5177(01)00048-6

Waters, R. D., Burnett, E., Lamm, A., & Lucas, J. (2009). Engaging stakeholders through social networking: How nonprofit organizations are using Facebook. *Public Relations Review*, *35*(2), 102–106. doi:10.1016/j.pubrev.2009.01.006

Weiermair, K., & Mathies, C. (2004). *The tourism and leisure industry: Shaping the future*. New York: Haworth Hospitality Press.

Woodman, J. (2008). *Patients beyond borders: Everybody's guide to affordable, world class medical tourism*. Chapel Hill, NC: Healthy Travel Media.

Wulf, V., Misaki, K., Atam, M., Randall, D., & Rohde, M. (2013). On the Ground. In Investigating Social Media use during the Tunisian Revolution. Social Networks During Major Transitions (Personal and Political). Academic Press.

Yates, D., & Paquette, S. (2010). Emergency knowledge management and social media technologies: A case study of the 2010 Haitian Earthquake. *International Journal of Information Management*, *31*(1), 6–13. doi:10.1016/j.ijinfomgt.2010.10.001

Yeoh, E., Othman, K., & Ahmad, H. (2013). Word-of-mouth and virtual marketing as potent marketing tools. *Tourism Management*, *34*, 196–201. doi:10.1016/j.tourman.2012.04.010

ADDITIONAL READING

Beesley, L. A., & Cooper, C. (2008). Defining knowledge management (KM) activities: Towards consensus. *Journal of Knowledge Management*, *12*(3), 48–62. doi:10.1108/13673270810875859

Boulos, M. K., Hetherington, L., & Wheeler, S. (2007). Second Life: An overview of the potential of 3-D virtual worlds in medical and health education. *Health Information and Libraries Journal*, *24*(4), 233–245. doi:10.1111/j.1471-1842.2007.00733.x PMID:18005298

Buhalis, D., & Law, R. (2008). Progress in information technology and tourism management: 20 years on and 10 years after the Internet - The state of e-Tourism Research. *Tourism Management*, *29*(4), 609–623. doi:10.1016/j.tourman.2008.01.005

Lee, R. G., & Garvin, T. (2003). Moving from information *transfer* to information *exchange* in health and health care. *Social Science & Medicine*, *56*(3), 449–464. doi:10.1016/S0277-9536(02)00045-X PMID:12570966

Lober, W. B., & Flowers, J. L. (2011). Consumer's empowerment in healthcare amid the internet and social media. *Seminars in Oncology Nursing*, *27*(3), 169–182. doi:10.1016/j.soncn.2011.04.002 PMID:21783008

Medhekar, A. (2010). Growth of Medical Tourism in India and Public-Private Partnerships. In the proceedings of the Seventh Indian Institute of Development Studies (IIDS) Australia, International Conference on Development, (pp. 1-25) Calcutta India.

Quintas, P., Lefrere, P., & Jones, G. (1997). Knowledge management: A strategic agenda. *Journal of Long Range Planning*, *30*(3), 385–391. doi:10.1016/S0024-6301(97)90252-1

Smith, B. G. (2010). Socially, distributing public relations: Twitter, Haiti, and interactivity in social media. *Public Relations Review*, *36*(4), 329–335. doi:10.1016/j.pubrev.2010.08.005

Trung, V. D. (2014). Social Marketing: A systematic review of research 1998-2012. *Social Marketing Quarterly*, *20*(1), 15–34. doi:10.1177/1524500413517666

KEY TERMS AND DEFINITIONS

Knowledge Management: Knowledge Management is the process of critically managing knowledge to meet existing needs of the global patients as medical tourists. To identify, create, existing and acquired knowledge assets and to develop new opportunities for firms in healthcare.

Medical Tourism: Medical Tourism is a phenomenon where a patient travels with or without a companion interstate within or outside his /her country of residence, for medical surgery. It can be risky, invasive and involves complex surgical procedures with the use of highly specialised medical equipment, technology and experienced surgeons, for the improvement of overall physical health and quality of life, and may be combined with a vacation, pre-surgery or post-surgery for recuperation at an exotic destination, only if medical condition and physician permits.

Social Media Tools: Is a set of Internet-based applications that allow the creation and exchange of user generated content (UGC) by the patients as medical tourists and the healthcare providers/hospitals. For example, Facebook, TripAdvisor, Twitter, LinkedIn, Blogs, P-interest, Discussion Forums, Flickr, Chatroom, Wikis, YouTube video testimonials, Google Plus, Peer-to-peer social network and photo and video sharing websites.

Web 2.0: Web 2.0 applications are Internet based technologies intended to be consumer-centric where the users can interact with others, share information, create content, collaborate and have extensive control over content that is subsequently shared through these channels by using social media as creators of user-generated content in healthcare virtual community.

Word-of-Social-Media: Word-of-social-media (WoSM) is a situation where a medical tourist, based on the personal experience of medical tourism can recommend a specialist doctor, hospital, hotel and a country of medical tourism to friends, relatives and strangers via various social media tools.

Chapter 3
Exploring Knowledge Sharing over Social Media

M. Natarajan
Jimma University, Ethiopia

ABSTRACT

The role of Knowledge Sharing (KS) in an academic environment, with the framework of KS has been explored in this chapter. The role played by social media (SM) as a technology for KS has been discussed. The different aspects of human attitude towards sharing have been expressed with the role of library professionals, in order to support the research activity of the students within the knowledge management cycle. Few examples like the use of blogs, Facebook, and YouTube in different types of institutions /organizations and the value, purpose and challenges are highlighted. The use of social networking tools by cataloguers as a necessity for current awareness information is also emphasized. It is found that the use of social media in education, health, and other domains is mostly used to enhance reaching out to users. The advantages of KS with the need for sharing of knowledge to enhance the role by the administrators in universities and by the professionals are provided. Further research in the field of SM by specific disciplines can be carried out.

INTRODUCTION

The World Wide Web enables people to gain access to information, create content and disseminate ideas more efficiently. It optimizes the social networks in which individuals are connected through widening communication channels and lowering costs (Barsky & Purdon, 2006). Social networking sites first emerged for Internet users to find long-lost friends and classmates, link with each other and share profiles. An increasing number of individuals have become members of one or more social networking sites leading to soaring membership numbers, largely because these sites are free and easy to use. Lately, these social networking sites have gained a foothold among companies, organizations, and even politicians who want to reach out to their target populations (Read, 2006). The wide application of social networking in different contexts appears to have included universities and libraries as well (Boyd & Ellison, 2007). It has been suggested that academic libraries could take the opportunity of using these social networking

DOI: 10.4018/978-1-5225-0495-5.ch003

tools to disseminate information, market services and promote new releases (Burkhardt, 2010). Social media (SM) employ mobile and web-based technologies to create highly interactive platforms via which individuals and communities share, co-create, discuss, and modify user-generated content. The use of social networking is rapidly increasing at an alarming rate. Facebook had 150 million users early last year whereas the latest figures reveal the number of users to be 500 million (Chugh, 2012; Gordon, 2010). A growth of 350 million users in over a year demonstrates the increasing popularity of social networking. Some sites are for the general masses, like Friendster, Hi5 and Facebook. Other sites, like LinkedIn, are more focused professional networks. Media sharing sites, such as MySpace, YouTube and Flickr concentrate on shared videos and photos. Knowledge sharing (KS) can be considered an important process in organizations, because it is fundamental to generating new ideas and developing new business opportunities through socialization and the learning process of knowledge workers. KS among university students has been recognized as an important and interesting area of study in the academic world. With the increasing emphasis on collaborative work in organizations, universities have been structuring its curriculum to engage students in collaborative learning which allows them to reflect and teach more effectively (Walker, 2002). Such an approach has been proven to benefit students in terms of cognitive gains and positive learning outcomes (Rafaeli & Ravid, 2003). To increase the ability to manage KS within and across the organization is thus one of the major challenges facing contemporary organizations. The organizational value of employee knowledge increases when it is shared. Only when employees are willing to share knowledge with colleagues can organizations begin to manage knowledge resources effectively. KS among students is very important both for research and practice. A review of prior studies indicated that this topic has received considerable research attention (Khyzer et al., 2009; Oosterlinck, 2004; Parekh, 2009; Wangpipatwong, 2009; Yaghi et al., 2011).The purpose of this chapter is to explore the KS practices and the use of social media for it in different types of environment including libraries.

Knowledge Management (KM)

Knowledge is increasingly being seen as the most important strategic asset in organisations and an important resource for achieving sustainable competitive advantage. Davenport and Prusak (1998) described knowledge as a blend of experience, values, contextual information, and expert insight that provides a framework for evaluating and incorporating new experience and information. Knowledge evolves continuously as the individual and the organisation adapt to influences from the external and the internal environment (Siakas & Georgiadou, 2006). Knowledge management (KM) is defined as the process by which knowledge needed for an organisation to thrive is created, captured, shared and leveraged. Tiwana (2002) classifies KM in three different processes: knowledge acquisition, knowledge sharing and knowledge utilization. Knowledge acquisition is the process of development and creation of insights, skills, and relationships. Knowledge sharing is the act of disseminating and making available knowledge that is already known and knowledge utilization is where learning is integrated into the organization. The recent KM literature has emphasized the importance of interactive KM technologies (manifested widely in virtual communities) in bringing the human side into the KM equation (Ardichvili et al., 2003). The most recent of these technologies are blogs, wikis and other social media collectively dubbed as Web 2.0 technologies or Web 2.0 platforms (Levy, 2009; Weinberger, 2007). It is argued that such technologies have distinct technical features that unleash passion for engaging in knowledge sharing and addresses drawbacks in the current technologies used within organizations.

Knowledge Sharing

Knowledge Sharing (KS) can be defined as:

- A social interaction culture, involving the exchange of employee knowledge, experiences, and skills through the whole department or organization.
- The provision or receipt of task information, know-how and feedback regarding a product or procedure' and has been tied to a variety of managerial desirable outcomes including productivity, task completion time, organizational learning and innovativeness.
- A set of behaviors about knowledge exchange which involve the actors, knowledge content, organizational context, appropriate media, and societal environment.
- The action in which employees diffuse relevant information to others across the organization (Bartol & Srivastava, 2002).
- It is the process where individuals mutually exchange both tacit and explicit knowledge, and jointly create new knowledge (Georgiadou & Siakas, 2009b).

Social Media

The term 'social media' commonly refers to the use of the internet for collaboration and sharing of content through a variety of social networking tools, news sites and services. Social media (SM) can denote any Internet-based technology that facilitates rapid communication and collaboration through data networks. SM includes text, images, audio and video. It uses web-based technologies to transform broadcast media monologues (one-to-many) into social media dialogue (many-to-many). SM media have the potential of supporting the democratization of knowledge and information, transforming people from content consumers into content producers. The policy of SM includes under its purview different forms including magazines, Internet forums, weblogs, social blogs, microblogging, wikis, social networks, podcasts, photographs or pictures, video, rating and social bookmarking. There are six different types of social media: collaborative projects (e.g., Wikipedia), blogs and microblogs (e.g., Twitter), content communities (e.g., YouTube), social networking sites (e.g., Facebook), and virtual game worlds (e.g., World of War craft) and virtual social worlds (e.g. Second Life). Technologies include: blogs, picture-sharing, vlogs, wall-postings, email, instant messaging, music-sharing, crowd sourcing and voice over IP, to name a few. Many of these social media services can be integrated via social network aggregation platforms. SM network websites include sites like Facebook, Twitter, Bebo and MySpace. As one could understand from the above different types of SM, people are sharing, showing their presence, identity of self with others, conversations and relationships are normally done by anyone who is using SM. This can be seen from the honeycomb framework which defined all social media services in seven functional building blocks - identity, conversations, sharing, presence, relationships, reputation and groups.

RESEARCH METHOD

The study is aimed to investigate the knowledge sharing activities in different types of institutions, particularly from the universities / educational institutions / libraries as they all use social media tools. The investigation is based on a descriptive method, which is centered on a review of the existing literature.

The use of social networking sites, led to the introduction of social media marketing and presented new ways of communicating to expanse audiences on various Internet platforms. Marketers can no longer rely on mass media channels alone to communicate with their consumers. They must adopt new strategies if they wish to succeed (Kotler & Armstrong, 2011). Also Iyer and Sengupta (2010) have reported that Accenture, the world's second largest technology consulting firm, plans to recruit nearly 40% of their workforce over the next few years via SNS such as LinkedIn. So as social networking becomes more pervasive, it is vital to adapt recruitment practices to fit SNS and this will also lead to a reduction in the cost of hiring. On the other hand, it is also important for candidates to leverage SNS for advertising their skills, experience and keeping a positive online image to increase their chances of being hired. This descriptive study also is used to frame a KS cycle and explore the KS activities in libraries.

NEED FOR KS

The goal of KS can either to create new knowledge by differently combining existing knowledge or to become better at exploiting existing knowledge. KS is defined as the process intended at exploiting existing knowledge, and hence defined as being about identifying existing and accessible knowledge, in order to transfer and apply this knowledge to solve specific tasks better, faster and cheaper than they would otherwise have been solved. Hendriks (1999) suggested a conceptualized model which consists of two main activities for effective KS: transmission and absorption. The knowledge owner externalizes the knowledge through the skills of codification, elaboration and presentation. Knowledge is subsequently transmitted to the recipient (reconstructor) by the appropriate media or channels, and then the reconstructor internalizes this knowledge through the capabilities of reading, learning, interpreting and absorbing. Nancy (2000) proposed the concept of "sharing" and suggested that sharing is awareness, which is the conveyance of information or knowledge owned by individuals to others, which enables others to possess the same information and knowledge. Ruggles (1997) found that the important impediments for knowledge sharing include culture (54%), organizational structure (28%), information communication technology (22%), incentive system (19%), and staff turnover (8%), by investigating 431 US and European organizations (Table 1).

Table 1. Summary of knowledge sharing factors

Dimension	Sub-Dimension	Factors
Organizational level	Culture	Sharing culture/Cooperation and collaboration culture/ Knowledge-centered culture/Learning culture
	Structure	Incentive and reward/Work design/Management support/Norm/Political directives
	People	Arduous relationship/Shared understanding/ Similar knowledge frame/Social interaction
	Technology	IT infrastructure/IT know-how/IT support
Individual level		Motivation/Prior experience/Absorptive capacity/Source credibility
Knowledge level		Explicit and tacit knowledge/Causal ambiguity/Knowledge articulability/Knowledge embeddedness

Technology can also be used to catalogue expertise of organizational members and as a result facilitating access to the right people and enhancing KS.

KM Cycle

The processes of KM can be represented with KM cycles (e.g., Bukowitz & Williams (2000), McElroy (1999), Wiig (1993)). An integrated KM cycle with three major stages of KM has been described by Dalkir (2011) as:

1. Knowledge capture and/or creation;
2. Knowledge sharing and dissemination; and
3. Knowledge acquisition and application.

The three stages of KM supported by technologies are facilitated by a favorable organizational culture that promotes information and knowledge sharing. A framework has been formulated by me as below for KS on the use of SM (using Honeycomb framework) by the university students and users (Figure 1).

SOCIAL NETWORKING TOOLS

Social networking can encompass almost all collaborative environments employing Web 2.0 technologies (Alexander, 2006). The promise of Web 2.0 technologies is that they foster collaboration among users, which generates new thinking and strategies to meet the demands of the changing society (Chu & Kennedy, 2011; Glassman & Kang, 2011). Web 2.0 provides a new way of using the Internet for interactive purposes (McLean, Richards & Wardman, 2007). These tools include blogs, wikis, RSS (Really Simple Syndication), podcasting, social bookmarking, social networking, feeds and Google utilities (Churchill 2007). Social networks transmit media such as video, web logs (blogs), ratings and reviews, podcasts and audio among a group of people who are linked by a common characteristic, such as friends and family,

Figure 1.

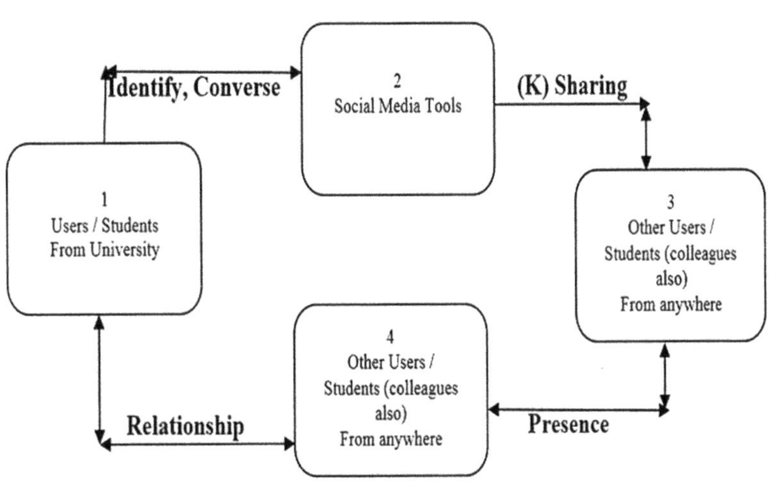

profession, school, residence and even likes and dislikes. They rely on networked users' connectivity and the Internet's ability to breach time and place to form communities and disseminate information. Although social networks are considered primarily a recreational tool, they are becoming increasingly important to businesses and organizations. Figure 2 shows the launch of various social networking tools.

Social networking websites are free and allow users to easily create personal pages filled with content in the form of images, music, and videos. Such websites function as a social network because members are able to share web pages with friends and search for new friends who have similar interests. Some websites allow photo/video sharing, while others allow blogging and private messaging. Social networks have been described to possess three functions:

1. Allow socialization among individuals,
2. Generate participation opportunities, and
3. Facilitate decisions (Passy, 2003).

Sites such as YouTube and Flickr allow users to construct profiles and share connections, buy they have been identified to be primarily for sharing videos and images, rather than for social networking (Hoffman 2009). While the use of social media has been suggested to be all about sharing, learning, ability to have conversations and giving (Burkhardt 2010), sites such as Flickr and YouTube are focused on content-sharing with limited social networking potentials. Similarly, Slideshare, Issuu and blogs are also content-sharing tools with limited potential for conversations between users.

Figure 2. Launch dates of various social networking tools
Chu & Du, 2013.

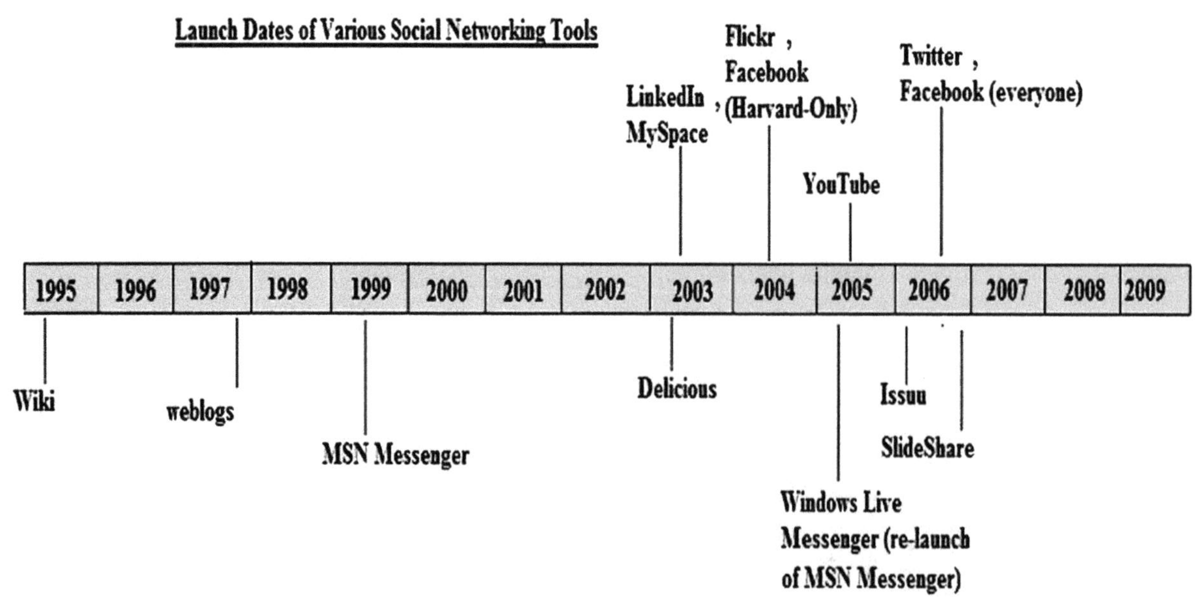

KNOWLEDGE SHARING USING SOCIAL MEDIA

Chan, et al. (2013) found that blogging and Facebook have gained increasing recognition as tools to support online information sharing and management. It also examined if, and in which aspects, blogs and Facebook scaffold and/or consolidate student users' knowledge capture, sharing and application during their internship. A mixed-methods design was employed to investigate users' practices and perceptions of blogs and Facebook in online information management and found that users generally hold positive perception on using blogs and Facebook for online knowledge management. In particular, Facebook appears to be a more facilitating platform for users to reflect upon prior knowledge, capture new experiences and provide feedback that is constructive to cultivating knowledge sharing environment. It was found that Facebook support the expression of social support among users, thereby reinforcing their motivation in participating in knowledge management processes.

Social Networks in Hospitals

Hospitals are increasingly using social networks for promotional purposes. More than 700 of the U.S. (5,000) hospitals have a social media and social networking presence to enhance their ability to market services and communicate to stakeholders. (Bennett, Ed). Cancer centers such as MD Anderson are developing health care communities to understand how their patients view their care experiences. (Li & Bernoff, 2008). Government agencies including the Food and Drug Administration (FDA) and the CDC are using social networks to engage the public during product recalls and in H1N1 flu pandemic preparations (HIN1). Another study by Griffis et al. (2014) investigated the relationship between hospital social media extent of adoption and utilization relative to hospital characteristics. They conducted a cross-sectional review of hospital-related activity on 4 social media platforms: Facebook, Twitter, Yelp, and Foursquare. All US hospitals were included that reported complete data for the Centers for Medicare and Medicaid Services Hospital Consumer Assessment of Healthcare Providers and Systems survey and the American Hospital Association Annual Survey. They determine the extent of adoption relative to hospital characteristics, including geographic region, urban designation, bed size, ownership type, and teaching status. Social media utilization was estimated from user activity specific to each social media platform, including number of Facebook likes, Twitter followers, Four square check-ins, and Yelp reviews. Adoption of social media varied across hospitals with 94.41% (3351/3371) having a Facebook page and 50.82% (1713/3371) having a Twitter account. A majority of hospitals had a Yelp page (99.14%, 3342/3371) and almost all hospitals had check-ins on Foursquare (99.41%, 3351/3371). Large, urban, private nonprofit, and teaching hospitals were more likely to have higher utilization of these accounts. This preliminary investigation of social media adoption and utilization among US hospitals provides the framework for future studies investigating the effect of social media on patient outcomes, including links between social media use and the quality of hospital care and services.

Social Networks in Education

Social media tools provide unique opportunities for meeting online and blended education's collaboration and student-to-student communication needs. The "Learning 2.0 has been used to describe a social media technology that requires a demand-pull rather than a supply-push educational approach (Whitehouse, Reynolds & Caperton, 2009). Some of the researchers have identified several benefits in using social software tools in supporting the development and activities of online and blended learning (Dron & Anderson, 2009; Maddux & others, 2007). Wikis, blogs, forums, and online media sharing sites are examples of the types of social software that are being explored as tools for professional learning and education (Brownson, 2009; Ferdig, 2007; Karabulut & others, 2009). According to Dron and Anderson (2009), one reason that social software has considerable potential for online learning is due to the networking capability of social software in that social media essentially leverages knowledge contained in the minds of others. Through sharing and construction of shared artifacts, knowledge passes into and through the network.

Several kinds of social media tools have already begun to show promise in supporting specific educational activities and many, such as blogs and wikis, have been extensively used in educational contexts for well over a decade. For example, Ferdig (2007) describes this potential for blogging as a virtual place in which collaborative and cooperative learning can occur. The potentials of social networking sites (SNS) where students are provided with the opportunity for publication and feedback are becoming more evident. The potential for social software tools grouped together on one website, as an SNS, for a platform in which to provide learning support is also being recognized (Dron, 2012). The use of Facebook in formal learning (Munoz & Towner, 2009) reports that push message technologies may be one way to support learners using SNS tools. Ning, a social platform where people can (for a price) create private social networks, has been studied as a learning management system for education (Karabulut, et al., 2009). Results of this study in indicated that using Ning provides "opportunities for community building by means of features that allow personalization, socialization, communication among class members, as well as organization of the classroom by allowing a convenient access to assignments, readings and resources.

Recently, 30 educators (approx) are interviewed, including teachers, principals, superintendents, directors of curriculum and learning and consultants at the Texas Association for supervision and curriculum development conference, held in Dallas in order to out the role – if any in social media (Facebook, Twitter, You Tube, etc.) plays in the classroom, in the school, or in the district. The answers were quite interesting. Of those interviewed, 46 percent said that social media plays a limited role in their school or district, primarily to keep parents and the community abreast of activities, schedules and developments taking place at the school or district level. For some schools and districts, social media plays a much more prominent role, with 29 percent said that they actively use social media in their school to fully engage with students, parents and the community. Twenty-five percent do not use social media in any capacity (Tad Druart, 2013).

YOUTUBE AND EDUCATION

YouTube is a video sharing website that started in 2005 and has since exploded into worldwide popularity. YouTube videos can be uploaded by virtually anyone and video content can range from animation, to vlogs, to instructional videos about cooking, artwork, makeup and an assortment of other specialties. When YouTube first launched it was mostly used by people who wanted to share information on a specific hobby or talent but as the website gained substantial audiences, bigger organizations noted its potential and signed on. It has also been noted as being one of the most famous social media platforms for showcasing new and creative work for all age ranges. The educational use of video is accelerating rapidly in departments across all disciplines—from arts, humanities, and sciences to professional and

Figure 3. Learn English: 3 easy ways to get better at speaking English: a guide to critical thinking
By JamesESL English Lessons (engVid) 1,099,693 views - 1 year ago by Mr. Beat's Social Studies Channel, 39,850 views - 1 year ago.

vocational curricula. Youtube is allowing educational institutions and for-profit and non-profit organizations to readily engage new audiences and share valuable information. It is acting as a helpful learning tool and those who value learning should take time to explore the site and see what content fits their specific needs in order to enhance their educational experience. There are plenty of educational videos are available now. Some of the videos available for different educational purpose are shown in Figure 3.

Most of the people are using YouTube as it can be easily utilized for creating as power point presentation or by giving link from there. It is easy to embed as a Flash object so that they can appear on actual slide. Also one can bookmark it, paste the URL as a hot link onto the slide or create an "action" that will open YouTube and take you directly to the video.

VALUE OF SOCIAL MEDIA

The value of social media for education is in the potential that these tools can be used by designers of education to support three key successful educational elements. Instructional designers report that discussion, collaboration, and bringing real-world experiences into the classroom space are the elements (Harasim, 2012) where social media can support learning. These three elements can be described as follows:

1. Social Media supports peer-peer active learning and learning that takes place between lectures and other classroom activities. Discussion about educational content, using communication tools that are part of their day-to-day interactions with others, allows students to express themselves, enhancing their learning experience (Frechette, 2012).
2. Social Media sites like wikis, blogs, Twitter, YouTube support both collaboration and cooperation. The social networking sites like Facebook or LinkedIn provide students with opportunities to learn from and with each other. Students begin to see themselves as authentic producers of knowledge, sharing their student voice and representing their world view.
3. Social Media bridge the real-world and classroom spaces. Online tools provide effective ways to connect to resources and people outside the classroom. They offer opportunities for engaging with data, people, and situations adding meaning and context for learning experiences. In many ways, the simple act of engagement in a network can be a profoundly educational experience, whether intentional or otherwise (Siemens, 2005).

Table 2. Social media uses in higher education

Social Media	Use in Higher Education
Microblog (Twitter, Hotseat)	Engaging students in lectures, information sharing
Photo/Video sharing (YouTube, Flickr)	Examples, course content, student assignments
Blogs & Journals	Reflection activities, Lecturer blogs to support course activities
Wiki	Group work, scaffolded assessments
Interactive Media (Voice thread, EtherPad, YouTube)	Lecturer and tutor feedback for assessments, student-created products
Social Networking Sites (Facebook, LinkedIn)	Lecturer and tutor profiles, connect point with some students, share information & resource links, develop student portfolio and online presence

Table 2 provides an overview of the types of social media and how they are being used in higher education settings.

Some of the successes of incorporating social media into blended and online courses include the use of:

1. Facebook pages to disseminate information to large enrolment courses.
2. LinkedIn to connect students to professionals in the field.
3. Twitter to send short messages to students providing them with news articles relevant to the course content.
4. YouTube to provide examples relating to business and culture from around the world.
5. Voice thread to provide instructor and tutor feedback on assessments.
6. Wikis to provide places for groups of students to work on collaborative activities.
7. Blogs to provide a teacher presence in the online space relevant to the course content and activities.
8. Wikipedia editing as a learning activity to encourage both engagement with a broader community and an active learning process that provides motivation and feedback from beyond the classroom.

These uses of social media represent some of the emerging practices for incorporating social media into formal educational settings.

SOCIAL NETWORKING TOOLS IN LIBRARIES

Social Networks in Libraries

Social networking tools that were within this social media study's operational definition were reportedly used for marketing and publicity, enhancing reference services, and knowledge sharing among staff (Chu & Du, 2013). It was found that Facebook and Twitter have been used for marketing among the respondents, while an earlier study had reported that libraries were indifferent towards marketing through Facebook (Charnigo & Barnett-Ellis, 2007). Instant messaging was reportedly used for handling enquiry-related services and internal staff communication. This tool has been shown to enhance users' social presence and to facilitate a sense of connection, which was not provided by emails and conventional Web 1.0 websites (Boulos & Wheelert, 2007). Wikis were also reportedly used to handle enquiries and frequently asked questions (FAQ), which is consistent with earlier findings by Chu (2009) that wikis have enabled communication between librarians and users. Wikis have also been used to create, capture, share and transfer knowledge (Chu, 2008). That social networking tools were helpful in promoting library services was consistent with the finding that the two most reported purposes for which libraries used social networking tools were promotion of library events (e.g., exhibitions, competitions, talks, seminars, workshops, tutorials, training courses) and dissemination of news (e.g., events alert, library updates).

Set of Guidelines of Social Media Usage in Libraries

Social media plays an important role now-a-days in every field, including libraries. Social media is key to 21st century communication with library users, and enables the academic library to pursue its mission and goals online, while promoting library resources and services (Johnson & Burclaff, 2013b). Libraries use social media to fulfill a range of objectives, with most focused on promotion (visibility for and usage of the library service and resources). However, broadcast/ informational communications are increasingly being supplemented with two-way communications designed to solicit feedback (e.g. for collection development), offer real-time customer service and build engagement with users. Social media is also increasingly being seen as a collection management tool, offering flexible ways to present resources (e.g. YouTube for video delivery) and categorize them (e.g. folksonomies). Outreach is also seen as important – for example, helping librarians increase their visibility and connections within the broader library community; also, for assisting in the promotion of the work of their faculty. Use of social media for enhancing teaching and learning is currently a lower priority, but this will likely become an important activity in the near future, and librarians with their growing experience of using social media tools are well-placed to help develop institutional capabilities. (Taylor & Francis, whitepaper, Oct 2014). Therefore, there are organizations like American Libraries Association, Online Computer Library Center and others that have framed guidelines to be followed by the librarians in order to be associated with the users / organizational members. Some of the guidelines are as follows:

1. Library should have a policy to have social media interaction.
2. Key themes to be followed in social media.
3. Determine how the Social media will be used.
4. Provide that content that facilitates literacy.
5. Checklist for social media posts.

Facebook and Libraries

Facebook became a topic of research in library and information science scholarship in 2007 (Scale, 2008), thus representing scholars' interest in the emerging social phenomenon. Most of the articles found in library publications are written from a librarian's perspective, explaining the essence of Facebook and describing different ways in which Facebook might be used by librarians to promote library services (Bates & Can, 2007; Breeding, 2007). Mack et al. (2007) present the results of research that compared the number of reference inquiries received through Facebook, e-mail, phone, instant messaging and traditional person-to-person questions, outside of normal reference desk shifts. They found that the most questions were asked through Facebook, with e-mail as a close second. Charnigo and Barnett-

Ellis (2007) conducted a survey of academic librarians, in which participants were asked about their awareness of Facebook, their attitudes towards Facebook and the day-to-day impact of Facebook on the everyday workings of their library.

Facebook and MySpace

A study in mid 2000s indicated that most of the library directors and the general public from the United States did not think that libraries had a role in social networking. But the potential of using social networking in libraries has been demonstrated through the use of Facebook and MySpace (Chu & Nalani-Meulemans 2008). By displaying their status (whether they are online or not), available librarians were easily identified by users to address their enquiries. Librarians also found it advantageous when they wished to communicate with colleagues to answer users' enquiries, thus providing answers to users' enquiries more efficiently. Furthermore, Facebook and MySpace were found to be helpful in enhancing libraries' social visibility through profiles that showed a uniform identity. It was also found that MySpace allowed different librarians to contribute knowledge and information, maintain a profile together and promote new library collections. A number of librarians have suggested that Facebook could be a feasible way to deliver library services and communicate with users (Charnigo & Barnett-Ellis, 2007). In the case of Kimbel Library of the Coastal Carolina University, Facebook has been used to provide reference assistance and library tours, and promoting services (Graham, Faix, & Hartman, 2009) and also Facebook helped colleagues become closer and to personally know each other better.

While social networking websites appear to have benefits for libraries, their use has not been pervasive, partly due to librarians' perceived limitations in their abilities to set up profiles and time dedicated for maintenance (Hendrix et al. 2009). Students have reported that they felt more comfortable and interested in using social networking tools to communicate with people whom they regarded as friends, which would not likely include librarians. Some college students have also shown negative feelings about the librarians using Facebook and MySpace as outreach tools since it may infringe on their sense of personal privacy (Connell, 2009).

The Role of a Community of Cataloguers in Informal Further Education

For many, the need to access cataloguers with experience and knowledge of new developments in cataloguing practice is met by an online community of cataloguers. Hopkins (2002) focused on the role of a community of cataloguers with reference to the use of technology for communication; specifically, electronic discussion lists, websites and blogs. She argued that a cataloguer's immediate colleagues as sources of information and further education have, through technology, been expanded to an international network of cataloguers. Eustis (2011) discussed the role of blogs in providing cataloguers with access to specific information, as well as information about cataloguing and related fields. In addition, she suggested that blogs offer the opportunity to engage with colleagues about the present and future of the profession. McElfresh's (2010) article, "Catalogers and social media: a whole lotta movin' and shakin' going on", concentrates on the use of Twitter and, like Eustis, she touches on Hopkins' categories of use, such as assigning subject headings or classification numbers to difficult items for immediate and specific current awareness for use and providing links to blog posts and articles which she referred to as general current awareness.

ADVANTAGES OF KS USING SM IN LIBRARIES

Some of the benefits of KS are as follows:

- KS makes the captured expertise available to all people serving in an organization uniformly.
- As KM is to capture knowledge and make it accessible to all service and support agents, it no longer stays with those who hold or discover it; becomes an organization asset available to all who need it.
- KS enhances contacts with other people either local, regional, national or at international and develops a knowledge networks.
- KS reduces the costs of repeated mistakes or re-inventing the wheel.
- KS enhances functional effectiveness.
- SM tools and services are mostly applied in different section of library. The user service section used Library 2.0 technology to promote their newsletter and library programs. The technical section used Library 2.0 tools to develop the tags cloud to help user to find materials easier.
- Web 2.0 help people to use the web and publish information online easier. In the same time, they use library online service is easier.
- Communicating with users as a broadcasting service, e.g. pushing out information, promoting library events or highlighting library resources (new books, interesting items in the existing collection, or expertise of library staff).
- Engaging in dialogue with users – monitoring social media feeds for mentions or comments in order to keep an eye on what is being said about the library, responding to queries or complaints, and providing reference services or readers advisory services. For example, clarifying research projects, or as one respondent identified, using social media in school libraries to engage parent groups.
- Networking and engaging with clients who are staff within a parent organisation e.g. council or university.
- Communicating with distance or remote users.

Thus, libraries are able to use social media to respond to users and also to build relationships among them (Bradley & McDonald, 2011; Golden, 2010).

CHALLENGES IN IMPLEMENTING SOCIAL NETWORKING TOOLS

A number of challenges in using social networking tools in libraries were identified, the most pressing of which appears to be limitations associated with inadequate time. This may be problematic since using social networking tools have not been given priority due to insufficient time to learn how to use them and also noted that these tools were very technical to learn, explore and implement in the library. Generally, monitoring the social networking tools was perceived to require additional time and manpower in the library. Besides time, the 'aging and shrinking staff' of the library also found it difficult to follow the technological innovations of the tools. Furthermore, some difficulty was perceived in 'understanding how each tool worked and how to align it to their specific business model'. The process of determining which tool users might welcome more was perceived to be challenging as a consequence of the continuous evolution of social media.

CONCLUSION

This study explored and found that social networking tools were being used by a number of institutions /organizations and academic libraries. They were perceived to be helpful in promoting library services and interacting with students. Moreover, the tools were also reported to be helpful for internal staff communication. However, the implementation of these tools by library staff was found to be challenged by limited time and perceived inadequacy of the staff to keep pace with the development of technology. There is a need to be researched in the area of social media use in education, and the potentials of these technologies to enhance learning. As Dahlstrom (2012) points out, the development of lecturer/designer knowledge about which technologies are more effective for specific types of student-teacher interactions can lead to the development of strategic pedagogical investments of lecturers' time and resources. In the twenty-first century new educational professionalism is needed to deal with lifelong learning, knowledge development and knowledge sharing. It can be seen that nature of knowledge, working culture, staff attitude, motivation to share and opportunities to share play important role in enhancing KS among teaching staff in universities. Sharing of knowledge could also be enhanced if the university administrators play a positive role by encouraging their teaching staff to share knowledge by organizing open discussions, forums, seminars or colloquiums. It has been emphasized that KS is – or should be – part of ongoing organizational activities, and therefore it is fruitful to consider the process as one of bridging situations of interdependencies. Now-a-days, in the field of medicine many social networking sites have been created specifically for the use of doctors, medical practitioners, nurses and others. Similar efforts can be done by all other disciplines to share their specific subject interest on those sites. Further studies can also be done taking specific subject oriented social networking sites. A number of libraries, which have not been using these tools, indicated plans to adopt them in the future, depending on the response of library patrons. The phenomenon of social networking tools is likely to continue evolving rapidly.

REFERENCES

H1N1 Web and Social Media Metrics Cumulative Data Report April 22, 2009– December 31, 2009. (n.d.). Division of eHealth Marketing (DeHM) National Center for Health Marketing (NCHM) Centers for Disease Control and Prevention (CDC).

Alexander, B. (2006). A new wave of Innovation for Teaching and Learning? *EDUCAUSE Review*, *41*(2), 32–44.

Ardichvili, A., Page, V., & Wentling, T. (2003). Motivation and barriers to participation in virtual knowledge-sharing communities practice. *Journal of Knowledge Management*, *7*(1), 64–77. doi:10.1108/13673270310463626

Barsky, E., & Purdon, M. (2006). Introducing Web 2.0: Social networking and social bookmarking for health librarians. *Journal of the Canadian Health Libraries Association*, *27*(3), 65–67. doi:10.5596/c06-024

Bartol, K. M., & Srivastava, A. (2002). Encouraging knowledge sharing: The role of organizational reward system. *Journal of Leadership & Organizational Studies*, *9*(1), 64–76. doi:10.1177/107179190200900105

Bennett, E. (n.d.). *Hospital Social Network Data & Charts.* Retrieved May 02, 2015 from http://ebennett.org/hsnl/data

Boyd, D. M., & Ellison, N. B. (2007). Social network sites: Definition, history, and scholarship. *Journal of Computer-Mediated Communication, 13*(1), 210–230. doi:10.1111/j.1083-6101.2007.00393.x

Bradley, A., & McDonald, M. (2011). *The Social Organization.* Boston: Harvard Business Review Press.

Brownson, S. (2009). *A study of the integration of wikis and blogs into an online course on student interaction and satisfaction* (Doctoral dissertation). Retrieved from Dissertations & Theses: Full Text. (Publication No. AAT 3371718)

Bukowitz, W., & Williams, R. (2000). *The Knowledge management fieldbook.* London, UK: Prentice-Hall.

Burkhardt, A. (2010). Social media: A guide for college and university libraries. *College & Research Libraries News, 71*(1), 10–24.

Chan, R. C. H., Chu, S. K. W., Lee, C. W. Y., Chan, B. K. T., & Leung, C. K. (2013). Knowledge management using social media: A comparative study between blogs and Facebook.*Proceedings of the ASIS&T 2013 Annual Meeting*. doi:10.1002/meet.14505001069

Charnigo, L., & Barnett-Ellis, P. (2007). Checking Out Facebook.com: The Impact of a Digital Trend on Academic Libraries. *Information Technology & Libraries, 26*(1), 23–34.

Chu, M., & Nalani-Meulemans, Y. (2008). The Problems and Potential of MySpace and Facebook Usage in Academic Libraries. *Internet Reference Services Quarterly, 13*(1), 69–85. doi:10.1300/J136v13n01_04

Chu, S.K.W. & Du, H. (2013). Social Networking Tools for Academic Libraries. *Journal of Librarianship & Information Science, 45*(1), 64-75.

Chu, S. K. W., & Kennedy, D. (2011). Using online collaborative tools for groups to co-construct knowledge. *Online Information Review, 35*(4), 581–597. doi:10.1108/14684521111161945

Chugh, R. (2012). Social networking for business: Is it a boob or bane? In Cruz-Cunha et al. (Eds.), *Handbook on Research on business Social networking: Organisational, managerial, and Technological dimensions.* Hershey, PA: IGI Global. doi:10.4018/978-1-61350-168-9.ch032

Churchill, D. (2007). Web 2.0 and possibilities for educational applications. *Educational Technology, 47*(2), 24–29.

Connell, R. S. (2009). Academic Libraries, Facebook and MySpace, and Student Outreach: A Survey of Student Opinion. P*ortal. Libraries & the Academy, 9*(1), 25–36. doi:10.1353/pla.0.0036

Dahlstom, E. (2012). *Study of Undregraduate students and Information Technology 2012 (Research Report).* Luiosville, CO: EDUCAUSE.

Dalkir, K. (2011). *Knowledge Management in Theory and Practice.* Cambridge, UK: The MIT Press.

Davenport, T., & Prusak, L. (1998). *Working Knowledge: How Organizations Manage What They Know.* Boston, MA: Harvard Business School Press.

Dron, J. (2012). Self-paced and Social. In T. Bastiaens, & G. Marks (Eds.), *Proceedings of World Conference on E-Learning in Corporate, Government, Healthcare, and Higher Education 2012* (p. 962-976). Chesapeake, VA: AACE.

Dron, J., & Anderson, T. (2009). How the Crowd Can Teach. In S. Hatzipanagos & S. Wartburton (Eds.), *Handbook of Research on Social Software and Developing Community Ontologies* (pp. 1–17). Hershey, PA: Information Science Reference. doi:10.4018/978-1-60566-208-4.ch001

Eustis, J. M. (2011). Blogs and their place in the continuing education of catalogers. In E. R. Sanchez (Ed.), *Conversations with Cataloguers in the 21st Century* (pp. 219–225). Santa Barbara, CA: Libraries Unlimited.

Ferdig, R. E. (2007). Editorial: Examining Social Software in Teacher Education. *Journal of Technology and Teacher Education*, *15*(1), 5–10.

Frechette, J. (2012). Learning beyond the classroom walls: Keeping students engaged in Class 2.0. *Journal of Media Literacy*. Retrieved on 3rd Sep 2015 from http://journalofmedialiteracy.org/index.php/current-issue/98-david-considines-ten-technology-tips-for-principals

Georgiadou, E., & Siakas, K. (2009b). *Collaborative projects: a bottom-up approach to European integratio*. International Technology, Education and Development Conference (INTED 2009), Valencia, Spain.

Glassman, M., & Kang, M. J. (2011). The logic of wikis: The possibilities of the Web 2.0 classroom. *Computer-Supported Collaborative Learning*, *6*(1), 93–112. doi:10.1007/s11412-011-9107-y

Golden, M. (2010). *Social Media: Strategies for Professionals and Their Firms*. Hoboken, NJ: John Wiley and Sons.

Gordon, S. (2010). *Facebook notches up 500 million members.* Retrieved July 27, 2010, from http://news.sky.com/skynews/Home/Business/ Facebook-To-Hit-500-Million-Users-WorldwideJust-Six-Years-After-Mark-Zuckerberg-CreatedIt/ Article/201007315668531

Graham, J. M., Faix, A., & Hartman, L. (2009). Crashing the Facebook party: One library's experiences in the students' domain. *Library Review*, *58*(3), 228–236. doi:10.1108/00242530910942072

Griffis, H. M., Kilaru, A. S., Werner, R. M., Asch, D. A., Hershey, J. C., Hill, S., & Merchant, R. M. et al. (2014). Use of Social Media Across US Hospitals: Descriptive Analysis of Adoption and Utilization. *Journal of Medical Internet Research*, *16*(11), e264. doi:10.2196/jmir.3758

Harasim, L. (2012). *Instructional Design & Social Media Panel*. World Conference on Educational Media & Technology 2012.

Hendriks, P. (1999). Why share knowledge? The influence of ICT on the motivation for knowledge sharing. *Knowledge and Process Management*, *6*(2), 91–100. doi:10.1002/(SICI)1099-1441(199906)6:2<91::AID-KPM54>3.0.CO;2-M

Hendrix, D., Chiarella, D., Hasman, L., Murphy, S., & Zafron, M. L. (2009). Use of Facebook in academic health sciences libraries. *Journal of the Medical Library Association: JMLA*, *97*(1), 44–47. doi:10.3163/1536-5050.97.1.008

Hopkins, J. (2002). The community of cataloguers: Its role in the education of cataloguers. *Cataloging & Classification Quarterly*, *34*(3), 375–381. doi:10.1300/J104v34n03_09

Iyer, S., & Sengupta, D. (2010, July 5). Top IT firms log on to social networking sites to hire middle & senior-level staff. *The Economic Times*.

Johnson, C., & Burclaff, N. (2013). Making Social Media Meaningful: Connecting Missions and Policies. In *Imagine, Innovate, Inspire* (pp. 399–405). Indianapolis, IN: American Library Association. Retrieved 1 Oct 2015, from http://www.ala.org/acrl/sites/ala.org.acrl/files/content/conferences/confsandpreconfs/2013/papers/JohnsonBurclaff_Making.pdf

Karabulut, A., et al. (2009). Student Level of Commitment and Engagement with Ning as a Learning Management System. In C. Maddux (Ed.), Research Highlights in Technology and Teacher Education (pp. 43-49). SITE.

Khyzer, M. D., Asim, K. M., Zulfiqar, A., Zafar, A., Musarrat, M. N., Ishraf, A., & Naveed, A. et al. (2009). Interpersonal factors and tendencies to knowledge sharing among students: A case of Punjab University. *The Knowledge Economy*, *1*(1), 519–525.

Kotler, P., & Armstrong, G. (2011). *Principles of Marketing* (14th ed.). Pearson Prentice Hall.

Levy, M. (2009). WEB 2.0 implications on knowledge management. *Journal of Knowledge Management*, *13*(1), 120–134. doi:10.1108/13673270910931215

Li, C. & Bernoff, J. (2008). *Groundswell: Winning in a World Transformed by Social Technologies.* Academic Press.

Maddux, C., Sprague, D., Ferdig, R., & Albion, P. (2007). Editorial: Online Education: Issues and Research Questions. *Journal of Technology and Teacher Education*, *15*(2), 157–166.

Marshall, L. (1997). Facilitating Knowledge Management and Knowledge Sharing: New Opportunities for Information Professionals. *Online*, *21*(Sept/Oct), 92–98.

Marwick, D. (2001). Knowledge management technology. *IBM Systems Journal*, *40*(4), 814–830. doi:10.1147/sj.404.0814

McElfresh, L. K. (2010). Catalogers and social media: A whole lotta movin' and shakin' going on. *Technicalities*, *30*(4), 2–5.

McElroy, M. W. (2003). *The New Knowledge Management: Complexity, Learning and Sustainable Innovation*. Burlington, MA: KMCI Press/Butterworth-Heinemann.

McLean, R., Richards, B. H., & Wardman, J. I. (2007). The effect of Web 2.0 on the future of medical practice and education: Darwikinian evoluation or folksonomic revolution? *The Medical Journal of Australia*, *187*(3), 174–177.

Munoz, C., & Towner, T. (2009). Opening Facebook: How to use Facebook in the college classroom. In *Society for Information Technology & Teacher Education International Conference* (No. 1, p. 2623-2627).

Nancy, M. D. (2000). *Common Knowledge: How Companies Thrive by Sharing What They Know*. Boston, MA: Harvard Business School Press.

Oosterlinck, A. (2004). *Knowledge management in post-secondary education: universities, OECD working paper*. Retrieved 4th Sep 2015, from www.oecd.org/dataoecd/46/21/2074921.pdf

Parekh, R. A. (2009). Knowledge sharing: collaboration between universities and industrial organizations. In *Globalizing Academic Libraries: Vision 2020: Pre-conference Volume:The International Conference on Academic Libraries*. University of Delhi.

Passy, F. (2003). Social movements and networks. In M. Diani & D. McAdam (Eds.), *Relational Approaches to Collective Action*. New York: Oxford University Press.

Petrides, L., & Nodine, T. (2003). *KM in Education: Defining the Landscape*. Half Moon Bay, CA: Institute for the Study of Knowledge Management in Education.

Rafaeli, S., & Ravid, G. (2003). Information sharing as enabler for the virtual team: An experimental approach to assessing the role of electronic mail in disintermediation. *Information Systems Journal*, *13*(2), 191–206. doi:10.1046/j.1365-2575.2003.00149.x

Read, B. (2006). To the Chagrin of Its Clientele, Facebook Expands Its Membership. *The Chronicle of Higher Education*, *53*(5), A35.

Ruggles, R. (Ed.). (1997). Knowledge Management Tools. Boston: Butterworth Heinemann.

Siakas, K., & Georgiadou, E. (2006). Knowledge sharing: cultural dynamics. In *Proceedings of 7th European Conference of Knowledge Management (ECKM06)*. Public Academic Conferences Ltd.

Siemens, G. (2005). Connectivism: A learning theory for the digital age. *International Journal of Instructional Technology and Distance Learning*, *2*(1).

Taylor & Francis. (2014). *Use of social media by the library: Current practices and future opportunities.* Retrieved 6th Sep 2015, from http://www.tandf.co.uk/journals/access/white-paper-social-media.pdf

Tiwana, A. (2002). *The Knowledge Management Toolkit: Orchestrating IT, Strategy and Knowledge Platforms*. Englewood Cliffs, NJ: Prentice-Hall.

Townley, C. T. (2001). Knowledge Management and Academic Libraries. *College & Research Libraries*, *62*(Jan), 44–55. doi:10.5860/crl.62.1.44

Walker, J. W. (2002). Research, knowledge sharing and you. *Human Resource Planning.*, *25*(2), 10–13.

Wangpipatwong, S. (2009). Factors influencing knowledge sharing among university students. *17th International Conference on Computers in Education.* Asia-Pacific Society for Computers in Education.

Weinberger, D. (2007). The real difference between the two 2.0s. *KM World*, *16*(2). Retrieved 10 May, 2015, from www.kmworld.com/Articles/Column/David-Weinberger/The-real-difference-between-the-two-2.0s-19130.aspx

Whitehouse, P., Reynolds, R., & Caperton, I. (2009). Globaloria Pilot Year One: New Directions for 21st Century Teacher Professional Development. In I. Gibson et al. (Eds.), *Proceedings of Society for Information Technology & Teacher Education International Conference 2009* (pp. 1590-1597). Chesapeake, VA: AACE.

Wiig, K. (1993). *Knowledge management foundations.* Arlington, TX: Schema Press.

Yaghi, K., Barakat, S., Alfawaer, Z. M., Shkokani, M., & Nassuora, A. (2011). Knowledge sharing degree among the undergraduate students: A case study at applied science private university. *International Journal of Academic Research, 3*(1), 20–24.

KEY TERMS AND DEFINITIONS

Knowledge Management (KM): Defined as the process by which knowledge needed for an organisation to thrive is created, captured, shared and leveraged. Therefore KM means that knowledge is generated within the organization that has to be captured, shared and preserved for future use.

Knowledge Sharing (KS): The process where individuals mutually exchange both tacit and explicit knowledge, and jointly create new knowledge. KS is nothing but sharing any type of knowledge which may create new knowledge by assimilation of the receivers.

Social Media (SM): Commonly refers to the use of the internet for collaboration and sharing of content through a variety of social networking tools, news sites and services. SM can denote any Internet-based technology that facilitates rapid communication and collaboration through data networks.

Social Networking (SN): Social networking can encompass almost all collaborative environments employing Web 2.0 technologies. It is nothing but sharing with friends and others and exchanging is also possible in social networking.

Chapter 4
Facilitating Knowledge Sharing on Social Media for Students of International Relations and Conflict Studies in Nigeria

James Okolie-Osemene
Wellspring University, Nigeria

ABSTRACT

This chapter has examined ways of facilitating knowledge sharing for the benefit of students of international relations and conflict studies in Nigerian universities. It is evident that tertiary institutions' students of the 21st Century cannot study now without the use of social media which serves as a platform for information sharing and knowledge production. It is a medium through which knowledge is transferred to users by think tanks and organisations across the world. Given that not only students benefit, people from all walks of life are not also left out as social networks record large number of users daily. This explains how social media serves as data bank for scholars and why students now need to continuously search to find related materials on social media. Using qualitative data the author used observation method in the classroom setting in the University of Ibadan and Wellspring University, Benin City, Nigeria. It should be stated that the type of digital device used by students can as well determine their level of access to the social media in Nigeria. Observations show that social media is very relevant for students especially in the study and teaching of international relations and conflict studies given the number of global courses like new states in world politics, democracy and human rights, post-cold war politics, global refugee regimes, international law problems of peacemaking and peacekeeping, among others which all generate issues on daily basis that need to be shared as relevant academic materials for among students.

DOI: 10.4018/978-1-5225-0495-5.ch004

INTRODUCTION

We need to reach out to social media, those who know the story better than Journalists – #Africa Summit, 2014.

The information revolution that emerged in the 21st Century was heralded by most people across the world, a situation that manifested in the embrace given to new media technologies which facilitate social networking and development of new platforms/applications. The 21st Century is replete with various technological innovations that now facilitate the coverage of terrorism as there are satellites, mobile phones, Ipad and Iphones. That is why acts of terrorism now trend on social media. In contemporary international socio-economic and political system, we have not only social networks' but also the networks of terror most of which operate beyond their continents of origin as they export their acts of terror. Social networks have become critical tools for addressing issues of concern on terror in the public sphere to the extent that people visit their pages/accounts or status to learn the trending issues.

Social media has increasingly become so relevant in contemporary international relations where intergroup and inter-state relations are characterised by disputable issues. International relations and conflicts studies are disciplines that require adequate utilisation on the social media considering its potency in offering timely information discrimination and knowledge management. The question is how many students of the two disciplines under investigation are aware of the potentials of social media in enhancing their studies? The issue is that most final year students even write their projects to complete their degrees and end up not benefiting from the rich information and data available on social media especially in the areas of international relations and conflict studies.

Knowledge management has increasingly become a notable attribute of the social media which gives users the opportunity to share information need to enhance their understanding. The nature of international relations and conflict studies are in such a way that collaborative information retrieval makes studies and understanding more interesting. In collaborative information retrieval sharing of information becomes easier given that no man is an island of knowledge.

As earlier noted by Smith (2014, p.9) 'partnership and collaboration are key to achieving set vision'. This is based on the fact that the global village phenomenon as contained in globalisation agenda, 'is facilitated by the modern information and communications technologies' (Odejobi, 2015, p.748). The revolution in the information and communication technologies (ICT) has transformed the global landscape for conducting governance, doing business and trade as well as managing international relationships (Eboh, 2009, p.24). There is no disputation that the growth of knowledge-intensive technologies has not only facilitated the transition to a new qualitative level of development of knowledge economy but has also enhanced the awareness of people on the relevance of such technologies (Vlasov & Panikarova, 2015, p.475). Also, the availability of distributed data collection, communication and control channels in institutions and think tanks led to the creation of a platform for suitable environment that gives room for collaboration. This means that non-governmental organizations, governments and individuals would definitely work in isolation in solving if we must address issues of global academic significance. According to London (1995) collaboration is a synergy between two or more organizations, or other agents to produce a combined effect greater than the sum of their separate effects. Through collaboration, individually generated information becomes general and people-oriented data for further research both in the area of affairs and activities of nation states and the conflict that involve state actors and non state actors.

Indeed, people can share information through various channels and not limited to mobile devices, published patent applications, working notes and smart boards. Documents which are usually paper based stickers, catalogues, comment books, instructional papers and rules of engagement. In addition, there are electronic data including those viewed through the instrumentality of drop box, team viewer, Skype and Yahoo messenger among others.

In their study, Amana and Attah (2014, p. 24) rightly pointed out that "foundational to the understanding of the notion of social media is the notion of the new media which refers to a platform that has been enhanced by digitization." Digital technologies led to the emergence of social media platforms which Kaplan and Haenlein (2009), describe as to "a group of Internet-based applications that build on the ideological and technological foundations of Web 2.0, and that allows the creation and exchange of User Generated Content" (cited in Barrons, 2012). That is why Feldman (1997) sees digital satellite television as an example of new media technology which uses digital compression to dramatically increase the number of television channels that can be delivered to viewers. Significantly, Osazee-Odia (2008, p.347) new digital technology refers to computer mediated systems which are enhanced by the internet and satellite technology. Interestingly, their applications to text delivery, communication, facilitated by transmission hardware are very significant to information sharing and knowledge development. It is the technology behind the digital devices that power the entire social media most of what do not necessarily need to be physically connected to each other to function well.

It is the activities of network providers and the regulatory agencies that have sustained the use of internet and all digital devices even in rural areas where there were no communication gadgets in the past. According to Ezike (2015, p.80):

The availability, accessibility, and frequency of use of laptops, desktops, palm held devices, tablets, telephones and other devices have increased over the last ten years in Nigeria. Telecommunication companies have tremendously boosted internet connectivity and access as it is observed that 2G and even 3G browsing networks are available even in remotest communities in Nigeria.

Notably, social networks are sites that allow people to create communities on the internet around shared relationships, interests and activities (Okolie-Osemene, 2012, p.257; Chugh, 2012). Social networking has been enhanced by the use of computer-mediated communication in the form of internet connectivity that now links different people (Chugh, 2012:603). According to Masuku and Moyo (2014, p.131) 'social networking sites are a category of sites that are based on user participation and user-generated content.' This user-generation of content entails that the presence of users, males and females also offers them a platform and opportunity to share updates, send requests, make comments on issues and invite friends to join discussion groups. It should be noted that every creation of group/online pages and content generation must be preceded by creation of profiles in the users' names. Such name (s) therefore becomes an identity. In the world of Dlodlo and Dhurup (2013, p.330) 'typical social media tools such as social networking sites allow a user to build and maintain a network of friends for social, professional or business interaction which could include a brand of communities.' Digital satellite television, global satellite telephones, internet websites, mobile telephony, whatsapp-internet enhanced telephones, short message service facilities, multimedia equipments such as video, audio and pod casts facilities have rapidly enhanced the use of social media in recent times.

The force of knowledge sharing (KS) has been noted: "there is an amount of abstinence from risky sexual behavior in the rural areas as a result of the available knowledge at their disposal" (Ikenwe &

Igbinovia, 2015, p.28). The missions and concerns of this chapter are obvious. The role of social media in knowledge development and management cannot be underplayed. This makes it crucial for scholars at all levels to harness the social media and digital devices in managing knowledge.

In fact, the social media has become a crucial determinant of the ability of students to learn more by being adequately informed when they were in the past. In this era, all we see is social media and collaborative knowledge management manifesting. This study was inspired by the divergence of students' awareness of the opportunities offered by social media in enhancing their studies especially in the areas of knowledge sharing specifically in international relations and conflict studies. The problematic is that majority of them have access to social networks and digital devices in particular but with little attention given to knowledge sharing which indeed is a panacea for knowledge development in every field of study. Not many Nigerian students are aware of the relevance of the social media in enhancing their studies. Only those that are aware attempt to share their focus, questions on this platform. This is based on the fact that people do no longer need to travel to institutions in order parts of the world to gain access to academic resources in those areas. As we all know, the study of international relations and conflict /peace studies demands networking and sharing of information / materials as they are produced or generated

Using participant observation, key informant interviews, secondary and primary sources of literature relevant to the study, this chapter responds to the following research questions:

1. How do we enhance students' awareness on ways of harnessing social media as a knowledge management tool?
2. How can students participate in the act of knowledge sharing?
3. What digital devices and social networks can facilitate knowledge sharing in international relations and conflict studies in Nigeria?
4. What do students stand to benefit from information shared on social media?

CONCEPTUAL AND THEORETICAL EXPLANATIONS

Indeed, social networks are sites that allow people to create communities on the internet around shared relationships, interests and activities (Okolie-Osemene, 2012, p.257). While some are open groups for people from all walks of life, others are closed groups usually meant for a specific class or category of people, community or profession. According to Masuku and Moyo (2014, p.131) 'social networking sites are a category of sites that are based on user participation and user-generated content.' This user-generation of content entails that the presence of users, all gender groups offers them a platform and opportunity to share updates, send requests, make comments on issues for more to be uncovered and invite friends to join their discussion groups. It should be noted that every creation of group/online pages and content generation must be preceded with the creation of profiles in the users' names. Thereafter, they are identified with the names as long as they continue using them.

In addition, social media belongs to the category of new media. Amana &Attah (2014, p. 24) noted that "foundational to the understanding of the notion of social media is the notion of the new media which refers to a platform that has been enhanced by digitization." In the words of Curca (2013, p.10) it can also be said that the new tools of communications pave way for messages to be amplified and communication flows to become increasingly horizontal and democratizing. In essence, Medium theory explains how media are themselves social contexts that foster certain forms of interaction and social identities, this is based on the experience of technologically - mediated communication manifesting in social networks (Meyrowitz, 1985; Okolie-Osemene, 2012). The interaction facilitated in this regard is aimed at promoting learning. In addition, with the availability of social media, people easily connect with others in other parts of the globe and the internet remains the driving factor facilitating the online connections (Chugh, 2012, p.603).

LITERATURE REVIEW: ELEMENTS OF KNOWLEDGE MANAGEMENT

This section of the article reflects on some issues that point to the existence of literature in the area of knowledge management which Modebelu and Duvie (2015, p.264) maintain, "protects intellectual assets from delay, seeks opportunities to enhance decisions, services and products through adding intelligences, increasing value and providing flexibility." It has been established that 'knowledge is a very critical and valuable resource in the international political system and human endeavours, considering the fact that individuals and groups or institutions that use properly utilise knowledge in their activities or programs seem to have an edge over those that do not (Troshani & Rao, 2005).

The main essence of teaching at any level or context is to enable the individual meet new situations of various degrees of relatedness and similarities effectively (Akinbobola, 2015, p.85). This chapter is in line with the finding of some scholars who revealed that both students and lecturers require access to upgraded, functional computers and high speed Internet facility to enable them connect without hindrances to various sites and social networks (Yasmeen et al, 2015, p.6). With this kind of academic friendly development, departments and faculties alike would easily gain access to the institution's network without having to go and access the internet at the information and communication technology department of their institutions.

According to Den Hoof and De Ridder (2004) "knowledge sharing is the process where individuals mutually exchange their knowledge and jointly create new knowledge" (cited in Ikenwe & Igbinovia, 2015, p.21). It is this creation of new knowledge that contributes to knowledge development for the benefits of present generation and to be transferred to future generations.

It is evident that knowledge management focuses on the sharing of information that is aimed at enlightening the target groups by way of communicating ideas through exchanges that would produce needed result (Ikenwe & Igbinovia, 2015). Research on social network sites has concentrated on the internet although these are also available on mobile telephony as a delivery platform (Acholonu, 2013, p.136). The use of technology at large scale is changing the pattern of life that includes working, learning and communicating with each other to the extent that the impact of technology devices on education usually manifest in teaching and learning (Yasmeen et al, 2015, p. 1). With the creation of new platforms for social engagement, it now possible for people to contribute in the development process in the society and benefit from variety of opinions by participating audience (Dunu & Uzochukwu, 2015, p.10). Knowledge is shared among students when a lecturer delivers his/her lecture and offers them links to access, while the students work together towards accessing and distributing, discussing the findings from the investigation. By implication, they are expected to dish the information out to their absent course mates.

On the need for international collaboration, Smith (2014, p.4) notes thus:

There is a whole world out there and we have to both prepare our students to be active participants in it and ensure that our researchers are tackling the challenges which face it. Knowledge does not recognise national borders. If a university is to achieve its aims in a holistic way, it simply has to operate in the international sphere.

The foregoing means that social media also offers students and their lecturers the opportunity to operate in the international sphere in studying international relations and conflict studies. This made Ezike (2015, p.80) to argue that "social networking is the grouping of individuals into specific groups, like small rural communities or a neighbourhood subdivision", and this engagement can empower students with needed skills for the life after schooling. It is obvious that communities can also be formed online in the classroom. There is no disputation that materials or reports domiciled on social media are sources of research which would aid teaching and learning.

Ikenwe and Igbinovia (2015) reiterate that knowledge sharing has influential impact in the lives of youth, offering the opportunity to get adequate information as well as the capacity to reduce the spread of HIV/AIDS among adolescents in the rural areas. It then means that knowledge sharing is instrumental to the shaping of people's lifestyles and in determining the programmes they participate in.

This explains why every business requires knowledge development. Every knowledge management initiative usually requires effective infrastructure that needs high professionalism. Knowledge management tackles the problems of learning in tertiary institutions given that it is the rationale for acquiring education (Modebelu & Duvie, 2015). According to Biloslavo and Zornada (n.d.) the processes of knowledge management must be in tandem with the objectives of the exercise, especially when assets, businesses, and orderliness are the strategic pillars, with notable knowledge management processes, namely creation, storing, transfer, and application of knowledge. In fact, the foregoing is apt considering the truism that until knowledge is created and stored, sending them to target users for proper utilisation would remain a mirage.

Given that "knowledge exists in both explicit (tangible) and tacit (intangible) forms", knowledge management and transfer are critical (Chugh, 2013, p.24). Davies (2013) highlights the notable elements of knowledge management, thus: document storage with word documents, PDFs, spreadsheets, presentations, knowledge of publishing and discussion among others. Because experts share opinions and respond to issues on social media, Nigerian students of international relations and peace / conflict studies have a lot to benefit from this media which responds to most of their questions.

Also, the collaboration element of knowledge management as identified by Marquardt (1996) suggests that individuals need to as a matter of fact, utilize social media to mine all available data for sharing purpose with different groups of people including friends (Das, 2013). This aspect of information discrimination can only be effective when the users subscribe for data that would enable them access the internet, log on to the global village which houses various internet platforms and contribute to knowledge development. A crucial thing to note is that information can only be appreciated when the right users and receivers receive them for proper utility. For instance, students of a particular course in the university can engage their counterparts in other universities in this act of knowledge sharing based on the contents of their course as taught by different lecturers.

In the context of this study, it is believed that the essence of knowledge management is to empower people and use the associated information to make them better people. As revealed by Troshani and Rao (2005), the contributions of people and the force of technological devices in facilitating knowledge management must be prioritised to enable information be sent from the source to the receivers. The students are the receivers in this regard. No doubt, adequately funding scientific research by universities structure is a way of empowering the lecturers with wealth of knowledge to the benefit of students they teach (Modebelu & Duvie, 2015, p.267). The foregoing is practicable because sound lecturers are those that actively participate in the search for knowledge through research, presentation of conference papers, symposia and workshops which enable scholars to network and interact with colleagues within an academic community.

KNOWLEDGE SHARING AND ACADEMIC BENEFITS OF INFORMATION SHARED ON SOCIAL MEDIA

There is no disputation that knowledge sharing is the raison d'être of universities across the world considering their capacity in facilitating knowledge transfer for the benefit of students and society at large (Chugh *et al*, 2015, p.2; Chugh, 2013). This section presents ways of facilitating knowledge sharing on social media for the benefit of students of international relations and conflict studies. The areas of enhancing students' awareness on ways of harnessing social media as knowledge management tool are numerous in the fields of international relations and peace/conflict studies. Understanding the evolution of events in the international political system requires timely sharing of reports produced by think tanks most of which are non-profit organisations by scholars and students.

As far as teaching is concerned, transfer of knowledge through learning can enhance students' understanding (Akinbobola, 2015). It should be stated that every student that desires to benefit from the information and resources deposited on social media must become an active user of social networks used by various think tanks to like their pages and or follow their user accounts.

In international relations, areas that information can be shared are the nature of responses to international sanctions such as aggressive and diplomatic responses. Another is the issues of veto and politics of abstention in the United Nations Security Council as well as the resurgence of Russia and her foreign policy objectives since the end of the Cold War.

Social media has reported how Russia threatens global stability through her ambition in Eastern Europe, her show of strength toward the West, military drills, and Putin's political statements, including how Russia merged its air force and aerospace defense forces, at a cost of $60 billion. Other crucial areas are the international political system and post-Cold War politics which are scholarly relevant for students are the manifestations of sanctions namely commodity embargo, verbal condemnation and threat to use the instrument of sanction, imposition of travel ban on foreign nationals or top government officials, arms embargo, freezing of assets belonging to top government officials.

The foregoing reveal that lack of access to social media can limit students' knowledge about the various issues in international relations, most of which are not in books and can only be published in journals and books after a long period of time. It becomes even more pertinent when such students are determined to learn more about international law as well as the activities of International Criminal Court which investigates various allegations of crimes against humanity and war crimes. Live updates of such investigations are reported by journalists on social media and need to be shared by scholars for the benefit of students.

It then means that engaging students in the act of knowledge sharing on social media requires them to identify the technological devices as noted by Troshani and Rao (2005) to enable them also contribute to discussions as demanded by think tanks to sample their opinions in this regard. It is realistic given that the number of internet users in Nigeria is more than 48, 366, 179 while the internet penetration in the country is 28.4% as revealed by Terragon's State of Digital Media Nigeria report of 2013. And the foregoing further shows that the problem is no longer the lack of internet service providers or high cost of network access which has reduced appreciation over the years.

In the area of conflict studies, a lot have been happening across the world. From inter-state and intra-state armed conflicts to global terrorism has emergence of militant groups with the rising need for insurgent containment, these events have made it necessary for students to also be actively engaged in the dominant discourses in the international community.

An interesting area is the menace of modern terrorism in developing and developed countries, considering the associated counterterrorism threats to prevent more coordinated attacks by the groups. There are social media reports on how terrorism is directly responsible for the nasty nature of life in Somalia which made her to be synonymous with failed state and a host of terrorist groups since the first decade of the 21st Century (Kagwanja, 2012). This is because underlying the menace of terrorism is that communities in the Horn of Africa now struggle to overcome the security challenges occasioned by persistent threats of violent extremism and transnational terrorism with attendant internal displacements (Turbiville, Meservey & Forest, 2014; Schwartz, Shetret & Millar, 2013). Through social media, students can understand better the shift toward civilian-oriented donor counterterrorism assistance especially in the form of foreign security assistance (Schwartz, Shetret, & Millar, 2013, p.100).

According to Cordano (2015, p.1) "the Al-Shabaab which formally pledged allegiance to al-Qaeda in February 2012 professes a quasi-Salafist ideology with a notable Wahhabist inflection." The United States Department of State (2010, p.31) revealed that al-Shabaab consists of a disparate grouping of armed clan militias who undergo training usually led by al-Qa'ida affiliated foreign fighters; and knowing more about this group which is even sophisticated having carried out attacks that made Somalia prone to human rights abuses requires the use of social media which report events.

Notably, terrorism assumed a debilitating proportion in Nigeria's Fourth Republic and influenced the dynamics of intergroup relations in the country. Boko Haram terrorism is a modern form of terrorism which has scathed interreligious harmony especially between the major religions in the country. The situation is heightened by Boko Haram's radicalisation which threatens human security with attendant human rights violations and psychological trauma across the country. Presumably, the foregoing occasioned scenarios of physical violence. The recent proliferation of terrorist activities especially in the northern parts of the country made the church one of the targeted areas for terrorist activities. Historically, religion has been a significant sector in peacemaking and conflict prevention. Nigerian Churches belong to the umbrella body called the Christian Association of Nigeria that is headed by an elected president. The social media is relevant for informing people about the strategies adopted to prevent various attacks in places of worship and the effectiveness of such innovations, spiritual impact and how the Christian Association of Nigeria and their Muslim counterparts work towards promoting human security.

Furthermore, there are many issues that students need to update their knowledge with case studies. One of them is the need to identify the main objectives of human trafficking (HT) such as slavery, forced labour and forced marriage for sexual exploitation and selfish purposes. They would comprehend the forced/compulsory labour perspective which contravenes the Forced Labour Convention of 1930; as well as the debt bondage associated with those trafficked for sexual purposes, especially how trafficking in persons is a heinous crime which is one of the sources of human rights violations. They can have a grasp of how inequalities result in the migration of the vulnerable women and girls to the well developed countries that serve as receiving markets for sexual exploitation. There are reports on social media on the patterns of this illicit business which often leaves the trafficked persons at the receiving end. Of course, human trafficking continues to scar Nigeria despite the ratification of a Protocol on Trafficking attached to the UN Convention against Organized Crime, signed by 80 countries and the European Union in December 2000, establishment of the Compact Coalition Pact by the Nigerian Police, the Immigration Service and National Agency for the Prohibition of Trafficking in Persons (NAPTIP) and Other Matters, and the passing into law of the Trafficking in Persons (Prohibition) Law Enforcement and Administration Act of 2003. It is not disputable that perennial poverty and greed are the sources of human trafficking. Through reports on social media, students can be encouraged to investigate beyond the poverty induced trafficking for sexual exploitation (TSE) given that there are other parameters like the erosion of the family values, decline in community brotherhood/values, bad orientation, deceit, cultural disconnect among others.

Such information will make them to find out whether victims are trafficked by consent, coerced or even deceived to accept payments to gain consent of the targets. However, understanding the voluntary or coercive aspect of this phenomenon will offer more insight into the modalities of enrolment and options for eradication as far as the networks of trafficking for sexual exploitation are concerned. That is why it is crucial to investigate the nexus between brothels and the prostitution networks. The social media reports would make them conduct vulnerability assessment of the trafficking for sexual exploitation, from the identification of demographic features of those recruited into the business especially age group and level of education.

The academic benefits of information sharing on social media cannot be downplayed. In the field of international relations and conflict studies, it can enhance students' understanding of the courses and give them timely information needed to give them up to date developments in various states across the world. For instance, in the field of new states in international relations, it is the use of social media tools and platforms that can aid students with the knowledge of various contemporary events especially concerning these states that are mainly transitional democracies and with different leadership and development challenges, as well as intra-state conflicts that have attracted the attention of regional and international organisations. Through the use of social media, students easily get acquainted with some information about the prevailing context of the conflicts, parties, third parties, shadow parties, stakeholders, conflict management approach and the intervention of the international community. At the University of Ibadan, the author observed that most students of peace and conflict studies at the Institute of African Studies were already well informed about the communication relevance of social media, but unfortunately, not many were actively involved in using it search for materials in doing their assignments. If assuming most of them are aware that all they need are also available on Twitter and Facebook by following some think tanks, they would not find it difficult in this regard.

Also, while teaching in class in the university, the author interacted with the students to identify some of the courses they easily find materials on social media to enhance their understanding and in aiding their assignments. It was found that most of the students were only searching for materials on topics that relate to diplomacy, half of them gpot materials on African Studies, others are International Political System, Introduction to International Relations, Political Science, Political Science and the Study of Politics. Materials on Introduction to Political Science, History of World War 1 & 2, Introduction to Political Science, Niger Delta Development, Political Science, Politics and Problems of the OAU/African Union, Religion and The Structure of International Relations were accessed by few of them that were in class.

What this means is that most of them have different reason for using social media ranging from research purposes, networking with friends, for reconnecting with old friends among others. However, a very high number of students, more than half of them in class use social media for every purpose (research, network and reconnect with friends) as far as the device they use has facilities that are compatible with such purposes.

The factors responsible for the foregoing are not farfetched. Of course there are devices that are compatible with the internet and the ones commonly used by most of the students the author interacted with show that they are using social media. More than half of them use android devices, Black Berry, laptop while very few use iphone. This is mainly because of the availability and affordability of android phones and tablets in markets across Nigeria. Most people who cannot afford the high cost of original and durable iphones settle for Android phones. Obviously, this section has demonstrated the relevance of social media in the study of international relations and conflict studies.

Embracing these sites would enhance their information sources and network of knowledge. An example is the academia.edu which is a platform where institutions and conference conveners upload papers and publicise call for papers for conferences, symposia, colloquia, workshops, journal articles among others. While carrying out this study, information was retrieved on academia.edu about the special edition on religious violence in Africa to be published by the Journal of Religion.

Most students who use different social media platforms are opportuned to acquire knowledge from the available information uploaded by think tanks. When they log in, there are many things that would see, especially the update features to user friendly sharing platforms with the ability to even search for individual and organizational accounts or usernames to be added, liked or followed to extract data. For instance, Journal Peace & Development, Allfor Peacebuilding, Heritage Institute, Sahan Journal, Transparency International, UNICEF Education, all have Twitter accounts including United Nations which is the custodian of international relations.

On Twitter, Building Peace Forum 5th Annual Academic Symposium on innovation in Graduate Peace & Conflict Resolution Education was uploaded in March 2015, Beverley Sackville reported that the United Nations adopted the Arms Trade Treaty on 2 April, 2013 as favourited on Twitter by Control Arms on 2 April, 2015.

Social media has many reports on geopolitical issues, activities of international / regional organizations as far as global security, democratization and human rights promotion are concerned. The United Nations' peace process strategies in Syria since 2011 are readily available on social media through the pages/status of various think tanks. The Norwegian Peacebuilding Resource Centre publishes its policy brief every month and this would be relevant to students of international relations and diplomacy in Nigerian universities and others in Africa.

Classification of Information that Can Be Shared by Students

The information available for students to share can be classified as follows: Perspectives on maintaining international peace and security, democracy and human rights, gender and peacebuilding, foreign policy of nations, activities of international organisations, mediation and negotiation, nuclear weapons, border studies matters, labour movement and politics of mobilisation, conflict mapping, third party intervention, impact assessment, monitoring and evaluation, sustainable development goals, identity and ethnicity, national integration, government policies, international development and Millennium Development Goals (MDGs), the role of the media in international relations and conflict reporting among others, like public awareness in terms of facilitating students' awareness of academic events in other parts of the world requires engaging them in the knowledge sharing endeavour.

It is recommended that students of international relations visit Nigeria Watch in University of Ibadan, to enable them learn more about collaborative information retrieval which is an aspect on knowledge sharing. This is because the organization has a unified data management system through Opsomai Media which enables researchers to have easy access to the database in line with the rules and operational oversight of the company. Most time, users can only get all the needed data when they demand for them through the request for a special password and username before being able to extract all the data on cases of violent deaths, protagonists, locations, among other. While at Nigeria Watch, students would comprehend the differences between human-related as well as document-related collaborative tasks aimed at sharing all information that appear on published patent applications, working notes and smart boards; which usually has a connection with the processed knowledge by team members. The organization has two projects namely, visible and invisible violence projects which have the following areas of focus: Oil companies and lethal violence, Political parties, Land Pressure, Car accidents, Maritime Piracy, Witchcraft and Cult Societies, Community Violence, Political Violence and violence against women.

As a member of the Peace and Security Working Group (PSWG), Nigeria Watch which also partners with the Nigeria Stability and Reconciliation Programme, works with other members of the PSWG to generate and share updates on conflict and violent deaths through social media. Some of them are Fund for Peace, Mercy Corps, Nigeria Stability and Reconciliation Programme, IFRA/Nigeria Watch, FFP/PIND (The Fund for Peace/Partners for Peace in the Niger Delta), Search for Common Ground, and Working Group on Armed Violence. Students need to know more about the activities of these organizations.

CONCLUSION

Based on the findings, which are highly scholarly relevant, this chapter argues that considering how social media is designed to facilitate interpersonal and intergroup relations, enabling people create groups on virtual basis with the aim of analysis relevant issues of global significance, students of Wellspring University and their counterparts in other parts of the world cannot be left behind. This is based on the fact that classroom settings or activities are not adequate if students desire to know more in international relations and conflict studies. It is because international affairs are both contemporary and historical issues that require extensive investigation of available data. Given that social media provides opportunities for learning experiences, with new data generated daily, knowledge sharing in this context would aid violence research, and also make teaching and learning easier. Any student that cannot participate to benefit from knowledge sharing cannot be an informed student.

The limitations of this study are conspicuous. The issue is that there is no specific methodology to carry out a study of this nature is obvious considering the fact that not all students always visit social media due to internet access complexities and power supply challenges in the country. The stability of the network was an issue while conducting this study as the use of different network service providers could not guarantee easy access to the internet. Additionally, existing literature on knowledge management in Nigeria is not adequate and even most studies on social media have not given adequate consideration to the use of social media in the teaching and learning of international relations and conflict studies in the country. Therefore, future research should give more priority to the courses that can be shared on social media especially in the sciences and social science disciplines, as well as examine how the incessant power failure affects students' use of social media in Nigerian universities.

REFERENCES

Acholonu, R. (2013). Social media and the social behaviour of Caritas University students. In D. Wilson (Ed.), *Communication and the new media in Nigeria: Social engagements, political development and public discourse* (pp. 133–151). Nigeria: Africa Council for Communication Education.

Akinbobola, A. O. (2015). Enhancing transfer of knowledge in physics through effective teaching strategies. *Information and Knowledge Management, 5*(6), 85-92. Retrieved from http://iiste.org/Journals/index.php/IKM/article/view/23149/23661

Amana, D., & Attah, C. (2014). Social media and security challenges: The relationship between security messaging, believability and social alarm. *International Journal of Media, Security and Development, 1*(1), 22–30.

Barrons, G. (2012). Suleiman: Mubarak decided to step down #egypt #jan25 oh my God': examining the use of social media in the 2011 Egyptian revolution. *Contemporary Arab Affairs (London, England), 5*(1), 54–67.

Biloslavo, R., & Zornada, M. (n.d.). *Development of a knowledge management framework within the systems context.* Retrieved August 15, 2015, from http://www2.warwick.ac.uk/fac/soc/wbs/conf/olkc/archive/oklc5/papers/h-3_biloslavo.pdf

Chugh, R. (2012). Social networking for businesses: Is it a boon or bane? In M. M. Cruz-Cunha, G. D. Ptnik, N. Lopes, P. Goncalves, & E. Miranda (Eds.), Handbook of Research on Business Social Networking: Organizational, Managerial, and Technological Dimensions. Hershey, PA: IGI Global. Retrieved from http://www.researchgate.net/publication/275771610_Social_Networking_for_Businesses_Is_it_a_Boon_or_Bane

Chugh, R. (2013). Workplace dimensions: Tacit knowledge sharing in universities. *Journal of Advanced Management Science, 1*(1), 24–28. doi:10.12720/joams.1.1.24-28

Chugh, R., Wibowo, S., & Grandhi, S. (2015). Mandating the transfer of tacit knowledge in Australian Universities. *Journal of Organizational Knowledge Management*. Retrieved from http://www.ibimapublishing.com/journals/JOKM/2015/297669/297669.pdf

Cordano, D. (2015). The conflict between Al-Shabaab and the Federal Government of Somalia. *Bradbury's Global Risk Partners*. Retrieved September October 10, 2015, from http://www.bradburys.co.uk/wp-content/uploads/2015/01/The-conflict-between-al-Shabaab-and-the-Federal-Government-of-Somalia.pdf

Curca, M. (2013). The peace process will not be re-tweeted. *The Peace Journalist, 1*(2), 10–11.

Das, S. (2013). *Elements of knowledge management*. Retrieved September 15, 2015, from http://knowmgt.blogspot.com/2013/07/elements-of-knowledge-management.html

Davies, A. (2013). Four key elements of successful knowledge management. *Ntegra, Newbury*. Retrieved September 10, 2015, from http://ntegra.com/blog/2013/01/16/four-elements-for-successful-knowledge-management/

Den Hooff, V. B., & De Ridder, J. (2004). Knowledge sharing in context: The influence of organizational commitment, communication climate and CMC use on knowledge sharing. *Journal of Knowledge Management*, *8*(6), 117–130. doi:10.1108/13673270410567675

Dlodlo, N., & Dhurup, M. (2013). Examining social media dimensions among a cohort of generation Y consumers in South Africa. *Mediterranean Journal of Social Sciences*, *4*(14), 329–338.

Durnu, V. I., & Uzochukwu, C. E. (2015). Social Media: An Effective Tool for Social Mobilization in Nigeria. *IOSR Journal of Humanities and Social Science*, *20* (4), 10-21. Retrieved from http://www.iosrjournals.org/iosr-jhss/papers/Vol20-issue4/Version-3/C020431021.pdf

Eboh, E. (2009). Developing Owa clan in the 21st Century: Opportunities & challenges. Enugu: El' Demak Publishers.

Ezike, C. O. (2015). Adoption of social networking technology in teaching and learning process in Nigeria tertiary institutions. *International Journal of Science and Technology*, *1*, 79–93.

Feldman, T. (1997). *An introduction to digital media*. London: Routledge. doi:10.4324/9780203398401

Ikenwe, I. J., & Igbinovia, M. O. (2015). Influence of knowledge sharing in reducing the spread of "HIV/AIDS" among adolescents in rural areas in Delta State, Nigeria. *Kuwait Chapter of Arabian Journal of Business and Management Review*, *4*(12), 18-31. Retrieved from http://www.arabianjbmr.com/pdfs/KD_VOL_4_12/3.pdf

Kagwanja, C. (2012, July-August). *Religious pockets of conflict – dealing with resurgence of radical Islamism and terrorism in Kenya. Horn of Africa Bulletin.*

Masuku, C., & Moyo, P. (2014). An Assessment to the use of Facebook as a communication tool by Midlands State University students from 2012 to 2013. *Journal of Media and Communication Studies*, *6*(8), 130–143. doi:10.5897/JMCS2014.0391

Meyrowitz, J. (1985). *No sense of place: The impact of electronic media on social behaviour*. New York: Oxford University Press.

Modebelu, M. N., & Duvie, A. N. (2015). Knowledge management creativity elements expected of academics in Nigerian universities. *American Journal of Educational Research*, *3*(3), 263–267. Retrieved from http://pubs.sciepub.com/education/3/3/2

Odejobi, O. A. (2015). Self – knowledge and intellectualism: A perspective from Yoruba Cosmology. In Y. K. Salami, J. O. Famakinwa, & G. Fasiku (Eds.), *Nationalism and Economic Justice in Nigeria*. Ile – Ife: Obafemi Awolowo University Press.

Okolie-Osemene, J. (2012). Social media and the question of cultural identity in Nigeria. *African Notes: Journal of the Institute of African Studies*, *36*(3).

Osazee-Odia, O. U. (2008). Assessing the Relevance of New Media Technology in Globalisation of Broadcasting. In E. M. Mojaye, O. O. Oyewo, R. M'Bayo, & I. A. Sobowale (Eds.), *Globalisaion and Development Communication in Africa*. Ibadan: Ibadan University Press.

Schwartz, M., Shetret, L., & Millar, A. (2013). Rethinking international counterterrorism assistance to the greater Horn of Africa: Toward a regional risk reduction strategy. *Perspectives on Terrorism*, *7*(6), 100–112.

Smith, M. E. (2014). *Internationalization, partnership and research collaboration in tertiary education.* Convocation Lecture, University of Benin.

Terragon Limited. (2013). *State of Digital Media Nigeria 2013.* Retrieved September 5, 2015, from http://twinpinenetwork.com/publications/Nigeria-%20State%20of%20Digital%20Media.pdf

Troshani, I., & Rao, S. (2005). Key elements in an effective knowledge management system: A case study approach. In *Proceedings of the Fifth International Conference on Electronic Business* (pp. 563-564). Retrieved August 5, 2015, from http://iceb.nccu.edu.tw/proceedings/2005/563-564.pdf

Turbiville, G., Meservey, J., & Forest, J. (2014). *Countering the al-Shabaab insurgency in Somalia: Lessons for U.S. special operations forces.* Joint Special Operations University. Retrieved from http://jsou.socom.mil/JSOU%20Publications/al_Shabaab_Feb_2014%20PDF.pdf

Vlasov, M., & Panikarova, S. (2015). Knowledge creation in state-owned enterprises. *Mediterranean Journal of Social Sciences, 6*(4), 475-480. Retrieved from http://www.mcser.org/journal/index.php/mjss/article/view/6954/6658

Yasmeen, S., Alam, M. T., Mushtaq, M., & Bukhari, M. A. (2015). Comparative study of the availability and use of information technology in the subject of education in Public and Private Universities of Islamabad and Rawalpindi. *Sage Open*. Retrieved from: http://sgo.sagepub.com/content/spsgo/5/4/2158244015608228.full.pdf

KEY TERMS AND DEFINITIONS

Conflict Studies: A field of studies in the social sciences and humanities which focuses on the management of social relations between groups and individuals who usually struggle over values and adopt ways of achieving their goals in the society.

International Relations: The study of the relationship between nation states in the international political system, including the foreign policies and national interests of states.

Internet: The technology that makes people to gain access to the social media.

Knowledge Production: The process of promoting the generation of new data for academic purposes especially when cutting edge research is involved.

Knowledge Sharing: The process of disseminating the produced academic data that would inform students and scholars.

Online: A virtual platform where internet users visit to be live on the internet. When people are online, their real identity can hardly be known due to lack of face-to-face conversation.

Social Media: A platform that offers users the opportunity to get timely information on different global issues.

Students: People that are enrolled to undergo training in character and learning, in the tertiary institution or other institutions of learning.

Section 2

Application of Social Media as an Aid for Knowledge Management Activities

Chapter 5
A Social Knowledge Management Platform for Universal Primary Education Online

Somprakash Bandyopadhyay
Indian Institute of Management Calcutta, India

Shrabastee Banerjee
Indian Institute of Management Calcutta, India

Arina Bardhan
Indian Institute of Management Calcutta, India

Srimoyee Das
Indian Institute of Management Calcutta, India

Priyadarshini Dey
Indian Institute of Management Calcutta, India

Kalyan S. Mandal
Indian Institute of Management Calcutta, India

ABSTRACT

Social knowledge management is a framework that allows its users to create and modify content collaboratively using social media and web 2.0 technologies. Social knowledge management can also be defined as the management of social knowledge where it is aimed towards social development. India today is facing a huge rural-urban divide with regard to poor learning achievement at the elementary level in remote rural areas. Remote rural schools are engulfed with problems such as the unavailability of good quality teachers and a poor learning environment. In this context, the chapter seeks to utilize a robust social knowledge management framework to impart universal education in the form of both formal and informal knowledge to the masses in remote rural areas by mobilising free online knowledge resources and the dormant knowledge capital of educated senior citizens. It further illustrates the design and development of a social media based knowledge management platform named OwlishOracle that addresses issues of exclusion and unequal educational attainment through "connecting generations".

INTRODUCTION

Knowledge management (KM) is the process of applying a systematic approach to capture, structure, manage and disseminate knowledge throughout an organization in order to work faster, reuse best prac-

DOI: 10.4018/978-1-5225-0495-5.ch005

tices, and reduce costly rework from project to project (Dalkir, 2005). As Clarke (2001) says, knowledge management, which is often a source of competitive advantage for firms, provides the means to generate, distribute, and use knowledge in ways that add value to business activity and provide new opportunities for enterprise. With the growing popularity of the Social Media and Web 2.0 technologies, the concept of "Knowledge Management 2.0 (KM 2.0)" has evolved to allow individuals to create and modify content collaboratively. This enables improvements in connectivity, resultantly weaving a relationship of trust, improvement in communications and knowledge transfer (Semple, 2012). In this context, *Social Knowledge Management* is defined as a knowledge management framework that allows us to create and modify content collaboratively using social media and web 2.0 technologies.

Social Knowledge Management can also be defined from a social perspective as the management of social knowledge where the aim is more towards social development and not just promoting competitive advantages for companies (Laszlo, 2002, 2006). The issues of disparity in the quality and access of primary education in remote rural areas of developing countries is the primary motivation behind the structure of the *Social Knowledge Management Platform* discussed in this chapter. In our context, social knowledge management is a framework for holistic learning and knowledge dissemination to children in remote rural areas through digital connections and social collaboration using web 2.0 technologies. The framework ensures delivery of holistic education to underprivileged children by mobilizing the vast pool of dormant knowledge capital of educated senior citizens and free digital educational resources available in the cyber-space.

India today is facing huge rural-urban divide with regard to poor learning achievement at the elementary level in remote rural areas. Remote rural schools are mired with problems such as the unavailability of qualified teachers, lack of good teaching-learning materials and a poor learning environment. The objective of this work is to architect a social knowledge management platform that would act as an online learning environment to not only improve access to quality education for underprivileged youth in remote rural areas using effective and interesting on-line teaching-learning methods, but also to improve learning outcomes and students' well-being. In this research initiative, educated senior citizens who have acquired a lifetime of skills, knowledge and wisdom would share them with younger generations, contributing to the knowledge capital of the society (Bandyopadhyay, 2013; Bardhan, 2014). Our framework addresses the issues of exclusion and inequality in educational attainment through "connecting generations", where educated senior citizens train underprivileged children using synchronous distance e-learning.

To achieve this, our work proposes a social knowledge management platform, OwlishOracle (www.owlishoracle.com), that captures and disseminates formal and non-formal knowledge and wisdom of the elderly to educate underprivileged youth online by mobilising a group of experienced senior citizens and quality teaching learning materials. This social knowledge management platform is not only a medium of knowledge dissemination but also a facilitator in bringing together educators and learners disregarding geographical boundaries and thus creating a global socio-cultural phenomenon. This is a space where people interact and collaborate with each other, establish community norms and values, share resources and build trustful relationships, which are the core values of social capital: a relational resource composed of a variety of elements, most notably social networks, social norms, values, and trust and shared physical resources (Bourdieu, 1992; Putnam, 2000).

Social capital refers to the network of social relations that may provide individuals and groups with access to resources and supports (Policy Research Initiative, 2005). Social capital is a concept that refers to connectedness within and between social networks. It has been considered by researchers to be an important link between development and education – it has been further seen that open distance education can affect quality and quantity of social capital in the country (Sadegh, 2011). Regarded originally as being a relatively immutable endowment, inherited from a distant past (Putnam, 2000), researchers have argued and demonstrated that social capital can be created and built up (Krishna, 2002).

OwlishOracle can help redefine the roles of the senior citizens in today's global society for educating the youth (especially marginalised children who stay in remote rural areas) through video based interactive remote-teaching methods. In this research, the senior citizens are treated as an asset and not as a "hindrance" towards the future sustainability of a nation. Elderly citizens can play a critical role in shaping the future of our society, if they choose not to withdraw as they age, instead to nurture themselves as active elders. Those who are generally less mobile but knowledgeable can act as mentors to children using this e-platform (Bandyopadhyay, 2013; Bardhan, 2014). This approach will help enhance the quality of living of the senior citizens by making them responsible teachers and active agents in changing the current scenario of school education in remote rural areas.

BACKGROUND

Problems of Primary Education in India

The indicator of the Millennium Development Goal (MDG) of Achieving Universal Education is based on the net enrolment ratio in primary education. However, it is also important to identify the obstacles learners encounter in attempting to access opportunities for quality education. In this context the UNESCO Convention against Discrimination in Education and other international human rights have pointed out: "If the right to education for all is to become a reality, we must ensure that all learners have access to quality education that meets basic learning needs and enriches lives. But in reality, millions of children, youth and adults continue to experience exclusion within and from education around the world" (United Nations Educational, Scientific and Cultural Organization [UNESCO], 2014). Asia-Pacific education ministers to guide the region's learning sector over the next 15 years have identified some priority action areas such as ensuring inclusive, lifelong learning for all, and improving the quality of education (UNESCO, 2015). A study undertaken by the World Bank (Dundar, Beteille, Riboud & Deollikar, 2014) pointed out that the poor quality of education in South Asia is an obstacle to the region's future economic development. The study thus emphasized on the need to improve quality of education in schools in South Asia.

India has undergone significant educational expansion in recent years with regard to physical infrastructure of schools and enrolment of students, both at the primary and secondary levels of education. However, the dropout rates at rural areas are still high at 57% at the primary level of education. In 2001, the Government of India launched the *Sarva Shiksha Abhiyan* (SSA, or education for all) to achieve universal elementary education. In 2009, the Indian Parliament passed the Right to Education (RTE) Act, guaranteeing free and compulsory education to all children ages 6–14 years. The RTE sets minimum school infrastructure standards (e.g., building, library, toilets kitchen), pupil-teacher ratios, and teacher hours, in all of which there has been notable progress. Both SSA and RTE have led to impressive increases in enrolment, in part because of significant increases in public spending for education. As a result, the government has largely met its objective of ensuring access to elementary schools even in rural areas where, the government estimates, 99 percent of the population lives within one kilometer of a school (Dundar, Beteille, Riboud & Deollikar, 2014).

Despite focus on access to education and improving infrastructure in schools across India, the nation still struggles to improve learning achievements both at the primary and secondary level. According to Annual Status of Education Report [ASER], (2014), the quality of learning as measured by reading, writing, and arithmetic has either shown no improvement or has worsened in the last nine years. However, the enrolment level in schools has significantly increased: now 97% children are in schools, compared with 93% in 2005. The proportion of all children in Class 5 who can read a Class 2 level text has declined by almost 15% since 2005. Similarly, the portion of students in Class 8 who can do divisions has declined by almost 23% during the same period (Sarva Siksha Abhiyan Report [SSA], 2014).

Taking note of the problem of poor educational outcome in remote rural schools, the focus of the policy framework in India for elementary education has shifted to examining learning outcomes, and not just school enrolment. This led the Twelfth Five Year Plan (Government of India, Planning Commission [GOI], 2013) to emphasise on improving learning outcomes at all levels. Poor learning achievements in spite of large investments at rural classrooms are results of teacher absenteeism, poor quality of teaching due to non-availability of good teachers at remote areas, non-availability of attractive teaching methods including teaching-learning materials in remote areas, teacher-centred teaching, low skill attainment, and a stagnant daily routine. Teaching methods are quite often dominated by mindless rote learning, including repetition without comprehension – of what has been read, and endless chanting of multiplication and other tables (ASER, 2014; Dreze & Sen, 2013). Dreze and Sen (2013) pointed out that neither the pedagogy, nor curriculum, has been adapted to take into account the influx of children and their characteristics: many of these children are first generation learners whose parents are not in a position to follow what is happening in school or react if their child falls behind. Increasing dissatisfaction with the quality of public schooling has given rise to calls for increasing the involvement of the private sector in education. Despite the rise of private schools with high teacher accountability, low-cost private schools in many remote rural areas concentrate more on profits through low-cost schooling rather than on enhancing quality learning (Nambissan, 2014). The actors in this Bottom-of-Pyramid (BoP) education market include individual 'edupreneurs' and, more recently, corporate groups which have entered the schools' business in developing countries. However, private entrepreneurs attempting to improve the quality of education provided to the BoP face unique challenges in a new but growing market where quality, scale and sustainability are desired but rarely attained outcomes (Deutsche Gesellschaft für Internationale Zusammenarbeit [GIZ report], 2014).

In this context, our social knowledge management platform, OwlishOracle, aims at mobilising effective and interesting teaching learning materials from free cyber resources and a group of educated senior citizens from urban areas who have the potential of becoming mentors and teachers. OwlishOracle thus wishes to enhance learning outcomes of underprivileged children from those remote rural schools that have the availability of basic infrastructures but a poor learning environment (Dundar, Beteille, Riboud & Deolalikar, 2014). Improving quality learning implies focusing on the holistic development of underprivileged children in remote rural areas (Ilona, 2012). Holistic learning of each child can be achieved by exposing them to the form of learning which is both formal and non-formal comprising of value inculcation, story-telling, recitation, singing etc. which is a component of life-long learning. Knowledgeable senior citizens who have acquired valuable experiences and wisdom throughout their lives can play the role of 'grand-parents' by disseminating both formal and informal knowledge to underprivileged children.

Related Work

In recent years, the interaction model of the World Wide Web has dramatically transformed e-learning systems with the emergence of the Web 2.0 interaction paradigm. Web 2.0 refers to web applications that facilitate interactive information sharing, social networking, collaboration and user-centred social software (Laschewski, 2011). Educators are now engaged with Web 2.0, with significant interest in the use of social networks in formal education, leading to a new paradigm of Education 2.0 (Selwyn, 2008; Waks, 2013). There is a wealth of literature that discusses Web 2.0's potentials as a technology for transforming education (Alexander, 2006; Brown & Adler, 2008; Bonk, 2009; Downes, 2005; Richardson, 2009; Waks, 2013). Web 2.0 facilitates 'interactive' rather than 'broadcast' forms of exchange, in which information is shared 'many-to-many' rather than being transmitted from one to many. Web 2.0 applications are built around the appropriation and sharing of content amongst communities of users, resulting in various forms of user-driven communication, collaboration and content creation and recreation (Selwyn, 2008).

Education 2.0 can thus play an important role in disseminating quality education to children in remote rural areas by transforming knowledge to an 'interactive' one rather than a 'broadcast' one. Education 2.0 offers learners, even those in rural areas, a more participatory experience of learning in which they have increased opportunities to interact with more learners and with more learning resources. Active and authentic learning takes place best where knowledge can be constructed actively by learners who are supported in communal social settings (Selwyn, 2008). At OwlishOracle too, active learning can happen when the group of underprivileged children from remote rural areas participate in the learning process with a group of educated senior citizens, disseminating knowledge in various forms. In this context, senior citizens act as virtual grandparents of young children, participating in collaborative exchange of formal and non-formal knowledge.

Social knowledge management has the potential of using OER (Open Educational Resources) and Creative Commons, an initiative to utilize widely accessible and online learning resources based on the collaborative economy. Pioneers of this initiative, such as Khan Academy and Rice University's Openstax, have brought free education to the mainstream, providing access to quality educational resources. These initiatives along with some not-for-profit organizations focus on transforming the education landscape in rural and remote regions using digital e-learning environments that are based on sharing and collaboration. These organizations aim to inspire and empower the rural generations by providing standardized lesson plans and remote guidance for a consistent educational ambience. A few other initiatives are:

- **Share My Lesson (www.sharemylesson.com):** Share My Lesson is a place where educators can come together to create and share their very best teaching resources. Developed by teachers for teachers, this free platform gives access to high-quality teaching resources and provides an online community where teachers can collaborate with, encourage and inspire each other. Share My Lesson was developed by the American Federation of Teachers and TES Connect, the largest network of teachers in the world.
- **Edmodo (www.edmodo.com):** Edmodo is an educational technology company offering communication, collaboration, and coaching tools to K-12 schools and teachers. The Edmodo network enables teachers to share content, distribute quizzes, assignments, and manage communication with students, colleagues, and parents. It is the world's largest K-12 social learning community.

- **My Big Campus (www.mybigcampus.com):** My Big Campus makes it easy to engage students, develop lessons, track and improve academic progress and connect with a learning community. My Big Campus makes learning collaborative and fun. Parents can communicate with teachers, view assignments and events, and monitor their child's grades and progress.

In order to transform these initiatives into a systematic social knowledge management practice, it is necessary to devise a process of applying a "systematic approach to the capture, structure, management, and dissemination of knowledge" throughout society in a decentralized manner in order to achieve social development through inclusive education.

SOCIAL KNOWLEDGE MANAGEMENT LIFE CYCLE

Knowledge management refers to efforts to capture, store, and deploy organizational knowledge using a combination of information technology and business processes. Knowledge management is a conscious strategy of getting knowledge to the right people at the right time and putting it into action to improve organizational performance (Alavi & Leidner, 2001; Al-Hawamdeh, 2003; Choo, 2006). So, the companies trying to implement knowledge management (KM) require a coherent and comprehensive KM life cycle model or framework. Wiig (1993) was among the first to address the need for a 'coherent and practical framework for KM' through identification of a set of organizational knowledge processing phases. His approach was based on the principle that knowledge must be organized, to be useful and valuable (Dalkir, 2011). Dalkir (2005) investigated four life cycle models (Wiig, 1993; Meyer & Zack, 1999; Bukowitz & Williams, 1999) with respect to their scholarly adoption and frequency of use by practitioners. Dalkir (2011) formulated an integrated life cycle model that incorporated most of the elements of the above models. The intent was to simplify the KM life cycle as much as possible by combining phases where possible and by identifying key activities before linking them to major phases. It included the following phases: *create/capture*, *assess*, *share/disseminate*, *contextualize*, *apply/use*, *update*. By integrating the major KM life cycles developed thus far, Evans (2013, 2014) proposes a model, the Knowledge Management Cycle (KMC) model, containing seven phases: *identify*, *store*, *share*, *use*, *learn*, *improve*, and *create*.

Although there is a plethora of research dealing with different models of KM life cycle in the context of business organization to enhance the organizational performance, there is no explicit proposal for the KM life cycle in the context of *social knowledge management* where the objective is to manage *social knowledge* for social development. Building on existing models, a social knowledge management life cycle model is proposed below with four phases:

1. Identification/creation,
2. Organization and storage for universal access,
3. Sharing/Interactive Dissemination (dissemination of both explicit and tacit knowledge),
4. Evaluation.

In the context of imparting universal education through connecting generation, the activities corresponding to different phases of the Social KM Life Cycle model are:

- **Identification/Creation:** Social knowledge management aims to *identify* if appropriate knowledge assets exist in the cyberspace, or if appropriate knowledge assets need to be *created.* There are plenty of digital teaching-learning-materials for primary and secondary students available in the web. Also, depending on needs and local preferences, free teaching / training material can be created through crowd-sourcing.
- **Organization and Storage for Universal Access:** Once identified, the knowledge assets are to be stored and organized in the Social KM system for universal access. The platform that supports the social KM initiative needs to organize in a systematic manner all the available teaching/training material class-wise / subject-wise.
- **Sharing/Interactive Dissemination:** In this phase, knowledge assets are retrieved and shared (disseminated/communicated) in pre-determined time slots using fully supervised or semi-supervised learning through video conferencing. This would require the social KM system to have in-built video-conferencing facilities that would help the knowledge providers to disseminate both explicit and tacit knowledge to the knowledge recipients. Here, knowledge sharing and dissemination of knowledge is viewed as an active process that is intimately associated with human interaction.
- **Evaluation:** This phase leads to further refinement of the knowledge assets. This involves not only students' performance evaluation but also evaluation of students' well-being and holistic development. The United Nations Convention on the Rights of the Child stated that "the education of the child shall be directed to: the development of the child's personality, talents and mental and physical abilities to their fullest potential". So, it becomes imperative to periodically measure students' well-being in order to modify / re-build knowledge assets and dissemination mechanisms.

The scope of social knowledge management is not restricted with these activities; in fact there is a lot of concern with regard to the stake-holders who are responsible towards the functioning of these activities. The social knowledge management framework aimed towards social development needs to have an ecosystem to autonomously support KM activities through decentralized mobilization of necessary resources. The social knowledge management platform, OwlishOracle proposed in this chapter thus revolves around the activities mentioned above. The platform also requires certain agents who would initiate the process of knowledge dissemination and sharing.

Figure 1 shows the ecosystem needed to architect the social knowledge management platform described earlier. The five agents that contribute to the activation and utilization of the dormant knowledge resource of the elderly community and quality teaching learning materials for creating a social learning environment are as follows:

- **Provider of Knowledge, the Senior Citizens:** This geographically dispersed group are generally not involved in any mainstream productive activities but their knowledge and wisdom can be activated as a resource to be harnessed to create a social learning environment;
- **Recipient of Knowledge, the Underprivileged Children:** Children from remote rural areas who are in need of access to quality education;
- **Digital Knowledge Capital of the Cyber-World:** Quality teaching learning materials that are necessary for improving learning environment in remote rural schools, are freely available in cyber space that can be used by knowledge providers as well as recipients;
- **Skill Capital of Cyber-Citizens:** This is a group of volunteers who provide:

Figure 1. The ecosystem for the social knowledge management framework

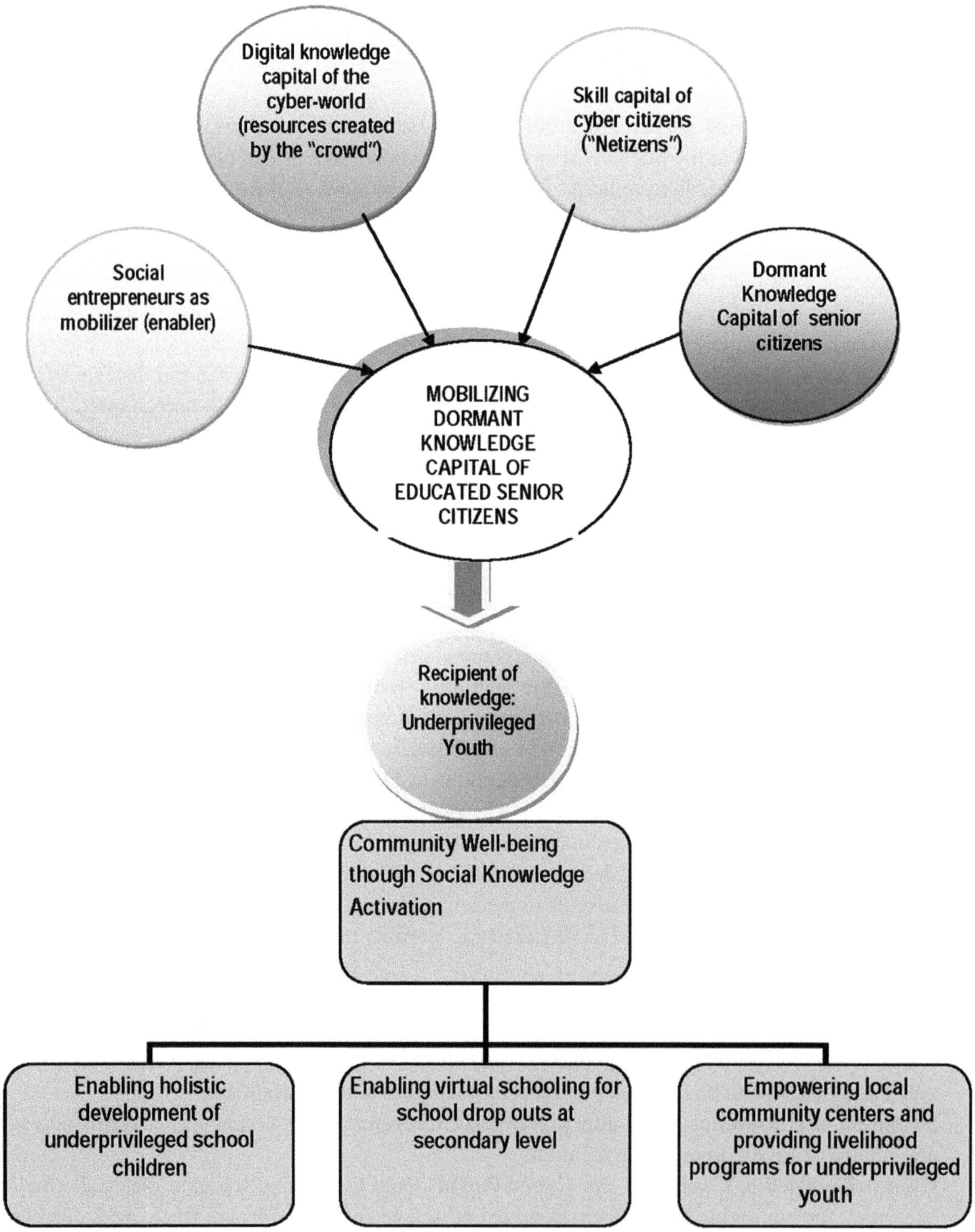

    - Digital teaching-learning materials to augment the digital knowledge capital of the cyber-world;
    - Training to elderly knowledge providers on internet/computer usage; and, finally
- **Social Entrepreneurs:** This group creates the Social Knowledge Management platform to mobilize the other four agents mentioned above and provide web based social networking together with an online virtual classroom where the actual interactions take place between the provider of knowledge and its recipients using a synchronous distance learning paradigm. Owlish Oracle (described in the next section) is one such initiative.

Thus, dormant knowledge capital of the experienced elderly teachers in urban areas can be mobilized to enhance the overall well-being of the community though knowledge, innovation and transformative action. These benefits may be summarized as (Figure 1):

- Holistic development of underprivileged school children by filling gaps in the conventional learning model by utilizing the virtual knowledge providers.
- Virtual schooling for drop outs.
- Harnessing dormant knowledge capital to empower local community centers and impart livelihood programs for underprivileged youth.

HARNESSING KNOWLEDGE CAPITAL OF SENIOR CITIZENS: CROWD CAPITAL

Sharing and collaboration as important components in the social knowledge management framework posits the importance of another related concept which is Crowd Capital. Traditionally, the term 'crowd' is used in the context of a self-organized collection of people around a common purpose or experience. Today, firms often try to engage the power of the "crowd" for organizational benefits. Crowdsourcing, defined as the use of information technologies to outsource business responsibilities to crowds, can now significantly influence a firm's ability to leverage previously unattainable resources to build competitive advantage. As a result, firms build *crowd capital*: organizational resources acquired through crowdsourcing (Prpic, 2015). C*rowd capital* can thus be explained a heterogeneous knowledge resource generated by an organization, through its use of crowd capability, which is defined by the structure, content, and process by which an organization engages with the dispersed knowledge of the *crowd* (Prpic, 2013).

The use of crowd-sourcing as a productive tool has increased significantly in recent times. Benkler and Nissenbaum (2006) in explaining crowd-sourcing, says, Commons-based peer production is a socio-economic system of production that is emerging in the digitally networked environment. Facilitated by the technical infrastructure of the Internet, the hallmark of this socio-technical system is collaboration among large groups of individuals who cooperate effectively to provide information, knowledge or cultural goods without relying on either market pricing or managerial hierarchies to coordinate their common enterprise (Benkler, 2006).

However, use of crowd-sourcing as an effective tool for societal development is a relatively less explored area. In this context, the chapter explores the use of crowd-sourcing as an effective tool for promoting universal primary education. Wisdom of the crowd which is the dormant knowledge capital of experienced elderly teachers and the vast cyber-knowledge-resources available over the Internet can be extensively crowd-sourced in order to strengthen dissemination of quality education in remote rural areas through the social knowledge management platform. Crowdsourcing education on the web which is a comparatively new topic for research and development, finds its expansion through numerous e-learning platforms where learners connect with the larger world of knowledge providers (Corneli & Mikroyannidis, 2012). Crowd-capital is related to F.A. Hayek's concept of dispersed knowledge which is described as a "body of very important but unorganized knowledge… the knowledge of the particular circumstances of time and place" (Hayek, 1945). In context to architecting a social knowledge management framework, OwlishOracle crowd capital acts as a heterogeneous social knowledge resource, derived from dispersed knowledge of the elderly (the *crowd*), and facilitating their productive activity by educating children.

OWLISHORACLE: A SOCIAL KNOWLEDGE MANAGEMENT PLATFORM

Overview

In context to the importance and relevance of a social knowledge management platform in improving the current situation of educational disparity and poor quality of learning in remote rural schools despite availability of infrastructures, OwlishOracle (www.owlishoracle.com), a unique e-learning platform plays an important role in disseminating both formal and informal knowledge to underprivileged children by the senior citizens.

Figure 2 illustrates the framework where underprivileged children are connected to remote elderly teachers over the internet using their personal tablet or classroom video conferencing system through OwlishOracle. The objective is to create an impact on the learning process of underprivileged children by:

1. Providing accessibility in an organized manner to the free on-line teaching-learning materials available in the cyber-space.
2. Utilizing the vast pool of knowledge resource of the educated senior citizens as on-line virtual teachers, who are currently not involved in any mainstream productive activities.

The primary hypothesis is that, a social knowledge management platform such as this can help senior citizens play a critical role in improving quality of education (both formal and informal) and holistic development of underprivileged children in remote areas by becoming responsible teachers / mentors / grandparents.

Based on this framework of social knowledge management, the OwlishOracle Platform (Figure 3) facilitates three agents that contribute to the activation, utilization and creation of the knowledge resource. These agents as follows:

- **Provider of Knowledge, Senior-Citizens:** Population ageing and poor implementation of policies for old people in India has led to lack of meaningful opportunities in later life. OwlishOracle aims at providing those educated elderly who are no longer a part of the labour market directly, an opportunity to be productive in society through dissemination of knowledge (both formal and informal) to underprivileged children in remote rural areas. Basset (2009) says wisdom as a form of informal knowledge is present in older people. This informal knowledge to be acquired from educated senior citizens is beneficial in the holistic development of children in rural areas. Elderly who are generally less mobile and more enthusiastic and knowledgeable can thus act as remote

Figure 2. The model: the students are connected to remote teachers over the internet using their personal tablet or classroom video conferencing system

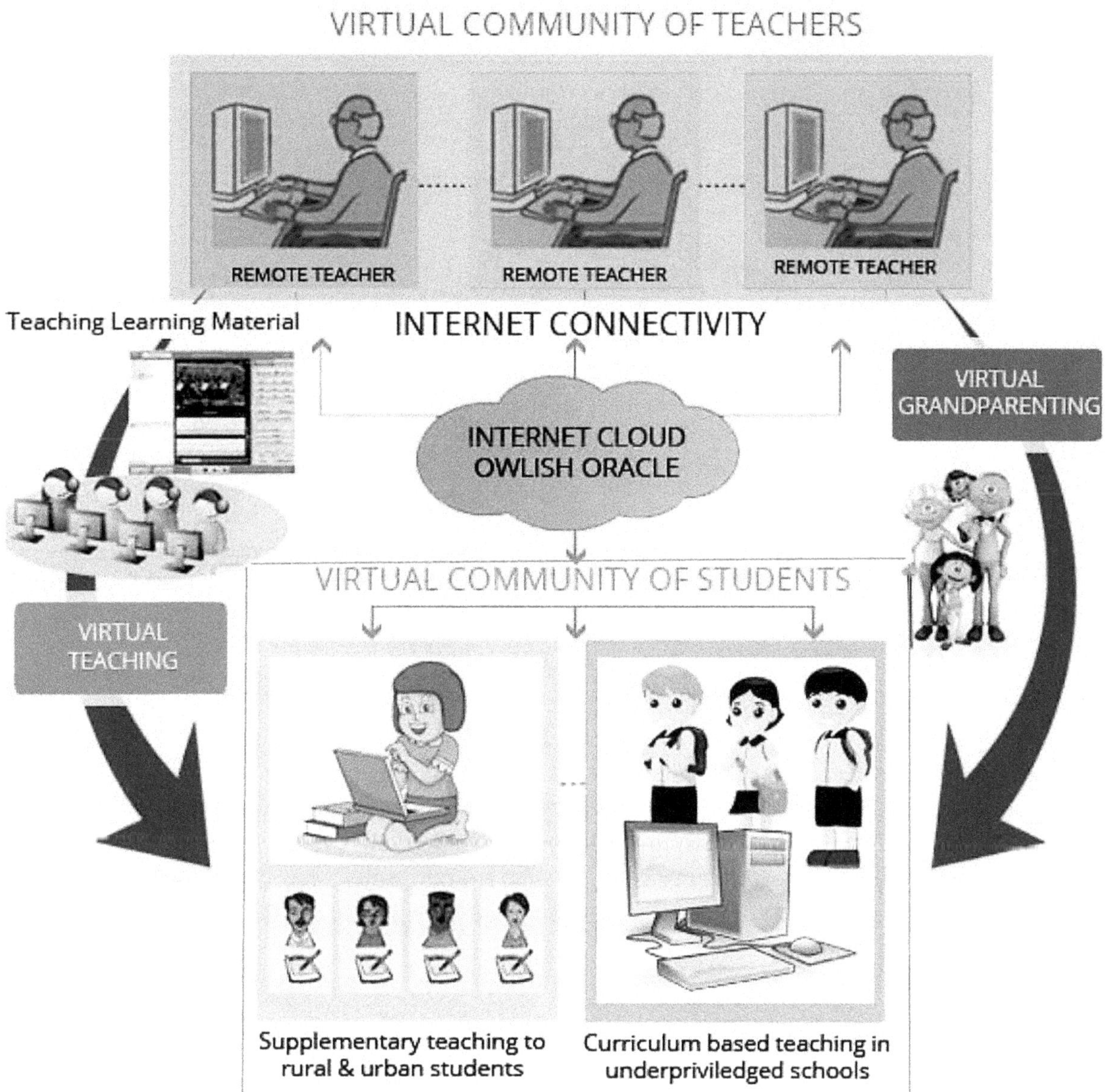

teachers, mentors and virtual grand-parents to the underprivileged children working towards their enhancement of learning outcome.

- **Recipients of Holistic Education, Underprivileged Children in Remote Rural Schools:** Owing to lack of quality teaching and learning environment despite availability of infrastructures in many remote rural schools of India, the learning outcome of the children in these schools lack far behind in comparison to that of the children in urban schools. These children can find quality TLMs with components of holistic learning along with enthusiastic teachers who are educated senior citizens

Figure 3. OwlishOracle: connecting teachers and students synchronously

in urban areas. The formal and informal modes of learning received by senior citizens through this platform would help these children to develop a bond with the older adults who would become virtual grand-parents along with enhancing their learning.

- **Volunteers from Urban Areas:** Interesting teaching learning materials are an important component of quality education. OwlishOracle as a Social knowledge management platform aims to utilise a group of volunteers including teachers who would collaborate, create and share interesting video based teaching learning materials (TLMs) from free cyber resources, enabled by crowd-sourcing. They would also train the elderly knowledge providers to use the platform.

A Functional Description

The agents described above need to be further clarified with respect to their specific roles here. These agents are inter-dependent and play important roles in disseminating quality education with components of holistic development in the remote rural areas of the country by using all components of social knowledge management including sharing, collaboration, crowd-sourcing and finally leading to social capital building.

Senior Citizens

At OwlishOracle, the senior citizens register as a 'grandparent' in order to be a part of the learning space. After becoming a member, they can:

1. Provide curriculum teaching using teaching learning materials (TLMs) to a class of underprivileged children from remote rural schools,
2. Provide one to one supplementary teaching to each underprivileged child from remote rural areas who needs help with studies,
3. Provide grand-parenting sessions to both classrooms and individual underprivileged child by reading stories, reciting poems, singing, sharing values etc. These sessions indicate holistic development of children with elements of informal learning,
4. Establish connections with the underprivileged children by exchanging messages through this platform and
5. Establish connection with other teachers on this platform and share their best-practices of teaching online.

Qualified senior citizens on Owlish Oracle can create their own TLMs using free cyber resources. The TLMs that are to be shared are in the form of video or images that will support learning of the children and/or sharing the best practices for fellow grand-parents. Teaching / grand-parenting sessions are conducted using a video conferencing software (*Adobe Connect),* which has been integrated with Owlish Oracle (Figure 4).

Underprivileged Children

On this platform, a representative of a remote rural school in need of quality teaching, including teachers and TLMs, can register as a virtual classroom. Here the underprivileged children can:

1. Receive curriculum support from enthusiastic senior citizens who would be the teachers disseminating both formal and informal knowledge to a class of underprivileged children in remote rural areas,
2. Receive supplementary teaching in the form of one-to-one tuition by helping them in their studies by experienced senior teachers,
3. Receive extra-curricular help in the form of story-telling, recitation, music etc. called 'grand-parenting' from the senior-citizens leading to the possibility of enhancing holistic development,
4. Be a part of learning which is enjoyable, activity-based and communication oriented,
5. Establish connection with other senior citizens by exchanging messages.

Figure 4. One-to-one online teaching

This would lead to informal modes of communicating with the senior-citizens and in turn observing the component of 'virtual grand-parenting'.

Volunteers from Urban Areas

A group of volunteers would facilitate the initial operationalization of OwlishOracle as a social knowledge management platform. These volunteers, depending on their expertise, perform certain functions of:

1. Collaborating, creating and sharing teaching learning materials by following the principles of the National Curriculum Framework (NCF) of India and using free cyber resources and finally uploading them on OwlishOracle,
2. To monitor and mobilize the use of these TLMs as curricula, used in the targeted remote rural schools with the help of online elderly teachers,
3. To assist the senior citizens using the platform and assist the class coordinators in helping the students connect with the former on OwlishOracle.

Pilot Study

OwlishOracle, a social media platform after initial level of developments, has been pilot-tested in a school for underprivileged students named Ma Sharada Shishu Tirtha at Krishnanagar, West Bengal. Two elderly teachers from urban areas taught a class of 32 students of 5 to 7 years of age (class I) using this platform of remote learning (Figure 5). The elderly teachers, both home-makers used their acquired knowledge and experiences in teaching English and Maths lessons for one month using Adobe Connect video conferencing software integrated in OwlishOracle. The teachers used some TLMs that were prepared through crowd sourcing with the help of some volunteers while teaching the children remotely.

Initial trials with OwlishOracle suggested positive outcomes with children showing interest in learning new concepts and ideas through this unique method of teaching. The TLMs that were created and shared from free cyber resource were used while teaching. The teachers showed them interesting videos while explaining the concepts and the underprivileged students in turn learned with lot of patience and cooperation despite the physical absence of the teachers. OwlishOracle as a social media platform thus

Figure 5. Virtual classroom teaching

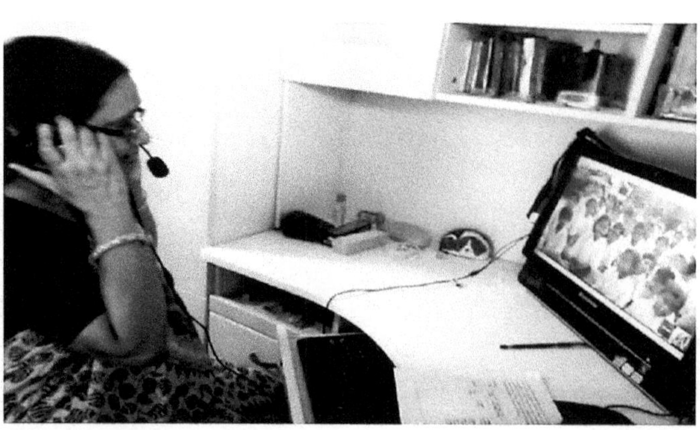

aims at initiating children to connect to any senior-citizen already registered on the platform and share their stories or problems. The children also shared their stories and anecdotes with the teachers who in turn shared theirs leading to exchange of learning in an informal manner. Six more senior citizens from urban Kolkata taught six children from rural parts of West Bengal in a supplementary basis of teaching. The teachers taught on a one to one basis two subjects such as Mathematics and Mentoring (EVS). These teachers have shown interest in interacting and sharing knowledge, both formal and informal, to the underprivileged children by explaining various concepts such as the feature of birds or developing concept of time through daily routine. They have shared videos using the Teaching Learning Materials (TLMs) and also narrated stories of their childhood while teaching. Children took interest in learning new things from the elderly teachers and were very enthusiastic to participate in the Adobe Connect Classroom. These underprivileged children in remote rural areas are generally used to viewing teachers in schools perform the role of teachers alone. These sessions in Adobe Connect helped the children look at a set of teachers as their virtual grandparents and mentors with whom they can share anything and in return get invaluable guidance. There was mutual reciprocity in the form of support and guidance in these sessions.

Problems of OwlishOracle and Future Work

Internet connectivity and network bandwidth are the primary set back of this entire initiative. Most of the elderly teachers are not acquainted with the usage of social media hence would often find the navigation at OwlishOracle a little complicated primarily because of the various functions of this social media platform. These problems could be successfully overcome by ensuring a stable internet connection so that this platform facilitating synchronous learning could be easily availed in remote rural areas, which is the primary target. In case of curriculum teaching of underprivileged schools, the presence of a coordinator is desirable as it is often seen that the children cannot connect the internet or follow proper instructions from their online teachers. Presence of coordinators would also help monitor the entire process of remote teaching. The elderly teachers who are new to this e-learning process would need full guidance from a group of trainers which would solve navigation problems in OwlishOracle eventually.

CONCLUSION

In this chapter, a social KM framework has been discussed and several design issues have been highlighted in order to make an acceptable, usable and beneficial social KM platform for the targeted community, the underprivileged children from remote rural schools that have infrastructural facilities. The purpose of developing the platform is thus enhancing learning outcomes of underprivileged children in remote rural areas, and holistic development using informal and formal knowledge disseminated by a group of educated senior citizens. In developing countries like India, where qualified teachers and good teaching-learning materials are not available in remote classrooms, Internet-enabled social KM platform may be the primary choice in future. Two major obstacles in implementing OwlishOracle are:

1. Convincing the school authorities in rural areas about the effectiveness of a virtual classroom, and
2. Training the elderly on the usage of computer, so that they can operate OwlishOracle independently.

These obstacles may be overcome through demonstration of on-line teaching activities to the school authorities and training the elderly on the usage of computer. Additionally, this initiative is dependent on the regular availability of committed and motivated on-line teachers; so, a carefully planned business model is needed to sustain this initiative.

REFERENCES

Al-Hawamdeh, S. (2003). *Knowledge management*. Oxford, UK: Chandos Publishing. doi:10.1533/9781780631936

Alavi, M., & Leidner, D. E. (2001). Review: Knowledge management and knowledge management systems: Conceptual foundations and research issues. *Management Information Systems Quarterly*, *25*(1), 107–136. doi:10.2307/3250961

Alexander, B. (2006). Web 2.0: A new wave of innovation for teaching and learning? *EDUCAUSE Review*, *41*(2), 33–44.

Annual Status of Education Report. (2014). *Annual Status of Education Report (Rural) 2013: Provisional*. New Delhi: ASER Centre.

Bandyopadhyay, S., Shaw, V., & Banerjee, A. (2013). Social Knowledge Management: Use of Social Media for Disseminating Informal Wisdom of Elderly to the Youth. *International Journal of Knowledge, Innovation and Entrepreneurship*, *1*, 107–115.

Bardhan, A., Bandyopadhyay, S., & Mandal, K. S. (2014). *Redefining the role of elderly as facilitator to educate young generation through Information and Communication Technology*. Paper presented at International Conference on Ageing Well-Social and Managerial Challenges (ICAW), Kochi, Kerala, India. Retrieved from https://facultylive.iimcal.ac.in/sites/facultylive.iimcal.ac.in/files/2-Ageing-IIMC-Paper-final.pdf

Bassett, C. (2009). Elder Wisdom. *Second Journey*. Retrieved February 15, 2015, from http://www.secondjourney.org/itin/09_Fall/Bassett_09Fall.htm

Benkler, Y., & Nissenbaum, H. (2006). Commons-based peer production and virtue. *Journal of Political Philosophy*, *14*(4), 394–419. doi:10.1111/j.1467-9760.2006.00235.x

Bonk, C. J. (2009). *The World Is Open: How Web Technology Is Revolutionizing Education* (1st ed.). San Francisco, CA: JosseyBass, a Wiley Imprint.

Bourdieu, P., & Wacquant, J. D. (1992). *An Invitation to Reflective Sociology*. Chicago: The University of Chicago Press.

Brown, J. S., & Adler, R. P. (2008). Minds on fire: Open education, the Long Tail, and Learning 2.0. *EDUCAUSE Review*, *43*(1), 16–32.

Bukowitz, W. R., & Williams, R. L. (1999). *The Knowledge Management Field Book*. Financial Times Prentice Hall.

Choo, C. W. (2006). *The knowing organization: How organizations use information to construct meaning, create knowledge, and make decisions* (2nd ed.). New York: Oxford University Press.

Clarke, T. (2001). The Knowledge Economy. *Journal of Education and Training*, *43*(5), 189–196. doi:10.1108/00400910110399184

Corneli, J., & Mikroyannidis, A. (2012). Crowdsourcing education on the Web: a role-based analysis of online learning communities. In A. Okada, T. Connolly, & P. Scott (Eds.), *Collaborative Learning 2.0: Open Educational Resources* (pp. 272–286). Hershey, PA: IGI Global. doi:10.4018/978-1-4666-0300-4.ch015

Dalkir, K. (2005). *Knowledge management in theory and practice*. Boston: Routledge.

Dalkir, K. (2011). *Knowledge management in theory and practice* (2nd ed.). Cambridge, MA: Massachusetts Institute of Technology.

Deutsche Gesellschaft für Internationale Zusammenarbeit (GIZ Report). (2014). *The BoP Education Entrepreneurship Ecosystem in India.* Retrieved from http://responsiblebusinessindia.com/downloads/bop-education-entrepreneurship-ecosystem-india/

Downes, S. (2005). *Elearning 2.0.* Retrieved from http://www.elearnmag.org/subpage.cfm?article=291&section=articles

Dreze, J., & Sen, A. (2013). *An Uncertain Glory – India and Its Contradictions*. Penguin.

Dundar, H., Beteille, T., Riboud, M., & Deolalikar, A. (2014). *Student Learning in South Asia: Challenges, Opportunities, and Policy Priorities*. Washington, DC: The World Bank. doi:10.1596/978-1-4648-0160-0

Evans, M. M., & Ali, N. (2013). Bridging knowledge management life cycle theory and practice. In *Proceedings of 10th International Conference on Intellectual Capital, Knowledge Management and Organisational Learning (ICICKM '13).* Washington, DC: George Washington University.

Evans, M. M., Dalkir, K., & Bidian, C. (2014). A Holistic View of the Knowledge Life Cycle: The Knowledge Management Cycle (KMC) Model. *Electronic Journal of Knowledge Management*, *12*(2), 85–97. Available online at http://www.ejkm.com/volume12/issue2

Government of India, Planning Commission (GOI). (2013). Twelfth Five Year Plan 2012-17, Social Sectors (vol. 3). New Delhi: SAGE Publications.

Hayek, F.A (1945). The use of knowledge in society. *The American Economic Review*, *35*(4), 519-530.

Kickbusch, I. (2012). Learning for Well-being: A Policy Priority for Children and Youth in Europe. A process for change. *Learning for Well-being Consortium of Foundations in Europe: Universal Educational Foundations.*

Krishna, A. (2002). *Active Social Capital: Tracing the Roots of Development and Democracy*. Columbia University Press.

Laschewski, L. (2011). *Innovative E-learning in rural areas.* Retrieved from http://ssrn.com/abstract=1861912

Laszlo, K., & Laszlo, A. (2006). Fostering a sustainable learning society through knowledge based development. In *Proceedings of the 50th Annual Meeting of the ISSS*. Sonoma State University.

Laszlo, K. C., & Laszlo, A. (2002). Evolving knowledge for development: The role of knowledge management in a changing world. *Journal of Knowledge Management*, *6*(4), 400–412. doi:10.1108/13673270210440893

Meyer, M. H., & Zack, M. H. (1999). The design and development of information products. *Sloan Management Review*, *37*.

Nambissan Geetha, B. (2014). *Poverty, Markets and Elementary Education in India.* Working Papers of the Max Weber Foundation's Transnational Research Group India. Retrieved from http://www.cprindia.org/sites/default/files/events/Geetha%20Nambissan%20paper.pdf

Policy Research Initiative. (2005). *Social Capital as a Public Policy Tool Project Report*. Ottawa: Policy Research Initiative.

Prpic, J., & Shukla, P. (2013). The theory of crowd capital. In *Proceedings of the 46th Annual Hawaii International Conference on Systems Sciences*. Washington, DC: IEEE Computer Society.

Prpić, J., Shukla, P. P., Kietzmann, J. H., & McCarthy, I. P. (2015). How to Work a Crowd: Developing Crowd Capital through Crowdsourcing. *Business Horizons*, *58*(1), 77–85. doi:10.1016/j.bushor.2014.09.005

Putnam, R. D. (2000). *Bowling Alone: The Collapse and Revival of American Community*. New York: Touchstone. doi:10.1145/358916.361990

Richardson, W. (2009). *Blogs, Wikis, Podcasts, And Other Powerful Web Tools for Classrooms* (3rd ed.). Thousand Oaks, CA: Corwin Press.

Sadegh, B. I. (2011). Relationship between Education and Social Capital. *International Journal of Humanities and Social Science*, *1*(12), 52–57.

Selwyn, N. (2009). The Digital Native-myth and reality. *Aslib Journal of Information Management*, *61*(4), 364–379.

Semple, E. (2012). *Organizations Don't Tweet, People Do: A Manager's Guide to the Social Web*. Wiley.

SSA Report. (2014). *Sarva Shiksha Abhiyan (SSA): A Critical Review of SSA*. Retrieved from https://socialissuesindia.files.wordpress.com/2014/03/ssa-report-2014.pdf

UNESCO. (2014). *Addressing Exclusion.* Retrieved from http://www.unesco.org/new/en/education/themes/strengthening-education-systems/inclusive-education/

UNESCO. (2015). *Asia-Pacific Statement on Education Beyond 2015*. UNESCO. Retrieved from http://www.unesco.org/new/en/education/themes/strengthening-education-systems/inclusiveeducation/single-view/news/inclusive_quality_lifelong_learning_for_all_asia_pacific

Waks, J. L. (2013). *Education 2.0: The Learning Web Revolution and the Transformation of the School*. Paradigm Publishers.

Wiig, K. M. (1993). *Knowledge Management Foundations: Thinking About Thinking - How People and Organizations Represent, Create and Use Knowledge*. Schema Press.

KEY TERMS AND DEFINITIONS

Asynchronous E-Learning: Asynchronous e-learning involves coursework delivered via web, email and message boards that are then posted on online forums. In such cases, students ideally complete the course at their own pace, by using the internet merely as a support tool rather than volunteering exclusively for an online interactive classes.

Computer Aided Learning: CAL is where someone makes use of a specially designed software application in order to learn about a subject or practice a new set of skills. Computer Aided Learning is not only used in schools but is also widely used in industry to teach employees about the things they need to know about.

Connectivism: Connectivism is the integration of principles explored by chaos, network, and complexity and self-organization theories. Connectivism expounds that learning (defined as actionable knowledge) can reside outside of ourselves (within an organization or a database) and is focused on connecting specialized information sets, and the connections that enable us to learn more are more important than our current state of knowing.

Crowd Capital: Crowd capital refers to a heterogeneous knowledge resource generated by any organization or group which is accumulated through the capabilities and contribution of the dispersed knowledge of individuals –the Crowd.

Knowledge Capital: Knowledge capital refers to an intangible asset that comprises the knowledge and skills of people that they share with each other in order to improve efficiencies, and abilities of the society as a whole.

Social Capital: Social capital refers to the collective value of all "social networks" [who people know] and the inclinations that arise from these networks to do things for each other ["norms of reciprocity"].

Social Media: Social media refers to a variety of web-based platforms, applications and technologies that enable people to socially interact and share contents with one another online. Some examples of social media sites and applications include Facebook, YouTube.

Synchronous E-Learning: Synchronous e-learning involves online studies through chat and video-conferencing. This kind of learning tool is real-time. It is like a virtual classroom which allows students to ask, and teachers to answer questions instantly, through instant messaging, which is why it is called synchronous.

Teaching Learning Materials: In the field of Education, TLM is a commonly used acronym that stands for "teaching/learning materials." Broadly, the term refers to a spectrum of educational materials that teachers use in the classroom to support specific learning objectives, as set out in lesson plans.

Virtual Classroom: A virtual classroom is an online learning environment. Just like in a real-world classroom, a student in a virtual classroom participates in synchronous e-learning, which means that the teacher and students are logged into the virtual learning environment at the same time.

Web 2.0: Web 2.0 refers to a second generation in the development of the World Wide Web. It is combination of concepts, trends, and technologies that focus on user collaboration, sharing of user-generated content, and social networking. In web 2.0 the web applications go beyond displaying individual pages of static content and allow a community of users to interact with the site and each other by adding or updating the content.

Chapter 6
Knowledge Workers' Social Media Usage as a Personal Knowledge Management Tool

Oya Zincir
Istanbul University, Turkey

ABSTRACT

This chapter aims to provide a theoretical framework for "profiling knowledge workers' mainstream social media usage" and "investigating knowledge workers' mainstream social media usage for personal knowledge management purposes". For this purposes, it seeks to analyse the social media usage for personal knowledge management purposes of 365 knowledge workers who work in private sector organisations in Turkey. Frequency statistics and factor analysis are conducted on to the data collected on SurveyMonkey. Two factors emerge from this analysis which are named as 'Sharing and Creating New Knowledge' and 'Harnessing Professional Knowledge'.

INTRODUCTION

...There is a central difference between the old and new economies: the old industrial economy was driven by economies of scale; the new information economy is driven by the economics of networks...
– Shapiro & Varian; 1993:173

Famous futurist Alvin Toffler (1980) describes the post-industrial society as 'The Third Wave' which grounds on 'knowledge' as the primary resource. According to him, all organisations are operating and employees are working not only in the infosphere, but also in the technosphere and the sociosphere. By infosphere, Toffler refers to the global knowledge and information dissemination network. Toffler defines technosphere as all the elements of technological ecosystem and by sociosphere, he refers to interrelated social institutions. People are effected by these changing environments and change their workplace behaviours hereunder to these environments.

DOI: 10.4018/978-1-5225-0495-5.ch006

According to Naisbitt (1994), technological revolution is the driving power of the new economy. Thus, in the 21st century, work-based paradigm shifted to individual-based paradigm. As the global economy grows day by day without restriction of the technological developments, individuals -as global actors of the new economy- gain relative importance and power compared to the other actors. New knowledge is created from the existing knowledge by common sharing activities on the digitalsphere and individuals who have internet connection can reach all the open source information and knowledge easily on this digitalsphere. As a fact that, from Industrial Age to Information Age; capability, learning and flexibility became the essential facets of individuals to compete in the global workplace. Also some authors (Anderson, 2012; Rifkin, 2011; Rifkin 2014) define this new age as "Third Industrial Revolution" and explain it as 'the industrialization of information age'. Anderson (2012) also mentions knowledge as a open source in a futurist paradigm and explains how people will use and share knowledge to create new ideas, methods, techniques and productions.

Peter Drucker (1989), one of the management gurus, describes today's employees as 'knowledge workers' -which are called as gold-collars- by explaining them as the main factors of the modern economy. Knowledge workers work in the global knowledge economy, Drucker (1989) described it as 'the information capitalism', which is creativity-based. And by creativity, he refers to generating new knowledge from existing knowledge and using it in the work-related activities. The global dynamic and ever-changing environment, with technological resources, brings continuous change, transformation and development. Having knowledge and using it effectively are the key factors of 'staying alive in the dynamic workplace' and 'competing to others'. Technological developments and innovations empower employees. These developments also challenge them to go further, harness new innovative ways of thinking, working and being creative. In this multi-sphere, dynamic and challenging world, collecting information, processing and turning it into 'knowledge' is survival and essential for both organisations and individuals who work for organisations. Thus, it is essential to understand social media usage for knowledge management purposes as investigated in this chapter by individual level.

This chapter provides a comprehensive view of the literature background of Web 2.0, social media and personal knowledge management (PKM). It also has a relevant research study on the topic. Data have been collected from 365 knowledge workers in Turkey who work in various private sector organisations such as manufacturing, health services etc. Their usage of mainstream social media platforms for PKM purposes are discovered by using Sigala and Chalkiti's (2015) scale with additional items. The study first covers the relevant literature background on social media and PKM followed by methodological design of the study. With the findings, implications and concluding remarks of the study, it is aimed to provide a useful insight, to determine the current state and to shed a light on the future opportunities for both researchers and practitioners in the academia and the industry.

BACKGROUND

In today's world, individuals live in a network society that enhances organisational and personal knowledge, creativity and learning capacity. The most important charachteristic of this network society is that knowledge can easily be harnessed and shared. To understand the relationship between social media and PKM, first, it is important to understand the concept and context of the topics.

An Overview of Social Media Literature

From Web 1.0 to Web 2.0 so much has changed; users abilites and online behaviours has changed, internet connection velocity has increased, devices have been updated, connectivity has been increased and so on. But, what is Web 1.0 and Web 2.0? And on what features do they differ from each other? Table 1 briefly shows the characteristics and differences between Web 1.0 and Web 2.0.

Tim Berners-Lee, who first used the term Web 1.0 (WWW/W3), defines it as "a pool of knowledge which would allow collaborators in remote sites to share their ideas and all aspects of common project" (Berners-Lee et al., 1994, p. 76). Tim O'Reilly, who used the term of Web 2.0 on a conference and made it 'popular', defines it as; "a continually-updated service that gets better the more people use it, consuming and remixing data from multiple sources, including individual users, while providing their own data and services in a form that allows remixing by others, creating network effects through an 'architecture of participation', and going beyond the page metaphor of Web 1.0 to deliver rich user experiences" (O'Reilly, 2005, para. 1). In this case, Web 1.0 had a half-static and one-way communication-based structure. On the contrary, Web 2.0 has a dynamic and two-way communication-based structure.

According to Şahin and Turan (2012), Web 2.0 is a network which is beyond global and local structures and has changed knowledge sharing and flow processes widely. Web 2.0 provides an online open source platform to reach out all kinds of information via internet. It changed the user profile as well. Table 2 briefly shows the differences between Web 1.0 and Web 2.0 users.

User 1.0 (on Web 1.0) is a person that is 'just a reader' on the web and can be defined as a 'passive user'. User 2.0 (on Web 2.0) can be defined as an 'active user' which interacts and creates user generated contents on web platforms such as all kinds of work and non-work related information and knowledge.

Since addressing Web 2.0 as the grounding concept of social media, it will be useful for this study to represent this topic widely. Social media -today's way of exchanging information, knowledge and thoughts- became a part of our everyday lives. It effects all the dynamics of societal structure by chang-

Table 1. Characteristics of Web 1.0 and Web 2.0

Feature	Web 1.0	Web 2.0
Metaphor for the Internet	Information superhighway	Platform for interaction
Metaphor for the World-Wide-Web (WWW)	Web of information resources stored on a global network of servers where what matters is retrieval and display.	Human web where what matters is human contacts and relations between individuals.
Major Sites	Information portals	Online social networks
Tools	Oriented to display and retrieve information stored on the Internet.	Designed to enable collaboration and content creation on the Internet.
Strategy Pursued	Efficiency	Effectiveness
Economies Sought	Economies of scale	Network effects
Software Used	Software as a product	Software as a service
Computing Model	Client-server	Cloud computing
Communication Range	Wide and local area networks	Mobile communication also considered
Issues	Technological	Social

Source: Mata and Quesada, 2014, p. 58.

Table 2. Differences between Web 1.0 users and Web 2.0 users

User 1.0	User 2.0
Searches out content only. Is "just a reader" on the web.	Supports to create and share online content.
Is contingent upon the person who supplies the content. Cannot share own ideas openly.	Share ideas on web and changes the content.
Usually connects to internet by first generation network devices.	Usually connects to broadband internet connection with new generation devices.
Uses web pages the way they are, cannot edit them or develop them.	Can edit web pages and content.
E-mail is the main communication tool.	Person-to-person communication programs are the main communication tools.
The main access point is computer.	Can connect with many devices such as smartphones.
Connects to internet with time restriction.	Is on-line all day.

Source: Odabaşı et al., 2012, p. 91.

ing our communication processes and types. Social media has created its own cultural and economic system and has been a driving power for new social and individual relationship styles, cultural values and economic environment mechanisms (Kara, 2013). There are many terms which can be used to identify social media and often in use interchangeably with the terms of social technology, social computing etc. These terms are general to define such technologies but they are different from one another at the base. Specifically, social media, is the set of platforms such as Facebook, Twitter, LinkedIn etc. that enables people to connect, communicate and collaborate. It can be defined as "a complex and interconnected knowledge, communication and interaction ecosystem" (Jue, Marr & Kassotakis, 2009, p. 43).

Many authors identify different types of social media platforms (Mayfield, 2008; Kaplan & Haenlein, 2011; Safko, 2010; Zarella, 2010). In this study, in general, six types of social media platforms are explained below (Kaplan & Haenlein, 2010; Jue, Marr & Kassotakis, 2009; Holotescu & Grosseck, 2010; Boyd & Ellison, 2007):

- **Social Networking Sites (e.g., Facebook, LinkedIn):** Social Networks or Social Networking Sites (SNSs) can be explained as communications among a group of people. SNSs are online communities that allows people to share their profile and connect each other. SNSs are web-based services that allow individuals to:
    - Construct a public or semi-public profile within a bounded system,
    - Articulate a list of other users with whom they share a connection, and
    - View and traverse their list of connections and those made by others within the system.
    - With online information sharing easily and effective social interactions, SNSs are the most popular social media platforms among all.
- **Blogs (e.g., Blogger):** Short term of 'web log', blogs are special types of websites that usually display date-stamped entries in reverse chronological order and can have various forms from personal diaries to corporate blogs. Blogs are different from personal websites; a blog can be updated easily, allows more personal ideas to share and interactions between owner(s) and visitors by comments.

Figure 1. Basic types of social media platforms

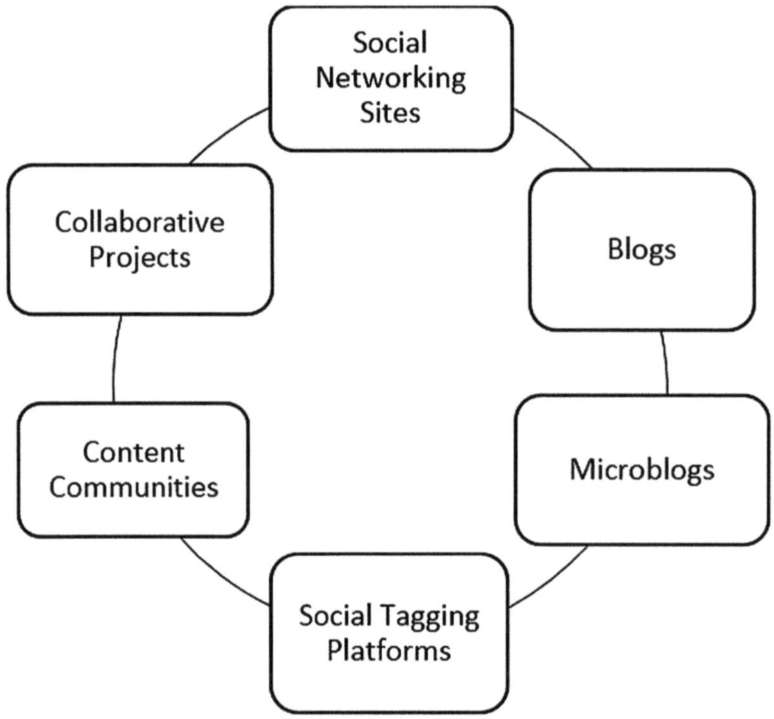

- **Microblogs (e.g., Twitter):** Microblogs are web diaries allows people to share short and instant contents. Microblogging offers the opportunity to discuss/practice different types of online discourse, to organize ideas, reflections; creates instant communities in unexpected environments; promotes a collaborative virtual environment which foster process-oriented learning; is used in the convergence of knowledge and facilitates the creation of a personal learning network etc.
- **Social Tagging Platforms (e.g., del.icio.us):** Social Tagging Platforms enables users add and use tags (some kind of keywords; e.g. "social media") to find/be found more easily on the web which the subjects they are searching for. Also, with social tags, it is easy to find new information sources and to develop new informations. Thus, social tagging allows users to link contents, have a common sense and collaborate more easily on the web.
- **Content Communities (e.g., Flickr, Pinterest, YouTube):** The main objective of this platforms is sharing media contents between users such as images, presantations, videos, audios etc. Users of this communities are not required to create a personal profile page; if they do, these pages usually only contain basic information such as 'the date they joined the community'.
- **Collaborative Projects (e.g., Wikipedia):** Collaborative projects enable the joint and simultaneous creation of content by many end-users and the main idea underlying it is that the joint effort of many actors leads to a better outcome than any actor could achieve individually. Collaborative projects allow users to add, remove, and change text-based content and enables the group-based collection and rating of internet links or media content.

Table 3. Benefits of using social media platforms for the individuals

Social Media Platforms	Benefits for the Individuals
Social Networking Sites (SNSs)	• Personal knowledge sharing • Help career advancement • Promotion of projects • Facilitate keeping up with previous colleagues, and with many looser connections
Collaborative Projects	• Personal knowledge management • Share knowledge, lessons learned • Share problems with others • Motivation (reputation, sense of having an impact) • "Self-served" knowledge for new employees
Microblogging	• Knowing what other employees are working on • Updated with news • Follow relevant contacts • Easy access to experts • Promoting their own work
Blog	• Getting/sharing information • Engaging in dialogue • Gaining perspective and "company pulse" • Collaborating • Support more informal communication
Content Communities	• Engagement and fun • Gaining better knowledge of other team members • Accessing the know-how and ideas

Source: Razmerita et al., 2014, p. 87.

When explaining social media platforms, some of the features has been mentioned. It will be useful to indicate the benefits of using some mainstream social media platforms for individuals (considering the subject of this study) which can be seen in Table 3.

Indicating to all these benefits, it can be said that social media platforms allow people to develop and maintain social relationships in ways that appear to differ in quality and quantity than face-to-face relationships by its very nature. These tools enable building and maintaining large social networks (e.g. Twitter, LinkedIn, Facebook, Tumblr) which "is a novel way of increasing a person's business and/or social acquaintances by connecting with other people" (Chugh, 2012, p. 603). These tools also enable self-publishing as a way of sharing knowledge with anyone who has a similar interest (e.g. blogs, YouTube, Flickr, Pinterest). With these tools, one can collaborate with friends and strangers around the world as evidenced by the collaborative co-production of the largest single source of dynamically evolving knowledge (e.g. Wikipedia) (Hemsley & Mason, 2013, p. 141). Social media, in this manner, gives opportunity to individuals to have an online network, to collaborate, and to gather information and knowledge about various subjects.

Theoretical Base of Personal Knowledge Management

Knowledge is basically defined as "know-what" and "know-how"; it refers to personalized information. Knowledge emerges through "interpretation of raw information, through deeper engagement with an activity, social process and justification of beliefs" (Von Krough, 2012, p. 155). Knowledge is not the same as data or information. Data means information in raw or unorganized form (such as alphabets, numbers, or symbols) that refer to, or represent conditions, ideas or objects and is limitless and present everywhere in the universe (BusinessDictionary.com, 2015). Information, on the other hand, can be explained as processed/interpreted data.

A large category of highly skilled professionals (knowledge workers) including consultants, lawyers etc. use knowledge as a central resource for most of their daily tasks. At the base, all knowledge workers need to think through what information is for them, what data they need. First, they need to know what they are doing; then, to be able to decide what they should be doing; and finally, to appraise how well they are doing (Drucker, 1988). In this manner, to understand social media usage for personal knowledge management purposes, first it is essential to define it. Personal knowledge management (PKM) is defined as "managing and supporting personal knowledge and information to make it accessible, meaningful and valuable to the individual; maintaining networks, contacts and communities; making life easier and more enjoyable; and exploiting personal capital" (Higgison, 2004, para. 3).

PKM, which was introduced in a working paper by Frand and Hixon (1999), focuses on the individual's quest to learn, work efficiently or socialise. One of the aspects of PKM is to allow the individuals to better manage their knowledge processes and interaction, collaboration and knowledge exchanges with others. PKM reflects the goal of supporting individual knowledge workers rather than establishing an organisational approach (Razmerita et al., 2009). PKM is a framework to organise the knowledge of individuals that is important for them (Frand & Hixon, 1999), and now the concept evolved into organising personal information, making sense of information, negotiating meaning, creating new ideas, developing networks, collaborating, sharing and interacting (Efimova, 2004; Wright, 2005). PKM environments integrate individual work environments (in this study, it is the mainstream social media platforms) and infrastructures to support joint creation, distribution, sharing and application of knowledge (Maier & Sametinger, 2004). PKM on Web 2.0 is implemented by a set of tools that allow people to create, codify, organise and share knowledge. It also provides opportunities to socialise, extend personal networks, collaborate on organising knowledge and create new knowledge. It represents the sub-domain of knowledge management that emphasises the crucial importance of the individual in every knowledge process. PKM proposes a model of knowledge management which is focused on the individual use (Razmerita et al., 2009).

A literature overview about PKM can be seen with the main ideas of some articles in Table 4. The main goals of the studies are basicly to investigate these questions: "Do using computers, Web 2.0 and other PKM tools help knowledge workers to manage information and knowledge effectively? If so, how?". In this manner, it can be said that web pages, e-mails, Web 2.0 platforms etc. are important tools for managing information and knowledge effectively. These platforms support knowledge workers to harness information and knowledge through online activities such as participating in online discussions/forums and social networks; distributing information in social networks, placing tags to their bookmarks, to their documents; posting comments to online discussions; sense-making and learning-by-doing processes (e.g. participate in simulations on virtual worlds); passive learning by reading others' comments and online discussions; keeping notes of what it was read; writing reflections of reading or discussions; building a collective knowledge; uploading information on a social network or a wiki etc.

Table 4. Personal knowledge management literature overview

Specific Issues of Knowledge Work	Article	Main Ideas
How can computers be better utilised to help the knowledge worker to manage information and knowledge effectively; or how can the knowledge workers' tasks be better supported?	Benson and Standing, 2001; Sellen et al., 2002	Improving access to documents, files, webpages, e-mails, etc. An analysis of the type of activities the knowledge workers undertake on the web in order to better improve web tools and better support web tasks.
	Schwarz, 2005	An explicit model of the knowledge worker's context can better support the user's tasks
	Cutrell et al., 2006	Search systems can alleviate the need to organise information search help, no matter where it was encountered or how much of it is remembered
	Oren et al., 2006; Jiang et al., 2007	Social software is useful for PKM, but it does not fully satisfy all requirements of PKM. Semantics could help to improve the software towards better support of PKM
	Phipps et al., 2000; Apshvalka and Grundspenkis, 2006; Grundspenkis, 2007	There is considerable potential for using intelligent agents to develop more intelligent KM solutions
How to better organise and store your own ideas; how to improve problem-solving skills; how to improve learning skills	Apshvalka, 2004; Davies et al., 2006	The issue of how to store personal knowledge and insights is addressed as a necessary supplement and extension to human memory
	Cartelli, 2008	Personal strategic thinking is useful for complementing PKM in helping people to obtain and select knowledge, develop new knowledge and improve problem solving skills.
	Li and Liu, 2008; Fang et al., 2008	PKM tools may have far-reaching effects on e-learning, and the management of personal knowledge may be a key element for lifelong learning
What is the benefit of a PKM tool; how people can be motivated to use PKM tools?	Kjellin and Stenfors-Hayes, 2007; Lin et al., 2007; Völkel and Abecker, 2008	The benefit of using a PKM system is the summarisation of successfully retrieved knowledge items. The cost is the sum of all effort of authoring and structuring knowledge. Organisations should put more effort into amending knowledge management. The effects could be measured from a personal level.
How can Web 2.0 tools improve PKM?	Kirchner et al., 2009	Web 2.0 tools simultaneously support individual and collective knowledge processes

Source: Razmerita et al., 2009, p. 1025.

METHODOLOGY

Data for the study were gathered through an online survey which consisted of a 18-item scale about knowledge workers' usage of mainstream social media platforms and how they use these platforms for PKM purposes. Since online surveys are easy for sharing to collect responses from many based on the network effect, this method has been used. The items used in the scale translated in Turkish which has been controlled for not to have any misunderstandings for respondents. The survey is included "social media usage" (Sigala & Chalkiti, 2015) and "social media usage for PKM purposes" (Sigala & Chalkiti, 2015) scales. Also, three item added to the scale from Zincir's (2014) social media usage scale items (e.g. "Search for collecting information about current issues", "Search for collecting information about competitors", "Search for collecting sectoral information") for enhancing Sigala and Chalkiti's "search for collecting information" item. These three items had been gathered by the literature and interview results which has been used in the study. The reason to add this items is to enhance the "search for collecting information" item which is weak for measuring different usage purposes when search for collecting information.

The collected data for the study were gathered through an online survey which consisted of a frequency and usage profile of the respondents' mainstream social media platforms usage such as blogs, Facebook, Twitter, LinkedIn etc. In order to reach knowledge workers who are working at private sector organisations; Google, Facebook, Twitter and LinkedIn search engines were used to find Turkish business groups and pages such as "Turkish Business Network", "Network for White Collars in Turkey" and other sectoral groups and pages. The notification of the survey was sent to the moderators/owners of these online e-groups and sent to the main page of the groups and pages. On the moderators/owners' approval, an e-mail with the survey link was delivered to the members of selected online groups. The e-mail message explained the purpose of the study, guaranteed confidentiality of respondent information and included a link to the survey site. The contact information of the author was also provided. In the survey link which was put on SurveyMonkey website, firstly social media, knowledge worker and personal knowledge management terms have explained; then responses requested. With the survey, the respondents' demographic and job profile; their usage frequency of mainstream social media platforms and their social media usage for PKM purposes has been collected.

Online surveys can occasionally be criticized for lack of reliability due to possible multiple entries by the same respondent(s) and missing responses of some respondents. In order to prevent this, internet protocol (IP) addresses of the respondents were saved and the respondents with the same IP addresses were excluded from the data gathered. Initially, the total number of respondents was 401. However, 36 of them were deleted since they gave missing responses to the questions. Thus, the final sample size of the study is 365.

Demographic characteristics of the respondents are presented as frequencies and percentages in Table 5. The distributions of gender is quite fairly distributed; 178 of them is female, 187 of them is male - almost equal number of each group. In terms of education level, those with a bachelor and master degree dominate the sample. This is because of the fact that the survey has been performed online and internet users, especially those who are actively participating in online communities and groups, mostly have such an education profile in Turkey. Most of the respondents are high educated and young professionals (could be called as 'Gen Y[1]' based on their age and education).

As can be seen on Tables 6 and 7, most of the respondents work in big size companies (168 people), 84 of them work in medium size companies, 113 of them work in small size companies[2]. Respondents mostly work in Information and Communication sector (12.9%). Turkish Statistical Institute (TUIK) (2015) grouping of the sectors has been used for grouping sectors. In "other" lines, which can be seen the last line of the Table 7, include Business Development department and E-Commerce sector. According to this information, it can be said that respondents mostly work in big size companies where networking and harnessing knowledge is an important part of their work. When sending the survey link, online groups' page profile, sharings and some members' personal pages have been examined. It has been seen that an important amount of members of these online groups work in big size companies in Turkey. The respondents represent professionals with a varied experience in several sectors and departments. They work mainly in human resources department (18.9%), while least amount of them work in public relations and quality control (2.5%).

Table 5. Demographic profile of respondents

	n	%
Age		
20-29	136	37,3
30-39	136	35,7
40-49	60	16,4
>= 50	33	9
Gender		
Female	187	48,8
Male	178	51,2
Education		
High School	12	3,3
Vocational School Degree (2 year collage)	19	5,2
Bachelor	195	53,4
Master (MsC)	124	34
Doctoral (PhD)	15	4,1

Table 6. Company size of the respondents' work for

Company Size	n	%
Small Size Company (<50 Staff)	113	31
Medium Size Company (50-250 Staff)	84	23
Big Size Company (>250 Staff)	168	46
Total	365	100%

Table 7. Sectoral and departmental profile of the respondents

Sector	n	%	Department	n	%
Manufacturing	44	12,1	Human Resources	69	18,9
Energy	33	9	Marketing	42	11,5
Construction	33	9	Sales	37	10,1
Health Services	10	2,7	Research and Development (R&D)	53	14,5
Information and Communication	47	12,9	Production	23	6,3
Technologic Services	36	9,9	Accounting	12	3,3
Financial Services	36	9,9	Finance	18	4,9
Education	34	9,3	IT	24	6,6
Tourism	13	3,6	Supply Chain & Procurement	18	4,9
Research & Councultancy	51	14	Public Relations	9	2,5
Textile	10	2,7	Management	30	8,2
FMCG	13	3,6	Quality Control	9	2,5
Other (E-Commerce)	5	1,4	Other (Business Development)	21	5,8
Total	365	100%	Total	365	100%

The collected data were analysed by using Statistical Package for the Social Sciences (SPSS) 21.0. Frequency statistics and factor analyses have been employed in the study.

FINDINGS

According to the frequency statistics' results, Facebook, LinkedIn, Twitter and Instagram are the mainstream social media platforms that respondents use widely. %40,5 of the respondents 'almost always' use Facebook, % 25,8 of them use LinkedIn and %19,2 of them use Twitter. Xing is the most seldomly at use of these platforms (never used; 75,9%). It can be said that it is because LinkedIn is more popular and globally in use. Also, Tumblr is one of the most seldomly at use (never; 75,1%). It can be said that because it has a blogging form, hence, Twitter is more popular and effective at microblogging. As can be seen at Table 8, respondent's usage of Xing's mean value is 1,16. It means that respondents rarely use this social media platform (as explained above). On the other hand, according to the results, the respondents mostly use Facebook. Its mean value is 3,87. It means that respondents mostly use this social media platform. Facebook is the most widely at use for many reasons across the world. It is a leading social networking site for several usage purposes. In this study, one can see this based on the results.

Most of the respondents do not have a personal blog (75.6%), but read others' blogs (72.6%). Using blog is an extra-effort demanding activity, so reading others' blogs, which can be useful for job-related information and knowledge gathering, is possibly more useful and easy for users. They mostly use collaborative authoring tools such as Wikipedia (79.2%) to get information; content sharing networks (70.1%) such as Instagram, Pinterest; and any text, audio, video-conferencing sharing tools (86%) such as YouTube, Skype, Periskop. The adoption of the various social media tools by the respondents reveal that personal blogs and collaborative tagging websites are the least used tools. On the other hand, social networks, (reading other users') blogs, microblogs, collaborative authoring tools, content sharing networks and text, audio, video-conferencing sharing tools represent the most highly used social media tools.

Sigala and Chalkiti's scale is been revised for making the scale more certain for understanding the statements. With this purpose, when the scale is transleated in Turkish, "...as a member of the platform?" wording has been used in Turkish. Hence, one can see in Table 9, this wording has been added to the four items in the scale.

Before analysing the scale, reliability statistics has been applied to test the reliability of the scale which is adapted from the items of Sigala and Chalkiti's (2015) and Zincir's (2014) scale items together. The test shows that "SM-PKM (named by the author as 'Social Media Usage as a Personal Knowledge Management Tool')" scale is highly reliable (see Table 10). With KMO and Bartlett's Test, validity of the scale has been tested and result shows that the scale is valid (see Table 11).

Table 8. Respondents' usage of mainstream social media platforms

	SD[3]	Mean
Facebook	1,24294	3,87
LinkedIn	1,18941	3,55
Twitter	1,42648	3,01
Foursquare	1,28287	1,94
Instagram	1,54478	3,04
Xing	0,54425	1,16
Tumblr	0,78329	1,25

Table 9. Adoption and use of social media tools

Types of Social Media Tools	Yes		No	
	n (%)		n (%)	
Do you have a personal blog?	89	24,4	276	75,6
Do you read the blogs of other users?	265	72,6	100	27,4
Are you a member of a microblog? e.g. Twitter, Tumblr, Identi.ca	245	67,1	120	32,9
Do you use a collaborative authoring tool as a member of the platform? e.g. Wikipedia	289	79,2	76	20,8
Do you use a content sharing network as a member of the platform? e.g. Flickr, Instagram, Pinterest	256	70,1	109	29,9
Do you use any collaborative tagging website as a member of the platform? e.g. Delicious, StumbleUpon, Citeulike, Digg	33	9	332	91
Do you use any text, audio, videoconferencing sharing tool as a member of the platform? e.g. YouTube, Skype, Periscope	314	86	51	14

Table 10. Reliability statistics

Cronbach's Alpha	Cronbach's Alpha Based on Standardized Items	N of Items
.879	.881	10

Table 11. KMO and Bartlett's test

Kaiser-Meyer-Olkin Measure of Sampling Adequacy.		.875
Bartlett's Test of Sphericity	Approx. Chi-Square	1599.930
	df	45
	Sig.	.000

SM-PKM scale items (which adopted to analyse the usage of mainstream social media platforms for PKM purposes) can be seen on Table 12: collecting information about current issues, competitors, sectoral information (has been adopted from Zincir's knowledge workers' social media usage scale items) and uploading information online for storing it for public use, updating personal profile and status, sharing information for discussing it, becoming a member of professional networks, identifying experts for debating information, participating in online discussions for creating new knowledge, comparing information for creating new knowledge (has been employed from Sigala and Chalkiti's scale items).

Finding information on social media is easy. It requires only a network connection and if necessary 'a login process'. For example, when needing expertise, to find a relevant piece of information one can look at knowledge repositories such as wikis, online forums or blogs. Also, to find an expert, blogs, corporate social networks, platforms such as Twitter, LinkedIn, Yammer and Xing are very useful. Getting information from colleagues and other social contacts and finding broader perspectives on work and professional interests on social media can be efficacious for a knowledge worker. It is essential to transform it to 'knowledge'.

According to the results, the respondents least use these platforms for collecting information for participating in online discussions for creating new knowledge. In this manner, new knowledge creation by participating in online discussion is not mostly selected as a way of PKM by the respondents because it requires time and extra-effort. As can be seen in Table 12, "Participate in online discussions for creating new knowledge" item's mean value is 3.37. Considering the 5 point Likert scale, it can be said that this value is relatively good. On the other hand, according to the results, the respondents mostly use these

Table 12. SM-PKM scale items

Items	SD	Mean
Participate in online discussions for creating new knowledge	1,11598	3,37
Share information for discussing it	1,09219	3,55
Compare information for creating new knowledge	1,03827	3,69
Upload information online for storing it for public use.	1,10549	3,70
Update my personal profile and status	1,02283	3,75
Become a member of professional networks	1,00630	3,73
Search for collecting information about competitors	1,03622	3,70
Search for collecting sectoral information	,91620	4,06
Search for collecting information about current issues	,98397	4,13
Identify experts for debating information	,82740	4,19

platforms for collecting information for "identifying experts for debating information". The item's mean value is 4,19. Considering the 5 point Likert scale, it can be said that this value is relatively very good. Since experts such as consultants, CEOs, managers etc. are more and more use these platforms, when they share work-related information and knowledge on their online social media platform pages, it is possible and considered as an important online activity for knowledge workers to debate information with them.

Factor analysis -which is exploratory factor analysis- on SPSS (Rotated Component Matrix) can be seen on Table 13. Results of the analysis, different from the original one, present two factors which are named as (1) sharing and creating new knowledge and (2) harnessing professional knowledge. When considering the items of the scale profoundly, on the basis of the cultural and user differences of the knowledge workers, it can be said that the scale differs from the original one. First factor is more related to sharing and creating knowledge and the second one is more related to "harnessing" professional knowledge of business environment (called as stakeholders). "Participate in online discussions for creating new knowledge", "share information for discussing it", "compare information for creating new knowledge", "upload information online for storing it for public use", "update my personal profile and status", "become a member of professional networks" items mainly represent of sharing and creating new knowledge. "Search for collecting information about competitors", "search for collecting sectoral information", "search for collecting information about current issues", "identify experts for debating information" mainly represent harnessing professional knowledge of business environment. Such business environment, by other means stakeholders, are the main work-related information and knowledge resources considering the usage purposes.

CONCLUSION

The major purpose of this study is to understand the knowledge workers' mainstream social media platforms usage for PKM purposes. Furthermore, presenting a profile of knowledge workers' usage of social media in Turkey is another purpose of this study. For this purposes, a 18 items scale -with three items added from another scale- adopted. Frequency statistics and factor analysis are conducted on to the data collected. Two factors emerged from this analysis which are named as 'Sharing and Creating New

Table 13. Factors of SM-PKM scale

Scale Items	**Item Loadings**	
	Sharing and Creating New Knowledge	**Harnessing Professional Knowledge**
Participate in online discussions for creating new knowledge	.829	
Share information for discussing it	.812	
Compare information for creating new knowledge	.775	
Upload information online for storing it for public use.	.617	
Update my personal profile and status	.632	
Become a member of professional networks	.533	
Search for collecting information about competitors		.828
Search for collecting sectoral information		.826
Search for collecting information about current issues		.766
Identify experts for debating information		.538
Variance Explained	48.52%	11.82%

Knowledge' and 'Harnessing Professional Knowledge'. Sample of this study shows that knowledge workers mostly use social media for the purpose of 'identifying experts for debating information'. They least use these platforms for the purpose of 'participating in online discussions for creating new knowledge'. This finding clearly shows that at individual level, knowledge workers are aware of the digital-sphere and they are most likely to use it for PKM purposes.

Social media platforms are effective tools for searching, reading, sharing and discussing information. Social media can be used to support conversational and collaborative knowledge management processes. By searching, storing and reading information, individuals can enhance their personal knowledge. And, by sharing, discussing, debating and synthesising information from various platforms, they can contribute to create knowledge as well. Social media is on the junction of people, technology and communication. It grounds on interactions between multiparts including individuals, organisations and other interest groups called as stakeholders. By its interactive nature, it is very easy to collect and share information from and with others. In everyday life, whether a work-day or off-day, knowledge workers can be online and seek, share and harness knowledge and information, and collaborate each other within and beyond the organisational boundaries. Individuals' behavior of seeking knowledge, sharing user created content which contains both knowledge and information have been affected by social media and its features. Social media and PKM concepts are been enhanced with many theoritical and emprical studies. Thus, a deeper understanding of both personal and collective knowledge harnessing processes by using social media platforms is very important.

From a technology-centric to a people-centric approach, the literature shows that social media usage supports PKM. Social media, as a PKM tool, changes the ways of working by its participative, collaborative, collective and creative nature. Digital tools advance very rapidly. The way people interact with the digital tools is also changing. Hence, further and continuous research is required in order to better understand the dynamic human–digital tools interactions and their influence on people's cognitive and creative processes, especially for work-related activities. By adopting a PKM approach, this study tries to explain and examine the role of social media on PKM usage of knowledge workers in Turkey. With this study, it is expected to make a significant contribution to the field. Further, by explaining the individual level of use, emprical studies can enhance meso-level (group-team level) and organisational level of use social media for knowledge management purposes. In addition, it will be useful if the scales would adopted, refined and tested within other countries, cultural and industrial-professional contexts.

REFERENCES

Anderson, C. (2012). *Makers: the new industrial revolution*. New York, NY: Crown Business.

Berners-Lee, T., Cailliau, R., Loutonen, A., Nielsen, H. F., & Secret, A. (1994). The world-wide web. *Communications of the ACM*, *37*(8), 76–82. doi:10.1145/179606.179671

Boyd, D. M., & Ellison, N. B. (2007). Social network sites: Definition, history, and scholarship. *Journal of Computer-Mediated Communication*, *13*(1), 210–230. doi:10.1111/j.1083-6101.2007.00393.x

Chugh, R. (2012). Social networking for businesses: is it a boon or bane? In M. M. Cruz-Cunha, G. D. Putnik, N. Lopes, P. Gonçalves, & E. Miranda (Eds.), *Handbook of Research on Business Social Networking: Organizational, Managerial and Technological Dimensions* (pp. 603–618). Hershey, PA: IGI Global. doi:10.4018/978-1-61350-168-9.ch032

Data. (n.d.). In *Business Dictionary online*. Retrieved from http://www.businessdictionary.com/ definition/data.html

Drucker, P. (1988). The coming of the new organization. In *Harvard Business Review on Knowledge Management* (pp. 3–11). Boston, MA: Harvard Business School Press.

Drucker, P. (1989). *The new realities: in government and politics, in economics and business, in society and world view*. New York, NY: Harper & Row.

Efimova, L. (2004). Discovering the iceberg of knowledge work: a weblog case. In *Proceedings of 5th European Conference on Organizational Knowledge, Learning and Capabilities (OKLC)*. Innsbruck (Austria).

Frand, J., & Hixon, C. (1999). *Personal knowledge management: who, what, why, where, when, and how*. Retrieved 15 September, 2015 from www.anderson.ucla.edu/faculty/jason.frand/researcher/ speeches/PKM.htm

Hemsley, J., & Mason, R. M. (2013). Knowledge and knowledge management in the social media age. *Journal of Organizational Computing and Electronic Commerce*, *23*(1-2), 138–167. doi:10.1080/10919392.2013.748614

Higgison, S. (2004). Personal knowledge management. *Inside Knowledge*, *7*(7). Retrieved 15 September, 2015 from http://www.kmmagazine.com/xq/asp/sid.7551F69D-2683-471C-A18C-C3365B30C312/articleid.DDDD6EE3-47C6-49CD-9070-F1B1547FD29F/qx/display.htm

Holotescu, C., & Grosseck, G. (2010). Learning to microblog and microblogging to learn: a case study on learning scenarios in a microblogging context. In *Proceedings of 6th International Scientific Conference eLearning and Software for Education (eLSE)*. Bucharest (Romania).

Jue, A. L., Marr, J. A., & Kassotakis, M. E. (2010). *Social media at work: how networking tools propel organisational performance*. San Francisco, CA: Jossey-Bass.

Kaplan, A. M., & Haenlein, M. (2010). Users of the world, unite!: The challenges and opportunities of social media. *Business Horizons*, *53*(1), 59–68. doi:10.1016/j.bushor.2009.09.003

Kaplan, A. M., & Haenlein, M. (2011). The early bird catches the news: Nine things you should know about micro-blogging. *Business Horizons*, *54*(2), 105–113. doi:10.1016/j.bushor.2010.09.004

Kara, T. (2013). *Sosyal media endüstrisi: insan, toplum ve ekonomi*. Istanbul: Beta Yayınları.

Maier, R., & Sametinger, J. (2004). Personal knowledge management in a peer-to-peer environment. In *Proceedings of the 5th European Conference on Knowledge Management*. Paris (France).

Mata, F. J., & Quesada, A. (2014). Web 2.0, social networks and e-commerce as marketing tools. *Journal of Theoretical and Applied Electronic Commerce Research*, *9*(1), 56–69. doi:10.4067/S0718-18762014000100006

Mayfield, A. (2008). What is social media? *iCrossing*. Retrieved 12 June, 2015 from http://www.icrossing.com/uk/sites/default/files_uk/insight_pdf_files/What%20is%20Social%20Media_iCrossing_ebook.pdf

Naisbitt, J. (1994). *Global paradox: the bigger the world economy, the more powerful its smallest players*. New York, NY: Avon Books.

O'Reilly, T. (2005). *Web 2.0: compact definition?* Retrieved 14 June, 2015 from http://radar.oreilly.com/2005/10/ web-20-compact-definition.html

Odabaşı, H. F., Mısırlı, Ö., Günüç, S., Timar, Z. Ş., Ersoy, M., Som, S., & Erol, O. et al. (2012). Eğitim için yeni bir ortam: Twitter. *Anadolu Journal of Educational Sciences International*, *2*(1), 89–103.

Razmerita, L., Kirchner, K., & Nabeth, T. (2014). Social media in organisations: Leveraging personal and collective knowledge processes. *Journal of Organizational Computing and Electronic Commerce*, *24*(1), 74–93. doi:10.1080/10919392.2014.866504

Razmerita, L., Kirchner, K., & Sudzina, F. (2009). Personal knowledge management. *Online Information Review*, *33*(6), 1021–1039. doi:10.1108/14684520911010981

Rifkin, J. (2011). *Third industrial revolution: how lateral power is transforming energy, the economy, and the world*. London: Palgrave Macmillan.

Rifkin, J. (2014). *The zero marginal cost society: the internet of things, the collaborative commons, and the eclipse of capitalism*. London: Palgrave Macmillan.

Safko, L. (2010). *The social media bible: tactics, tools, and strategies for business success*. Wiley.

Şahin, K., & Turan, B. O. (2012). The impact of social networks on designing education. *Journal of Information Technology in Construction.*, *17*, 485–501.

Shapiro, C., & Varian, H. R. (1993). *Information rules: a strategic guide to the network economy*. Boston, MA: Harvard Business School Press.

Sigala, M., & Chakiti, K. (2015). Knowledge management, social media and employee creativity. *International Journal of Hospitality Management*, *45*, 44–58. doi:10.1016/j.ijhm.2014.11.003

Toffler, A. (1980). *Third wave*. New York, NY: William Morrow & Co.,Inc.

Turkish Statistical Institute (TUIK). (2015). Retrieved from: http://www.turkstat.gov.tr/

Von Krogh, G. (2012). How does social software change knowledge management? toward a strategic research agenda. *The Journal of Strategic Information Systems*, *21*(2), 154–164. doi:10.1016/j.jsis.2012.04.003

Wright, K. (2005). Personal knowledge management: Supporting individual knowledge worker performance. *Knowledge Management Research and Practice*, *3*(3), 156–165. doi:10.1057/palgrave.kmrp.8500061

Zarella, D. (2010). *The social media marketing book*. O'Reilly Media Inc.

Zincir, O. (2014). *Yöneticilerin sosyal medya kullanım amaçları: bir kuramsal çerçeve önerisi*. (Unpublished master dissertation). Istanbul University, Istanbul, Turkey.

KEY TERMS AND DEFINITIONS

Information Age: Information Age is a period of human history that grounds on information which is the primary source.

Knowledge: Knowledge is a mix of data and information which requires a complex process of interpretation of individuals, groups or organizations.

Knowledge Worker: Knowledge worker is a person whose main work-related source is knowledge such as engineeers, scientists etc.

Personal Knowledge Management: Personal Knowledge Management is sub-domain category of Knowledge Management with the primary focus on individual knowledge searching, collecting and storing.

Social Media: Social Media is computer-mediated community of platforms (e.g. Facebook, Twitter) that allow people to create, share or exchange information, ideas etc. in digital-sphere.

User 2.0: User 2.0 is a person who basicly uses Web 2.0 platforms and ability to use interactive web-based tools.

Web 2.0: Web 2.0 is a web based paradigm – can be called as 'interactive web'- that allows individuals to create user-generated content and share to the world which also gives opportunity to share and collect information and transform it into new information and knowledge.

ENDNOTES

1 Generation Y people: Born in between 1980 to 2000, good at using technology comparing to other generations before.

2 The size of the companies is being determined by Small and Medium Enterprises Development Organisation in Turkey: http://www.kosgeb.gov.tr/Pages/UI/Default.aspx.

3 Standard Deviation.

Chapter 7
Social Media and Knowledge Management in a Crisis Context:
Barriers and Opportunities

Terri Toles Patkin
Eastern Connecticut State University, USA

ABSTRACT

The role of social media in managing and disseminating organizational knowledge is illustrated in this case study of a local government's response to a natural disaster. The interplay of technological, organizational and ecological factors was magnified as town officials utilized both social media and traditional media to disseminate information to the public during and after the crisis. As organizations embrace social media, managers must recognize that in addition to the organization educating the public, social media features the public talking to the organization, and perhaps more resonant, the public talking to the public.

INTRODUCTION

Knowledge, information, and data are central to all organizations, and most especially in the postmodern context. Whether rooted in action, content, people, or process, most discussion of knowledge management understandably focuses on KM within the organization. As organizations increasingly embrace social media, however, communication with external publics and the associated challenge to KM becomes an area of consequence. An organization's knowledge management strategy consists of orientation (organizational proactivity/reactivity to knowledge gathering and development), milieu (emphasis on tacit or explicit knowledge; embedding knowledge in technology or personnel), and scope (the breadth of topics for which knowledge is sought), and these are interdependent (Kasten, 2008). In most organizations, strategic knowledge management is reflected in the tactical day-to-day actions in the organization.

DOI: 10.4018/978-1-5225-0495-5.ch007

Employee knowledge can be utilized as a strategic input that can shape culture, but knowledge creation and sharing is not always directly tied to compensation and reward structures (Pasher & Ronen, 2011).

Knowledge is much more than the information created, transformed, disseminated, or embedded in products, systems, or individuals (Bodhanya, 2008).

The cognitive-possession, or first order, positivist approach to knowledge management conceptualizes knowledge as static and reified, while the systems theory and complexity theory perspectives recognize the dynamic and adaptive properties of a knowledge ecology. Increasingly, the KM discourse has come to distinguish between knowledge as a resource or commodity and knowledge as a process (Bodhanya, 2008).

A pyramid of knowledge exists, beginning with "data" as the foundation, the processed raw material of the data becomes "information," and that is in turn transformed into "knowledge." This emerges through action and the capability to solve problems that arise. At the next level, "intellectual capital" combines the knowledge of the entire organization both intangible and tangible, and finally at the peak comes "wisdom," which allows the identification of the most effective use of knowledge and intellectual capital for organizational success (Pasher & Ronen, 2011). Knowledge management leaders identify increased internal knowledge sharing, increased employee collaboration, and improved decision-making as key factors in effective KM. One significant challenge, however, stems from communication barriers (Croteau & Dfouni, 2008). These may be social or technological in origin, and in either case, can limit organizational effectiveness if not addressed in a timely manner.

The first stage of KM focused on intellectual capital and finding the best use of technology for coordination and sharing of knowledge. The second stage included a new focus on communities of practice, recognizing the importance of human factors in the KM process. The third stage emphasized content management and retrievability. A fourth stage may now be emerging that extends information and knowledge to an extra-organizational context (Koenig, 2008). A prerequisite for future knowledge management is documenting and codifying existing knowledge efficiently (Pasher & Ronen, 2011).

Following a systems perspective that views organizations as dynamic and complex entities interacting with their environment, it becomes clear that the flow of information and knowledge occupies a central position in determining the organization's success. A hierarchically-ordered interdependent system allows information and resources to enter and exit via permeable boundaries (Miller, 2015). This process is challenged when social media is added to the mix, accelerating and intensifying the exchange and feedback processes. In systems theory, the focus is on holistic relationships and the permeable boundaries between the organization and its environment. The positive and negative feedback processes contribute to the system's stability or turbulence. In this perspective, the manager is placed firmly within the dynamic system rather than as an external observer; in an emergent system both information and human identity are constantly emergent (Bodhanya, 2008).

As demonstrated in this case study, an organization's environment extends beyond the physical to encompass the information environment. An organization's information environment is constructed and enacted by organizational members as their actions allow them to engage in sensemaking, or the reduction of equivocality. Since unpredictability is inherent in any information environment – and heightened during periods of crisis – organization members utilize procedures and processes to select key informational inputs and utilize them in sensemaking (Miller, 2015). Even in a relatively small organization, such as the local government examined here, best practices in knowledge management and crisis communication are required for organizational success.

BACKGROUND

A crisis is marked by several factors: it appears suddenly, often without warning, escalates in intensity, causes threats to the organization and its reputation, and creates stress and uncertainty. Crisis management demands four communication functions: uncertainty reduction, coordination, information dissemination, and strategic ambiguity. Each of these works in conjunction with the others to provide a holistic foundation for crisis resolution (Seeger, Sellnow, & Ulmer, 2003). Unpredictability is not sufficient for an event to be classified as a crisis; it must also threaten important institutional values (Fishman, 1999; Millar, 2004). The difference between information and knowledge as elements in the crisis context must be remembered as the nexus of social media and knowledge management (of which knowledge dissemination is an important part) becomes crucial in a crisis context. The use of social media creates particular challenges as external publics may not only demand organizational transparency and knowledge transfer, but may actively participate in knowledge creation and transfer themselves as extra-organizational actors.

Crisis communication is event-centered, often spontaneous and reactive, and typically emphasizes a short-term focus. In order to fully understand an organization's response to crisis, it is important to comprehend the dynamic, multidimensional relationships and public relations strategies that emerge in response to a rapidly changing communication environment (Fishman, 1999). This need becomes magnified when social media is added to the picture.

Social media reaches approximately 80% of the 272 million active internet users in the United States (Nielsen, 2011). "Social media are the various electronic tools, technologies, and applications that facilitate interactive communication and content exchange, enabling the user to move back and forth easily between the roles of audience and content producers" (Tinker & Fouse, 2013, p.1). The benefits of an organizational online presence such as a blog, Twitter account or Facebook page include enhanced relationships with important target audiences and an additional platform for positioning the organization in a positive light (Zhang & Ma, 2008).

Laad and Lewis (2012) offer examples of a wide variety of social media tools currently available, including social networking sites (Facebook, LinkedIn) that permit people to group in communities-of-interest, social bookmarking sites (Reddit, StumbleUpon) that allow users to share favorite online content with one another, blogs (WordPress, Tumblr) featuring online journals, microblogging sites (Twitter) that facilitate abbreviated information sharing, collaborative projects (Wikipedia, Google Docs) that permit multiple users to join forces in content creation, photo sharing (Flickr, Photobucket), video and music sharing (YouTube, Spotify), presentation sharing (Slideshare, Scribd), intellectual property sharing (Creative Commons), and Questions-and-Answers sites (Yahoo questions, Formspring). The most common tools used in crisis situations have been social networking, blogs, microblogging, and photo/video sharing (Laad & Lewis, 2012). With over 800 million active Facebook users, each of who has an average of 130 "friends," (Leavesley & Hemus, 2013), it seems clear that any information shared via social media is going to spread rapidly.

CASE STUDY: SOCIAL MEDIA AND CRISIS

The Blizzard of 2013 ("Winter Storm Nemo") struck the town of "Grancesso" particularly hard, dumping a season's worth of snow on the community in a single day, and blocking roads for almost a week. This crisis situation is perhaps unique due to the importance of social media throughout the storm. In many ways, the banality of the crisis in comparison to more dramatic natural disasters such as earthquakes, tsunamis, or hurricanes would seem to disqualify it for serious consideration: citizens were not displaced; in fact, they were forced to shelter in place. They were not facing grave physical threat; despite the heavy snowfall, almost everyone in town had electricity and internet available as they waited for the snowplows to arrive. Those conditions created the perfect storm, so to speak, for social media use, and the significance of that outcome provides fertile ground for understanding the role of knowledge management in a crisis situation. Those affected by the crisis were home-bound, and the use of communication technology was for most the only way to make contact with others not living in close proximity. In fact, membership on the Facebook page doubled during the storm, and the page hasn't been that active before or since (C. Leng, personal communication, June 16, 2015). What the organization first identified as a natural disaster crisis morphed into a social media crisis as events unfolded.

Methodology

This research utilizes a narrative approach to case study through an examination of the town's communication strategies during the storm, focusing on the use of social media. Using deep description, it offers a qualitative evaluation of real-time unfolding of discourse throughout the storm following a rhetorical approach to crisis communication that stresses message development and presentation. Public discourse about the storm was primarily tracked through a content analysis of interactions on the town's official Facebook page during the week of the crisis. The repetition of those official statements via other forms of media was noted, but not included in the analysis as radio, television, and newspaper releases were identical to those posted on Facebook. Other forms of social media, such as Twitter, were not in use by the town at the time of the study. The 132 Facebook postings from town officials and 4,249 comments and responses from members of the public appearing over the course of the ten-day crisis were categorized according to the rhetorical themes of uncertainty reduction, coordination, information dissemination, and strategic ambiguity, and correlated with the chronological stages of the crisis. In order to protect privacy, individual identities and the actual name of the community have been anonymized.

Private and internal knowledge management processes that shaped the public discourse were revealed via a series of personal interviews with town officials responsible for public communication during the storm, especially the administrator of the town's Facebook page at the time. The intertwining of public and private illuminates the ways in which the interactive nature of the social media platform shaped organizational rhetoric and knowledge management during the crisis.

Context

Grancesso is a mostly middle class community with about 60,000 residents living in neighborhoods characterized as urban, suburban, and rural, and it is home to people of a range of socioeconomic statuses, ethnicities, and education. The town already had a functional knowledge management system in place at the time of the storm (C. Leng, personal communication, June 16, 2015). Statistically, the total average annual snowfall in Grancesso is 33.97 inches, so when Nemo dumped 40 inches on the town on a single day in February of 2013, it created a challenge even for well-prepared local services. The ordeal was magnified by the intensity of the blizzard: eleven of the town's fifteen snow removal trucks got stuck during the whiteout conditions at the height of the storm (Bellmore, 2013). Snow began falling on Friday, February 8, and the last street was finally cleared almost a week later. Any severe weather event has the potential to create an organizational crisis for a town's Public Works Department and the Mayor's Office, and Storm Nemo was no exception. As the storm – and more important, the storm cleanup – progressed, the town as an organization faced a public image crisis in addition to the crisis caused by the natural disaster. Frustrated residents demanded immediate attention to their needs and threatened political action against town officials, especially when they were perceived as inadequately managing the situation.

The Town of Grancesso activated its crisis management team in anticipation of the storm, bringing together representatives from the Mayor's Office, Department of Public Works, Police and Fire Departments, Risk Management, Purchasing, and other relevant departments for a pre-storm meeting. Grancesso had experienced hurricanes, wind storms, and an unseasonably early winter storm in previous months, so the team was well-prepared for what promised to be a serious weather event (C. Leng, personal communication, June 16, 2015). The town typically uses multiple traditional media platforms, including radio, television, and newspaper reports, to update the public, and town officials continued to utilize all of these throughout the crisis. The mayor served as the official spokesperson for the town, giving interviews to local and national broadcast and print media concerning the storm. Indeed, the national news coverage of the town following the National Weather Service's identification of Grancesso as the title-holder for most snowfall in the region created in itself another mini-crisis for town officials.

In recent years, Grancesso, like many organizations, has begun to supplement its use of traditional media with social media, creating what Leng (2015), who was responsible for information management at the time, called an "old school – new school mix." Starting in September 2010, the town has hosted a Facebook page titled "Town of Grancesso." A Facebook page is essentially a community of practice, a collaborative learning community that shares common ground and common purposes for knowledge sharing. Typically, a community of practice is evolutionary, incorporating and socializing new members over time (Zhang & Ma, 2008). The page is administered by the Town Administrator, although there is no indication of this person's identity on the Facebook page, since all posts are made from the anonymous Town of Grancesso (although anyone may comment on a Town posting). In fact, the profile picture features an image of the historic Town Hall, an important local landmark, giving the impression that an abstract entity called "The Town" is behind the messages. Until the storm, the page had not been very active, but during Winter Storm Nemo, it became a central piece in the communication puzzle. Before the storm, announcements had included relatively mundane yet diverse community-related content including discussions about on a spending freeze for nonessential items, construction of an all-abilities playground, business incentive packages, tax and pension issues, suggestions for community movie night, equipment for police officers, an announcement of a genealogy workshop at the public library, school security, a link to the governor's "state of the state" address, a lecture by a local college professor, and an invitation to the maple sugaring demonstration at a town park. Some of these garnered a handful of comments while most simply served as unidirectional announcements. Many residents discovered the page during the storm by clicking on the link to "Storm Clearing Updates" on the town's webpage, which brought up the Facebook page. Indeed, after the storm, activity on the page subsided, except for once several months after the storm when the town mandated that citizens begin using new trash and recycling bins provided by the town. Some citizen protest occurred at that time, but it did not begin to compare to the Nemo outcry, and in fact the town effectively utilized the KM strategies learned during the snowstorm in dealing with the considerably less significant trash bin debate on social media.

Town officials utilized the web page and Facebook group during the storm to share limited organizational knowledge with citizens. The town's web page included a link to the town's established snow removal policy and included general information about plowing priorities and division of responsibilities within the Department of Public Works. For example, two of the town's major thoroughfares are state roads, and those roads are cleared on a different schedule than other streets, since the town is not responsible for them. For town roads, the plowing pattern for each of the 15 routes focuses on main roads followed by residential streets, and finally culs-de-sac and other dead-end roads. In the event of major snow accumulation, the first pass clears a single lane, and curb-to-curb plowing follows at a later time. This knowledge has been developed over a long period within the organization, but may not have been explicitly shared with the public previously. What many citizens wanted, however, was an even more precise identification of which specific streets were on the plowing agenda for a particular day, and that information was not released.

In addition, the town's web page provided telegraph-style updates throughout the storm, with messages announcing general information such as school closings, delayed trash pickup, and a continuation of the parking ban. As the storm progressed, the discourse changed from information-based to knowledge-based as exemplified in the Day 4 message that ended with a plea for patience, detailing the town's tandem use of plows and loaders to clear streets, noting that "it is a slow but effective process" (C. Leng, personal communication, June 16, 2015). Town postings tended to be informational or provide crisis advice, as well as forwarding material from other sources, especially local news media. Citizens, however, were less objective: comments from residents ran the gamut from concerns about unplowed streets, some rants about generalized town incompetence, praise for the public works crews, and requests for information. There seemed to be a bandwagon effect in place to a degree: one positive comment was often followed by several other supportive comments. The truly negative comments appeared for the most part to be directed at other users, not the town itself.

A significant barrier was created by a technological breakdown; the mayor's plan to make reverse-911 calls to all town residents was delayed by a full day due to technical difficulties with the reverse-911 system, forcing the town to quickly identify a backup provider. Although the new system, which was provided at low cost by a different provider for the duration of the crisis, could only reach registered voters, town officials encouraged recipients to contact friends and family who didn't receive the call and share the information. The town also made it possible for citizens to call a central number and hear the recording, as well as posting the script of the message on the town website and Facebook page. This was received positively; "people loved getting calls with information during the crisis," reports the current mayor (C. Leng, personal communication, June 16, 2015).

Stages of the Crisis

The town's response to the storm crisis most closely mirrored Fink's (1986) Natural History Approach to crisis. This divides the evolution of a crisis into a series of chronological stages, each with their own demands for organizational action and communication.

Stage One, the prodromal or precrisis phase, was marked by announcements that severe weather was predicted and the dissemination of standard emergency management advice. Day 1 (Friday), when the snow began late in the day, can be classified as precrisis. Little social media activity occurred during this stage, and whatever messages were posted were largely unidirectional reminders of typical emergency preparedness advice. Residents of Grancesso are accustomed to severe winter weather, so these messages were taken in stride by most people. Behind the scenes, the town's crisis management team was quietly gearing up for the storm (C. Leng, personal communication, June 16, 2015). During this time, the ratio of public comments to town postings was roughly 2:1; as the storm began, for instance, the town posted 24 announcements, and there were 48 comments posted.

Stage Two, the Acute Crisis Phase, was marked by the rapid unfolding of events. This included the heaviest period of the snowstorm on Friday night into Saturday morning, when multiple plows got stuck (some for several hours), some residents lost power, and town plowing had to be suspended to assist with traffic and other emergencies (C. Leng, personal communication, June 16, 2015). Fink (1986) identifies multiple elements that may arise at this stage, including increased public attention and media attention, increased intensity of the crisis, distractions from the crisis interfering with normal business activity, impacts on the financial well-being of the organization, as well as threats to the organization's reputation. All of these occurred in Grancesso, and they eventually sparked a secondary social media crisis marked by citizen resistance to the official communication provided by the town. At this point, plow drivers were working day and night, and the mayor was coordinating with state and federal officials to obtain emergency relief resources (Bellmore, 2013). Ironically, the social media crisis did not correlate directly with the storm crisis, but rather lagged behind it. There was some minimal social media activity during Stage Two, but most residents were trying to find a way to open their doors that were blocked by 40 inches or more of drifting snow, and some began the slow process of clearing their driveways and making paths from their homes to the street. Some residents shared social media content in person with neighbors who had lost power or did not have internet connectivity during the storm (C. Leng, personal communication, June 16, 2015). By the end of this phase, however, citizen social media comments had soared to 521 on Day 3, compared with the 24 postings made by the town that day.

In Fink's third stage, the Chronic Crisis Phase, the organization is working to recover from the crisis but may experience self-doubt and self-analysis. This appeared in the Nemo crisis as road clearing slowly continued, from Sunday (Day 3) through Wednesday (Day 6). The highest level of social media use occurred during this period. On Day 4, there were 922 comments to the town's 33 postings; on Day 5, 1,697 citizen postings were made while the town made 22 postings; by Day 6, citizen postings had diminished to 725, while the town only made 9 postings. During this time, town officials monitored social media and coordinated resources as necessary; individuals who posted messages about needing to get out for a personal emergency such as a scheduled surgery, for example, were assisted whenever possible. Town officials and plow drivers would meet the individual at the nearest cleared intersection and assist them in arranging transport to the hospital, for instance. One plow driver even drove a man having a heart attack to the nearest cleared street to meet an ambulance (C. Leng, personal communication, June 16, 2015). A thematic analysis of these comments details information seeking, advice providing, positive and negative reinforcement, references to other media, and social interaction frames.

The town's postings were consistent throughout the storm, and were largely informational in nature, with information dissemination accounting for 58.6% of all posts made on the Facebook page N=132). General advice about best practices for handling the blizzard (make sure your elderly neighbors are all right, check that your furnace vent isn't blocked by snow) made up only 9% of the town's total postings, but each individual post tended to be lengthy and detailed. Links to other media and references to social media sites accounted for an additional 25% of the postings, while positive responses acknowledging helpful citizens covered 6.9% of the town's postings. Postings peaked on Day 4 (Monday). On Tuesday (Day 5), there were notable increases in positive comments, where the town provided positive reinforcement to those posters urging others to remain calm and patient as the town does its best to help them as the immediacy of the crisis receded. Most of the postings were unidirectional in nature; for the organization, it was less a conversation than a broadcast.

Finally, Stage Four, or Crisis Resolution, identifies the point at which the organization makes a full recovery. Day 7 (Thursday) marked the beginning of this stage, as all town roads were made passable by late Wednesday night. Although a full recovery had yet to occur, the promise of federal and state disaster relief resources provided hope for the future. The rhetoric from the Mayor's Office and Town Hall became more personal, with the mayor responding to individual citizens directly rather than using media to broadcast information to a wider public (R. Lion, personal communication, February 20, 2013). Social media use dropped as people returned to work and other daily activities, and both the storm crisis and the social media crisis receded. On Day 7, the town made nine postings and citizens made 179; on Day 8, the town's two postings netted 37 comments; by Day 9, the town's five postings received 79 comments; and on Day 10, the town made a single post indicating that crews were continuing to work on clearing the streets, which received 23 comments.

Post crisis communication continued the town's agenda of openness. The Friday following the storm (Day 8), a poster complained that, while he was in general pleased with the job that had been done by the town, he was concerned about damage caused by the snow plow. The response from the town appears to offer redress for the situation, while providing information about how the citizen should proceed.

Citizen: *I am not unhappy with the job that has been done by the Town, the contractors and the National Guard. I know that it is a monumental task. I want to share that the snow was dumped on my front lawn directly onto a very expensive ornamental tree. I am not sure if it will die this spring as a result. The payloader driver got so close to my driveway that they scooped up and destroyed a very expensive flower pot. There were many other places on my lawn where the snow could have been dumped safely. When we called the Town to ask them to tell the drivers to be more careful they were extremely rude and didn't offer an apology. I wasn't calling to complain I was just calling to ask them to be careful and the response I got was pretty shocking.*

Town of Grancesso: *Please call the Town's Risk Manager for damage to your property. Take pictures please. Please accept the Town's apology.*

Social media use, both positive and negative, hit its peak on Days 4 and 5 of the storm crisis (Monday and Tuesday), the point at which people had begun to run out of patience with the plowing delay. This marked the high point of the social media crisis, while the town had the storm crisis well in hand, even if not completely resolved. By this time, the town had gotten into a pattern of updating the Facebook page multiple times each day, with several updates in the evening hours, including links to media coverage and the text of the mayor's daily phone message. Bruni, Francalanci and Giacomazzi (2012) report that Facebook users "like" posts as a means of showing support for the individual or the content of the comment, and this was the case in Grancesso, where "likes" peaked from an average well below 500 per day to over 2,000 likes on Day 4. Day 4 was a busy social media day as reader response via comments also peaked around Day 4, falling off sharply once most streets were plowed and residents returned to their daily routines.

The problem with social media, of course, is that it is *social.* People used the Facebook page as a place to vent about their frustrations with being snowed in: all that cabin fever was released in a series of complaints that their street had not yet been plowed. Reasons citizens cited for needing their particular street plowed included: a sick or elderly resident living in the home, essential employee (health care workers especially), pregnant person, broken furnace needing repair or oil delivery needed, and "the state police payroll will be in jeopardy." The bandwagon effect veered to the negative: 60.3% of reader comments

(N=4,249) focused on complaints and requests, while only 19.4% of comments were positive. Anecdotal observations indicate that comment valence was influenced by other nearby postings: one "support the hard working plow drivers" post typically inspired five or six similar comments within a short period of time. Approximately 8.1% of the reader comments provided information, 6.2% represented negative interactions among users or irrelevant comments ("Hi Bob, I didn't know you lived in Grancesso"), 2.6 asked a question, and the remaining 3.4% was split among offering advice, references to other media, and references to social media (such as the twitter account providing information).

Grancesso effectively used communication tactics to prevent and mitigate the natural disaster crisis throughout the event, but efforts to mitigate the social media crisis were less effective. In the midst of a crisis, communicative attempts to exert control and define the meaning of a crisis can be blocked on social media platforms. Post-crisis communication that restores organizational control and brings the crisis to closure (Heath & Millar, 2004) were effective in large part because citizens lost interest in the Facebook page once they were able to return to normal everyday routines.

One contributing factor may have been a disconnect between the Town's media choices and the ambiguity of the content communicated during the event. A "rich" medium is one that closely mimics face-to-face communication; it offers instant feedback, uses natural language and multiple cues, and has a personal focus. The more ambiguous the situation and the greater the need for personalized information, the richer the medium should be (C. Leng el & Daft, 1988; Miller, 2015). While the Town employed multiple media platforms ranging from print to electronic to social media, no change was made to the message communicated; the identical information was merely broadcast via different channels. Such a "lean" approach may have been suitable for traditional media, such as a radio "closings list" announcement, but its use on social media had a boomerang effect. Rather than mitigating the situation, the impersonal message irritated the audience and in some cases even sparked an extremely negative response. The mismatch did not create a complete communication failure, but it contributed to data starvation in a time of rapidly unfolding events, and led to a less-than-optimal result.

Rhetorical Themes

The four interdependent communication functions necessary for crisis management identified by Seeger, Sellnow, and Ulmer (2003) include uncertainty reduction, coordination, information dissemination, and strategic ambiguity. The Town of Grancesso Facebook page utilized each of these strategies over the course of the Nemo crisis.

Uncertainty reduction is key for the organization's ability to maintain control over the interpretation of the event as it unfolds; it permits the organization to frame the meaning of the crisis in terms favorable to the organization (Seeger, Sellnow, & Ulmer, 2003). The town's consistent provision of information was perhaps the strongest element of its communication strategy. Some residents expressed concerns about the town's handling of this storm in comparison to other snow events. This post, for example, expresses both high levels of cognitive and affective uncertainty.

This storm was no surprise everyone knew it was coming and should have had an emergency plan in effect. I am sick of hearing how the plows were stuck in the storm. Their plows would not have gotten stuck in the storm if each one plowed their route regularly throughout the storm, they would have only had a few inches at a time to plow but, no, they waited until there was too much snow to move, so now nothing is done! Did they ever hear of plowing with the storm, anyone who knows anything about plow-

ing knows that. I never saw a plow down my street or in my neighborhood throughout the duration of the storm, where were they? I still have not seen a plow. But, the last snow storm when we only had a couple of inches the plow came down my street continuously even when there was no snow left on the ground. Who made that decision? Why didn't they make that decision this time? This is totally unacceptable! The town wants to continue to increase taxes and give us less and less service. We the residents need to get together and do something about this! Someone needs to be held accountable for this horrific situation! We have all been put at risk because of the incompetence of the person or persons in charge of the plowing?! We cannot get out to go to work, no mail, no oil deliveries, cannot get to a store if we need something important and hope there is no emergency.

As residents struggled to make sense of the storm, several compared it to other natural disasters, such as hurricanes or man-made crises such as school shootings, but these posts found a negative reception from other posters. Such comparisons were called "disgusting" and phrases like "shame on you for mentioning that" were used. Others made jokes or snarky remarks, such as this parody of people's pleas for why their street need to be plowed out in a hurry: *My pet goldfish has swimming lessons at the Y on Monday, my street better be plowed.* However, these tended to be dismissed as relatively inconsequential.

The real-time availability of data and information dissemination via social media can provide valuable information for managing a crisis as well as enabling mobilization of resources from around the globe. Situational awareness can be heightened, and it offers an effective way for the organization to defend its brand and reputation (Laad & Lewis, 2012). The continued presence of Town of Grancesso on the Facebook page was effective, but at the cost of considerable effort on the part of the administrator, who clearly was putting in additional hours to keep the public updated (many posts were made late at night or very early in the morning). Uncertainty reduction was a strength for the town's use of social media in the crisis.

Coordination is the second key area for crisis communication (Seeger, Sellnow, & Ulmer, 2003), and Grancesso accomplished this by coordinating message strategies across traditional and social media. Multimedia content plays an increasingly important role in social media: posts with links to multimedia content receive more user attention (in the form of retweets and sharing) than do posts with no such link. This is especially true when the link contains a photo or video (Bruni, Francalanci & Giacomazzi, 2012). The town posted links to news reports and photos of road crews at work as the storm progressed, in an effort to establish credibility in light of the accusations that "no one is doing anything." A visual narrative is often the more effective means of transferring the richness of tacit knowledge (Hawamdeh & Refai, 2008). From the town's perspective, the photos far outstripped words as a means of communicating proactive crisis management to the public (C. Leng, personal communication, June 16, 2015). The photos met their goal on one level, but also experienced a boomerang effect as some residents began to comprehend how low on the priority list their street might be, based on the location of the photos.

Message consistency in radio, television, print, reverse-911 telephone calls, the official town web page, and Facebook messages was seen throughout the crisis. People were following the news, not just in Grancesso, but also in surrounding towns, and comparing the local situation to the bigger picture, and the town's consistency made for a more effective information dissemination strategy. The clean-up timeline in nearby towns were mentioned, and media remarks by both Grancesso's mayor and leaders of other communities were shared, with a state-wide context being emphasized.

The expectation of coordination among agencies also was a theme. Many posters attempted to make it clear that any criticism of decision making was separate from their support of the public works staff busy clearing the streets, echoing some of the "support the troops even if you disagree with the war" discourse that has been observed in recent years on the national scene.

It's just a frustration with Grancesso in general as their plowing/clearing of the roads are horrible in any amount of snow - you have to admit that's true. The lack of communication and the misguided information is what is getting residents frustrated. Understanding that the Public Safety is doing the best they can BUT they NEED HELP!

Not every posting reflected a calm and reasoned approach to the problem; some became quite heated.

*Im so tired of hearing people whine about how they are the only ones who haven't been plowed out yet... WAKE THE F*** UP YOU SELF CENTERED MORONS...THERE ARE THOUSANDS OF PEOPLE IN THE SAME BOAT AS YOU ALL OVER GRANCESSO AND THE REST OF THE STATE...GROW UP BE PATIENT SIT BACK AND BE GRATEFUL YOU HAVE HEAT ELECTRICITY CABLE AND A STAYCATION WITH YOUR FAMILY*

Clearly, only extra-organizational participants may indulge in such emotional communication, a disparity that can cause frustration for organization members. Only one negative comment was made by the town; this occurred after the storm when the town posted that it would have been nice to not have been criticized while trying to do their job.

The third rhetorical element in crisis management is information dissemination. The appointment of a single credible spokesperson who handles both internal and external communication is key (Seeger, Sellnow, & Ulmer, 2003). Grancesso accomplished this by directing all media inquiries to the mayor as well as having only one identifiable poster on the town Facebook page, identified only as "Town of Grancesso" with the avatar image of an easily-recognized town landmark. The anonymity of the poster generated both positive and negative results: it allowed for the appearance of official objectivity while at the same time garnering a kind of "Wizard of Oz" effect in which ordinary citizens questioned the identity of the source of the information. General weather preparedness information, emergency management tips, and data regarding reports of power outages formed a substantial portion of the information dissemination category.

While the town didn't respond to every single negative posting, posts that indicated a true emergency often received attention, such as this exchange with a mother who had previously posted several comments about her fears concerning her son's health.

Citizen: *B******* [road] not touch if emergency happens they will have to come fast my son has had several asthma out burst!! better come fast!! (sic)*

Town of Grancesso: *If you have medical conditions, please call the Emergency Operations Center at 555-555-5555 to give them information and to assist the Town in prioritization of clearing efforts!*

Town of Grancesso: *If you have a medical emergency, please call 911.*

Note that the town gives two levels of information to the parent, as well as modeling appropriate levels of concern, while providing useful data to any other readers who may experience a parallel situation in the course of the crisis.

Grancesso also provided textbook handling of the final rhetorical theme, strategic ambiguity, the art of providing sufficiently vague information that will both protect the organization and permit the continued management of the crisis (Seeger, Sellnow, and Ulmer, 2003). However, the lack of specific information in part created a vacuum, sparking a negative response among those who demanded to know the town's internal timeframe for plowing.

If you go to the town website there is a link to Clearing Updates- this link brings you to Facebook- I am fine waiting to be cleared but where is the LIST of streets done and why is it not being updated minute to minute for the town to see- this would cut down on the frustration of not knowing...my neighbor just went out driving around to "explore" since we have no updates on what is happening- again I am happy to wait so this is done safely however some SPECIFIC updates from the town would be helpful.

The information demanded by frustrated citizens came into direct opposition to the town's internal KM procedures on occasion. The mayor announced on Monday that he hoped to have 90% of the town's roads passable by Wednesday evening, and they actually were cleared just ahead of schedule, thanks to resources provided by the state, other communities, and the National Guard. This did not, however, prevent disgruntled residents from demanding even faster service to their own area, or complaining about plow drivers moving slowly or taking breaks. In fact, while most residents cheered the arrival of plow drivers to their street (sometimes even offering hot coffee and homemade treats), one angry man attacked a snowplow with a shopping cart, dislodging its bumper (Bellmore, 2013).

Despite public calls for transparency, the town chose to provide only selected information that essentially reiterated the general plowing policy. Over the third and fourth days of the crisis (Sunday and Monday), there was a growing groundswell of insistence that the town post maps showing streets that had been cleared, and potentially even list the priority plan for clearing other roads. Some residents recognized that releasing this information would only lead to increased conflict, as every resident would identify his or her own street as more important than someone else's. One frequent poster, "Jon," whose posts often appeared confrontational, mocked several people's requests that the town plow their street soon.

Jon (several times): *Everybody: "ME. ME. ME. ME. Take care of ME, ME, ME."*
Other Poster: *No Jon, it's "information", "information", "information" that's what most of us want and Grancesso is not giving it to us.*
Jon: *The "information" you want is "when will you get to ME, ME, ME?"*

Perhaps in response to these concerns, the town did post some maps very early Tuesday morning, but quickly deleted them from the page after a couple of hours when it was discovered that one map included a worker's home phone number. Amid concerns about employee privacy (and several phone calls to the worker's home), all of the maps were removed (C. Leng, personal communication, June 16, 2015). Additionally, since the maps were being updated manually twice a day by the head of DPW, there were complaints from some that the information was "old" and the town was "doing nothing" to clear the snow (C. Leng, personal communication, June 16, 2015). Naturally, the removal of the maps itself sparked a controversy – some might call it a conspiracy theory – about where the maps had gone. In the absence of information, some posters took on the responsibility of putting information out themselves. This included citizens opening a twitter account titled GrancessoIsOpen and the creation of an interactive google map, both of questionable accuracy, that alleged to show cleared and blocked streets. Both were unofficial, and neither was addressed by the town. In fact, town officials claim no knowledge of these efforts even after the storm (C. Leng, personal communication, June 16, 2015). This is a prime example of how information will rush to fill a void, and the town would have been better advised to provide sufficient information to prevent the grassroots effort based on unsubstantiated information, perhaps by reposting the maps after removing individually identifiable information.

Much of the communication via social media in the Nemo crisis illustrated Weick's theory of sensemaking. Enactment, choosing to notice a specific informational input, and selection, choosing a sensible interpretation for that input, can both clearly by seen in the Facebook comments (Miller, 2015). Much was made of the announcement that Grancesso got the highest snowfall total in the region; indeed, this specific data point served to calm many people down about the fact that their street had not been plowed. The depth of the snowfall served as a rationale for many, many comments defending the public works handling of the crisis: this wasn't just "a" big snowstorm, it was "the" biggest snow storm ever. The reduction of equivocality, central to Weick's thesis (Seeger, Sellnow & Ulmer, 2003), similarly played a significant role. A vast majority of the Facebook comments demanded information in the form of maps or a plan for plowing; when the town did not provide such information, private citizens took on the job of maintaining an unofficial twitter feed to fill the gap. Residents engaged in personal sensemaking dialogues, which they then freely shared via Facebook. Frustrations spread from the immediate problems of the storm to complaints that only tangentially related to the crisis, e.g.

*I just want to make it clear, Mayor Jackson the town is made up of more than just M*****, R**** Road, and W********** [wealthy areas]. I understand that this is where the titans of industry, and the millionaires live but we people on the other end of D****** [economically challenged area] need plowing too.*

Or this posting, which seems to encompass issues far beyond the snowstorm:

Mayor Jackson and Obama doesn't care about white people

Some of the town's attempts at transparency in information dissemination resulted in a boomerang effect. When Town of Grancesso posted a link to a newspaper article stating "Grancesso mayor says half the town's roads still not passable as of Sunday evening," the town received negative responses including complaints that the town's postings were not current and that the strategy seemed to be one of appeasement.

SOLUTIONS AND RECOMMENDATIONS

The use of social media in crisis communication can be challenging due to the circulation of non-verified information and the lack of confidentiality in a public forum. Social media forcibly democratizes institutional communication. Where traditional media feature a structured sharing of gatekeeper-monitored information bound to fixed deadlines, social media's unstructured, unmonitored, and continual and instant information flow creates an entirely different information environment (Laad & Lewis, 2012). Barczyk and Duncan (2012) warn that the interactive nature of social media can be a double-edged sword: the organization must monitor social media to ensure that unreliable content does not overtake supportable evidence. As Grancesso's mayor (C. Leng, personal communication, June 16, 2015) puts it, "Technology *can* be very helpful." In a crisis, it is important that an organizational spokesperson continually curates the social media information available and serves as a liaison between internal and external knowledge communities. Social media not only accelerates the speed at which crises emerge and spread, it also compels higher standards of transparency; there is no way to hide incidents in today's social media environment (Leavesley and Hemus, 2013). This creates serious challenges for an organization's knowledge management, and especially knowledge dissemination, strategy when external players become part of the organization's information environment.

"Knowledge is only generated in the act of knowing; everything else is information" (Bodhanya, 2008, p. 10). This becomes even more true is a crisis context.

Best practices include recognition of the interactive nature of social media; in addition to the organization educating the public, social media features the public talking to the organization, and perhaps more resonant, the public talking to the public. Tinker and Fouse (2013) recommend that social media content be message-driven rather than channel-driven, and Grancesso did this. Similar messages were shared via traditional media (television, newspapers), reverse 911 calls, tweets and Facebook messages. The message was unified. Grancesso appeared to follow much of the standard advice for managing social media: monitor online content, respond to comments, engage with audiences in a positive manner, restrict unauthorized access to social media accounts, engage with the community to explain the issue (Leavesley & Hemus, 2013).

One of the strengths of the Town of Grancesso Facebook page was its responsiveness to comments. According to Tinker and Fouse (2013), only a small percentage of emergency managers use social media for anything other than traditional unidirectional communication, even though interaction is the strength of social media. Whenever Town of Grancesso would post a response to a comment, several people immediately "liked" the response, either because of the content, or as a way of praising the town's perceived expression of concern, or to give support to the town officials. Even with this effort, some citizens demanded even more of a media presence. The immediacy of social media creates strong expectations from the public that may not be in sync with the organization's KM perspective or capabilities. Had the town not been focused on the primary crisis of snow removal, officials might have averted the social media crisis by incorporating knowledge from extra-organizational participants, perhaps even co-opting more posters to support town initiatives. Building such communication structures during non-crisis periods could provide a stronger infrastructure for crisis management in future situations.

One of the first lessons learned from crisis is "communicate early and often." Responding to a crisis requires reducing uncertainty, coordinating activities and disseminating information (Ulmer, Sellnow & Seeger, 2007). Social media accelerates a crisis either for the positive or the negative. Grancesso faced not only a natural disaster crisis, where town officials had to resolve serious physical problems such as finding a way to transport people with medical emergencies through deep snow, but also an image crisis fueled by social media. The instant information and immediate gratification associated with digital media, aided and abetted by the social connections facilitated by social media, created a secondary crisis for the town. It seems clear that organizations committed to using social media as part of a total communications package will also need to commit personnel and resources to counter its dangers as well as harnessing its strengths. While angry mobs with pitchforks and torches may rarely appear in the physical world, the nature of social media facilitates their formation in cyberspace. The ways in which the uses of text in practice reflect general and enduring patterns of thought and communication is exemplified in this case study. Social media content during the crisis offered clues to the larger systemic and institutional patterns of communication embodied in the organization and its knowledge management strategies and practices. Some of the angry comments relating to economic disparities in the community, for example, indicate that deeper concerns may lurk beneath the surface of citizen complaints about superficial problems like snow removal. The town would do well to explore the development of such perceptions and counter them if appropriate.

"Strategic conversation is the sum total of all exchanges and interactions (which may be mediated by artifacts), both formal and informal, taking place between members of the organization and external actors that stimulate cognitive re-interpretations of their organisational world and its relation to the environment" (Bodhanya, 2008, p. 18). By limiting organizational information to largely dry information dissemination, the town missed the opportunity to calm citizen concerns with messages utilizing a more personal and emotional tone. Because many citizens associate social media with noninstrumental communication, using it to engage in activities such as connecting with friends, sharing photographs, or telling stories, social media tends to fill an affective need for the user rather than a cognitive one. The potential disconnect between an organization's use of social media for cognitive purposes of knowledge management and knowledge dissemination and the audience's predisposition toward an affective use can create problems. To the extent that Town of Grancesso acknowledged citizen frustration with the storm delays, that barrier was breached, but such acknowledgements only came after the initial emphasis on cognitive data and information sharing. Earlier attention to this nontraditional organizational focus could have mitigated some of the conflict seen on the social media site.

Social media extends the intellectual capital of an organization, fundamentally shifting not only knowledge dissemination but also knowledge creation, preservation of existing knowledge, and knowledge sharing within the organization. The problem is that the connectivity made extra-organizational members connected via social media misperceive the importance of their own role in the communication network and led them to develop an expectation of greater transparency in knowledge sharing than the organization intended. The result was that the citizen users essentially staged a coup d'état by using the social media outlet for creating and acquiring knowledge, and attempted to leverage that knowledge to their own advantage. Such a resistance narrative thrives in a social media environment which emphasizes participatory and vernacular communication.

FUTURE RESEARCH DIRECTIONS

Clearly, any discussion of social media is already out-of-date by the time it is published. Noting that limitation, however, there are nevertheless numerous lines of research that are suggested by this case. While the specifics of communication flow vary according to the particular channel employed, it seems clear that organizational adherence to time-tested rhetorical principles including transparency, openness, and proactive communication during crisis have the potential to contribute positively to both internal and external communication. Research correlating specific communicative content with emerging technologies will in the future provide direction for continued positive development within the knowledge management sphere.

CONCLUSION

The extension of knowledge to an extra-organizational context is accelerated when social media is added to the mix. The permeability of the information environment is accentuated both during crisis and when the response of the public must be factored into organizational decision-making. Indeed, public demand for information may come into conflict with an organization's established knowledge management procedures. The interactive nature of organizational rhetoric and public response in a modest and relatively trivial crisis points to the need for recognition of the complexities associated with these intertwined elements when serious crisis looms in order to avoid the development of a social media crisis in addition to the original crisis situation.

Marshall McLuhan (1976) famously said that Americans are the only people in the world who go outside to be alone and inside to be social. He was talking about television, but his statement was prophetic for today's era of 24/7 connectivity. Organizations wish to engage customers and share information through websites and social media, but managers must be aware that today's media environment is a two-way street. Not only has the unidirectional model of information dissemination gone the way of the dinosaur, so has the bidirectional model. In the age of social media, all communication is multidirectional. This has both positive and negative implications whenever an organization must weather a crisis.

REFERENCES

Barczyk, C. C., & Duncan, D. G. (2012). Social Networking Media as a Tool for Teaching International Business. *Journal of Teaching in International Business*, *23*(2), 98–122. doi:10.1080/08975930.2012.718703

Bellmore, M. (2013, March 3). Working Together to get the job done. *New Haven Register*, p. B1.

Bodhanya, S. (2008). Knowledge Management: From Management Fad to Systemic Change. In E. Abou-Zeid (Ed.), *Knowledge Management and Business Strategies* (pp. 1–26). Hershey, PA: Information Science Reference. doi:10.4018/978-1-59904-486-6.ch001

Bruni, L., Francalanci, C., & Giacomazzi, P. (2012). The Role of Multimedia Content in Determining the Virality of Social Media Information. *Information*, *3*(4), 278–289. doi:10.3390/info3030278

Croteau, A., & Dfouni, M. (2008). Knowledge Management Leaders' Top Issues. In E. Abou-Zeid (Ed.), *Knowledge Management and Business Strategies* (pp. 47–68). Hershey, PA: Information Science Reference. doi:10.4018/978-1-59904-486-6.ch003

Fink, S. (1986). *Crisis Management: Planning for the inevitable*. New York: American Management Association.

Fishman, D. A. (1999). ValuJet Flight 592: Crisis Communication Theory Blended and Extended. *Communication Quarterly*, *47*(4), 345–375. doi:10.1080/01463379909385567

Hawamdeh, S., & Refai, H. (2008). Video Management and the Transfer of Knowledge through Audiovisual Material. In T. K. Srikantaiah & M. E. D. Koening (Eds.), *Knowledge Management in Practice* (pp. 223–238). Medford, NJ: Information Today Inc.

Heath, R. L., & Millar, D. P. (2004). A Rhetorical Approach to Crisis Communication: Management, Communication Processes, and Strategic Responses. In D. P. Millar & R. L. Heath (Eds.), *Responding to Crisis: A Rhetorical Approach to Crisis Communication* (pp. 1–17). Mahwah, NJ: Lawrence Erlbaum Associates.

Kasten, J. (2008). Knowledge Strategy: The Linkage Between Business Strategy and Knowledge Management. In T. K. Srikantaiah & M. E. D. Koening (Eds.), *Knowledge Management in Practice* (pp. 115–124). Medford, NJ: Information Today Inc.

Koenig, M. E. D. (2008). KM Moving into Stage IV? The Extra-Organizational Stage. In T. K. Srikantaiah & M. E. D. Koening (Eds.), *Knowledge Management in Practice* (pp. 9–16). Medford, NJ: Information Today Inc.

Laad, G., & Lewis, G. (2012). *Role of Social Media in Crisis Communication.* Retrieved June 12, 2013, from http://geraldlewis.com/publications/Role_of_Social_Media_in_Crisis_Communication_Jan_2012_Gitanjali_Laad.pdf

Leavesley, J., & Hemus, J. (2013). *Braving the Social Media Crisis.* Retrieved June 12, 2013, from http://www.slideshare.net/Insignia_Communications/braving-the-social-media-crisis

Lengel, R. H., & Daft, R. L. (1988). The selection of communication media as an executive skill. *The Academy of Management Executive*, *2*(3), 225–232. doi:10.5465/AME.1988.4277259

McLuhan, M. (1976). Inside on the Outside, or the Spaced-Out American. *Journal of Communication*, *26*(4), 46–53. doi:10.1111/j.1460-2466.1976.tb01935.x PMID:7577

Millar, D. P. (2004). Exposing the Errors: An Examination of the Nature of Organizational Crises. In D. P. Millar & R. L. Heath (Eds.), *Responding to Crisis: A Rhetorical Approach to Crisis Communication* (pp. 9–31). Mahwah, NJ: Lawrence Erlbaum Associates.

Miller, K. (2015). *Organizational Communication* (7th ed.). Boston, MA: Wadsworth.

Nielsen & NM Incite. (2011). *The Social Media Report: Spending Time, Money and Going Mobile.* Retrieved June 13, 2013, from http://blog.nielsen.com/nielsenwire/social/2012/

Pasher, E., & Ronen, T. (2011). *The Complete Guide to Knowledge Management.* Hoboken, NJ: Wiley. doi:10.1002/9781118983782

Seeger, M. W., Sellnow, T. L., & Ulmer, R. R. (2003). *Communication and Organizational Crisis.* Westport, CT: Praeger.

Tinker, T., & Fouse, D. (2013). *Expert Round Table on Social Media and Risk Communication. During Times of Crisis: Strategic Challenges and Opportunities.* Retrieved June 13, 2013, from http://www.boozallen.com/media/file/Risk_Communications_Times_of_Crisis.pdf

Ulmer, R. R., Sellnow, T. L., & Seeger, M. W. (2007). *Effective Crisis Communication: Moving from Crisis to Opportunity.* Thousand Oaks, CA: Sage Publications.

Zhang, Q., & Ma, S. (2008). Corporate Blogs and Communities of Practice. In T.K. Srikantaiah & M.E.D. Koening (Eds.), Knowledge Management in Practice (pp. 303-320). Medford, NJ: Information Today Inc.

KEY TERMS AND DEFINITIONS

Boomerang Effect: Communication has the opposite effect of the communicator's intent.
Crisis: Events that threaten an organization's goals.
Discourse: Speech or writing about a topic.
External Public: Group outside an organization to which communication is directed.
Internal Public: Group inside an organization to which communication is directed.
Rhetoric: The act of effective or persuasive speech or writing.
Social Media: Digital platforms designed to enable users to share content with one another.
Strategic Ambiguity: Avoiding specifics in the presentation of information.

Chapter 8
Principles and Good Practices for Using Wikis within Organizations

Eli Miron
Ben Gurion University of the Negev, Israel

Adi Palmor
Rafael Advanced Defense Systems Ltd., Israel

Gilad Ravid
Ben Gurion University of the Negev, Israel

Avigdor Sharon
Tel Aviv University, Israel

Ariel Tikotsky
Bar Ilan University, Israel

Yehuda Zirkel
Elta Systems Ltd., Israel

ABSTRACT

This chapter discusses the basic properties of corporate Wikis that make them an effective learning and knowledge management tool. Wikis offer a user-friendly environment that enhances informal knowledge sharing and the collaborative creation of new knowledge. Enterprise-wide adoption of Wikis promotes the reuse of existing know-hows and prevents employee re-invention of the wheel. Four cases of successful implementations of Wikis in large, hi-tech global organizations are described in detail including their goals, design considerations, implementation and actual use for formal and informal knowledge creation and sharing. The adoption and long-term sustainability of Wikis is attributed to perceived business outcomes by managers and to perceived usefulness and ease of use by individual contributors and users. Good practices based on one or more of these use-cases can provide practical guidance to organizations that wish to use a Wiki for KM purposes.

INTRODUCTION

Hi-tech companies operate in a global, highly competitive and rapidly changing environment (Henselewski, Smolnik, & Riempp, 2006). Survival in this "Darwinian system" largely depends on the ability of the companies to learn, in order to develop new technologies or innovative solutions as a response to new market demands, as well as to adopt emerging technologies or adapt to new regulations.

DOI: 10.4018/978-1-5225-0495-5.ch008

Knowledge management (KM) in organizations incorporates all aspects of knowledge under one umbrella and allows employees in a high-paced, knowledge-intensive, multi-project work environment to share and find valuable knowledge, avoid repeated mistakes and provide quicker responses to customer needs. All these issues are essential to ensure business agility and a competitive edge.

KM initiatives include the creation of new knowledge, the re-use of existing knowledge, and the organization of learning products and knowledge assets, such as intellectual property, for safe-keeping and easy retrieval.

A corporate Wiki is a multi-purpose KM tool (Sousa, Aparicio & Costa, 2010) "that has been developed to capture organizational knowledge and make it available" (Meloche et al., 2009), to "support innovation processes" and to "address challenges of knowledge management and collaboration" (Standing & Kiniti, 2011). However, many obstacles may obstruct the way to successful deployment of corporate Wikis (Garcia-Perez & Ayres, 2010).

This chapter describes the principles of Wiki-based organizational KM solutions and provides detailed descriptions of successful implementations in four global organizations where each Wiki serves a different KM-related purpose. The chapter reviews methodological, technical (platform), cultural and implementation aspects of these Wikis. Good practices and key success factors for Wiki adoption are discussed in a way that can help organizations wishing to harness the power of a corporate Wiki.

LEARNING ORGANIZATIONS

The notion of a learning organization was developed by De Geus (1988) who claimed that "the ability to learn faster than your competitors may be the only sustainable competitive advantage" for companies. Lunenburg (2011) stresses the strategic element of learning organizations: "A learning organization is a strategic commitment to capture and share learning in the organization for the benefit individuals, teams, and the organization". Garvin (2000) defined a learning organization as follows: "An organization skilled at creating, acquiring, and transferring knowledge, and at modifying its behavior to reflect new knowledge and insights". Senge (2006) details five learning disciplines that constitute a learning organization. This chapter describes techniques that are relevant to two disciplines: personal mastery and team learning. Every profession expands in such a way that an expert may be familiar just with a section of this profession. An organization must therefore exercise team learning in order to lead in existing and emerging technologies. Lunenburg (2011) combines Garvin's and Senge's observations: "It does this through alignment and the collective capacity to sense and interpret a changing environment; to input new knowledge through continuous learning and change; to imbed this knowledge in systems and practices; and to transform this knowledge into outputs". Garvin, Edmondson and Gino (2008) define three building blocks of a learning organization: "A supportive learning environment, concrete learning processes and practices and leadership behavior that provides reinforcement". One of the 'managerial' requirements from the organizational knowledge management team, from a learning perspective, is to provide environments in which organization members can converse with each other, share existing knowledge and views and work together to create new knowledge (team learning in Senge's lexicon). Nonaka, Toyama and Konno (2000) define 'ba' as a learning environment: "Ba is a place where information is interpreted to become knowledge" "ba works as the platform of knowledge creation by collecting the applied knowledge of the area into a certain time and space and integrating it". A Wiki-based KM solution constitutes a "virtual KM ba" as will be discussed in detail in the use cases.

WEB 2.0, ENTERPRISE 2.0, AND KM 2.0

Web 2.0: Basic Principles

The basic principles of Web 2.0 are as follows: The web is just a platform accessible by any standard browser, where the users can not only read content but also contribute to it in a very simple way (UGC = user generated content). The emergence of Web 2.0 brought about a major change in the habits of internet users and enabled the fulfillment of the four principles of the *wisdom of crowds*: diversity of opinion, independence, decentralization and aggregation (Surowiecki, 2005). Examples of Web 2.0 platforms that offer UGC include:

- **Blog:** A single person (or company) online publication environment. Blogs are basically a one-man band, with a built-in commenting option. Readers cannot change the original posted material; only add comments to the original content.
- **Internet Forums:** Online discussion sites where people can hold conversations in the form of posted messages. A discussion forum is hierarchical or tree-like in structure. Within a forum's topic, each new discussion started is called a thread, and can be replied to by many people (Wikipedia – forums). Discussion forums tend to be devoted to a certain general subject.
- **Wiki:** A collaborative workspace in a web site where many authors write collectively on a subject or a multitude of subjects.
- **Social Networking Services (or Social Networking Sites = SNS):** An SNS is a platform for building social networks or social relations among people who share interests, activities, backgrounds or real-life connections (Boyd & Ellison 2010). Facebook, YouTube and LinkedIn are familiar examples of the multitudes of SNSs. In terms of KM, SNS platforms provide easy access to experts, a convenient way to share professional news and enable 'groups'- another type of discussion forum (for discussion on groups see Miron & Ravid, 2015).

Enterprise 2.0

Web 2.0 applications have been widely used on an individual level by millions of users. Organizations therefore endeavored to utilize to social platforms to increase their creativity, knowledge sharing, and collaboration to better perform and innovate in their field (O'Reilly & Battelle, 2009).

McAfee (2006) defines and explains Enterprise 2.0 as follows: "Enterprise 2.0 is the use of emergent social software platforms within companies, or between companies and their partners or customers. Platforms are digital environments in which contributions and interactions are globally visible and persistent over time. Emergent means that the software is freeform, and that it contains mechanisms to let the patterns and structure inherent in people's interactions become visible over time. Freeform means that the software is most or all of the following: optional; free of up-front workflow; indifferent to formal organizational identities; accepting of many types of data".

KM 2.0

Cook (2008) lists four general primary functions of social enterprise platforms (the 4Cs): "Communication, Cooperation, Collaboration and Connection". The 4Cs enhance organizational knowledge flow, especially with regard to tacit knowledge. They do not replace existing knowledge-related organizational functions - their purpose is to augment and empower previous existing functionalities.

Okimoto (2007) notes that "Organizations are considering how they will shift from private and controlled environments to public and dynamic collaboration but as new sources and methods to share knowledge appear, none of the old disappear". A survey of measured benefits gained by using Web 2.0 technologies in enterprises showed that the top benefit for internal purposes and for working with external partners or suppliers was "increasing speed of access to knowledge" (Bughin & Chui, 2010).

KM 2.0 is therefore an example of Enterprise 2.0 utilization as defined by McAfee, for purposes of knowledge management. An enterprise social network platform can provide a virtual ba – a digital environment for knowledge creation and knowledge sharing. In addition to the creation of new knowledge it can also provide easy access to existing knowledge, thus enabling knowledge reuse and preventing the re-invention of the wheel (Nonaka, Toyama & Konno, 2000).

The four use cases that are described in detail in this chapter provide excellent examples for using a KM 2.0 tool (Wiki) as a building block for organizational learning by knowledge sharing, co-creation of new knowledge, accessing and re-using existing knowledge, articulation of implicit knowledge and improving cross-organizational knowledge flow.

KNOWLEDGE AND COLLABORATION NEEDS OF HI-TECH COMPANIES AND OTHER LEARNING ORGANIZATIONS

Most organizations today, including global hi-tech companies, are structured in a hierarchical system of divisions, departments, units and teams. This structure is well-suited for political organizations, militaries and industrial-age companies, but less suited to the quick-response and agile development needs of the internet age. When factoring in the global distribution of the workforce across continents and time zones, and the multitude of work locations that range from corporate offices to customer sites, home offices or on the go, people in very large corporations would feel disconnected from fellow employees if not for modern communications technologies that bridge the barriers of distance and time.

In large organizations, parallel competencies, experience, and concurrent active projects are most likely to exist in different parts of the organization. Quite often widespread distribution of disconnected units that have similar targets, needs and competencies still work in ineffective and inefficient isolation because of the distributed and hierarchical structure, without sufficiently getting to know and collaborate with relevant peers. As a result, it can be tempting to work as small teams or even as individuals. Thus, the organization is forced to work as a multitude of disconnected islands rather than as truly coherent body of activity, know-how and experience.

Providing communication, content management and project management tools cannot fully bridge these gaps. Specific tools that suit the different needs and preferences of different groups may be incompatible and result in the implementation of many disparate workgroups - a huge archipelago of disconnected islands.

In high-tech organizations this issue can be even more aggravated, wasting the expertise of professionals such as software engineers and other knowledge workers. Each team might not only adopt a different media or work platform, but may also be tempted to create a new one altogether, showcasing their ingenuity, but at the same time creating additional, unnecessary barriers within the organization, wasting valuable time, effort and resources.

Organizations need a consistent, connected and efficient work platform, to save time and resources in order to become a continent of efficacy and productivity, while at the same time catering to the particular needs and preferences of each team and every professional.

CORPORATE WIKI AS A LEARNING AND KNOWLEDGE MANAGEMENT TOOL

Basic Properties

A Wiki is an application which allows easy modification, extension, or deletion of its content and structure by its users. Cunningham, the developer of the first wiki, described it as "the simplest online database that could possibly work" (Ebersbach, Glaser, Heigl & Warta, 2008). The Wiki is a web site organized in pages. "While a wiki is a type of content management system, it differs from a blog or most other such systems in that the content is created without any defined owner or leader, and Wikis have little implicit structure, allowing structure to emerge according to the needs of the users" (Wikipedia -Wiki). All Wikis share some common characteristics that make them suitable tools for knowledge management. Some of the characteristics are:

- **No Need to Predefine the Content Structure:** Contrary to many content management systems. In Wikis the content structure emerges from the pages and hyperlinks formed over time.
- **Hypertextuality:** The pages are linked by contextual hypertext links, this kind of links increase learning and retrieval performance (Dillon & Gabbard, 1998).
- **Multimediality:** Wiki pages can include many types of media including text, pictures, video, audio and more.
- **Transparency:** The ability to see and analyze any action performed enables users to assess the knowledge in the Wiki and evaluate it in the right frame.
- **Archive:** Every page and edit action are archived and can be retrieved later. One can compare and see the evolution of pages over time since any two versions can be easily compared.
- **Markup Language:** Wiki pages are edited and formatted with simple markup language. Each Wiki platform has its unique language but all share the ability of bulk editing and automatic page processing. This freedom and ease of writing in a shared organizational content platform does not breach content security principles and any careless or unintentional deletion of content contributions by peers can easily be undone.
- **Meta-Content:** A "chat" mechanism that allows for discussing a point which is in dis-agreement or otherwise requires discussion. Chats are also automatically saved.
- **Elasticity:** Each Wiki characteristic can be implemented in a different level, for example one can choose to implement side by side an open Wiki and a closed one where access is restricted only to designated personnel or to a specific department.
- **User Interface:** The only tool users and managers need to operate in Wiki environments is a web browser. "Informational content can be created and easily organized within the wiki environment and then reorganized as required" (Stephens, 2009, p.4). No special tools and no special skills are required. These properties can be successfully used for collaborative learning and for group knowledge creation.

Wiki is unique among social software as, in addition to editing the content itself, it also allows users to edit the structure of the contributions. The open encyclopedia project, Wikipedia, is the most popular and successful Wiki to date.

Corporate Wikis vs. Public Wikis

Corporate Wikis differ from public Wikis in that they must operate in an organizational environment, which excludes anonymous contributions and in some cases requires modifications and add-ons to cope with business needs.

Wiki properties that enhance organizations can be used for aggregating various knowledge types (existing and new) and offer the following: easy collaborative content creation (no need to use check-in / check-out procedures common in document management systems); incremental content creation – (no need to submit a complete document; any content can be further improved by the original writer or by other workers); dynamic knowledge structure that is automatically built by itself; minimum requirements for content approval by superiors or by experts; unlimited version history including the identity of the version changer; easy comparison of any two versions; notification of changes by email; built-in chat option to discuss controversial issues (these discussions are also automatically saved); easy maintenance; connectivity to other organizational systems such as enterprise portal, ECM, ERP etc., and finally, the ability to enforce security or content confidentiality requirements or regulations by controlling and restricting access to certain content areas.

The clear identification of the original creator of any content eliminates the problematic addition of non-professional content or spam on the part of anonymous writers, as may happen in Wikipedia or other public Wikis. Grudin and Poole (2010) argue that "enterprise wiki is a blanket term describing three different genres of wiki: single contributor wikis, group or team wikis, and internal-use encyclopedias emulating Wikipedia". Examples of organizational uses of Wikis are: shared professional repository, organizational encyclopedia, technical documentation tool, knowledge sharing, call centers, and many more.

KM Related Wiki Properties and Usage

Pfaff and Hasan (2006) discuss KM related advantages of using a Wiki in an organization: "a. capability to co-create and co-evolve a knowledge repository. b. promotion of organizational learning that leverages the collaborative efforts of all members of the organization to create an effective library of knowledge".

Wagner (2006) claims that "much of today's organizational knowledge still exists outside repositories of formal information and often exists only in people's heads". Wagner proposes the use of wikis "as software that enables Bazaar style, more effective knowledge acquisition by collaborative, conversational knowledge management". Cress and Kimmerle (2008) stress the contribution of a Wiki to personal knowledge management. They suggest that "people process the information available in the Wiki and integrate it into their individual knowledge. Through this internalization people develop new knowledge".

Sousa, Aparicio and Costa (2010) discuss the usefulness of organizational Wikis as a knowledge management tool according to the SECI model (Nonaka, Toyama & Konno, 2000). They found that "the internalization process is the prevalent knowledge conversion process as most users access the wiki seeking information. The wiki also makes it easy to identify specialists through the information available in the system". They also examined Wikis in view of the four competencies of a learning organization (Kerkhof, Ende & Bogenrieder, 2003). They conclude that "diffusion of knowledge within the organization is the most developed one, and efforts must be made in order to promote generation of new knowledge through the conversion from tacit to explicit knowledge".

Liebowitz (2011, p.9), regards Wikis as "Collaborative Editing Logs" with the following learning and knowledge related advantages: shortening the individual or organizational learning curve and reducing the time required to find specific information and knowledge. Analysis of a few case studies by Grace (2009) showed that the "strongest push for organizations embracing wiki technology is its ease of use and ability to facilitate knowledge sharing".

Standing and Kiniti (2011) discuss the importance of Wikis for innovation processes. They argue that "innovation processes require the support of collaborative technologies because they help in the efficient storage and retrieval of codified knowledge, bring people together to innovate". Therefore, "wikis have significant potential as collaborative and knowledge management tools in organizations" and hence can support the knowledge requirements for innovation processes. They list knowledge processes that can be efficiently performed for various stages of the innovation process. These knowledge processes include "individual knowledge conversion into group knowledge which can be shared; facilitation of external knowledge sharing as well as a place to combine the knowledge of multiple experts; common repository where knowledge can be centrally stored and retrieved; a transparent environment letting users see what others contribute and more".

Bolisani, Scarso and Giuman (2014) analyzed a Wiki used as a knowledge management system at a small ICT company with 30 employees and five external collaborators. Their Wiki is in a form of a portal and can be accessed by all employees, including from home. They report that the Wiki was considered the most important information source in the company and that the motivating factor for its use was the improvement of both individual and company performances. The most important perceived advantages for the company were: "improvement of internal knowledge sharing and enhancement of internal collaboration". An organizational Wiki is a feasible technological platform that can perform as a virtual 'ba' where workers can share knowledge and create new knowledge collectively. The collective buildup of a technical subject gradually improves the contents unlike documents that can be updated only by authoring a new version.

Knowledge Use and Reuse

Knowledge provides the ability to perform effectively. Practically, this means that the right people need the capability to retrieve the relevant knowledge at the right place and at the right time. "The overriding purpose of enterprise KM is to make knowledge accessible and reusable to the enterprise" (O'Leary, 1998).

Schubmehl and Vesset (2014) quote the results of a survey performed by IDC - the time percentage a worker spends on KM related tasks: "Searching/gathering information 16.2%; Communicating with customers/suppliers/partners/colleagues 12.0%, Collaborating with group members and others 10.3%". These KM related tasks can be performed by Wikis since they serve as a context-wise knowledge repository. Wikis are organized by topics and subtopics (unlike blogs or forums where discussions are listed chronologically). Each topic is a different website, and each subtopic is a page on this site which provides logical access to knowledge, in addition to a search option.

Personal Motivation to Participate: WIIFM (What's in It for Me?)

Participation in public Web 2.0 applications is considered to follow the 1-9-90 thumb rule: for every active contributor who writes new content, 9 comment on this content and 90 just read it, (Nielsen, 2006). This ratio is unacceptable in corporate environments.

Personal motivators have been examined by Majchrzak, Wagner and Yates (2006) who conducted a survey of 168 corporate Wiki users and discovered two types of personal benefits that are achieved through the participation in corporate wikis: "benefits to enhanced reputation and benefits to making work easier. Benefits are more likely perceived when work tasks require novel solutions (rather than routine tasks), and when other wiki contributors are believed to provide credible information". These benefits were the triggers for workers' contribution to the corporate Wiki.

Razmerita and Kirchner (2011) discussed a case study where a Wiki was used to manage knowledge in an SME with 50 employees that develop business software. The Wiki included a template and specific guidelines on where and how people can add their contributions to the system as well as full text search functionality. "The wiki system has been used regularly by half of the employees, but only 10 per cent of them take an active role by adding content". From our experience active contributions by 10% of the employees is usually considered successful.

Organizational Culture

Organizational culture of knowledge sharing is an essential requirement for successful Wiki implementation. Lau (2009) wrote about "an organization that, after implementing an enterprise-wide employee wiki, realized it didn't exactly have the right culture to bring it to life... Employees were allowed to contribute through profiles with pictures but the organization had a conservative culture so no one actually wanted to make visible what they were working on right now."

Fostering a corporate knowledge sharing culture is a high priority task for top management, as evident in the case of Buckman Laboratories, where cultural change was brought about by the leadership. (Buckman, 2004). Implementation of knowledge sharing culture can be enhanced by utilizing gamification principles. A comprehensive solution is embedding the Wiki in organizational procedures. In such cases the employees' use of the Wiki is embedded in their daily work routines, and this in turn, helps make the best use out of the knowledge provided by the Wiki.

Wiki Platforms Requirements

There are two basic requirements from a Wiki platform in an organizational environment:

1. Perform the tasks required by the users, adapted to their work needs.
2. Work side by side with the current IT platform - a separate Wiki platform is required if the current IT platform does not include a Wiki, or its Wiki does not provide the required functionality and modifications are difficult to implement.

Extensive use of organizational Wikis often requires developing add-ons (as will be demonstrated in the cases studies). General and technical information for a number of Wiki software packages is listed at Wikipedia (Wiki platforms). A choice wizard that helps finding Wikis that match specific needs is available at http://www.wikimatrix.org/. Companies weigh various considerations when choosing a Wiki platform; for example, when Frankfurt airport decided to provide individual Wikis to their divisions they switched to Confluence, "where it is easy to manage several Wikis at the same time" (Bhasin, 2015).

Wiki ROI

In general, it is difficult to quantify ROI with any tool that provides mostly intangible benefits, or is used as a reference and facilitator in a large number of other activities in the organization by multiple groups and persons (research, sales, engineering, production, delivery, support, etc.), where revenue and ROI are measured separately for each resulting outcome.

Grace (2009) notes that "the usage of wikis as a knowledge management tool has provided intangible value to the users, but there was difficulty to show truly quantifiable Return-on-Investment".

Kaske, Kügler and Smolnik (2012), suggest a method to assess the profitability of social media in organizations.

ROI has not been examined in our sample use cases.

Wiki Sustainability

Grudin and Poole (2010) present basic requirements for sustainability in enterprise Wikis, including, "aligning the expectations of managers and individual contributors; content organization and flexibility over time and positioning the wiki in an existing information ecology and corporate culture". Majchrzak, Wagner and Yates (2006) assessed the sustainability of corporate Wikis by examining a relatively large set of users. They confirmed that "corporate wikis are sustainable and that sustainability is based on the length of wiki existence, the number of participants, the number of lurkers, and the frequency of accesses".

Key Success Factors for Wiki Adoption and Use by Employees

Garcia-Perez and Ayres (2010) studied a Wiki which had been implemented to support a group of researchers. They analyzed its success both quantitatively (by the number of logins) and qualitatively (using a questionnaire). "More than two thirds of the total number of visits originated from the same computer" and "most visits lasted less than 2 minutes". The reasons given by 8 interviewees were: "lack of time", "the information on the Wiki did not motivate them" and "not having an easy, direct link to the Wiki". A similar long tail phenomenon is described at Ravid, Kalman and Rafaeli (2008), who also emphasize the ability to empower the writers.

Yeo and Arazi (2012) analyzed the reasons that make corporate Wikis work based on examination of "Wiki affordances", where affordance is defined as "an action that an individual can potentially perform in their environment" (EdutechWiki - affordance). They "investigated five wiki affordances - collaborative authoring norms, unregistered editing, automatic publishing, non-attribution, and peer-based quality control - and have reported on users' perceptions regarding the extent to which altering these wiki affordances - by either modifying the wiki system or by changing work practices - is likely to increase users' participation". In addition to modifying Wiki capabilities they also note that "corporate wiki users desire recognition for their efforts, highlighting the need for both a mechanism that can estimate and publicize users' contributions as well as to provide clear guidance on the collaborative authoring process while not attempting to impose controls on wiki's automatic publishing affordances".

Hanrahan et al. (2010) claim that "Corporate wikis have suffered from low adoption rates, preventing them from reaching the critical mass required for a sustainable and useful repository. We contend that the lack of support for collaborative knowledge management is a contributing factor to this problem".

Holtzblatt, Damianos and Weiss (2010) list "Factors Impeding Wiki Use in the Enterprise". Most of these factors are addressed in the successful use cases described below.

USE CASES

Four use cases of global organizations that successfully use a Wiki as a knowledge management tool are presented and analyzed. Goals, design considerations, implementation and actual utilization are discussed in detail for all cases.

All four Wikis are sustainable according to Majchrzak, Wagner and Yates (2006) criteria. The reasons for success are presented, along with conclusions and recommendations.

Amdocs

Amdocspedia: The Cross-Corporate Wiki

The Company

Amdocs is a global market-leader in customer experience solutions and services for the world's largest communications, entertainment and media service providers. As of early 2015, Amdocs has more than 24,000 employees worldwide that serve customers in over 90 countries. Amdocs had revenues of $3.6 billion in fiscal 2014 and is listed on the NASDAQ Global Select Market (Amdocs, 2015).

The Business Need

Amdocspedia, the cross-corporate Wiki at Amdocs, was created by the knowledge management team to address actual knowledge sharing and collaboration needs of many groups within the organization. It was designed to be a knowledge work environment that allows project teams and professional centers of excellence to work locally and affect globally by facilitating knowledge sharing between groups and making professional information easier to find.

The process that led to the creation of Amdocspedia was the result of the convergence of three initiatives:

1. **Workgroups within the Delivery and Products Organizations:** Required workspaces to share information and insights that were more agile and flexible than writing documents, yet more robust and efficient than emails or forums.
2. **Senior Managers:** Defined the ability of professional groups to easily share practical, non-confidential know-how and experience as a business need.
3. **The Information Technology (IT) Department:** Sought to create a consistent cross-corporate platform that would effectively enhance collaboration among groups while at the same time satisfy the unique needs, structure and identity of each group.

The convergence of these initiatives into a collaborative effort among the groups via mutual meetings and roundtables, discussions and compromise was the golden key to success.

The groups for this matter are any of the three types of stakeholders mentioned above and additional workgroups within the organization. They are organizational or professional entities, either formal or informal. They can vary greatly in the number of related employees and they can be spread globally. For example, the Java development experts of a specific project unit or the core competency center of a specific product line are both "groups" that took part in the effort.

Design Considerations

While the confidentiality of customer and business information was considered a top content security principle, it was also clear that the sharing of professional information would help maintain prime-quality standards, avoid repeated development efforts, and prevent errors by encouraging learning from peer experience and reusing good practices. A solution was needed to share professional information and experience, or other types of information, which would improve the work experience of employees within the organization while maintaining the sacred confidentiality of business information.

Collaboration was not the easy approach. It could have been all too easy for each group to work on its own, in the way that it saw fit. IT could have adopted the all too easy, "build-it-and-they-will-come" approach, which resulted in failure for several KM projects in other organizations. Senior managers could define rules and professional experts could just go about their own business, never minding anyone else. In all those cases, synergy and useful collaboration would not have happen.

Collaboration between senior managers, project managers and subject-matter experts proved essential. The planning, design and implementation were done in close collaboration between the IT department, senior managers, experts and user groups within the organization and the KM team. Working together in synergy prevented common pitfalls and helped to ensure success.

The knowledge management team sought to provide a service that would allow achieving these goals, using a centralized cross-organization environment that is easy to maintain and manage yet allows each group to use and express their own unique identity and work style as they had prior to its introduction.

After evaluating different knowledge and content management platforms, Wiki was chosen as most appropriate for this purpose. A Wiki has a flat structure that sidesteps the pitfalls of rigid hierarchical directory structures. All Wiki pages are of equal rank and can all be cross-linked by a flexible network of keywords, expressions and categories.

Implementation

A new concept or role was introduced: "knowledge champions". Senior experts or technical writers within each group that would drive sharing and writing, organize content and oversee content quality, a similar role to that of a Wikipedia content administrator. The Wiki was designed to allow each knowledge champion to organize and administer the content in their own field of expertise with ease.

Each group could have one or more knowledge champions who work with additional experts and local trustees within the groups to ensure not only that valuable professional content, experience and insights are written and shared, but also that the Wiki is maintained up-to-date in the long run knowledge champions create and structure the main pages while others gradually add tips and in formation. Each person that creates a new page would automatically be defined as its owner. The Wiki system would then send periodical reminders to check the page every few months or so, to make sure the pages are kept informative and up-to-date.

The knowledge champions and the local trustees were not dedicated exclusively to this. It was not a new job assignment. They were all working professionals within the product and delivery teams that had their own projects and goals. Amdocspedia was available for them as a work tool. A Wiki has the great benefit that it does not require a large time investment. It does not need to be painstakingly and carefully authored as a blog or a document would need to. One could just quickly open the Wiki to share just one bit of information, write it quickly and finish it in a matter of 1-5 minutes. The bits of information and additional sentences could be added later at any time. The Wiki adopts intuitive writing and a cross-linking approach on the go. Thus, the 'knowledge champions' assignment did not require a great deal of effort. It was just a matter of care, responsibility and recognition of effort and contribution.

The requirement that groups would keep their own close-knit collections and express their own identities was solved by creating page templates, tags and breadcrumbs to be used by the content editors or the knowledge champions in each group. (Breadcrumbs is a backtracking method that simulates a hierarchical taxonomy. Example: *UK* > *England* > *Bristol* is a breadcrumbs structure).

Technology

Each group could design its own template and create a special Wiki page that would serve as their "homepage". This required a dedicated design and development effort, as they were not available in the out-of-the-box Microsoft Office SharePoint Server (MOSS) 2007 Wiki platform.

Although the KM team had a great group of internal developers who were working on a number of projects, it has decided to focus on the design and functionality of the new Wiki platform and on user engagement and to carry out the actual development that was required to provide the enhanced functionality, content management and user experience in collaboration with an external development team. The KM project leader and the internal development team leader would work in collaboration with the external development team.

Having done so, Amdocspedia was developed as a joint project between Amdocs and KWizCom, a company that specializes in the development of SharePoint related products and add-ons. It was agreed that KWizCom could then have the license to offer the enhanced Wiki platform as a product that it could sell to other organizations as well. The result of this fruitful collaboration was KWizCom WikiPlus (http://bit.ly/pSx7te). Technically, it was an extension of the Microsoft Office SharePoint Server (MOSS) 2007 out-of-the-box Wiki. Adoption was indeed successful. Many organizations worldwide have purchased KWizCom's WikiPlus.

This collaboration and open approach had of course the financial benefits of both sales and internal cost reduction. However, it had other major benefits as well, as it ensured the continued development and improvement of the Amdocspedia-WikiPlus platform (Figure 1), introducing new capabilities and fresh ideas that turned it into a sustainable development platform.

The entire project of Amdocspedia implementation was broken-down into 2 phases.

Phase I: the new Wiki was designed and custom-developed on the basis of the existing wiki platform in SharePoint 2007 and delivered only to the product and technology experts in one major group.

Phase II: Amdocspedia went corporate-wide. The process included again close work with managers and local knowledge champions, merging separate professional tip collections into shared collections.

Figure 1. Amdocspedia home page

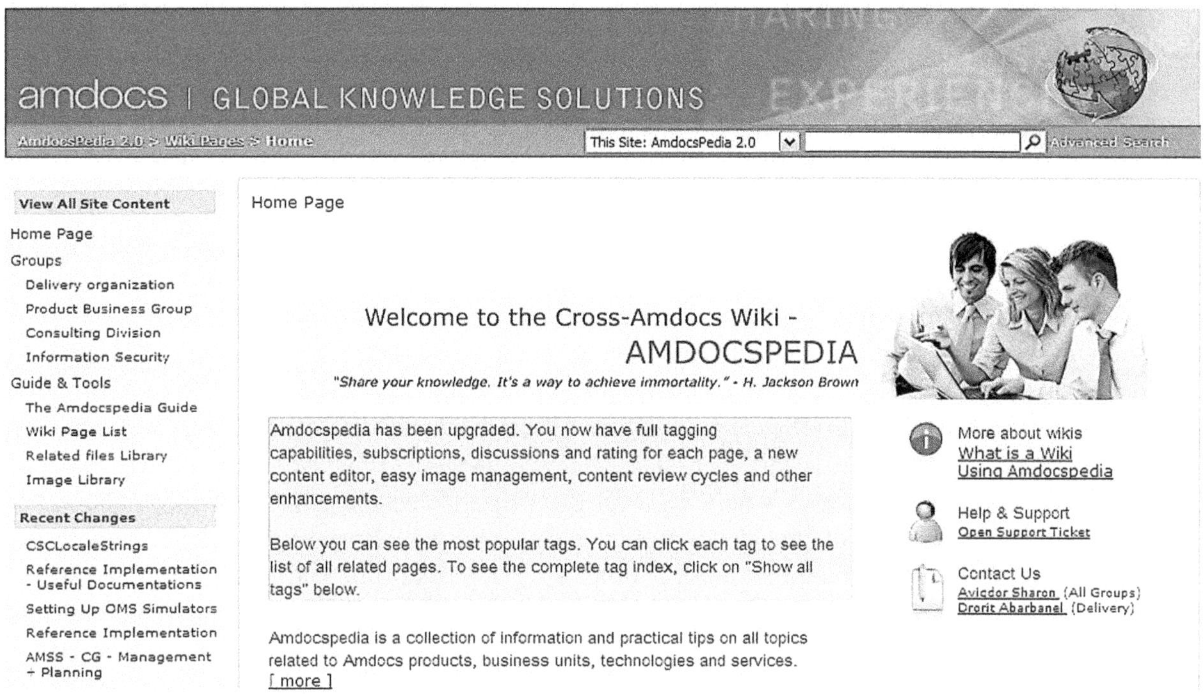

The journey to create Amdocspedia began in early 2007 with a study of company needs, the mapping of groups, support from upper management, the emergence of knowledge champions and with numerous meetings and brainstorming sessions.

It then continued with a pilot of 'out of the box' SharePoint Portal 2007 wiki, followed by step-by-step implementation within with groups. 'Amdocspedia 1.0' was born.

Just a few teams performed in the pilot phase to create a base content "critical mass". The entire group followed thereafter. During this process, specific requirements were discussed and defined with knowledge champions and users.

Adoption

Adoption was enthusiastic. "Amdocspedia 1.0" saw 18,000 monthly visits monthly by 1,500 professionals, and over 400 new content pages created each month.

This process took place during Feb-May 2007 and resulted in the WikiPlus specification in June. Development was then conducted and by the end of the year "Amdocspedia 2.0" was ready to be piloted with leading knowledge champions and "power users". This was done alongside ongoing use of Amdocspedia 1.0, and resulted in fine tuning of usability and configuration elements of the new Wiki.

In April of 2008, Amdocspedia 2.0 was ripe and ready to be implemented. Content was transferred to the new system, and Amdocspedia 2.0 was launched. Amdocspedia 1.0 was still kept available but only as a read-only copy for reference.

This ensured a smooth transition process and offered both a sense of control and trust that allowed the managers, knowledge champions and knowledge consumers all to adapt to the new platform with ease. This set the stage for Phase II of the Amdocspedia implementation as a cross-corporate platform for any group that sought to use it as a knowledge sharing and insight management tool.

The knowledge champions' roundtables discussions and video conferences stimulated the implementation and adoption journey by increasing professional collaboration and co-learning, as well as incentive and enthusiasm.

Content navigation ease of access and the desire to showcase the work and identity of specific groups were achieved by providing 'homepages' for corporate units and by simulating a hierarchical content structure in a flat content realm.

Using the Wiki with such work methods provided even more unexpected benefits for the company; it provided knowledge consolidation for different groups. For example, several development groups wrote sets of Java development tips and related knowledge and their local knowledge champions nurtured these local 'knowledge bases' of Java development insights, each one at its separate 'world'. It was expected that at the roundtable meetings they would discover that other teams and other knowledge champions were creating similar Java development 'knowledge bases' and would want to use them. This indeed was the case; as such, they agreed that these parallel efforts wasted time and valuable knowledge, as each instance offered limited access and use. Surprisingly--or rather not, they agreed to collaborate and share these great resources together and to interlink their work to create one large and rich set of tips and insights, while still continuing to work on their own pages and in their own comfort zones. It was truly a 'have the cake and eat it too' achievement. Thus, as one of the outcomes of these meetings, it was deciding to craft together these gems of insights and practical information into shared resources by cross-linking and by editing shared pages. It also made it very easy for Java developers and project managers, the consumers of all this information, to walk through shared content rather than having to deal with many incompatible collections.

Summary

The initial top goal of Amdocspedia was to bridge the gaps between the disparate islands of know-how and experience separated by a sea of miscommunication, into one continent of rich information, where experts and content consumers could roam easily. Collaboration, care, mutual trust and willingness to adopt other people's ideas in harmony were the drive. The attention of senior managers and knowledge champions, together with the user-oriented, exceed- expectations approach of the KM team enabled success. The friendly and highly usable Wiki platform paved the road and facilitated a smooth transition. The technology was the enabler for this process to happen in a global, distributed work environment.

The adoption of Amdocspedia benefited the participant groups and the organization as a whole in a number of ways. It saved time, simplified information management, promoted know-how reuse, avoided redundant efforts and supported quality assurance. It offered quick access to valuable, practical information without having to resort to time-consuming phone calls or email threads. It thus provided business benefits to both professional workers who were sitting the entire day at an office, to employees working on the road or to implementation experts visiting a customer site.

Rafael Advanced Defense Systems Ltd.

I^{2} - ('yeda baribua' =>> 'Knowledge Squared' in Hebrew) - Wiki-based Knowledge Management System.

The Company

Rafael is a government-owned corporation that develops advanced, state-of-the-art defense systems for land, sea, air & space applications. Rafael is divided into six divisions: Air Superiority Systems, Air and C4ISR (Command, Control, Communications, Computers, Intelligence, Surveillance and Reconnaissance) Division, Land Systems Division, Manor (engines & warheads) and Technologies, R&D and Engineering Division, Ordnance and National Infrastructure Division (http://bit.ly/1e83OKL).

The defense industry is a highly competitive, fast-evolving and knowledge-intensive business. Successful operation of such a knowledge-based enterprise requires effective knowledge creation processes and efficient use of this knowledge for new product development and for the reduction of manufacturing costs. The mission of the knowledge management initiative is to promote the creation of professional knowledge and technologies and to simultaneously provide the full documentation required for projects in accordance with customer requirements as well the organization's internal needs. The goal is to prevent employee re-invention of the wheel, to enable rapid entry to new markets, to quickly adapt to new technologies and to provide flexible responses to clients' new requirements.

The Business Need

Knowledge may be broken down to two categories: formal and informal. Formal knowledge is explicit knowledge such as contracts, procedures, specifications, records, designs etc. Formal knowledge is necessary for projects throughout their life-cycles. Most formal knowledge is created and saved by specific information systems such as DMS (Document Management System) or ERP. The use of formal knowledge is a requirement embedded in the organizational procedures. Formal knowledge is thus considered "managed" knowledge. Even though the creation of formal knowledge is regarded as 'solved', creating a multi-author document is still an issue since it is a serial task that requires check-in and check-out procedures.

Informal knowledge consists of tacit knowledge as well as some types of explicit content, such as engineering guides, software manuals and usage tips, documented and undocumented best practices, etc. Informal knowledge is not project-specific and it applies to various projects in more than one division; hence, this knowledge should be handled in a cross-organizational manner. Informal knowledge is not "managed" in the way that formal knowledge is. An attempt to handle informal knowledge took place by establishing communities of practice (CoPs) and blogs for creation and preservation of informal knowledge. However, the CoPs were mostly used as platforms for questions and answers, which was a real need, but provided only a partial solution.

In general, the communities (and blogs) have not been widely adopted at Rafael due to three operational issues:

1. The scope of questions and answers is relatively limited and it covers the subject only partially.
2. The frequency of questions asked was low.
3. The community facilitator had to prompt the users and frequently ask them to contribute.

These findings are consistent with the findings of Retna and Tee (2011): "The key factors that nurture CoPs to promote innovative learning and knowledge-sharing environments are leadership, culture and individual motivation".

A Wiki does not have the types of problems described above that had prevented the adoption of CoPs for the following reasons:

1. A Wiki platform can function as an organizational encyclopedia, thereby fully covering a subject. Furthermore, any part of the contents can be linked to other items, which gives a broader coverage or exposure to complementary articles. Questions can be asked under the proper heading. The contents can include updated instruction manuals, best practices, access to organizational procedures, etc.
2. The amount of content is not determined by the number of questions. The multi-author option offered by Wikis enabled the creation of content on a particular subject that could be improved with time. On the other hand, blogs enable only one author to make changes in the 'body', while all other contributors could only comment.
3. Unlike CoPs, Wikis do not require a facilitator for ongoing operation.

These reasons motivated the creation of I^2 - a cross-organizational Wiki platform to facilitate the creation and sharing of informal and formal knowledge. I^2 is capable of managing all types of informal knowledge and is not affected by the issues that led to CoPs failure. The goal was to potentially see participation on the part of all Rafael employees since "knowledge sharing between employees and within and across teams allows organizations to exploit and capitalize on knowledge-based resources" (Wang & Noe, 2010).

Compliance with the strict authorization policy (*need to know*) typical for this type of enterprise was a basic preliminary design constraint. Best (2011) discussed the problem of *Need-to-Know* (everything is restricted, only those with specific authorization can access) vs. *Need-to-Share* (everything is open except sensitive material). Clapper (2012) recommends finding a "the ideal sweet spot for classifying: We shouldn't either over classify or under classify". The sweet spot for Rafael's knowledge management platform was to have it open to all employees, which means that it does not contain any restricted items; these reside in the document management system.

Design Considerations

I^2 organizational Wiki can be viewed as a large shared informal knowledge "notebook" that everyone with proper authorization can easily access and use.

I^2 is non-hierarchical. It connects managers, R&D personnel, production engineers, marketers, etc. I^2 major sections are: suppliers list (with attached catalogues), book club (reviews and summaries of technical literature), marketing (a separate Wiki page for each product), how-to guides, professional forums (replacing existing communities of practice), publications and conference proceedings, and e-learning material. The sections are easily accessed via clickable icons on the $\mathbf{I^2}$ home page.

I^2 Basic Characteristics

- **Dual Type Categories:** Both a content tree and a hierarchical tree.
- Wiki pages can be retrieved using the organizational portal search engine.
- **Authorizations:** The Wiki does not contain any proprietary knowledge and is practically open to all Rafael's employees.

- **DMS Connectivity:** The Wiki is connected to the organizational document management system, so that relevant documents could be included via hyperlinks without duplication. The linking is performed by a toolbar that has been specifically developed for this purpose. Sensitive documents that are stored in the document management system are accessible only to personnel with proper authorizations.
- **Author Identity:** All Wiki pages and individual entries include the full name of the original author and of the authors of all subsequent entries.
- **Technical Approval**: Any entry may be submitted for pre-approval by one of a few designated experts. Pre-approval is similar to quality assurance and authors are free to use it at will.
- **Tagging:** Each page is tagged by the original author and by readers. The author is assisted by an automatic tag suggestions add-on and by an auto-complete mechanism.
- Babylon Enterprise connectivity enables fast and effective one-click access to essential information stored in enterprise systems such as CRM, ERP and organizational portals, as well as to external content sources that have been previously downloaded (the internal network is disconnected from the internet).
- The questions and answers that were used in the forums have been replaced by requests to open new pages. In this case the 'answers' are continuously improved by the users and there is no need to sift through the chronological list of comments to get updated.

Special attention was given to keep confidential material out of I^2. Automatic word-check flags a warning when suspicious words or phrases are encountered. This add-on enables smooth operation without the need to receive security approval for each publication. Due to the highly technical nature of the content, an advanced equation editor has been developed to enable presentation of engineering derivations and calculations. The equation editor is shown in Figure 2, and a sample derivation and calculation in Figure 3.

Figure 2. Equation editor

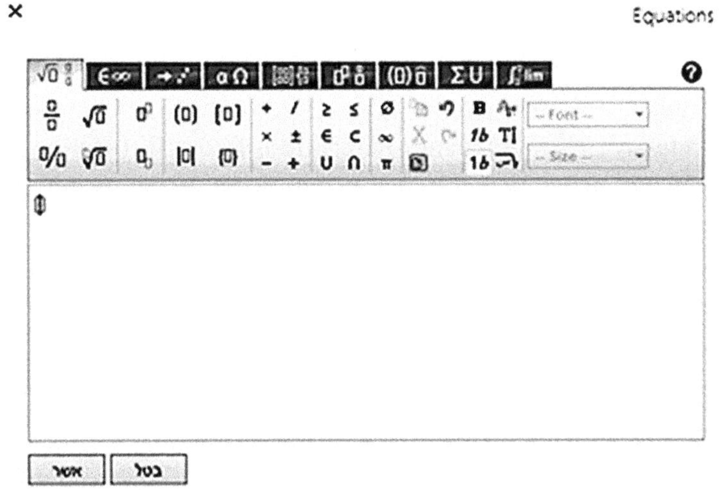

Figure 3. Sample derivation

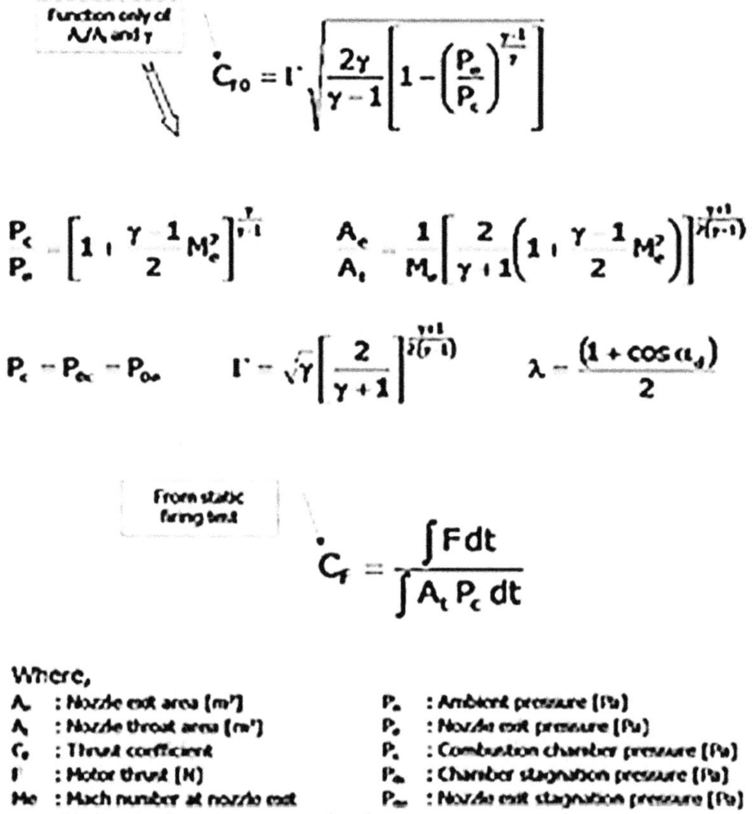

Technology

In principle there were three options: a freeware platform such as MediaWiki, a commercial Wiki platform or the Wiki segment of Microsoft Office Sharepoint Server that already existed at Rafael. The decision was to refrain from adding another organizational software, i.e. to stay with SharePoint, but upgrade to SharePoint 2013. SharePoint 2013 has new capabilities as compared to previous Sharepoint versions, including social capabilities such as activity feeds, following, like and reputations features. Most of the required features for $\mathbf{I}^2$ were available out of the box; a few such as the tag suggestion mechanism, equation editor, alert for possible use of restricted terms and a document toolbar, were developed separately. The Wiki connects seamlessly to MS Office as SharePoint is a part of this Microsoft product suite.

Implementation

The first step was to convince a C-level executive that the organization had to solve the issue of informal knowledge and that a Wiki is a viable solution. This step was crucial for cross-organizational support and for allocation of resources (monetary and man-hours). The second step was to convince leading experts and convert them to be Wiki 'torch bearers'. These Wiki champions served both as members of the steering committee (headed by a senior scientist that belongs to Rafael's management) and also as representatives of the users.

Pre-launch marketing activities included:

- Detailed instructions – over 70 meetings were held with potential users prior to fielding.
- Internal conferences.
- Banners in the company's home page.
- Articles in Rafael's newsletter and in the public media.
- Email alerts.

Adoption

After 3 years of operation, I^2 currently contains about 2,200 Wiki pages. About 2 new pages are added each day. The pages are distributed across the organization and are used for different technologies as shown in Figure 4 (each column represents a technology, e.g. electro-optics).

About 8% - 10% of Rafael's employees have created Wiki pages, a percentage that exceeded expectations by far. Figures on the number of employees that updated existing pages were not determined. There are two types of motivations for workers to participate. 1. Internal motivation: the employees create pages in order to brand themselves as experts or to seek out help. 2. External motivation: the management promotes involvement by awarding certificates of excellence for page quality, number of pages per author and number of readers per article.

I^2 has become firmly embedded in Rafael's procedures and in its organizational culture. I^2 is regarded as the main knowledge management system and is considered a great success by both the employees and the management.

Summary

- Exposes all Rafael employees to relevant informal knowledge.
- Stimulates intra-departmental collaborations.
- Enables cross-organizational knowledge and information flow.
- Promotes personal branding via quality contributions.
- Highlights departmental work across the organization.

Figure 4. Number of Wiki pages per main technology subject

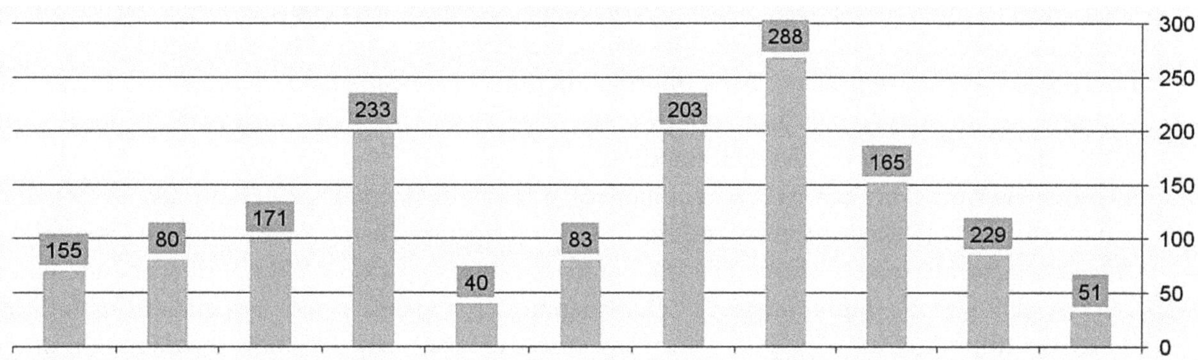

As a consequence, I^2 is regarded as the ultimate knowledge management system in Rafael. It continues to evolve each year. Rafael's internal procedures are continuously incorporated into I^2. Future plans of enhancing its capabilities include adding on fresh social media features such as blogs, forums, chats, and news feeds.

I^2 has been jointly developed by Rafael's IT department and eWave.

Elta Systems Ltd.

EltaWiki

The Company

Elta Systems Ltd. is an Israeli manufacturer and subsidiary of Israel Aerospace Industries. Elta has 3,500 employees and operates in the Intelligence, Defense & HLS global markets and specializes in RADAR, C4ISR, Communication, Cyber, SIGINT and Electronic Warfare products.

EltaWiki was established in 2006 and has since served as the organizational brain of the company's CI (competitive intelligence) department.

The Business Need

EltaWiki is designed to perform the following functions:

1. Accumulate all the information relevant to the business-competitive market in which the company operates.
2. Provide easy access to the accumulated information.
3. Enable associative retrieval of relevant items that have not been explicitly searched for.

Design Considerations

EltaWiki home page is a Wiki Portal (Wikipedia, Portals) - a visual dashboard where users can navigate to a category and then drill down (via subcategories) to the specific issue of interest.

- EltaWiki can be visualized as a multi-layered network of the competitive business information relevant to Elta.
- The knowledge map has been continuously built over the years and includes a huge variety (many thousands) of information objects such as companies, competitors, cooperations, countries, organizations, systems, sensors, platforms, weapons, technologies, product lines, projects, opportunities, people, events, trends, etc. Each information object is documented in a separate Wiki page and assigned to a few association groups (categories). The knowledge map includes more than twelve thousand categories and their interlinks.
- The associative navigation method is enabled by a detailed ontology system and association groups that include extensive relationships between the groups, using the MediaWiki categories.
- Advantages of associative navigation: the homepage offers access to Wiki portals and the users can navigate step by step to interesting information items via their own associations as well as directives from the EltaWiki system. In many cases, the user may not know the definition of an

object he is searching for; for example, a user who is looking for a specific product without knowing its exact name can set different parameters to navigate to it, such as:
  - The company that manufactures the product.
  - The platform that the product is installed on.
  - The problem that the product solves.
  - The product user.
  - The technology implemented in the product.
- Another advantage of this approach is that the user often stumbles upon important information without searching for it, and even without knowing about its mere existence, as a result of connections between data entities and system categories.

Technology

- In order to bridge the wide range of users' associations, rich common language (professional company jargon) is continuously maintained, using taxonomy, vocabulary (thesaurus), shortcuts (abbreviations), keywords, related words etc. for each subject and theme. The rich language allows users to easily navigate the multi-dimensional and otherwise nebulous category tree. One may navigate various ways to reach the same specific piece of information (all roads lead to Rome).
- EltaWiki is growing and is maintained by the introduction of timely and relevant information within the appropriate context (precise categories). Tagging and filing the up-to-date information is completed manually.
- Most information is inserted by the CI team on an ongoing basis (hoping for more and more contribution from the users in the future). Updates consist of new pages or addition of files (reports, studies, presentations, tables, charts, pictures, video clips, etc.) to existing pages. All updates are added to the relevant category and appropriately tagged.
- In addition to the navigational approach of EltaWiki, all the information is indexed and retrievable by the organizational Google search engine, or by using the Wiki's internal search engine.
- EltaWiki is powered by the MediaWiki software platform.

Planned Improvements

- Addition of access authorizations to sensitive information.
- Monitoring mechanism to produce operational logs (who looked at what and when).
- Automatic mechanisms for filing and tagging.

Adoption

Users:

- More than 3,000 workers have logged in.
- More than 500 people use EltaWiki regularly (mostly for retrieving information).

Contents

- More than 4,000 entities (Wiki pages).
- More than 12,000 categories.
- More than 30,000 attached files (reports / studies / articles / tables / external and internal publications).

Summary

- EltaWiki has been serving as the corporate memory (database) for competitive intelligence topics for the last 10 years.
- EltaWiki is unique in that it is highly accessible for gathering information and that it is easy to navigate through it to find relevant information via association.
- The rich ontologies, including thousands of inter-connected categories and the coherent professional and rich language (folksonomy) are the result of an ongoing effort; any new information accumulated in the system is tagged and filed within the appropriate context in the multi-dimensional category tree.

ClickSoftware

The Company

ClickSoftware is a leader in the area of field service management (FSM), recognized as such by leading analysts such as Gartner (for four consecutive years), IDC and Frost and Sullivan. Its products are used to manage the work of some 750,000 service personnel around the world, who provide services to around 700 million consumers.

The Business Needs: Knowledge Challenges at ClickSoftware

ClickSoftware operates in a fast-pace field that needs to cater to ever-evolving changes, and to make use of the best and most cost-effective technologies. Technology trends such as wearable computing, the internet of things (IoT), Software as a Service (SaaS) are being quickly adopted in the FSM field. Combined with numerous projects and products, this leads to large amounts of volatile knowledge which needs to be shared among a global organization. Another dimension of the knowledge challenge is the domain expertise required both by the development and professional services teams; for instance, scheduling shifts and allocating resources varies greatly within a gas company and a telecommunication enterprise. ClickSoftware engineers need to master the domain knowledge (best practices and even the respective jargon) of such domains. Under these circumstances, a lot of tacit knowledge is gathered by ClickSoftware's developers and implementers. Recently, as the company continues to focus on providing cloud services (in addition to its on-premise, project-based offerings), another dimension emerged, that is the creation and management of knowledge regarding the company's evolving best practices in cloud operations.

Another challenge which arises is that of the need to empower a large ecosystem of partners with high quality (highly relevant, detailed, accurate, up-to-date) knowledge in order to support their technical teams in deploying ClickSoftware products to their customers.

Design Considerations

ClickSoftware had used another knowledge system for years before embarking on a Wiki solution. That knowledge system was record-based and was considered to be hard to use and manage, and thus, despite its inherent importance, had not seen significant participation (both in the knowledge contribution and the knowledge consumption aspects). These deficiencies rendered that system ineffective, and made it clear to management that a participatory and usable system was in need.

To ensure knowledge is stored, shared and harnessed towards effective product development and project delivery, a Wiki was introduced in 2011, with the following foci:

- Document vertical-specific (e.g.: Utilities, Telecommunication, etc.) knowledge, relevant to project delivery to respective customers.
- Collaboration and sharing of knowledge around effective techniques for the planning, installation and configuration of ClickSoftware software products with customers.

The main target users are professional service teams (amounting to about a third of the company's headcount), with support engineers and developers constituting additional beneficiaries of that knowledge. In recent years an emphasis has been placed on sharing major parts of the Wiki's content with ClickSoftware's partners and customers (more details are provided below).

Technology: Structure and Content Management

The Wiki is organized in Hubs – each hub corresponds to a main product and/or service that ClickSoftware provides. Each hub is managed by one or two hub owners, who are responsible for helping the individual contributors, if such help is needed. However, their main role is to maintain the quality of the hub pages, so they can be shared not only within the company but also with its immediate ecosystem – its customers and partners.

Due to confidentiality concerns, the Wiki is structured in such a way that the content shared with partners is a subset (some 40%) of the overall ~4,500 Wiki pages. Along the same lines, the company's customers have access to a subset (50%) of the content shared with the partners. Partners and customers currently have read-only permissions, but a planned upgrade to the Wiki platform will allow them to comment (but not to edit pages or create new ones).

Simple guidelines are provided to content contributors and to hub owners to ensure quality. The basic approach is that content quality is critical while format is of much less importance, thus the content control processes are more stringent than those for format. Specifically, while every employee is encouraged to contribute content (i.e.: author new pages, edit existing ones, provide comments and ratings), the publication of Wiki pages to the partner and customer ecosystem is delegated to hub owners and the KM team only.

Another process that is used in order to ensure content quality is a periodic review of existing content. This review (which takes place every 18 months or so) is useful mainly for finding outdated pages, thus prompting their update or archival. Another benefit of this process is that when an old page is found to still be accurate and up-to-date, flagging the "Reviewed on" field assures the readers that the content is still relevant and trustworthy.

Adoption

Continued high-quality and high-volume participation is crucial to the Wiki success. Engrained within the Wiki concept, knowledge is contributed by ClickSoftware employees, on top of their regular responsibilities. To ensure participation, a few measures have been implemented:

In knowledge intensive groups (such as the support group), Wiki usage and contribution have been established as part of the standard work procedure. For example, support engineers are required to document in the case management system which Wiki pages they consulted when working on a case, and are also required to create a new Wiki page (or update an existing one) when they came up with a new or undocumented solution.

Wiki hub owners have an essential part in the Wiki's success. This mission is a part of their job description and 2-4 weekly hours are specifically allocated for this role. In their mid-year performance review, they agree with their direct managers and with the company's KM manager on hub-specific objectives (e.g.: increase the portion of pages published to partners from 40% to 45%), which serves as a motivator and helps to calibrate expectations and set base levels.

Lastly, and probably most importantly, a "respect point" system has been introduced, in which contributors receive respect points for their contribution (e.g.: four points for creating a new page, three points for editing a page). In every page, next to the page owner's name and picture, the associated number of respect points is displayed, and a hall of fame (per hub and a cross-hub one) is highly prominent within the Wiki. Every six months the most valuable wiki contributors are announced, and they receive a certificate of appreciation and a prize (generally in an 'all-hands meeting').

Summary: The Wiki as Part of the Overall Knowledge Services Stack

While the Wiki is arguably the most effective knowledge service within ClickSoftware, it certainly is not the only one the company uses. It is important to understand the relationships between the Wiki and the other knowledge services in order to understand some of the challenges.

The company's internal portal provides not only specific services (such as a channel for disseminating news and updates, a container for team document management, and more), but it also provides an (almost) one-stop-shop for other knowledge services, including the Wiki. Wiki content, like content from other knowledge services, can be accessed (mostly via search, but also via various links), from the portal.

Another relevant knowledge service is the company's enterprise social network (Salesforce Chatter based), which is used not only for sharing social information, but also for sharing technical knowledge (in designated groups that focus around technical domains). The main differences between a Chatter group used for sharing knowledge about a certain ClickSoftware product on the one hand, and the respective Wiki hub on the other, is the nature of the information and the type of interaction in those two channels. In the case of the Chatter group, one expects to see very short tips, or a question and its respective answers. Meanwhile, in the respective Wiki hub, one expects to see lengthier, more organized content. Additionally, while many employees get immediate notifications about new posts into their Chatter groups of interest, and in so are able to respond immediately, Wiki content is less volatile and is mostly accessed via search. A typical interrelation we see is a post in Chatter pointing to newly created (or newly found) Wiki content, or an answer to a Chatter question providing a brief answer and a reference to the full information as documented in the respective Wiki page(s). Hub owners are encouraged to identify knowledge gaps via the communication in Chatter, and create the corresponding Wiki content. They are also encouraged to harvest various Chatter posts and incorporate them into Wiki pages. Finally, hub owners use Chatter to notify their target audience on new, or otherwise important, Wiki content.

ClickSoftware also provides its partners and customers with a forum, used by technical staff to ask questions and get answers and tips from their fellow experts. The relationship between this forum and the Wiki resembles that between the Wiki and Chatter (see above).

Finally, another important knowledge service the company provides both internally and externally is product documentations, which are formal manuals, guides and technical references organized in a library that is provided to partners and customers along with each product release, and is available in various formats and languages. While this content is highly extensive (consisting of what amounts to dozens of books, or some 15,000 pages), and is of the highest caliber, its production and update processes are inherently slower in pace than that of the Wiki pace. ClickSoftware aims to harness knowledge from the Wiki into the respective product documentation guides. The technical writer in charge of documenting a specific product is requested to follow the respective Wiki hub, and incorporate relevant content (after careful review and approval, as product documentation requires), into the respective guide. To date, ClickSoftware is migrating its product documentation into a Wiki platform, so that the company's technical writers and internal reviewers may benefit from the full range of Wiki features, and so that end-users will be able to not only read content, as they did until now, but also comment on it. This will enable the company to get immediate feedback (and thus improve product documentation), in a much faster pace than it currently does, where product documentation is updated only a few times per year. Moreover, it will grant the end-users with the ability to help and be helped by their peers.

DISCUSSION

Meloche et al. (2009) listed 12 critical Wiki success factors (CSFs) based on a study of corporate Wikis with limited scope (technical encyclopedia only). The use-cases described in this chapter demonstrate how these CSFs are met in Wikis with much broader scope.

Meloche et al. (2009) and many others studies referenced here, focus primarily on user adoption. The use cases in this chapter demonstrate also the important contribution of the Wiki in attaining business goals.

Garcia-Perez and Ayres (2010) claim that: "Although technologies such as Wiki have great potential there are also pitfalls in undertaking such projects which are not yet well understood". Organizations that wish to use a Wiki for KM purposes can avoid the pitfalls by learning from the successful use-cases detailed above. Practical guidance as to what can be achieved as well as good practices on how to approach such a project, can be obtained from one or more of these use-cases. The following part of the discussion elaborates on major issues including implementation, from a KM vantage point.

Implementation Points of View

Four examples of successful and sustainable Wiki implementations in large companies have been described in detail. The first success criterion assessed was Grudin and Poole's (2010) major challenge relevant to Wiki adoption and long-term sustainability: "aligning the expectations of managers and individual contributors". The expectations of managers are usually related to business outcomes. However, none of the four firms attempted to measure or calculate ROI, a difficult task as previously noted. For this reason, managers of knowledge-based companies usually "accept anecdotes about successful (or failed) knowledge reuse, stories of productive (or unproductive) collaborative projects, and surveys of employee and customer satisfaction as the best indicators of value" (Cohen, 2006). In all four cases, the management was satisfied with the direct or perceived business outcomes, as per Cohen's definition. This led to continuous managerial support and allocation of resources (monetary and manpower) for the Wiki to thrive.

The expectations of individual contributors can be analyzed using TAM - the Technology Acceptance Model (Davis, 1989). TAM is based on the insight that users' attitudes toward a technology are critical factors in their acceptance and use of new technologies: "*Perceived usefulness* and *perceived ease of use* are the most fundamental determinants for formulating positive attitudes toward technology and behavioral intention to use technology and, therefore, ultimately define actual use". Users' participation logs provided general insight into how they perceived the Wiki.

Yeo and Arazi (2012) discuss Wiki affordances in an attempt to determine what makes corporate Wikis work. Studying Wiki affordances is not feasible in the context of the four different Wikis since an affordance "focuses on the suitability of the tool for supporting a specific task", and each Wiki of the four described uses different, specifically-developed, add-ons that provide additional capabilities for responding to each company's needs and contribute to the perceived ease of use.

All four Wiki implementations were geared to achieve both usefulness and ease of use. Rafael, ClickSoftware and Amdocs are using the integral SharePoint Wiki which provides basic capabilities. All three companies made specific modifications, mostly in response to business needs. These add-ons did affect the actual usefulness (business needs), but simultaneously contributed both to the *perceived usefulness* and to the *perceived ease of use* of the users. It should be noted that the ease of use is double pronged (for writers and for readers): the ease to contribute knowledge on one hand and the ease to retrieve knowledge on another. Enhanced personal reputation as an outcome of contents contribution served as another motivator; see Majchrzak, Wagner and Yates, (2006).

In Elta, most Wiki users are just readers and their contribution to EltaWiki contents is mostly vicarious and not direct – they provide relevant information to the Wiki team that categorize and publish it accordingly. The perceived usefulness of EltaWiki is high since reading the competitive intelligence information is an important business need and there is no other way to access all relevant information. Retrieving the information in EltaWiki is quite straightforward in the 'out of the box' MediaWiki so there was no need to develop add-ons for this purpose. The conclusions about user attitude (acceptance) in all four cases were drawn from user logs and not from questionnaires.

The Updated DeLone and McLean Model of Information Systems Success (Urbach & Müller, 2012) points to six success dimensions for information systems: System Quality, Information Quality, Service Quality, Intention to Use/Use, User Satisfaction and Net Benefits (to the different stakeholders). Subjective judgment of each dimension in the cases of the four organizations was high, thus resulting in successful Wiki implementations.

In most use cases employees' participation is on voluntary basis since the Wikis do not constitute a required part of the organizational workflows. This model can therefore serve also as an inductive tool in conjunction with the TAM model (Davis, 1989). System quality, service quality and information quality contribute to user satisfaction (perceived personal benefits by the employees) which results in their active usage.

The contribution of the Wikis to business goals (DeLone and McLean's sixth dimension - organizational benefits) is difficult to measure since "benefits in terms of numeric costs are not possible because of intangible system impacts" (Urbach & Müller, 2012). The use of knowledge management systems in organizations is not mandatory and not required by any regulation or standard (except documents and records management in some cases). The continuous support by the managements in the four use cases can therefore only be interpreted by perceived contribution of the KM systems to the business.

- **Basic Considerations:** A Wiki should be considered in relation to the other knowledge systems within the same organization. In the four examples presented here, the Wiki has different levels of prominence and importance as compared to other knowledge systems in the respective organization. Knowledge architects should ensure that the boundaries and the interrelationships among the knowledge systems they provide to employees are well laid out and clear to users and owners, to ensure effectiveness and to minimize uncertainties.
- **Implementation:** Even though Wiki is a familiar web 2.0 application, its learning curve is not zero, especially for employees who are expected to author new pages. All potential users should receive training prior to implementation; special attention should be given to the use of the new developed add-ons and to company-specific rules.

Onboarding has to be carefully planned. An important issue is preparation of preliminary content prior to formal launch. Readers that start using a new system that is empty will regard it as useless. Examples of pre-launch marketing activities were given for Rafael's Wiki. ClickSoftware has gone a step further from the traditional KM 2.0 where the contribution is voluntary and for a few key personnel, as well as for all technical support engineers and implemented their Wiki in some organizational procedures - i.e. the employees must use the Wiki to accomplish their tasks. Wiki-related activities are formally included in job descriptions and/or designated work procedures.

Securing the support of top management and prominent users is an essential component for success.

- **Alignment with Company's Culture:** Rafael is in the defense business and employs a "need to know" policy which usually precludes cross-company knowledge sharing. This has been overcome by opening the Wiki to all employees, while keeping the restricted material in the document management system only. In addition, the management awards active participation. ClickSoftware policy encourages cooperation, via gamification and by including contribution to and use of the Wiki in job descriptions and company procedures. At Amdocs confidentiality is sacred; hence Amdocspedia was strictly not customer specific.
- **Company Size:** In principle, a Wiki can be implemented in any organization, regardless of size. Razmerita & Kirchner (2011) discuss Wiki implementation in SMEs; their case study is of a company with 50 employees. Ling (2011) and Wiewiora, Murphy, Trigunarsyah and Brown (2014) claim that smaller companies generally enjoy more internal trust since the employees know each other; in turn, interpersonal trust has positive impact on knowledge sharing. A systematic discussion of Wiki adoption in SMEs is given by Stieglitz and Dang-Xuan (2011).
- **Motivating Employees to Contribute Contents by Gamification:** Both Rafael and Clicksoftware use game mechanics to reward employees for active involvement. Various types of contributions are ranked according to some criteria (ClickSoftware established a special 'respect point' system for this purpose). Employees receive awards according to their accumulated points. The incen-

tives are not monetary following Pink (2011) who described the effect of monetary reward on knowledge workers: "for tasks that require even rudimentary cognitive skill, a larger reward lead to poorer performance". The motivational aspect in Wiki adoption is extensively discussed by Gears (2012).

- **Training:** Wiki is a Web 2.0 application which can be self-taught. However, an organization should provide basic training, such as how to create new Wiki pages. Special attention should be given to corporate-specific rules such what should be published on the Wiki and what should be documented elsewhere, and how to link the Wiki to other organizational applications.

KM Points of View

- **Findability:** EltaWiki uses a unique information architecture (combining labeling and navigation schemes) not only to improve findability but also to enable locating information that was not explicitly searched for. The retrieved information is already filtered, analyzed and focused on the subject, in contrast to search that may provide multitude of irrelevant items. Items in the other three Wikis can be located by searching from the organizational portal's home page, which enhances ease of use, especially for readers. Rafael developed the option of backtracking Wiki pages, i.e. readers can not only drill down but also go back to an originating page, a function absent from most Wikis.
- **Document Handling:** The direct connection to the document management system in Rafael and to several types of documentation systems in Amdocs and ClickSoftware eliminates the need to save documents within the Wiki while preserving the rule of saving documents in a single physical place and obeying strict authorization policy.
- **Knowledge Sharing and Creation of New Knowledge:** The corporate Wiki in Rafael, Amdocs and ClickSoftware provide a virtual 'ba' for the creation (and sharing) of new knowledge using the collective experience and knowledge of individual employees. It is important to note that employees play a dual role: they are both content contributors and content consumers. Although sharing is not a goal by itself, it paves the road to business goals by preventing employees from 're-inventing the wheel', supporting reuse of latent organizational knowledge by using existing practices and tools rather than re-inventing them and by combining disparate islands of knowledge to a single, richer and higher-quality repository.
- **Embedding Knowledge Processes in Business Procedures:** "The need to align KM strategy with business strategy was identified as critical to the success of KM" (Oliukpe 2012). The ClickSoftware use case is an example of how this strategy may be implemented. ClickSoftware moved from the totally voluntary mode, common to most Enterprise 2.0 technologies to a mode in which usage and contribution became an integral part of standard work procedures. In addition, the job descriptions of key Wiki personnel include Wiki-related work and their performance in the field is measured.
- **Overall Utility:** Wiki is a tool that can be effectively used for various organizational processes that support the attainment of concrete business objectives. Indeed, Wiki has become the most prominent knowledge service within ClickSoftware and Rafael.

CONCLUSION

1. The use of a Wiki as a KM 2.0 media for organizational learning and knowledge management has been demonstrated in four corporations. In two cases the Wiki has evolved into the main organizational KM tool.
2. The successful Wikis described in this chapter offer the groundwork for an organization wishing to implement a corporate Wiki by adopting good practices from these use cases.
3. Successful adoption requires agreement and cooperation among three involved parties: stakeholders (usually management), users (usually employees, in some cases also clients and business partners), and the IT department. Sophisticated uses may require modifications to the out-of-the-box Wiki platform, in the spirit of those that have been made by Amdocs, Rafael or ClickSoftware.
4. Organizational culture plays an important role as an enabler to a Wiki's success. It is possible to resolve culture-related obstacles by the top management that can define cooperation as a part of the organizational vision, reward employees for their contributions to the Wiki and support gamification as a means to foster collaboration.
5. Overall success: the use of non-mandatory KM systems in general, stems from both perceived contributions to the organizational goals by the management (deduced from continuous support and allocation of resources), and from perceived usefulness to the employees (deduced from active contribution or use by the employees). The best indicator of the success of a Wiki, from a KM point of view, is when the Wiki becomes an integral part of a business process, as demonstrated in the use case of ClickSoftware.

REFERENCES

Amdocs. (2015). *About Amdocs*. Retrieved June 26, 2015, from: http://www.amdocs.com/about/pages/default.aspx

Bhasin, R. (Frankfurt Airport Innovation and Knowledge Management Executive) (2015). Private communication.

Best, R. A., Jr. (2011). *Intelligence Information: Need-to-know vs. Need-to-share*. CRS Report for Congress R41848. Retrieved June 26, 2015, from: https://www.fas.org/sgp/crs/intel/R41848.pdf

Bolisani, E., Scarso, E., & Giuman, L. (2014). Wiki as a Knowledge Management System in a Small Project-Based Company: Benefits, Issues and Managerial Challenges. In *Proceedings of the 15th European Conference on Knowledge Management ECKM 2014*.

Boyd, D., & Ellison, N. (2008). Social Network Sites: Definition, History, and Scholarship. *Journal of Computer-Mediated Communication*, 13.

Buckman, R. H. (2004). *Building a Knowledge-Driven Organization*. McGraw-Hill. Retrieved from http://www.who.int/kms/resources/Building_a_knowledge_driven_organization_bookreview.pdf

Bughin, J., & Chui, M. (2010). The Rise of the Networked Enterprise: Web 2.0 Finds its Payday. *The McKinsey Quarterly*, *4*, 3–8.

Clapper, J. (2012). *Information Sharing*. Speech in the Center for Strategic and International Studies (CSIS). Retrieved June 26, 2015, from: https://csis.org/files/attachments/120126_info_sharing_clapper_transcript.pdf

Cohen, D. (2006). What's Your Return on Knowledge? *Harvard Business Review*, *84*(12), 28. PMID:16649692

Cook, N. (2008). *Enterprise 2.0: How Social Software Will Change the Future of Work*. London: Gower Publishing, Ltd.

Cress, U., & Kimmerle, J. (2008). A Systemic and Cognitive View on Collaborative Knowledge Building with Wikis. *International Journal of Computer-Supported Collaborative Learning*, *3*(2), 105–122. doi:10.1007/s11412-007-9035-z

Davis, F. D. (1989). Perceived usefulness, perceived ease of use and user acceptance of information technology. *Management Information Systems Quarterly*, *13*(3), 319–339. doi:10.2307/249008

De Geus, A. P. (1988). Planning as learning. *Harvard Business Review*, *66*(2), 70–74.

Dillon, A., & Gabbard, R. (1998). Hypermedia as an educational technology: A review of the quantitative research literature on learner comprehension, control, and style. *Review of Educational Research*, *68*(3), 322–349. doi:10.3102/00346543068003322

Ebersbach, A., Glaser, M., Heigl, R., & Warta, A. (2008). *Wiki: web collaboration* (2nd ed.). Berlin: Springer.

Edutech Wiki – affordances. (n.d.). Retrieved June 26, 2015, from: http://edutechwiki.unige.ch/en/Affordance

Garcia-Perez, A., & Ayres, R. (2010). Wikifailure: The limitations of technology for knowledge sharing. *Electronic Journal of Knowledge Management*, *8*(1), 43–52. Available online at http://bit.ly/1I1js2O

Garvin, D. A. (2000). *Learning in Action: a Guide for Putting the Learning Organization to Work*. Harvard Business School Press. Retrieved from http://bit.ly/1WZubE7

Garvin, D. A., Edmondson, A. C., & Gino, F. (2008). Is yours a learning organization? *Harvard Business Review*, *86*(3), 109. PMID:18411968

Gears, D. A. (2012). Corporate wikis underground: An investigation of motivation and collaborative engagement. *Journal of Management and Marketing Research*, (9). Available online at: http://www.aabri.com/manuscripts/11894.pdf

Grace, T. P. L. (2009). Wikis as a knowledge management tool. *Journal of Knowledge Management*, *13*(4), 64–74. doi:10.1108/13673270910971833

Grudin, J., & Poole, E. S. (2010). Wikis at work: success factors and challenges for sustainability of enterprise Wikis. In *Proceedings of the 6th international symposium on Wikis and open collaboration* (p. 5). ACM. doi:10.1145/1832772.1832780

Hanrahan, B., Quintana-Castillo, R., Stewart, M., & Perez-Quinones, M. A. (2010). *WikiAtoms: Contributions to Wikis as Atomic Units*. Available online at: https://www.parc.com/content/events/attachments/Hanrahan_revised_Group10.pdf

Henselewski, M., Smolnik, S., & Riempp, G. (2006). Evaluation of knowledge management technologies for the support of technology forecasting. In *System Sciences, 2006. HICSS'06. Proceedings of the 39th Annual Hawaii International Conference on System Sciences*. IEEE.Available online at: http://www.researchgate.net/publication/4216329_Evaluation_of_Knowledge_Management_Technologies_for_the_Support_of_Technology_Forecasting

Holtzblatt, L. J., Damianos, L. E., & Weiss, D. (2010, April). Factors impeding Wiki use in the enterprise: a case study. In CHI'10 Extended Abstracts on Human Factors in Computing Systems (pp. 4661-4676). ACM. doi:10.1145/1753846.1754208

Kaske, F., Kügler, M., & Smolnik, S. (2012). Return on Investment in Social Media--Does the Hype Pay Off? Towards an Assessment of the Profitability of Social Media in Organizations. In *System Science (HICSS), 2012 45th Hawaii International Conference on System Sciences* (pp. 3898-3907). IEEE. Available online at: https://www.wiwi.uni-augsburg.de/en/bwl/paul/Downloads/Publications_Kaske/Kaske-Kuegler-Smolnik_2012.pdf

Kerkhof, C., Ende, J. V. D., & Bogenrieder, I. (2003). Knowledge management in the professional organization: A model with application to CMG software testing. *Knowledge and Process Management*, *10*(2), 77–84. doi:10.1002/kpm.167

Lau, K. (2009). Three myths of enterprise wiki deployment. *Computerworld*, *28*(Jan). Retrieved from http://www.computerworld.com/article/2530642/networking/three-myths-of-enterprise-wiki-deployment.html

Liebowitz, J. (Ed.). (2011). *Beyond Knowledge Management*. Boca Raton, FL: Taylor & Francis Group/CRC Press. doi:10.1201/b11511

Ling, C. T. N. (2011). Culture and trust in fostering knowledge-sharing. *Electronic Journal of Knowledge Management*, *9*(4), 328–339.

Lunenburg, F. (2011). Systems Thinking and the Learning Organization: The Path to School Improvement. *Schooling*, *2*(1), 1–6.

Majchrzak, A., Wagner, C., & Yates, D. (2006). Corporate wiki users: results of a survey. In *Proceedings of the 2006 international symposium on Wikis* (pp. 99–104). ACM. doi:10.1145/1149453.1149472

McAfee, A. (2006). *Enterprise 2.0*. Retrieved June 26, 2015, from: http://andrewmcafee.org/2006/05/enterprise_20_version_20/

Meloche, J. A., Hasan, H. M., Willis, D., Pfaff, C., & Qi, Y. (2009). Co-creating corporate knowledge with a wiki. *International Journal of Knowledge Management*, *5*(2), 22–50. doi:10.4018/jkm.2009040103

Miron, E., & Ravid, G. (2015). Facebook Groups as an Academic Teaching Aid: Case Study and Recommendations for Educators. *Journal of Educational Technology & Society*, 18 (4), 371-384.

Nielsen, J. (2006). *The 90-9-1 Rule for Participation Inequality in Social Media and Online Communities*. Available online at: http://www.nngroup.com/articles/participation-inequality/

Nonaka, I., Toyama, R., & Konno, N. (2000). SECI, Ba, and Leadership: A Unified Model of Dynamic Knowledge Creation. *Long Range Planning*, *33*(1), 5–34. doi:10.1016/S0024-6301(99)00115-6

O'Leary, D. E. (1998). Enterprise knowledge management. *Computer*, *31*(3), 54–61. doi:10.1109/2.660190

O'Reilly, T., & Battelle, J. (2009). *Web Squared: Web 2.0 Five Years On*. Web 2.0 Summit Special report. Retrieved June 26, 2015, from: http://assets.en.oreilly.com/1/event/28/web2009_websquared-whitepaper.pdf

Okimoto, J. (2007). *Industry Trends: the evolution of knowledge management (KM 1.0 vs. KM 2.0)*. IBM Global Business Services. Retrieved June 26, 2015, from: http://www.slideshare.net/elsua/the-evolution-of-knowledge-management-km-10-vs-km-20

Oluikpe, P. (2012). Developing a corporate knowledge management strategy. *Journal of Knowledge Management*, *16*(6), 862–878. doi:10.1108/13673271211276164

Pfaff, C. C., & Hasan, H. (2006). Overcoming organisational resistance to using Wiki technology for Knowledge Management. In *Proceedings of the 6th international symposium on wikis and open collaboration* (p. 14). ACM.

Pink, D. H. (2011). *Drive: The surprising truth about what motivates us*. Edinburgh, UK: Canongate Books Ltd. Retrieved from http://www.ted.com/talks/dan_pink_on_motivation

Ravid, G., Kalman, Y. M., & Rafaeli, S. (2008). Wikibooks in higher education: Empowerment through online distributed collaboration. *Computers in Human Behavior*, *24*(5), 1913–1928. doi:10.1016/j.chb.2008.02.010

Razmerita, L., & Kirchner, K. (2011). How wikis can be used to manage knowledge in SMEs: A case study. *Business Information Review*, *28*(3), 175–178. doi:10.1177/0266382111420354

Retna, K. S., & Tee Ng, P. (2011). Communities of practice: Dynamics and success factors. *Leadership and Organization Development Journal*, *32*(1), 41–59. doi:10.1108/01437731111099274

Schubmehl, D., & Vesset, D. (2014). *The Knowledge Quotient: Unlocking the Hidden Value of Information Using Search and Content Analytics*. IDC white paper. Retrieved, June 26, 2015, from: http://www.coveo.com/~/media/Files/WhitePapers/Coveo_IDC_Knowledge_Quotient_June2014.ashx

Senge, P. M. (1990). The Fifth Discipline: The Art & Practice of The Learning Organization. New York: Doubleday

Standing, C., & Kiniti, S. (2011). How can organizations use wikis for innovation? *Technovation*, *31*(7), 287–295. doi:10.1016/j.technovation.2011.02.005

Stieglitz, S., & Dang-Xuan, L. (2011). Adoption and Use of Corporate Wikis in German Small and Medium-sized Enterprises. In *AMCIS 2011 Proceedings – all submissions*. Paper 235. Available online at: http://bit.ly/1WZuDCc

Stephens, R. T. (2009).Empirical analysis of functional Web 2.0 environments. In *Web 2.0 - the Business Mode*. Springer.

Sousa, F., Aparicio, M., & Costa, C. J. (2010). Organizational wiki as a knowledge management tool. In *Proceedings of the 28th ACM International Conference on Design of Communication* (pp. 33-39). ACM. doi:10.1145/1878450.1878457

Surowiecki, J. (2005). *The wisdom of crowds*. Anchor books.

Urbach, N., & Müller, B. (2012). The updated DeLone and McLean model of information systems success. In *Information systems theory* (pp. 1–18). New York: Springer. doi:10.1007/978-1-4419-6108-2_1

Wagner, C. (2006). Breaking the knowledge acquisition bottleneck through conversational knowledge management. *Information Resources Management Journal*, *19*(1), 14. doi:10.4018/irmj.2006010104

Wang, S., & Noe, R. A. (2010). Knowledge sharing: A review and directions for future research. *Human Resource Management Review*, *20*(2), 115–131. doi:10.1016/j.hrmr.2009.10.001

Wiewiora, A., Murphy, G., Trigunarsyah, B., & Brown, K. (2014). Interactions Between Organizational Culture, Trustworthiness, and Mechanisms for Inter-Project Knowledge Sharing. *Project Management Journal*, *45*(2), 48–65. doi:10.1002/pmj.21407

Wikipedia. (n.d.a). *Forums*. Retrieved June 26, 2015, from: https://en.wikipedia.org/wiki/Internet_forum

Wikipedia. (n.d.b). *Wiki*. Retrieved 26 June 2015, from: https://en.wikipedia.org/wiki/Wiki

Wikipedia. (n.d.c). *Wiki platforms*. Retrieved June 26, 2015, from: https://en.wikipedia.org/wiki/Comparison_of_wiki_software

Wikipedia. (n.d.d). Wiki Portals. Retrieved June 26, 2015 from: https://en.wikipedia.org/wiki/Portal:Contents/Portals

Yeo, M. L., & Arazy, O. (2012). What makes corporate wikis work? Wiki affordances and their suitability for corporate knowledge work. In *Design Science Research in Information Systems. Advances in Theory and Practice* (pp. 174–190). Berlin: Springer. doi:10.1007/978-3-642-29863-9_14

KEY TERMS AND DEFINITIONS

Associative Navigation: Retrieval of information that is associated with the main search item.

Good Practice: A practice that has been proven to work well and produce good results.

Informal Knowledge: Tacit or explicit knowledge that is not a part of any organizational procedure; e.g. – best practices, user manuals.

Knowledge Champions: Senior workers who are recognized leaders in their field.

Organizational Wiki (Corporate Wiki): Organizational website based on the Wiki platform which allows collaborative knowledge creation.

Perceived Usefulness: The attitude of an individual worker that using the Wiki brings about personal benefits.

Wiki Adoption and Sustainability: The process of prompting workers to continuously use and contribute contents to the Wiki.

Chapter 9
The Internet, Social Media, and Knowledge Production and Development of Political Marketing

Nyarwi Ahmad
University of Gadjah Mada Yogyakarta, Indonesia

ABSTRACT

Though the use and development of the Internet, World Wide Web and social media and their impacts on politics have been robustly investigated, specific attention has not yet been paid to explore the impact of adaptation and use of social media by political actors and organizations on the knowledge production and generation of political marketing. In order to fill this knowledge gap, a conceptual framework to explore modes of knowledge production and generation of political marketing has been proposed. The transcendental realism approach postulated by Bhaskar (1998, 2008) and the meta-theoretical assumptions of political marketing proposed by Henneberg (2008) were adopted. A content analysis of 320 articles of Journal of Political Marketing published in between 2002 and 2015 was carried out. This work reveals that the adaptation and use of the Internet and social media have been accounted for in producing and generating the operational or the rudimentary-conceptual or the established-conceptual knowledge of political marketing.

INTRODUCTION

The adaptation and use of Information and Communication Technologies (ICTs), especially the Internet, various websites and social media, have provided various impacts on individuals, society and organisations at large. These developments and their impacts on knowledge management—in general—and knowledge production, and sharing—in particular—have been studied. Nonetheless, such developments and their effects on politics, political communication and campaigning have been robustly undertaken

DOI: 10.4018/978-1-5225-0495-5.ch009

as well. However, a specific research has not yet been undertaken to discuss the impact of the adaptation and use of social media platforms on knowledge production and generation of political marketing.

In addressing this issue, this work postulates following propositions. *Firstly,* the development of media, as a medium of political exchange and interaction and the adaptation and use of ICTs and the Internet by political actors and organisations, as a strategic communication tool and platform in the political sphere, have influenced the knowledge production and generation of political marketing. *Secondly,* there have been two-fold dynamic conditions that determine on how and the extent to which social media have impacted on the knowledge production and development of political marketing. The first one is modes and degrees of the adaptation and use of the Internet, websites and social media by political actors and organizations, while the second one is the ways political marketing scholars have captured and theorised these actors and organisations when they have adopted and used the Internet, websites and social media during the elections and post the elections. *Thirdly,* political marketing scholars whose work has been published in Journal of Political Marketing have been considered to assess the adaptation and uses of social media. The focus was to explore whether they have created and generated the practical or the rudimentary-conceptual or the established-conceptual knowledge of political marketing. However, they have not yet accounted for the various modes of adaptation and use of social media for producing and generating the systemic knowledge of political marketing.

Based on these propositions, the following points will be discussed in this chapter. The first section will examine the media, ICT developments and their impact on political marketing. The second section will propose a conceptual framework that examines modes of knowledge production and generation and its application in the field of political marketing. The third section will spell out the transcendental realism perspective, meta-theoretical assumptions of political marketing and research design. The fourth and fifth sections will explore how, in which ways and the extent to which the Internet and social media has been accounted for in knowledge production and generation of political marketing. The last section will present the conclusions and research recommendations.

THE MEDIA, ICT DEVELOPMENTS, AND POLITICAL MARKETING

The changing landscapes of the media, the development of ICT and the adaptation of the Internet have carved a huge impact on politics, political marketing and campaigning. They have been widely seen of being important as essential factors that determine not only the strategies and practices of political marketing, but also the development of theories and concepts of political marketing (Lees-Marshment, 2001, 2004, 2008; Stromback, 2007; Stromback, et.al, 2012; Ormrod, 2005, 2007, 2009, 2011; Ormrod & Henneberg, 2009, 2010a, 2010b). Some researchers have suggested that they need to be taken into further account practices of political marketing and to develop theories and concepts of political marketing (Harrop, 1990: 227; Lock & Harris, 1996: 21; Henneberg & O' Shaughnessy, 2007: 22; Henneberg, 2008: 171; O'Shaughnessy, 2010: 1050-1051; Temple & Savigny, 2010; Temple, 2013).

Political marketing scholars so far have accounted the development of ICT and the adaptation of the Internet using diverse political marketing perspective. Collins and Butler (1996) and Butler and Collins (1999) have considered the media as a vital element for developing the positioning strategies of political parties in the political market. Moreover, Wring (1997, 2005), and Lilleker (2006) have placed the media as an important element when political parties have followed either the selling-orientation or the market-orientation. Additionally, Lees-Marshment (2000; 2001, 2004, 2008) and Lilleker and Lees-

Marshment (2005) have positioned the media and the Internet as a strategic element of communication and campaigning when political parties have advanced whether it is from a product-orientation, sales-orientation or market-orientation perspective.

In a different vein, Savigny and Temple (2010) and Temple (2013) have highlighted the pivotal roles and powers of the media in shaping political messages and determining whole processes of exchanges and interactions in the political sphere. Moreover, Newman (1994: 12) has placed the media as well as the changing information, communication and technology (ICT) as one of what he called 'environmental-forces' that determine the stages, strategies and processes of political marketing and campaigning of presidential candidates. Furthermore, Stromback (2007, 2009) and Stromback (et.al, 2012) have placed the media as a type of political market arena, while Johansen (2012) has positioned the media as a political sub-market. In addition, Ormrod (2005, 2007, 2009, 2011) and Ormrod and Henneberg (2009, 2010a, 2010b) have considered the media as an external stakeholder.

As evident, these authors have conceptualised the position and role of media and their impact on political marketing and campaigning. However, whilst the landscape of media continues to change, ICT developments and adaptation and usage of the Internet transform modes of political marketing and campaigning, these authors have lacked in offering sufficient theoretical frameworks to explain the impact of these developments on knowledge production and generation of political marketing. More importantly, since various forms of social media platforms have been widely adopted in the political spheres soon after Web 2.0, they have not yet specifically discussed on how, in which ways and the extent to which political marketing scholars have considered the uses of these social media platforms by political actors and organizations for the knowledge generation of political marketing and campaigning.

MODES OF KNOWLEDGE PRODUCTION AND GENERATION OF POLITICAL MARKETING

As an emanating study, political marketing has originated from its mother disciplines, which are: marketing, political science and communication science (Scammell, 1999; Egan, 1999; Lees-Marshment, 2001a, 2001b, 2001c, 2004, 2008). Political marketing so far has offered the normative, prescriptive and predictive theories, concepts and models, which have been seen of being helpful to understand the whole attitude and behaviour of political actors and organizations within the contexts of policy development in governments or internal organizations or elections (Henneberg, 2004; Savigny, 2004, 2007, 2008; Hennerberg & O'Shaughnessy, 2007; O' Shaughnessy, 2010). Moreover, political marketing has also provided a set of strategies and practices, which have been adopted and developed by political parties, parties' leaders, members, activists and candidates when they have dealt with the changing political environments and addressed the needs, demands and wants of political markets in order to get elected during the elections or be successful in government (Newman, 1999a, 1999b; Lees-Marshment, 2001b, 2004, 2008; Lilleker & Lees-Marshment, 2005; Lilleker, et.al, 2007; Lees-Marshment, et.al, 2012).

So far two-fold elements have determined the development of political marketing. The first one is the ways in which political marketing scholars have realized, captured and understood political marketing and campaigning phenomena and then adopted and constructed the wide or the narrow interpretations of political marketing theories and concepts as they have underpinned and or explored these phenomena (Ormrod, 2012; Ormrod, et.al, 2013). The second one is the way in which political actors and political organizations have considered and adopted concepts, principles and procedures of marketing and advanced a set of practices and strategies of political marketing management when they have dealt with political markets and political market environment (Newman, 1999a, 1999b; Henneberg & O' Shaughnessy, 2007; Butler & Harris, 2009). Whilst such elements have been seen of being closely connected each other (Henneberg, 2002, 2004, 2008; Hennebrg & O'Shaugnessy, 2007; Savigny, 2007, 2008; Butler & Harris, 2009), a specific conceptual framework that explores the relationships between these elements and their impact on knowledge production and generation of political marketing has been still under-developed. In order to untangle this issue, following points would discuss and scrutinize the existing literature that theorise modes of knowledge creation and development.

Generally speaking, knowledge production that has been taking place in modern society in general or groups of (professional) societies in particular are indeed complex and multi-layered processes. Investigations so far have been commonly directed to understand three main sub-topics, which are the knowledge about society, the knowledge of society and the knowledge produced and generated by individual and groups of societies. Although these themes seem closely related to each other, each of them however, typically belongs to a particular field of study. In this respect, the first and the second themes have been recognized as the research domain of sociology of knowledge, while the last theme has been considered as the research domain of knowledge management.

Since 1990s, various perspectives and conceptual frameworks have been introduced to explore diverse issues of knowledge management in general and knowledge creation in particular. Moreover, various terms have been introduced to categorize the types and forms of knowledge (Baskerville & Dulipovici, 2006; Heisig, 2009). Since a specific conceptual lens to understand modes of knowledge creation and generation in the study of political marketing has not yet been advanced, the ideas of other researchers would be adopted in order to tackle this knowledge gap.

Nonaka (1994) has postulated some basic concepts and models of organisational knowledge creation. He has stated that 'knowledge is a multifaceted concept with multi-layered meanings' (Nonaka, 1994: 15). He has clarified the differentiation between knowledge and information. Moreover, as informed by idea of Polanyi (1966), he has outlined two kinds of knowledge, which are *tacit knowledge* and *explicit knowledge*. The first one is a type of knowledge, which is deeply rooted in human skills, mind, ideas, judgments, actions, experiences, commitments and involvements in a specific context, but very hard to be formulated in a formal language and transferred through communication activities. Slightly contrasting, the second one is a type of knowledge, which is much easier to be codified, communicated, reported and transmitted through a formal and systemic language (Nonaka, 1994: 16; Nonaka & Kono, 1998: 42; Chugh, 2013: 25; Chugh, et.al, 2015: 2-3).

Nonetheless, he has proposed four modes of knowledge creation and conversion wherein *the tacit knowledge*, which is produced through socialisation, could be transformed to *the explicit knowledge* through the four types of processes of what he called as socialisation, internalisation, externalisation and combination (Nonaka, 1994: 19-20). Socialisation is a self-transcending process of individuals and involves tacit to tacit knowledge transfer, while externalisation involves converting tacit knowledge into an explicit form. Internalisation focuses on converting explicit knowledge into a tacit form while the combination focuses on organising and integrating explicit into other explicit knowledge forms (Nonaka & Konno, 1998: 43). In types of processes, he has posited that under a certain condition (such as intention, chaos/fluctuation, requisite variety and redundancy), the individual knowledge can be shared, conceptualized, crystalized, justified and generated as the networking knowledge (Nonaka, 1994: 27).

Knowledge production is determined by not only the existing social base of society, but also the dynamic interactions between various agencies and (social) structures that exist in the society (Berger

& Luckmann, 1966; Gidden, 1984). As adopted ideas of Gidden (1984) and Polanyi (1966), Nonaka and Toyama, (2003: 4) have voiced that practical consciousness produces *the tacit knowledge*, while the discursive consciousness generates *the explicit knowledge*. They have also highlighted that knowledge creation is a dialectic process, which is directed by the 'dualistic nature' of interactions between the agents and structures and between the tacit and the explicit knowledge (Nonaka & Toyama, 2003: 9).

Meanwhile, Baskerville and Dulipovici (2006: 91), in line with the ideas of Nonaka and Takeuchi (1995) and Nonaka (et al., 2000), have outlined modes of the knowledge creations wherein four types of knowledge are created and generated. The first one is *sympathized knowledge*, which is realized and approved by the individual and created based on the socialization processes. The second one is *operational knowledge*, which is produced based on the internalization processes. The third knowledge type is *conceptual knowledge*, which is shaped based on the externalisation processes. In addition, the last one is *systemic knowledge*, which is constructed based on the combination processes. They have grouped the first and third types of knowledge as the tacit knowledge, while the second and fourth types as the articulated knowledge.

Based on the work of the previously outlined authors, this work proposes modes of knowledge productions and generations of political marketing as charted in Figure 1. This work assumes that political marketing scholars consider the roles and position of the media, ICT developments and the adaptation and use of the Internet and social media by political actors and organisations as a political marketing phenomenon. This work proposes that these scholars have gradually accounted the adaptations and use

Figure 1. Modes of knowledge productions and generations of political marketing
Source: Adapted from Nonaka (1994), Baskerville and Dulipovici (2006) and Nonaka and Toyama, (2003).

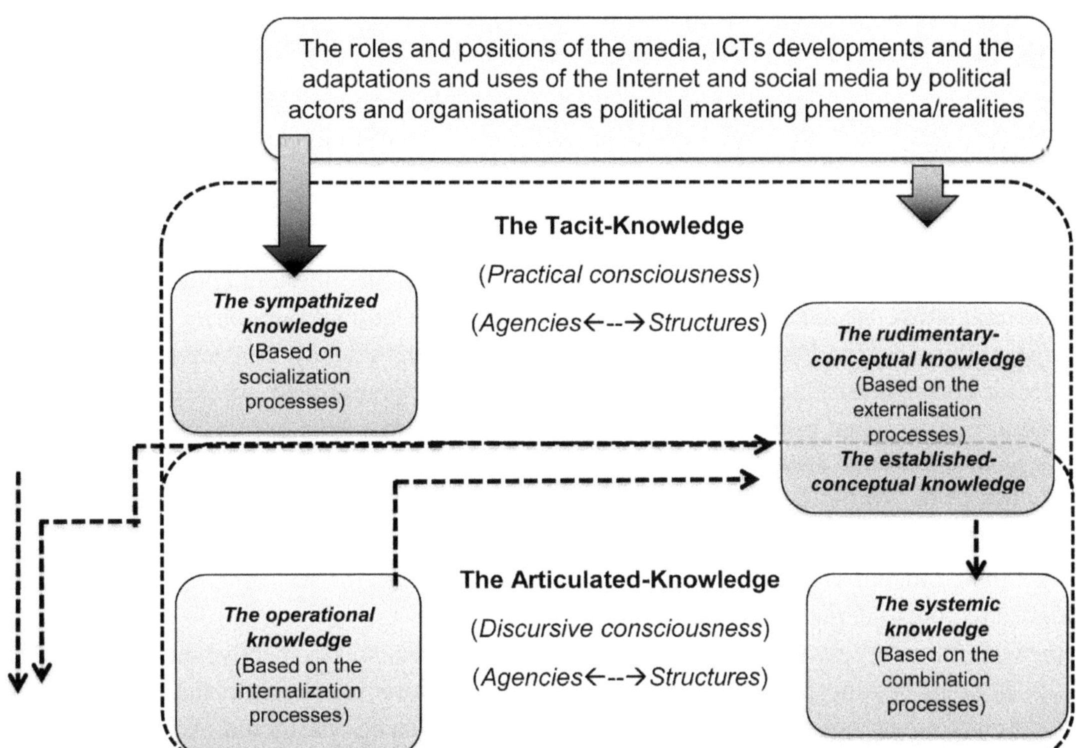

of social media for knowledge production and generation of political marketing soon after web 2.0 and various social media platforms have been widely adopted and deployed by political actors and organisations during the elections and post elections.

Social media is a type of web-based service, which is characterized by the controlled-networking activities, the visibility of users' profiles and deliberative discussion and sharing advanced by those who have got connected in various social media network systems. Slightly different from the old fashioned way of web-based services, social media has offered the handiest and the more interesting online communication facilities that provide various advantages for users. They allow individuals to develop a public or semi-public profile located in a bounded system, get connected with a list of other users with whom they possibly share and discuss the information and opinion, evaluate and distribute their list of connections to those who have entered within the system (Boyd & Ellison, 2007; Chugh, 2012). Having offered interactive web-based communication features, social media has been widely embraced by political actors and organizations, including by those who have run, involved in, engaged and participated in policy development in government or elections.

Having realized and accounted these phenomena, they then produce *the tacit-knowledge* and *the articulated-knowledge*. This work conjectures that formulation of *tacit-knowledge* is driven by individual practical consciousness, while construction of *the articulated-knowledge* is directed and stimulated by individual and collective discursive consciousness. Knowledge production is also determined by the 'dualistic nature' of interactions between the *agents* and *structures* and between *the tacit-knowledge* and *the articulated-knowledge*. Five types of knowledge are then produced and generated. As led by practical consciousness, *sympathized knowledge* of political marketing is created. Being directed by discursive consciousness, *operational knowledge* is produced. As followed by practical consciousness, *rudimentary-conceptual knowledge* is constructed. Meanwhile, as stimulated by discursive consciousness, *established-conceptual knowledge* is constructed. In this respect, as formulated from *sympathized knowledge*, *rudimentary-conceptual knowledge* would be considered as *the tacit knowledge*, while as produced from *the operational knowledge, established-conceptual knowledge* would be accounted as *articulated knowledge*. Despite stimulating the production of operational *knowledge*, the discursive consciousness also paves the way for *the systematic knowledge*.

This work postulates that these aforementioned knowledge creation and generation steps take place as a sequential process. As approved, accepted and acknowledged by peer and/or professional groups of people, *the sympathized knowledge*, which is created through the individual practical consciousness, could be leveraged as *conceptual knowledge*. *Conceptual knowledge* could also be modified as *operational knowledge*, as these peer and/or professional groups of people have widely considered this knowledge as the applicable conceptual frameworks or the better role models. As approved, accepted and acknowledged by peer and/or professional groups of people and organisations that exist in society, *the operational* and *the conceptual knowledge* could be possibly produced to *the systemic knowledge*. This work assumes that there would be only a small amount and particular kind of *sympathized knowledge* that could be generated to formulate either *the conceptual knowledge or the operational knowledge.* There would be also only a small amount and particular type of *the operational* and *the conceptual knowledge* that could be advanced to construct *the systematic knowledge.*

In line with this conceptual framework, the transcendental realism perspective introduced by Bhaskar (1998, 2008) would be adopted as a philosophical standpoint. Moreover, the meta-theoretical assumptions of political marketing proposed by Henneberg (2008) would also be considered. Additionally, an appropriate research design would be advanced as well. The next section further elaborates on these issues.

TRANSCENDENTAL REALISM PERSPECTIVE, META-THEORETICAL ASSUMPTIONS, AND RESEARCH DESIGN

Transcendental realism perspective is one of the philosophical school of thought, which is innovative, based on the argument that see there have been *'two-sides of knowledge'* that cannot be simply understood using either the naturalist or the anti-naturalist perspective (Bhaskar, 1998: 16-18, 2008: 11-14). Bhaskar (2008:15-16) highlights that it is the real structures, mechanisms and events which eternally exist and keep existing and evolving independently outside our knowledge and experience on the one hand and how our minds have addressed, defined and understood these structures, mechanisms and events on the other that have really generated the body knowledge of science. Though there is no consensus among social scientists, some called it as 'scientific realism' or 'relational realism' or 'critical realism' or 'empirical realism' perspectives (Sayer, 2000: Moses & Knutsen, 2012).

Bhaskar (1998, 2008) has claimed that this perspective offers a new insight. It ontologically and epistemologically accounts the complexity of the relationships between what Bhaskar (1998, 2008) called as the 'two-sides of knowledge', which are the 'structures and mechanisms that generate phenomena' on the one hand and the 'knowledge' produced in the 'social activity of science' on the other. For realists, they cannot be simplified and being seen as neither the reality that is separable with the human mind (following the *empiricism*) nor the reality that is being constructed by the human mind (following the *idealism*). Rather, being recognized of having the 'categorical distinctness', these 'two-sides of knowledge' have to be ontologically and epistemologically considered as being dialectically existent and eternally transformed within the whole processes of the *'social construction'* of the body of knowledge of science (Hartwig, 2008: xi). The use of realism perspective therefore allows us to avoid of what Bhaskar (1997:40, 2008:30) called as the 'epistemic fallacy' when we have understood the reality. More interestingly, as accounted these intransitive and transitive knowledge dimensions, it would be much more possible for realists for going further into what Bhaskar (1998:xii; 2008: 32) called as the 'trans-factuality (universality) of laws', regardless the complexity and differentiation of the world. It is possibly accomplished because of the existence of what Bhaskar (1998: xix) named as the 'ceteris paribus' condition, which is 'a condition for moving from fact to fact in the open-systemic world to which the laws of nature trans-factually apply as much as it is to moving from fact to value in the practical social world of belief, judgment and action' (Bhaskar, 1998: xix). In addressing these the nature of 'trans-factuality of laws' on the one hand and the 'value in the practical social world of belief, judgment and action' on the other, those who have stood for the philosophical orthodoxy, either the 'naturalist'/'positivist' or the 'anti-naturalist'/'anti-positivist', tend to understand them as the 'radical dichotomies'. Instead, for the realist, they could be seen as the 'exact parallels' (Bhaskar, 1998:xix). This perspective is essentially needed with relevance to the fact that sciences have been created based on the 'imaginative' and 'disciplined work' of scientists. This was determined by *what theories and concepts were given to them* on the one hand and *the ways they have understood the real, the actual and the empirical of levels and forms of reality* on the other (Baskhar, 2008: 176-177).

The transcendental scientific realism perspective would be helpful to tackle the innate weaknesses of the empiricism, positivism and relativism perspectives. Going beyond the naturalist and the anti-naturalist approaches, this perspective has been widely seen of being helpful to understand the multidimensional, multi structure and multi layers of social phenomena (Bhaskar, 1998, 2008; Hartwig, 2008: xi-xv: Moses & Nutsen, 2012:12-14). Since this perspective holistically analyses social phenomena using the methodological approach of natural science on the one hand and the interpretative approach on the other

(Sayer, 2000: 2-3), it allows us to leverage the research paradigm that goes beyond the naturalism and constructivism paradigms (Moses & Knutsen, 2012:12) and resolve the controversial debates between and among those who have followed the behavioralist (positivist) and social constructivist (interpretativist) paradigms (Savingy, 2007:36-37). Therefore, Pavitt (1999) has suggested that this perspective needs to be considered as *the third way* for developing theories and concepts in the field study of communication. Savigny (2007: 36-36) has also echoed this perspective would be useful to develop the theories and concepts of political marketing and formulating models of political marketing. It is utmost ultimate when we want to scrutinize on how far the existing theories and concepts or the new theoretical and conceptual propositions of political marketing can be employed to generate new knowledge in the political sphere (Henneberg, 2008:161). To such ends, we need to consider the ontological and epistemological assumptions of the exchanges and interaction processes of political marketing (Henneberg, 2008: 160-161; Savigny, 2007: 36; Henneberg & Ormrod, 2013: 97).

In specifically addressing the meta-theoretical assumptions of political marketing, Henenberg (2008: 62) has proposed four aspects. They consist of: a) the nature and structure of the exchange and interaction processes of political marketing; b) the conditions of political markets and interactions between political markets and political players of political marketing; c) the social embededness of political system and its relationships with social and the other narrative models of political representation; and d) the structural connectedness of managements of politics and the interdependent of political marketing activities in the political spheres (Henneberg, 2008: 161-163).

Based on the ideas of these authors, a scrutiny of the existing literature published by *Journal of Political Marketing*, which has released articles that cover theories, concepts and practices of political marketing and campaigning would be helpful. To this end, a mixture of qualitative and quantitative methods (Bryman, 2008; Tashakkori, 2009; Tashakkori & Creswell, 2007b; Creswell and Clark, 2007, 2011, Lunde, et.al, 2013) would be deployed. The 'concurrent research design' of these methods (Guest, 2013) would be adopted. Moreover, the quantitative and the qualitative contents analyses would be concurrently undertaken with the thematic analysis (Butler-Kisber, 2010). In this respect, the quantitative analysis using the statistical descriptive analysis would be carried out simultaneously with the thematic analysis. Such analyses are directed to map out how and the extent to which the authors of the articles published in Journal of Political Marketing in between 2002 and 2015 have considered the developments of ICTs and the use of the Internet/new media, websites and various forms of social media and their impact on politics, political marketing and campaigning as a research theme in the field of political marketing. Moreover, the qualitative content and thematic analyses would be utilized together to explore how and in which ways these authors have advanced either the existing or the new theories and concepts of political marketing and campaigning when they have investigated these issues. Further, research synthesis by aggregation and configuration (Sandelowski, et.al, 2012: 324-326) would be undertaken in order to holistically discuss how, in which ways and the extent to which the use of social media and their impact on politics, political marketing and campaigning have been taken into account for knowledge production and development of political marketing. The following section will outline the research findings.

THE ADAPTATION AND USE OF THE INTERNET AND SOCIAL MEDIA AS POLITICAL MARKETING PHENOMENA AND RESEARCH THEMES

The increasing number and forms of social media and the adaptation of social media as interactive communication platforms is closely related with the innovations and developments of the Internet and information and communication technologies (ICTs). For more than two decades, we have witnessed that the Internet has provided a Web platform, which has evolved from Web 1.0 to Web 2.0. Since the Web 2.0 has taken shape, various forms of social media sites have emerged. Such developments have been considered as an interesting theme in the field studies of politics, political marketing and campaigning by those who have published their works in social science and technology journals, including in *Journal of Political Marketing*.

Before this journal was established in 2002, there was potentially no journal that specifically discussed perspectives, theories, concepts, models and practices of political marketing. Scholars interested in such issues have favoured publishing their ideas in the *European Journal of Marketing* and *Journal of Public Affairs* and some edited-books. Most of those who have studied political marketing, released their works in these two journals and disseminated their ideas through various international conferences and edited handbooks since 1996 up to 2010 and have explored either the key concepts used in the political marketing study or boundaries of political marketing research (see Harris and Lock, 2010). Though both of these journals since 2012 up to 2015 have published plenty of articles that cover contemporary issues in political marketing, most of these articles have not yet specifically explored the uses of social media in relations with the knowledge production and development of political marketing.

As *Journal of Political Marketing* established in 2002, a number of authors who have published their works in this journal have gradually considered the development of information, communication and technologies (ICTs) and its impact on politics, political marketing and campaigning. Williams (2012) has run the qualitative content analyses of 214 articles released by this journal in the first five years (2002-2006) and the second five years (2007-2011) to explore how and the extent to which these authors have selected topics of investigation. Williams (2012: 5) has found that following topics such as election campaigns, candidates, political parties and political consultants have emerged as central themes of political marketing research. The uses of the Internet and the adaptations of Web campaigns have been gradually investigated and theorized especially when professionalization of political communication campaigning has taken shape in the US as well as European countries (Williams, 2012: 5-6). Williams (2012), however, has not yet fully detailed on how and the extent to which those who have released their works in this journal have accounted the development and the uses of social media and their impacts on politics, political marketing and campaigning as research themes in the study of political marketing.

Based on this caveat, this work then runs concurrently the quantitative, qualitative and thematic content analyses of 320 articles published by this journal in between 2002 and 2015. The analysis reveals some interesting findings, as displayed by the following figures. As seen from Figure 2 the total number of articles that discuss the development of communication technologies (ICTs) and the use of the Internet and their impact on politics, political marketing and campaigning has gradually rocketed from 2.81% in 2002 to 19.68% in 2015. Moreover, as charted by Figure 3, the percentage of articles that cover such issues has increased from 22.25% in 2002 to 51.21% in 2003. However, it has then dramatically declined from 14.24% in 2014 to 0% in 2007. Though, it escalated from 12.00% in 2008 to 38.09 in 2011, it has then dramatically decreased to 9.52% in 2012. Even though it rose from 14.28% in 2003 to 18.75% in 2014, it has slightly dropped to 17.04% in 2015. Furthermore, these articles cover four main research themes, which are: e-government and e-politics (6.87%), cyber-democracy (3.75%), the Internet and new media (5.94%) and the Internet and social media (2.81%), as seen from Figure 4.

Figure 5 then details per cent of a total number of these articles that focus on these themes. As seen, 12.5% of total articles published in 2002, 39.02% of total articles released in 2003 and 4% of articles published in 2008 have focused on e-government and e-politics. Meanwhile, 7.50% of the total articles

Figure 2. A sum of articles (in %) published in Journal of Political Marketing in between 2002 and 2015 that cover the ICTs development and the uses of the Internet and their impacts on politics, political marketing and campaigning
Source: Journal of Political Marketing, 2002-2015.

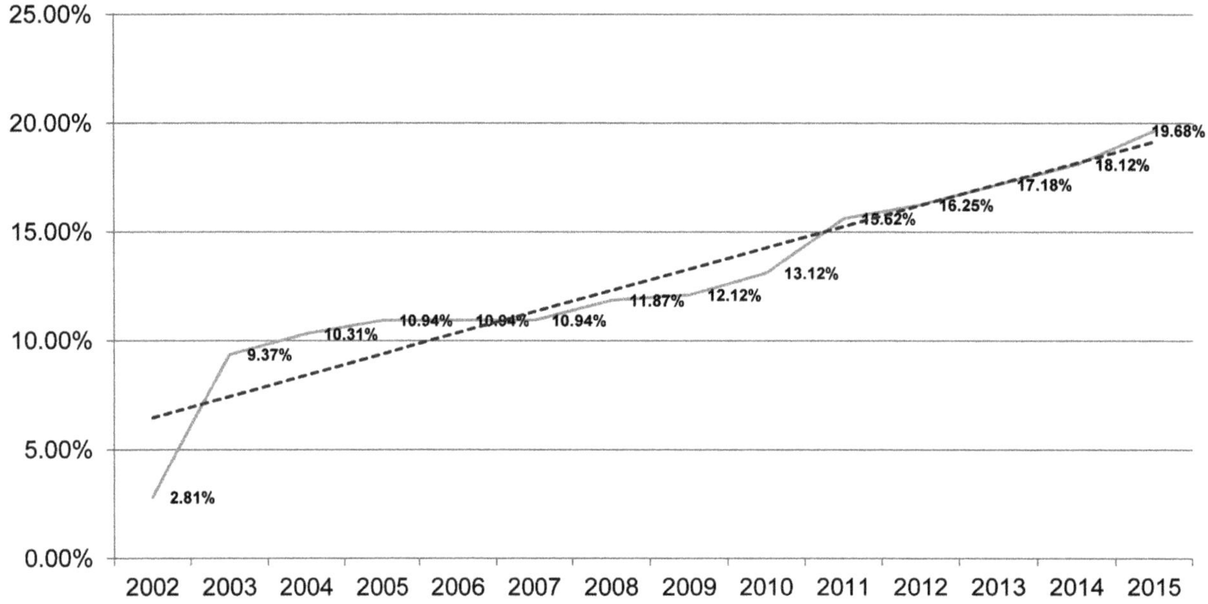

Figure 3. A percent of articles published in Journal of Political Marketing in between 2002 and 2015 (vol 1-14) that cover the ICTs Development and the uses of the Internet and their impacts on politics, political marketing and campaigning
Source: Journal of Political Marketing, 2002-2015.

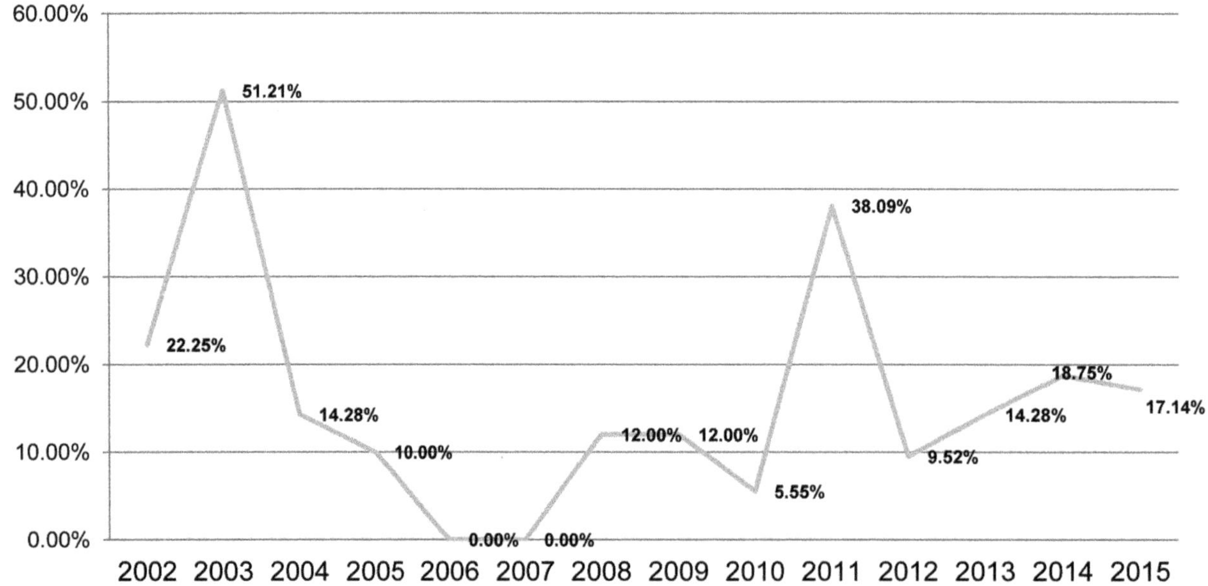

Figure 4. A sum of articles (in %) published in Journal of Political Marketing in between 2002 and 2015 that Focus on e-government and e-politics, cyber-democracy, the Internet and new media and the Internet and social media network as a research theme
Source: Journal of Political Marketing, 2002-2015.

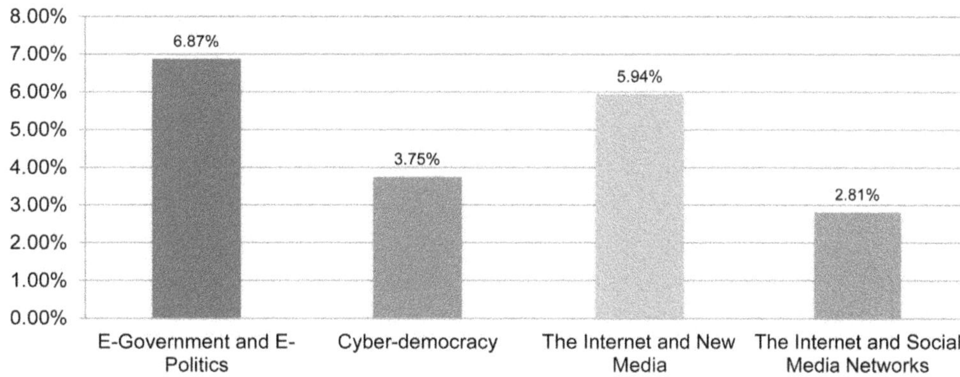

published in 2002, 7.3% of total articles released in 2003, 4.76% of articles released in 2004, 10% of articles released in 2005, 4% of articles released in 2008, or 8% of total articles released in 2009, 5.55% of total articles released in 2010, 14.28% of total articles published in 2011, 4.79% of total articles published in 2012, 4.79% of total articles published in 2013, 12.50% of total articles published in 2014 and 2.85% of total articles published in 2015 have discussed the uses of Internet and the new media as a tool of political marketing and campaigning. In the meantime, 2.50% of total articles released in 2002, 4.87% of total articles published in 2003, 9.52% of total articles published in 2004, 4% of total articles published in 2008, 4% of total articles published in 2009, 19.04% of total articles published in 2011 and 4.79% of total articles published in 2012 have explored the uses of the Internet and the new media and their impact on the practices of political marketing.

A sum of articles, which cover e-government, e-politics and cyber-democracy, is positively correlated with a sum of articles that discusses the Internet/new media and social media uses and their impact on politics, political marketing and campaigning. There is a linear relationship between these articles. As charted by Figure 6, this relationship is numerically significant. Whilst the first one has increased from 6 articles (1.87% of total articles) to 34 articles, the second one has escalated as well stretching from 0.94% in 2002 to 9.37% in 2015. However, while the first one has remained stagnant since 2012 up to 2015, the second one has rocketed dramatically from 18 articles (or 5.6% of total articles) to 30 articles (or 9.37% of total articles). Overall, the first one however, has been higher over the second one.

While those who have published their ideas in this journal in between 2002 and 2010 have shown interest in exploring the ICT developments and the use of the Internet and Web campaigns, as a central theme—in relations with e-government, e-politics, cyber-democracy, e-campaign, web-based marketing and campaigning and online political marketing, whilst those who have published their works in this journal in between 2011 and 2015 have gradually accounted for the use of the Internet and social media and their impact on political marketing and campaigning as a primary theme. As seen from Figure 5, 4.76% of articles published in 2011, 9.52% of total articles published in 2013, 6.25% of total articles released in 2014 and 14.28% of total articles released in 2015 have explored this issue.

Scholars who have released their works in *Journal of Political Marketing* in between 2012 and 2015 have adopted less of the broad and rudimentary concepts, such as e-government, e-politics and cyber-

Figure 5. A percent of articles published in Journal of Political Marketing in between 2002 and 2015 that discuss e-government and e-politics, cyber-democracy, the Internet and new media and the Internet and social media network as research themes
Source: Journal of Political Marketing, 2002-2015.

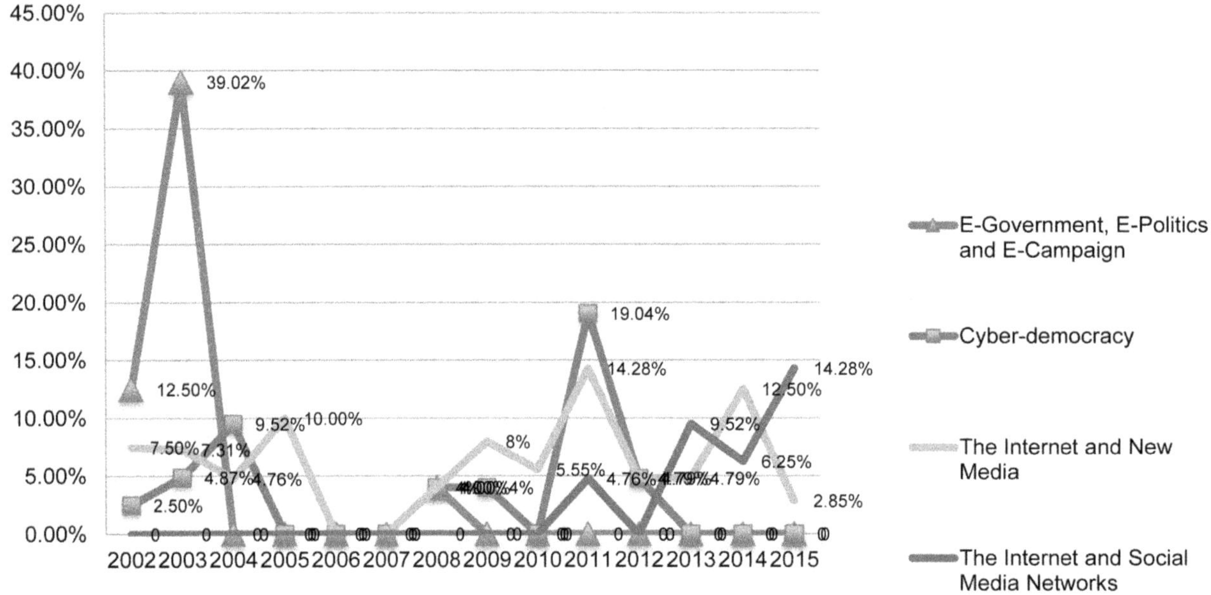

Figure 6. The numerical relationships between a commulative number of articles that examines e-government, e-polititics and cyber-democracy and a sum of articles that assesses the Internet, new media and social media networks
Source: Journal of Political Marketing, 2002-2015.

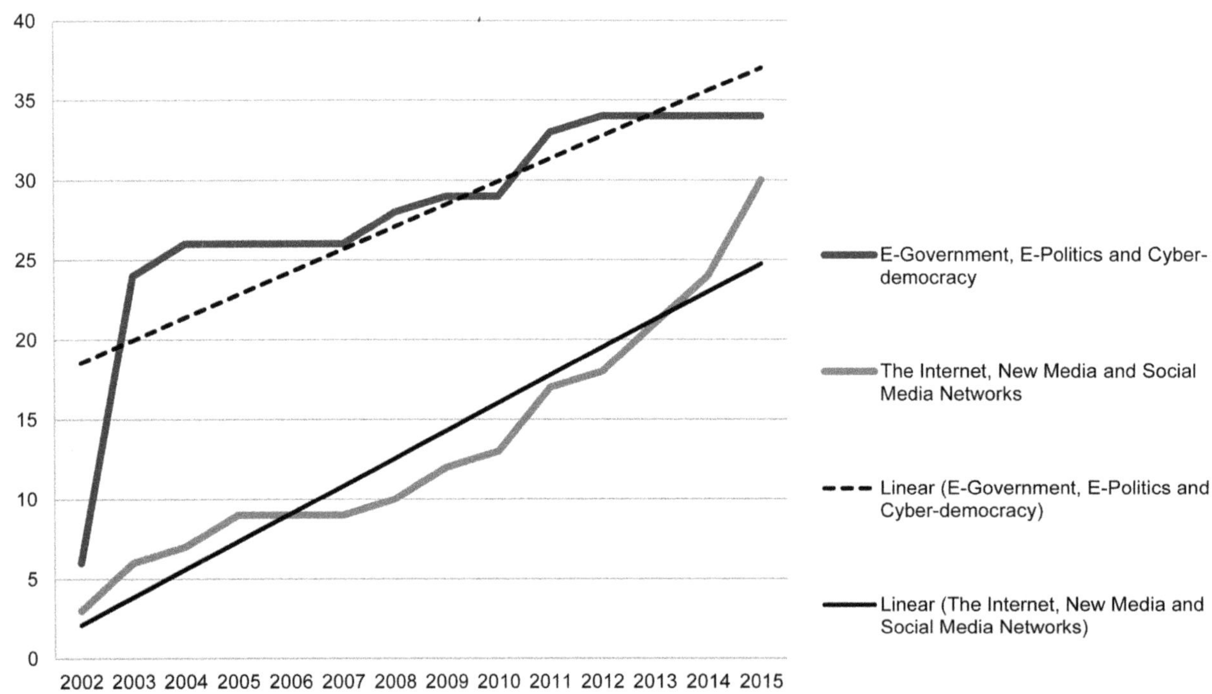

Figure 7. A percent of articles published in Journal of Political Marketing in between 2011 and 2015 that Specifically focus on the uses of social media networks and their impacts on politics, political marketing and campaigning
Source: Journal of Political Marketing, 2011-2015.

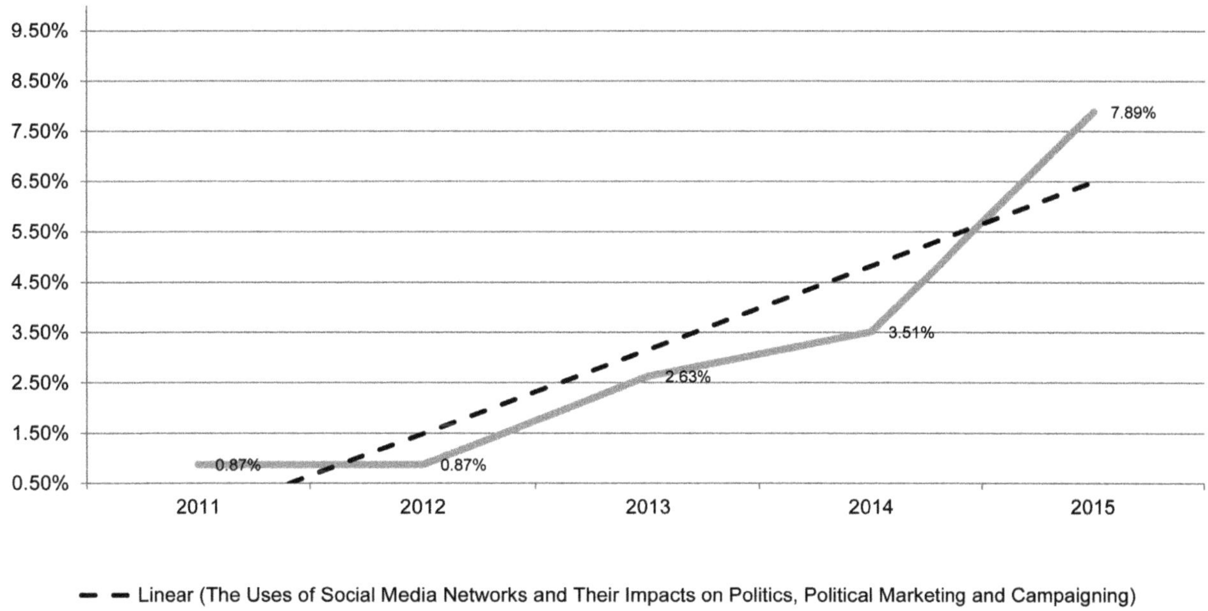

democracy. Rather, they have favoured adopting and developing the more advanced and specific concepts such as e-campaign, web-based marketing and campaigning, online/e-political marketing and e-branding and interactive political communication. More importantly, some of them have strongly shown interest in exploring social media use and its impact on politics, political marketing and campaigning as primary research. A sum of articles that specifically focuses on social media therefore has substantially increased As seen from Figure 7, it has been gradually soaring from only 0.87% in 2011 to 7.89% in 2015.

Generally speaking, a total number of those who have published their works in *Journal of Political Marketing* in between 2002 and 2015 and explored the adaptation and the use of Internet, new media and websites in political sphere have substantially increased cumulatively stretching from 2.81% in 2002 to 19.68% in 2015. However, a sum of those who have released their work in this journal and specifically focused on social media use and its impact on political marketing and campaigning has remained at a low level, which is cumulatively only 1.56%. There was no article published by this journal in between 2002 and 2010 that has specifically addressed the adaptation and use of social media as a central theme since social media platforms and the advanced-native social bottoms of these social media, as we see today, were still under-developed.

FROM THE SYMPHATIZED AND THE RUDIMENTARY-CONCEPTUAL KNOWLEDGE TO THE OPERATIONAL AND THE ESTABLISHED-KNOWLEDGE

The qualitative and thematic content analyses of 320 articles published in *Journal of Political Marketing* in between 2002 and 2015 reveals the following findings. Led by the practical consciousness, Curtin and Sommer (2003: 108) have come up with *the sympathised knowledge*, which was then transformed to *the rudimentary-conceptual knowledge* as their work was published in *Journal of Political Marketing*. They have proposed that the uses of the Internet and Web Campaigns have taken place in the US politics during 1996 US presidential election. As Bush and Gore campaigns were strongly interested in adopting Web Campaign during the 2000 US presidential election, the development of ICTs and Internet and the use of the Internet and Web Campaign and their impacts on politics have been gradually accounted for to capture transformations of strategies and practices of political marketing and campaigning. Moreover, Sherman and Schiffman (2002) who have released their work in the first volume of *Journal of Political Marketing* have highlighted that the advancement of Web Campaigns not only has transformed the US politics, in general, and practices and strategies of political marketing and campaigning, in particular, but also has opened fertile political marketing research. As directed by the practical consciousness, Sherman and Schiffman (2002) have suggested developing *the established-conceptual knowledge*.

Slightly different to these authors, Johnson (2002a) has advanced a new *rudimentary-conceptual knowledge*, which is *a cyber-democracy*. This conceptual knowledge has been deployed to explore the adaptations and uses of the Internet and Web Campaigns during the 2000 US presidential election. He has optimistically viewed that the Internet uses in political sphere has carried out a similar impact as the television did during the 1960 US election (Johnson, 2002a: 214). Regardless of the existing plenty of pessimistic views related to the impacts of the adaptation of the Internet and Web Campaigns in politics, he has outlined that Websites as new communication and campaign platforms have offered political benefits. He has stated as follows:

.... Electronic campaigns could use their Websites to persuade and inform voters twenty-four hours a day...electronic campaigns could use e-mail; polling could be conducted online, volunteers could be activated and informed, and fundraising could be conducted online. Websites could level the playing field: a campaign, short on funds but with dedicated volunteers, could fight against a well-funded professionally based campaign by hiring a college kid to design a simple Website, and thus get the message out to voters eager for issues papers and persuasion (Johnson, 2002a: 214).

Johnson (2003a, 2003b, 2004a, 2004b) has then advanced this knowledge as *the established-conceptual knowledge*. Johnson (2003a) has deployed this knowledge to examine electronic voting. Moreover, Johnson (2003b, 2004a) has also deployed it to explore the ways members of the US Congress have responded to the online communication environment using the interactive web and e-mail. Jonson (2004b) has scrutinized the development of the Internet uses and its impact on transformation of campaigning during the 2004 US Presidential election. More importantly, as roughly evaluated on how and in ways political parties, parties' candidates and interest groups have harnessed Web Campaigns during this election, Johnson (2004b: 111-112) come up with *operational knowledge* and voiced the following:

Candidates, political parties, and interest groups have come to rely on electronic communications, and there is no going back. But consider this: No successful presidential campaign can function without electronic communications, but no presidential campaign can be successful if it relies solely on it. Campaign websites, blogs, discussion groups, pop-up advertising, instant messaging and e-mail are all vital; but they cannot replace the seemingly old fashioned techniques of grassroots organizing and television campaigning. (Johnson, 2004b: 111-112)

Nonetheless, Johnson (2002b), in addressing the adaptation of Web Campaign by those who have ruled the government, has introduced the subsequent *rudimentary-conceptual knowledge*, which is *e-government*. This conceptual knowledge has also been advanced as *the operational knowledge* to describe several potential advantages offered by State and local government Websites, as follows:

State and local government Web sites, while varying considerably, are now providing an extraordinary amount of information that was unavailable in the pre-online days. But there is still far to go. (Johnson, 2002b: 102)

Likewise Johnson (2002b), the other authors such as Curtin (2002), Curtin (et.al, 2002) and Vis-Sommer (2003) have also advanced this knowledge as *the established-conceptual knowledge* to portray the rise of electronic government in the US politics. Though implicitly hinted that this concept could be furthered especially when voters via the state and local government websites have easily retrievable political information, these authors has detailed less the definition and operationalization of this concept in order to be accepted as *the systematic knowledge*. While Johnson (2002a) has not yet sufficiently explained the extent to which *e-government* has taken shape in the US politics, Curtin (et.al, 2002) has adopted this knowledge to explore on how and the degree of which 223 major American cities populated by 100000 citizens or more have advanced the online services through Websites. This knowledge has been also adopted by Vis-Sommer (2003) as well to explore the development of Web Campaign taken by five ministries of UN members.

Shaw (2002) and Williams (et.al, 2002) have created *the established-conceptual knowledge*, which is 'e-campaign', while Curtin and Sommer (2003) and Sommer and Tavlin (2003) have introduced the rudimentary-conceptual knowledge, which are 'online politics' and 'e-politics'. As used concept 'e-campaign', Shaw (2002) has attempted to explore how and the degree of which: a) voters seek political information from party websites and perceive political information displayed in these websites; and b) political parties and parties' candidates have adopted the Internet/Web Campaign during the 2000 Presidential Election for internal communication and grassroots mobilization. Moreover, Williams (et. al, 2002) has deployed this concept to assess the increasing number of the Website Campaigns of party' candidates those want to get elected as members of US Senate during the 2000 election. Unlike wise to these authors, Curtin and Sommer (2003: 108) have favoured utilizing concept 'e-politics' to portray the emergence and developments of what they called as 'online campaigning' since the 1996 election up to the 2000 election. Though this remains existing as *a rudimentary-conceptual knowledge*, this concept however, has been advanced as *the operational knowledge*. He has stated the following:

The 1996 election cycle was the earliest that anyone can honestly say online campaigning really occurred...During the 1998 election cycle, an increasing number of congressional and gubernatorial candidates, and even a good number of state and local candidates, had moved their campaigns online in one form or another–although in reality one could hesitate to call many of them more than a mere online presence. It was the 2000 presidential election cycle that really sparked the birth of online politics, or e-politics as we now know it...The 2000 election was also noteworthy for a range of online experiments beyond the typical brochure type site, although even then the cost of the more innovative technology was still prohibitive for all but the largest and richest political campaigns. (Curtin & Sommer, 2003: 108)

Likewise, Curtin and Sommer (2003), Sommer and Tavlin (2003) have also deployed this knowledge to assess the emergence of e-politics and its impact on political campaigns in the US politics. They have then also generated this knowledge as the operational knowledge. He has spelled out as follows.

After 2000, we stopped working normal political campaigns to concentrate on and create new, useful alternative Internet political options. We weren't alone. Others were just as smart and had caught the wind. Most of us were betting that sooner or later, citizens might be so energized with their own e-involvement and voter disgust, they might actually use the convenience of the Web to chase away the dominance of fat-cat politics, and help to create confidence in a fair, long overdue, fresh, new grassroots-energized citizen democracy, changing America for the better. (Sommer & Tavlin, 2003: 88)

Unlike these authors, some have favoured the development of American campaign model during the 2000 US presidential election (Espindola, 2002; Holtz-Bacha, 2002). As the Internet and new electronic communication have been vigorously innovative and widely adopted across the globe, Espindola (2002) and Hotz-Bacha (2002) have introduced the new rudimentary-conceptual knowledge, which are 'Americanization' of campaigning and 'professionalization' of political communication and campaigning. Espindola (2002) has favoured using the second concept to assess the changing nature of campaigning in Argentina, Chile and Uruguay during the 1999 elections. Meanwhile, Holtz-Bacha (2002) has utilized this second concept to capture the campaign transformation of Germany political parties. As a rudimentary-conceptual knowledge, 'professionalization' of political communication and campaigning has carried out various interpretations (see Mancini, 1999; Plasser & Plasser, 2002) and entailed disputable debates that need to be sufficiently clarified (see Lilleker & Negrine, 2001, 2002; Negrine, et.al, 2007, 2008). Anumber of authors have leveraged this knowledge as whether the operational or the established-conceptual or the systematic knowledge by proposing its definitions, indicators and measurements to understand the ways and the degrees of which political parties have adopted the Internet and Web Campaigns during the elections and in between the elections (see Gibson & Rommele, 2001, 2009; Esser & Tenscher, 2005a, 2005b; Stromback, 2007, 2009; Tenscher, et.al. 2012; Tenscher, 2013; Tenscher & Mykkanen, 2013, 2014; Vergeers, et.al, 2013). Unlikewise 'Americanization' of campaigning that remains exists as the rudimentary-conceptual knowledge, 'professionalization' of political communication and campaigning has been advanced not only as the operational knowledge, but also as the established conceptual and the systematic knowledge.

Despite introducing new frameworks, most of those who have published their ideas in *Journal of Political Marketing* in between 2004 and 2014 have also considered the existing theories and concepts of marketing management when political parties and parties' politicians and candidates to gain electorates' support during the elections have gradually harnessed the Internet and Web Campaigns. For example: Demenrtzis (et.al, 2005) have taken into account ideas of Kotler and Kotler (1999) to generate the rudimentary-conceptual knowledge, which are online political marketing and e-political marketing. Moreover, a number of authors have also developed the existing theories of political communication and political sciences to generate the rudimentary-conceptual knowledge, which was then deployed to understand not only the ways American voters have accessed and used the Internet in between 1997-2007 and in between 2004 and 2008 (Hall & Sinclair, 2011), but also how and the degree to which various forms of social media have impacted on political attitudes of American young electorates during the 2008 US presidential election (Towner & Dulio, 2011). Additionally, though advanced, the rudimentary-conceptual knowledge of online political marketing and campaigning, the other authors have investigated various themes, such as the level of adaptation of Web campaign technologies (Foot, et.al, 2009), campaign websites of candidates and endorsement of organizations (Williams, et.al, 2009), the uses of Internet and political blog, online videos and YouTube as campaign platforms during the elections (Wallsten, 2011; Jackson, 2011; Vesnic-Alujevic & Bauwel, 2014) and websites of female candidates and gender-based strategies (Schneider, 2014)

Generally speaking, articles published in *Journal of Political Marketing* in between 2002 and 2011 have discussed the ICTs development and adaptation of the Internet in the fields of politics, political marketing and campaigning, but covered less the uses of social media and their impact on political marketing and campaigning. In slightly contrast, articles published in *Journal of Political Marketing* Vol. 9 (2011) that have focused on this issue have been framed using a broad theme 'money and technology'. In this respect, the emergence of social media networking facilitated by the Internet has been gradually accounted as a leading research theme to produce *the rudimentary-conceptual, the operational knowledge* and *the established-conceptual* of political marketing. *The rudimentary-conceptual knowledge* has taken shape when the 2008 Obama campaign during the 2008 US presidential election has been widely seen of being successfully harnessing the websites (My.BarackObama.com), Facebook and YouTube as a strategic online tool, which is combined with the offline strategies directed either to attract campaign donators or persuade and mobilize some groups of electorates (Hassell, 2011; Lipsitz & Panagopoulos, 2011: 47; Christenson & Smidt, 2011: 24; Garcia-Castanon, et.al, 2011: 33-34). In addressing online campaigning during the 2008 US presidential election, Panagopoulus (2011) has formulated *the rudimentary-conceptual knowledge.* He has stated as follows:

Of the many noteworthy, and even historic, aspects of the 2008 presidential election campaign cycle, developments related to money and technology in political campaigns were especially significant...A wide range of developments in online communications, including but by no means limited to the proliferation of social networking (Facebook) and video sharing (YouTube) Web sites, have essentially revolutionized political campaigns, creating unparalleled opportunities for interaction and information acquisition and helping to make 2008 a watershed year in the trajectory of political campaign history. (Panagopoulos, 2011: 1)

A year later, Towner and Dullio (2012) have strongly called political scholars to further conduct innovative studies that address the developments of technology and new media and their impact on campaigning and relationships among journalists, candidates and citizens. They have implicitly called for developing *the established-conceptual, the operational and the systemic knowledge* that holistically capture and theorise the adaptations and uses of new media and their impacts on political campaigning. In addressing this issue, they have voiced as follows:

These rapid changes in technology and new media require scholars to update the design and direction of future research. Clearly, new media are altering the process of campaigning for political office, changing the relationships among journalists, political candidates, and citizens. Scholars are just beginning to inquire into the empirical links between new media and political attitudes, leaving many questions unanswered and theories untested...In a way, this article is a call to new media researchers to grasp some of these changes and develop innovative research that builds up our empirical evidence and expands our theoretical understanding. (Towner & Dullio, 2012: 112)

Though they advocated the importance of developing these types of knowledge, Towner and Dullio (2012) have not yet specifically suggested to develop the *well-established-conceptual* and *systemic knowledge* that can be deployed to capture and explain the developments and uses of social media and their impact on politics—in general—and political marketing and campaigning—in particular. Political marketing scholars have paid much more attention to social media uses and their impacts on politics when various groups of social media users have successfully triggered political revolution in the Middle East. This has indicated the pivotal roles of social media in shoring up a political movement and campaign against the authoritarian regime. In addressing this issue, Newman (2012) has outlined *the rudimentary-conceptual knowledge*. He has stated as follows:

The world has recently witnessed a series of political revolutions in the Middle East that have resulted in authoritarian leaders who had been in power for decades being overthrown by a coalition of citizens. These revolutions stemmed from political movements and grassroots efforts that relied on the use of social networks and social media tools to organize and plan demonstrations as well as public responses to government initiatives to stop these actions. These tools are one part of the arsenal of hi-tech political campaigns carried out in democracies around the world that are studied by political marketers. (Newman, 2012: 2)

Despite of highlighting the pivotal roles of social media on the Middle East revolutions, Newman (2012) has postulated *the operational knowledge*, which is derived from the uses of social media during the 2008 Obama campaign. He has spotlighted that social media as a campaign tool of Obama to support political movement has led him get elected during the 2008 US presidential election.

The 2008 Obama campaign has been widely seen as a role model of online political marketing and campaigning. Since widely acknowledged on successfully harnessing social media, especially Facebook, this model has been gradually adopted across the globe (Miller, 2013). Further research has been vigorously conducted to explore Web Campaign and social media use within the context of the 2010 UK General Election. For example, in addressing mode of campaigning of parties during this election, Higgins and Smith (2013) have examined on how and in which ways leaders of Conservative and Labour Parties have attempted exploiting various new media platforms that combine official party websites, personal blogs and webcasts. Slightly different with these authors, Lilleker and Jackson (2013) have postulated a new *established-conceptual knowledge*, which is *Obama-ization of e-campaign*. As informed by ideas of O'Reilly (2005), Anderson (2007), Chadwick (2007), Anstead and Chadwick (2008) and Lilleker (et. al, 2010), Lilleker and Jackson (2013) have deployed this conceptual knowledge to understand mode of online campaign strategies of the UK political parties the (main parliamentary parties—Conservative, Labour, and Liberal Democrat—and three non-parliamentary national challengers—Green, UK Independence, and British National) during the 2010 general election. This conceptual knowledge is also advanced as *the operational knowledge*, as it is used to explore the 'Internet selling and campaigning' and the 'marketing communication mix' strategies of these parties during this election.

Meanwhile, since theoretical debates related to political branding have been gradually accounted for, some authors have then considered the importance of social media to develop theories and concepts of political branding (Busby and Cronshaw, 2015; Lilleker, 2015; Rutter, et.al, 2015). Busby and Cronshaw (2015) have simply highlighted that new and social media potentially pave the way for creating a type of *political branding* directed by consumers. Slightly different with these authors, Lilleker (2015) has theorized a conceptual lens to understand how UK parties and these parties' members elected to the House of Commons in the period 2007 to 2010 have harnessed the Internet and social media, such as Facebook, Twitter and YouTube, as interactive platforms for developing of what he called as the *e-branding strategies*. Slightly contrasting, Rutter (et.al, 2015) have favoured adopting idea of Aaker (1997) to explore the ways in which the five UK political parties have differentiated themselves using the *brand personality*, which is constructed through their websites. These new understanding of political branding so far has remained exist as *the rudimentary-conceptual knowledge* and has not yet been properly advanced as whether *the established-conceptual* or *the operational or the systematic knowledge*.

Some authors have specifically addressed developments and uses of social media in the fields of politics, political marketing and campaigning. Cogburn and Espinoza-Vasquez (2011) have created *the rudimentary-conceptual knowledge*, which is called as 'a networked nominee' and 'a networked nation'. The first one has been deployed to understand the role of Web 2.0 and social media in a presidential campaign, while the second one has been deployed to explore the role of Web 2.0 and social media on generating new social movements that shore up the 2008 Obama presidential campaign. Moreover, Cameron (et.al, 2014) has produced the other *rudimentary-conceptual knowledge*, which is *the networks effect of social media on the election results*. It is derived from the types and the degrees of the relationships between the size of candidates' social media on Facebook and Twitter and a total number of voters those who have casting their votes to these candidates during the 2011 New Zealand general election. Furthermore, Bode and Dalrymple (2014) have proposed the effects of Twitter, as a popular social media, on political interest, political knowledge, trust to the media, political engagement and online and offline political participation. While these authors have favoured generating *the rudimentary-conceptual knowledge*, Harris and Harrigan (2015) have been interested in developing *the operational knowledge*. They explored the uses of social media by political parties in the UK politics during the 2010 UK General Election and by the Obama campaign during the 2008 US presidential election, and have scrutinized the extent to which the social media can be considered for establishing the long- or the short-terms online and offline relationship strategy. Similarly, Parsons and Rowling (2015) have also proposed *the operational and the established-conceptual knowledge*, which is called as e-*relationship marketing*. This knowledge discusses the inherent challenges of the uses of social media by politicians when they have favoured an interest in developing political relationship with the electorates.

Generally speaking, either the wider or the narrow interpretations of political marketing (see Ormrod, 2012; Ormrod, et.al, 2013), *the rudimentary-* and *the established-conceptual knowledge* have been introduced to capture and understand the ICTs development and the use of Internet/new media, web campaigns and social media in the fields of politics, political marketing and campaigning. In this respect, those who have published articles in this journal in between 2002 and 2003 have been much more interested in advancing *the rudimentary-conceptual knowledge*, such as *cyber-democracy* (Johnson, 2002a; 2003a, 2003b, 2004a, 2004b), *e-politics* (Curtin and Sommer, 2003), *e-government* (Johnson, 2002b; Curtin, et.al, 2002; Vis-Sommer, 2003) and *e-campaign* (Shaw, 2002; Williams, et.al, 2002). Though widely adopted by political marketing scholars, *cyber-democracy* and *e-politics* have remained existent as *the rudimentary-conceptual knowledge*. Meanwhile, *e-government and e-campaign* as *the rudimentary-conceptual knowledge* have then been advanced as *the established-conceptual knowledge* and modified as *the operational knowledge* since they have been strongly accepted and acknowledged as pivotal and fruitful concepts to explain the ICTs development and the adaptation and use of the Internet and social media by political actors and organisations in political sphere.

Meanwhile, following the narrow interpretation, those who have released their studies in *Journal of Political Marketing* in between 2004 and 2015 have advanced *some conceptual knowledge*—such as *online/e-political marketing* (Demenrtzis, et.al, 2005), *Web campaign* (Yannas & Lappas (2005), *Web campaigning* (Carlson, 2007) and *The Obama-ization of e-campaigning* (Lilleker & Jackson, 2013) and some *operational knowledge* such as *Web-based advocacy* (Williams, et.al, 2007), *Web-based marketing* (Williams, et.al, 2010), *Web-based political campaign* (Wu & Dahmen, 2010), and *e-branding and interactive political communication* (Lilleker, 2014) and *e-relationship marketing* (Parsons & Rowling (2015). The authors however have not yet fully advanced *the systematic knowledge* based on *the operational knowledge* they have proposed. For example, Demenrtzis (et.al, 2005) who have introduced the concept *online/e-political marketing* has not yet further clarified both the similarities and the differences between this concept and the other concepts such as *e-government* (Johnson, 2002b; Curtin, et.al, 2002; Vis-Sommer, 2003), *e-politics* (Curtin & Sommer, 2003) and *e-campaign* (Shaw, 2002; Williams, et.al, 2002). Moreover, Lilleker and Jackson (2013) who have proposed the concept *e-campaigning* have not yet sufficiently discussed this concept with the other concepts such as *Web campaign* (Yannas & Lappas (2005), *Web campaigning* (Carlson, 2007), *Web-based advocacy* (Williams, et.al, 2007), *Web-based marketing* (Williams, et.al, 2010) and *Web-based political campaign* (Wu & Dahmen, 2010). Furthermore, Parsons and Rowling (2015) have advanced the concept *e-relationship marketing* have not yet fully scrutinized the relationships between this concept and the other concepts, such as e-*branding and interactive political communication* (Lilleker, 2014). In addition, Lilleker (2014) who has attempted conflicting concepts of *e-branding* and *interactive political communication* has not yet systematically delineated dimensions and indicators of e-branding and interactive political communication. Nonetheless, though authors of these articles have accounted the developments and the uses of social media by political parties and parties' leaders, candidates and politicians as well as by electorates/voters, most of them however, have much more preferred accounting the social media as part of an extension of Web Campaigns facilitated by the Internet/new media. In this sense, the use, adaptation and development of the Internet and new media have been widely accounted for as a central theme when they have discussed the strategies, practices and activities of online political marketing and campaigning of these parties and parties' leaders, candidates and politicians.

In the meantime, those who have published their works in this journal since 2011 up to 2015 have highlighted the important roles of social media on driving political revolutions and transforming the election campaigning (Newman, 2012) and theorized the uses of social media and their impacts on politics, political marketing and campaigning (Cogburn & Espinoza-Vasquez, 2011; Cameron, et, al., 2014; Bode & Dalrymple, 2014; Parsons and Rowling, 2015; Harris and Harrigan, 2015). Most of them have not yet offered *the established-conceptual knowledge, the operational knowledge* and *the systematic-knowledge* to capture such issues however. For example, though Cogburn and Espinoza-Vasquez (2011) have introduced concepts 'a networked nominee' and 'a networked nation' when they have captured the 2008 Obama presidential campaign, these authors however have not yet fully detailed these concepts. As derived from their subjective views, these authors have offered a less sufficient theoretical explanation and measurements. Such proposed knowledge seems difficult to be adopted and universally accepted and applied as *the systematic knowledge*. Moreover, although some authors have proposed *the rudimentary-conceptual knowledge* to understand the networks effects of social media on the election results (Cameron, et, al., 2014) and the effects of Twitter uses on political interest, political knowledge, trust to the media, political engagement and online and offline political participation (Bode and Dalrymple, 2014), they however have attempted less to develop *the systematic knowledge* that can be used to quantitatively and qualitatively analyse the effects of the social media uses on strategies and practices of political marketing and campaigning of political party and party' leaders, candidates and politicians on the one hand and on political knowledge, engagement and participation of the electorates/voters on the other. Additionally, even though sufficiently constructed, *e-relationship marketing* (Parsons and Rowling, 2015) and the long- or the short-terms of *the online and offline relationship strategy* (Harris & Harrigan, 2015) as the established-conceptual knowledge have not yet been properly advanced as *the systematic knowledge*.

CONCLUSION AND FURTHER RESEARCH RECOMMENDATIONS

Knowledge always takes shape as a multifaceted concept with multi-layered meanings (Nonaka, 1994:15). Knowledge is also produced and generated by scholars from particular point of view and stemmed from particular context wherein the multi dimensions of (social) realities and information have been realized and accounted (Nonaka & Toyama, 2003: 3). As there has always been a social base, the dynamic interactions between the agencies and structures to determine these realities and information that exist in society (Berger & Luckmann, 1966; Gidden, 1984), appropriate conceptual frameworks that can be deployed to holistically understand the knowledge creation and generation are deemed important. Since such frameworks have not yet been advanced within the specific field of political marketing, this work has proposed a specific theoretical framework to capture and explore modes of the knowledge production and generation of political marketing.

The quantitative, qualitative and thematic content analyses of 320 articles published in *Journal of Political Marketing* in between 2002 and 2015, this work highlights the following conclusions. *Firstly,* the quantitative and thematic content analyses of these articles, this work reveals that political marketing scholars who have published their works in this journal have gradually considered the ICTs development and the adaptation and use of the Internet and social media by political actors and organisations in political sphere for the knowledge creation and generation of political marketing. It is indicated by a sum of articles that cover issues related to the Internet/new media, Web Campaigns and social media, which have been substantially increased from 2.81% in 2002 to 19.68% in 2015; though a sum of article that specifically discusses social media use and its impacts on politics, political marketing and campaigning has still been low, at only 1.56% of total articles.

Secondly, the qualitative and thematic content analyses of these articles uncovers that the ICT development and the adaptation and use of the Internet and social media by political actors and organisations in political sphere have stimulated political marketing scholars who have published their works in *Journal of Political Marketing* in between 2002 and 2015 to produce the rudimentary-conceptual or the operational or the established-conceptual knowledge of political marketing. Most of these scholars have advanced the rudimentary-conceptual knowledge; some of them transformed this knowledge into *the* operational knowledge and or the established-conceptual knowledge. There have been a small number of these scholars who have been strongly interested in generating the established-conceptual and the operational knowledge and attempted developing the systematic knowledge. Though acknowledged as a useful conceptual framework to capture and understand the ICT development and the adaptation and use of the Internet and social media by political actors and organisations in political sphere, these kinds of knowledge have not yet been fully advanced as systematic knowledge.

Thirdly, the qualitative and thematic content analyses of these articles indicates that the leading social media platforms, such as Facebook and Twitter, have been gradually accounted for knowledge production and generation of political marketing since the 2008 Obama presidential campaign has succeeded. Harnessing Facebook and Twitter as a campaign platform and strategic tools to raise campaign funds and mobilize electorates have been important for political change in the Middle East revolution. Most of the political marketing scholars who have released their works in *Journal of Political Marketing* in between 2011 and 2015 however have still considered various social media platforms as part of Web 2.0. There have been only some of these scholars who have specifically addressed the adaptation and use of social media by political actors and organisations as a primary research theme to produce either *the rudimentary-conceptual* or *the operational* or *the established-conceptual knowledge*. Though various forms of social media have been robustly adopted in political sphere and vigorously investigated since 2008s, none of them have substantially considered the adaptation and use of social media platforms by political actors and organisations to formulate *the systematic knowledge* surprisingly.

As the research findings presented in this work still entails some innate weaknesses, this work suggests the following further research recommendations. Firstly, this work has strongly relied on articles published in *Journal of Political Marketing* as primary data. Comparative content analyses of articles published in several peer-reviewed journals and edited-book written by scholars those who have different educational background needs to be conducted since these scholars commonly use different philosophical standpoints and meta-theoretical assumptions when they have studied the ICT developments and the adaptation and use of the Internet and social media and their impacts on knowledge production and generation of political marketing.

Secondly, though this study has used the quantitative and the qualitative content analyses, which are combined simultaneously with the thematic content analysis as a mixture of the quantitative and qualitative method, it has taken into account less the other qualitative and quantitative methods. For further research, it is suggested to deploy the other qualitative and quantitative methods, such as survey, in-depth interviews and focus group discussion. These methods need to be properly deployed not only to holistically understand the impacts of social media uses on advancement of political marketing management, but also to explore various views among political marketing scholars on assessing the degrees of importance of the Internet and social media for the knowledge production development of political marketing. These methods would also help in assessing whether the sympathized or the rudimentary-conceptual or the established-conceptual or the systematic knowledge of political marketing is important.

Thirdly, though this work offered a new conceptual framework to understand modes of knowledge production and generation and its application in the field study of political marketing, it has not fully clarified conceptually and empirically demarcated between and among the systematized, the rudimentary-conceptual, the practical-operational and the established-conceptual knowledge. With regards to this limitation, further research needs to be undertaken to examine not only the conceptual boundaries between and among these types of knowledge, but the empirical border and crosscutting lines between and among these types of knowledge. In this respect, a strong theoretical proposition needs to be properly advanced to theoretically define the border and crosscutting lines between and among these types of knowledge. More importantly, an appropriate research method and sufficient data also need to be holistically collated to conceptually and empirically evaluate these border and crosscutting lines.

Fourthly, this article has only focused on how, in which ways and the extent to which political marketing scholars who have published their works in *Journal of Political Marketing* accounted the adaptation and use of the Internet and social media by political actors and organisations as political marketing phenomena to create and generate knowledge production and generation of political marketing. This work has not yet explored the impact of adaptation and use of the Internet and social media on the knowledge production and generation of political marketing among political actors and organisations those who have run in the elections or those who have ruled in the government. Further investigation needs to be conducted to uncover this issue. A holistic research needs to be undertaken to explore the adaptation and use of the Internet and social media on the knowledge production and generation of political marketing among these actors and organisations on the one hand and among political marketing scholars who have studied these actors and organisations on the other. To such ends, a collaborative project involving peer groups of scholars from various disciplines, social science and technology needs to be advanced.

REFERENCES

Baskerville, R., & Dulipovici, A. (2006). The Theoretical Foundations of Knowledge management. *Knowledge Management Research & Practice*, *4*(2), 8M–105. doi:10.1057/palgrave.kmrp.8500090

Berger, P. L., & Luckmann, T. (1966). *The Social Construction of Reality: A Treatise in the Sociology of Knowledge*. London: Penguin Books.

Bhaskar, R. (1998). *The possibility of naturalism: A philosophical critique of the contemporary human sciences* (3rd ed.). London: Routledge.

Bhaskar, R. (2008). *A Realist Theory of Science* (2nd ed.). London: Verso.

Bode, L., & Dalrymple, K. E. (2014). Politics in 140 Characters or Less: Campaign Communication, Network Interaction, and Political Participation on Twitter. *Journal of Political Marketing*. doi:10.1080/15377857.2014.959686

Boyd, D. M., & Ellison, N. B. (2007). Social network sites: Definition, history, and scholarship. *Journal of Computer-Mediated Communication*, *13*(1), 11. doi:10.1111/j.1083-6101.2007.00393.x

Bryman, A. (2008). *Social Research Methods* (3rd ed.). Oxford, UK: Oxford University Press.

Busby, R., & Cronshaw, S. (2015). Political Branding: The Tea Party and Its Use of Participation Branding. *Journal of Political Marketing*, *14*(1-2), 96–110. doi:10.1080/15377857.2014.990850

Butler, P., & Collins, N. (1994). Political Marketing: Structure and Process. *European Journal of Marketing*, *28*(1), 19–34. doi:10.1108/03090569410049154

Butler, P., & Collins, N. (1999). A Conceptual Framework for Political Marketing. In B. I. Newman (Ed.), *Handbook of Political Marketing* (pp. 55–72). Thousand Oaks, CA: Sage Publications.

Butler, P., & Harris, P. (2009). Considerations on the evolution of political marketing theory. *Marketing Theory*, *9*(2), 149–164. doi:10.1177/1470593109103022

Butler-Kisber, L. (2010). *Qualitative Inquiry: Thematic, Narrative and Arts- Informed Perspectives*. London: Sage Publications Ltd.

Cameron, M. P., Barrett, P., & Stewardson, B. (2014). Can Social Media Predict Election Results? Evidence From New Zealand. *Journal of Political Marketing*, 1–17. doi:10.1080/15377857.2014.959690

Christenson, D. P., & Smidt, C. D. (2011). Riding the Waves of Money: Contribution Dynamics in the 2008 Presidential Nomination Campaign. *Journal of Political Marketing*, *10*(1-2), 1–2, 4–26. doi:10.1080/15377857.2011.540189

Chugh, R. (2012). Social Networking for Business: Is it a Boon or Banes?. In Handbook of Research on Business Social Networking: Organizational, Managerial, and Technological Dimensions. IGI Global.

Chugh, R. (2013). Workplace Dimensions: Tacit Knowledge Sharing in Universtities. *Journal of Advanced Management Science*, *1*(1), 24–28. doi:10.12720/joams.1.1.24-28

Chugh, R., Wibowo, S., & Grandi, S. (2015). Mandating the Transfer of Tacit Knowledge in Australian Universities. *Journal of Organizational Knowledge Management*, *2015*, 297669. doi:10.5171/2015.297669

Cogburn, D. L., & Espinoza-Vasquez, F. K. (2011). From Networked Nominee to Networked Nation: Examining the Impact of Web 2.0 and Social Media on Political Participation and Civic Engagement in the 2008 Obama Campaign. *Journal of Political Marketing*, *10*(1-2), 1–2, 189–213. doi:10.1080/15377857.2011.540224

Collins, N., & Butler, P. (1996). Positioning Political Parties: A Market Analysis. *The Harvard International Journal of Press/Politics*, *1*(2), 63–77. doi:10.1177/1081180X96001002006

Creswell, J. W., & Plano Clark, V. L. (2007). *Designing and Conducting Mixed Methods Research*. Thousand Oaks, CA: Sage.

Creswell, J. W., & Plano Clark, V. L. (2011). *Designing and Conducting Mixed Methods Research* (2nd ed.). Thousand Oaks, CA: Sage.

Creswell, J. W., & Tashakkori, A. (2007). Editorial: Differing Perspectives on Mixed Methods Research. *Journal of Mixed Methods Research*, *1*(4), 303–308. doi:10.1177/1558689807306132

Curtin, G., McConnachie, R., Sommer, M., & Vis-Sommer, V. (2002). American E-Government at the Crossroads. *Journal of Political Marketing*, *1*(1), 149–191. doi:10.1300/J199v01n01_08

Curtin, G. G., & Sommer, M. (2003). Is the Campaign Web Site Really "Dead"? *Journal of Political Marketing*, *2*(1), 107–111. doi:10.1300/J199v02n01_07

Curtin, G.G., Sommer, M.H., & Vis-Sommer, V. (2003) The World of E-Government. *Journal of Political Marketing, 2*(3-4), 1-16. DOI: 10.1300/J199v02n03_01

Demertzis, N., Diamantaki, K., Gazi, A., & Sartzetakis, N. (2005). Greek Political Marketing Online. *Journal of Political Marketing*, *4*(1), 51–74. doi:10.1300/J199v04n01_04

Egan, J. (1999). Political Marketing: Lessons from the Mainstream. *Journal of Marketing Management*, *15*(6), 495–503. doi:10.1362/026725799785045806

Espíndola, R. (2002). Professionalised Campaigning in Latin America. *Journal of Political Marketing*, *1*(4), 65–81. doi:10.1300/J199v01n04_04

Esser, F., & Tenscher, J. (2005a). *The Professionalization Dilemma: Exploring a 'Strategic Approach' for Political Communication Experts*. Paper prepared for presentation to the Political Communication Division at the ICA conference.

Esser, F., & Tenscher, J. (2005b). *Measuring The Professionalization of Political Campaign*. Paper prepared for presentation to the Political Communication Division at the ICA Conference.

Foot, K., Schneider, S. M., Xenos, M., & Dougherty, M. (2009). Candidates' Web Practices in the 2002 U.S. House, Senate, and Gubernatorial Elections. *Journal of Political Marketing*, *8*(2), 147–167. doi:10.1080/15377850902813519

Garcia-Castañon, M., Rank, A. D., & Barreto, M. A. (2011). Plugged In or Tuned Out? Youth, Race, and Internet Usage in the 2008 Election. *Journal of Political Marketing*, *10*(1-2), 1–2, 115–138. doi:10.1080/15377857.2011.540209

Gibson, R. K., & Rommele, A. (2001). Changing Campaign Communications: A Party-Centered Theory of Professionalized Campaigning. *The Harvard International Journal of Press/Politics*, *6*(4), 31–43. doi:10.1177/108118001129172323

Gibson, R. K., & Rommele, A. (2009). Measuring the Professionalization of Political Campaigning. *Party Politics*, *15*(3), 265–293. doi:10.1177/1354068809102245

Giddens, A. (1984). *The Constitution of Society: Outline of the Theory of Structuration*. Oxford, UK: Polity Press.

Guest, G. (2013). Describing Mixed Methods Research: An Alternative to Typologies. *Journal of Mixed Methods Research*, *7*(2), 141–151. doi:10.1177/1558689812461179

Hall, T. E., & Sinclair, B. (2011). The American Internet Voter. *Journal of Political Marketing*, *10*(1-2), 1–2, 58–79. doi:10.1080/15377857.2011.540194

Harris, L., & Harrigan, P. (2015). Social Media in Politics: The Ultimate Voter Engagement Tool or Simply an Echo Chamber? *Journal of Political Marketing*, *14*(3), 251–283. doi:10.1080/15377857.2012.693059

Harris, P. (2000). *To Spin or not to Spin that is the Question: The Emergence of Modern Political Marketing*. Westburn Publishers Ltd.

Harris, P., & Andrew, L. (2010). "Mind the gap": The rise of political marketing and a perspective on its future agenda. *European Journal of Marketing*, *44*(3/4), 297–307. doi:10.1108/03090561011020435

Harrop, M. (1990)*... Political Marketing. Parliamentary Affairs. Oxford University Press, 1990*, 227–291.

Hartwig, M. (2008). *Introduction. In A Realist Theory of Science* (2nd ed.; pp. ix–xxiv). London: Verso.

Hassell, H. J. G. (2011). Looking Beyond the Voting Constituency: A Study of Campaign Donation Solicitations in the 2008 Presidential Primary and General Election. *Journal of Political Marketing*, *10*(1-2), 1–2, 27–42. doi:10.1080/15377857.2011.540192

Heisig, P. (2009). Harmonisation of knowledge management: Comparing 160 KM frameworks around the globe. *Journal of Knowledge Management*, *13*(Issue, 4), 4–31. doi:10.1108/13673270910971798

Henneberg, S. C. M. (2002). Understanding Political Marketing. In N. J. O'Shaughnessy & S. C. M. Henneberg (Eds.), *The Idea of Political Marketing*. Westport, CT: Praeger.

Henneberg, S. C. M. (2004). The Views of an Avocatus Dei: Political Marketing and Its Critics. *Journal of Public Affairs*, *4*(3), 225–243. doi:10.1002/pa.187

Henneberg, S. C. M. (2008). An Epistemological Perspective on Research in Political Marketing. *Journal of Political Marketing*, *7*(2), 151–182. doi:10.1080/15377850802053158

Henneberg, S. C. M., & O'Shaughnessy, N. J. (2007). Theory and Concept Development in Political Marketing. *Journal of Political Marketing*, *6*, 2–3, 5–31. doi:10.1300/J199v06n02_02

Henneberg, S. C. M., & O'Shaughnessy, N. J. (2009). Political Relationship Marketing: Some macro/micro thoughts. *Journal of Marketing Management*, *25*(1-2), 5–29. doi:10.1362/026725709X410016

Henneberg, S. C. M., & Ormrod, R. P. (2013). The triadic interaction model of political marketing exchange. *Marketing Theory*, *13*(1), 87–103. doi:10.1177/1470593112467269

Holtz-Bacha, C. (2002). Professionalization of Political Communication. *Journal of Political Marketing*, *1*(4), 23–37. doi:10.1300/J199v01n04_02

Jackson, N. (2011). Perception or Reality: How MPs Believe the Internet Helps Them Win Votes. *Journal of Political Marketing*, *10*(3), 230–250. doi:10.1080/15377857.2011.588099

Johansen, H. P. M. (2005). Political Marketing. *Journal of Political Marketing*, *4*(4), 85–105. doi:10.1300/J199v04n04_05

Johnson, D. W. (2002a). The Electronic Information Candy Store. *Journal of Political Marketing*, *1*(4), 101–102. doi:10.1300/J199v01n04_07

Johnson, D. W. (2002b). Campaign Website. *Journal of Political Marketing*, *1*(1), 213–215. doi:10.1300/J199v01n01_11

Johnson, D. W. (2003a). Anthrax and Digital Mail. *Journal of Political Marketing*, *2*(1), 113–115. doi:10.1300/J199v02n01_08

Johnson, D. W. (2003b). The U.S. Congress Responds to Online Communication Needs. *Journal of Political Marketing*, *2*(3-4), 3–4, 235–254. doi:10.1300/J199v02n03_13

Johnson, D. W. (2004a). the 2004 U.S. Presidential Elections. *Journal of Political Marketing*, *3*(4), 111–113. doi:10.1300/J199v03n04_06

Johnson, D. W. (2004b). Rethinking Electronic Voting. *Journal of Political Marketing*, *3*(3), 107–109. doi:10.1300/J199v03n03_07

Kotler, P., & Kotler, N. (1999). Political Marketing: Generating Effective Candidate, Campaigns and Causes. In Handbook of Political Marketing. London: Sage Publication.

Lappas, G., Chatzopoulos, S., & Yannas, P. (2008). Parliamentary Candidates Running on the Web for the 2004 Greek National Elections. *Journal of Political Marketing*, *7*(3-4), 3–4, 256–277. doi:10.1080/15377850802008327

Lees-Marshment, J. (2001a, September). The Marriage of Politics and Marketing. *Political Studies*, *49*(4), 692–713. doi:10.1111/1467-9248.00337

Lees-Marshment, J. (2001b). The product, sales and market-oriented party: How Labour learnt to market the product, not just the presentation. *European Journal of Marketing*, *35*(9/10), 1074–1084. doi:10.1108/EUM0000000005959

Lees-Marshment, J. (2001c). *Political Marketing and British Political Parties: The Party's Just Begun*. Manchester, UK: Manchester University Press.

Lees-Marshment, J. (2004). *The Political Marketing Revolution: Transforming the Government of the UK*. London: Routledge Publication.

Lees-Marshment, J. (2008). *Political Marketing and British Political Parties* (2nd ed.). Manchester, UK: Manchester University Press.

Lees-Marshment, J. (Ed.). (2012). *Routledge Hanbook of Political Marketing*. London: Routledge Taylor & Francis Group.

Lees-Marshment, J., & Lilleker, D. G. (Eds.). (2005). *Political Marketing: A Comparative Perspective*. Manchester, UK: Manchester University Press.

Lees-Marshment, J., Stromback, J., & Rudd, C. (Eds.). (2010). *Global Political Marketing*. London: Routlegde.

Lilleker, D. G. (2014). Interactivity and Branding, Public Political Communication as a Marketing Tool. *Journal of Political Marketing*. doi:10.1080/15377857.2014.990841

Lilleker, D. G., & Jackson, N. A. (2013). Reaching Inward Not Outward: Marketing via the Internet at the UK 2010 General Election. *Journal of Political Marketing*, *12*(2-3), 2–3, 244–261. doi:10.1080/15377857.2013.781475

Lilleker, D. G., Jackson, N. A., & Scullion, R. (2007). *The Marketing of Political Parties*. Manchester, UK: Manchester University Press.

Lilleker, D. G., & Lees-Marshment, J. (Eds.). (2005). *Political Marketing: A Comparative Perspective*. Manchester, UK: Manchester University Press.

Lilleker, D. G., & Negrine, R. (2002). Professionalization: Of What? Since When? By Whom? *The Harvard International Journal of Press/Politics*, *7*(4), 98–103. doi:10.1177/108118002236354

Lipsitz, K., & Panagopoulos, C. (2011). Filled Coffers: Campaign Contributions and Contributors in the 2008 Elections. *Journal of Political Marketing*, *10*(1-2), 1–2, 43–57. doi:10.1080/15377857.2011.540193

Lock, A., & Harris, P. (1996). Political marketing – *vive la différence! European Journal of Marketing*, *30*(10/11), 14–24. doi:10.1108/03090569610149764

Lunde, A., Heggen, K., & Strand, R. (2013). Knowledge and Power: Exploring Unproductive Interplay Between Quantitative and Qualitative Researchers. *Journal of Mixed Methods Research*, *7*(2), 197–210. doi:10.1177/1558689812471087

Mancini, P. (1999). New Frontiers in Political Professionalism. *Political Communication*, *16*(3), 231–245. doi:10.1080/105846099198604

Miller, W. J. (2013). We Can't All Be Obama: The Use of New Media in Modern Political Campaigns. *Journal of Political Marketing*, *12*(4), 326–347. doi:10.1080/15377857.2013.837312

Moloney, K. (2008). Is Political Marketing New Words or New Practice in UK Politics? *Journal of Political Marketing*, *6*(4), 51–65. doi:10.1300/J199v06n04_03

Moses, J. W., & Knutsen, T. L. (2012). *Ways of Knowing: Competing Methodologies in Social and Political Research* (2nd ed.). New York: Palgrave Macmillan.

Needham, C., & Smith, G. (2015). Introduction: Political Branding. *Journal of Political Marketing*, *14*(1-2), 1–6. doi:10.1080/15377857.2014.990828

Negrine, R. (2008). *The Transformation of Political Communication: Continuities and Changes in Media and Politics*. New York: Palgrave Macmillan.

Negrine, R., & Lilleker, D. G. (2002). The Professionalization of Political Communication: Continuities and Change in Media Practices. *European Journal of Communication*, *17*(3), 305–323. doi:10.1177/0267323102017003688

Negrine, R., Mancini, P., Holtz-Bacha, C., & Papathanossopoulos, S. (Eds.). (2007). *The Professionalization of Political Communication*. Bristol: Intellect.

Newman, B. I. (1994). *The Marketing of the President: Political Marketing as Campaign Strategy*. Thousand Oaks, CA: Sage Publications.

Newman, B. I. (1999a).Preface. In *Handbook of Political Marketing*. Thousand Oaks, CA: Sage.

Newman, B. I. (Ed.). (1999c). *Handbook of Political Marketing*. Thousand Oaks, CA: Sage.

Newman, B. I. (1999b). *The Mass Marketing of Politics: Democracy in an Age of Manufactured Image*. London: Sage Publication.

Newman, B.I. (2012). The Role of Marketing in Politics: Ten Years Later. *Journal of Political Marketing, 11*. DOI: 10.1080/15377857.2012.642697

Nonaka, I. (1994). Dynamic Theory of Organisational Knowledge Creation. *Organization Science*, *5*(1), 14–37. doi:10.1287/orsc.5.1.14

Nonaka, I., & Kono, N. (1998). The Concept of "Ba': Building a Foundation for Knowledge Creation. *California Management Review*, *40*(3), 40–54. doi:10.2307/41165942

Nonaka, I., & Toyama, R. (2003). The knowledge-creating theory revisited: Knowledge creation as a synthesizing process. *Knowledge Management Research & Practice*, *1*(1), 2–10. doi:10.1057/palgrave.kmrp.8500001

Norris, P. (2000). *The Virtuos Circle–Political Communication in Postindustrial Societies*. Cambridge, UK: Cambridge University Press. doi:10.1017/CBO9780511609343

O' Schaughnessy, N. J., & Hanneberg, S. C. M. (2002). *The Idea of Political Marketing*. London: Praeger Series in Political Communication.

O'Cass, A. (2001a). Political Marketing: An Investigation of the Political Marketing Concept and Political Market Orientation in Australian Politics. *European Journal of Marketing*, *35*(9/10), 1003–1025. doi:10.1108/03090560110401938

O'Cass, A. (2001b). The Internal-External Marketing Orientation of a Political Party: Social Implications of Political Party Marketing Orientation. *Journal of Public Affairs*, *1*(2), 136–152. doi:10.1002/pa.59

O'Shaughnessy, NJ. (2010) The marketing of political marketing. *European Journal of Marketing*, *35*(9-10), 1047-1057.

Omrod, R. P. (2011). *Product-, Sales- and Market-Oriented Parties: Literature Review and Implications for Academics, Practitioners and Educators.* Working Paper Series in Management 2011/2 Institute for Economics and Management Aarhus University, Denmark.

Ormrod, R. P. (2005). A Conceptual Model of Political Market Orientation. *Journal of Nonprofit & Public Sector Marketing*, *14*(1/2), 47–65. doi:10.1300/J054v14n01_04

Ormrod, R. P. (2006). A Critique of the Lees-Marshment Market-Oriented Party Model. *Politics*, *26*(2), 110–118. doi:10.1111/j.1467-9256.2006.00257.x

Ormrod, R. P. (2007). Political Market Orientation and Its Commercial Cousin. *Journal of Political Marketing*, *6*(2-3), 2–3, 69–90. doi:10.1300/J199v06n02_05

Ormrod, R. P. (2009). *Understanding Political Market Orientation.* (Doctoral Thesis). Aarhus School of Business, University of Aarhus, Denmark.

Ormrod, R. P. (2012) *Defining Political Marketing.* Management Working Papers. Institut for Økonomi, Aarhus Universitet. 22 Oct 2012

Ormrod, R. P., & Henneberg, S. C. M. (2008). *Understanding Political Market Orientation.* Paper presented at International Conference on Political Marketing, Manchester, UK.

Ormrod, R. P., & Henneberg, S. C. M. (2009). Different Facets of Market Orientation: A Comparative Analysis of Party Manifestos. *Journal of Political Marketing*, *8*(3), 190–208. doi:10.1080/15377850903044742

Ormrod, R. P., & Henneberg, S. C. M. (2009). Different Facets of Market Orientation: A Comparative Analysis of Party Manifestos. *Journal of Political Marketing*, *8*(3), 190–208. doi:10.1080/15377850903044742

Ormrod, R. P., & Henneberg, S. C. M. (2010). Strategic Political Postures and Political Market Orientation: Toward an Integrated Concept of Political Marketing Strategy. *Journal of Political Marketing*, *9*(4), 294–313. doi:10.1080/15377857.2010.518106

Ormrod, R. P., & Henneberg, S. C. M. (2010, February). Understanding voter orientation in the context of political market orientation: Is the political customer king? *Journal of Marketing Management*, *26*(1–2), 108–130. doi:10.1080/02672570903574270

Ormrod, R. P., & Henneberg, S. C. M. (2011). Political Market Orientation and Strategic Party Postures in Danish Political Parties. *European Journal of Marketing*, *45*(6), 852–881. doi:10.1108/03090561111119949

Ormrod, R.P., Henneberg, S.C.M., & O'Shaughnessy, N. J. (2013). *Political Marketing: Theory and Concepts.* London: Sage Publication.

Panagopoulos, C. (2011). Introduction: Money and Technology in the 2008 Elections. *Journal of Political Marketing, 10*. DOI: 10.1080/15377857.2011.540188

Parsons, M., & Rowling, M. (2015). Social Media and the Paradox of Fear: An Exploratory Study of Political Relationship Marketing Within South Wales. *Journal of Political Marketing*, 1–23. doi:10.1080/15377857.2015.1039746

Pavitt, C. (1999). The Third Way: Scientific Realism and Communication Theory. *Communication Theory*, *9*(2), 162–188. doi:10.1111/j.1468-2885.1999.tb00356.x

Plasser, F., & Plasser, G. (2002). *Global Political Campaigning: A Worldwide Analysis of Campaign Professionals and Their Practices*. Westport, CT: Praeger.

Polanyi, M. (1966). The Tacit Dimension. London: Routledge & Kegan Paul.

Rutter, R. N., Hanretty, C., & Lettice, F. (2015). Political Brands: Can Parties Be Distinguished by Their Online Brand Personality? *Journal of Political Marketing*, 1–20. doi:10.1080/15377857.2015.1022631

Sandelowski, M., Voils, C. I., Leeman, J., & Crandell, J. L. (2012). Mapping the Mixed Methods–Mixed Research Synthesis Terrain. *Journal of Mixed Methods Research*, *6*(4), 317–331. doi:10.1177/1558689811427913 PMID:23066379

Savigny, H. (2004). *Political Marketing: A Critical Assessment-Caveat Emptor*. (Doctoral Thesis). The University of Birmingham.

Savigny, H. (2007). Ontology and Epistemology in Political Marketing. *Journal of Political Marketing*, *6*(2-3), 2–3, 33–47. doi:10.1300/J199v06n02_03

Savigny, H. (2008). *The Problem of Political Marketing*. New York: Continuum.

Savigny, H. & Temple, M. (2010). Political Marketing Models: The Curious Incident of the Dog that Doesn't Bark. *Political Studies, 58,* 1049–1064.

Sayer, A. (2000). *Realism and Social Science*. London: Sage. doi:10.4135/9781446218730

Scammell, M. (1999). Political Marketing: Lessons for Political Science. *Political Studies*, *67*(4), 718–739. doi:10.1111/1467-9248.00228

Schneider, M. C. (2014). Gender-Based Strategies on Candidate Websites. *Journal of Political Marketing*, *13*(4), 264–290. doi:10.1080/15377857.2014.958373

Shaw, D. R. (2002). How the Bush and Gore Campaigns Conceptualized and Used the Internet in 2000. *Journal of Political Marketing*, *1*(1), 39–65. doi:10.1300/J199v01n01_04

Sherman, E., & Schiffman, L. G. (2002). Political Marketing Research in the 2000 U.S. Election. *Journal of Political Marketing*, *1*(2-3), 2–3, 53–68. doi:10.1300/J199v01n02_05

Sommer, M., & Tavlin, B. (2003). Notes on the California E-Politics Campaign Trail. *Journal of Political Marketing*, *3*(1), 87–96. doi:10.1300/J199v03n01_05

Stromback, J. (2007). Political Marketing and Professionalized Campaigning'. *Journal of Political Marketing*, *6*(2), 49–67. doi:10.1300/J199v06n02_04

Stromback, J. (2009). Selective Professionalisation of Political Campaigning: A Test of the Party-Centred Theory of Professionalised Campaigning in the Context of the 2006 Swedish Election. *Political Studies, 57,* 95–116.

Stromback, J. (2010). A Framework for Comparing Political Market-Orientation. In Global Political Marketing. London: Routledge Taylor & Francis Group.

Stromer-Galley, J. (2000). On-line interaction and why candidates avoid it. *Journal of Communication, 50*(4), 111–132. doi:10.1111/j.1460-2466.2000.tb02865.x

Tashakkori, A. (2009). Are we there yet? The State of the Mixed Methods Community. *Journal of Mixed Methods Research, 3*(4), 287–291. doi:10.1177/1558689809346151

Tashakkori, A., & Creswell, J. W. (2007a). Editorial: Exploring the Nature of Research Questions in Mixed Methods Research. *Journal of Mixed Methods Research, 1*(3), 207–211. doi:10.1177/1558689807302814

Tashakkori, A., & Creswell, J. W. (2007b). The new era of mixed methods. *Journal of Mixed Methods Research, 1*(1), 3–7. doi:10.1177/2345678906293042

Temple, M. (2013). The Media and the Message. *Journal of Political Marketing, 12*(2-3), 2–3, 147–165. doi:10.1080/15377857.2013.781479

Tenscher, J. (2004, September). 'Bridging the Differences': Political Communication Experts in Germany. *German Politics, 13*(3), 516–540. doi:10.1080/0964400042000287482

Tenscher, J. (2013). First-and second-order campaigning. *European Journal of Communication, 28,* 241.

Tenscher, J., & Mykkänen, J. (2013). Transformations in second-order campaigning: A German-Finnish comparison of campaign professionalism in the 2004 and 2009 European parliamentary elections. *Central European Journal of Communication, 2,* 171–187.

Tenscher, J. & Mykkänen, J. (2014). Two Levels of Campaigning: An Empirical Test of the Party-Centred Theory of Professionalisation. *Political Studies, 62*(S1), 20–41. DOI: 10.1111/1467-9248.12104

Tenscher, J., Mykkänen, J., & Moring, T. (2012). Modes of Professional Campaigning: A Four-Country Comparison in the European Parliamentary Elections, 2009. *The International Journal of Press/Politics, 17*(2), 145–168. doi:10.1177/1940161211433839

Towner, T. L., & Dulio, D. A. (2011). The Web 2.0 Election: Does the Online Medium Matter? *Journal of Political Marketing, 10*(1-2), 1–2, 165–188. doi:10.1080/15377857.2011.540220

Towner, T. L., & Dulio, D. A. (2012). New Media and Political Marketing in the United States: 2012 and Beyond. *Journal of Political Marketing, 11*(1-2), 1–2, 95–119. doi:10.1080/15377857.2012.642748

Vesnic-Alujevic, L., & Bauwel, S. V. (2014). YouTube: A Political Advertising Tool? A Case Study of the Use of YouTube in the Campaign for the European Parliament Elections. *Journal of Political Marketing, 13*(3), 195–212. doi:10.1080/15377857.2014.929886

Vis-Sommer, V. (2003). Surveying Government Web Sites. *Journal of Political Marketing, 3*(1), 97–103. doi:10.1300/J199v03n01_06

Wallsten, K. (2011). Many Sources, One Message: Political Blog Links to Online Videos During the 2008 Campaign. *Journal of Political Marketing*, *10*(1-2), 1–2, 88–114. doi:10.1080/15377857.2011.540203

William, C. B. (2012). Trends and Changes in Journal of Political Marketing Titles 2002–2011. *Journal of Political Marketing*, *11*, 1–2, 4–7. doi:10.1080/15377857.2012.642702

Williams, C. B., Aylesworth, A., & Chapman, K. J. (2002). The 2000 E-Campaign for U.S. Senate. *Journal of Political Marketing*, *1*(4), 39–63. doi:10.1300/J199v01n04_03

Williams, C. B., Gulati, G. J., & Foxman, E. R. (2009). What's In an Endorsement? An Analysis of Web-Based Marketing in the 2004 Presidential Campaign. *Journal of Political Marketing*, *8*(3), 173–189. doi:10.1080/15377850903048214

Wring, D. (1997). Reconciling Marketing with Political Science: Theories of Political Marketing. *Journal of Marketing Management*, *13*(7), 651–663. doi:10.1080/0267257X.1997.9964502

Wring, D. (2005). *The Politics of Marketing the Labour Party*. Hampshire, UK: Palgrave MacMillan.

Wu, H. W., & Dahmen, N. S. (2010). Web Sponsorship and Campaign Effects: Assessing the Difference Between Positive and Negative Web Sites. *Journal of Political Marketing*, *9*(4), 314–329. doi:10.1080/15377857.2010.522454

Yannas, P., & Lappas, G. (2005). Web Campaign in the 2002 Greek Municipal Elections. *Journal of Political Marketing*, *4*(1), 33–50. doi:10.1300/J199v04n01_03

Section 3

Knowledge Management and Social Media Frameworks and/or Models

Chapter 10
Managing Social Knowledge Management:
Balancing the Gatekeeping vs. Crowdsourcing Requirements

Ashish Kumar Jha
IIM Calcutta, India

Varun Jain
Star India Pvt. Ltd., India

ABSTRACT

In a knowledge driven economy, the ability of a firm to grow and gain competitive advantage is defined by its ability to realize economic value from its knowledge assets. In one form or the other, firms have attempted to capitalize on the power of knowledge based economy. Multiple steps were taken by various firms to capture the knowledge and create knowledge bank in form of KM tools and other propriety media. Social media has provided firms with a very powerful tool to appropriate the benefits of such codified knowledge. Social media, in form of both public social network sites and propriety social media tools has enabled collaborative creation and storage of knowledge like never before in human history. Availability of these media has lowered the barrier of entry in a knowledge driven economy by democratizing collection and organization of knowledge. In this chapter, we present an exploratory framework to analyze the implications of use of various types of social media based KM tools on the firm's knowledge collection and sharing strategies.

INTRODUCTION

We live in a knowledge economy (Powell & Snellman, 2004). Knowledge is the new critical resource of firms. In a knowledge-driven economy, the ability of a firm to grow and gain a competitive advantage is defined by its ability to realize economic value from its knowledge assets. Various researchers have termed it as an extension of the resource-based theory of firm (Lavie, 2006; Siemens, 2014). The power

DOI: 10.4018/978-1-5225-0495-5.ch010

of knowledge-based economy was realized by firms quite early and steps were taken by various firms to capture the knowledge and create knowledge bank in form of KM tools and other propriety media, but the true revolution was brought into this sector by advent of social media.

At a very generic level knowledge management has been termed to be the process of acquiring, managing, distributing and enabling the usage of knowledge within the firm (Alavi & Leidner, 2001; Dalkir, 2013). A firm may gather knowledge in multiple ways. It can either be the traditionally stored knowledge, which is nothing but processed information (Bhatt, Pankaj, & Rodger, 2014) or a formal record of tacit knowledge available with skilled workers or other stakeholders. A knowledge management system is the overarching system which manages all potentially beneficial information available within the firm or its stakeholders in utilizable form (knowledge). It can be understood to be the complete spectrum of the process by which the firm manages all the information necessary currently or in future for its successful operation. One important aspect needed to be understood in handling knowledge for firms is that there exist two kinds of knowledge within the firms, tacit and explicit (Dixon, 2000; Polyani, 1966). Careful thought needs to be given for handling both these types of knowledge as the processes for storing the two kinds of knowledge and its impacts differ vastly.

One of the issues that firms deal with today while managing their Knowledge Management (KM) processes is how to collect and disburse the information essential for firm's continued growth. Social media, in form of both public social network sites and propriety social media tools like wiki etc., has enabled collaborative creation and storage of knowledge like never before in human history (Kaplan & Haenlein, 2010). Availability of these media has lowered the barrier to entry in a knowledge-driven economy by democratizing collection and organization of knowledge. On one hand while these media have enabled quicker sharing of information and easier storage of firm's knowledge, it has also increased the possibility of making tacit knowledge of a firm public and explicit (Allee, 2004). Such an event has the capability to severely affect the competitive advantage of the firm.

There is a definite and critical need to understand and reflect on the implications of KM in social media age. Both scale and scope of KM implementations have changed dramatically in recent times. Not only have KM tools become much more pervasive than in past allowing small and new firms to grow much more quickly but also the stakeholders of standard KM engagements have changed. KM engagements now do not necessarily rely on information management of firm's employees (Hislop, 2013). Firms gather information from customers, suppliers etc. Some of the firms as discussed in the following sections even use crowdsourcing techniques to build their information bases. The term crowdsourcing literally implies collecting from a crowd but has become popular for collection of information or funds through online channels (Zhao & Zhu, 2014). The database storing critical information can be publicly accessible as well. This approach, although still in infancy and practiced by few firms, is a far cry from the days of old when firm's knowledge database was one of most fiercely protected infrastructure. This brings us to the important aspect of 'Gatekeeping' which has been covered in this article. Gatekeeping is defined as the mechanism of controlling access to certain information available with a select group of entities or individuals. In the context of this study, the essential question is determining the extent of gatekeeping for firms with varying degree of KM integration with social media.

In this work, exploratory research methods are employed to understand the complex relationship between firm's knowledge management strategies and the implications of the use of various kinds of social media tools. Social media in the context of this article stands for a medium which allows for networked interactions and could be any of either propriety tools or public social media tools including the likes of Facebook® and Linkedin®. This article shows how modern KM systems based in an increasingly social world with different types of social media interactions can be best utilized by the firms for their benefit. The organizational foundations are still the KM tools and social media is an additional way which enhances the capacity of these KM tools.

Through the use of intelligence gathered through case studies and expert interviews in India, one of the fastest growing economies in the world, this article illustrates how the interference of social media has enabled the smaller firms to quickly build their knowledge bases and increase the pace of their growth. However, as is evident in the case studies, not all social media based KM tools, suit all firms. The social media based KM intervention has to match the firm's requirement based on its knowledge management strategy.

The paper presents an exploratory framework to better analyze the implications of KM implementations on firm's codified knowledge. The framework attempts to provide a ready reckoner to both practitioners and academicians on understanding the circumstances and the kind of firms where strict gatekeeping of information is required and firms which would do well by having a seamless integration with social media for their KM implementations. The research would plug an important gap in fast evolving KM literature on implications of social media mediated KM implementations.

LITERATURE REVIEW

The definition of Knowledge that is implied in this work is the most commonly used and understood definition. Knowledge in the context of this work would mean "processed information which can be of potential use to the entity" (Klein, 1971). Processing information from various sources and storing them as utilizable knowledge is the core tenet of all knowledge management systems. Knowledge management has always been considered as a very important aspect of firm success (Chen & Huang, 2009; Darroch, 2005; Hislop, 2013). For a firm, using IT to enhance organizational learning has been established to be a very significant contributor to enhancing its performance (Senge, 2014). Most of this learning happens through organizational KM initiatives where knowledge, both tacit and explicit, is codified and passed on to all corners of the organization. Knowledge management initiatives aimed at creating such knowledge banks for firms lead to a higher firm performance (Cohen & Olsen, 2015). Such efforts create additional value for all entities associated with a firm (Weaven, Grace, Dant, & Brown, 2014) and hence the efforts to generate and nurture all forms of organizational knowledge have always been encouraged by top management of the firm.

The core reason why better KM capabilities lead to higher firm performances were illustrated by Darroch (2005) where it was found that "firm with a knowledge management capability will use resources more efficiently and so will be more innovative and perform better". Knowledge management not only leads to higher firm performance but also a significantly higher level of innovativeness in a firm (Darroch, 2005; Lai, Hsu, Lin, Chen, & Lin, 2014). In today's world, where continuous innovation is one of the prime factors for a firm's long term survival and success, its KM capabilities become a much more strategically significant resource (Kim, Lee, Chun, & Benbasat, 2014).

Firms invest a large amount of money on building such capabilities to achieve competitive advantage in the industry. Huge expenses are not only due to the technology costs but in part also due to incentivizing the users to create the knowledge bases (Kulkarni, Ravindran & Freeze, 2007). The greatest impact of social media and associated tools has been felt in this domain by lowering the barrier of entry. This has happened due to lowering of the cost of creating a KM system based on social media tools. To completely understand the impact that social media has had on firms' KM policies, there is a need to understand the impact that easy collation of information can have on firms and humans alike.

The amount of influence, access to information can have on society, is tremendous. More so in an information economy where access to information can be the difference between a mediocre and a top performing firm (Dewett & Jones, 2001). From public systems to firms, almost all aspects of human lives have in some way been impacted by easier availability and dissemination of information (Castells, 2011). Easier collation and dissemination of information has always inspired human society to enable to take next step in development. In recent times, social media has emerged as one of the greatest information collation tools. It has enabled the next leap in the codification of not only explicit but also tacit information available with humans. Katz and Rice (2002) in their work on social consequences of internet use have stated that societies are evolving to respond to the much easier availability of information with individuals. A lot of innovation in firms can be credited to the fact that all the information of the world is available to people via mobile and internet (Zack, 2003). Katz and Rice (2002) also state that the knowledge revolution due to easier availability of information in an information economy is providing opportunities to people in locations that were not possible earlier like people in developing economies and rural areas. This in some sense can be construed to be the democratization of knowledge and opportunities.

Social media is having similar consequences for KM systems of firms and in turn for firm performance as well. One of the most important things is that the definition of KM itself is changing in the current scenario. A few decades ago the only information that firms stored and considered as important for firm performance was day to day functioning information of firms collected from the employees working directly with the product or service offerings of the firm (Wiig, 1997). This information was easier to assign a value to and hence considered worthy of spending firm resources on. The next stage was the associated processes of the firm including firm's support processes that were carefully documented and stored and the era evolved towards firms with large KM systems, standardized processes. KM systems were considered important for ensuring standardization of processes and outcomes in large multinational firms (Lievrouw & Livingstone, 2002). This enlargement of the scope of KM systems put a lot of pressure on smaller firms. This occurred as creating a comprehensive and high quality data based KM system was a very expensive affair and smaller firms many times could not afford such costly implementations (Fuller, 2012).

This gap between large and small firms or between firms in developed economies and emerging economies is what has been tremendously reduced by the advent of social media based KM systems (Lievrouw & Livingstone, 2002). As an example it can be seen how the knowledge management system has developed over the years in two different settings. Nerolac®, a paints company, used dedicated propriety KM tools to store the preferences of its customers. This was done through their customer feedback team which collected feedback from select customers and dealers. Nerolac® could process the information in terms of change in requirements as per customer preferences, success stories etc. Such strong KM database can be a huge asset for a firm in a competitive market space. However, in Indian market Asian paints®, an Indian firm which is leader in domestic decorative paints segment, expanded its knowledge base at much larger pace. It deployed distributed terminals at all their dealerships without interference of customer feedback team where customers could see what other customers had chosen for their homes, give their feedback on the products and demand new products. This was instantly visible to all other dealers as well as to warehouse which could dispatch related products. This system can be understood to be one of the closest approximations of social media enabled KM tools in pre-social media era. Such knowledge gathering system enabled Asian paints to quickly gather a much larger intelligence of customer preferences and eventually led them to being the dominant player in Indian paints market (Vrat, 2014).

Starting from such examples till today social media and associated technologies have fundamentally impacted the way the KM systems of firms are visualized. This has happened in two ways:

1. **Network Effect:** The speed and information collection abilities in firms have increased tremendously by the use of network tools that create network effect (Lerman, 2007). KM tools are more likely being modelled on systems like Wiki or a personal social media as against central database systems controlled by the Information departments. The right to create information has passed on from some people at Information Systems (IS) department of firms to all stakeholders of the firm. This has increased employee involvement in development and maintenance of knowledge base. Use of a social media like KM tool has created a system where everyone has the rights to enter their tacit information in a KM tool which was difficult earlier. Firms like TCS® have even "gamified" their propriety social media styled KM systems by giving titles of "star knowledge creator", "chief knowledge creator" etc. This creates a situation where the friends of knowledge creator also come aboard such KM tools and fill in the details. Bringing of such a social effect where everyone can see how much people in their network have contributed leads to the network effect by challenging all people in the network to contribute equally if not more. Such fast growing KM systems brings a much required standardization across the divisions of the firm and leads to lower costs of standards compliance.
2. **Increased Stakeholders:** The second way is by integration with public social media tools to connect with a wider array of stakeholders. The information is not just collected about the firm's offerings and its processes but about its suppliers and also its clients (Alavi & Leidner, 2001).It can be seen that by the integration of public social media tools like Facebook to its KM systems, amazon has included the end consumers as a vital stakeholder whose likes/dislikes and comments are being stored and analysed for stock management. Such information bank enables the higher involvement of firm with all stakeholders and brings the firm closer to its stakeholders who might be in any part of the globe. The difference in location or age of firm or even its resources has started to matter for little with the ability of firms to collect information from all across the globe at an unprecedented pace (Bloom, Garicano, Sadun, & Van Reenen, 2014).

The question that is most pertinent for firms, in this context, is deciding when and how to tap into the vast information space available. Security is one of the burning issues in this domain. Levy (2009) in his work has stated that CIOs regard the security of firm information as one of the most critical detrimental factors stopping from a transition towards a more socially integrated KM system. A delicate balance needs to be maintained between security issues of firm's critical information and enabling faster and more effective social media enabled KM systems. New age startups and small firms in remote locations of the world, without the baggage or security considerations of larger and more established rivals, have developed unique KM solutions built entirely on social media enabled systems. These systems are fast eroding the gaps between large and small firms on a global scale.

Our current work evaluates the factors that are critical in enabling a CIO to decide on the level and type of integration of KM system with social media. This article proposes a framework for enabling the decision making and also presents some unique case studies in this domain.

RESEARCH METHODOLOGY

The research in the field of social knowledge management is still in its nascent stage with multiple theoretical developments still taking place (Geisler & Wickramasinghe, 2015). As such, to advance the theoretical foundations of the field, the article intends to present a conceptual framework for the field. This is an exploratory work and hence exploratory methods for theory advancement as proposed for social sciences researchers have been employed in this work (Tashakkori & Teddlie, 2010; Yin, 2011). Exploratory works are considered to be one of the primary tools for theoretical advancements in the field and case study based research is the preferred method of choice for researchers for developing new theoretical frameworks (Eisenhardt, 1989).

A two stage research method has been employed for collecting data for this work (Richards, 2014). A two-stage research method is suggested for collecting data while indulging in research in little understood areas. This helps the researcher in building the background information on the research question when delving deep in the final data collection stage (Richards, 2014; Tellis, 1997). We use semi-structured interviews with area experts at the first stage to collect the information and identify the major themes in the field, new developments and innovations in the area of social knowledge management. We follow this up with the in-depth case studies of social knowledge management implementations.

At both stages of the research design, the choice of sample selection is done using purposive sampling. It is a non-probabilistic sampling technique popularly used in social sciences and medical sciences research to collect information and data about a phenomenon that is rare but requires in-depth information (Ritchie, Lewis, Nicholls, & Ormston, 2013). Given the nascent stage of the phenomenon of study itself and the even smaller sample of success stories and experts in the field location, India, this sampling technique was the best solution for our work (Ritchie et al., 2013; Yin 2014).

Semi-Structured Interviews

Semi-structured interviews help a researcher develop intricate understanding of a topic from the interviewee. The free-flowing interview format is a preferred interview technique to collect information about various aspects of the phenomenon under study (Kvale & Brinkmann, 2009). Semi-structured interviews with field experts help the research in two ways by a) exposing the researchers to the internal dynamics, facts, norms and other tacit information of the phenomenon available with the expert and b) in helping the researchers to design the next stage of the research to identify the deep-diving issues of the phenomenon (Opdenakker, 2006; Wengraf, 2001).

For our study, the interviewees were industry practitioners in the field of KM solutions development, social media integration etc. The snapshot of the profile of interviewees is given in Table 1. The interaction with the domain experts was free flowing to get maximum understanding of the industry practices without any leading questions (Kvale & Brinkmann, 2009; Wengraf, 2001). To apprise the interviews and remove any misgivings about the discussion, the interviewees were contacted beforehand by email and a brief note on the topics around with the discussion would be structured was informed (Opdenakker, 2006). The discussion was broadly structured around the following themes:

1. **Changes in Knowledge Management Practices:** This section was with a special focus on social media implications. The interviewees talked about the differences in implementation of KM tools

Table 1. Description of the interviewees

Identifier	Experience (in Years)	Details of Experience (Specialization)	Major Points of Discussion
Interviewee 1	5	Game Developer/Technical entrepreneur. Worked with multiple Tech-startups including Safecity	Novel social media KM based startups, Why social media integration
Interviewee 2	8	Social media consultant, Cofounder social media advisory firm	The impact of social media on firm's strategies.
Interviewee 3	4.5	Technical lead developer of KM consulting firms. Deployed KM system at various firms	Traditional and evolving nature of KM at firms
Interviewee 4	6	Knowledge management systems consultant at a leading consulting firm	Change in approach to social media with respect to KM systems

and methods in different enterprises post the social media boom of mid 2000's. The discussion revolved around the use of public social media forums like Linkedin®, Facebook® etc. or development of custom social media applications in-house by firms using propriety or open source tools like Wikis.

2. **Involvement of Multiple Stakeholders in Developing the Knowledge Base:** The changing role of various stakeholders in KM in a firm was discussed. The aim was to identify the enlargement of the scope of stakeholders of a KM initiative.
3. **Future of Knowledge Management Practices:** We inquired about practitioner's views about the future of changing nature of KM initiatives. The aim was to collect information about how the industry sees the KM initiative evolve over next decade. We attempted to understand the new age KM initiatives under development or conceptualization and their motives at various firms.
4. **Firms with Innovative KM Initiatives Using Social Media:** We attempted to identify the most innovative firms with novel implementations of KM. The firms which according to industry practitioners are using novel ideas to develop cutting edge technologies for KM and also changing the scope of traditional KM implementations.

CASE STUDY

Case based theory development research is one of the most widely accepted theory advancement methods. "…a new generalization may emerge from case study's findings alone. The analytic generalization may be based on corroborating, modifying, rejecting or otherwise advancing theoretical concepts" (Yin, 2014, p. 42). In our case, after understanding the intricacies of the industry and various factors associated with KM implementations in different firms we conducted multiple case studies on the novel KM implementation. The analyses in sections below are based on 4 case studies performed on firms with unique KM tools and methods. Three of the firms are technology SMEs based out of India and fourth is a large Indian multinational software services giant, one of the largest in the world. Table 2 gives a summary of the characteristics of the four firms studied in the case studies. We analyzed their KM tools in-depth to draw learning's and generalizable implications from them.

Table 2. Description of KM implementations studied

S. No.	Firm	Industry	Size (No. of Employees)	Novelty
1	Tata Consultancy Services	IT Services	More than 300000	Developed a large KM tool in-house
2	ApartmentAdda	Closed service provider to apartment complexes	30-50	Sources information from a closed network of users
3	Roposo.com	Fashion deals online	55-70	Uses information from consumers to serve another set of consumers. Typical crowdsourcing
4	SafeCity	Crowd mapping of sexual harassment issues	10-25	Sources information to build knowledge base from public at large

The choice of these firms for case study was based on the following factors as prescribed by (Benbasat, Goldstein, & Mean, 1987; Patton, 2005):

1. **Having Maximum Diversity and Extremes in the Cases:** The ability to draw meaningful and generalizable results from small sample case studies is best possible with the diverse sample. The sample was diverse in terms of size of employees as well as in terms of different industries to which they belonged. Having cases from different ends of the spectrum allowed us to analyze the phenomenon in much more depth from different angles.
2. **Having Maximum Novelty:** Another factor that was looked into while choosing the case studies was "novelty". New and exciting interpretations of KM methods provide a wider learning opportunity with the possibility of new insights being unearthed. We attempted to find cases with different forms of modern KM implementations using social media.
3. **Ability to Get Maximum and In-Depth Information:** Ability to draw generalizable results and insights from case studies relies on the fact that the case studies are in-depth. We used those firms as cases to be studied from which we got maximum information about their KM implementation, purpose and intent. This allowed us to draw learning from those cases and develop a framework for the same.

Research Validation

A case study based research framework is considered to be rigorous if it satisfies three conditions i.e. a) high internal validity, b) construct validity and c) analytic generalizability (Gibbert, Ruigrock, & Wicki, 2008).

1. Yin (2011) states that for an exploratory work, the internal validity is established by its strong sense of logic building for the theoretical foundations of the phenomenon under study. To achieve the same, we draw from various strands of literature to position the relevance and theoretical basis for our proposed framework.
2. Construct validity ensures the presence of "….a clear chain of evidence to allow readers to reconstruct how the researcher went from the initial research questions to the final conclusions" (Gibbert et al., 2008, p. 1468). Data triangulation technique that entails collecting data from more than one

source to validate the findings is used for the same. We draw our data not only from expert interviews and company analysis but also from independent third party news from websites, corporate magazines etc.

3. The third is the external validity of the research. According to Cook and Campbell (1979) "… researchers should provide a clear rationale for the case study selection, and ample details on the case study context to allow the reader to appreciate the researchers' sampling choices" (Cook & Campbell, 1979, p. 83). In our sections on research methods explained above, we provide the complete description of the field settings and data collection methods to enable the future researchers to derive their own conclusions from the evidence presented in our work.

CROWDSOURCING VS. GATEKEEPING: THE CHOICE TO BE MADE

"The rise of social media has made the question of whether to integrate social media redundant. The question is how and when to integrate." This statement made by a social media entrepreneur during one of our interview sessions perfectly describes the situation of KM systems evolution as of today. Today the most important decision to be made by management teams at all firms is to settle the "Gatekeeping vs. Crowdsourcing" debate. These two philosophies represent the two extremes of the KM system integration with social media (Albors, Ramos, & Hervas, 2008). Although most firms base their KM systems somewhere in the continuum between a truly crowdsourced one and a fully protected one, understanding the intricacies of these philosophies and its impact on firm's own information strategy is the fundamental step in design of the KM system.

Knowledge Gatekeeping

Gatekeeping is a security term implying protecting entry or exit to something of value (Barzilai-Nahon, 2005; Lewin, 1947; Mitchell, Boyle, Burgess, & McNeil, 2014). The term was first used for information protection in human systems by psychologist Kurt Lewin (Lewin, 1947). Higher the perceived value of the item being protected; higher is the effort in ensuring robust gatekeeping mechanisms. In terms of KM system, it would translate to protecting the access to the institutional knowledge of firms to a select few (Macdonald & Williams, 1994). These may be the only the employees of the firm and in some extreme cases a select group of employees of the firm. In information intensive industries, such gatekeeping is more prevalent. More and more firms are easing the access to KM systems gradually due to the problems posed by them. As one of our interviewees with wide KM experience commented:

In past some firms protected institutional knowledge so much that to get information about the past project you needed to visit the KM department and get a copy of the information. Something like this not only slowed the outcome, it also discouraged employees from using past experiences of projects to develop better solutions.

The major problem posed by such gatekeeping is that gatekeeping entails significant cost (Chen & Liu, 2013; Macdonald & Williams, 1994). The benefits of stringent gatekeeping have to be enormous to offset the costs of gatekeeping and also discouraging the usage of such systems. Today the incentive to have a greater control is decreasing due to easier availability of information on public sources from the internet or otherwise. Creation of information banks and KM systems is also difficult in such systems where employees feel it to be an additional task to develop this. This statement by an interviewee illustrates the problem with this system "when you know that there is very little chance that you would ever refer to a document again, you practically have no incentive to create that document in first place".

Crowdsourcing

It is the other extreme end of KM philosophy where all the information is sourced from the public at large. The institutional information is not internal to institute which is collected from few select employees (Vouri, 2012). Information is readily available to all in a firm and sometimes even outside firm. This leads to interesting business models, models that were not possible earlier are now possible and being implemented by some firms in various corners of the world. One of the technical developers of Safecity stated "without the power of social media, creating a website and service like ours was not possible. It would take years before we could build a database worth deploying publicly. We source information from people and let other people access it. That's our business model at the core".

The second important consequence of having a crowdsourced information model, even within the firm is that it creates a peer pressure to generate and store knowledge that was a very difficult task earlier (Brzozowski, Sandholm, & Hogg, 2009). The impact of such models on quantity and quality of information being generated can best be understood by the following statement elucidating simple human psychology where social media creates maximum effect.

When employees see that their peers are generating information that they use, it creates a mental pressure on them to contribute or be seen as the odd one out. It generates information quickly. Even quality of information goes up as people get likes and ratings on their articles, a phenomenon that was possible due to social media tools only.

Information Management Framework

Figure 1 shown here is the proposed framework wherein most of the KM systems of the firms can be categorized. These classes are along two axes of the need for speed of information collection on y-axis and criticality of information to be managed on the x-axis. Although the firms' KM efforts may lie anywhere in the solution space represented by the two axes, four major categories are represented for ease of understanding.

The first one is the category wherein the need for speed of information collation is low but the information is very critical. Firms need to maintain a very strict control on where the information is sourced from and who accesses it. This is very critical for firms in industries like pharmaceuticals or telecom where the performance depends on the quality of information which is also a critical factor for maintaining the competitive advantage of the firms. This style of KM system is termed as "Insourcing". It is implemented by having a strict gatekeeping regime with access control at both data entry and data reading points. Most of such systems have little to no integration with social media or even rely on the network effect.

The second style of KM system is for those firms where the information is not very critical for core operations of firm and errors in reliability of information can be acceptable to a certain degree but the

Figure 1. The matrix of information management

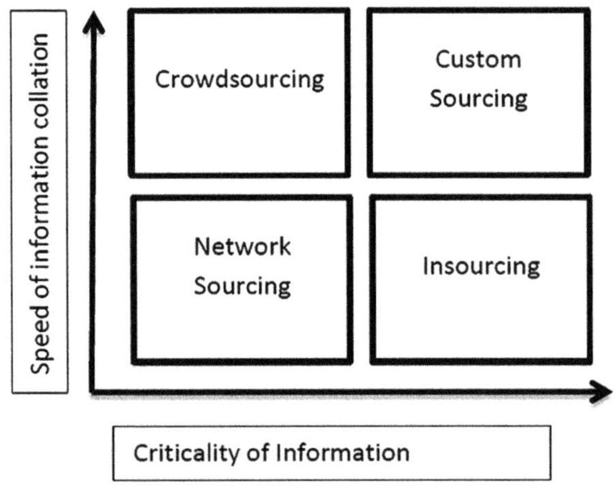

information is required to be built up very fast. For emergent firms that need to scale up quickly or collect a large amount of non-critical data such KM systems are very useful. Such KM systems termed as "crowdsourcing" is obtained by having a close network of public media through channels like Facebook etc. Such KM system are becoming very popular now and is even leading to development of new business models

Another style of networked KM system is "network sourcing". This style is most beneficial when the requirement for speed of data collection or criticality both is low to medium. In such systems, information is sourced from networks open or closed. Most of such networks are however closed or limited. An example might be a firm level network where a firm uses Facebook closed group to enable employee interaction and generate ideas. Some firms have even used such channels for getting ideas about new products by invoking network of their customers over public media like Facebook or Twitter.

The final KM style is one of the most critical ones and something that traditional firms use more often now. This KM style is "Custom Sourcing" or sourcing information from a large set of pre-determined networks deploying network effect but also maintaining the quality of information by having control on the sources from which the information is drawn. A typical example can be the KM of a large retailer that sources its information from a targeted group of suppliers and customers along with reviewers to decide the stock of the products to keep. This method builds a large credible database of information very quickly but requires considerable expertise and investment to develop.

LESSONS FROM IMPLEMENTATIONS: ANALYSIS OF CASE STUDIES

As stated in previous sections, 4 case studies were conducted on live implementations of innovative KM initiatives by firms to validate our framework and draw additional learning for firms to cope with the growing impact of social media. The aim of this practical case analysis is to see some of the unique implementations of KM systems and their varying interaction and evolution from social media tools. These examples do not focus on the technical aspect of the implementations but rather draw learning for the managerial audience to illustrate which kind of approach works best under what circumstances.

Such case study based analysis of the discussed framework would provide a powerful tool for CIOs of firms to engage the power of social media in their KM initiatives.

Knome: A Specialized Social Media for a Large Firm

The first case in point is of one of the largest IT services firm of the world. Tata Consultancy Services (TCS) is a 13.5 billion dollar firm with a presence in over 46 countries. TCS has an employee count of over 300,000. For such a large firm codifying organizational knowledge is of paramount information, more so because the industry and firm dynamics which include:

1. A very high rate of attrition (11-20%);
2. High learning curve to keep abreast with evolving technologies;
3. Very high degree of competition.

These factors force TCS to have a highly evolved KM solution. Without a highly efficient KM solution, managing organizational knowledge for a firm with high attrition in a highly volatile industry is extremely difficult.

To achieve codification of all organizational information, TCS uses a two-tiered KM system. The first tier is a social media developed in-house for organizational employees called Knome®. This allows employees at TCS to connect with each other and share information amongst one another. The information includes information on projects, latest technologies projects, IP etc. The second layer is the knowledge bank where all codified information is stored in a wiki like structure (the system is not a wiki though). The authors of these knowledge bases are the employees themselves who have been given access to edit the information based on role, hierarchy and project. This codified information is available to all employees of the firm to access for any future project.

Crowdsourcing Information: Roposo.com1

Roposo is a product cataloguing and aggregating service which displays wares from more than 100 online retailers. It offers deals and discounts on the most popular product combinations. For services like Roposo, survival and excellence is dependent on it acquiring a huge amount of intelligence and knowledge database of popular fashion styles, colors popular among various age groups etc. Such knowledge bases have been built over years by large online retailers like Amazon successfully. The big players use these knowledge bases to offer interesting and relevant offers to their clients.

For Roposo the success depends on being able to develop such a knowledge base quickly and without a very high cost. This is an extremely trying challenge for firms like Roposo. It is in such instances where the power of social knowledge creation and collation can be best utilized. Roposo creates a recommender system by asking its users to develop a combination or bucket of products to mimic a roving fashion czar.

The products, styles, designs and brands on offer at this website are recommended by users who create their own lists with their names and photographs. This is social recommendation engine that collects/creates knowledge through crowdsourcing and share it with like-minded people. Social media helps in better scrutinizing of data based on the number of followers/comment/reviews. A user can see the products, designs and fashion combinations suggested by their favorite fashion czars.

The KM challenge for Roposo is very different from firms like TCS. It has to develop a knowledge base very quickly and keep updating it. Its complete business model depends on the quality, quantity and reliability of information that it can crowdsource.

Custom Sourcing Information from Consumer for Consumer: SafeCity

It is a platform that documents personal experiences of sexual harassment and abuse in public spaces. It further creates a visualization of that information on a map in the form of hotspots or location based trends. It facilitates crowd mapping of information that is inspired by a startup based out of Egypt named "Harassmap". The service has about 4000 reports from over 50 cities of India and almost 500 from Nepal. They are creating a database of information that currently does not exist as most of these reports have never been officially published.

This firm's existence and business model is dependent on it collecting information and building a huge and reliable information bank. They use an open-information collecting mechanism for gathering information from users. This method of collecting information and building a knowledge bank can be termed a sort of "information crowdsourcing". The major issue of using crowdsourcing is evaluating the authenticity of the information coming in.

According to Safecity, their information collection model does nothing to ensure authenticity. So they connect with their users to ensure high quality of incoming information.

There is almost no chance of validating the incoming information. The only way to ensure integrity here is to sensitize people and connect with them on an emotional level so that misuse of the platform for feeding faulty information can be prevented from the very beginning. It is more about projecting the sincerity in our project rather than just operating as an online reporting system. Hence, we are conducting regular workshops and making sure that this sincerity is being organically spread through people.

In this case, although the information generating stakeholders are external to the system, regular meetings and sensitizing endeavors connects with these stakeholders and ensures the maximum integrity of data.

Business to Consumer Knowledge Network: ApartmentAdda.com

It is a unique concept of developing dedicated services for specific apartments and housing complexes. Such a group for a single complex is called an "ADDA". An ADDA can be understood as a secure and private portal for an apartment/villa Complex. Each ADDA has integrated web based software system for communication among residents, facility management, and society accounting. The challenge for such a service to flourish is to develop intelligence about each housing complex uniquely. Given the security and privacy concerns of various residents, it is also essential that information and kind of services being offered to a particular housing complex be kept secret from other complexes.

The two possible approaches for such data collection and information warehouse development are explained below:

1. **Traditional Method:** Where the service offering firm (ApartmentAdda) gathers all the information from different societies and develops its offerings.

2. **The Social Method:** The social method that the firm has employed capitalizes on the information available to its users to build its knowledge base. The residents of a society contribute information for the service. This can be construed to be a system of knowledge development from consumers. The incentive for consumers to give authentic information is high as the firm modifies its service based on the information available. Also, small communities of closed network and peer identification prevent falsification of any information.

The social method is not just cost-efficient for the firm but also provides an external validity of data and thus is more trustable. People found data contributed by other like them more trustable and hence the transactions based on such data led to a much higher traction amongst the customer base of ApartmentAdda.

Discussion and Analysis

To analyze the four distinct cases, lenses of social media and KM interaction has been used. The aim as always is to find the generalizable patterns from the case and also the places where the cases show distinctive behavior not explained by the framework. The cases have been analyzed on four factors i.e. uniqueness of the platform, criticality of information being managed, the pace of knowledgebase creation and integration with public social media tools.

Uniqueness of the Platform

A platform's uniqueness can have both negative and positive implications. On the positive side, it may offer multiple features that may not be present in any of the off-the-shelf products for knowledge management. While this may improve the quality of knowledge being collected and make it focused, it comes with a risk of alienating the users. In an age of massive social media presence dominated by few ubiquitous media outlets like Facebook, LinkedIn etc. people may not be too comfortable or willing to learn new platforms. This has been the bane of various traditional KM tools that have failed to pump enthusiasm in the target user base to use them. Offering a unique and customized platform is thus a risky venture and firms should carefully evaluate their objectives before going for it.

A unique platform will serve a better purpose if the dependency of the users on the platform is huge and also if the number of potential users is large enough to justify such a large scale development. As seen in these cases TCS has a unique platform that is used by over 300,000 users and the high turnover of employees there make it almost imperative for users to fall back on the platform, hence a very high usage of their tool.

Criticality of Information Being Stored

Criticality of information being stored is one of the most important factors determining the choice of KM system as well as its integration with the outside world through social media. For firms like TCS the KM system stores very critical information, most of the information is critical for the business and also frequently consists of intellectual property. On the other hand, the information content of Safecity is not that critical. It is contributed by the users and is collected to be released to public only. The integration with public media does not pose any security risk for the firm. Somewhere in the middle there exist firms like ApartmentAdda where the criticality of data is not zero but not very huge either.

Firms should be careful while integrating social media with their KM systems. While a large knowledge base is essential for fast scaling up and offering better and standardized services, information leaks for firms can quickly erode that value and also shake the stakeholder confidence.

Pace of Knowledge Creation

The speed at which social media generates knowledge is possibly its most revolutionary impact. The need of having a KM system based on social media principles promoting network effects or drawing from social tools depends on the required pace of knowledgebase creation. A social media enabled system by its network structure would create a lot more information at a much higher pace. Roposo, as an instance, used the network structure to create a huge amount of fashion database from external users. Creation of such a database without a network structure or social interaction would take ages and would require many experts.

Integration with Public Social Media

With public social media, the article implies mean social networking websites and tools available freely over the internet like Twitter®, Facebook®, Linkedin® etc. As explained above the pace of knowledgebase creation is very high with social tools promoting network effects, but interaction with public social networks leads to an even more phenomenal speed. This is because these networks have a large user base that are online for a large part of the day on these tools and are highly familiar with this tool. Firms like Safecity and Roposo have social media interconnection tools to build up the database by connecting to public social media. However, as explained earlier, firms with data criticality issues shy away from collecting data from public forums for two reasons. One this isolates their KM system from the influx of a lot of unverifiable information and also that it helps in not exposing their KM system to the outside world.

The analysis on these four counts for the four firms can be summarized below and the four firms can be seen to be belonging to different categories of KM system developing firms.

Table 3 was created after a careful evaluation of the four firms on these four counts. As we can see the four types of KM tools are not in black and white but rather in various shades of grey. The needs of different firms differ widely and firms often create a KM system best suited to their needs. In our case, TCS is a typical example of a firm using insourcing for information creation and storage. Their needs are such due to the criticality of information. There is no pressing need for high speed KM development for them. KM development is an outcome and not a requirement for TCS. However, for other firms that are small startups, a robust KM is needed for growing and their pace of growth is limited by quality and breadth of the knowledge base. Firms like ApartmentAdda use network sourcing to source information about housing complexes and tailor their offerings while firms like Safecity and Roposo use something between Crowd and custom sourcing to get the kind of information they are seeking.

An important lesson that lies here for all CIOs planning evolution of their KM tools is testing their requirement on the two parameters of criticality and need for pace. Social media integration rarely goes well with highly critical information. A way out for many firms can be a custom social media tool development like TCS. This approach though very costly might be immensely helpful for large firms with

Table 3. Comparison of the KM implementations

S. No.	Factor	Score			
		TCS	SafeCity	Roposo	ApartmentAdda
1	Uniqueness of platform	High	Low	Low	High
2	Criticality of Information	Very High	Low	Low	High
3	Need for Pace of Creation	Medium	High	Very High	Medium
4	Social Media Integration	Very Low	Very High	Very High	Low
Type of KM at the Firm		Insourcing	Custom Sourcing	Crowdsourcing	Network Sourcing

huge KM requirements. The very fact that social system brings with it a high degree of external validity and peer pressure to be a part of the system solves dual issues that have plagued KM systems for long. These dual issues were incentivizing people to develop the knowledge base and second ensuring the correctness of the collected data. Though the correctness of data for very open KM systems with high connectivity with public social media tools will also be difficult but refuge in such situations can be taken in high number of users like Wikipedia, where the average information is safely assumed to be correct.

CONCLUSION

Social media as an information gathering tool has truly revolutionized the way information generated, collected and analyzed in the world. This has profound implications not only for public systems but also for all the knowledge management systems of firms. The most important implication that a social media enabled KM system has, is the increase in the pace of the KM development. It has additional benefits of generating interest in the use of KM by involving peers. Incentivizing employees at a firm to develop knowledge base has always been a huge challenge for firms and social media enabled systems can solve this to a huge extent. The network effect that social media enabled system generates has an additional benefit of the certain amount of external validation of data. However, one of the most important concerns in initiating a modern social media enabled KM system for firms has been to decide the extent of usage, the benefits to be derived from such integration and the access levels. The criticality of private data and quality and reliability of information collected as such are other concerns that hinder its more widespread usage.

Through our analysis, the article has presented a matrix structure indicating the extent and type of social media interaction based KM that would be most beneficial for firms. The matrix is on a scale of need for pace of information collected and criticality of information. The cases presented in this chapter analyses some unique KM implementations at firms and how they have made use of social media aspects in their KM implementations. The framework presented here has been drawn from intensive literature review and experience of practitioners in this niche field. This paper builds on their expertise and presents a generalizable framework for use by the top management of the firm.

The work presented in this chapter is not without its fair share of drawbacks which comes from the choice of methodology primarily. Being a very niche and emerging field, the generalizability of the framework needs to be further established and relevant cultural context needs to be understood before implementation. Some cultures are more open to social interaction while others are not. Behavior of firm's employees on online social media tools and KM systems needs to be viewed through this cultural lens. Such cultural context needs to be better understood both as a research problem as well as an implementation problem by the management team. The framework presented here is a starting point in understanding the delicate balance between various issues plaguing higher usage of social media in KM systems and how to increase this usage.

REFERENCES

Alavi, M., & Leidner, D. E. (2001). Review: Knowledge management and Knowledge Management Systems: Conceptual Foundations and Research Issues. *Management Information Systems Quarterly*, *25*(1), 107–136. doi:10.2307/3250961

Albors, J., Ramos, J. C., & Hervas, J. L. (2008). New Learning Network Paradigms: Communities of Objectives, Crowdsourcing, Wikis and Open-source. *International Journal of Information Management*, *28*(3), 194–202. doi:10.1016/j.ijinfomgt.2007.09.006

Allee, V. (2004). The future of knowledge. *The Learning Organization*, *11*(1), 94–95. doi:10.1108/09696470410515751

Barzilai-Nahon, K. (2005). Network Gatekeeping Theory. In K. E. Fisher, S. Erdelez, & L. McKechnie (Eds.), *Theories of information behavior* (pp. 247–254). American Society of Information Science and Technology.

Benbasat, I., Goldstein, D. K., & Mead, M. (1987). The case research strategy in studies of information systems. *Management Information Systems Quarterly*, *11*(3), 369–386. doi:10.2307/248684

Bhatt, G. D., Pankaj, P., & Rodger, J. A. (2014). Managing Knowledge in Shared Spaces. *Intelligent Information Management*.

Bloom, N., Garicano, L., Sadun, R., & Van Reenen, J. (2014). The distinct effects of information technology and communication technology on firm organization. *Management Science*, *60*(12), 2859–2885. doi:10.1287/mnsc.2014.2013

Brzozowski, M. J., Sandholm, T., & Hogg, T. (2009). Effects of feedback and peer pressure on contributions to enterprise social media. In *Proceedings of the ACM 2009 international conference on Supporting group work* (pp. 61-70). ACM. doi:10.1145/1531674.1531684

Castells, M. (2011). *The rise of the network society: The information age: Economy, society, and culture* (Vol. 1). New York: John Wiley & Sons.

Chen, C. J., & Huang, J. W. (2009). Strategic human resource practices and innovation performance—The mediating role of knowledge management capacity. *Journal of Business Research*, *62*(1), 104–114. doi:10.1016/j.jbusres.2007.11.016

Chen, J., & Liu, Q. (2013). Information Markets, Product Markets and Vertical Merger. *Journal of Economics and Finance*, *37*(1), 33–61. doi:10.1007/s12197-010-9169-0

Cohen, J. F., & Olsen, K. (2015). Knowledge Management Capabilities and Firm Performance: A Test of Universalistic, Contingency and Complementarity Perspectives. *Expert Systems with Applications*, *42*(3), 1178–1188. doi:10.1016/j.eswa.2014.09.002

Cook, T. D., & Campbell, D. T. (1979). *Quasi-Experimental Design: Design and Analysis Issues for Field Settings*. Skokie, IL: Rand McNally.

Dalkir, K. (2013). *Knowledge Management in Theory and Practice*. Burlington, MA: Routledge.

Darroch, J. (2005). Knowledge Management, Innovation and Firm Performance. *Journal of Knowledge Management*, *9*(3), 101–115. doi:10.1108/13673270510602809

Dewett, T., & Jones, G. R. (2001). The Role of Information Technology in the Organization: A Review, Model, and Assessment. *Journal of Management*, *27*(3), 313–346. doi:10.1177/014920630102700306

Dixon, N. M. (2000). *Common Knowledge: How Companies Thrive by Sharing What They Know*. MA: Harvard Business Press.

Eisenhardt, K. M. (1989). Building Theories from Case Study Research. *Academy of Management Review*, *14*(4), 532–550.

Fuller, S. (2012). *Knowledge Management foundations*. Burlington, MA: Routledge.

Geisler, E., & Wickramasinghe, N. (2015). *Principles of Knowledge Management: Theory, Practice, and Cases*. Burlington, MA: Routledge.

Gibbert, M., Ruigrok, W., & Wicki, B. (2008). Research Notes and Commentaries What Passes as a Rigorous Case Study. *Strategic Management Journal*, *29*(13), 1465–1474. doi:10.1002/smj.722

Hislop, D. (2013). *Knowledge Management in Organizations: A Critical Introduction*. Oxford: Oxford University Press.

Kaplan, A. M., & Haenlein, M. (2010). Users of the World, Unite! The Challenges and Opportunities of Social Media. *Business Horizons*, *53*(1), 59–68. doi:10.1016/j.bushor.2009.09.003

Katz, J. E., & Rice, R. E. (2002). *Social Consequences of Internet Use: Access, Involvement, and Interaction* (pp. 1–463). Cambridge, MA: MIT press.

Kim, T. H., Lee, J. N., Chun, J. U., & Benbasat, I. (2014). Understanding the Effect of Knowledge Management Strategies on Knowledge Management Performance: A Contingency Perspective. *Information & Management*, *51*(4), 398–416. doi:10.1016/j.im.2014.03.001

Klein, P. D. (1971). A Proposed Definition of Propositional Knowledge. *The Journal of Philosophy*, *68*(16), 471–482. doi:10.2307/2024845

Kulkarni, U. R., Ravindran, S., & Freeze, R. (2007). A Knowledge Management Success Model: Theoretical Development and Empirical Validation. *Journal of Management Information Systems*, *23*(3), 309–347. doi:10.2753/MIS0742-1222230311

Kvale, S., & Brinkmann, S. (2009). Interviews: Learning the craft of qualitative research interviewing. *Sage (Atlanta, Ga.)*.

Lai, Y. L., Hsu, M. S., Lin, F. J., Chen, Y. M., & Lin, Y. H. (2014). The Effects of Industry Cluster Knowledge Management on Innovation Performance. *Journal of Business Research*, *67*(5), 734–739. doi:10.1016/j.jbusres.2013.11.036

Lavie, D. (2006). The Competitive Advantage of Interconnected Firms: An Extension of the Resource-Based View. *Academy of Management Review*, *31*(3), 638–658. doi:10.5465/AMR.2006.21318922

Lerman, K. (2007). Social Information Processing in News Aggregation. *IEEE Internet Computing*, *11*(6), 16–28. doi:10.1109/MIC.2007.136

Levy, M. (2009). WEB 2.0 Implications on Knowledge Management. *Journal of Knowledge Management*, *13*(1), 120–134. doi:10.1108/13673270910931215

Lewin, K. (1947). Group Decision and Social Change. *Readings in Social Psychology*, *3*, 197–211.

Lievrouw, L. A., & Livingstone, S. (Eds.). (2002). *Handbook of New Media: Social Shaping and Consequences of ICTs*. Sage.

Macdonald, S., & Williams, C. (1994). The Survival of the Gatekeeper. *Research Policy*, *23*(2), 123–132. doi:10.1016/0048-7333(94)90049-3

Mitchell, R., Boyle, B., Burgess, J., & McNeil, K. (2014). "You Can't Make a Good Wine Without a Few Beers": Gatekeepers and Knowledge Flow in Industrial Districts. *Journal of Business Research*, *67*(10), 2198–2206. doi:10.1016/j.jbusres.2014.01.007

Opdenakker, R. (2006). Advantages and Disadvantages of Four Interview Techniques in Qualitative Research. In *Forum Qualitative Sozialforschung/Forum: Qualitative. Social Research*, *7*(4).

Patton, M. Q. (2005). *Qualitative Research*. New York, NY: John Wiley & Sons, Ltd. doi:10.1002/0470013192.bsa514

Polanyi, M. (1966). The Logic of Tacit Inference. *Philosophy (London, England)*, *41*(155), 1–18. doi:10.1017/S0031819100066110

Powell, W. W., & Snellman, K. (2004). The Knowledge Economy. *Annual Review of Sociology*, *30*(1), 199–220. doi:10.1146/annurev.soc.29.010202.100037

Richards, L. (2014). *Handling Qualitative Data: A Practical Guide*. London: Sage.

Ritchie, J., Lewis, J., Nicholls, C. M., & Ormston, R. (Eds.). (2013). *Qualitative Research Practice: A Guide for Social Science Students and Researchers*. London: Sage.

Senge, P. M. (2014). *The Fifth Discipline Fieldbook: Strategies and Tools for Building a Learning Organization*. London: Crown Business.

Siemens, G. (2014). *Connectivism: A Learning Theory for the Digital Age*. Working Paper Series. Accessed at http://er.dut.ac.za/handle/123456789/69

Tashakkori, A., & Teddlie, C. (Eds.). (2010). *Sage Handbook of Mixed Methods in Social & Behavioral Research*. London: Sage. doi:10.4135/9781506335193

Tellis, W. M. (1997). Application of a Case Study Methodology. *Qualitative Report*, *3*(3), 1–19.

Vrat, P. (2014). Systems Approach and Supply Chain Management. In *Materials Management* (pp. 357–378). New Delhi: Springer India.

Vuori, M. (2012). Exploring Uses of Social Media in a Global Corporation. *Journal of Systems and Information Technology*, *14*(2), 155–170. doi:10.1108/13287261211232171

Weaven, S., Grace, D., Dant, R., & Brown, J. R. (2014). Value Creation through Knowledge Management in Franchising: A Multi-Level Conceptual Framework. *Journal of Services Marketing*, *28*(2), 97–104. doi:10.1108/JSM-09-2013-0251

Wengraf, T. (2001). *Qualitative Research Interviewing: Biographic Narrative and Semi-Structured Methods*. London: Sage. doi:10.4135/9781849209717

Wiig, K. M. (1997). Knowledge Management: Where Did it Come From and Where Will it Go? *Expert Systems with Applications*, *13*(1), 1–14. doi:10.1016/S0957-4174(97)00018-3

Yin, R. K. (2011). *Applications of Case Study Research*. London: Sage.

Yin, R. K. (2014). *Case Study Research: Design and Methods*. London: Sage.

Zack, M. H. (2012, Spring). Rethinking the knowledge based organization. *MIT Sloan Management Review*.

Zhao, Y., & Zhu, Q. (2014). Evaluation on Crowdsourcing Research: Current Status and Future Direction. *Information Systems Frontiers*, *16*(3), 417–434. doi:10.1007/s10796-012-9350-4

KEY TERMS AND DEFINITIONS

Attrition: The cumulative rate of employee outgo from a firm. It is the sum total of employee outgo due to any reason.

Crowdsourcing: The process of collecting any desired input for a process through a number of people gathered through any means or platform.

Knowledge Gatekeeping: Process of filtering the dissemination of any information in a specific channel or platform.

Knowledge Management: Methods and techniques through which a firm manages the institutional knowledge within the firm.

Network Effect: Effect of an entity on the behavior of other entities in a connected network.

Social Network: A network of entities related through some mechanism that enables close interaction between the entities.

ENDNOTE

1 http://www.livemint.com/Leisure/BXUATmzUVCzf77oM0yZHSJ/Lounge-Review--Roposocom.html?utm_source=copy

Chapter 11
The Role of Social Media in Knowledge Management:
How SECI-SM Model Can Help

Syed Afzal Moshadi Shah
COMSATS Insititue of Information Technology, Pakistan

Shehla Amjad
COMSATS Insititue of Information Technology, Pakistan

ABSTRACT

The purpose of this chapter is to highlight the importance of social media and theoretically link it with Knowledge Management (KM). A massive increase in social media usage around the world and its enhanced role in everyday life of employees offer enormous opportunities to businesses. One of the most important challenges that management faces in today's dynamic business environment is knowledge management. This becomes the key concern in professional service firms that are knowledge intensive in nature. The chapter discusses the association between social media and knowledge management. A theoretical model (SECI-SM) proposed by Shah, Khan, and Amjad (2013) is presented and discussed which is an extension of the seminal work of Nonaka and Takeuchi (1995). The model puts social media at the heart of knowledge management system and processes. It purports social media as an ideal vehicle for knowledge sharing and retaining. The chapter discusses the superiority of SECI-SM Model and lays out some useful suggestions for businesses.

INTRODUCTION

Social media has become a central part of the daily life of most Internet users around the world. According to PewResearch (2014) around 74% of adults on the Internet use social networking websites. This has captured the interests of marketers and businesses around the world. To them social media is more than a socialization website where an individual interacts with his friends and family. Marketers approach towards social media is somewhat similar to the reaction of a hungry Tom (a cat) to Jerry (a mouse) in the "Tom and Jerry" Cartoons. A hungry Tom would not see the Jerry in his natural outfit rather he

DOI: 10.4018/978-1-5225-0495-5.ch011

would see an image of a roasted mouse. If the number of the rats increases in a particular scene, Tom's imaginations of roasted mice will also increase. Companies have already started to investigate different prospects enhancing sales volume via social media forums.

One of the key success factors of leading companies over the period of time has remained around understanding of their customers. Successful companies know their customers better than average companies. The range of the customers may vary from current, potential, past or competitors' customers. Social media offers them a unique opportunity to approach all sorts of customers on a single forum.

Organizations that have their hand on the pulse of the market can devise better strategies which will earn them competitive and sustainable advantages. The key is the knowledge creation, acquisition and utilization on an appropriate time. This can better be explained by the example of Walmart stores Inc. The company has written history in the business world by becoming the first retailer that is more powerful than the manufacturers. It has become the most promising retail business around the world. This was achieved by remaining in touch with customers around the clock through an effective use of technology. This enabled the company to unfold the likes and dislikes of the customers which in return help them to understand the ongoing trends, fads and fashions.

Technology is just one aspect, however in order to remain sustainable in the market, companies have realized the importance of retaining employees that are enriched with relevant and valuable knowledge. This knowledge may be regarding the understanding of the market, or the operations of the businesses or simply the skills and capabilities required to effectively undertake a particular job. Empson (2001) claims that two things have contributed towards enhanced importance to knowledge management around the world. Firstly, a decline in capital and labor intensive firms in developed countries has lead to investment in businesses that are more information intensive in nature. Secondly, the advancement in information technology enabled organizations to develop more systematic procedures of knowledge management. Professional service firms (PSF) employee a high range of educated knowledge workers (Lowendahl, Revang, & Fosstenløkken, 2001) and hence are considered to be an appropriate audience for the implementation of SECI-SM Model.

The massive use of Internet users around the world and the popularity of social media have further decreased the global communication boundaries and distances. Some researchers view this opportunity to learn and enhance formal learning useful for knowledge sharing. Social media will provide a platform where knowledgeable individuals will earn more respect by readily sharing their experiences and leanings.

This chapter discusses 'SECI–SM Framework' proposed by Shah, Khan & Amjad (2013), an extension of the work done by Nonaka and Takeuchi (1995). It asserts that media can play a pivotal in knowledge management efforts and the organizations that introduce their knowledge management efforts around social media will reap valuable outcomes and enhance sustainability. Knowledge workers are always difficult to retain but those who are engaged through social media will be more useful and more cooperative in sharing knowledge.

Social media is a reality now; people socialize and will keep on socializing.

Researchers have strongly condemned a sole reliance on technology while making efforts towards developing knowledge management systems. Social media on the other hand furnishes an environment where participants interact freely and voluntarily. They interact according to their personal convenience and desires. They choose their preferred interactions and their limits to interact, making such an environment very conducive for knowledge sharing.

Figure 1. Clock image

Social media is not a substitute for conventional knowledge management tools and techniques.

Managing knowledge on social media should be embraced as an opportunity not as a threat. SECI-SM model does not undermine the conventional efforts towards knowledge management, but it suggests a platform that will have more outreaching impact in such efforts.

The time to implement social media based knowledge management system is now, now, now…

SOCIAL MEDIA IS EARNING AN UNPRECEDENTED POPULARITY

The popularity of social networking has been unprecedented over the last decade. PewResearch (2014) reported around 74% of the Internet users are active users of social media as well. Figure 2 indicates 72% of male Mnternet users and 76% of female Internet users socialize over the Internet. A significant difference between the age of different users is found on the basis of social website usage. The report found around equal participation from different educational background with 72% of high school grads or less, 78% having some college degrees where 73% having colleges degrees and above. Figure 3 shows the stats of the age groups using social media while Figure 4 shows the stats of mobile phones users using social media websites.

KNOWLEDE WORKERS AND CHALLENGES TO MANAGEMENT

The business environment has become more dynamic as compared to a decade ago. Jobs have become more dynamic in nature; require a high level of technical and computer skills, and diversified workforce. Most technical jobs require an up to date understanding and experience of latest tools and techniques in that field. This, on one hand keeps the skilled workforce under immense pressure to keep themselves

Figure 2. Stats on users of social networking sites

Who uses social networking sites

% of internet users within each group who use social networking sites

All internet users	*74%*
a Men	72
b Women	76
a 18-29	89[cd]
b 30 49	82[cd]
c 50-64	65[d]
d 65+	49
a High school grad or less	72
b Some college	78
c College+	73
a Less than $30,000/yr	79
b $30,000-$49,999	73
c $50,000-$74,999	70
d $75,000+	78

Pew Research Centers Internet Project January Omnibus Survey, January 23-26, 2014.
Note: Percentages marked with a superscript letter (e.g., [a]) indicate a statistically significant difference between that row and the row designated by that superscript letter, among categories of each demographic characteristic (e.g., age).

PEW RESEARCH CENTER

Figure 3. Stats on age groups using social networking sites

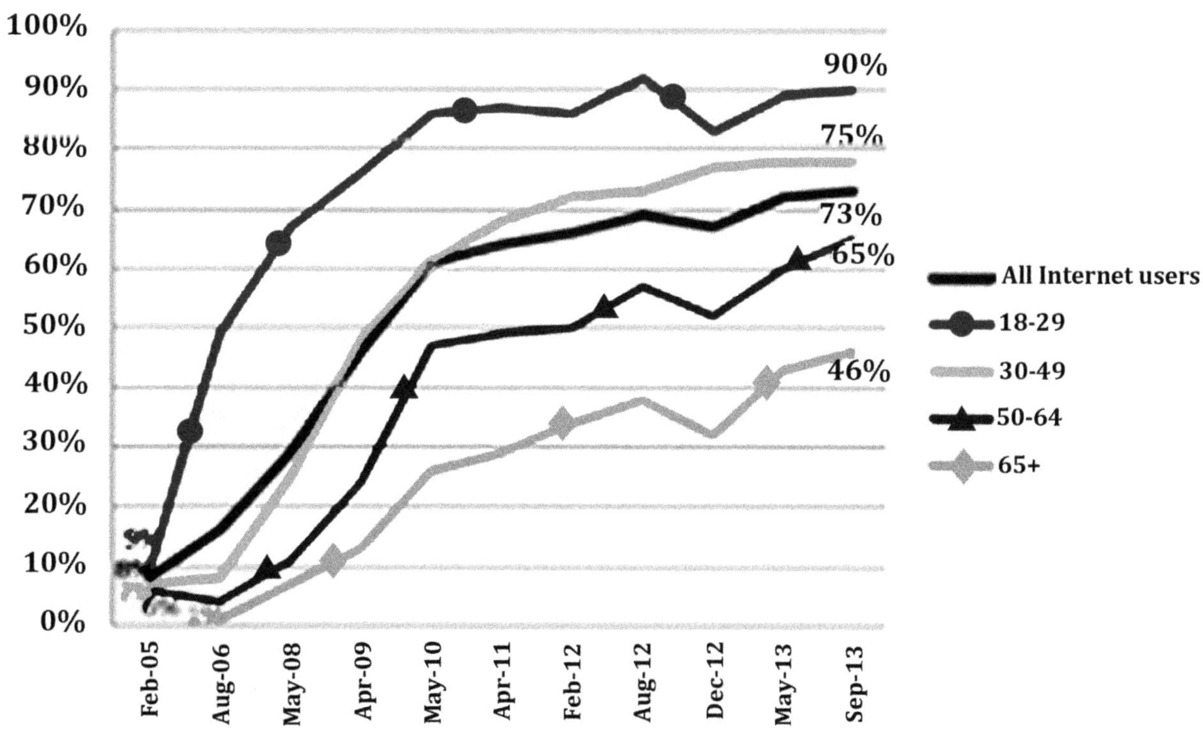

Figure 4. Stats on mobile users of social networking sites

Social Networking on Mobile Phones

% of cell phone owners who use a social networking site on their phone

	All cell phone owners (n=1,954)	40%
a	Men (n=895)	39
b	Women (n=1,059)	41
	Age	
a	18-29 (n=340)	67[bcd]
b	30-49 (n=562)	50[cd]
c	50-64 (n=587)	18[d]
d	65+ (n=429)	5
	Race/ethnicity	
a	White, Non-Hispanic (n=1,404)	36
b	Black, Non-Hispanic (n=234)	48[a]
c	Hispanic (n=180)	49[a]
	Annual household income	
a	Less than $30,000/yr (n=447)	38
b	$30,000-$49,999 (n=316)	40
c	$50,000-$74,999 (n=272)	48[a]
d	$75,000+ (n=538)	45[a]
	Education level	
a	No high school diploma (n=156)	33
b	High school grad (n=542)	37
c	Some College (n=490)	42[a]
d	College + (n=752)	43[ab]

Source: Pew Internet Spring Tracking Survey, March 15 – April 3, 2012. N=2,254 adults ages 18+. Interviews were conducted in English and Spanish and on landline and cell phones. Margin of error is +/- 3 percentage points for results based on cell phone owners.

Note: Percentages marked with a superscript letter (e.g., [a]) indicate a statistically significant difference between that row and the row designated by that superscript letter, among categories of each demographic characteristic (e.g. age).

abreast with latest developments made in their field, while on other hand poses a challenge to the management in the process of hiring, retaining and motivating the workforce. The demand of skilled workforce has become a boundary less phenomena where international players with the ease of Internet can quite easily approach, attract and hire skilled workforce around the world.

To company management, this triggers productivity concerns and creates a vacuum of knowledge also. Any company that has incurred a massive cost in the process of hiring, retaining, training and motivating such workforce faces a massive challenge of fulfilling this loss with replacement of expertise of the same level. Even if the company is able to hire a person of same skills and capabilities, still the knowledge in form of work experience, understanding of the company culture, work environment and so forth would be irreplaceable. Management is vigorously exploring the methods through which they can minimize this knowledge loss and to retain and enhance their knowledge base. Sometimes management finds out that the skilled and knowledgeable workforce is not very loyal to the company and is using the

Figure 5. A sinking boat

name of the organization to build their personal brand value and uses the organization as a vehicle to sell their skills and knowledgebase. Although these knowledge workers make their small boats, it is the responsibility of the management that it should not be at the cost of the organizational losses.

RELATIONSHIP BETWEEN SOCIAL MEDIA AND KNOWLEDGE MANAGEMENT

Social media to some researchers are websites that help to facilitate free interactions between individuals with an added feature of sharing contents (ConnectingPeople,2010), which to some is called social networking that includes web sites e.g. Facebook, Club Penguin, and Bebo (Huijster, 2008). MSN Messenger and Myspace can be added to this list, whereas Whatsapp and Viber can be added to mobile phone social networking tools. The individuals on these websites and mobile apps have a real time interaction experience. Individuals can leave instant messages, can have online discussion forums, interact with different individuals, and can exchange things through blogs, photos, videos and audios contents (Redecker et al., (2009). Dabbagh and Kitsantas (2012) have mentioned Blogs, Wikis, Google calendar, YouTube or Flickr, social networking sites, social bookmarking as effective tools for a personal learning environment.

Knowledge management according to IBM and Lotus is a systematic process for innovation, responsiveness, competency and efficiency by effective use of contents and expertise (Pohs, 2001). It is a tool that enables organizations to develop effective policies and actions to achieve desired goals (Horwitch & Armacost, 2002), which incorporates generating, extracting, transforming and storing correct knowledge. To some it is a process of generating knowledge, checking its validity, knowledge presentation and distribution to get the desired applicability (Bhatt, 2001).

Bradley and McDonald (2011a) have highlighted some similarities and differences between social media and knowledge management:

Similarities:

- The use of technology for accessing information.
- The need of individuals to generate information.
- Sharing of information with others.

Differences:

- Knowledge management is company driven (directed), whereas social media is self or peers driven.
- Knowledge management is what company considers is important for you, whereas social media is what an individual or his/her peers considers is important for him/her.

Reichental (2011) purports knowledge management system incorporating social media will be superior than the conventional methods. This will be ideal combination for managing behavioral and technical issues where the participants will feel more motivated towards knowledge sharing on social media and feel less threatened towards their knowledge or value loss (Reichental, 2011). Also, in the case of technical guidance, individuals seek the help from their social media friends.

Bradley and McDonald (2011b, p.2) highlighted major misconceptions towards the use of social media in organizations:

- Social media does not deliver real business value and can waste a lot of employee time.
- Social media poses unacceptable risks to privacy, IP protection, regulatory compliance, HR infractions, customer services and more.
- Social media is just another marketing channel.
- All you need to do is to provide social media technology and the rest will happen on its own. After all, that's how it happens on the internet.
- You don't need a business justification for social media because it's so cheap and you cannot anticipate or measure the benefits anyways.

ACADEMIC INVESTIGATION OF KNOWLEDGE MANAGEMENT AND SOCIAL MEDIA

Hughes, Rowe, Batey and Lee (2012) considered social networking sites (SNS) as an important platform for sharing information and social interaction. They reported a difference of personality of the users who opt different modes of SNS sites. Social media provides a platform for knowledge management where individuals can interact with technology and techniques that are most recommended and desired in order to secure a sustainable competitive advantage in the market (Bhutt, 2001). The informal sessions of leanings between learners used to take place between lunch breaks, study groups, brown bag sessions and student organizations (Martindale & Dowdy, 2010) have been replaced by social media interactions between them (Dabbagh & Kitsantas, 2012).

Massingham (2014) in his pioneering systematic study towards understanding the role of knowledge management within organizations has shared some interesting results over five years (2008-2013). The findings are that knowledge sharing can be promoted and enhanced through effective management of the knowledge and reject the mainstream criticism on the role of knowledge management on knowledge sharing. Knowledge strategy and knowledge measurement aspects are identified to be the most effective knowledge management toolkits. Swan, Newell, Scarbrough, Hislop, (1999) investigated the role of IT in developing an effective knowledge management system. They proposed that a "community based" model of knowledge management will produce higher results as compared to the one in which the focus is on IT called as "IT lead knowledge management initiatives".

Chua and Banerjee (2013) revealed some encouraging results for organizations managing knowledge management for their customers through social media. The customer knowledge management efforts put together by Starbucks through social media has played a vital role in enhancing their branding efforts and serving as an effective tool for marketing. The company has used social media as an effective tool to secure feedback from customers which contributes towards innovation. They have effectively engaged customers on social media and have overcome their reluctance to share knowledge.

Ardichvili, Page and Wentling (2003) in a qualitative study investigated the sources of motivation and barriers faced by the employees of Caterpillar Inc. while participating in virtual knowledge sharing communities. They identified two important aspects of knowledge sharing by employees on these forums. Firstly, if they consider the knowledge belongs to the organization or is beneficial for all, they would more readily share it on the forum. Secondly, employees refrain from sharing knowledge because of their certain fears i.e. the fear of misleading others and fear of being criticized by others. They recommended the company should eliminate such fears by introducing trust building measures in order to inculcate a healthy knowledge sharing platform.

Bradley and McDonald (2011b) call for developing an organizational vision for effective online community collaboration. They consider four activities as mandatory to achieve the desired objectives for social organizations:

1. Understanding when community collaboration is appropriate.
2. The knowledge of areas where community collaboration is more likely to deliver value.
3. The application of the understanding of organizational goals and culture.
4. Crafting an organizational vision for community collaboration.

A list of social media tools for inculcating personal learning environment by Dabbagh and Kitsantas (2012) is provided in Table 1.

Bhatt (2001) strongly recommended a totality of focus on all the three pillars of knowledge management i.e. people, technologies and techniques. A sole focus on one aspect while ignoring the others will have severe impact on organization's desire to remain competitive in the market (Bhatt, 2001). Dabbagh and Kitsantas (2012) considers the use of personal learning environment (PLE) facilitated by social media is establishing its grounds in the field of e-learning. The facility of social media to interact with participants in a real life and the ability to create, share and organize contents has given birth the concept of PLE (Martindale & Dowdy, 2010).

Four basic actions or stages of effective social media based collaborations are identified by Bradley and McDonald (2011):

1. **Contributions:** Community members enhance the knowledge through contributing thoughts, ideas, opinions, suggestions and even questions or problems.
2. **Feedback:** The knowledge gets enhanced and polished through the process of feedback from other participants in the group.

Table 1. Tools of social media to facilitate self-regulated learning in personal learning environment

	(Level 1) Personal Information Management →	(Level 2) Social Interaction and Collaboration →	(Level 3) Information Aggregation and Management →
Blogs	Instructor encourages students to use a blog as a private journal to set learning goals and plan for course assignments and tasks	Instructor encourages students to enable the blog comment feature to allow for instructor and peer feedback enabling basic interaction and sharing	Instructor demonstrates how to configure a blog to pull in additional content and how to add the blog to RSS aggregation services
Wikis	Instructor encourages students to use a wiki as a personal space for content organization and management	Instructor encourages students to enable the wiki's collaborative editing and commenting features for feedback	Instructor demonstrates how to view a wiki's history to promote student self-evaluation of their learning across time
Google Calendar	Instructor encourages students to use Google Calendar for personal planning	Instructor encourages students to enable the calendar sharing features to allow feedback and collaboration to complete course tasks	Instructor demonstrates how to archive personal and group calendars to promote student self-valuation regarding time planning and management
YouTube or Flickr	Instructor encourages students to use Flickr or YouTube to set up a personal media archive related to course content	Instructor encourages students to enable the sharing feature of the media archive and join similar media archives created by peers	Instructor demonstrates how to aggregate media from several media archives to refine their personal archive
Social networking sites	Instructor encourages students to create an academic and career profile on LinkedIn	Instructor encourages students to connect to online communities related to their professional goals	Instructor asks students to engage in self-reflection with the goal to restructure their profile and social presence
Social Bookmarking	Instructor encourages students to use a social bookmarking tool (e.g. Delicious) to organize course content	Instructor encourages students to collaborate with other classmates and create a shared list of bookmarks related to a specific learning topic or project	Instructor asks students to self-reflect on their personal and group bookmarks to enhance the desired learning outcome

Source: Adopted from Dabbagh and Kitsantas (2012).

3. **Judgment:** The community makes the judgment on the multisided discussions and subsequent feedbacks. The community endorses and validates the knowledge sharing process.
4. **Change:** Participant evaluates himself/herself and modifies his/her behavior which indicates his/her learning happened over the social media.

THE SECI Model

One of the most promising work in the field of knowledge management is by Nonaka and Takeuchi (1995), the famous SECI model. Knowledge management is a process of social interaction that involves four different types based on the nature of the knowledge being shared. A socialization process is required in order to convert tacit knowledge into another tacit knowledge, whereas converting tacit knowledge into explicit knowledge requires a process of externalization. Explicit knowledge can be converted to tacit knowledge through the process of internalization. The process of converting explicit knowledge into another type of explicit knowledge can be accomplished through combination process. The letters in SECI are Socialization, Externalization, Combination and Internalization. The authors claim that the model is universal in nature whereas few disagree (Andreeva & Ikhilchik, 2011) and believe that the claim can neither be accepted nor rejected on the basis of empirical findings. The model is presented in Figure 6. Firestone and McElroy (2003) strongly criticized the model as the implicit nature of the tacit knowledge is not transferable.

Yoshida (2015) proposed a design thinking methodology or soft system investigation following the SECI and reported that long term memory retention requires motivation by the management, curiosity

Figure 6. SECI model

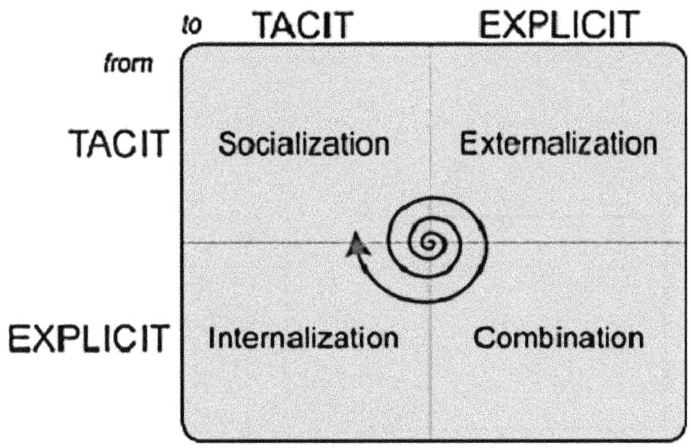

and inquiry ability of the participants. Liu, Zhou and Guan (2015) used SECI model to investigate the knowledge transfer between university and industry cooperation. They reported the impact of environmental factors and a multilevel knowledge acquisition, sharing and transformation have an impact on knowledge management system. Rabelo et al., (2015) studied knowledge management for software development activities and proposed a Competing Values Framework (CVF) in order to develop a conducive organizational cultural for knowledge management.

Cheng (2015) investigated knowledge management at schools using the SECI model at individual, group and organizational level. The role of strategies, processes, organizational culture, employees' competencies and information technology on knowledge management efforts discussed. Ahmad et al., (2015) utilized SECI model to develop a framework for enhance Students programming ability by combining it with pair programming. The results supported the theoretical framework and called for exploring other important determinants as well.

THE SECI-SM Model

Shah, Khan and Amjad (2013) have proposed a SECI-SM theoretical model that extends the work of Nonaka & Takeuchi (1995) by placing the social media in the heart of knowledge management process. The model is shown in Figure 7. It shows the spiral movement of the knowledge creation through Tacit to Explicit forms of knowledge interaction taking place over the Internet. The spiral loop in the middle of the SECI-SM model expresses the activity of knowledge sharing as a continuous activity. SECI-SM contains the following four dimensions by incorporating four stages in knowledge sharing:

- Combination over Social Media (C-SM).
- Externalization over Social Media (E-SM).
- Internationalization over Social Media (I-SM).
- Socialization over Social Media (S-SM).

The knowledge sharing over social media that facilitates conversion of explicit knowledge into explicit knowledge is termed as "Combination" and is referred as C-SM. This can be considered as one of the

Figure 7. SECI–SM model

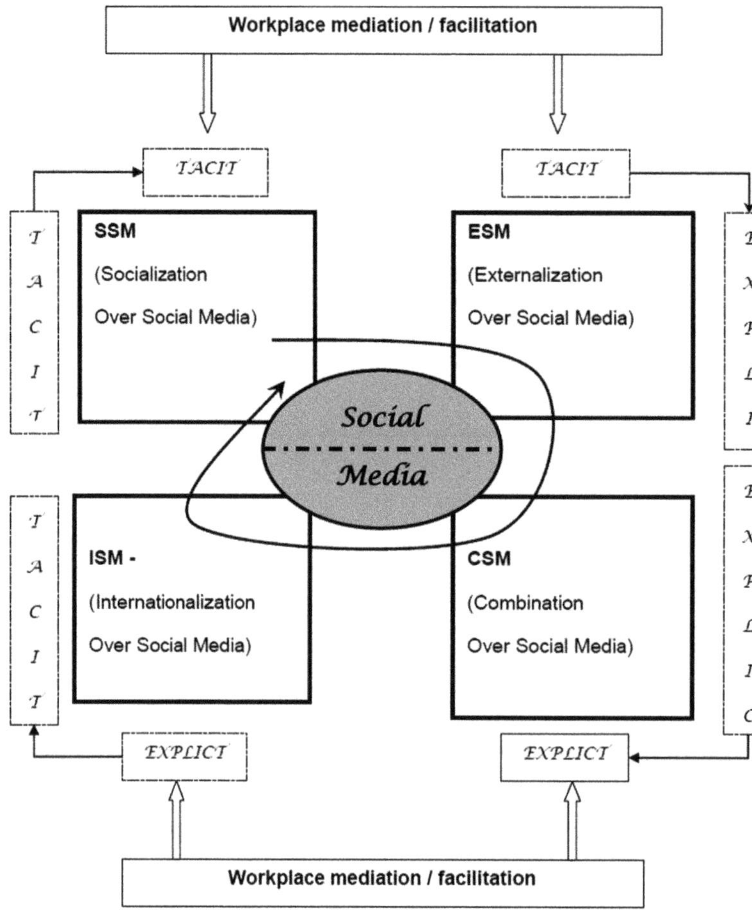

easiest form of knowledge sharing, which does not require much of experienced based tacit knowledge. E-learning courses devised around imparting general understanding about the company, rules and regulations, companies' health and safety policy etc. can be shared through C-SM.

The process of converting tacit knowledge into an explicit knowledge taking place over the social media is categorized as "Externalization" and is referred as E-SM. Experienced individuals normally finds such a knowledge sharing process much easier as compared to less experienced ones. This process should ideally involve indulging senior and experienced employees.

The process of converting explicit knowledge into tacit knowledge using social media as vehicle is termed as "Internationalization" and is expressed by I-SM. This can be achieved through introducing simulations, virtual games and group activities designed in such a way that these are interesting, interactive and purposeful.

Knowledge sharing process in which tacit knowledge is converted into another type of tacit knowledge and facilitated through social media is categorized as "Socialization" and is referred as S-SM. This can also be achieved by designing simulations, virtual games and group activities designed to be interesting, interactive and purposeful. The only difference between I-SM and S-SM activities will be the level of input from the participants. In I-SM the participants will actively participate, enjoy and learn whereas in

S-SM activities the participants will further add in their inputs, which then will be incorporated through simulation effects and will be shared by their brain child. This process will help to enhance their tacit knowledge and will facilitate organization to innovate and think outside the box.

Shah et al., (2013) claimed that SECI-SM Model offers a new dimension in knowledge management efforts by companies. It offers an extended form of knowledge sharing activities highlighted through SECI model to a whole new perspective. Knowledge intensive organizations mostly professional service firms (PSF) may capitalize upon social media in two ways, one through learning ways to share knowledge management over prevailing social networks, second by developing and marketing their own social media's for knowledge management purposes. It is important to note that the model does not undermine the importance of conventional knowledge management efforts rather adds a new dimension to it.

SECI-SM MODEL: IN THE LIGHT OF PREVIOUS RESEARCHES

It is well established in the literature that the knowledge management process is enabled through computing resources and especially the internet. The SECI-SM model is in line with the expectations of the most of the researchers who realized the importance of Internet and social media.

Redecker et al., (2011) envisages an immense impact of ICT on learning and knowledge sharing. To them, ICT will affect every aspect of learning. They considered the dynamic nature, high level of flexibility, facilitating virtual environment, and customized learning facilities of ICT are the key contributors to this change in knowledge sharing. SECI-SM model rightly fit in these characteristics.

The Bruges Communiqué (2010) considered the process of learning to be a lifelong process of personal development. This requires flexible mode of learning options that help and facilitate the learners. A revised method of evaluation for bothers formal and informal learning. SECI-SM seems to be a right answer to such needs highlighted by Bruges Communiqué (2010) and will facilitate the lifelong learning and knowledge sharing process.

Bradley and McDonald (2011a) identified the role of social media in the knowledge management process. According to them, KM requires a higher level of collaboration which was unprecedented in the history. Social media can serve an ideal place to fulfill this demand. To them a self-driven and uncontrolled collaboration serves requirements of effective KM where participants will make small groups / communities and interact freely. SECI-SM is a theoretical extension of such ideas that have been put forward by Bradley and McDonald (2011a).

SECI-SM MODEL: IN LIGHT OF FIRESTONE AND MCELROY (2003) CONCERNS

Firestone and McElroy (2003) have raised certain concerns over the future of knowledge management. These concerns have been discussed in light of the SECI-SM model and case is built in favor of an introduction of social media based knowledge management system that overcomes such concerns.

KM Independent of Strategy

Firestone and McElroy (2003) considered the future knowledge management would be independent of rigidly defined strategies. SECI-SM model furnishes the facility of evolving, evaluating and revising strategies on social media.

SECI Model and Oversimplification of Tacit Knowledge

One of the biggest criticisms on SECI model is the transfer of tacit knowledge. According to Firestone and McElroy (2003) it has over simplified tacit knowledge which is implicit in nature. SECI-SM model calls for devising online simulation exercises designed with a purpose of enhancing the leaning and knowledge sharing concept. Hence, it will help to develop a tacit knowledge through simulated environment. This process will help to elicit most of the tacit knowledge embedded in experienced and knowledgeable employees. When the employees will experience the difficulty of the task and other parameters of real like work environment they will bring into play their past leanings. During this time one can engaged them to share their feelings and their behaviors and actions will also worth examining. By this way, one of the crucial tasks of transfer of tacit knowledge would be resolved.

One of the simplest examples is when old friends meet each other after a long time they immediately call each other's with old names, start laughing and cherishing their old times. This is because they feel relaxed with each other. They have many things in common and easily share information in a relaxed manner. If companies, for instance wish to elicit the knowledge through its knowledge workers it has to provide them a relaxed environment where the individuals do not see themselves competing against others. As it is noted that social media provides a platform where individuals feel relaxed and share things with each other without being afraid of the loss of knowledge, the claim of SECI-SM seems quite appropriate.

Introducing Knowledge Portal

Firestone and McElroy (2003) consider that there should be a difference between Enterprise Information Portal (EIP) and Enterprise Knowledge Portal (EKP). This difference should be understood by the top management in order to develop effective KM strategies. EIP is more a static website whereas EKP is a more interactive. According to Feng (2010) EKP should contain knowledge resources, knowledge sharing, cross-platform retrieval system, virtual reference and user management systems. In this aspect, this is similar to social networking. Also O'Dell & Hubert (2011) believe that social networking equip individuals to create their profiles in online places, filter friends and experts who can participate and share in activities with confidence and trust. Hence, social media based initiative for developing EKP is the answer to effective knowledge management efforts.

Social media is a free economy of knowledge. A knowledge perceived higher in value will be demanded more than low perceived low value knowledge.

Some Lessons from Successful Marketing Campaigns

Organizations can learn from successful social marketing campaigns and replicate these within their particular organizations settings. This requires a paradigm shift in the strategy by viewing employees as their customers. Siu (2015) has highlighted few such examples where the participants helped organizations to achieve their objectives. We claim similar results can be achieved if organizations effectively engage their employees on social media activaties of knowledge sharing.

The marketing campaign of "Best Job in the World" by Tourism Queensland in order to draw tourists to a Queensland Island can have many learning lessons for organizations attempting to develop effective knowledge management system. The campaign offered a six month caretaker job with a staggering

Figure 8. Best jobs
Adopted from Siu, 2015.

$150,000 AUD payment in a most beautiful tourism spot in the world. Around 34,000 participants from over 200 countries submitted the videos and many others learned about the Queensland Island.

Employees can be encouraged to submit their ideas and share their knowledge like Heineken used a technique in 2012. The company upon discovering that customers' preference towards more original type of draught introduced a new campaign with name "Reinvent the Draught Beer Experience". This provided customers an opportunity to share videos, images and ideas to help change the experience. The company received hundreds of ideas to improve the product.

The campaign of Belkin and Lego in 2013, also give gives a very good example of how participants of social media can help improve product through their innovative and out of box ideas. In a quest to develop customizable iPhone cases, Belkin and Lego rolled down a campaign on social media for customers to share pictures of their cool news cases and to show others the benefits of making their own.

Figure 9. Heineken idea
Adopted from Siu, 2015.

Figure 10. Belkin
Adopted from Siu, 2015.

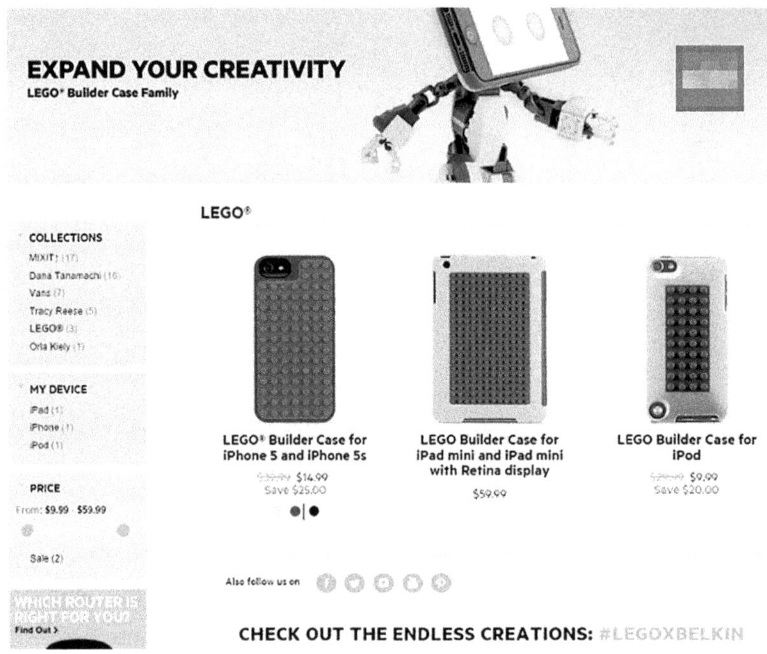

CONCLUSION

Businesses around the world are changing, developing countries are moving towards knowledge intensive businesses whereas developed countries are moving towards production related businesses. Knowledge intensive firms like professional service firms (PSF) firms endeavor to create, share and retain knowledge in order to remain competitive in the market.

This chapter has discussed the role of social media on knowledge management systems. A brief literature review on the relationship between knowledge management and social media was carried out in the beginning of the chapter. Later it presented the famous SECI Model by Nonaka and Takeuchi (1995) and SECI-SM model by Shah et al (2013). Towards the end the distinctive features of SECI-SM model was discussed in the light of previous researches.

Social Media based knowledge management system should be need based not requirement based…

In short, companies should adopt the strategy of social media based knowledge management systems aligned with their corporate needs. The key to this is employees' behavior towards social websites. Do they like to interact on social media? How often they interact on social media? What is their motive behind interaction? This should be followed by decisions regarding the amount of money and resources to be dedicated towards this strategy. The process should be need based not on the sole purpose to meet certain sanctioned requirements.

Social Media should be viewed as an opportunity rather than a threat.

Figure 11. Need vs. requirement

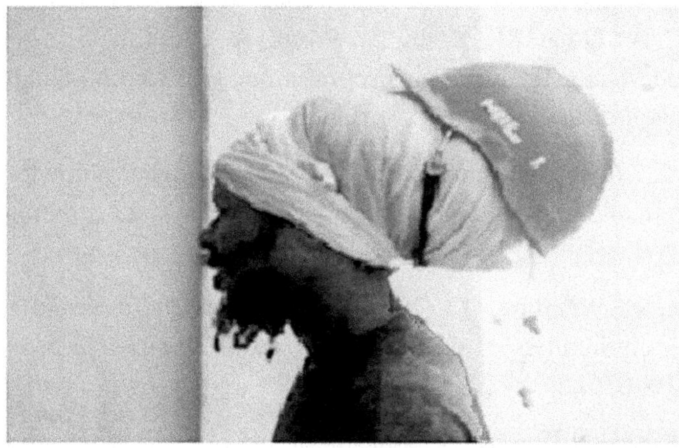

In conclusion, Social media offers a range of opportunities to business around the world, it is however the responsibilities of the business to avail the right opportunity. The organizations need to understand the nature of their businesses and conduct an appropriate SWOT analysis and then decide upon the strategies around capitalizing upon social media.

Organizations should paint a right picture to fetch real benefits of social media.

Figure 12. Self-portrait

REFERENCES

Ahmad, M., Razak, A. H. A., Omar, M., Yasin, A., Romli, R., Mutalib, A. A., & Zahari, A. S. (2015). The Impact of Knowledge Management in Pair Programming on Program Quality. In *Pattern Analysis, Intelligent Security and the Internet of Things*. Springer.

Andreeva, T., & Ikhilchik, I. (2011). Application of the SECI Model of Knowledge Creation in Russian Cultural Context: Theoretical Analysis, Knowledge and Process Management. *Wiley Online Library*, *18*(1), 56–66.

Ardichvili, A., Page, V., & Wentling, T. (2003). Motivation and barriers to participation in virtual knowledge sharing communities of practice. *Journal of Knowledge Management*, *7*(1), 64–77. doi:10.1108/13673270310463626

Bhatt, G. D. (2001). Knowledge management in organizations: Examining the interaction between technologies, techniques, and people. *Journal of Knowledge Management*, *5*(1), 68–75. doi:10.1108/13673270110384419

Bradley, A. J., & McDonald, M. P. (2011a). Social Media versus Knowledge Management. *HBR Blog Network, Harvard Business Review*. Retrieved from http://blogs.hbr.org/cs/2011/10/social_media_versus_knowledge.html

Bradley, A. J., & McDonald, M. P. (2011b). *The Social Organization: How to Use Social Media to Tap the Collective Genius of Your Customers and Employees*. Harvard Business Review Press.

Bruges Communiqué. (2010). Review the strategic approach and priorities of the Copenhagen process for 2011-2020. The European Social Partners and the European Commission, Communiqué of the European Ministers for Vocational Education and Training, Bruges.

Cheng, E. C. (2015). Knowledge Management for School Development. In Knowledge Management for School Education. Springer Singapore.

Chua, A. Y. K., & Banerjee, S. (2013). Customer knowledge management via social media: The case of Starbucks. *Journal of Knowledge Management*, *17*(2), 237–249. doi:10.1108/13673271311315196

ConnectingPeople. (2010). *Digital Learning Platforms, Research Series Paper No. 2, Education Policy and Research Division*. Research and Innovation Department of Education and Early Childhood Development Melbourne.

Dabbagh, N., & Kitsantas, A. (2012). Personal Learning Environments, social media, and self-regulated learning: A natural formula for connecting formal and informal learning. *The Internet and Higher Education*, *15*(1), 3–8. doi:10.1016/j.iheduc.2011.06.002

Empson, L. (2001). Introduction – Knowledge Management in Professional Service Firms. *Human Relations, Sage Publications.*, *54*(7), 811–817. doi:10.1177/0018726701547001

Feng, L. (2010). Research on the Construction of the Knowledge Service-oriented Learning Knowledge Portal System in Universities. *Information Studies: Theory & Application*, *1*, 29.

Firestone, J. M., & McElroy, M. W. (2003). The new knowledge management, special focus. *The new knowledge management.* Retrieved from http://www.kmci.org/media/New_Knowledge_Management.pdf

Horwitch, M., & Armacost, R. (2002). Helping knowledge management be all it can be. *The Journal of Business Strategy*, *23*(3), 26–32. doi:10.1108/eb040247

Hughes, D. J., Rowe, M., Batey, M., & Lee, A. (2012). A tale of two sites: Twitter vs. Facebook and the personality predictors of social media usage. *Computers in Human Behavior*, *28*(2), 561–569. doi:10.1016/j.chb.2011.11.001

Huijster, H. (2008). Exploring the educational potential of social networking sites: The fine line between exploring opportunities and unwelcome imposition. *Studies in Learning, Evaluation, Innovation and Development*, *5*(2), 45–54.

Liu, Y., Zhou, J., & Guan, Q. (2015). Study on University-Industry Cooperation Platform Construction Based on Knowledge Management. *LISS.* Springer Berlin Heidelberg.

Lowendahl, B., Revang, Ø., & Fosstenløkken, S. M. (2001). Knowledge And Value Creation In Professional Service Firms: A Framework For Analysis. *Human Relations, Sage Publications.*, *54*(7), 911–931. doi:10.1177/0018726701547006

Martindale, T., & Dowdy, M. (2010). Personal learning environments, G. Veletsianos (Ed.), Emerging technologies in distance education. Athabasca University Press.

Massingham, P. (2014). An evaluation of knowledge management tools: Part 1 – managing knowledge resources. *Journal of Knowledge Management*, *18*(6), 1075–1100. doi:10.1108/JKM-11-2013-0449

Nonaka, I., & Takeuchi, H. (1995). *The knowledge-creating company: How Japanese companies create the dynamics of innovation.* Oxford University Press.

O'Dell, C., & Hubert, C. (2011). *The New Edge in Knowledge: How Knowledge Management Is Changing the Way We Do Business.* John Wiley & Sons.

PewResearch Center. (2014). *Social Networking Fact Sheet.* Pew Research Center, Internet, Science & Tech. Retrieved from http://www.pewinternet.org/fact-sheets/social-networking-fact-sheet/

Pohs, W. (2001). Practical Knowledge Management: the Lotus Discovery System. IBM Press.

Rabelo, J. D. H., Oliveira, E. C. C. D., Santos, D. V. D., Braga, L. C. D. S., Souza, G. D. S., Steinmacher, I. F., & Conte, T. U. (2015). Knowledge Management and Organizational Culture in a Software Organization--A Case Study. *8th International Workshop on IEEE/ACM, Cooperative and Human Aspects of Software Engineering (CHASE).*

Rachel. (2008). *How Social Media Is Changing Communication + Organizations.* The Social Organization. Retrieved from http://www.thesocialorganization.com/2008/11/the-importance-of-social-networking-to-information-work.html

Redecker, C., Alla-Mutka, K., Bacigalupo, M., Ferrari, A., & Punie, Y. (2009). *Learning 2.0 The Impact of Web 2.0 Innovations on Education and Training in Europe.* JRC Scientific and Technical Report, Institute for prospective technological studies, European Commission. Retrieved from http://ftp.jrc.es/EURdoc/JRC55629.pdf

Redecker, C., Leis, M., Leendertse, M., Punie, Y., Gijsbers, G., Kirschner, P., . . . Hoogveld, B. (2011). The Future of Learning: Preparing for Change. JRC Scientific and Technical Reports, Institute for prospective technological studies, European Commission.

Reichental, J. (2011). Knowledge management in the age of social media, The days of the single, authoritative voice are coming to an end. *Oreilly Radar*. Retrieved from http://radar.oreilly.com/2011/03/knowledge-management-social-media.html

Shah, S. A. M., Khan, I., & Amjad, S. (2013). The Role of Social Media in Developing an Effective Knowledge Management Process in Professional Service Firms. *Mediterranean Journal of Social Sciences*, *4*(14), 775–782.

Siu, E. (2015). 10 User Generated Content Campaigns That Actually Worked. *Hubsopt Blogs*. Retrieved from http://blog.hubspot.com/marketing/examples-of-user-generated-content

Swan, J., Newell, S., Scarbrough¸, H., & Hislop, D. (1999). Knowledge management and innovation: Networks and networking. *Journal of Knowledge Management*, *3*(4), 262–275. doi:10.1108/13673279910304014

Yoshida, T. (2015). Cultivation of Perception and Creativity by Repeating Soft Systems Approach. *58th Annual Meeting of the ISSS-United States*, *1*(1).

KEY TERMS AND DEFINITIONS

Explicit Knowledge: A source indifferent knowledge that is easy to transfer to other forms and individuals.

Knowledge Management: An intentional effort towards the management of knowledge.

Knowledge Portal: An electronic facility developed for employees for the exclusive purpose of knowledge management in organization.

Knowledge Worker: A person in an organization who is directly or indirectly involved in the process of knowledge management.

SECI Model: A famous theoretical model by Nonaka and Takeuchi (1995) discussing different types of knowledge and their interactions.

SECI-SM Model: A theoretical model by Shah, Khan & Amjad (2013) discussing interactions of different knowledge types over the social media.

Social Media: An electronic facility enabling individuals to socialize.

Tacit Knowledge: A source specific knowledge that is difficult to transfer to other forms and individuals.

Chapter 12
Towards a Model of Social Media Impacts on Cybersecurity Knowledge Transfer:
An Exploration

Nainika Patnayakuni
Calhoun Community College, USA

Ravi Patnayakuni
University of Alabama – Huntsville, USA

Jatinder N. D. Gupta
University of Alabama – Huntsville, USA

ABSTRACT

Technical solutions to security have been suggested but found lacking and it has been recognized that security is a people issue as well, and behavioral research on information security is critical. Individual learning about cybersecurity is not formal and linear, but complex and network based. In this paper we develop a model of how social media characteristics impact cybersecurity knowledge transfer using technology threat avoidance theory. In developing the conceptual model we seek to answer the following questions. How do users discover cybersecurity knowledge on social media platforms? What are the platform and interaction characteristics that enable them to find cybersecurity knowledge and share this knowledge with others? In doing so we consider the impact of the threat and protection context on cybersecurity knowledge transfer which is different from knowledge transfer in the other contexts.

INTRODUCTION

Information Systems (IS) security is a major concern for organizations as cyber-attacks continue to escalate. Technical solutions to security have been suggested but found lacking and it has been recognized that security is a people and organizational issue as well (Hinde, 2003) and behavioral research on informa-

DOI: 10.4018/978-1-5225-0495-5.ch012

tion security is critical (Crossler et al., 2013). People in organizations perform actions that influence an organization cyber security posture and these actions are influenced by policies, procedures, and tools. These policies, procedures and guidelines constitute an organizations knowledge about cybersecurity which may be explicit and managed by a knowledge management systems or tacit and distributed at different horizontal and vertical levels of an organization.

The way knowledge is created and shared is changing in the digital age. While cyber security was the domain of experts and cyber-attacks on organizations were few and far between it was easier for organizations to control what and how cyber-attacks were reported. To believe that learning and behavior of individual and organizations about cyber security is primarily impacted by the formal mechanisms through which an organization approaches cybersecurity is to take objective approach to learning (Driscoll, 2000). New models of learning and knowledge creation suggest that learning is not linear, but complex and network based and "the capacity to form connections" between people, ideas and knowledge is the key to learning in the digital age (Siemens, 2014). At the same time as the half-life of knowledge is falling rapidly the role of social networks and weak ties in creating and distributing knowledge is being recognized (Siemens, 2005).

Social media provides us such affordances of linking with people and their ideas and just as the prevalence of cyber-attacks increases so do social media reports, rumor and hysteria about these attacks. While Edward Snowden and Wiki-Leaks used mainstream and online media for their security leak revelations, ISIS has continually used social media effectively to propagate their threats. And the role of social media in influencing political action such as the Arab Spring cannot be underestimated. As every teenage hacker and script kiddie can find information about creating new attacks online and through social media, and news of cyber-attacks spreads through social networks like wildfire, it becomes difficult to distinguish fact from rumor.

End users are key to information security and their actions are influenced by the information they consume, for example it has been reported that the NSA snooping program changed user online behavior (Hattern, 2014). However, research on the role of social media in influencing perception and actions related to information security does not exist. We develop an exploratory model of the influence of social media on cybersecurity knowledge transfer and how the characteristics of the social media as well as their social networks are likely to influence knowledge transfer. To develop this exploratory theoretical model we draw upon research on social media characteristics (Kietzmann, Hermkens, McCarthy & Silvestre, 2011), individual learning in the digital age (Siemens, 2005), theories on the process of knowledge creation (Nonaka, 1994; Nonaka & Takeuchi, 1995; Gao, Li, & Nakamori, 2002) and social network theories (Granovetter, 1973). In addition we draw upon the Technology Threat Avoidance Theory (Liang & Xue, 2009) to delineate how users' response to perceptions of threat, specifically threat appraisal and coping appraisal mediate the relationship between social media and knowledge transfer about cybersecurity.

In developing the conceptual model we seek to answer the following questions. How do users discover cybersecurity knowledge on social media platforms? What are the platform and interaction characteristics that enable them to find cybersecurity knowledge and share this this knowledge with others? Further what characteristics of the platform or the relational interactions enhance the ability of the users to personalize this knowledge which is likely to impact whether they will change their cybersecurity behaviors. We argue that social influences affect how users acquire cybersecurity knowledge and investigate the characteristics of the platform and relationships that enable knowledge transfer. In doing so, we consider the impact of the threat and protection context on cybersecurity knowledge transfer which is different than knowledge transfer in the other contexts. Consideration of the role of individual characteristics, knowledge characteristics such or the socio-cultural context as well as changes in cybersecurity behavior is outside the scope of our model.

This paper is organized as follows. In the next sections we explore the research on knowledge transfer, social media, individual learning theories as well as social influence in changing cybersecurity behavior. We then draw upon this research to explore the relationships between social media building blocks and knowledge transfer in the context of cybersecurity using technology threat avoidance theory. Based on our exploration we develop a parsimonious model of social media properties, threat avoidance and knowledge transfer. To the best of our knowledge, this is the first conceptual model that integrates threat avoidance and knowledge theories to identify how cybersecurity knowledge transfer take place over social media platforms.

PERSPECTIVES ON KNOWLEDGE, MEDIA, AND SECURITY

Knowledge Creation, Transfer, and Discovery

Research makes a distinction between information, data and knowledge. Information and data can be stored, transferred and disseminated, but knowledge is obtained when an individual applies that information to his existing knowledge frameworks in order to add to, or change what he or she already knows (Dretske, 1981). Knowledge is also defined as information and knowhow (Zander & Kogut, 1995). Research has also argued that there is no significance in distinguishing knowledge from information in knowledge sharing research, and knowledge is the information processed by individuals (Wang & Roe, 2010: Huber, 1991)

There is a differing perspective on whether it is only individuals in organizations that can learn or whether organizations can also learn (Prague, 1997; Bhatt, 2002). One view argues that only individuals can learn and individual learning is the basis of organizational learning (Nonaka, 1994) while the second perspective is that organizations can learn and evolve over time (Salomon & Perkins, 1998). We focus our attention on individual learning and knowledge acquisition. Recent research has defined knowledge as embedded in individuals (Brauner & Becker, 2006). Knowledge is therefore created by what people do actively while information or data can be considered as objects (Beesley & Cooper, 2008). Thus in order for knowledge to be transferred the person who receives the data or information objects must also actively participate in the process of knowledge creation by linking the new information with the existing knowledge that they already possess. Another definition suggests that creating new knowledge is different from sharing and transferring knowledge. A person may create new knowledge in response to that problem, and share that knowledge with others but a user would need to actively seek and engage with that information in order to acquire new knowledge. Acquiring new knowledge, as different from transferring and sharing knowledge is therefore a communication process (Beesley & Cooper, 2008, Davila; Epstein & Shelton, 2006). Some authors distinguish knowledge sharing from knowledge transfer and argue that transfer includes the acquisition of knowledge (Wang & Noe, 2010). Knowledge exchange has been another term that is used in a context similar to knowledge sharing (Cabrera, Collins & Selgado, 2006)

Communication between individuals is a necessary but not sufficient condition for the transfer of knowledge because in addition to interaction with people, the transfer of knowledge requires the development of mutual understanding (Schuetz, 1964; Beesley & Cooper, 2008). In order for such active knowledge transfer to take place, a distinction is made between single loop and double loop learning strategies (Argyris, 1977). Double loop learning is based on questioning basic assumptions so as to solve complex problems, and relies of two way communication and feedback loops. In one directional communication, for example, the interpretation of the message is based on the perspective of the receiver (Beesley & Cooper, 2008). Double loop learning also enables generative learning in which the learners explore, modify and add to their existing knowledge networks (Argyris, 1977).

In order for users to adopt new knowledge, cognitive, communication and social factors have to be in place (Beesley & Cooper, 2008). Cognitive factors relate to individual cognitive abilities and how they interact with the communicated knowledge and suggest that users engage in information processing activities when they acquire new knowledge. Communication factors are the directionality of communication, the way in which both meaning and values can be communicated. Social factors include things like relationship building, status, trust, power, politics, social structures, leadership (Beesley, 2003)

Knowledge management includes various processes such as personalization, codification, discovery, creation/innovation, combination, and socialization (Milton, Shadbolt, Cottam, & Hammersley, 1999; Nonaka 1994). Nonaka and Takeuchi (1995) argue that knowledge is created by individuals and the knowledge created by individuals get transformed into organizational knowledge. There are two dimensions of organizational knowledge creation epistemological and ontological. Epistemological dimension considers the interplay between explicit and tacit knowledge. Tacit knowledge arises out of individual experience and is difficult to articulate. Explicit knowledge, on the other hand, can be written down, codified and stored, distributed and shared through various means.

The ontological dimension refers to the level of social interaction. Since knowledge is created by individuals, organizations provide contexts to individuals so that their interaction amplifies the process of knowledge creation. Both formal and informal groups within and across organizations provide mechanisms for developing new associations to develop new knowledge. Interaction between individuals then enables the conversion of tacit knowledge to explicit knowledge and this is referred to as the spiral model of knowledge creation. There are four different "modes" of knowledge conversion from tacit knowledge to explicit knowledge, from explicit knowledge to explicit knowledge, from explicit knowledge to tacit knowledge, and from tacit knowledge to tacit knowledge.

The conversion of tacit knowledge to tacit knowledge through shared experience is the process of socialization. When organizations use primarily face to face interactions for the transfer of knowledge Hansen, Nohoria and Tierney (1999) refer to this as the personalization strategy. Combination is the process of recombining, restructuring and reorganizing several sources of explicit knowledge, in modern organizations mostly through technology. Tacit knowledge can be converted to explicit knowledge through the process of externalization while explicit knowledge can be converted to tacit knowledge through internalization. Socialization, internalization and combination can be compared to the theories of organizational culture, organizational learning and information processing (Nonaka, 1994). Tacit knowledge at the individual level is the key foundation of knowledge creation, but tacit knowledge is only usable when it amplified and converted to explicit knowledge through various organizational process. Socialization as a process of knowledge transfer does not create knowledge that is easily shareable while combination does not create knowledge that is specific and has contextual meaning. Externalization of tacit knowledge can be encouraged through the use of metaphors while internalization can be encouraged through experiential learning.

At an individual level commitment is required for knowledge creation and this commitment is enabled through individual intentions, level of autonomy and fluctuations in the environment such as randomness and crisis events. At the organizational level redundancy in information, creative rather than destructive chaos, and requisite variety in organizational information processing capabilities that match the information processing needs of the environment enable knowledge creation. Leadership styles that do not focus on top down management but on organizational designs that mimic the hypertext organization (Nonaka, Konno, Tokuoka, & Kawamura, 1992) also enable the process of organizational knowledge creation.

Trust has been a key determinant to knowledge sharing at an organizational level (Chiu, Hsu & Wang, 2006). A competitive climate inside the organization has been detrimental to knowledge sharing while a cooperative climate supports knowledge sharing (Schepers & Van den Berg, 2007). Knowledge sharing has been examined in communities of practice which consist of groups of individuals with common interests. Norms of reciprocity in social capital theory (Nahapiet & Ghoshal, 1998) have been used to study knowledge sharing in electronic communities with inconsistent results (Wang & Roe, 2010). Communities of practice are characterized by generalized reciprocity where knowledge shared by one person may be reciprocated by someone else in the community and not necessarily the original recipient (Ekeh, 1974; Wasko & Faraj, 2005). Chiu et al. (2006) found it norms of reciprocity to be positively associated with knowledge sharing while Wasko and Faraj (2005) found it to be negatively associated with knowledge sharing. Knowledge sharing happens in communities of practice not just in the basis on trust but also length of membership in teams with shared values (Bakker, Leenders, Gabbay, Kratzer, & Van Engelenl, 2006). The ties between individuals in communities of practice and the personal relationships between them can facilitate the transfer of knowledge (Chiu et al., 2006; Reagans & McEvily, 2003). Strong ties and likely to entail greater emotional closeness and increase the motivation to transfer information (Reagans & McEvily, 2003). Weak ties on the other hand are non-redundant and help in transfer of simple information with greater benefits reported by knowledge recipients (Levin & Cross, 2004; Hansen, 1999). Structural holes theory (Burt, 1992) has also been used to study knowledge transfer in networks (Ahuja, 2000). When non redundant information exists in two separate network clusters, structural holes are said to exist between the networks and employees in position to bridge these structural holes can facilitate the transfer of information between the two networks.

However when knowledge creation becomes a distributed process leveraged through the use of social media, managing the knowledge creation process becomes even more complex. In addition when systems are used to manage knowledge they also need to consider knowledge discovery (how users find security knowledge in social media), and personalization which indicate how users perceive an act upon the knowledge (Milton et al., 1999). In order to understand the process of knowledge creation we need to identify how various characteristics of social media impact knowledge discovery, personalization and the conversion of tacit knowledge to explicit knowledge.

Understanding Social Media

The social media framework developed by Kietzmann et al. (2011) characterizes social media in terms of the following building blocks - identity, presence, relationships, reputation, groups, conversations and sharing. Identity indicates the extent to which the users reveal their true identities in social media. Identity can include information like users' true name, location, gender etc. Identity may also include information about sexual and political orientation and users opinions on various topics. Research has shown that computer mediated environments increase the likelihood of self-disclosure (Joinson, 2001). Social media platforms also differ in the extent that they require a users' identity to be revealed. Since users may or may not be required to reveal their true identity on social media platforms, several services have emerged to verify identity across platforms such as OAuth and OpenID (Kaila, 2006).

Conversation indicates the frequency of communication between the members of social media as well as the bi-directionality of this communication and the length of the communication. Some platforms may enable long conversations while others like vine and twitter may control the length of your communications. At the same time the speed of communication varies, some communication is in real-time as in foursquare or mostly real-time such as updates on twitter (Kietzmann et al., 2011). Conversation has implications for development of trust, feedback loops and learning in social media sites.

Sharing indicates what is shared, whether it is information, feelings, products, images etc. Engeström (2005) presented the concept of object centered sociality to differentiate it from another definition of the social network which is simply a map of connections between the people, or the social graph. He argued that there are objects that connect these people and object centered sociality binds a social network together more than just the connections between people. Social media can thus also be characterized by what is shared, why it is shared and how much of it is shared.

Presence is the degree and granularity with which the users let others know whether they are accessible in real-time. Social media platforms allow users to control the degree to which they reveal their presence to part or all of their networks. How users interact with social media is related to the how immediate and intimate the platform is and greater levels of social presence increase influence in social media conversations (Kaplan & Haenlein, 2010). Kaplan and Haenlein (2010) also characterize social media in terms of social presence, media richness, and degree of self-disclosure. Ambient awareness, indeterminacy and push –pull communication have been other ways in which social media has been characterized (Kaplan & Haenlein, 2011). Ambient awareness is a combination of the level of social presence (Short, Williams, & Christie, 1976) and media richness (Daft & Lengel, 1986) such that a person can develop an understanding of the context based on, for example, short frequent tweets. When information from these tweets is combined together it can provide a significant amount of information. Many social media sites also encourage what is referred to as push-pull communication where information is pushed to the users and at the same time users can pull more information (Kaplan & Haenlein, 2011). Social media also encourages compulsive engagement amongst users because of indeterminacy (Vosgerau, Wertenbroch, & Carmon, 2006) in the sense that news and events that unfold in the media are more engaging because they are not pre-determined and orchestrated in advance.

Relationships in social media can be delineated in terms of structure and flow based on social network theory (Granovetter, 197; Borgatti & Foster 2003). Structure is the number of relationships and the centrality of the users place in the network of relationships. Flow describes the strength of the relationships. Strength can be due to the fact that users have multiple ties to each other. Some social media sites focus on increasing the strength of existing relationships by increasing interactions. Others such as LinkedIn work to expand the size of a users' network. Strength of relationship in networks have been characterized in terms of strong and weak ties (Granovetter, 1976). While according to Granovetter weak ties enable innovation, Krackhardt (1992) has argued that strong ties engender trust and a history of communication and help members deal with change and uncertainty. Social graph can be used to graph the relationship between nodes in a network. In addition to the social graph, an interaction graph has been presented as a means to better impart meaning to online social networks (Wilson, Boe, Sala, Puttaswamy, & Zhao, 2009). They argue that social links between users are not valid measures of user interactions.

Reputation indicates the degree to which users can identify the standing and trustworthiness of others and themselves in the social media space. Reputation not only may refer to the people that are connected to the social media (Wasko & Faraj, 2005) but it also refers to the objects of social media that are shared whether it is videos, or other content (Tavakolifard & Almeroth, 2012). Reputation of content can be enhanced by likes and user content rating systems that provide trending news on various sites. Complex recommendation systems such as Netflix try to connect users with content that would be of their interest based on algorithms that attempt to match them with users with similar profiles (Kietzmann et al., 2011). Groups indicate the degree to which users are allowed to create communities on social media platforms and the degree to which users can control the formation and sharing of objects and permissions in these groups (Kietzmann et al., 2011). In the next section we present research on individuals are influenced by sociality when it comes to threats and cybersecurity.

Individual Behavior on Cybersecurity

Users are continuously bombarded by IT security threats and it has been argued that simple safeguards implemented by users such as updating anti-virus software, using long and complex passwords and protecting private information on public sites can protect users from security risks. However users are either unaware of these safeguards or when they are aware they choose to ignore them. Users generally suffer from the perception that security attacks happen to other people (Schmidt & Arnett, 2005) but would not happen to them and avoid adopting security safeguards because they are too complex to implement and tend to slow down task performance (Warkentin, Shropshire & Johnston, 2007). While users may receive security advice from many sources, they tend to ignore it because either they do not believe that they have the knowledge to implement the safeguards or the cost of implementing the safeguards is too high (Herley, 2009). For example having multi-factor authentication on social media sites can slow down the speed with which you can get access to your friends' vacation updates.

Users' intention to adopt information security safeguards are positively impacted by fear appeals (Johnston & Warkentin, 2010). Researchers have used technology acceptance models to study the adoption of IT safeguards to protect against malicious threats but Liang and Xue (2009) argue that technology avoidance behaviors differ significantly from acceptance behaviors. Most research on individual avoidance of security risks focuses on the "rational actor" model weighing the costs and benefits of taking security risks and there is a lack of research on how individuals evaluate security risks (Wu et al., 2009). Liang and Xue (2009) argue that technology acceptance theories do not provide sufficient guidance of how users assess security threats and take action on them. They present the Technology threat avoidance theory which consists of two cognitive processes threat appraisal and coping appraisal. During threat appraisal users assess the likelihood and severity of the threat and during coping appraisal they evaluate the costs and benefits of implementing the coping technology and avoiding the risk as well as their self-efficacy in implementing the safeguards. Threat appraisal is impacted by the perceived probability of the threat occurring and the perceived magnitude of the negative impact from the threat. When evaluating threat the users consider the effectiveness of the avoidance measures, whether the benefits to them outweigh their costs and their self-efficacy in implementing the safeguard. Liang and Xue (2009) draw on cybernetic theory (Carver & Scheier, 1982), coping theory (Lazarus, 1966), risk analysis (Baskerville, 1991a), health protective behavior (Maddus & Rogers, 1983) and self-efficacy (Compeau & Higgins, 1995) to develop and test technology threat avoidance theory (Liang & Xue, 2010).

Johnston and Warkentin (2010) argue that social influence has a significant impact on the adoption of technology safeguards by individuals based on Theory of Reasoned Action (Fishbein & Ajzen, 1975), Theory of Planned Behavior (Venkatesh & Davis, 2000), social factors construct (Thompson, Higgins & Howell, 1991), technology acceptance model (Venkatesh, Morris, Davis & Davis, 2003), and the need to maintain a positive image with the group (Moore & Benbasat, 1991). Das, Kim, Dabbish, & Hong

(2014) study how social influence affects the decision to adopt or communicate about and use security tools. They refer to this as security sensitivity which consists of the "awareness of, motivation to use, and knowledge of how to use security and privacy tools" (Stanton, Mastrangelo, Stam & Jolton 2004, pp.32) Lack of awareness of security threats is a critical factor in both users and experts developing incorrect mental models of secure use practices (Adams & Sasse, 1999). Many users also do not consider that security threats are something that is likely to impact them personally (Adams & Sasse 1999, Herley, van Oorschot & Patrick, 2009). Other factors that impede users implementing these safeguards is that the benefits of implementing the safeguards is not visible (Herley, 2009) and the use of safeguards carries very high costs (Furnell, Jusoh, & Katsabas, 2006). Lack of knowledge is also a major detriment to users implementing security safeguards (Whitten & Tygar, 1999).

Security can also be modeled as a navigation task and social navigation based approaches have been used to study how users observes other users in an activity space to familiarize themselves with how to implement security safeguards (DiGioia & Dourish, 2005). Stories have also been used to increase users' awareness of security (Rader, Wash & Brooks, 2012). Social context can also impact how users perceive the implementation of security safeguards, for example, Gaw, Felten, and Fernandez-Kelly (2006) found that users found encryption of emails as a sign of paranoia. Redmiles, Malone and Mazurek (2015) study the sources of advice that users take into account when considering cybersecurity behaviors. In their small pilot study they found that the source of cybersecurity advice were more diffuse that sources of other security advice and users looked up to experts such as corporate IT and companies such as their bank or Apple for advice about cybersecurity. Hence there is some evidence that both experts and social influence processes play a significant role in users' cybersecurity knowledge and behavior.

Individual Learning and Knowledge

Research on organizational knowledge does not adequately address the relationship between learning and knowledge because they take an organizational rather than an individual centric view (Akbar, 2003). Organizational learning theories possess that tacit knowledge is possessed by the individual (Polyani, 1966) and then converted to explicit knowledge. The key individual learning theories are behaviorism, cognitivism and constructivism. Behaviorism connects learning with changes in observable performance while cognitivism focuses on the acquisition of knowledge (Leroy & Ramanantsoa, 1997). Constructivist learning theories argue that learning is not rational but occurs when meaning is created from experience (Bodner, 1986). Bandura's social learning theory (1977) suggests that people learn from others by observing behavior and the consequence of the behavior. People learn from modeling others behavior and such modeling can happen through live or symbolic means for example through electronic media. Social learning theory argues that three factors affect social learning, support present in the environment (situational support), feedback obtained from others (verbal persuasion) and the availability of vicarious learning opportunities. Warkentin et al. (2011) develop a model of the impact of informal social learning environment on information policy compliance using these attributes of social learning theory.

Connectivism as a theory of learning argues that accurate and current knowledge is the objective of all organizational action. Hence the "capacity to know more is more critical than what is currently known" (Siemens, 2005, pp. 5) since knowledge is constantly changing. The best way to acquire and share this current knowledge is to make connections between people and between knowledge management systems and databases and the people who use them. In addition, to complete a task knowledge has to be brought to bear on the task and increasingly this knowledge is neither present in the individual nor codified as a part of the organization. Resources and knowledge have to be collected from the distributed network and applied to the task in real-time. Connectivism as a learning theory is similar to social learning theory but it also adds that learning is distributed across the network and takes place by increasing network size and complexity and by connecting information sources across the network (Siemens, 2005). It argues that "know where", where to find the knowledge that one needs to know is more important than the "know what", the knowledge that you already possess (Downes, 2005). Connectivist theories of learning reinforce the idea that learning is acquired and propagated through social networks and the connections between social networks and technologies that enable the storage and sharing of knowledge.

TOWARDS A CONCEPTUAL MODEL

We begin by exploring the relationship between the building blocks of social media and their impacts on knowledge transfer in the context of cybersecurity. We characterize knowledge transfer as discovery of new knowledge (Milton et al., 1999), Externalization or codification of tacit knowledge (Nonaka, 1994), and Personalization which is to make the knowledge one's own, a process akin to Nonaka and Takeuchi (1995). Personalization is the process of adopting external knowledge in one's own knowledge frameworks, be it tacit or explicit knowledge. We use social exchange theory (Ekeh, 1974), structural holes (Ahuja, 2000) and strong and weak ties research in social networking (Granovetter, 1976; Krackhardt, 1992) and connectivist learning theory (Siemens, 2005) to hypothesize how the building blocks of social media will impact our dimensions of knowledge transfer. Finally we drawn upon technology threat avoidance theory (Liang & Xue, 2009; 2010) to understand how the role of threat avoidance rather than innovation diffusion impacts users' discovery, personalization and externalization of cybersecurity knowledge in social media contexts.

Users pay attention to cybersecurity knowledge only when they perceive threats in the environment. When users perceive cybersecurity threats, for example ransomware, large scale theft of identity information or the new Android Stagefright vulnerability that can hijack their phone through multimedia messaging they begin the process of threat appraisal and coping appraisal in the environment. This is

Figure 1. Towards a model of social media and cybersecurity knowledge transfer

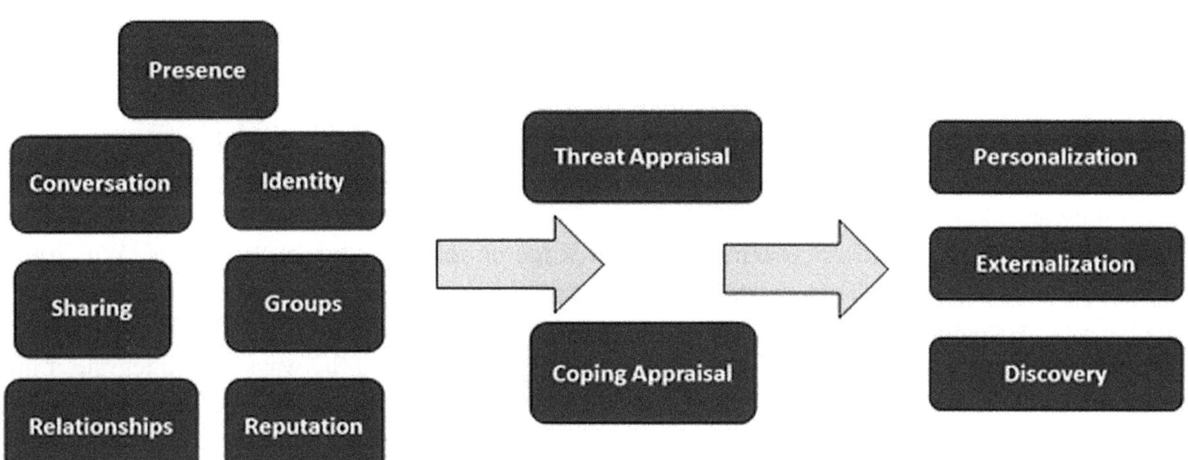

akin to the process whereby randomness and chaos in the environment increase individual commitment to knowledge creation (Nonaka & Takeuchi, 1995). Threat appraisal includes perceived severity and perceived susceptibility. Perceived susceptibility is a users' belief that the threat is likely to affect them and perceived severity is the extent of negative consequences that the users believe that they face as a result of the threat (Baskerville, 1991; Straub & Welke 1998). Users are unlikely to appraise the threat of the Stagefright vulnerability to them, if they do not own an android phone.

Coping appraisal measures the perceived avoidability of the threat from the user's point of view. It includes the perceived effectiveness of the measure, the costs of implementing that measure user's self-efficacy in implementing that security safeguard (Liang & Xue 2009). For example, if the users owns an android phone and considers Stagefright to be a threat, they still may not implement the safeguard because they might believe that it would not happen to them, that it would take too much time or that they could never figure out how to do it. We define coping appraisal as an internal process which consists of users perceptions of costs, effectiveness and self-efficacy in applying the cyber security knowledge that is appropriate to their effectiveness in their own environment. Perceived effectiveness is based on Bandura (1982) which is an outcome expectation that implementing a safeguard will protect the user from a threat. In this sense perceived effectiveness is similar to perceived usefulness in Technology Acceptance Model which was later renamed to performance expectancy (Venkatesh et al., 2003). This measure of coping appraisal deviates from Lue & Xang (2009) in that it is subjective rather than an objective measure. Coping appraisal also includes the costs to the user that is what time, effort and expense that the user believes that they have to undertake to obtain the cybersecurity knowledge. A significant component of coping appraisal includes self-efficacy a measure of users' confidence in applying the cyber security knowledge. Self-efficacy has been extensively studies in IT literature (Bandura, 1977; Compeau & Higgins, 1999).

Discovery of cybersecurity knowledge is defined as the degree to which the user scans the environment or passively encounters knowledge related to cybersecurity. Defined in this way discovery is a combination of push and pull and is much more than simply searching and retrieving knowledge from databases as defined in Milton et al. (2009). Personalization is not defined as socialization (Nonaka & Takeuchi, 1995) or use of face to face communication in the transfer of knowledge as defined by Hansen et al. (1999). Personalization is defined akin to its definition in learning theories as an adaptation of constructivism (Bodner, 1986). Personalization is the process when the users learn something and make it their own by ascribing to it meanings in their own specific context. Externalization is defined as the transfer and codification and explication of tacit knowledge (Nonaka & Takeuchi, 1994). Hence we define knowledge transfer as a process that is completed when knowledge is externalized, discovered and when users who receive the knowledge make it their own by actively personalizing it.

Drawing upon knowledge management literature we argue that threat appraisal is associated with discovery and externalization of knowledge. When users scan the environment and perceive significant threats they are likely to increase their efforts towards both externalizing what they know (Das, Kim, Dabbish & Hong, 2014) and discovering new knowledge or solutions to their problems (Wu, 2009). Coping appraisal impacts the personalization of knowledge. Since coping appraisal involves the creation of perceived expectancies about cost and effectiveness of the new knowledge as well as self-efficacy, it directly impacts the meaning that users ascribe to the knowledge and the ways they integrate it into their knowledge frameworks.

Connectivist theory of learning (Siemens, 2005) argues that learning and knowledge is distributed in the network and maintaining and expanding connections, and finding where to find knowledge is the key to learning in the digital age. Drawing on connectivist learning theory we develop insights into how each building block of social media will impact threat appraisal, coping appraisal and externalization, discovery and transfer.

The greater the degree of presence in a social media context the more likely users would receive rich media interaction, and location awareness of other users (Kaplan & Haenlein, 2010). Users are more likely to be engaged and committed to knowledge exchange because presence increases ambient awareness, and greater engagement due to indeterminacy. Presence would make it easier for users to personalize cybersecurity information that they encounter in social media because they have more opportunities for live, personal and rich exchange with the source of cyber security knowledge. Presence heightens the richness and timeliness of connections between nodes thus making it easier for them to use social navigation theory to help others walk them through learning about new security safeguards. Presence makes it easier for tacit knowledge to be transferred as tacit or explicit knowledge in social media contexts because it provides the greatest level of media richness as compared to face to face communication. Presence and the associated media richness reduces the cost of implementing the security safeguards by providing the user with direct access to the knowledge source in real time that would be able to walk them through the setup process. Presence also enables a more rapid feedback loop when it cofiguremes to evaluating threats. Media richness may increase the affective component during threat appraisal as rapid fire twitter feeds can give you a blow by blow account of rapidly unfolding cybersecurity threat. We propose that the degree of presence in social media platform is directly related to personalization of cybersecurity knowledge and to better coping appraisal which in turn is related to better personalization of cybersecurity knowledge.

The greater the degree of conversations in social media (Kietzmann et al., 2011) the greater the degree of personalization in knowledge transfer. Communication between people is required condition for knowledge transfer and a sine qua non of double loop learning. The more a social media platform allows frequent and bi-directional communication the more it will enable the feedback mechanisms that enable users to ask the why questions and integrate the new knowledge in their existing framework and adapt and modify them (Argyris, 1977). Sites that enable longer long form communication such security blogs will engender communities of practice and bi-directional communication and enable the transfer of more complex knowledge. At the same time, real time, high velocity communication can enable the spread of new cybersecurity threats as they develop as a cursory perusal of #cybersecurity hashtag on Twitter will reveal.

Conversation frequency can also aid in discovery of new cybersecurity threats and safeguards as they arise. The frequency of conversations can hasten the spread of paranoia and fear appeal in social networks thus enhancing threat appraisal events can take place. Long conversations increase a user understanding of the situation and thus increase the self-efficacy in implementing the cybersecurity safeguards. Frequency of communication is also likely to reduce the bias that "bad things cannot happen to me" because users frequently see and hear about cyber-attacks on social media. Thus degree of conversation in a social media platform is directly related to personalization and discovery of cybersecurity knowledge. The building block of conversations would include properties of frequency, bi-directionality and length. Bi-directionality and length of conversation in social media platforms is likely to be associated with personalization of cybersecurity knowledge. Frequency of conversation in social media platform is directly related to discovery of cyber security knowledge. Frequency of conversation in social media platform enables better threat appraisal which is likely to further enable discovery of cyber-security knowledge. Bi-directionality and length of conversation by enabling feedback provide better assessments of perceived effectiveness and self-efficacy and help in the personalization of cyber security knowledge.

Relationships in social media platforms signify the strength and flow of relationships (Borgatti & Foster, 2003). Strong ties enable the users to have long term relationships (Krackhardt, 1992) and shared goals with others that enables user commitment and personalization of knowledge. Weak ties on the other hand bridge structural holes and enable users to discover a much diverse array of cybersecurity knowledge (Granovetter, 1973). Strong ties increase self-efficacy and enable social navigation thus providing the users the confidence that they would be better able to cope with cyber security threats. Weak ties are likely to make users more aware of the different cyber security threats and tools and increase a user repertoire of threats knowledge especially when such knowledge originates from power influences with large network connections. Relationships in a social media platform are associated with both personalization and discovery of cyber security information. Strong ties in social media platforms enable the personalization of cyber security knowledge while weak ties in are directly related to discovery of cyber security knowledge. The larger the size of a persons' network in a social media platform, the more likely that the person is in a position of power or an influencer, the greater the association with discovery of cyber security knowledge. Strong ties in social media platforms are directly related to coping appraisal which in turn is related to personalization. Further weak ties in social media platforms enable greater awareness of cybersecurity events in the larger network allowing for better threat appraisal and discovery of cybersecurity knowledge.

Identity in social media platforms is related to user privacy, and the ability to access multiple applications and resources across the network (Kietzmann et al., 2011; Kaplan & Haenlein, 2010). Web sites that force users to reveal their true identities mitigate the problem that many users may not trust the cybersecurity information that they find on social media sites. A true identity clarifies the source of cybersecurity information and can help in discovery and search for cyber security knowledge. True identity on social media platforms validates perceptions of threat severity, threat susceptibility because the users trusts that the source of information is who they claim to be. However when users true identities are verifiable they are less likely to share information that may harm them or that they have not validated to be true. Identity in social media platforms thus reduces the spread of unstructured, uncertain and cutting edge knowledge about cybersecurity. Thus identity makes it easier to find information but makes it likely that users will share cybersecurity knowledge that is potentially dangerous and that may harm their position in the network because their true identities are visible to everyone. Revealing true Identity in social media platforms is positively associated with discovery of cybersecurity knowledge and negatively associated with externalization of cyber security knowledge.

Reputation in social media platforms includes both the reputation of the users (Wasko & Faraj, 2005) and the ranking and rating of the content on the web sites. Crowdsourcing and sharing of reputation information in sites such as Reddit makes it easier to find cybersecurity knowledge. Reputation management systems encourage the externalization of tacit knowledge so that the users can work on promoting their reputation. At the same time ranking and recommendation systems (Tavakolifard & Almeroth, 2012) imply that users have a greater confidence in the cybersecurity knowledge presented to them. As per the threat avoidance theory, users would have a greater confidence in the perceived threats and their implications when the user or content reputation score is high. Reputation in social media platforms is positively associated with discovery and externalization of cybersecurity knowledge. Threat appraisal partially mediates the relationship between reputation in social media platforms and discovery and externalization of cyber security knowledge. When perceived cybersecurity threats are high, it increases the likelihood that users with a high reputation score would seek to cement their reputation by further externalization of tacit knowledge.

Sharing in the context of social media indicates the object that is to be shared (Ozanne & Ballantine, 2010), and to what extent in the social graph it is shared (Kietzmann et al., 2011). Sharing does not imply direct reciprocity but may include norms of indirect reciprocity in that users who receive the benefits of sharing, share forward with other users. In the context of cybersecurity, sharing provides a direct connection with externalization of knowledge. The platform may allow sharing of audio, video or just text messages or it may be focused on explicitly sharing only cyber security related knowledge. The platforms may allow for the objects to be self-generated or allow users to share others objects, for example re-tweeting others security related tweets. Sharing increases the likelihood of discovery of cyber security knowledge. Thus, sharing in social media platforms is positively associated with discovery and externalization of knowledge. Shared objects make it easier for users to perceive severity of threats and evaluate their susceptibility to these threats. When users sees a video they are more likely to pay attention to new anti-virus tools. Thus threat appraisal partially mediates the relationship between sharing and discovery of cyber security knowledge. Users are more likely to share cybersecurity tips when they perceive threats in the environment and believe that they have the knowledge that can help others. Hence threat appraisal partially mediates the relationship between sharing and externalization of knowledge.

The last building block of social media is the degree to which users can form subgroups and the degree and granularity of control that they have over these groups (Kietzmann et al., 2011). When users can form more finely grained groups, they can create communities of practice with a shared interest, groups with strong ties and bonds of trust. Groups in social media platform are related to personalization of cybersecurity knowledge. Further it is in these close knit groups that users are emotionally committed and develop self-efficacy skills that reduce their perceived costs in implementing cybersecurity safeguards. Such close knit groups also provide affordances for social navigation to learn by example of new ways to deal with cybersecurity threats. Hence coping appraisal mediates the relationship between groups and personalization of cybersecurity knowledge.

DISCUSSION

Discussion of the theoretical implications of social media and cybersecurity knowledge leads us to the identification of some patterns. The building blocks of social media can be organized into the degree to which they enhance the strength of relationships, reduce positional ambiguity in the network and enable processes and objects of interaction. Presence, formation of small groups, strong ties in cohesive relationships, and conversation increase the strength of relationships in social media platforms. Frequent bi-directional conversation and sharing allows for processes that enable the sharing of media, and text. Identity, reputation and position in a network of relationships reduces positional ambiguity in the social media platform. Figure 2 presents the relationship between building blocks of social media and strength of relationships, positional ambiguity and processes and objects of interaction.

Strong relationships enable the personalization of knowledge and extension of knowledge frameworks in users. Reduction of positional ambiguity creates structures in social networks that enhance the discovery of new information. Processes and objects of interaction in social networks enable the externalization and discovery of knowledge. Technology threat avoidance theory indicates that adopting safeguards consists of two primary components threat appraisal and coping appraisal. We propose that while threat appraisal

Figure 2. Relationship between building blocks of social media and higher order constructs

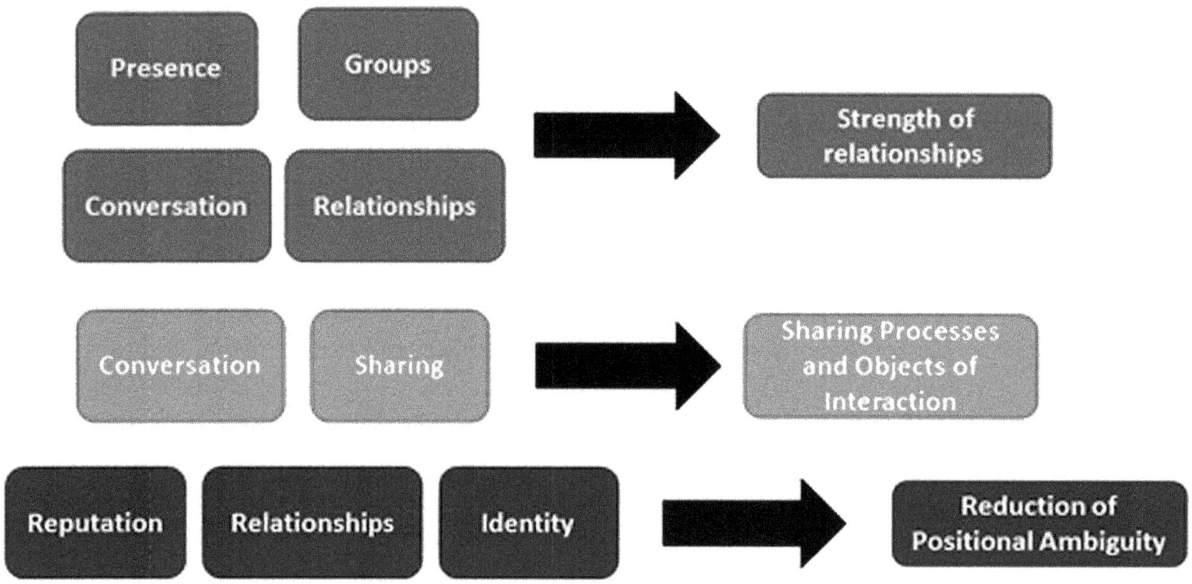

is primarily an environmental assessment process, coping appraisal is a self-appraisal process and an evaluation of the costs and benefits of cybersecurity knowledge with respects to the self's relationship with the environment. Threat appraisal enhances the processes of discovery and externalization while coping appraisal enables personalization in which the user evaluates the cybersecurity knowledge and provides meaning to this knowledge in the context of his or her own experience.

The greater the degree to which social media building blocks strengthen relationships, the greater the degree to which they enable the personalization of knowledge. Also strong relationships impact coping appraisal mechanisms in evaluating cybersecurity knowledge. When social media building blocks reduce positional ambiguity they strengthen the discovery of knowledge and increase the sharing of knowledge that builds on a personal brand reputation, while they weaken the sharing of ambiguous, or threatening knowledge that may have a negative impact in positional ambiguity. Further positional ambiguity reduces user confidence in the validity of the threat information that is being received.

Sharing objects and processes of interaction, enables the externalization and discovery of knowledge. Shared objects and processes of interaction also strengthen the processes of threat appraisal and coping appraisal. A video on a cybersecurity blog like that deals with cybersecurity safeguards will reduce user costs and increase their self-efficacy in personalizing cybersecurity knowledge. The conceptual model that follows explores the relationship between these constructs and personalization, discovery and externalization. Threat appraisal and coping appraisal mediate the relationship between social media constructs and personalization, discovery and externalization of cybersecurity knowledge. Figure 3 presents the conceptual model

Implications for Research

Measures of threat appraisal and coping appraisal have been developed and tested in a variety of contexts such as the adoption of anti-plagiarism software by faculty (Lee, 2011) and (Johnston et al., 2015). This

Figure 3. Conceptual model

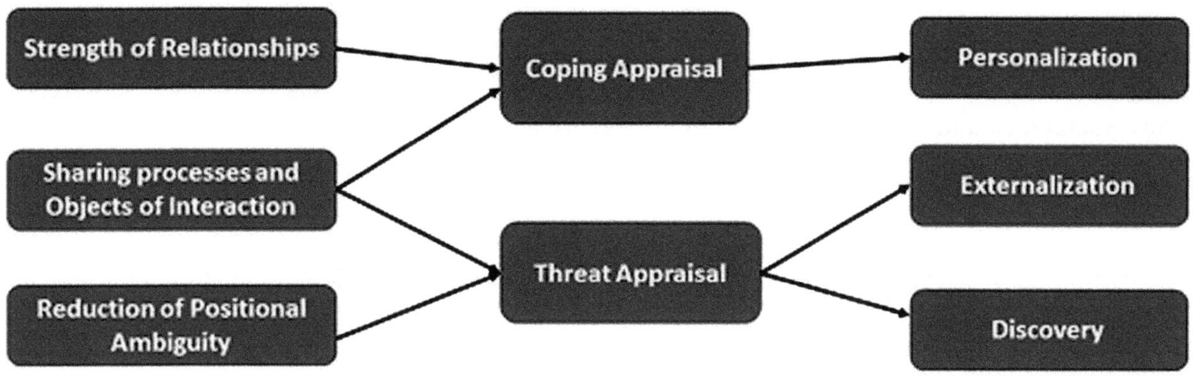

conceptualization proposes the development of a new framework for knowledge transfer in domains where protection from threats is a concern as compared to knowledge transfer in other domains. Our conceptual model is based on technology threat avoidance theory which has its basis in protection motivation theory (Rogers, 1975) that has been developed and used in health care fields. However as Johnston et al. (2015) point out there are limitations to the use of protection motivation theory in its application to information asset as compared to the human asset. The loss of information is likely to be perceived by employees differently as compared to the personal threat to health as in the case of previous protection motivation studies. They extend protection motivation theory to include the literature on sanctions as sanctions imposed by organizations in the context of security policy and compliance raise a threat to information asset to the level of a threat to the person, i.e. the human asset. In the context of this study, further investigations need to be conducted to identify how the influence was social media transforms what is perceived to be a threat to the information asset to be more of a threat to the human asset. We believe that relationship strength, sharing and positional ambiguity in the network have implications for the transforming perceptions of threat to the information asset into a threat to the human asset. While our theoretical discussions have looked at how these social media properties have in impact on discovery, personalization and externalization of security knowledge, further theoretical investigation needs to be conducted on the implication of social media knowledge transfer on the user perceptions of threat to information or human assets. To the extent that users perceive that such threats do not have direct impact on them, they are unlikely to pay attention to the knowledge in the first place.

In addition our model uses elements of social media (Kietzmann et al., 2011) to develop higher level properties that are likely to impact knowledge transfer and assesses the implications of these properties on knowledge transfer in the context not of adoption of new technologies but one where adoption is required for threat avoidance. Other measures and properties of differentiating social media design such as elements of visibility (Treem et al., 2012), awareness, and accountability (Erickson & Kellogg, 2000) need to be considered in terms of their impact on cyber security knowledge transfer.

This chapter has several limitations. While the model investigated discovery, externalization and personalization of knowledge, it does not include any measure of the skills acquired by the individual in dealing with cyber-security threats, in as much as such skills would be manifest in protective behaviors adopted by the users in protecting themselves of cybersecurity threats. Successful knowledge transfer is measured in terms of outcome variables which requires changes in behavior and one of the limitations of our model is that it does not consider any changes in behavior (Levin & Cross, 2004). Secondly, the measures and model used in the study have not been validated and tested empirically. Finally future work should further examine additional factors at the micro as well as the macro level such as the role of individual characteristics, cybersecurity knowledge characteristics and national culture differences in how social media impacts the transfer of cybersecurity knowledge.

Implications for Practice

The findings of this study will help security professionals within organizations and larger networks pay attention to the ways in which social media positions, relationships and sharing processes and objects are best used to enhance the discovery, personalization and externalization of knowledge. As managers, governments and private organizations seek to employ social media to disseminate cyber security knowledge they need to consider that each social media platform has different propensities when it comes to creating strong relationships, sharing of objects and processes and establishing and maintaining identities and positional hierarchies and each of these properties has implications for cybersecurity knowledge transfer. Further, over time community needs for knowledge transfer as well as the characteristics of the social media platform itself are likely to change and this necessitates a regular reappraisal of the best strategies for cybersecurity knowledge transfer in different contexts (Kietzmann et al., 2012).

In order to apprise users of the threats posed by a threat such as ransomware, for example, weak ties to multiple groups, users in positions of expertise or influence and social media platforms that enable sharing of threat information to the broader social network are likely to be useful. However discovery of such information is not likely to translate to protective behavior and knowledge personalization unless the users see their strong ties recommending it, they receive immediate and frequent instruction and feedback in the new safeguards from their close social network.

What implications does this have for changing the cybersecurity knowledge of the users? To increase awareness of cybersecurity threats, organizations would do well to identify influencers not just in cybersecurity space, but those whose expertise and influence spans multiple social groups with weak ties to each other. But when it comes to externalization of knowledge, it is necessary to provide platforms that simplify sharing of cybersecurity knowledge, and enable discoverability of both users and content based on their ranking in social media platforms. Finally to enable the personalization of knowledge and change of behavior we need to ensure that influencers in strong tightly knit groups with rich and frequent interactions on social media platforms have been trained in how to deal with cybersecurity threats.

CONCLUSION

This paper draws on research in the area of knowledge transfer, learning theories, and adoption of security safeguards to develop a conceptual model of how social media impacts knowledge transfer about cybersecurity. Based on research on the building blocks of social media, three higher level properties of social media are developed, strength of relationships, reduction in positional ambiguity and sharing of processes and objects of interaction. Knowledge transfer is defined in terms of personalization, discovery and externalization by drawing on knowledge and learning theories. Finally research on cybersecurity adoption is used to investigate how adoption of cybersecurity knowledge would be different from the transfer of other kinds of knowledge in social media domains. Our theoretical exploration reveals that there are two key properties that impact how users react to cybersecurity knowledge, threat appraisal and coping appraisal. Strength of relationships, position of users in social networks and processes and objects of sharing impact the threat appraisal and coping appraisal behavior. In addition they have direct effects on the discovery, personalization and externalization of cybersecurity knowledge.

In an increasingly digital world, users form majority of their opinions, gather information and gain knowledge through distributed social media networks that are outside the control of a single organization. As security becomes a bigger problem for organizations and users have a greater control of their devices through bring your own device policies, a study of how users gain cybersecurity knowledge through social media platforms has increased significance for organizational security. Further security is a human rather than a technical issue and policies and procedures tell only half the story of users' cybersecurity behavior. How users acquire cybersecurity knowledge can be the missing antecedent to understanding user cybersecurity behavior.

To our knowledge, this is the first theoretical exploration on cybersecurity knowledge transfer in social media platforms. We believe further insights into this problem have significant implications for research and practice.

REFERENCES

Adams, A., & Sasse, M. A. (1999). Users are not the enemy. *Communications of the ACM*, *42*(12), 40–46. doi:10.1145/322796.322806

Ahuja, G. (2000). Collaboration networks, structural holes, and innovation: A longitudinal study. *Administrative Science Quarterly*, *45*(3), 425–455. doi:10.2307/2667105

Akbar, H. (2003). Knowledge Levels and their Transformation: Towards the Integration of Knowledge Creation and Individual Learning. *Journal of Management Studies*, *40*(8), 1997–2021. doi:10.1046/j.1467-6486.2003.00409.x

Argyris, C. (1977). Double loop learning in organizations. *Harvard Business Review*, *55*(5), 115–125.

Bakker, M., Leenders, R. T. A., Gabbay, S. M., Kratzer, J., & Van Engelen, J. M. (2006). Is trust really social capital? Knowledge sharing in product development projects. *The Learning Organization*, *13*(6), 594–605. doi:10.1108/09696470610705479

Bandura, A. (1977). *Social learning theory*. Oxford, UK: Prentice-Hall.

Beesley, L. (2003). The challenge of emotion management in cooperative tourism research settings. In CAUTHE 2003: Riding the Wave of Tourism and Hospitality Research (85-106). Lismore, N.S.W.: Southern Cross University.

Beesley, L. G., & Cooper, C. (2008). Defining knowledge management (KM) activities: Towards consensus. *Journal of Knowledge Management*, *12*(3), 48–62. doi:10.1108/13673270810875859

Bhatt, G. D. (2002). Management strategies for individual knowledge and organizational knowledge. *Journal of Knowledge Management*, *6*(1), 31–39. doi:10.1108/13673270210417673

Bodner, G. M. (1986). Constructivism: A Theory of Knowledge. *Journal of Chemical Education*, *63*(10), 873–878. doi:10.1021/ed063p873

Borgatti, S. P., & Foster, P. C. (2003). The network paradigm in organizational research: A review and typology. *Journal of Management*, *29*(6), 991–1013. doi:10.1016/S0149-2063(03)00087-4

Brauner, E., & Becker, A. (2006). Beyond knowledge sharing: The management of transactive knowledge systems. *Knowledge and Process Management*, *13*(1), 62–71. doi:10.1002/kpm.240

Burt, R. S. (1992). *Structural holes: The social structure of competition*. Cambridge, MA: Harvard University Press.

Cabrera, A., Collins, W. C., & Salgado, J. F. (2006). Determinants of individual engagement in knowledge sharing. *International Journal of Human Resource Management*, *17*(2), 245–264. doi:10.1080/09585190500404614

Carver, C. S., & Scheier, M. F. (1982). Control theory: A useful conceptual framework for personality–social, clinical, and health psychology. *Psychological Bulletin*, *92*(1), 111–135. doi:10.1037/0033-2909.92.1.111 PMID:7134324

Chiu, C. M., Hsu, M. H., & Wang, E. T. (2006). Understanding knowledge sharing in virtual communities: An integration of social capital and social cognitive theories. *Decision Support Systems*, *42*(3), 1872–1888. doi:10.1016/j.dss.2006.04.001

Compeau, D., Higgins, C. A., & Huff, S. (1999). Social cognitive theory and individual reactions to computing technology: A longitudinal study. *Management Information Systems Quarterly*, *23*(2), 145–158. doi:10.2307/249749

Crossler, R. E., Johnston, A. C., Lowry, P. B., Hu, Q., Warkentin, M., & Baskerville, R. (2013). Future directions for behavioral information security research. *Computers & Security*, *32*, 90–101. doi:10.1016/j.cose.2012.09.010

Daft, R. L., & Lengel, R. H. (1986). Organizational information requirements, media richness and structural design. *Management Science*, *32*(5), 554–571. doi:10.1287/mnsc.32.5.554

Das, S., Kim, H. J., Dabbish, L. A., & Hong, J. I. (2014, July). The effect of social influence on security sensitivity. In *Proc. SOUPS* (Vol. 14).

Davila, T. M., Epstein, J., & Shelton, R. (2006). *Making Innovation Work: How to Manage It, Measure It, and Profit from It*. Upper Saddle River, NJ: Wharton School Publishing.

DiGioia, P., & Dourish, P. (2005, July). Social navigation as a model for usable security. In *Proceedings of the 2005 symposium on Usable privacy and security* (pp. 101-108). ACM. doi:10.1145/1073001.1073011

Downes, S. (2005). An introduction to connective knowledge. In T. Hug (Ed.), *Media, Knowledge & Education - Exploring new Spaces, Relations and Dynamics in Digital Media Ecologies*. Innsbruck, Austria: Innsbruck University Press.

Dretske, F. (1981). *Knowledge and the Flow of Information*. Cambridge, MA: MIT Press.

Driscoll, M. (2005). *Psychology of learning for instruction*. Needham Heights, MA: Allyn & Bacon.

Ekeh, P. P. (1974). *Social exchange theory: The two traditions*. London, UK: Heinemann.

Engeström, J. (2005). *Why some social network services work and others don't.* Or: the case for object-centered sociality. Retrieved from http://www. zengestrom. com/blog/2005/04/why_some_social. html

Erickson, T., & Kellogg, W. A. (2000). Social translucence: An approach to designing systems that support social processes. *ACM Transactions on Computer-Human Interaction*, *7*(1), 59–83. doi:10.1145/344949.345004

Fishbein, M., & Ajzen, I. (1975). Belief, attitude, intention and behavior: An introduction to theory and research. *Philosophy & Rhetoric*, *10*(2), 130–132.

Furnell, S. M., Jusoh, A., & Katsabas, D. (2006). The challenges of understanding and using security: A survey of end-users. *Computers & Security*, *25*(1), 27–35. doi:10.1016/j.cose.2005.12.004

Gao, F., Li, M., & Nakamori, Y. (2002). Systems thinking on knowledge and its management: Systems methodology for knowledge management. *Journal of Knowledge Management*, *6*(1), 7–17. doi:10.1108/13673270210417646

Gaw, S., Felten, E. W., & Fernandez-Kelly, P. (2006, April). Secrecy, flagging, and paranoia: adoption criteria in encrypted email. In *Proceedings of the SIGCHI conference on human factors in computing systems* (pp. 591-600). ACM. doi:10.1145/1124772.1124862

Granovetter, M. (1973). The strength of weak ties: A network theory revisited. *Sociological Theory*, *1*(1), 201–233.

Hansen, M. T. (1999). The search-transfer problem: The role of weak ties in sharing knowledge across organization subunits. *Administrative Science Quarterly*, *44*(1), 82–111. doi:10.2307/2667032

Hansen, M. T., Nohria, N., & Tierney, T. (1999). What's your strategy for managing knowledge? *The Knowledge Management Yearbook 2000–2001*.

Hattern, J. (2014). Many Say NSA News Changed Their Behavior. *The Hill*. Retrieved from http://thehill.com/policy/technology/202434-poll-nearly-half-say-nsa-news-affected-behaior

Herath, T., & Rao, H. R. (2009). Protection motivation and deterrence: A framework for security policy compliance in organizations. *European Journal of Information Systems*, *18*(2), 106–125. doi:10.1057/ejis.2009.6

Herley, C. (2009, September). So long, and no thanks for the externalities: the rational rejection of security advice by users. In *Proceedings of the 2009 workshop on new security paradigms workshop* (pp. 133-144). ACM. doi:10.1145/1719030.1719050

Herley, C., van Oorschot, P. C., & Patrick, A. S. (2009). Passwords: If we're so smart, why are we still using them? In Financial Cryptography and Data Security (pp. 230-237). Springer Berlin Heidelberg.

Hinde, S. (2003). The law, cybercrime, risk assessment and cyber protection. *Computers & Security*, *22*(2), 90–95. doi:10.1016/S0167-4048(03)00203-7

Huber, G. P. (1991). Organizational learning: The contributing processes and the literatures. *Organization Science*, *2*(1), 88–115. doi:10.1287/orsc.2.1.88

Johnston, A. C., & Warkentin, M. (2010). Fear appeals and information security behaviors: An empirical study. *Management Information Systems Quarterly*, *34*(3), 549–566.

Johnston, A. C., Warkentin, M., & Siponen, M. (2015). An enhanced fear appeal rhetorical framework: Leveraging threats to the human asset through sanctioning rhetoric. *Management Information Systems Quarterly*, *39*(1), 113–134.

Joinson, A. N. (2001). Self-disclosure in computer-mediated communication: The role of self-awareness and visual anonymity. *European Journal of Social Psychology*, *31*(2), 177–192. doi:10.1002/ejsp.36

Kaila, P. (2008). OAuth and OpenID 2.0. *From End-to-End to Trust-to-Trust, 18.*

Kaplan, A. M., & Haenlein, M. (2010). Users of the world, unite! The challenges and opportunities of Social Media. *Business Horizons*, *53*(1), 59–68. doi:10.1016/j.bushor.2009.09.003

Kaplan, A. M., & Haenlein, M. (2011). The early bird catches the news: Nine things you should know about micro-blogging. *Business Horizons*, *54*(2), 105–113. doi:10.1016/j.bushor.2010.09.004

Kietzmann, J. H., Hermkens, K., McCarthy, I. P., & Silvestre, B. S. (2011). Social media? Get serious! Understanding the functional building blocks of social media. *Business Horizons*, *54*(3), 241–251. doi:10.1016/j.bushor.2011.01.005

Kietzmann, J. H., Silvestre, B. S., McCarthy, I. P., & Pitt, L. F. (2012). Unpacking the social media phenomenon: Towards a research agenda. *Journal of Public Affairs*, *12*(2), 109–119. doi:10.1002/pa.1412

Krackhardt, D. (1992). The strength of strong ties: The importance of philos in organizations. In Networks and organizations: Structure, form, and action (pp. 216-239). Cambridge, MA: Harvard Business School Press.

Lee, Y. (2011). Understanding anti-plagiarism software adoption: An extended protection motivation theory perspective. *Decision Support Systems*, *50*(2), 361–369. doi:10.1016/j.dss.2010.07.009

Leroy, F., & Ramanantsoa, B. (1997). The cognitive and behavioral dimensions of organizational learning in a merger: An empirical study. *Journal of Management Studies*, *34*(6), 871–894. doi:10.1111/1467-6486.00076

Levin, D. Z., & Cross, R. (2004). The strength of weak ties you can trust: The mediating role of trust in effective knowledge transfer. *Management Science*, *50*(11), 1477–1490. doi:10.1287/mnsc.1030.0136

Liang, H., & Xue, Y. (2009). Avoidance of information technology threats: A theoretical perspective. *Management Information Systems Quarterly*, 71–90.

Liang, H., & Xue, Y. (2010). Understanding security behaviors in personal computer usage: A threat avoidance perspective. *Journal of the Association for Information Systems*, *11*(7), 394–413.

Maddux, J. E., & Rogers, R. W. (1983). Protection motivation and self-efficacy: A revised theory of fear appeals and attitude change. *Journal of Experimental Social Psychology*, *19*(5), 469–479. doi:10.1016/0022-1031(83)90023-9

Milton, N., Shadbolt, N., Cottam, H., & Hammersley, M. (1999). Towards a knowledge technology for knowledge management. *International Journal of Human-Computer Studies*, *51*(3), 615–641. doi:10.1006/ijhc.1999.0278

Moore, G. C., & Benbasat, I. (1991). Development of an instrument to measure the perceptions of adopting an information technology innovation. *Information Systems Research*, *2*(3), 192–222. doi:10.1287/isre.2.3.192

Nahapiet, J., & Ghoshal, S. (1998). Social capital, intellectual capital, and the organizational advantage. *Academy of Management Review*, *23*(2), 242–266.

Nonaka, I. (1994). A dynamic theory of organizational knowledge creation. *Organization Science*, *5*(1), 14–37. doi:10.1287/orsc.5.1.14

Nonaka, I., Konno, N., Tokuoka, K., & Kawamura, T. (1992). Hypertext organization for accelerating organizational knowledge creation. *Diamond Harvard Business*, 12-22.

Nonaka, I., & Takeuchi, H. (1995). *The knowledge-creating company: How Japanese companies create the dynamics of innovation*. Oxford, UK: Oxford university press.

Ozanne, L. K., & Ballantine, P. W. (2010). Sharing as a form of anti-consumption? An examination of toy library users. *Journal of Consumer Behaviour*, *9*(6), 485–498. doi:10.1002/cb.334

Polanyi, M. (1966). The logic of tacit inference. *Philosophy (London, England)*, *41*(155), 1–18. doi:10.1017/S0031819100066110

Prange, C. (1999). Organizational learning – desperately seeking theory? In M. Easterby-Smith, L. Araujo, & J. Burgoyne (Eds.), *Organizational Learning and the Learning Organization*. London: Sage. doi:10.4135/9781446218297.n2

Rader, E., Wash, R., & Brooks, B. (2012, July). Stories as informal lessons about security. In *Proceedings of the Eighth Symposium on Usable Privacy and Security* (p. 6). ACM.

Reagans, R., & McEvily, B. (2003). Network structure and knowledge transfer: The effects of cohesion and range. *Administrative Science Quarterly*, *48*(2), 240–267. doi:10.2307/3556658

Redmiles, E., Malone, A., & Mazurek, M. L. 2015 How I Learned To Be Secure: Advice Sources and Personality Factors in Cybersecurity. *Symposium on Usable Privacy and Security* Poster 2015

Rogers, R. W. (1975). A protection motivation theory of fear appeals and attitude change1. *The Journal of Psychology*, *91*(1), 93–114. doi:10.1080/00223980.1975.9915803

Ruppel, C. P., & Harrington, S. J. (2001). Sharing knowledge through intranets: A study of organizational culture and intranet implementation. *Professional Communication. IEEE Transactions on*, *44*(1), 37–52.

Salomon, G., & Perkins, D. N. (1998). Individual and social aspects of learning. *Review of Research in Education*, 23.

Schepers, P., & Van den Berg, P. T. (2007). Social factors of work-environment creativity. *Journal of Business and Psychology*, *21*(3), 407–428. doi:10.1007/s10869-006-9035-4

Schmidt, M. B., & Arnett, K. P. (2005). Spyware: A little knowledge is a wonderful thing. *Communications of the ACM*, *48*(8), 67–70. doi:10.1145/1076211.1076242

Short, J., Williams, E., & Christie, B. (1976). *The social psychology of telecommunications*. London: Wiley.

Siemens, G. (2005). Connectivism: A learning theory for the digital age. *International Journal of Instructional Technology and Distance Learning*, *2*(1), 3–10.

Stanton, J. M., Mastrangelo, P., Stam, K. R., & Jolton, J. (2004, January). Behavioral Information Security: Two End User Survey Studies of Motivation and Security Practices. In *10th Americas Conference on Information Systems, AMCIS 2004*.

Tavakolifard, M., & Almeroth, K. C. (2012). Social computing: An intersection of recommender systems, trust/reputation systems, and social networks. *IEEE Network*, *26*(4), 53–58. doi:10.1109/MNET.2012.6246753

Thompson, R. L., Higgins, C. A., & Howell, J. M. (1991). Personal computing: Toward a conceptual model of utilization. *Management Information Systems Quarterly*, *15*(1), 125–143. doi:10.2307/249443

Treem, J. W., & Leonardi, P. M. (2012). Social media use in organizations: Exploring the affordances of visibility, editability, persistence, and association. *Communication Yearbook*, *36*, 143–189.

Venkatesh, V., & Davis, F. D. (2000). A theoretical extension of the technology acceptance model: Four longitudinal field studies. *Management Science*, *46*(2), 186–204. doi:10.1287/mnsc.46.2.186.11926

Venkatesh, V., Morris, M. G., Davis, G. B., & Davis, F. D. (2003). User acceptance of information technology: Toward a unified view. *Management Information Systems Quarterly*, *27*(3), 425–478.

Vosgerau, J., Wertenbroch, K., & Carmon, Z. (2006). Indeterminacy and live television. *The Journal of Consumer Research*, *32*(4), 487–495. doi:10.1086/500478

Wang, S., & Noe, R. A. (2010). Knowledge sharing: A review and directions for future research. *Human Resource Management Review*, *20*(2), 115–131. doi:10.1016/j.hrmr.2009.10.001

Warkentin, M., Johnston, A. C., & Shropshire, J. (2011). The influence of the informal social learning environment on information privacy policy compliance efficacy and intention. *European Journal of Information Systems*, *20*(3), 267–284. doi:10.1057/ejis.2010.72

Warkentin, M., Shropshire, J., & Johnston, A. (2007). The IT security adoption conundrum: An initial step toward validation of applicable measures. *AMCIS 2007 Proceedings*, 276.

Wasko, M. M., & Faraj, S. (2000). "It is what one does": Why people participate and help others in electronic communities of practice. *The Journal of Strategic Information Systems*, *9*(2), 155–173. doi:10.1016/S0963-8687(00)00045-7

Wasko, M. M., & Faraj, S. (2005). Why should I share? Examining social capital and knowledge contribution in electronic networks of practice. *Management Information Systems Quarterly*, *29*(1), 35–57.

Whitten, A., & Tygar, J. D. (1999, August). Why Johnny Can't Encrypt: A Usability Evaluation of PGP 5.0. In Usenix Security (Vol. 1999).

Wilson, C., Boe, B., Sala, A., Puttaswamy, K. P., & Zhao, B. Y. (2009, April). User interactions in social networks and their implications. In *Proceedings of the 4th ACM European conference on Computer systems* (pp. 205-218). ACM. doi:10.1145/1519065.1519089

Wu, Y. (2009). Influence of social context and affect on individuals' implementation of information security safeguards. *ICIS 2009 Proceedings*, 70.

Zander, U., & Kogut, B. (1995). Knowledge and the speed of the transfer and imitation of organizational capabilities: An empirical test. *Organization Science*, *6*(1), 76–92. doi:10.1287/orsc.6.1.76

KEY TERMS AND DEFINITIONS

Coping Appraisal: Measures the perceived avoidability of the threat from the user's point of view and includes the perceived effectiveness of the measure, the costs of implementing that measure and user's self-efficacy in implementing it.

Discovery: A combination of push and pull and is defined as the degree to which the user actively scans the environment or passively encounters knowledge related to cybersecurity.

Externalization: Defined as the transfer, codification and explication of tacit knowledge.

Personalization: The process by which the users learn something about cybersecurity and make it their own by ascribing to it meanings in their own specific context.

Reduction of Positional Ambiguity: Identity, reputation and position in a network of relationships that reduces positional ambiguity in the social media platform.

Sharing Processes and Objects of Interaction: Sharing includes frequent bi-directional conversation and processes that enable the sharing of media, and text.

Strength of Relationships: Presence, formation of small groups, strong ties in cohesive relationships, and conversation constitute the strength of relationships in social media platforms.

Threat Appraisal: Perceived severity and perceived susceptibility where perceived susceptibility is a users' belief that the threat is likely to affect them and perceived severity is the extent of negative consequences that the users believe that they face as a result of the threat.

Section 4

Challenges of Social Media for Managing Knowledge

Chapter 13
Intranet Exploitation of Social Network Knowledge Intelligence

Mark Alan Underwood
Krypton Brothers LLC, USA

ABSTRACT

Intranets are almost as old as the concept of a web site. More than twenty-five years ago the text Business Data Communications closed with a discussion of intranets (Stallings, 1990). Underlying technology improvements in intranets have been incremental; intranets were never seen as killer developments. Yet the popularity of Online Social Networks (OSNs) has led to increased interest in the part OSNs play – or could play – in using intranets to foster knowledge management. This chapter reviews research into how social graphs for an enterprise, team or other collaboration group interacts with the ways intranets have been used to display, collect, curate and disseminate information over the knowledge life cycle. Future roles that OSN-aware intranets could play in emerging technologies, such as process mining, elicitation methods, domain-specific intelligent agents, big data, and just-in-time learning are examined.

INTRODUCTION

Today's intranets occupy a space within web technology. While some early implementations encompassed file sharing and other intra-organizational network resources, its principal connotation by 1996 was intimately connected to web technologies. Barbera (1996), writing that year, depicted "the intranet concept" as "derived from the present Internet as a natural step in its own evolution. The same TCP/IP communication protocols and applications are used, in particular the web server/client model." While some collaboration software had emerged that was initially less web browser-friendly (Falkner, 1997), Microsoft (Wynkoop, 1996) and Netscape (Budnick, 1996) had book-length proponents of their web technologies hoping to spur adoption.

In today's intranet concept, beyond access to broadband and computing devices, the boundaries of that space are defined as much by the ability of organizations to recognize the value of intranets as by technology. Similarly, types of intranets are best categorized by purpose and audience than by specific

DOI: 10.4018/978-1-5225-0495-5.ch013

technical features. For this reason, understanding their history and typical settings is essential to identifying the role intranets play in Online Social Networks (OSNs) and vice versa.

Intranets Defined

Early definitions of "intranet" defined it as "internal [organizational] versions of the internet" The general meaning of intranet is a web site that is intended to serve a specific group – typically an organization. Membership is centrally controlled, and access is mainly via a controlled subnet. Access to selected elements of an intranet is also possible through the public internet or a virtual private network (VPN). When intranet access is extended to suppliers, partners, customers and other groups, the term *extranet* is applied. For example, the New York City Housing Authority maintains an extranet for a regulated landlord group.

In the knowledge management community, intranets are seen as a structured knowledge repository of some sort, but organizations may use intranets for unstructured or even casual purposes, such as organizing events. It is also common to classify some intranets by their host content management software (CMS). Intranets can be deployed using commercial or open source software such as Confluence, Jostle, Plone, eXo Platform, IBM WebSphere Portal, Microsoft SharePoint, Dropbox Stream or Tibco tibbr. Other intranets may be hosted on homegrown platforms constructed from a variety of tools (e.g., WordPress, Django, Google Sites). While there are potentially steep challenges for smaller enterprises (Chan & Chao, 2008), organizations as small as a sole proprietorship can see benefits from intranets (Underwood, 2014).

An intranet implies a closed community, but there are useful exceptions, such as certain wikis which may serve a more specialized social role when used in connection with OSNs. Wikis have been studied by Majchrzak et al. (Majchrzak, Wagner, & Yates, 2012, Majchrzak, Wagner, & Yates, 2013) and others (Danis & Singer, 2008). Contributors to wikis can be studied both with respect to the type of knowledge interacted with, the knowledge life cycle stage, and also how they perceive wiki knowledge being used by others. This latter aspect is influenced by contributor perceptions of and position within in an organization's social graph.

A primary function for intranets dating from its earliest versions is enterprise search. Recently, tools such as those offered by SearchBlox (Anthony, 2014) and others allow for searching not only of documents and email – the early focus of most intranets – but also Big Data repositories, typically those stored using the Hadoop Distributed File System (HDFS). Searching HDFS and other unstructured repositories alongside structured information, such as document metadata, has created a new level of capability for search, discovery and retrieval. Significantly, analytics from OSN data itself, such as data mined from Facebook, LinkedIn, and public web traffic, can now comprise an important search target for intranet users, as Skeels & Grudin (2009) and Hansen, Shneiderman, & Smith (2010) showed.

Despite new opportunities such as these for intranet architects operating in greenfield scenarios, the scope of many intranets remains mostly within the bounds what was seen as its original mission decades ago. Writing about a study of Microsoft SharePoint, a widely used commercial "corporate" intranet application, investigators recently found that "the most popular functionalities among the customers are [still] document management, version control, co-writing, project rooms (team sites), and social networking facilities such as 'Mysite,' Yammer and blogging" (Hustad & Vikstøl, 2014).

Incremental real-world adoption aside, some researchers nonetheless see intranets as part of a family of collaboration products once simply called groupware (Szuprowicz, 1996), but now embracing the somewhat more descriptive term "Computer Supported Cooperative Work (CSCW)." [1] The CSCW community tends to emphasize organizational and psychological dimensions of Human-Computer Interactions (HCI) versus a focus on the enabling technologies.

Intranets will continue to co-evolve with the supporting web technology, as well as related developments in wearables, mobile communications and pervasive computing. There are some previously unanticipated uses for intranets that illustrate the pattern of technology diffusion from web technologies. Consider, for instance, the attempt to expand the concept of intranet to include wearables and sensor data aggregated and analyzed from the Internet of Things (IoT) as suggested by Zorzi, Gluhak, Lange, and Bassi (2010) and Rabaey (2015):

The Human Intranet operates in a dynamic world, subject to both slow evolution and extremely fast changes in needs, activity, conditions, and composition—both in the surrounding environment and in the Intranet itself. Therefore, the Human Intranet should be constructed as an adaptive and evolutionary system that combines local decision making with centralized global learning and optimization performed in hub nodes. (Rabaey, 2015 p. 82)

To achieve some of these newer objectives, intranets will likely be further animated by automated or human-guided connections to dynamic social graphs, a concept taken up later in this chapter.

Prior Work

The importance of informal social networks in facilitating strategic collaboration was studied by Cross, Borgatti, and Parker (2002), who concluded that such networks "provided strategic and operational value" to host organizations. Social networks can be particularly helpful in bridging functional or geographic boundaries in an organization and in supporting post-merger and post-reorganization assessments.

Such studies of the role of information sharing in social networks suggest that software collaboration frameworks might also serve a similar purpose (although by no means a proxy for social network analysis). The connection between such frameworks and findings from social network analysis (SNA) may be indirect, such as the insight that it is "important for groups to identify and work with people who are highly central." To the extent that collaboration software, such as an intranet, can enable access to "central" social connections, it may facilitate strategic collaboration.

Representing social networks through graphics or matrices, or as semantic webs was studied by Jamali and Abolhassani (2006), though their analysis did not address intra-organizational SNA. On the other hand, the corporate intranet "W3" at IBM played a more direct role in a study where the intranet was shown to have provided "a common user interface system that supports the company's knowledge management strategy" (Stafford & Mearns, 2010).

Intranet Social Graph Uses

Intranets can be used to get "relationship information," such as a better understanding of the org chart. This can be essential for large scale intranets, such as IBM's "W3," which reportedly has around 400,000 users and hosts "tens of millions of pages and documents" (Ward, 2015). Intranets can provide evidence for potentially useful sociological differences between users (Smith et al., 2009).

Figure 1. Atlassian confluence 4.3 network overview screenshot
(Used by permission of Atlassian)

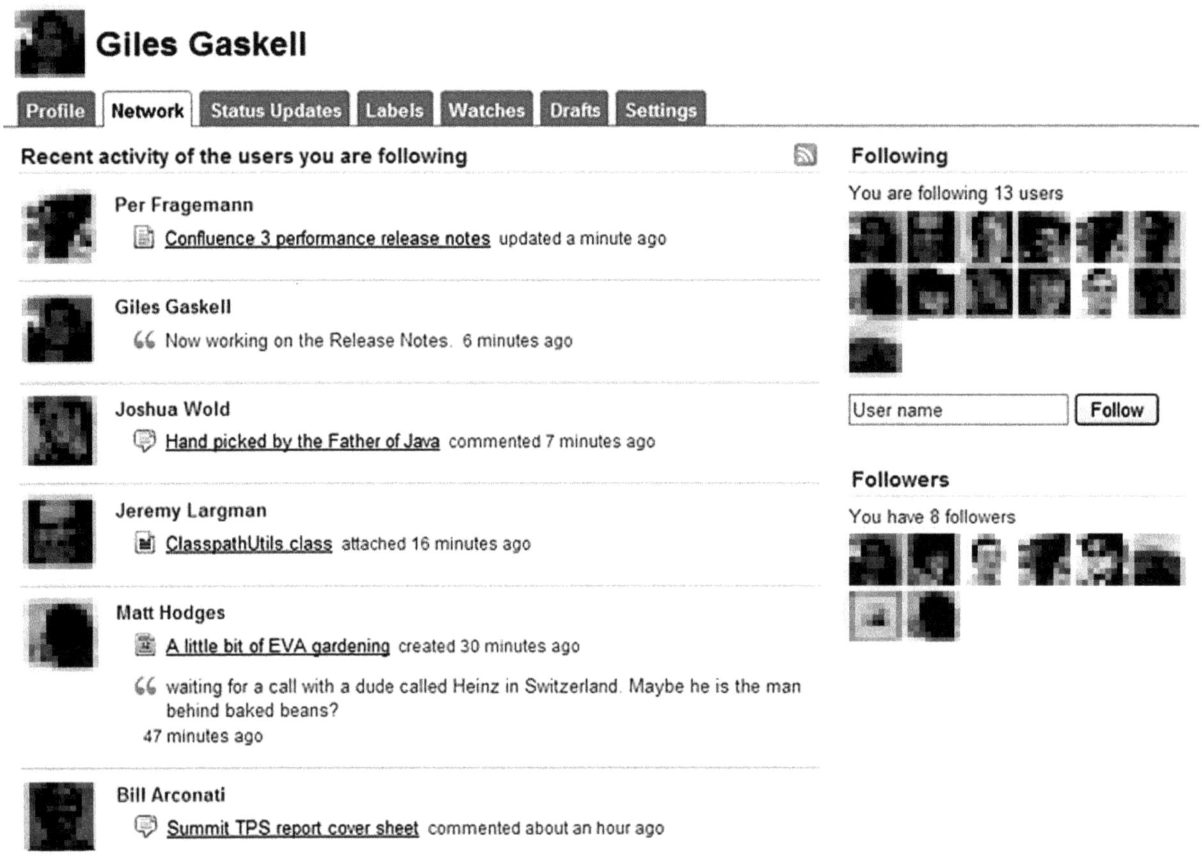

Used in conjunction with OSNs, intranets can foster a "learning commons" within organizational units, especially for product and cross-functional project teams (Somerville, Mirijamdotter, & Collins, 2006), or to facilitate sharing as part of Product Lifecycle Management,(Hwan, Youn-kyoung, & Do, 2009) . Analysts have proposed intranets as project management "enablers" (Roberta Lamb, 2003) that can assist in implementing enterprise-wide quality standards (Hussain, Barber, & Hussain, 2009) or as tools to facilitate "project-based integration" for inter-organizational teams and communities of practice (Roberta Lamb, 2003).

Some intranet service offerors (among them Prescient Digital) posit a subspecialty of intranets called "a social intranet." It is unclear whether this is a distinct category. Not long ago this belief was supported by the fact that only a few intranet platforms directly supported Facebook-like "follows," status tracking, chat, and timelines. An example from 2015 is shown in Figure 1, which depicts Atlassian's Confluence network view. This capability, however, is increasingly seen as a core feature for a CMS and for intranets.

These tools allow participants to interact with each other, through chat, shared bookmarks, annotated digital documents, FAQ editing and document creation. Participants do so inside the more secure perimeter of an intranet's controlled setting. Activities like social bookmarking of enterprise content as well as external web content annotation are only a few of the many interactions intranets powered by pairing with OSNs.

Logistical considerations can motivate intranet collaboration, but more effort may be needed in organizing tasks than most intranets support. Intranets could in principle be used to facilitate finely tuned process orchestration (Gupta, 2009), but few detailed examples of this level of implementation have been described. Instead intranets may serve less critical services, such as storing artifacts – i.e., serving as a sort of waystation between more mature automated systems, such as Enterprise Resource Planning, Human Resource Management, Customer Relationship Management (CRM), customer service or business intelligence.

However, these more mature software products tend to involve OSNs in a casual way. It is not surprising that CIOs may discover these uses for OSNs in enterprise are not easily unified, which discourages adoption.

Increasing complexity and the intrusion of stale information contaminates the perception of data quality in an intranet, so many have assumed that curatorial roles, perhaps C-level positions like Chief Knowledge Officer, would be needed to elevate the stature of intranet content. Scant evidence regarding this is available, but it is generally acknowledged that knowledge acquisition and curation has a cost, and that this cost affects the scope and quality of intranet social graphs. Even support for intranet search has a cost (Levine & Prietula, 2006).

After-the-fact curation only lightly integrated with business processes may not be only be costly, but may allow knowledge artifacts to "decay;" i.e., to become obsolete or incorrect. This is unsurprising. Imagine a business process represented using a Systems Modeling Language (SysML) model that omitted all references to actors. In many respects, intranets with weakly integrated OSNs resemble such a scenario.

Despite organizational headwinds, there are technology trends that would seem to facilitate social engagement through intranets. Unlike early efforts at knowledge management (e.g., (Davenport, De Long, & Beers, 1998), today's availability of video conferencing services (Webex, GoToMeeting, Google Hangouts, Adobe Connect, Microsoft Lync) allows intranet portals to supplement audio / chat collaboration with greater immediacy. It should be easier to connect to colleagues and their content, and to collaborate on common tasks.

Yet these services are often used as disposable, one-off resources whose artifacts are sometimes delivered as an afterthought: "Where can I get this PowerPoint presentation?" "Where should we put the chat log?"

Significant events in the course of employee skill acquisition are often social in nature, and also offer opportunities for intranet collaboration. For example, some research has investigated whether explicit mentor-mentee relationships can facilitate intranet use in job training settings (Yusof & Ahmad, 2012). Yet this expectation may instead be associated with a Learning Management System (LMS).

Taxonomies, Jargon, and Acronyms

Nascent or casual attempts at intranets in smaller organizations begin as FAQs, checklists, links to Wikipedia or document indexes. These simple schemes can have immediate benefits. But over time, especially with personnel turnover, classification schemes that worked at one point in time are no longer effective. Engagement with authors and users in a meaningful context – ideally in real time – may be essential to mature intranets beyond these initial stages.

An OSN can help by connecting, for example, the user of a confusingly worded or ambiguous FAQ entry with the author's OSN handle. The two can collaborate to improve the entry for the next user, rather than starting a potentially extended email thread that loses contextual richness. Also, the intranet can capture the whole process as a meta-event, which can be useful for future curators or automated processes.

The concept of a "proactive" intranet is an information system that actively utilizes intra-organizational knowledge to recommend content, interactive assets (e.g., a chat with a specialist) or e-learning. Automating this requires the use of a live person, or automatic aids built into the intranet.

Among potential automated aids are machine learning classifiers such as recommenders. These can facilitate maturation by providing prompts, cues or suggested edits to content, and to identify others in the organization – by leveraging a social graph – with whom collaborations might be sought. The SEEK!sem project is one such scheme. SEEK!sem works by ". . . automatically identifying and recommending related information resources to be added to a folder. The recommendations are based on rules, exploiting content and context similarity of information resources" (Lutz, Thonssen, & Witschel, 2013).

To the extent that such rules are OSN-aware, connections can be scored by most relevant "experts" as well as incorporating rules that take into account other OSN attributes – such as who is still working for the organization and actually available to help.

Spanning OSN Levels of Expertise

As Viaene explained in "Data Scientists aren't Domain Experts," subject matter experts (SME's or domain experts) are most effective operating in recognizable information spaces. To the extent that those information spaces are reflected on intranet repositories, domain experts can influence the effectiveness of corporate data retrieval by providing intranet signposts, such as annotations, taxonomies, tagging and other artifacts.

Their habitat is a space made up of real business transactions and interactions. (Viaene, 2013)

Viaene proposes activities that include modeling the business, discovering data, operationalizing insight and cultivating knowledge.

At characteristically low levels of OSN engagement, it is fair to assume that this level of abstraction is an endeavor undertaken infrequently on most intranets.

Intranets can be a source for learning. Examples of explicit worker outcomes include learning from failure (Hall, Nousala, & Kilpatrick, 2009) or by using intranet resources to frame the workplace as "a learning laboratory" (Mørch, Engen, & Åsand, 2004). To do so effectively, with or without an LMS, requires that content authors have recognizable levels of expertise that could, for instance, translate into the need for others to review material before it is made available across the intranet or extranet. For smaller organizations, greater reliance on automated curation and tagging may need to be the default action.

Intranet implementations that serve a clear purpose, especially when driven by institutional mandates, can improve adoption, and the reason this is the case may have as much to do with implicit OSNs as any other single aspect. For instance, a successful intranet used to deliver competency training for nurses incorporated supervisor and accreditation roles (Wolford & Hughes, 2001) Because the social graph is dynamic, intranets must be kept in sync in order to evolve in step with organizational changes.

Intranet successes often occur in regulated environments in which OSNs are explicit – even mandated by law. In other cases, OSNs orchestrate teacher/learner or expert/apprentice roles which are adopted as needed to meet competency goals. In a radiology intranet, a valued use was to post reference radiation dose estimates for common imaging examinations. Goals included improvements in radiation exposure risk, clarity in protocols and implications of radiation exposure risk in research settings (Brady, Mohaupt, & Kaufman, 2015). NeuPAT was an intranet "database" for assist in clinical and translational research on neuroblastic tumors (Villamón et al., 2013). The UK Building Information Modeling project was built to facilitate "collaborative web modeling of the built and natural environment" (Counsell, 2012).

Another example was Lighthouse, a coordination portal for software engineering aimed at overcoming senescence of design abstractions in software products (Proenca, Moura, & Van Der Hoek, 2009).

Each of these examples feature clear actor – beneficiary roles, and sometimes explicit knowledge coordinator-publishers. OSNs are thus shown to be context-specific. Intranets – including permissions for establishing reference material – must change as organizations. A student one day can become the instructor the next. Content, such as a proposed guideline, can shift from a guideline to an ISO standard that requires an IT governance role. After a corporate acquisition, a supervisor becomes a subordinate employee.

DECISION SUPPORT

Group decision-making is often viewed through the lens of a static organizational chart. This perspective is pervasive. An alternative view seeks to replace, or at least supplant the organizational chart with the social graph (Roberts, 2014). A contrasting approach uses a social graph-aware intranet that becomes part of orchestrated decision processes.

The social graph can have significant analytical value, even finding military uses that represent hypothetical enemy command structures. Business Intelligence tools such as Tableau or QlikView can be used to draw social graphs, as benign as identifying which philanthropists could be used to help guide nonprofits in decision-making as to where to seek funding for specific projects.

Box Inc. drew network graphs to represent flow characteristics such as degree of interconnectedness between employees, employees who tend to be information hubs, and interactions with external workers (Bouck, 2014).

"Smart enough" decision support can be paired with social intelligence. Organizations can improve through modest automation goals (Taylor & Raden, 2007). A Swedish study demonstrated that through the use of a clinical decision support system in emergency care settings, prehospital nurses were able to safely select the level of healthcare geriatric patients required (Vicente, Sjöstrand, Sundström, Svensson, & Castren, 2013). The study used data from electronic medical records and collaborative advice from medical experts.

In a 1998 survey of intranet decision support models, Sridhar used the "data-dialog-model framework of decision support systems" (Sridhar, 1998). This oft-cited framework originally proposed by Sprague and Carlson (Sprague & Carlson, 1982) predated intranets, and later adaptations often have not addressed avenues for incorporating social graph intelligence.

Decision-making processes by military planners have long used table-top exercises to rehearse and better understand processes. Military chain of command has an explicit social graph which must be adopted as policy (Walker et al., 2009). When military planners access shared workspace resources such as the Command Post of the Future (Shachtman, 2009), such protocols can be made explicit. Collaborations can even include virtual tabletop exercises (DeMatteis & Brown, 2008) or include rehearsed customer interactions for use in call centers.

Some have proposed using intranets for Big Data information summarization or visualization (McKinsey & Company, 2011), (Akerkar, 2014). Unstructured data can be structured for use in decision-making (Power, 2014), but may also involve Big Data variety. With variety may come a need to collaborate with other data owners and distributors, which could involve complex interactions with others in a social graph's subnet.

In this way, an intranet portal can address the need for knowledge "contextuality," as suggested by Majchrzak et al (2013).

An OSN can influence how intranets support information diffusion within an organization, as well as beyond it. This was studied by Aral, Brynjolfsson, & Van Alstyne (2007), but more properly belongs under an emerging category of software systems called Persuasive Systems; Oduor, Alahäivälä and Oinas-Kukkonen (2014a) suggest a class of software design patterns which facilitate social influence. Persuasive systems concepts are applied to intranets later in the chapter.

Reputation and Reward in Intranets

Some facets of OSN intranet integration may need further study prior to adoption. Using OSNs in an intranet may require adjustment from usage patterns familiar from experience with public OSNs like Facebook. Accurate information may not be "popular." Employee "crowdsourced" FAQs or checklists may reflect commonly held misbeliefs instead of fact unless they are properly vetted.

Some obvious social pitfalls with intranets can dilute their effectiveness. Anecdotal evidence suggests that on an intranet everyone may feel they must "follow" their supervisors and "like" what they say. Lack of anonymity for certain kinds of communications can be a problem, even though this can be overcome by a combination of policy and role-identified anonymity on an intranet.

A 2010 study of ePinions, Slashdot and Wikipedia (Leskovec, Huttenlocher, & Kleinberg, 2010) demonstrated that patterns of positive and negative social connections can be manifested in online settings. Using such information from social psychology could be integrated with Human Resource Management (HRM) practices to improve how participation in intranets can be nurtured. In one detailed study of a single organization, the intranet facilitated socialization of new workers (Chang & Lin, 2011), whereas another study of voice, text and email communications was able to infer "rich club effects" (Dong et al., 2015).

An intranet can serve a narrow purpose in this fashion, but that perspective is a management-centric, HRMS network with a limited focus – albeit still one driven by the need for intelligence about the enterprise and its workforce.

One possible approach to enhance engagement while establishing reputation involved an experiment in the banking industry (Morschheuser, Henzi, & Alt, 2015). Such in-situ intra-organizational experiments that use OSNs are best accomplished using intranet resources.

COMPLIANCE, INTELLECTUAL PROPERTY, AND RISK MANAGEMENT

R. Lamb (2001) proposed the notion of "the compliance intranet." Examples cited were quality management intranets designed to achieve an organization's certification level (e.g., ISO 9000) or to achieve address safety or health objectives. Seen from the perspective of social networks, what makes a compliance intranet different from others is a cross-organizational knowledge framework – often quite explicit – that can jumpstart and maintain intranet engagement.

For example, compliance in U.S. aviation maintenance is highly regulated. Content for an intranet within a jet engine repair facility must contain both compliance specifications as well as enterprise-specific workflow, roles and recommendations.

Defending information systems against insider threat is notoriously difficult. Because the incentives are so high, a highly integrated reliance on an intranet, as opposed to multiple, less regulated repositories, could enhance computer security. OSN profiles can be connected to an employee's or partner actual information access, which improves the opportunities to trigger alerts for unauthorized access or exfiltration (Ashley & Vandenwauver, 2013). This technique is helpful for detection algorithms that rely upon social graph as well as role-based access and organizational event triggers like access and tagging to improve anomaly detection (e.g., Manmadhan & Achuthan, 2014).

EXAMPLES

A few examples demonstrate how OSNs are typically integrated into intranets:

- An intranet can interoperate with Facebook for Work or LinkedIn, using shared logins with side panels to support live chat. Questions arise, as pointed out in previous studies of Facebook (Marshall & Shipman, 2015) as to knowledge ownership, or the reputation of its proponents.
- The WordPress plugin "Super Socializer" allows users to log into a WordPress site without separate registration by using their existing OSN credentials. Reasons why this class of plugins in preferred by some site administrators goes beyond the simplified login. They believe Facebook and Google have stronger enforcement for sham duplicate accounts, and because users will see posts made on a WordPress intranet on their OSN timeline, intranet content has another visibility opportunity.
- Microsoft SharePoint, probably the leading corporate portal product of its kind, is a multi-billion dollar business for Microsoft. For example, SharePoint 2013 supports OSN features through its own app store.
- An interview with the Chief Knowledge Officer of a 60,000+-member professional society (Underwood, 2015) showed that the association followed a common adoption pattern. While all employees were aware of its CMS-based commercial intranet, and while it had several compelling uses related to human resources, it was not used, for example, to systematically announce the start of new products, services or projects. Features to allow employee recommending, rating, following and likes was not currently in place, but the organization planned to implement these features. The society had deployed a LMS, but the intranet was not connected to it in any way.
- Integration of a chat system with an intranet provides a "hot link" between content and a company's social network. This feature lead to a series of reports on Microsoft's Yammer product by Deloitte (Townsend, 2012) and Pitney Bowes (Zhang, Qu, Cody, & Wu, 2010). Figure 2 shows Yammer installed with SharePoint through an embed function.

Figure 2. Example of a Yammer feed that has been embedded in SharePoint
(Used with permission from Microsoft)

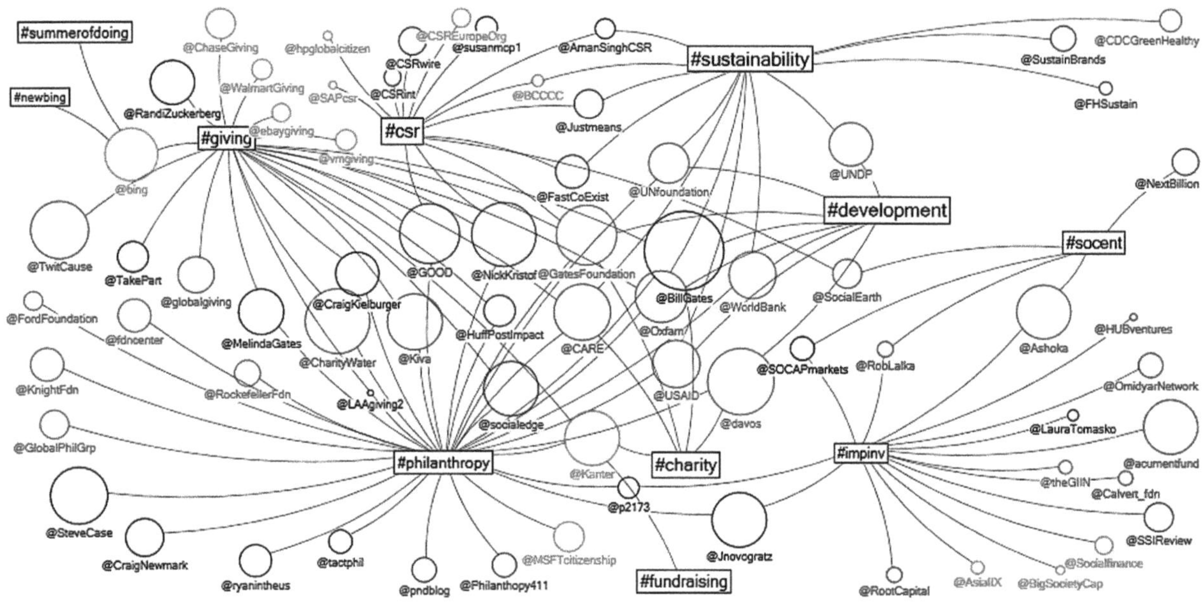

Similarly, Microsoft's Skype for Business (the previous Lync) now includes video calling. SharePoint can be configured to search Skype for Business data, and the concept of searching voice mail and image data cannot be far behind – similar to Facebook and Google's image recognition capabilities.

Intranet Image Recognition

It is worth examining a bit further why these new search and discovery features matter for OSNs operating in intranet contexts. Suppose the manager of an unfamiliar business unit snaps a few photos in a group meeting, including some whiteboard artifacts. She then posts these to the intranet – in a raw format. A utility in the intranet can examine the EXIF data in the images and determine which likely meeting appearing in the company calendar app was associated with those timestamps and location. Add to this a bit of image recognition and for some of the photos, intranet software would be able to perform the equivalent of Facebook's people tagging. Tagging is useful because it can improve engagement by connecting even the most passively involved to enterprise events and services.

The capability can be extended to non-employee partners, and even to improve competitive intelligence, which often neglects the importance of individual actors because it is difficult to gather such information about competitor employees. Stated differently, image data, rather than being treated as uninterpretable "blob," can, in some circumstances, serve as a common key to unite disparate data sources about people and organizations. This common key is a social one, ready to be hooked into either external or internal OSNs.

Storytelling, Narratology, and Discourse Support

The broad brush painted by the CSCW community includes HCI capabilities that encompass crowdsourcing, online gaming, collective intelligence (e.g., Delphi method) and virtual worlds – today represented by Linden Labs Second Life and Facebook's Oculus Rift (Vacca, 1996). These next-gen concepts offer tempting and new sources of social intelligence, such as crowdsourcing of project risk or cross-disciplinary folksonomies. One example from this latter category is LinkedIn skill and expertise tagging (Bastian et al., 2014). Trends such as these offer the prospect of amassing more knowledge on the intranet, but also strengthening ties within social graphs.

Group storytelling (Escalfoni, Braganholo, & Borges, 2011) can be encouraged using intranet resources, not only to leverage or strengthen OSNs but also identify strengths and weaknesses in projects and products (Bloomstein, 2012). Case studies, use cases, even anecdotes from employees, partners and sales can offer real life stories that sometimes represent priceless stories told in the safe, but also analytics-friendly community of the intranet. Just as importantly, sometimes key actors in these stories can be tagged and associated with these stories for vetting and other purposes.

Hosting a diversity of forum types and formats to support discourse and storytelling – whether for pedagogical purposes or persuasive computing – can serve to keep participants engaged. Perhaps more importantly, this allows for competitive surveillance or to identify market opportunities and product improvements in a setting that supports a curated give and take – plus has a digital footprint for post mortem analytics.

INTEROPERABILITY OPPORTUNITIES

There are numerous ways that OSNs can interoperate with an intranet. Some can be readily identified:

- Snips of email can be copied into relevant settings of an intranet, and vice versa, with full traceability.
- Hosted or OSN chat (e.g., ICQ, Gmail Chat, Google Hangouts, Apple FaceTime, Facebook Chat).
- Document editing with accountability for revisions.
- Online documentation such as user manuals, installation, troubleshooting guides, assembly, calibration that can be annotated.
- Host Bulletin Boards for quick-and-dirty list-making like checklists, useful for compliance or training.
- Twitter in the enterprise (Zhang et al., 2010).
- Capture discourse that might otherwise be lost in smartphone-only conversations.
- LMS.
- Connect local LAN-based document stores otherwise separately managed and potentially lost in the event of employee turnover.
- Connect to numerous other enterprise apps: CRM, Project Management, Product Lifecycle Management (PLM), ERP (e.g., purchasing), Information Technology Service Management (ITSM).

Table 1. Intranet involvement in the KMC life cycle model

KMC Life Cycle Model Phase	Example Intranet Involvement
Identify/Create	Identify and solicit knowledge requirements to peers; initiate a new email thread; receive new product or service feature announcements (internal or competitive); identify new regulatory or compliance requirements
Store	Add to document repository; curate content from email or other non-intranet channel; add FAQ item;
Share	share content on OSN; forward content to email; bookmarking of existing intranet content; share content with external subgroups (e.g., new pricelists or product availability);
Use	Integrate with workflow components in other enterprise software applications, e.g.: ERP, HR, project management, product data management, operations, audit, customer support, marketing
Learn	Enhance taxonomy; crosslink documents; expand ontology; incorporate into learning management systems;
Improve	Improve through socializing content, vetting with other specialists; combine with other non-intranet assets; apply canonical principles such as uniform taxonomies or adapt for lay uses such as non-expert public communication; link to related work elsewhere or to still-evolving intra-organization work

ROLE OF INTRANETS IN THE KNOWLEDGE MANAGEMENT LIFE CYCLE

Several models attempt to represent the life cycle of knowledge management. One of the latest, the Knowledge Management Cycle (KMC) approach, attempts to integrate the work of previous models as it proposes seven "non-sequential model phases" (Evans, Dalkir, & Bidian, 2014). The phases listed by these investigators include actions to be performed on knowledge: *identify, store, share, use, learn, improve* and *create*.

Intranet users participate in every phase of this KMC. Early work by Karl Wiig (1994) singled out knowledge pooling as central to collaboration and identified intranets as a technology enabler. Evans et al. make no further mention of it in their survey, but intranets support all phases of the KMC model, as enumerated in Table 1.

Ontology-Enabled Organizational Learning

The *Learn* phase of the KMC model can be further catalyzed through the use of ontologies in an intranet. Ontologies allow for machine-enabled translations across ontologies, as well as automating connections between knowledge islands. OIL, an early ontology framework (Fensel, van Harmelen, Horrocks, McGuinness, & Patel-Schneider, 2001), was seen as well suited to both intranet and internet needs. In addition to leveraging domain-specific ontologies, such as terminology shared across the oil and gas industries, Fensel. et al. noted that "ontology-based translation services [can] link different data structures in areas where standard ontologies do not exist or where a particular client needs a translation from his or her terminology into the standard. This translation service must cover structural and semantic as well as language differences" (p. 40).

STILL ON INTRANET DRAWING BOARDS

An optimistic forecast by O'Leary almost twenty years ago saw the potential for extensive exploitation of AI for intranets (O'Leary, 1997). Among other AI-exploiting capabilities, a bright future was seen for intelligent agents that could recognize patterns and similarities among social communities, pruning and preprocessing to enable faster delivery of more relevant information.

Elsewhere in this chapter multiple opportunities for workflow-enabled knowledge management have been identified. This is the single most often missed opportunity in most organizations. There is a good reason for this. Many enterprise apps do not have embedded workflow engines separate and open from their internal logic, and were not designed to share event triggering and handoffs from outside. Without workflow, many intranet interactions may be redundant or at least inconvenient.

Still on the drawing board, though its general outline has been mapped for some time, is the idea of enabling Just in Time Learning (Tucker & Winchester, 2009) using intranet resources. A reason that an LMS cannot substitute for this role is that this product is unlikely to ever be designed to execute – not only teach about -- mission critical tasks within an organization. By definition, this is a feature of enterprise grade intranets.

Leveraging and displaying task-relevant Big Data, such as IBM's SASH application performs on analytics platforms as part of IBM's intranet search (Sethi, Sachindran, & Raghavan, 2013), is an emerging capability. Social media datasets will often be part of the action. "Small Data" analytics could incorporate measures of effectiveness, influence, quality that take into account aspects of the social graph, such as frequency of interactions with customers, supervisors, regulators or other role-based actors.

Even more novel extensions for "people-centric sensing networks" have been proposed by Dürr and Wiesner (2011), such as the investigators' Vegas system (Durr, Maier, & Dorfmeister, 2012).

Knowledge Elicitation

In some settings, intranet frameworks for knowledge sharing should incorporate methods for highly interactive elicitation. Selection of recipients and form of such elicitation could take into account competency as measured by OSN, LMS activity and seniority. Elicitation opportunities were identified by analysts in the 90's (e.g., (Klooster, Brinkkemper, Harmsen, & Wijers, 1997). For large scale knowledge systems to grow, a combination of human and automated methods will be required, and natural language-based elicitation is the point of this spear.

Knowledge for Persuasive Systems Design

The knowledge required to influence and change human behavior is an important business objective. Development of effective marketing communications, for example, requires collaboration among multiple disciplines, drawing from expertise in social psychology, web development, competitive intelligence – plus strong knowledge of the product or service being sold. Before launching a promotional campaign to introduce a new product or service, and sometimes even before choosing to develop the product or service, an informed message must be crafted. As with other collaborative processes, this is typically accomplished by exchanging documents and commentary.

In a series of papers, Oinas-Kukkonen and co-investigators (Oinas-Kukkonen & Harjumaa, 2009), (Oinas-Kukkonen, 2012), (Oduor, Alahäivälä, & Oinas-Kukkonen, 2014b), (Oduor et al., 2014a) argue for a sub-discipline they term Persuasive Systems Design. The complete rationale for this proposal, as well as the suggested framework, is beyond the scope of the present analysis, but this line of inquiry highlights the importance of social elements in human-computer interactions:

Any interactive system provides some degree of system feedback to its users, potentially via verbal information or other kinds of summaries. There are several design principles related to implementing computer-human dialogue support in a manner that helps users keep moving towards their goal or target behavior. They include praise, rewards, reminders, suggestion, similarity, liking, and social role. (Oinas-Kukkonen & Harjumaa, 2009, p. 10)

An OSN-enabled intranet provides a vehicle for human-human as well as computer-mediated praise, reward, suggestions and the like. Utilized in connection with the other intranet capabilities explored in this chapter, organizations can utilize an intranet's connected OSNs to support focused personnel enrichment initiatives and directives. When the goal is collaborate on developing effective marketing communications, judging and – to the extent possible, managing -- intranet, extranet and public OSN social valence can be critical.

Citing earlier work by Fogg (2002), Oinas-Kukkonen and colleagues identified software features that support persuasion, but did not acknowledge unique opportunities offered by the relatively controlled environment of an intranet. Not only is an intranet OSN a comparatively closed system, but various software aids can be tapped for intranet settings that are not feasible, or possibly not even legal, in public OSNs. For example, task sequencing, event timelines, org charts, regulatory constraints, approvals and other workflow components aware of fine-grained project role assignments can inform the nature of an intranet-OSN interaction.

Questions for Chief Knowledge Officers

Table 2 presents a list of questions for use by analysts and system architects seeking to understand (or specify) the extent of social engagement in their own intranets.

Intranet Automation Frontiers

Increased intranet automation is needed to improve intranet value, maintain relevance, and remain abreast of other automation-accelerated events in the organization. A partial list of future-leaning activities that may be considered intranet OSN frontiers follows:

- Revisit agent technology, which some have given up for dead. Consider domain-specific virtual agents, such as the "social-affective agent" which uses the Web Ontology Language to provide semantic interoperability between agents (Boff, Santos, & Vicari, 2006).
- Implement e-coaching agents for trainees and for interactions with new customers. If the LMS supports this, start there.
- Add intranet support for all types of visualization (Trainer & Redmiles, 2012).
- Automate selected classification and tagging with integration to enterprise-wide metadata management.
- Integrate with enterprise-wide search (Sethi et al., 2013), at least initially with Google Search.

Table 2. Assessment questions for intranet social engagement

How well integrated is the intranet into other social processes within the organization, such as onboarding, termination, HR reviews, meetings, party planning, event planning (annual meeting / convention attendance, travel planning, polls?
Is the intranet connected to project launches or terminations?
Is it possible for OSNs to move content bidirectionally from email to chat to intranet page or application portlet?
What patterns exist between major contributors and curators and their position in the org chart?
Are external roles included, such as key partners, Boards of Directors or Boards of Trustees?
How congruent is the org chart with the contributor / influencer / curator trends (social graph) on the intranet?
Is there a connection to a learning-enabled Learning Management System? Are there other Single SignOns?
Is the intranet used to post strategic planning documents? Annotate drafts? Can changes be tied to the OSN?
Does the intranet host other communication functions, such as blogs, RSS, chat?
Are intranet user metrics gathered for analysis for continuous improvement?
Does the intranet support rating, recommending, "following" functions?
Can the intranet be accessed through employee mobile devices?

- Integrate with other enterprise apps by creating communicating portals (not portal islands juxtaposed on a common screen).
- Collect intranet usage metrics for "social optimization" and engagement at least as good as those collected for public-facing web properties.
- Promote close integration with HRMS. While an HRMS is just another enterprise application, it is the one with the most direct link to enterprise OSNs.
- Connect to online brand communities. Significant knowledge exists in partner and customer communities.
- Mine and analyze intranet information. For example, analysis can produce more intelligent intranet search by identifying shifts in user search requirements over time (Dignum et al., 2010). Others have used SharePoint event logs to help evaluate results of content or organizational initiatives in an industrial safety setting (Chaves & Cordoba, 2014).
- Integrate with workplace management systems, such as smart buildings, customer- or patient-flow monitors.

SEVEN NEXT STEPS

What are the most innovative ideas taken from the literature on OSN-enhanced intranets? Seven of the most compelling are listed below for ambitious intranet managers to consider.

1. Review corporate knowledge management initiatives suggested by Schneider and others (Schneider, 2005).
2. Nurture knowledge worker cultural integration, such as that proposed for CSCW and proactive health (Chamberlain et al., 2015).
3. Implement technological innovations aimed at specific workplace collaborations, e.g., "collaboration personas" (Matthews, Whittaker, Moran, & Yuen, 2011).

4. Promote process transparency (Dabbish, Stuart, Tsay, & Herbsleb, 2013) and use the intranet to advertise it.
5. Automate workflow "fabrics," e.g., B'fabric, or service architectures for e-science e.g., iData (Kalyanam et al., 2013). These services exploit pragmatic, near-term capabilities, especially useful for orchestration of cloud offerings.
6. Allow for self-articulated employee workflows and user-initiated intranet enhancements. See how far personalization can be taken to surface specialized knowledge areas. It may be possible to discover canonical principles among the idiosyncratic.
7. Transition from tags to ontologies. Look at agile, lightweight ontologies, such as Sem T++, used by teams for annotating shared digital resources (Goy, Magro, Petrone, Picardi, & Segnan, 2015).

PRAGMATIC STEPS USING EXISTING TECHNOLOGIES

Neatly proscriptive formulas for intranet success are not possible, and perhaps not appropriate. Most agree that empirical research on intranets is not sufficiently deep, nor do existing studies control adequately for important organizational differences. In addition, specific communities of interest employing more limited tools such as project intranets or project wikis can serve modest goals that would not be appropriate at enterprise-level scale. Consequently, experts are less confident in making prescriptive recommendations. Still, while research in the preceding frontier areas advances, there are pragmatic steps that can be taken:

- **Model Exploitation:** There is evidence from domain-specific solution areas that intranets can facilitate computer-aided deliberation by exploiting digital model management design patterns (Nunamaker, Applegate, & Konsynski, 1988). For instance, business intelligence applications can provide access to their resources via intranet portals, but just as importantly, those applications must be connected to underlying knowledge models. As Puerta & Eisenstein (1999) noted, frameworks such as domain models, application models and user-task models are among those which have been tapped to coordinate model-based interface development. A related approach focuses on the functions, activities or processes of a system (Hara, Matsutsuka, Kanaya, Ookubo, & Uehara, 1997), or domain-specific business processes (Ryan, 2014). Exemplars have been developed in fields such as chemoinformatics (Ertl, Selzer, & Mühlbacher, 2004).
- **Identify, Focus in Important Roles:** Role-dependent approaches examine ways to better utilize intranet resources based on the some concept of role. Unfortunately, "role" tends to have a somewhat loose meaning in some settings, and as a result translating work in one setting to another is not straightforward. Their approach did not use a formal definition of role, such as in the Business Process Modeling Language (BPMN), but Chang et al. emphasized the importance of newcomers to an organization (Chang & Lin, 2011). The same limitation affected an investigation of IT governance by Wilkin and Riddett in a healthcare setting.
- **Innovate:** Other intranet innovations have been tried, though on small or at experimental scale. For example, gamification has been tried in an experimental intranet setting, and this approach increased time spent reading intranet-hosted articles and improved answers to quizzes (Morschheuser et al., 2015). Gamification has been suggested for e-learning settings such as electronics design automation (Marasco, Mehjat, & Rosehart, 2015) and collaborative search, such as may be imple-

mented on an intranet using Google Site Search, Apache Nutch or Apache Solr (Fernández-Luna, Huete, Rodriguez-Avila, & Rodriguez-Cano, 2014).

- **Unify Communications around Knowledge Frameworks:** Some enterprises have moved toward more unified communications technologies. These digital offerings make it easier to present as well as to save content from phone calls and meetings. Making these items discoverable on intranets is an enterprise-wide need, even though there is a tendency for "a 'long tail' of small teams' intranet sites" to spring up (Seide, Thambiratnam, Lu, & Yu, 2009). Reuse and integration are seen as key to making these steadily accumulating resources attractive elements in intranet-hosted social networks.

Whether visualized via intranet connections or other sources of social network data, network analysis can help contribute to collaboration. For example, the NodeXL Excel add-in was motivated by the observation that

Analysis of social media populations and artifacts can create a picture of the aggregate structure of a user's social world. Network analysis tools can answer questions like: What patterns are created by the aggregate of interactions in a social media space? How are participants connected to one another? What social roles exist and who plays critical roles like connector, answer person, discussion starter, or content caretaker? What discussions, pages, or files have attracted the most interest from different kinds of participants? How do network structures correlate with the contributions people make within the social media space? (Smith et al., 2009)

Intranet administrators and content creators across all social media platforms can use information gathered by such tools. OSN representation can be gathered by intranet tools themselves, but also by marketing tools which are capable of click analytics. The Google Analytics tool, widely used for monitoring traffic patterns on public web sites, can also be deployed on intranets. By correlating Google Analytics data with internal network topologies and organizational roles, complex intranet usage patterns can be measured and optimized.

To summarize, intranet pragmatists can:

- Exploit existing models, either within the enterprise or as adopted across a discipline, such as traffic engineering or radiology.
- Identify relevant roles involved in key business processes, then connect these to existing or potential social networks.
- Innovate using new techniques such as gamification, polls, quizzes and collaborative search.
- Leverage unified communications, from phone networks to chat (such as Slack and Yammer) and meeting spaces to engage social networks across multiple platforms. Then store and index using scalable intranet resources, especially big data.
- Measure intranet usage and optimize its value using techniques analogous to those used for web marketing intelligence.

CONCLUSION

Empirical evidence about intranet use continues to be limited when compared to research about web site use more generally. Market forces and Big Data analytics push for a deeper understanding of how site technologies, visitor social behavior, and content – knowledge in this context – interact. Less powerful forces are arrayed to drive equivalent understanding of how organizations can marshal corporate knowledge and OSNs to create efficiencies or to foster innovation. This suggests a near term future which incremental improvements are likely to carry the day – for a time.

Advances in web standards development, such as cross-organizational identity management APIs, have been made in part been made to support public OSN technologies. For example, a single LinkedIn credential can be used as a single login across otherwise unrelated web sites. Evidence suggests that similar incentives to support the use of OSNs for intranets are few. For example, Microsoft Dynamics CRM 2015 allows for sharing documents in Microsoft SharePoint. The Insightly CRM / project management cloud app allows for integrated access to Google Docs when operating on Google's platform. But the granularity of this "sharing" is low; the two applications do not share a common understanding of the social roles of users, and leverage that information to deliver role-appropriate data in formats that take into account richly dynamic information available from social graphs.

The result is a confluence of contradictions. While the organizational incentives for intranet collaboration are clearer for OSN use in intranets than for public OSNs alone, and despite the massive explosion of participation in public OSNs like Facebook and LinkedIn, the impact on intranets has been underwhelming.

Whether worldwide public OSN adoption can stimulate greater use in intranets is unclear. However, there are uses which could expand beyond their limited scope to wider deployment. Project management, clinical decision support, Big Data analytics, e-learning and e-science are disciplines where intranets can impact quality, productivity and profitability. Large organizations with robust R&D investments will find new machine learning capabilities that will not be possible without ontologies curated by active social networks across the entire knowledge life cycle. Meanwhile, the gradual evolution of domain ontologies will create potential efficiencies that may stimulate adoption in firms whose intranets semantic web-ready.

A different story may unfold for small – even tiny enterprises. For them, support for new opportunities may be found in the emergence of numerous cloud applications which enable smaller enterprises to access powerful tools once only available to giant enterprises. Entrepreneurs may go the extra mile to recruit and nurture a talent base for which OSNs are second nature. The result may be intranets fully integrated with highly customized products and services that rely on employee- and customer-driven interactions, and do so more seamlessly than has been seen thus far. Smaller enterprises, operating on a shoestring, with strong incentives to maximize the output of a few knowledge workers, may be the vanguard of those to recognize the uncultivated land at their feet.

As on other knowledge management fronts, further advances depend more on shifts in the ability of a workforce to embrace abstract models and canonical frameworks that are intranet enablers. The technology likely already awaits them.

REFERENCES

Akerkar, R. (2014). *Big Data Computing*. Boca Raton, FL: CRC Press.

Anthony, A. (2014). *Guest Post: SearchBlox Makes Sense Out of Multiple Data Sources*. Retrieved October 5, 2015, from https://channel9.msdn.com/Blogs/AzurePartner/Guest-Post-SearchBlox-Makes-Sense-Out-of-Multiple-Data-Sources

Aral, S., Brynjolfsson, E., & Van Alstyne, M. W. (2007). *Productivity Effects of Information Diffusion in Networks*. SSRN Electronic Journal. doi:10.2139/ssrn.987499

Ashley, P., & Vandenwauver, M. (2013). *Practical Intranet Security: Overview of the State of the Art and Available Technologies*. Springer Publishing Company, Incorporated.

Barbera, J. (1996). *The intranet: a new concept for corporate information handling*. Retrieved from http://cat.inist.fr/?aModele=afficheN&cpsidt=2726592

Bastian, M., Hayes, M., Vaughan, W., Shah, S., Skomoroch, P., & Kim, H., … Lloyd, C. (2014). LinkedIn skills. In *Proceedings of the 8th ACM Conference on Recommender systems - RecSys '14* (pp. 1–8). New York: ACM Press. doi:10.1145/2645710.2645729

Bloomstein, M. (2012). *Content Strategy at Work: Real-world Stories to Strengthen Every Interactive Project*. Academic Press.

Boff, E., Santos, E. R., & Vicari, R. M. (2006). *Social Agents to Improve Collaboration on an Educational Portal*. Academic Press.

Bouck, W. (2014). *The Information Economy: A Study of Five Industries*. Academic Press.

Brady, S. L., Mohaupt, T. H., & Kaufman, R. A. (2015). JOURNAL CLUB: A Comprehensive Risk Assessment Method for Pediatric Patients Undergoing Research Examinations Using Ionizing Radiation: How We Answered the Institutional Review Board. *American Journal of Roentgenology*, *204*(5), W510–8. doi:10.2214/AJR.14.13892 PMID:25905957

Budnick, L. (1996). *Official Build a NetScape Intranet*. Ventana Communications Group, Incorporated.

Chamberlain, A., Schraefel, m. C., Poole, E., Munson, S., Danis, C., & Churchill, E. (2015). Moving Beyond e-Health and the Quantified Self. In *Proceedings of the 18th ACM Conference Companion on Computer Supported Cooperative Work & Social Computing - CSCW'15 Companion* (pp. 273–276). New York: ACM Press. doi:10.1145/2685553.2685555

Chan, I., & Chao, C. (2008). Knowledge management in small and medium-sized enterprises. *Communications of the ACM*, *51*(4), 83–88. doi:10.1145/1330311.1330328

Chang, L.-E., & Lin, S.-P. (2011). Newcomers' Socialization by Intranet System. In *2011 10th IEEE/ACIS International Conference on Computer and Information Science* (pp. 239–243). IEEE. doi:10.1109/ICIS.2011.45

Chaves, M. A., & Cordoba, E. R. (2014). Deciphering event logs in SharePoint Server: A methodology based on process mining. In *2014 XL Latin American Computing Conference (CLEI)* (pp. 1–12). IEEE. doi:10.1109/CLEI.2014.6965174

Counsell, J. (2012). Beyond Level 2 BIM, Web Portals and Collaboration Tools. In *2012 16th International Conference on Information Visualisation* (pp. 510–515). IEEE. doi:10.1109/IV.2012.88

Cross, R., Borgatti, S. P., & Parker, A. (2002). Making invisible work visible: Using social network analysis to support strategic collaboration. *California Management Review*, *44*(2), 25–46. doi:10.2307/41166121

Dabbish, L., Stuart, C., Tsay, J., & Herbsleb, J. (2013). Leveraging Transparency. *IEEE Software*, *30*(1), 37–43. doi:10.1109/MS.2012.172

Danis, C., & Singer, D. (2008). A wiki instance in the enterprise. In *Proceedings of the ACM 2008 conference on Computer supported cooperative work - CSCW '08* (p. 495). New York: ACM Press. doi:10.1145/1460563.1460642

Davenport, T., De Long, D., & Beers, M. (1998). Successful Knowledge Management Projects. *Sloan Management Review*.

DeMatteis, P., & Brown, J. (2008). *Tabletop Exercises: Cost Effective*. Verifiable, Practical.

Dignum, S., Kruschwitz, U., Fasli, M., Kim, Y., Song, D., Beresi, U. C., & de Roeck, A. (2010). Incorporating Seasonality into Search Suggestions Derived from Intranet Query Logs. In *2010 IEEE/WIC/ACM International Conference on Web Intelligence and Intelligent Agent Technology* (Vol. 1, pp. 425–430). IEEE. doi:10.1109/WI-IAT.2010.258

Dong, Y., Tang, J., Chawla, N. V., Lou, T., Yang, Y., & Wang, B. (2015). Inferring social status and rich club effects in enterprise communication networks. *PLoS ONE*, *10*(3), e0119446. doi:10.1371/journal.pone.0119446 PMID:25822343

Durr, M., Maier, M., & Dorfmeister, F. (2012). Vegas -- A Secure and Privacy-Preserving Peer-to-Peer Online Social Network. In *2012 International Conference on Privacy, Security, Risk and Trust and 2012 International Confernece on Social Computing* (pp. 868–874). IEEE. doi:10.1109/SocialCom-PASSAT.2012.42

Dürr, M., & Wiesner, K. (2011). *A Privacy-Preserving Social P2P Infrastructure for People-Centric Sensing*. doi:10.4230/OASIcs.KiVS.2011.176

Ertl, P., Selzer, P., & Mühlbacher, J. (2004). Web-based cheminformatics tools deployed via corporate Intranets. *Drug Discovery Today: BIOSILICO*, *2*(5), 201–207. doi:10.1016/S1741-8364(04)02413-8

Escalfoni, R., Braganholo, V., & Borges, M. R. S. (2011). A method for capturing innovation features using group storytelling. *Expert Systems with Applications*, *38*(2), 1148–1159. doi:10.1016/j.eswa.2010.05.008

Evans, M., Dalkir, K., & Bidian, C. (2014). A Holistic View of the Knowledge Life Cycle: The Knowledge Management Cycle (KMC) Model. *Electronic Journal of Knowledge Management*, *12*(2), 85–97.

Falkner, M. (1997). *Using Lotus Notes as an Intranet*. New York, NY: John Wiley & Sons, Ltd.

Fensel, D., van Harmelen, F., Horrocks, I., McGuinness, D. L., & Patel-Schneider, P. F. (2001). OIL: An ontology infrastructure for the Semantic Web. *IEEE Intelligent Systems*, *16*(2), 38–45. doi:10.1109/5254.920598

Fernández-Luna, J., Huete, J., Rodriguez-Avila, H., & Rodriguez-Cano, J. (2014). Enhancing Collaborative Search Systems Engagement Through Gamification. In *Proceedings of the First International Workshop on Gamification for Information Retrieval SE - GamifIR '14* (pp. 42–45). New York: ACM. doi:doi:10.1145/2594776.2594785

Fogg, B. (2002). Persuasive technology: Using computers to change what we think and do. *Ubiquity*, *2002*(December), 2. doi:10.1145/764008.763957

Goy, A., Magro, D., Petrone, G., Picardi, C., & Segnan, M. (2015). Ontology-driven collaborative annotation in shared workspaces. *Future Generation Computer Systems*. doi:10.1016/j.future.2015.04.013

Gupta, A. (2009). The 24-Hour Knowledge Factory: Can It Replace the Graveyard Shift? *Computer*, *42*(1), 66–73. doi:10.1109/MC.2009.25

Hall, W., Nousala, S., & Kilpatrick, B. (2009). One company – two outcomes Knowledge integration vs corporate disintegration in the absence. *VINE: The Journal of Information and Knowledge Management Systems*, *39*(3), 242–258. doi:10.1108/03055720911003996

Hansen, D., Shneiderman, B., & Smith, M. (2010). *Analyzing Social Media Networks with NodeXL: Insights from a Connected World.* San Francisco, CA: Morgan Kaufmann Publishers Inc.

Hara, H., Matsutsuka, T., Kanaya, N., Ookubo, T., & Uehara, S. (1997). Model-Based Architecture for the Intranet. In *Proceedings of the 21st International Computer Software and Applications Conference SE - COMPSAC '97* (pp. 182–187). Washington, DC: IEEE Computer Society.

Hussain, Z., Barber, K., & Hussain, N. (2009). An Intranet based system as an enabler in effective project management and implementation of quality standards: A case study. *Journal of Engineering and Technology Management*, *26*(3), 196–210. doi:10.1016/j.jengtecman.2009.06.003

Hustad, E., & Vikstøl, T. (2014). Implementing Intranet 2.0: A Study of Knowledge Requirements for External Consultants in Enterprise Systems. *Procedia Technology*, *16*, 694–703. doi:10.1016/j.protcy.2014.10.018

Hwan, K. J., Youn-kyoung, J., & Do, N. S. (2009). Product Information Exchanges between CAD/PDM systems and the Collaboration Portal System using PLM Services. In *2009 WRI World Congress on Computer Science and Information Engineering* (pp. 718–721). IEEE. doi:10.1109/CSIE.2009.962

Jamali, M., & Abolhassani, H. (2006). Different Aspects of Social Network Analysis. In *Web Intelligence, 2006. WI 2006. IEEE/WIC/ACM International Conference on* (pp. 66–72). doi:10.1109/WI.2006.61

Kalyanam, R., Zhao, L., Song, C. X., Wong, Y. L., Lee, J., & Villoria, N. B. (2013). iData. In *Proceedings of the Conference on Extreme Science and Engineering Discovery Environment Gateway to Discovery - XSEDE '13* (p. 1). New York: ACM Press. doi:10.1145/2484762.2484813

Klooster, M., Brinkkemper, S., Harmsen, F., & Wijers, G. (1997). Intranet facilitated knowledge management: A theory and tool for defining situational methods. In A. Olivé & J. Pastor (Eds.), *Advanced Information Systems Engineering SE - 22* (Vol. 1250, pp. 303–317). Springer Berlin Heidelberg; doi:10.1007/3-540-63107-0_22

Lamb, R. (2001). Tracing influence through intranets of compliance. In *Proceedings of the 34th Annual Hawaii International Conference on System Sciences* (p. 10). IEEE Comput. Soc. doi:10.1109/HICSS.2001.926354

Lamb, R. (2003). Intranet Boundaries as Guidelines for Systems Integration. *International Journal of Electronic Commerce*, *7*(4), 9–35. Retrieved from http://dl.acm.org/citation.cfm?id=1288207.1288210

Leskovec, J., Huttenlocher, D., & Kleinberg, J. (2010). Predicting positive and negative links in online social networks. In *Proceedings of the 19th international conference on World wide web - WWW '10* (p. 641). New York: ACM Press. doi:10.1145/1772690.1772756

Levine, S. S., & Prietula, M. (2006). *Towards a Contingency Theory of Knowledge Exchange in Organizations*. Retrieved from http://papers.ssrn.com/abstract=2378060

Lutz, J., Thonssen, B., & Witschel, H. F. (2013). Breaking free from your information prison: A recommender based on semantically enriched context descriptions. In *Proceedings of the First International Conference on Enterprise Systems: ES 2013* (pp. 1–9). IEEE. doi:10.1109/ES.2013.6690092

Majchrzak, A., Wagner, C., & Yates, D. (2012). *The Impact of Shaping on Knowledge Reuse for Organizational Improvement with Wikis*. Retrieved from http://papers.ssrn.com/abstract=2536091

Majchrzak, A., Wagner, C., & Yates, D. (2013). Knowledge Reuse for Organizational Improvement. *Management Information Systems Quarterly*, *37*(2), 455–469.

Manmadhan, N., & Achuthan, K. (2014). Behavioural analysis for prevention of intranet information leakage. In *2014 International Conference on Advances in Computing, Communications and Informatics (ICACCI)* (pp. 1535–1537). IEEE. doi:10.1109/ICACCI.2014.6968644

Marasco, E., Mehjat, L., & Rosehart, W. (2015). Enhancing EDA education thruogh gamification. In *IEEE International Conference on Microelectronics Systems Education (MSE)* (pp. 25–27). Pittsburgh, PA: IEEE Press. doi:10.1109/MSE.2015.7160009

Marshall, C. C., & Shipman, F. M. (2015). Exploring the Ownership and Persistent Value of Facebook Content. In *Proceedings of the 18th ACM Conference on Computer Supported Cooperative Work & Social Computing - CSCW '15* (pp. 712–723). New York: ACM Press. doi:10.1145/2675133.2675203

Matthews, T., Whittaker, S., Moran, T., & Yuen, S. (2011). Collaboration personas. In *Proceedings of the 2011 annual conference on Human factors in computing systems - CHI '11* (p. 2247). New York: ACM Press. doi:10.1145/1978942.1979272

McKinsey & Company. (2011). Big data: The next frontier for innovation, competition, and productivity. *McKinsey Global Institute*. doi:10.1080/01443610903114527

Mørch, A. I., Engen, B. K., & Åsand, H.-R. H. (2004). The workplace as a learning laboratory. In *Proceedings of the eighth conference on Participatory design Artful integration: interweaving media, materials and practices - PDC 04* (Vol. 1, p. 142). New York: ACM Press. doi:10.1145/1011870.1011888

Morschheuser, B., Henzi, C., & Alt, R. (2015). *Increasing Intranet Usage through Gamification -- Insights from an Experiment in the Banking Industry*. doi:10.1109/HICSS.2015.83

Nunamaker, J. F., Applegate, L. M., & Konsynski, B. R. (1988). Computer-Aided Deliberation: Model Management and Group Decision Support. *Operations Research*, *36*(6), 826–848. doi:10.1287/opre.36.6.826

O'Leary, D. E. (1997). The Internet, intranets, and the AI renaissance. *Computer*, *30*(1), 71–78. doi:10.1109/2.562929

Oduor, M., Alahäivälä, T., & Oinas-Kukkonen, H. (2014a). Persuasive software design patterns for social influence. *Personal and Ubiquitous Computing*, *18*(7), 1689–1704. doi:10.1007/s00779-014-0778-z

Oduor, M., Alahäivälä, T., & Oinas-Kukkonen, H. (2014b). Persuasive software design patterns for social influence. *Personal and Ubiquitous Computing*, *18*(7), 1689–1704. doi:10.1007/s00779-014-0778-z

Oinas-Kukkonen, H. (2012). A foundation for the study of behavior change support systems. *Personal and Ubiquitous Computing*, *17*(6), 1223–1235. doi:10.1007/s00779-012-0591-5

Oinas-Kukkonen, H., & Harjumaa, M. (2009). Persuasive Systems Design: Key Issues, Process Model, and System Features. *Journal of the AIS Electronic Library*, *24*(1). Retrieved from http://aisel.aisnet.org/cais/vol24/iss1/28

Power, D. J. (2014). *Using "Big Data" for analytics and decision support*. Retrieved from http://www.tandfonline.com/doi/abs/10.1080/12460125.2014.888848

Proenca, T., Moura, N. T., & Van Der Hoek, A. (2009). *On the use of emerging design as a basis for knowledge collaboration*. Retrieved from http://dl.acm.org/citation.cfm?id=1881958.1881972

Puerta, A., & Eisenstein, J. (1999). Towards a general computational framework for model-based interface development systems. *Knowledge-Based Systems*, *12*(8), 433–442. doi:10.1016/S0950-7051(99)00037-4

Rabaey, J. M. (2015). The Human Intranet--Where Swarms and Humans Meet. *IEEE Pervasive Computing / IEEE Computer Society [and] IEEE Communications Society*, *14*(1), 78–83. doi:10.1109/MPRV.2015.20

Roberts, D. (2014). *Move over Org Chart, make way for the Social Graph: Collaborative Decision Making for the Agile Enterprise*. Academic Press.

Ryan, J. (2014). A Business Process Management Approach to Perioperative Supplies/Instrument Inventory and Workflow. In C. Lewis, B. Doster, & S. Daily (Eds.), *2014 47th Hawaii International Conference on System Sciences* (Vol. 0, pp. 2868–2877).

Schneider, H. (2005). *Rapid ICT Change and Workplace Knowledge Obsolescence*. SSRN Electronic Journal, doi:10.2139/ssrn.870084

Seide, F., Thambiratnam, K., Lu, L., & Yu, R. (2009). Multimedia Retrieval Through Indexing Speech: An Enterprise Perspective. In *Proceedings of the Third Workshop on Searching Spontaneous Conversational Speech SE - SSCS '09* (pp. 1–2). New York: ACM. doi:10.1145/1631127.1631128

Sethi, M., Sachindran, N., & Raghavan, S. (2013). SASH: Enabling continuous incremental analytic workflows on Hadoop. In *2013 IEEE 29th International Conference on Data Engineering (ICDE)* (pp. 1219–1230). IEEE. doi:10.1109/ICDE.2013.6544911

Shachtman, N. (2009). *"Command Posts of the Future" Readied for Afghan Surge*. Wired.

Skeels, M., & Grudin, J. (2009). When Social Networks Cross Boundaries: A Case Study of Workplace Use of Facebook and Linkedin. In *Proceedings of the ACM 2009 International Conference on Supporting Group Work SE - GROUP '09* (pp. 95–104). New York: ACM. doi:10.1145/1531674.1531689

Smith, M. A., Shneiderman, B., Milic-Frayling, N., Mendes Rodrigues, E., Barash, V., Dunne, C., … Gleave, E. (2009). Analyzing (social media) networks with NodeXL. In *Proceedings of the fourth international conference on Communities and technologies - C&T '09* (p. 255). New York: ACM Press. doi:10.1145/1556460.1556497

Somerville, M., Mirijamdotter, A., & Collins, L. (2006). Systems Thinking and Information Literacy: Elements of a Knowledge Enabling Workplace Environment. *HICSS, 7*.

Sprague, R. W., & Carlson, E. D. (1982). *Building Effective Decision Support Systems*. Englewood Cliffs, NJ: Prentice Hall Inc.

Sridhar, S. (1998). Decision support using the Intranet. *Decision Support Systems*, *23*(1), 19–28. doi:10.1016/S0167-9236(98)00033-5

Stafford, C., & Mearns, M. A. (2010). *What happens when organisations embrace social networking? Knowledge sharing at a multinational business solutions corporation*. SA Journal of Information Management. doi:10.4102/sajim.v11i4.414

Szuprowicz, B. O. (1996). *Intranets and Groupware*. Charleston, SC: Computer Technology Research Corp.

Taylor, J., & Raden, N. (2007). *Smart Enough Systems: How to Deliver Competitive Advantage by Automating Hidden Decisions*. Prentice Hall PTR.

Townsend, S. (2012). What Are You Working On? *eLearn, 2012*(1), 1. doi:10.1145/2090108.2090109

Trainer, E. H., & Redmiles, D. F. (2012). Foundations for the design of visualizations that support trust in distributed teams. In *Proceedings of the International Working Conference on Advanced Visual Interfaces - AVI '12* (p. 34). New York: ACM Press. doi:10.1145/2254556.2254566

Tucker, T. G., & Winchester, W. W. (2009). Mobile learning for just-in-time applications. In *Proceedings of the 47th Annual Southeast Regional Conference on - ACM-SE 47* (p. 1). New York: ACM Press. doi:10.1145/1566445.1566469

Underwood, M. (2014). *A One-Person Firm Still Needs an Intranet*. Academic Press.

Vacca, J. (1996). *Virtual Reality: Strategies for Intranet and World Wide Web Applications*. Charleston, SC: Computer Technology Research Corp.

Viaene, S. (2013). Data Scientists Aren't Domain Experts. *IT Professional*, *15*(6), 12–17. doi:10.1109/MITP.2013.93

Vicente, V., Sjöstrand, F., Sundström, B. W., Svensson, L., & Castren, M. (2013). Developing a decision support system for geriatric patients in prehospital care. *European Journal of Emergency Medicine : Official Journal of the European Society for Emergency Medicine*, *20*(4), 240–247. doi:10.1097/MEJ.0b013e328356452d PMID:22759990

Villamón, E., Piqueras, M., Meseguer, J., Blanquer, I., Berbegall, A. P., Tadeo, I., & Noguera, R. et al. (2013). NeuPAT: An intranet database supporting translational research in neuroblastic tumors. *Computers in Biology and Medicine*, *43*(3), 219–228. doi:10.1016/j.compbiomed.2012.11.011 PMID:23290604

Walker, G. H., Stanton, N. A., Revell, K., Rafferty, L., Salmon, P. M., & Jenkins, D. P. (2009). Measuring Dimensions of Command and Control Using Social Network Analysis: Extending the NATO SAS-050 Model. *The International C2 Journal, 3*(2), 1–49.

Ward, T. (2015). IBM's new intranet represents change in intranet design. *Intranet Blog*.

Wiig, K. M. (1994). *Knowledge Management Foundations: Thinking about Thinking - how People and Organizations Represent, Create, and Use Knowledge*. Schema Press, Limited.

Wolford, R. A., & Hughes, L. K. (2001). Using the hospital Intranet to meet competency standards for nurses. *Journal for Nurses in Staff Development : JNSD : Official Journal of the National Nursing Staff Development Organization*, *17*(4), 182–189. doi:10.1097/00124645-200107000-00004 PMID:12760000

Wynkoop, S. (1996). *Building an Intranet with BackOffice*. Indianapolis, IN: Que Corp.

Yusof, A. N. M., & Ahmad, N. (2012). Quality and effectiveness of knowledge management transfer using of Mentor-mentee Program and on Job Training in work place. In *2012 International Conference on Innovation Management and Technology Research* (pp. 50–55). IEEE. doi:10.1109/ICIMTR.2012.6236359

Zhang, J., Qu, Y., Cody, J., & Wu, Y. (2010). A case study of micro-blogging in the enterprise. In *Proceedings of the 28th international conference on Human factors in computing systems - CHI '10* (p. 123). New York: ACM Press. doi:10.1145/1753326.1753346

Zorzi, M., Gluhak, A., Lange, S., & Bassi, A. (2010). From today's INTRAnet of things to a future INTERnet of things: A wireless- and mobility-related view. *IEEE Wireless Communications*, *17*(6), 44–51. doi:10.1109/MWC.2010.5675777

KEY TERMS AND DEFINITIONS

Agent-Based System: Software built using multiple interacting intelligent agents within an environment. Related to Agent-Based Models, a class of computational models for simulating the actions and interactions of agents, such as those in an organization.

Extranet: Subset of an intranet that is accessible to authorized persons or applications outside of an organization.

Human Resource Management System: A suite of software applications that combines human resource functions, such as payroll, benefits administration, performance analysis, etc.

Intranet: A computer network with restricted access, as within an organization, that typically uses software and protocols developed for the Internet.

Learning Management System: A learning management system is software for administering, documenting, tracking, reporting and delivering educational content.

Narratology: For software systems, a branch of knowledge engineering that deals with the structure and function of narrative, including themes, conventions and symbols. It is more loosely referred to as storytelling in some circles.

Online Social Network: A social networking computer service that serves as a platform to build social networks between people who share interests, activities or real-life connections.

Persuasive Systems Design: An approach to communication using technologies that is designed to shape attitudes or change behaviors through persuasion or social influence.

Social Graph: A representation of relationships between people (or other entities) in an online social network.

ENDNOTE

1 The Association for Computing Machinery currently supports an annual conference on Computer-Supported Cooperative Work and Social Computing.

Chapter 14
Challenges of Knowledge Management amidst Rapidly Evolving Tools of Social Media

Ritesh Chugh
Central Queensland University, Australia

Mahesh Joshi
RMIT University, Australia

ABSTRACT

Social media technologies have been embraced by individuals and organizations on such a massive scale in the last decade that knowledge sharing and application has molded into a totally new paradigm. It has not only changed the social discourse of communication but also affected the knowledge management strategies of organizations. This raises quite a number of fundamental challenges out of which three are being dealt in this chapter. The first challenge is whether knowledge management has fully embraced social media as a channel of mass reach the way it did in case of other means of mass communication. The second one is the question of speed and extent of knowledge sharing in social media. The third challenge is whether social media strategy can provide a high advantage to smaller and newer companies in comparison to older but larger organizations. It is apparent that the commercial aspect of social media is easy for a tête-à-tête but difficult to articulate and design the right strategy because it needs a lot of refinements owing to inherent complexities in the process.

INTRODUCTION

When Procter and Gamble (2008) and General Electric (2008) introduced social media as a part of their integrated media communication strategy, little could be said about the impact that social media tools left on knowledge management. In much less than a decade, blogs, vlogs, instant messaging, virtual communities, videos, mobile advertising and others have become predominant tools of social media strategy. Something that began as a way of information processing, transferring, codification and reuse got evolved into a formal practice of knowledge creation and sharing. It kept growing with transformation

DOI: 10.4018/978-1-5225-0495-5.ch014

of knowledge into social capital as well as a critical resource for value creation and innovation. Every organization should realize the importance of creating and applying knowledge (Chugh, 2012), in this case via social media. In a short history of less than two decades, the mesh of knowledge management and social media has deepened as well as broadened rapidly to acquire an unavoidable and important status in organizational processes. Knowledge management is a process through which organizational intellectual capital and information can be managed (Chugh, 2013). When an organization builds a comprehensive relationship with knowledge processes, it has a challenging opportunity of assimilating social media tools in its knowledge management strategy. Similarly, a complete definition of a learning organization cannot be pictured without involving social media channels in its knowledge sharing activities. This is typically important because such periphery practices have now graduated into mainstream organizational activities. Not only the notion of hierarchy and knowledge transmission is under a shift but the role of knowledge managers has to assume a lot of flexibility inside the consumer-to-consumer communication space. Currently, no business strategy can exist by ignoring social media. So, how knowledge is managed in an organization can actually reflect on the business potential too. The top-down structures of knowledge management in the Information Technology field took nearly two decades to settle its conceptual contours but social media technologies have diversified at such a fast pace in less than a decade that their assimilation via the knowledge management route is full of both risks and opportunities.

A brief look at the technology scenario in 2014 and 2015 presents some unique developments in social media. The sudden emergence of personal broadcast apps like Meerkat[1] and Periscope[2] through Twitter has taken the Twitterati on to a new level. To all the followers of a Twitter account, it changes the definition from an individual-led textual communication into an audio-video one. The emergence of Skype translator[3] has brought multi-lingual speakers on to a common platform as the human task of translation is going to be replaced by cloud-based machine languages. This creates a possibility of so many unexpected advances in business communication that organizations can create a totally new definition of knowledge management. The revenue disruption of voice calling telecom networks by the launch of voice-calling by OTT[4] players like WhatsApp, Facebook Messenger, Line and Viber has created much better and cheaper means of social interaction. Crowd-sourcing of ideas and crowd-funding of projects is turning into a reality because of widespread use of social media. The business models that were dependent on traditional sources of capital and knowledge are suddenly able to find an alternative space that was non-existent some years back. Physical cash is being replaced by digital cash and that too not through traditional bank-led or government-led networks. The widespread launch of retail payment networks through new platforms like Apple Pay[5], Android Pay[6] and particularly through message apps like Snapcash[7], seems to be driving new ways of linking social media with revenue streams and advertising. The number of people joining this bandwagon is so enormous that this new wave of social media throws interesting challenges of managing knowledge too. Within a large organization, it creates exciting opportunities for communication between staff of different departments, hierarchies and geographical status but for all organizations, and it may fulfill some requirements that were earlier assigned only to mass media. Despite that, social media does not work inside the traditional top-down hierarchical structures of knowledge management rather most of it works as well as emerges from a bottom-up "rhizomatic[8] form of communication" where customers, suppliers and partners may share a space that is both inviting and disruptive. Though some new terms like Enterprise 2.0, Enterprise social software or even social business have emerged to define this trend, it has not been an easy task to assimilate such forms of new communication inside the available strategies of knowledge management.

AIMS OF THE CHAPTER

In the backdrop of this difficult but creative relationship between social media and knowledge management, it can be said that any researcher who works in this territory would have to be permanently on toes. Social media is not a closed container rather it is changing very fast and along with this, consumer behavior is changing too. Now, it is not possible to rest with a conventional understanding of social media that equates it with a conglomeration of social media technologies like e-mail, chatting, instant messenger and emerging social networking tools such as blogs, wikis, public social networking sites (i.e., Facebook, Twitter, and LinkedIn) and enterprise social networking technologies. From a knowledge management perspective, this is a very inadequate insight as it simply scratches the surface and nothing more. Levy (2013) looked into the role that social media can play inside an organization as an enabler of knowledge management. Levy's analysis shows that "implementing social media in organizations is more than a yes/no question" (pg. 1). The extent of implementation with respect to the technologies used is a critical factor. In many cases, the implementation may be simply partially confined to some specific tools or it may simply be a case of visibility. A simple application of a social media tool does not mean that an organization has fully embraced it in terms of the overall knowledge management strategy. It may exist in multiple levels beginning from simple visibility to partial use and to full implementation. As this domain may be too large for the scope of one chapter, we tend to narrow down our focus to only three inter-related challenges of knowledge management amidst the rapidly evolving tools of social media.

The first challenge that is explored in the following section is whether knowledge management practices have fully embraced social media as a channel of mass reach the way it did in case of other means of mass communication and if not, what are the areas where some sort of theoretical catch-up is required by the proponents of knowledge management. Looking at customers requires a firm to know what the customers think about the products, prices, services, markets, trends, offers, discounts and so forth. There has to be a way to access such information. To enable that, a firm also needs to tap into its inner resources- its own employees as they are both the source of quality suggestions as well as the backbone of organizational processes. In such a context, how to accommodate a diverse set of social media tools/platforms? What should be the factors that decide the pick-and-choose policy for any social media tool for an organization?

The second challenge is the question of speed of communication sharing in social media, which is explored in section four. The most common term of something spreading so fast is "a viral event". Grass-root viral events can connect with masses at an explosive pace that may force an organization that is totally unprepared and hence driven into a vulnerable spot. Virality puts an organization before a sudden emergence of a social network with an ephemeral bond drawn from a ground-swelling of crowd emotions. The sudden emergence of this phenomenon may be both an asset and a liability for an organization. It can be deliberately created or accidental. It is an issue of large audience management too. In the context of an organization, it is an issue of customer relations management. The resources needed to engage such an event are drastically different from any traditional approach in knowledge management. That is why it raises many questions. Can virality be different from the sudden emergence to a pre-calculated creation of knowledge capital that is in line with the organizational growth? Can it be redirected or exclusively extended to a product or a utility? In terms of connectivity, virality appears to have a potential output equivalent to that of mass media advertisement but the question is whether the customer knowledge managers in an organization have the competence to manage the saturation point of virality.

The third challenge under exploration, in section five, is whether social media strategy can give disproportionately high advantage to smaller and newer companies in comparison to older but larger organizations. Does consumer-to-consumer communication within a social network allow level-playing field to all organizations, big or small, thus creating better access to the mindshare and hence market share of consumer segment? As financial tech innovation is fast catching up with newer forms of search and advertisement in social media tools, what is the potential of emerging link-up of "Buy Button" on social media driven advertisement and retail payment networks as being proposed on YouTube by Google. This is particularly important because now, the predominant device in the hands of a consumer is not a TV or a desktop/laptop rather it is a smartphone which stays with an individual during the entire waking time within the 24 hours of a day. This mobile bias is growing in size and mediates almost all the screen-based interactions of a consumer. With the quarterly growth of smartphone shipments rising from 332.6 million in the third quarter of 2014 to 355.2 million in third quarter of 2015 (IDC, 2015), more than a billion users are hopping on to the app ecosystem. Social media seems to be gaining a much larger space in the discipline of knowledge management (knowledge creation and sharing) than what has been traditionally given to it. In a world with soon-expected universal ownership of connected smartphones with widespread 3G and 4G networks, social media may assume the dominant priority for knowledge managers within and outside organizations. After exploring and discussing the three above mentioned challenges, this chapter concludes with broad suggestions vis-à-vis the interaction of social media and knowledge management.

MISSING LINKS BETWEEN KNOWLEDGE MANAGEMENT AND SOCIAL MEDIA

Before analyzing the integration aspect of social media with knowledge management, it is crucial to contextualize how social media actually entered the knowledge management space. It is important to understand the range of social media tools that are under use presently as well as the others that are available for future use. To get into the thick of the issue, some real examples of its implementation are analyzed. In a case study by Anderson and Mohan (2011) involving four companies in different sectors, the implementation of multiple social media tools was explored. The first company was a legal entity with 1,00,000 employees across many countries and it used Microsoft SharePoint as a platform for social networking. The second company was a pharmaceutical company that used a group of social media tools like SharePoint, a wiki and the company's website. The third company, an insurance organization, used a wiki only and the fourth company, a software unit, used both Yammer and SharePoint. In the case of the legal company, the search functions improved while in the pharmaceutical company, research and design processes and marketing directly to the consumers and partners improved. In the case of the insurance company, IT staff used wiki but stopped without leadership motivation and in the case of the software company, both the technologies were used by the staff. The legal and pharmaceutical company did not share information outside the company and even within the organization, restricted its use because of privacy concerns. In all the cases, the role of the leadership within an organization and within a sector or a department was seen as being very important.

In another study by Murphy and Salomone (2013), an interesting dimension came out. The authors suggest that use of social media does not mean acceptance of a wide set of tools rather specific kind of networks can bring relevant advantages to the organization in terms of intra-organizational communication, collaboration and knowledge sharing. They used two illustrations of Lockheed Martin and Pfizer to show "how social media technologies can link groups and provide a neutral space to begin defining the scope and nature of the issue." Lockheed Martin used an internally developed tool for enabling employees' communication and interaction and used Microsoft SharePoint for generative purpose. They also used other tools like feeds, webcast and mash-ups to supplement their social media strategy. Pfizer adopted a wiki route by creating a large wiki known as Pfizerpedia supported by regular supply of news and audio messages. This led to a drastic reduction in the use of e-mail and provided other socialization and externalization opportunities. Lockheed Martin was quite focused upon the issues regarding their ageing employees but Pfizer wanted to enhance the research and development potential of their employees by promoting a collaborative culture through social media technologies. The authors suggested that in large organizations, there is a serious problem of information lock-up within the departmental specializations. Social media applications could nullify such blocks in information flow. Though this example did work in an engineering context but its lessons may work beyond the sector.

Seebach (2012) conducted a study by analyzing the content of 15,505 enterprise microblogging messages (EMB) created by 1,166 employees of an international financial institution. The primary target was to find how knowledge is managed successfully between those who seek it and those who provide it and how pertinent is the use of a social media platform in this context. This EMB platform was similar to Twitter where users could post their short messages that appeared in a chronological order on the users' interface. With nearly 27% users using the platform, the promise of finding the right link was there. The results of this analysis show that communication in a traditional tool like e-mail happens when both the seeker and the contributor of knowledge know each other but in the social media domain, this need is transcended. The demand and supply of knowledge within an organization is always there but the ties between multiple departments or sections of an organization may be very weak but social media actually manages to capitalize on these weak links and creates a steady stream of information flow that fill the gaps whenever and wherever they arise. This also results in lowering of knowledge search costs.

With these three examples in the background, it can be seen that social media can touch nearly all the dimensions of knowledge management. This is in line with what Pettenati, Cigognini, Mangione and Guerin (2007) highlight by their focus on the recognized and growing importance of social software as an "educational middleware" in formal learning. There may not be a universal definition of knowledge management but a broad consensus does exist around this. It is a set of strategies, procedures or processes that enable an organization "to generate value from knowledge-based assets." Social media technologies share both the fundamental traits i.e. knowledge communication as well as value creation. Hemsley and Mason (2013) highlight that social media platforms form a communication infrastructure that enables three important social mechanisms:

1. All the users get self-organizing skills to build their own social networks.
2. Users' interact for building both trust and reputation in a community.
3. Content sharing by users on a regular basis.

This theoretical functional congruence makes it natural that both knowledge management and social media strategies should coalesce into one discipline but this merger is a deep and a continuous process. What is necessary is to identify the areas where this match-making is happening and how far things are yet to move up.

The traditional strategies of knowledge management were more focused on the explicit knowledge. As the distance between the top and the bottom of a hierarchy increases, it was quite possible that explicit knowledge gets reduced down into strict rules or isolated principles but with social media, even the last employee in the chain can communicate back as social media does not maintain any superficial boundary between tacit and explicit knowledge. From a rather formal structure of knowledge management, it has now moved to a mix of formal and informal elements of a knowledge ecosystem. What has happened as a result is that social media technologies have got aggregated into a system where communications costs are substantively lowered for people if they want to self-organize to share knowledge or self-publish or share resources on a large scale. What happens to the knowledge status of an organization beyond this procedural explanation is also important.

Several studies (Hsia, Lin, Wu, & Tsai, 2006; Abidi, Hussini, Sriraj, Thienthong, & Finley, 2009; Steininger, Ruckel, Dannerer, & Roithmayr, 2010; Panahi, Watson, & Partridge, 2013) highlight that with the arrival of multiple online initiatives, social media technologies provide newer opportunities for tacit knowledge sharing. Tacit knowledge, a term coined by Polanyi (1958) is the knowledge that accrues to people in the process of executing tasks both as individuals and groups. This kind of knowledge is different from the explicit forms of learning that is received through books, documents and other forms of formal articulation. Social media can be used to aid the knowledge creation model (also called the SECI model) developed by Nonaka and Takeuchi (1995). It states that there are four stages through which knowledge gets converted:

1. Socialisation (tacit to tacit);
2. Externalisation (tacit to explicit);
3. Combination (explicit to explicit); and
4. Internalisation (explicit to tacit).

Razmerita, Kirchner and Nabeth (2014) also point that knowledge, in both personal and group terms, can be transformed into social collaboration through the tools of social media. However, the type of social media tools that could be used for different interactions also needs some sort of categorization. In some cases, the level of control tilts towards the individual and with some others, it does towards the group. This is where some conventional distinctions of the discipline of knowledge management actually merge. These are known as PKM (Personal Knowledge Management) and CKM (Complete Knowledge Management). These two anchors have remained the core focus in knowledge management studies. CKM, analogous to organizational knowledge creation, can be defined as "the process of making available and amplifying knowledge created by individuals as well as crystallizing and connecting it to an organizational knowledge system" (Nonaka and Von Krogh 2009, pg. 635). Razmerita, Kirchner and Nabeth (2014) outline that PKM deals with the development of skills and attitudes that lead to improved communication, collaboration and social networking. This in turn also helps an individual to be effective in personal, organizational, and social settings. A lot of PKM tools were developed earlier in the form of e-mails, chats and calendars, which improved productivity on a personal front but it never went beyond that to support social interaction or collaboration. The social and community/group aspect of interaction was not fully served by them and hence large scale spontaneous as well as designed collaborations could not be achieved. The trends in social networking sites show a shift towards specialization of the social networks as they are segmented according to the types of market segment and need they serve (Chugh, 2012).

Based upon this insight, the choice of a tool or a technology is very important. For example, one of the first social networks used in an organization was Beehive in 2007 by IBM (DiMicco et al., 2008).

The objective for providing social networking at work was that employees should express themselves to build a current flow of information across them. All of them upload their information, views and emotions on the group platform though they are not connected geographically. The clear goal was to enable them to share tacit knowledge. When data was analyzed, there emerged individual motives behind the sharing of tacit knowledge. These motives were personal career growth prospects, enlarging the circle of influence, status of projects and other details of promotion. Phosaard and Wiriyapinit (2011) chose a much liberal social media platform that is Facebook. They rely on the immense popularity of this tool and ease of use. Their findings suggest that organizations need to develop a model or framework to merge the knowledge gaps across employees, partners and suppliers. They need to develop their IT and business models in line with the focused use of social media platform. Bharati, Zhang and Chaudhury (2015) explore a similar domain and suggest that social media affects structural capital and cognitive capital of the organization directly.

But knowledge sharing is not an automatic process and is augmented by a sharing culture. There are factors that encourage or discourage the sharing culture. Vuori and Okkonen (2012) highlight there are motivational factors that work behind it. Their study suggests that organizational culture is also a critical factor in terms of deciding how employees would treat knowledge as well as the sharing process of knowledge. In case of a weak culture, knowledge sharing would be severely hampered even if there is a good channel deployed for social media interaction. If somebody shares information and that gesture is equally reciprocated, it lightens daily work and enhances both the ease and speed of sharing too. A collective co-working of these factors make social media use a success inside the domain of knowledge management but again, there is a word of caution regarding the use of technologies as there is something inherent in them that attracts people for specific purposes. Jarrahi and Sawyer (2013) have studied workplace usage of social media tools for knowledge sharing. They have focused upon both common wide-spread tools like those of e-mails, short messaging services and upcoming social networking tools like Facebook and Twitter as well as blogs and enterprise social network technologies. There is a distinctive kind of competition that happens within these technologies as to which technology gets maximum attention and users' attention. In the domain of knowledge society, the pros and cons of a particular tool are being continuously determined in term of functional capabilities they add to employees' knowledge portfolio. A technology would eventually win out if it proves relevant in this domain and others might fizzle out.

But there is still a lack of clarity about how the issue of output would be understood. All knowledge sharing cannot produce expected results. That is where a study by Lang (2004) comes to forefront where it highlights that knowledge is not identical to information. Despite information flows being continuous and perpetual, knowledge may not flow similarly as it faces multiple kinds of friction. The technology aspect of social media may create multiple contexts of collaborations but social relationships play a critical role in establishing them in the existing scheme of knowledge flows in an organization. Lang (2004) identifies four different forms of knowledge integration, which are dependent upon the social context and social capital. The four forms of knowledge integration are based on the diversity of knowledge streams, tacitness of the knowledge and the value created:

1. **Frontier Knowledge Integration:** It creates newer forms of insights and discoveries but with a lack of certainty as to how they would be reliable and usable on the quality front. This kind of knowledge can be achieved by highly specialized research activity or it may happen as a spillover of existing efforts. This kind of integration is inter-disciplinary and builds intuitive leads for new

applications. It happens in an environment where organizations provide social bonds as well as loose inter-organizational work flows.

2. **Incremental Knowledge Integration:** It takes place in a social environment where organizational work flows are very tight and knowledge acquisition works with a sense of collective reciprocal support.
3. **Instrumental Knowledge Creation:** This happens when organizations work with explicit knowledge and all interactions take place on the basis of pre-determined set of transactional expectations. It works with a low quality of social embeddedness and limited but prescribed use of existing facilities.
4. **Combinative Knowledge Integration:** It happens where collective expectations are tightly controlled by a single goal of solidarity but within a group with very low degree of social embeddedness.

Looking at the above mentioned issues, it is evident that social media and knowledge management need to be looked at with an integrated reflective approach. There is no easy way to define their relationship. There are many factors that can create differentiated results: choice of social media technology, motivational factors behind knowledge sharing, role of leadership and intra-organizational culture.

CAN KNOWLEDGE MANAGEMENT STRATEGY COPE UP WITH THE SPEED OF SOCIAL MEDIA?

A knowledge ecosystem is not always a set of controlled segments and processes particularly in the context of social media. There can be unpredictable situations too. For example, Yates and Paquette (2011) studied the role of social media during the 2010 Haiti Earthquake where relief operations were coordinated by U.S. with support from United Nations, Haiti and many other countries. It was a large and complex operation that was accomplished using Knowledge Management Systems (KMS). That is where the use of social media tools were applied via wikis and multiple collaborative workspaces as key means of knowledge sharing.

Panagiotopoulos, Shan, Barnett, Regan and McConnon (2015) highlight that "for organizations, that interface with a large audience (i.e. governments, businesses, consumer bodies, non-profits), there are expectations that engagement on social media can improve responsiveness" (pg. 394). They developed a framework of social media engagement based on a case study with food governance and consumer bodies of the UK and Ireland and identified the following three capabilities that can frame the contribution of social media engagement in this context:

1. The levels of consistency as to how social interactions are managed.
2. In the case of specific audience, how engaging content is created.
3. How the entire network is kept alert by social media use.

These capabilities highlight the importance of organizational resources behind the knowledge management issues in the context of social media tools. Decision-makers need to decide on many new issues i.e. how to design a new campaign on Facebook or Twitter or how to back up this campaign with steady flow of inputs, the timing of such an event and quality of the information and so forth. Chua and

Banerjee (2013) conducted a very insightful study in this context in which they studied the use of social media tools in existing bricks-and-mortar business model as to how customer knowledge was managed in the case of Starbucks, an international coffee house chain that operates around 19,000 stores in 59 countries. Four social media tools were used by Starbucks:

1. **Twitter:** Starbucks posts regular tweets with text and photos to approach their customers for promoting their latest products, offers and discounts. With this, Starbucks has immediate feedback mechanism about what they do and that is continuous. Starbucks is quick to respond to the knowledge assimilated from its customers, averaging ten tweets per day.
2. **Facebook:** Very prominent for Starbucks as their Facebook page has over 31 million likes.
3. **Foursquare:** A popular local search service that helps users find the nearest place of interest (geographical location) and help them check-in. Based on the number of check-ins, users earn reputation in the form of badges and mayorships. After checking in, users can also leave comments (tips). Foursquare is currently supported by over 800,000 users.
4. **Corporate Discussion Forum Services (CDS):** Known as MyStarbucksIdea. This works as a platform of customers to enquire, comment, ideate or even express their negative feedback about the organization.

With this kind of vast base of social media-driven relationships, Starbucks was able to design advertising strategies for larger business goals as it came out with a short video advertisement just before the presidential race started in 2008 wherein it offered a free cup of coffee to every voter. It added this video on both video-sharing websites and other social networks like Facebook and Twitter to augment its reach. This video was viewed 419,000 times by Election Day, attracted over 400,000 comments on Facebook and customers were found tweeting on Starbucks every eight seconds (Chua and Banerjee, 2013).

Upon reflection, it can be said that social media is not just a communication tool rather it can replace the traditional advertising route with new forms of promotional means on social networks. This is unlike the traditional methods where a high degree of control was asserted. That is why managers need to evaluate and comprehend the new changing landscape of social communication. They need to understand that the scale of social media tools can be very large or nearly unlimited. To offset any negative fallout, the durability of a social network is of paramount importance. Once achieved, social media can be leveraged to improve a firm's business activities to gain business value (Aral, Dellarocas and Godes, 2013) and disseminate organizational knowledge relevant to customers.

This kind of business opportunity is not a one-way affair. Durability of such a network is a serious issue. There is difficulty in mastering social media channels because it is not one central hub talking to all the spokes rather all the spokes are also talking to one another. In such a new architecture of communication, any kind of promotional activity may not be a fully zero-risk activity. Mangold and Faulds (2009) find that managers can be in a difficult territory as far as managing social media interactions of customers are concerned. The speed, content and timing of these can be beyond the control of a manager particularly if they are not trained to shape such discussions in line with the goals of their organizations. This needs some kind of sustainable and repetitive use of customer networking with social media tools like blogs, social networks, short messaging and other similar channels, supplemented with training of managers.

Ford and Mason (2013) take this issue to another dimension that lies within an organization. They discuss the tensions that are perceived in organizations by the use of social media platforms such as Facebook and Twitter. They study its effect on four key organizational factors:

1. Roles,
2. Ownership,
3. Control,
4. Value.

There may exist some tensions when managers tend to maintain the legacy institutional frameworks at the macro level whereas the rise of social media universe need a micro-level and meso-level handling of issues. A lot more flexibility is expected as far as the notion of organizational boundaries are concerned. In a way, this study hints at wider possibility of changes at the level of the theory of a firm because of social media.

The core of the challenge is to have a nuanced approach to social media. Speed of communication can be an asset but only in conjunction with a situation at hand and organizational strategy. The use of the new media tools needs a kind of mastery of resources that may not be available within a traditional set up. It can take the shape of either a technology or a human resource challenge or even both. It can affect not only the employees but also the ownership and the management levels too.

DECODING THE NATURE OF LEVEL-PLAYING FIELD OFFERED BY SOCIAL MEDIA TECHNOLOGIES

Asur and Huberman (2010) raise the issue that social media platforms generate a lot of content but how this content is to be tapped, is an issue. They demonstrate how social media content can be used to predict real-world outcomes by attempting a smaller study. They used live feed about movies from Twitter.com to predict collections at box-office. Their study shows that a model worked out on the basis of tweets per second can actually prove better than market-based prediction mechanisms. However, they have not yet realized any further potential in terms of predicting real-world outcomes. The commercial aspect of social media is easy for a tête-à-tête but difficult to articulate and design the right strategy because it needs a lot of refinements owing to inherent complexities in the process.

It seems true that social media does have a disruptive relationship with knowledge management in certain contexts. This disruption is uniquely placed in a digital and mobile world. What is important to understand is that social media brings an organization very close to its customers. It is so close that it can simply be one click away! This kind of possibility gains a critical importance when most of the consumers spend a considerable time on smartphones, tablets or laptops. Brand building is a dominant element of knowledge management but the future of brands in the era of open and instant communications is an issue. Kohli, Suri and Kapoor (2015) endorse the managers' problem at this sudden shift in the traditional method of brand building within the controlled regimes of the past. They suggest that brand management has to change substantively. It has to be relocated in terms of how markets are targeted and products are delivered. The realities of a new marketplace have been changed by the advent of social media. Lai (2010) highlights the need of understanding the burgeoning use of social media and its subsequent effects on the emerging social commerce. Kaplan and Haenlein (2010) explore the predominant concern of business executives as to how they can make profitable use of applications like Wikipedia, YouTube, Facebook, Second Life and Twitter but despite an active interest; it is not easy to find the precise methods of monetization. Kwahk and Ge (2012) examine how social media influences the users' visit intention and purchase intention. This kind of technological shift makes knowledge management a very powerful tool as it knocks the door of e-commerce. Having a social media presence is not only important but its connection with e-commerce is also a possibility. It is a double windfall for the strategists of knowledge management but Pereira, Maria and Mateus (2014) suggest that it is not an easy affair. While investigating the role of Facebook in the establishment of relationships between brands and their fans, the information sharing is not the only point. The main goal is to use a strategy to involve a user to extend this culture to other consumers. This is quite similar to what Waters, Burnett, Lamm and Lucas (2009) derived that users' participation is difficult to achieve in such a context. Solely having a Facebook profile will not increase the range and effectiveness of an organization. Zhao and Benyoucef (2013) take this issue to the next level where they mention that design of a social platform is paramount to any sustained brand relationship with the user. These design features must involve a user's journey from social engagement to e-commerce. In a way, social media must have certain elements that should lead to social commerce too. This problem is not actually in the social media rather it belongs to the realm of knowledge management. This brings a totally unexpected territory of technology design into knowledge management. The development of a good web interface is not an easy affair. Even, the big companies hire great design teams at great salaries today to attract consumers on to their brands with excellent displays, content placements and many new features. Liang and Turban (2011) identify the need for research into key issues of social commerce. This area is not a stand-alone one rather it needs quite a number of future efforts. Without recognizing the potential research problems, it is not possible to find any genuine answers.

The size of a company is also an issue to be resolved in terms of social media strategy. Knowledge managers need to sense that small firms may have a much larger business opportunity in social media domain in comparison to the traditional advertising. Gomez, Amado and Montes (2015) discuss how social media can be leveraged to improve the firm's business activities to create value. They try to develop the constituent elements of a social media design and strategy for small firms. Social media capabilities are more important for smaller firms over larger ones because small firms have less financial resources to compete effectually in the market. After testing a model over 100 small U.S. firms included in the 2013 Forbes America's Best Small Companies ranking, they suggest, in this order of importance, "IT infrastructure capability, social competitor pressure, marketing management and innovation management are key mechanisms through which small firms learn to develop a social media competence." (pg. 443) While the complete picture may not be known yet but things are changing very rapidly and these mechanisms become important. The recent talk of YouTube coming out with a "Buy" button on its advertisements is a big indicator of things to come. The sudden and big appearance of too many payment platforms like Apple Pay, Android Pay, Square is a sure signal of what has been missing for quite some time. Yet, there is not any clear sight as to how technology would actually merge social media with e-commerce that is embedded with designs of payment platforms. This raises many interesting questions that are currently beyond the scope of this chapter.

CONCLUSION

Having studied the challenges of knowledge management amidst the explosive expansion of social media, it seems that any strategy in the field cannot survive and exist without the inclusion of social media. However, the advent of social media cannot be pinned down to any one technology or platform like Facebook or Twitter. It is so dispersive and rapidly evolving that to keep pace with only the technical side of social media is itself a big challenge. It is also raising the issues of mastery of skills needed for these new tools. Organizations need to achieve their goals using these new tools, which may create not only a lot of cost saving and enhanced opportunity but also restructuring of human resource strategy as well as organizational management. Secondly, organizations work in a pre-existing work culture and adding new tools and methods would necessitate either a critical review of past practices or totally changing them. This is not an easy task for knowledge managers as they are still grappling with the legacy issues. They are not yet comfortable and conversant with the new methods of business. Apart from internal customers of an organization for whom social media can be used to share knowledge, there is a changing trend in external customers too. External customers have partially shifted from mortar shops into the online domain. A customer is in the mode of evaluation (search for knowledge) of multiple choices that are available now and evaluate both online and offline options before making a purchase. The actual reality is somewhat mid-way. Legacy institutions and practices have an adaptability issue at stake. A customer's online behavior needs research as it brings new tools of engagement. Online media and e-commerce players do not have a large space to traverse if they align their strategies with social media tools. Yet, it is not fully evident on the horizon. It is such a historical stage that brings small scale businesses at par with big ones in some sectors or at least choice of strategies. A framework that connects with customers utilizing social media, can transform an existing business model. That is why knowledge management for current business practices or fast evolving organizations becomes very challenging and frameworks can be devised in future studies. What is needed is an open and flexible approach that can accommodate and embrace whatever changes come into the sector.

REFERENCES

Abidi, S. S. R., Hussini, S., Sriraj, W., Thienthong, S., & Finley, G. A. (2009). Knowledge sharing for pediatric pain management via a Web 2.0 framework. *Studies in Health Technology and Informatics, 150*, 287–291. PMID:19745315

Anderson, S., & Mohan, K. (2011). Social networking in knowledge management. *IT Professional, 13*(4), 24–28. doi:10.1109/MITP.2011.68

Aral, S., Dellarocas, C., & Godes, D. (2013). Social media and business transformation: A framework for research. *Information Systems Research, 24*(1), 3–13. doi:10.1287/isre.1120.0470

Asur, S., & Huberman, B. A. (2010). Predicting the future with social media.*IEEE/WIC/ACM International Conference on Web Intelligence and Intelligent Agent Technology (WI-IAT).*

Bharati, P., Zhang, W., & Chaudhury, A. (2015). *Better knowledge with social media? Exploring the roles of social capital and organizational knowledge management.* Management Science and Information Systems Faculty Publication Series *Paper, 48*, 1–40.

Chua, A. Y. K., & Banerjee, S. (2013). Customer knowledge management via social media: The case of Starbucks. *Journal of Knowledge Management, 17*(2), 237–249. doi:10.1108/13673271311315196

Chugh, R. (2012). Knowledge sharing with enhanced learning and development opportunities.*IEEE International Conference on Information Retrieval and Knowledge Management.* doi:10.1109/InfRKM.2012.6205014

Chugh, R. (2012). Social Networking for Businesses: Is it a Boon or Bane? In M. M. Cruz-Cunha, G. D. Putnik, N. Lopes, P. Gonçalves, & E. Miranda (Eds.), *Handbook of research on business social networking: organizational, managerial, and technological dimensions.* Hershey, PA: IGI Global. doi:10.4018/978-1-61350-168-9.ch032

Chugh, R. (2013). Workplace dimensions: Tacit knowledge sharing in universities. *Journal of Advanced Management Science, 1*(1), 24–28. doi:10.12720/joams.1.1.24-28

DiMicco, J., Millen, D. R., Geyer, W., Dugan, C., Brownholtz, B., & Muller, M. (2008). Motivations for social networking at work.*Proceedings of CSCW'08.*

Ford, D. P., & Mason, R. M. (2013). A multi-level perspective of tensions between knowledge management and social media. *Journal of Organizational Computing and Electronic Commerce, 23*(1-2), 7–33. doi:10.1080/10919392.2013.748604

Gomez, J. B., Amado, J. B., & Montes, F. J. L. (2015). How do small firms learn to develop a social media competence? *International Journal of Information Management, 35*(4), 443–458. doi:10.1016/j.ijinfomgt.2015.04.003

Hemsley, J., & Mason, R. M. (2013). Knowledge and knowledge management in the social media age. *Journal of Organizational Computing and Electronic Commerce, 23*(1-2), 138–167. doi:10.1080/10919392.2013.748614

Hsia, Z. L., Lin, M. N., Wu, J. H., & Tsai, H. T. (2006). A framework for designing nursing knowledge management systems. *Interdisciplinary Journal of Information, Knowledge, and Management, 1*, 14–21.

IDC. (2015). *Smartphone Shipments Reach Second Highest Level for a Single Quarter as Worldwide Volumes Reach 355.2 Million in the Third Quarter.* Retrieved December 1, 2015, from http://www.idc.com/getdoc.jsp?containerId=prUS25988815

Jarrahi, M. H., & Sawyer, S. (2013). Social technologies, informal knowledge practices, and the enterprise. *Journal of Organizational Computing and Electronic Commerce, 23*(1-2), 110–137. doi:10.1080/10919392.2013.748613

Kaplan, A. M., & Haenlein, M. (2010). Users of the world, unite! The challenges and opportunities of Social Media. *Business Horizons, 53*(1), 59–68. doi:10.1016/j.bushor.2009.09.003

Kohli, C., Suri, R., & Kapoor, A. (2015). Will social media kill branding? *Business Horizons, 58*(1), 35–44. doi:10.1016/j.bushor.2014.08.004

Kwahk, K. Y., & Ge, X. (2012). The effects of social media on e-commerce: A perspective of social impact theory.*45th Hawaii International Conference on System Sciences.* doi:10.1109/HICSS.2012.564

Lai, L. S. (2010). Social Commerce – E-Commerce in Social Media Context. *World Academy of Science. Engineering and Technology*, *4*, 12–27.

Lang, J. C. (2004). Social context and social capital as enablers of knowledge integration. *Journal of Knowledge Management*, *8*(3), 89–105. doi:10.1108/13673270410541060

Levy, M. (2013). Stairways to heaven: Implementing social media in organizations. *Journal of Knowledge Management*, *17*(5), 741–754. doi:10.1108/JKM-02-2013-0051

Liang, T. P., & Turban, E. (2011). Introduction to the Special Issue - Social Commerce: A research framework for social commerce. *International Journal of Electronic Commerce*, *16*(2), 5–13. doi:10.2753/JEC1086-4415160201

Mangold, W. G., & Faulds, D. J. (2009). Social media: The new hybrid element of the promotion mix. *Business Horizons*, *52*(4), 357–365. doi:10.1016/j.bushor.2009.03.002

Murphy, G. D., & Salomone, S. (2013). Using social media to facilitate knowledge transfer in complex engineering environments: A primer for educators. *European Journal of Engineering Education*, *38*(1), 70–84. doi:10.1080/03043797.2012.742871

Nonaka, I., & Takeuchi, H. (1995). *The knowledge-creating company*. New York, NY: Oxford University Press.

Nonaka, I., & von Krogh, G. (2009). Tacit knowledge and knowledge conversion: Controversy and advancement in organizational knowledge creation theory. *Organization Science*, *20*(3), 635–652. doi:10.1287/orsc.1080.0412

Panagiotopoulos, P., Shan, L. C., Barnett, J., Regan, A., & McConnon, A. (2015). A framework of social media engagement: Case studies with food and consumer organizations in the UK and Ireland. *International Journal of Information Management*, *35*(4), 394–402. doi:10.1016/j.ijinfomgt.2015.02.006

Panahi, S., Watson, J., & Partridge, H. (2013). Towards tacit knowledge sharing over social web tools. *Journal of Knowledge Management*, *17*(3), 379–397. doi:10.1108/JKM-11-2012-0364

Pereira, H. G., Maria, M. D. F., & Mateus, I. (2014). Say yes to Facebook and get your customers involved! Relationships in a world of social networks. *Business Horizons*, *57*(6), 695–702. doi:10.1016/j.bushor.2014.07.001

Pettenati, M. C., Cigognini, E., Mangione, J., & Guerin, E. (2007). Using social software for personal knowledge management in formal online learning. *Turkish Online Journal of Distance Education*, *8*(3), 52–65.

Phosaard, S., & Wiriyapinit, M. (2011). Knowledge management via Facebook: Building a framework for knowledge management on a social network by aligning business, IT and knowledge management. *Proceedings of the World Congress on Engineering 2011*.

Polanyi, M. (1958). *Personal knowledge: towards a post-critical philosophy*. Chicago University of Chicago Press.

Razmerita, L., Kirchner, K., & Nabeth, T. (2014). Social media in organizations: Leveraging personal and collective knowledge processes. *Journal of Organizational Computing and Electronic Commerce*, *24*(1), 74–93. doi:10.1080/10919392.2014.866504

Seebach, C. (2012). Searching for answers - Knowledge exchange through social media in organizations. *45th Hawaii International Conference on System Sciences*. doi:10.1109/HICSS.2012.514

Steininger, K., Ruckel, D., Dannerer, E., & Roithmayr, F. (2010). Healthcare knowledge transfer through a Web 2.0 portal: An Austrian approach. *International Journal of Healthcare Technology and Management*, *11*(1/2), 13–30. doi:10.1504/IJHTM.2010.033272

Vuori, V., & Okkonen, J. (2012). Knowledge sharing motivational factors of using an intra-organizational social media platform. *Journal of Knowledge Management*, *16*(4), 592–603. doi:10.1108/13673271211246167

Waters, R. D., Burnett, E., Lamm, A., & Lucas, J. (2009). Engaging stakeholders through social networking: How nonprofit organizations are using Facebook. *Public Relations Review*, *35*(2), 102–106. doi:10.1016/j.pubrev.2009.01.006

Yates, D., & Paquette, S. (2011). Emergency knowledge management and social media technologies: A case study of the 2010 Haitian earthquake. *International Journal of Information Management*, *31*(1), 6–13. doi:10.1016/j.ijinfomgt.2010.10.001

Zhao, H., & Benyoucef, M. (2013). From e-commerce to social commerce: A close look at design features. *Electronic Commerce Research and Applications*, *12*(4), 246–259. doi:10.1016/j.elerap.2012.12.003

KEY TERMS AND DEFINITIONS

Blogs: A condensed form of the words "Web Log". Blogs are informational text entries made online and can be made public or private and comments can be invited from the intended audience.

Knowledge: Knowledge is an awareness or understanding of facts, information and skills, which can be acquired through practice, familiarity, experience, observation or study.

Knowledge Management: Knowledge management is the process of acquiring, organizing, disseminating, applying and reusing knowledge.

Rhizomatic: Spreading out laterally and horizontally with no defined boundaries and no distinct centre, beginning or end.

Social Media: Social media is the use of collaborative online applications and technologies for the creation, sharing and application of information by facilitating a social environment amongst users.

Vlogs: Akin to a blog but the posts are made in a video format.

Wiki: A website that can be developed, edited or altered by a collaborative group of users.

ENDNOTES

1 Meerkat is an app that turns a Smartphone into a live broadcasting tool to all the twitter followers of a particular account.

[2] Periscope is almost like Meerkat but with better rates of acceptance across the Twitterati.

[3] Skype Translator is enhanced version of web service Skype where the language of the interacting users can be different and unknown to them. The job of translation is done in real time by the in-built software. Currently, this is available in four languages but Microsoft appears to be working on dozens of more language options for users to choose from.

[4] OTT means Over the Top. It refers to all those players particularly in the telecom market who do not follow a route of formal licensing procedures from government of a particular country. They simply thrive on viral public acceptance that is hinged on to free service model.

[5] Apple Pay was launched in 2014. It converts the iPhone into a digital wallet. By simply tapping or displaying the phone before retail counter Point-of-Sale machine, one can pay for a product or a service. It saves a person's credit card or debit card information in the background and saves this through an encrypted system.

[6] Android Pay is like Apple Pay though it works with all kinds of Android devices. It was launched in May, 2015.

[7] Snapcash is meant for funds transfer between the users of message app, Snapchat. This is an app that gives a unique advantage of messages self-destroying within ten seconds.

[8] A term used in the book "A Thousand Plateaus", by Deleuze and Guattari, 1980.

Chapter 15
Social Media and Big Data: A Conceptual Foundation for Organizations

Meena Jha
Central Queensland University, Australia

Sanjay Jha
Central Queensland University, Australia

Liam O'Brien
Geoscience Australia, Australia

ABSTRACT

The introduction of new and the evolution of existing social media technologies have enabled efficient and broader communication through online social interaction. Today consumers' thinking has shifted towards their trusted network for guidance rather than simply accepting what organisations tell them. With the advent of social interaction, knowledge management paradigms are being stretched beyond their ability to deliver useful results, which is forcing change within organisations globally. Using only transactional and internal data will result in mistaken conclusions or missed opportunities. Social media helps organisations acquire and manage massive amounts of data to better understand their customers, products, competition, and markets and make better decisions using Big Data solutions. These solutions enable organisations to decide on the basis of evidence rather than intuition. This chapter introduces Big Data, Big Data technologies used for capturing knowledge from social media and discusses Big Data Solutions for organizations.

INTRODUCTION

Knowledge management is about managing the knowledge of and in organizations. According to Duhon (1998), "Knowledge management is a discipline that promotes an integrated approach to identifying, capturing, evaluating, retrieving, and sharing all of an enterprise's information assets. These assets may

DOI: 10.4018/978-1-5225-0495-5.ch015

include databases, documents, policies, procedures, and previously un-captured expertise and experience in individual workers". Traditional Knowledge management is about two ideas:

1. To capture explicit knowledge from people and
2. To consistently find the right knowledge at the right time.

The introduction of new technology, such as social media, and the evolution of existing technology have enabled efficient and broader communication and have introduced a significant source of data. Social media is changing organizations around the globe and is increasingly being used as an information source. Social media has sparked thinking and behaviour of people on a massive scale. Today, consumers thinking has shifted towards their trusted network guidance rather than simply accepting what brands tell them.

Social media data can be captured from web-tracking, blogs, discussion forums, chat rooms, social networking websites, video sharing websites, photo sharing websites, collaborative websites, social bookmarking websites and virtual worlds. Social media platforms used by organizations are increasingly being used to engage with employees and the public (National Archive, 2013). The U.S. Navy describes the importance of using social media in its Social Media Handbook as helping (American Council, 2011) "fulfill your obligation to communicate with all of your stakeholders. It also provides another, often richer, means of sharing information with internal and external audiences. Your stakeholders are increasingly using social media, and you're better off reaching them there than not at all". Organizations have described social media tools as a "multiplier of resources" where "more audiences can be reached with fewer resources needed on the part of the organization" (National Archive, 2010).

Social media is impacting knowledge management and decision making. Traditional knowledge management paradigms, focuses primarily on creating structured mechanisms to provide a repeatable process for effective knowledge management. With the advent of social interaction, these knowledge paradigms are being stretched beyond their ability to deliver useful results. Using only transactional data and internal data will result in mistaken conclusions or missed opportunities.

Big Data solutions can help organizations acquire and handle massive amounts of social media data to better understand and make decisions about their customers, products, competition, and markets. The data captured from social media include reposting information available on organizations' websites, posting information not available on publicly accessible organization websites, soliciting and responding to comments, and providing links to other websites. Social media also includes data from communication and interaction with the public or collaborating with other organizations.

Using Big Data solutions enables managers to decide on the basis of evidence rather than intuition. Data-driven decisions are better decisions. For Big Data solution the organization is required to define what Big Data is, the domains of data that need to be considered, characteristics of Big Data and the technologies used for Big Data Solutions. Data integration captures and integrates both structured and unstructured Big Data within the enterprise. Big Data solutions enable data from social media to be captured, stored, processed and analyzed.

Knowledge about customers is a critical source of competitive advantage for an organization. Data generated from customer interaction will be rich in tacit content and can be a source of insights for product innovation, competitive intelligence and consumer behaviour. Such data can be captured through social media where interaction or socialization between people is done. Social media is one such technology that has seen increased usage as an information source (Westerman et al, 2013). For example, social media is being used to seek information about topical and important issues, such as circulating up-to-the minute information about cholera outbreaks in Haiti and identifying clean water sources during this outbreak (Slutter, 2010).

Knowledge management over the years has integrated information from multiple perspectives to provide the insights required for valid decision-making. Organizations do not make decisions based on just one factor, such as revenue, employee salaries or interest rates for commercial loans. The total picture is what should drive decisions, such as where to invest marketing dollars, how much to invest in R&D or whether to expand into a new geographic market. Automated collection of data and the reduced cost of storage storage have made data accessible. Data can be stored, processed and analyzed in abundance. However, relational databases are reaching the limits to store, process and analyze data. New solutions have emerged to deal with this so called Big Data. Big Data solutions help us to manage the increasing velocity, variety, and volume (the three Vs) of the data.

This chapter provides an introduction and background to Big Data and the technologies used for Big Data solutions, so that data from social media can be harnessed. An overview of the analytical approaches used in Big Data is outlined. Big Data solutions for knowledge management for organizations are discussed. The impact that Big Data solutions have on the Technology and Data Architectures of an organization are highlighted. A Data Management Framework will be outlined that identifies many areas within an organization's data and knowledge management capabilities that will be impacted by Big Data.

BACKGROUND

Big Data refers to datasets whose size is beyond the ability of typical database software tools to capture, store, manage and analyze. Big Data ranges from a few dozen terabytes to multiple petabytes of data. Big Data is data whose scale, diversity, and complexity require new architectures, techniques, algorithms, and analytics to manage it and extract value and hidden knowledge from it. According to Gartner (2009), "Big Data is high volume, high velocity information asset that demands cost-effective, innovative forms of information processing for enhanced insight and decision making". Big Data is being generated from a variety of sources including social media and networks (all of us are generating data), scientific instruments (collecting all sorts of data), mobile devices (tracking all objects all the time), sensor technology and networks (measuring all kinds of data) as shown in Figure 1.

Every Big Data source (live data, data from internal sources, and data from external sources) has different characteristics, including the frequency, volume, velocity, type, and veracity of the data. Generally Big Data is characterized by 3V's: Volume, Velocity and Variety (Gartner, 2009). Volume means the

Figure 1. Sources of big data generation

large amount of data. Traditionally the amount of data stored by the average company a few years ago was in terabytes and now the scale of data collected and generated is increasing exponentially and is in zettabytes (Adduci et al., 2011). Variety is the complexity of data. Data comes in various formats, types and structures. It could be text, numerical, images, audio, video sequences, time series, and social media data. To extract knowledge all these types of data need to be linked together. A single application can be generating/collecting many types of data. Velocity is the speed of data. In today's world data needs to be generated fast and needs to be processed fast. Late decisions mean missing opportunities. The model of generating/consuming data has changed. In the traditional model few companies are involved in collecting and generating data while others are consuming data. Now consumers are also the generators of data.

Big Data applications span a broad range of domains including:

1. Intelligent mobility systems and services;
2. Intelligent energy support systems;
3. Smart personal healthcare systems and services;
4. Intelligent transportation and logistics services;
5. Smart environmental systems and services;
6. Intelligent systems and software engineering;
7. Intelligent engineering and manufacturing.

Today, in the age of the Internet, much of the focus is on faster delivery of more information (e.g., documents, medical images, movies, gene sequences, and sensor data streams) to systems, PCs, mobile devices, and living rooms. The challenge for organizations in the next decade will be finding ways to better analyze, monetize, and capitalize on all these information channels and integrate them into the business for knowledge management so that better decisions can be made.

The real value of Big Data is in the insight it produces when analyzed and integrated into the existing Business Intelligence. Through analysis patterns are discovered, meaning is derived, indicators for decisions are generated, and ultimately the ability to respond to the world with greater intelligence is increased. Social networking and information sharing are not just interpersonal phenomena, but inter-organizational as well. Knowledge gained through employees, customers, users as well as through heads of companies can affect the business. Making informed decisions about how competitors are operating can affect how well a business performs.

HARNESSING BIG DATA

Data generated from customer interactions can have a significant impact on an organization's products and business. Such knowledge can be captured from interaction of people using social media, surveys and focus groups. Organization's need to understand the problems associated with the traditional database management systems that collect transactional data. Traditional database management systems, which are commercially available and are in place in most organizations, are disk based SQL oriented database systems. The data inside these systems is stored in disk blocks, which are heavily encoded for a variety of technical reasons. This technology, due to the proven capabilities, starting in the nineties when it took over the database market, is considered to fit all requirements. However, the significant increase in the form of application domains, database sizes, as well as the variety of data began to cause problems for this technology as it started to be too robust and not able to answer the requirements of new demands. A traditional DBMS architecture, which is originally designed and optimized for business data processing, has been used to support many data-centric applications with widely varying characteristics and requirements. This concept is no longer applicable to the whole database market and that the commercial world needs to venture into a collection of independent database engines, some of which may be unified by a common front-end parser (Stonebraker, 2006).

The Big Data solution is about driving actionable insight and timely organizational decisions from the combination of different types of data – unstructured, semi-structured, and structured data. The idea of analysing data to make sense of what's happening in businesses has been around for a long time. Over the years the name and terminology for data analytics have changed because of advent of technology and the way data is processed for use. The activity of making sense of data has been called Online Transaction Processing (OLTP), Online Analytical Processing (OLAP), and now Real-Time Analytics Processing (RTAP). OLTP is characterized by a large number of online database transactions such as INSERT, UPDATE, and DELETE. In OLTP databases use detailed and current data. OLAP is characterized by a relatively low volume of transactions. Queries are often very complex and involve aggregations. In OLAP databases are aggregated, historical data stored on multidimensional schemas. RTAP is characterized by stream analytics and uses traditional, relational, non-traditional and non-relational data sources as shown in Figure 2.

In Figure 2 the Non-Traditional/Non-Relational data sources have data that is continually being captured (in motion) as an event is taking place and this data is streamed and the analytics (stream analytics) needs to occur as the data is being generated. The Traditional/Relational data sources have data that is captured after an event has taken place and the analytics (data analytics) can take place any time after the event.

Different types of data when combined provide true insight. Unstructured data consists of ideas and concepts that people communicate every day. Social media offers an opportunity to an organization to connect and interact with its customers, understand what customers are saying about a product or the organization, promote the brand, and special offers. Getting involved in social media can also create a more human face to the organization and be fun at the same time. Using social media is a great way to make the organization seem friendlier and to form closer relationships with their customers. By engag-

Figure 2. Harnessing big data

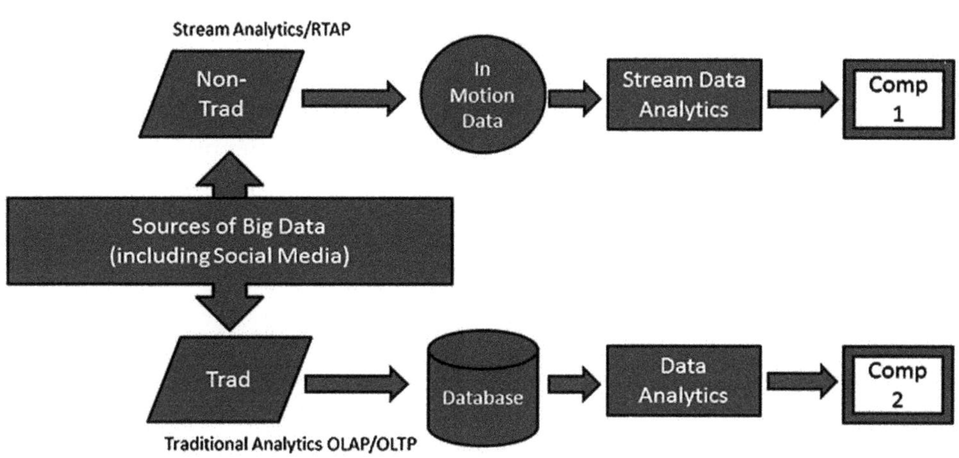

ing in social media, an organization can interact directly with customers and by creating interesting and useful content the organization can be in a more advantageous position than others in the same business.

Getting access to social media data can be achieved in a number of ways. Organisations using Big Data solutions can automatically extract data from social media sites through the use of Application Programming Interfaces (APIs). Many social media platforms provide APIs for free but impose restrictions on the amount and type of data. An alternative approach is to use a third party company to access greater quantities of data which then pass the data on to the organisation for a fee. This data can then be analysed using a variety of Big Data Analytics (including social media analytics) (HoP 2014).

Analytics using Big Data for decision making within an organization can be required to support critical operational processes of an organization. Organizations generate around one third of the data they use internally, and are responsible for around 56% of the remaining data, generated via consumers interacting with their services on the web. Every data point is potentially valuable, from the publicly available data such as social media on the Internet generates 60 trillion individual pages from consumer reviews, to internal data such as e-health records, smart cards and financial transactions (Adduci et al., 2011)

Many organizations have multiple databases and multiple database vendors, with terabytes or even petabytes of data. Some of these systems have accumulated data over several years. Many organizations build entire data warehouse and analytic platforms for this old data. For data to be useful to decision makers they must integrate data such as customers with finance and sales data, with product data, with marketing data, with social media data, with demographic data, with competitors data, and more.

BIG DATA AND TRADITIONAL ANALYTICS

It is important to understand different types of analytics and how Big Data has changed traditional analytics. There are three types of Analytics: Descriptive, Predictive and Prescriptive analytics. As an organization embraces Big Data and uses it to harness social media data it is important to understand what the analytics can do for them and the questions that the different types of analytics can answer.

Descriptive Analytics: Insight into the Past

Descriptive analytics depicts what has already happened and is the traditional analytics method. Until the advent of Big Data analytics this is the kind of analytics used in most organizations. Spreadsheets, financial statements, reports, bank statements, inventory reports are kind of data used for descriptive analytics. This enabled organizations to look back in time and evaluate what has already transpired. Descriptive analytics are useful because they allow us to learn from past behaviors, and understand how they might influence future outcomes. Descriptive analytics is used when there is a need to understand at an aggregate level what is happening in the organization, and to summarize and describe different aspects of the business. Today, descriptive analytics can be done by adding Big Data solutions which will give organizations more capability to consider more information which in turn provides more granular insights, to evaluate what has transpired.

Predictive Analytics: Understanding the Future

Predictive analytics is about looking forward. Predictive analytics is the practice of extracting information from existing data sets in order to determine patterns and predict future outcomes and trends and make appropriate decisions. Predictive analytics does not tell what will happen in the future. It only forecasts what might happen in the future. Financial organizations use predictive analytics to predict for example an individual's likelihood to default on a loan. Predictive analytics, a type of traditional analytics, are used to analyse historical data in order to better understand customers, products and partners and to identify potential risks and opportunities for a company.

With the advent of Big Data solutions current data can be analysed for predictive analytics as well. Predictive analytics is an enabler of Big Data. Businesses collect vast amounts of real-time customer data and predictive analytics uses historical data, combined with customer insight, to predict future events. Predictive analytics enable organizations to use Big Data (both stored and real-time) to move from a historical view to a forward-looking perspective of the customer. For example, stores that use data from loyalty programs can analyse past buying behaviour to predict the coupons or promotions a customer is most likely to participate in or buy in the future. Predictive analytics could also be applied to customer website browsing behaviours to deliver a personalized website experience for the customer, for example recommendations on book, DVD, or CD purchases.

Prescriptive Analytics: Advice on Possible Outcomes

Prescriptive analytics is the new frontier in analytics. Prescriptive analytics goes beyond descriptive and predictive analytics by recommending one or more possible courses of action. Results are accompanied by automated actions or a list of recommended actions with a likely outcome for each action. An organization may choose one of the choices and implement it. When implemented correctly, it can have a large impact on how organizations make decisions. Larger organizations are successfully using prescriptive analytics to optimize production; scheduling and inventory in their supply chain to make sure that they are delivering the right products at the right time and optimizing the customer experience. Once the past is understood and predictions can be made about what might happen in future, one needs to know what the best action will be, given the limited resources of the organization. In this class of analytics, results are accompanied with automated actions or a list of recommended actions with a likely outcome for each action. The user may pick one of the choices and implement it. Facebook uses prescriptive analytics to determine who to recommend to users as a friend on Facebook. Prescriptive analytics is based on the concept of optimization, which can be divided into two tasks:

- **Optimization**: How the best results can be achieved?
- **Stochastic Optimization**: How the best results can be achieved to tackle improbability in the data to make better decisions.

Prescriptive analytics is used in the maintenance of large systems such as road, water and cable TV systems. Prescriptive analytics can determine when a road will need widening or a stoplight should be added at an intersection based upon actual and expected traffic flows and other factors (Baker, 2015).

All the above stated three types of analytics can make use of Big Data. The difference between using Big Data for analytics and traditional data analytics is shown in Table 1. Using Big Data for analytics enables organizations to analyze a mix of structured, semi-structured and unstructured data from various data sources and gives valuable business information and insight which cannot be done using traditional analytics.

Table 1. Difference between big data and traditional analytics

	Big Data	Traditional Analytics
Types of Data	Structured Data Semi-structured Data Un-structured Data	Structured Data Formatted in rows and columns
Volume of Data	100s terabytes to Zettabytes	Tens of terabytes or less
Flow of Data	Constant flow of data Real-time data Historical data	Historical data
Analysis Methods	Machine learning	Hypothesis based
Primary Purpose	Decision support based on real-time data	Decision support based on historical data

BIG DATA TECHNOLOGIES

Traditional analytic technologies and approaches are hindering business transformation and provide challenges because they are incapable of managing the tsunami of social, mobile, sensor, and telemetry data, and consequently, they are unable to be used to make timely decisions (Schmarzo, 2013). Big Data technologies stack addresses these issues and challenges and comprises of three major layers: Foundation Layer, Analytics Layer and Application Layer. Big Data Storage and Processing, and Reporting are handled in the Foundation layer, Analytics is handled in the Analytics Layer and the result of Analytics Layer is visualized in Application Layer. The detail purpose of each layers is as follows:

- **Foundation Layer**: The foundation layer provides the infrastructure for storage and processing, access and management of Big Data. Depending on the nature of data, stream processing solutions ((Abadi et al., 2003), and (Salehi, 2010)), distributed persistent storage (Shvachko, 2010), cloud infrastructures (Cusumano, 2010) or a reasonable combination of these (Saker et al., 2011) are used for storing and accessing data in response to the upper-layer requests and requirements.
- **Analytics Layer**: This is middle layer and responsible for analytics. Here data warehousing technologies are currently exploited for extracting correlations and features from data and feeding classification and prediction algorithms (Thusoo et al., 2010).
- **Application Layer**: This layer is also called focused application layer and is at the top of the stack. The functionality of the application layer is based on the use of more generic lower-layer technologies and exposed to end users as Big Data solutions.

All three layers as shown in Figure 3 are the building blocks of Big Data solutions. According to its purpose, the Foundational Layer is concerned about being capable of processing as much data (volume) as possible as soon as possible (streaming). In particular, the faster the stream is (velocity), the more difficult it is to process the data. For the Analytics Layer volume, velocity, and variety are important and constitute the facets of efficiency. Big volumes of data which may change swiftly have to be processed in a timely manner so that it can be accessed by the Application Layer for end users of Big Data.

The functionality of all these layers is dependent on Technology Infrastructure and Data Architecture. Technology infrastructure is the cornerstone of Big Data solutions. Technology infrastructure relates to

Figure 3. Big data technology stack

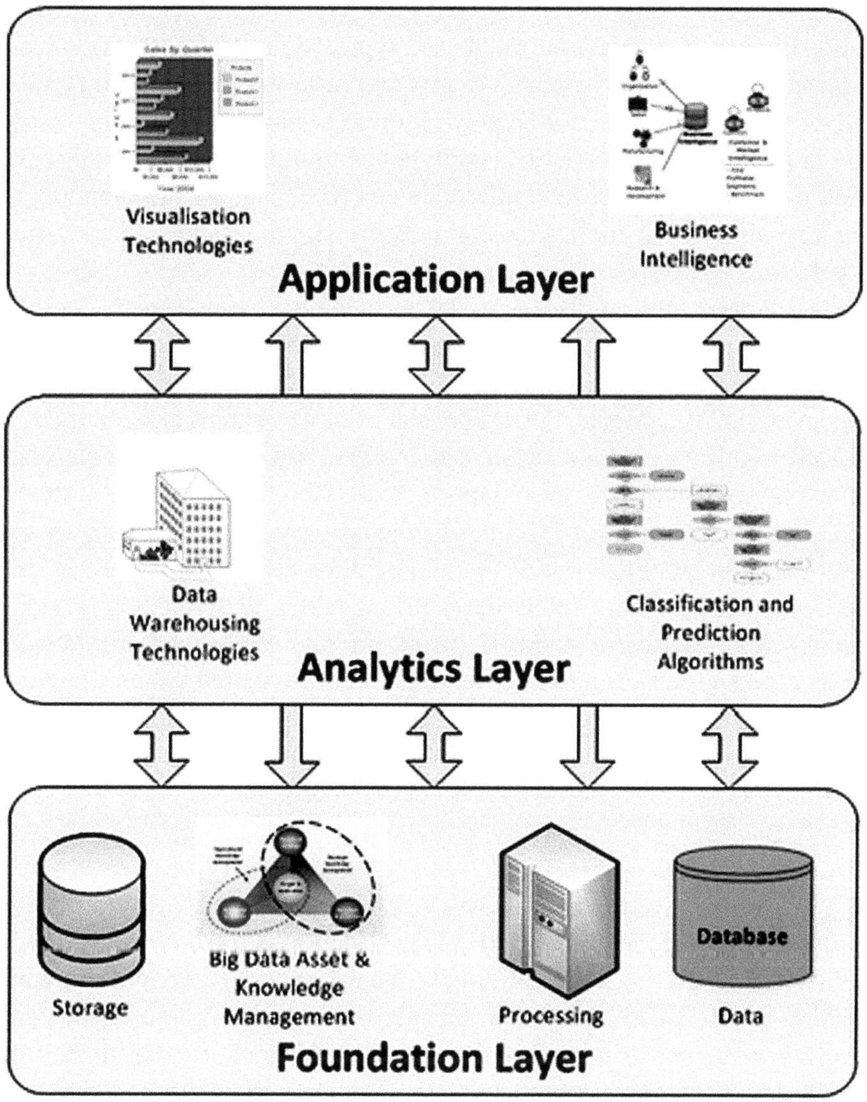

data storage, data steam processing, data management, and query planning and execution. Possessing the right tools for storing, processing and analysing data is crucial in Big Data solutions.

Introducing Big Data solutions will have an impact on the Data Architecture which is composed of models, policies, rules or standards that govern which data is collected, and how it is stored, arranged, integrated, and put to use in data systems and in organizations. Data sources and data access requirements should include a detailed plan and roadmap for prioritizing what Big Data to capture and where to store that data (both from a data access, as well as an analysis perspective). This plan will need to address both structured and unstructured data. It also needs to address external data sources, which means that the data plan will need to be updated every 4 to 6 months to accommodate the many new data sources that become available (Liebowitz, 2013).

Technology Infrastructure and Technology Architecture

For decades, enterprises relied on relational databases, typical collections of rows and columns, for processing structured data. However, the volume, velocity and variety of data mean that relational databases often cannot deliver the performance and latency required to handle large, complex data. The rise of unstructured data in particular meant that data capture had to move beyond merely rows and columns. Thus new technologies such as Hadoop, MapReduce emerged, capable of managing a vast variety of data, and making it possible to run applications on systems with thousands of nodes, potentially involving terabytes or petabytes of data.

Data integration in large organizations is a crucial but at the same time a costly, long-lasting, and challenging problem. While business-critical information is often already gathered in integrated information systems such as Enterprise Resource Planning (ERP), Customer Resource Management (CRM) and Supply Chain Management (SCM) systems, the integration of these systems as well as the integration with the abundance of other information sources (such as social media data) is still a major challenge. Large organizations often operate hundreds or even thousands of different information systems and databases.

After the arrival and proliferation of IT in large organizations, various approaches, techniques, and methods were introduced in order to solve the data integration challenge. In the last decade, the prevalent data integration approaches were primarily based on XML, Web Services, and Service Oriented Architectures (SOA). XML defines a standard syntax for data representation, Web Services provide data exchange protocols, and SOA is a holistic approach for distributed systems architecture and communication based on the use of services. However, these technologies are not sufficient to solve the data integration challenge in large organizations. In particular, overheads associated with SOA are still too high for rapid and flexible data integration (Halevy et al., 2006).

Hadoop

One of the key infrastructural technologies is Hadoop. Hadoop is a whole ecosystem of technologies designed for the storing, processing and analysing of data. The core Hadoop technologies work on the principle of breaking up and distributing data into parts and analysing those parts concurrently thus making it more efficient, rather than tackling one monolithic block of data all in one go. Hadoop is better suited to high-throughput, and in depth analysis. The main advantages of Hadoop are its cost and time effectiveness. Cost, because as it is open source, it is free and available for anyone to use, and can run on cheap commodity hardware. Time, because it processes multiple parts of the data set concurrently, making it a comparatively fast tool for in-depth analysis. The Apache Software Foundation are constantly updating and developing the Hadoop ecosystem such as Hadoop on Premium. Hadoop on Premium services such as Cloudera, Hortonworks and Splice offer the Hadoop framework with greater security and support, with added system and data management tools and enterprise capabilities. Some key components of Hadoop include:

- **HDFS**: Hadoop File System which is the default storage layer.
- **MapReduce**: This is composed of two components Map and Reduce. The Map job distributes a query to different nodes, and the Reduce gathers the results and resolves them into a single value.
- **Yet Another Resource Negotiator (YARN)**: Responsible for cluster management and scheduling user applications. YARN decouples MapReduce's resource management and scheduling capa-

bilities from the data processing component, enabling Hadoop to support more varied processing approaches and a broader array of applications. For example, Hadoop clusters can run interactive querying and streaming data applications simultaneously with MapReduce batch jobs.
- **Spark**: Used on top of HDFS, and promises speed up to 100 times faster than the two step MapReduce function in certain applications. This allows data to be loaded in memory and queried repeatedly, making it suitable for machine learning algorithms.
- **Not Only SQL (NoSQL)**: NoSQL is involved in processing large volumes of multi structured data. Most NoSQL databases are most adept at handling discrete data stored among multi structured data. Some NoSQL databases, like HBase, can work concurrently with Hadoop. NoSQL is better suited for operational tasks, interactive workloads based on selective criteria where data can be processed in near real time.

Hadoop and NoSQL products are sometimes marketed concurrently. Some big names in NoSQL field include Apache Cassandra, MongoDB, and Oracle NoSQL. Many of the most widely used NoSQL technologies are open source, meaning security and troubleshooting may be an issue. It also places less focus on atomicity and consistency than on performance and scalability. Premium packages of NoSQL databases (such as Datastax for Cassandra) work to address these issues. Hadoop and NoSQL are key components in a technology Architecture for processing and storage of social media data as there is a lot of data to be stored and processed and the timeliness of that processing especially for streaming data is critical.

Massively Parallel Processing (MPP) Databases

Massively Parallel Processing (MPP) Databases work by segmenting data across multiple nodes, and processing these segments of data in parallel. Hadoop usually runs on cheaper clusters of commodity servers (allowing for inexpensive horizontal scale out), whereas most MPP databases run on expensive specialised hardware (data warehouse appliances). MPP technologies process massive amounts of data in parallel. It may have hundreds (or potentially even thousands) of processors, each with their own operating system and memory, working on different parts of the same programme.

MPP uses SQL, and Hadoop uses Java as default (although the Apache Foundation developed Hive, a language used in Hadoop similar to SQL, to make using Hadoop slightly easier and less specialist). Many of the major players in the MPP market have been acquired by technology vendors. Netezza, for instance is owned by IBM, Vertica is owned by HP and Greenplum is owned by EMC.

Cloud Computing

Another key technology is Cloud computing, which refers to a broad set of products that are sold as a service and delivered over a network. The cloud computing paradigm builds on the premise that computational capacity can be consumed on-demand, thus reducing the cost at the demand side while improving the utilization of resources at the supply side. Virtualization via cloud computing can increase the utilization of computing infrastructures from an average of 15% up to 90% compared to traditional IT environments (Biocic et al., 2011). The traditional infrastructure setting requires hardware and software for each person involved with the processing and analyses of data. In cloud computing access to only one application (a web based service) is required. The expected benefits draw from flexible management of capacities to perform computational tasks without investing in new infrastructure, training of personnel, or licensing of software. This is very much relevant in the area of Big Data solutions where the increasing availability of heterogeneous data requires large amounts of storage capacities and computer intensive analytics to derive business value from cloud computing.

Case studies from market research and business literature suggest that Big Data storage system based on the principle of cloud computing coincide with massive savings in IT infrastructure and operation. Walt Disney lowered the company's IT expense growth from 27% to 3%, while increasing its annual processing growth from 17% to 45% after setting up Hadoop Cluster on the cloud (Gruman, 2010).

A Big Data ready cloud-computing platform provides the following key capabilities:

- **Agile Computing Platform**: Agility is enabled through highly flexible and reconfigurable data and analytic resources and architectures. Analytic resources can be quickly reconfigured and redeployed to meet the ever-changing demands of the business, enabling new levels of analytics flexibility and agility.
- **Linear Scalability**: Access to massive amounts of computing power means that business problems can be attacked in a completely different manner. For example, the traditional Extract, Transform and Load (ETL) process can be transformed into a data enrichment process creating new composite metrics, such as frequency (how often?), recent in time (how recent?), and sequencing (the order?).
- **On-Demand, Analysis-Intense Workloads:** Previously organizations had to be content with performing *after the fact* analysis. The organizations lacked the computational power to dive deep into the analysis as events were occurring or to contemplate all the different variables that might be driving the business. With a cloud platform, these computationally intensive, short burst analytic needs can be exploited. Business users can analyse massive amounts of data in real time. This means uncovering the relevant and actionable facts across hundreds of dimensions and business metrics.

Data Architecture

Information is called unstructured if it is not provided as a list of attribute value pairs for attributes with data types defined in a suitable schema. Typically for data types covering numbers, patterns of numbers, letters, and names. Structured information can be provided by a table as an instance of relation scheme fixing a set of attributes in a relational database. Examples of unstructured data are texts, sound, image, and multimedia data. Data Architecture design can be shown by following diagrams:

- **Class Diagrams**: The key purpose of the class diagram is to depict the relationships among the critical data entities (or classes) within the enterprise. This diagram is developed to present the relationships and to help understand the lower level data models for the enterprise.
- **Data Dissemination Diagrams**: The purpose of the data dissemination diagram is to show the relationship between data entities, business services, and application components. The diagram shows how the logical entities are to be physically realized by application components. This allows effective sizing to be carried out and the IT footprint to be refined. Moreover, by assigning business value to data, an indication of the business criticality of application components can be

gained. The diagram also shows data replication and system ownership of the master reference for data. This diagram can include services; that is, services encapsulate data and they reside in an application, or services that reside in an application and access data encapsulated within the application.

- **Data Life Cycle Diagrams**: The data lifecycle diagram is an essential part of managing business data throughout its lifecycle, from conception through disposal, within the constraints of the business process. The data is considered as an entity in its own right, detached from business processes and activities. Each change in state is represented in the diagram, which may include the event or rules that trigger that change in state. The separation of data from process allows common data requirements to be identified, thereby enabling more effective resource sharing to be achieved. Defining the lifecycle of business entities enables better formalization of these business entities, as well as the determination of the steps that are essential to their management. This very simple state model will be a guide in the definition of business processes, since these processes will themselves have to respect the constraints defined for transitions between states: if a business entity has not passed through all its states within the business processes that handle it, then these are incomplete. If the business processes transgress the lifecycle of the business entities, then they are incorrect.
- **Data Migration Diagrams**: The purpose of the data migration diagram is to show the flow of data from the source to the target applications. The diagram will provide a visual representation of the spread of sources/targets and serve as a tool for data auditing and establishing traceability. This diagram can be elaborated or enhanced as detailed as necessary. For example, the diagram can contain just an overall layout of migration landscape or could go into individual application metadata element level of detail.
- **Data Security Diagrams**: Data is considered as an asset to the enterprise and data security simply means ensuring that enterprise data is not compromised and that access to it is suitably controlled. The purpose of the data security diagram is to depict which actor (person, organization, or system) can access which enterprise data. This relationship can be shown in matrix form between two objects or can be shown as a mapping. The diagram can also be used to demonstrate compliance with data privacy laws and other applicable regulations (such as HIPAA andSOX). This diagram should also consider any trust implications where an enterprise's partners or other parties may have access to the company's systems, such as an outsourced situation where information may be managed by other people and may even be hosted in a different country.

Behind any knowledge management lies the core doctrine of data quality, data governance and metadata management along with considerations for privacy and legal concerns. Data governance helps an organization to take a holistic view and to manage data in the context of business process, and to support application integration needs. Big Data needs to be integrated into the organizations data architecture and not seen as a standalone effort. Data architecture requires information about master and reference data management, data warehousing business intelligence, transaction data management, structured technical data management, unstructured data management, metadata, analytical data, documents and contents, historical data, temporary data, and Big Data analytics. All these data sources need to be organized in an information framework which can support data governance and data asset planning.

Data Management Framework

The key element of organizational structure is the business functions. Organizations need to know the kind of data required, captured, acquired, stored and analyzed for business functions such as marketing, sales, supply chain, manufacturing, human resources, strategy making, finance and, information technology. Data is an asset to the organization and must be managed to ensure competitive advantage and managed in a way so as to reduce the complexity of the asset management in the organization. Figure 4 shows the components of a data management framework. Information Goals and Principles are top priority for any organization but this must be supported by Data Governance and Information Asset Planning. So while making a decision from knowledge management and extracting data from social media we require Data Governance, Information Asset Planning, Data Quality and Management, Data Integration, Information Life Cycle Management, Metadata Management, Data Models and Taxonomies and information about Master and Reference data Management, data warehousing business intelligence, transaction data management, structured technical data management, unstructured data management, Metadata, Analytical Data, Documents and contents, Historical Data, Temporal Data, and Big Data analytics.

For social media data it is important to determine the sources of the data and associated metadata, what forms the data will come into the organization, what processing is carried out on the data, what form the results will take, where they will be stored and managed and how they will be used to support decision making. It is important to keep a provenance records for results as if the results are used to support decision making it will be important to be able to track the results back to the inputs and what processing (algorithms and analytics) was applied. All of these data management activities are important pieces of the Data Management Framework.

Figure 4. Data management framework

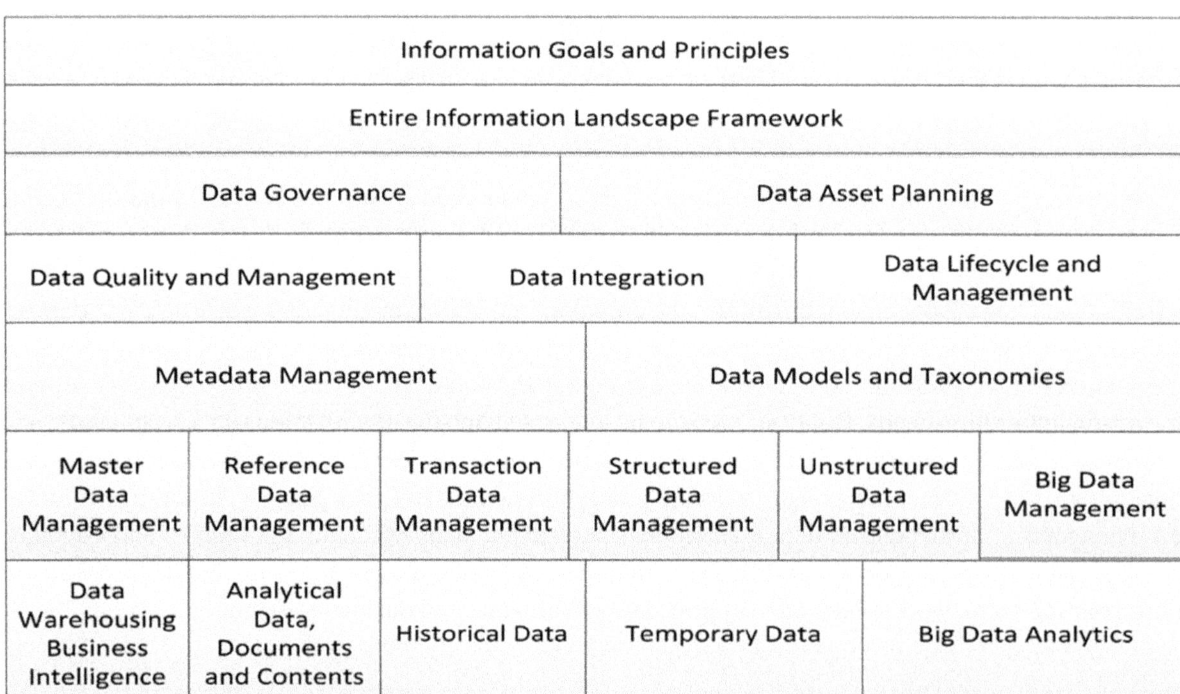

Data Sources

The data sources are heterogeneous involving more diverse unstructured and semi-structured data sets. The data sources are likely to be found both outside the organization (external social media platforms) and inside the organization (if the organization has its own social media environment). For Knowledge Management and Business Intelligence the external and internal data sources are required. In a high Information Technology consuming context such as a Big Data solution, data governance and data asset planning must be addressed. Data governance and data asset planning remove risk associated with operational/ transactional/in-motion data which removes the risk of poor Intelligence, reporting and poor decision making. The following (PWC, 2014) are the internal and external sources of Big Data which need to be integrated to Big Data solutions:

- **Open Data**: A key source of data from governments and private institutions. Open relates to how accessible a data set is in terms of allowing others to use it without restriction. Some social media platforms allow users to have public data where anyone can access and private data where user consent must be given to use such data.
- **Internal Enterprise Data**: Data that is collected by an organization about its own systems and processes. This data may not be digital, can consist of both quantitative and qualitative information, and can also be anonymised. A bank using anonymised customer transaction records to predict and proactively refill its ATMs is an example of this type of data.
- **Little Data**: Small businesses can also make use of data analytics across data that they have about their own business, similar to Big Data, but on a smaller scale.
- **My Data**: Internal data about a particular organization or individual, this type of data is typically held securely with strict rules regarding access; for example, a hospital holding an individual's health records for their health care professionals, which would also allow them to diagnose the patient on the basis of other aggregate data on medical conditions .
- **Web Logs**: Web Logs are personal web pages written in chronological order and maintained through specific software that helps their administration. A Web Log, sometimes written as Web Log or Weblog is a Web site that consists of a series of entries arranged in reverse chronological order, often updated frequently with new information about particular topics.

FUTURE RESEARCH DIRECTIONS

Businesses and organizations from all sectors began to gain critical insight from the structured data collected through various enterprise systems and analysed by commercial relational database management systems. Organizations should not let existing data warehouse and existing business intelligence processes, which are insufficient for today's deep, wide, and diverse data sources, hold the organization back. Big Data is the next generation of business analytics. Social media is impacting the way businesses run today. To extract the knowledge from social media and harness it for decision making requires new technologies.

New technologies should be leveraged, such as Hadoop, in memory computing, and in data analytics, to provide new knowledge management and advanced analytics capabilities, and open up new, more modern architectural options to leverage Big Data solutions. Organizations should be prepared to embrace open source technologies and tools. New ways of doing Data Analytics and Business Intelligence impact on technology infrastructure components and data architectures. Since most data including social media data is directly generated in digital format today these impacts and changes must be captured and documented by an organization's Enterprise Architecture for conducting enterprise analysis, design, planning, and implementation, using a holistic approach at all times, for the successful development and execution of organizational strategy and decision making by harnessing social media for knowledge management.

CONCLUSION

For businesses to be successful these days, creating a social media strategy is a must. Organizations are embracing social media for decision making. Social media is transforming group interaction and has a notable impact on how businesses reach their markets. Knowledge extracted from social media helps in making strategic decisions for the businesses. In this chapter, characteristics of Big Data and the existing technologies used for Big Data solutions and the Big Data Technology Stack have been outlined. Various types of data analytics have been outlined and the difference between Big Data analytics and traditional analytics has been summarized. The difference in capability between Big Data and traditional analytics is the major factor for adopting Big Data technologies in organizations.

Big Data technologies allow data from social media to be captured, stored, processed and analyzed to make timely decisions. The impact that Big Data solutions have on the Technology and Data Architectures of an organization have been highlighted. A Data Management Framework has been outlined that identifies many areas within an organization's data and knowledge management capabilities that will be impacted by Big Data. This Chapter has outlined a conceptual foundation for how Big Data could be used to harness social media. The limitation of this Chapter is that it does not describe in detail how a Big Data solution can be implemented within an organization, integrating social media data within that solution, processing the data to generate results and then using those results to support more informed decisions. This would be a significant and potentially costly undertaking for any organization but the results of doing so could be worth it.

REFERENCES

Abadi, D. J., Carney, D., Cetintemel, U., Cherniack, M., Convey, C., & Lee, S. (2003). Aurora: A new model and architecture for data stream management. *The VLDB Journal*, *12*(2), 120–139. doi:10.1007/s00778-003-0095-z

Adduci, R., Blue, D., Chiarello, G., Chickering, J., Mavroyiannis, D., Mirchandani, S., . . . Schleier-Smith, J. (2011). *Big Data: Big Opportunities to Create Business Value, Report and recommendations based on discussion with the Leadership Council for Information Advantage*. Retrieved January 15, 2015, from http://www.emc.com/microsites/cio/articles/big-data-big-opportunities

Baker, P. (2015). *Data Divination Big Data Strategies*. Cengage Learning.

Biocic, B., Tomic, D., & Ogrizovic, D. (2011). Economies of Cloud Computing, In *Proceedings of the 34th International Convention on Information and Communication technology, electronics and micro-electronics (MIPRO'11)*, (pp.1438-1442).

Cusumano, M. (2010). Cloud Computing and SaaS as New Computing Platforms. In Proceedings of Communications of the Association for Computing Machinery (ACM'10), (vol. 53, pp. 27-29). doi:10.1145/1721654.1721667

Duhon, B. (1998). It's all in our heads. *Inform (Silver Spring, Md.)*, *12*(8), 8–13.

Gruman, G. (2010). Tapping into the Power of Big Data: Making Sense of Big Data. In *Proceedings of Price Warehouse Coopers Technology Forecast.* Retrieved December 20, 2015, fromhttp://www.pwc.com/us/en/technology-forcast/2010/issue3/index.html

Halevy, A., Rajaraman, A., & Ordille, J. (2006). Data Integration: The teenage Years. In *Proceedings of the 32nd International Conference on Very Large DataBases (VLDB'06)*, (pp. 9-16). COEX.

Houses of Parliament (HoP) Parliamentary Office of Science and Technology. (2014). *Social Media and Big Data*. Retrieved March 16, 2015 from http://researchbriefings.files.parliament.uk/documents/POST-PN-460/POST-PN-460.pdf

Liebowitz, J. (2013). Big Data Business Analytics. Auerbach Publications. doi:10.1201/b14700

National Archives and Records Administration. (2010). *A Report on Federal Web 2.0 Use and Record Value*. Retrieved September 14, 2015 from http://www.archives.gov/records-mgmt/resources/web2.0-use.pdf

National Archives and Records Administration White Paper. (2013). *A report on Best Practices for the Capture of Social Media Records*. Retrieved January 20, 2015 from http://www.archives.gov/records-mgmt/resources/socialmediacapture.pdf

Price Water Cooper (PWC). (2014). *Deciding with data: How data-driven innovation is fuelling Australia's economic growth*. Retrieved October 20, 2015 from http://www.pwc.com.au/consulting/assets/publications/Data-drive-innovation-Sep14.pdf

Sakr, S., Liu, A., Batista, D. M., & Alomari, M. (2011). A survey of large scale data management approaches in cloud environments. In *Proceedings of IEEE Communications Society Surveys and Tutorials*. Retrieved February 14, 2015 from http://ieeexplore.ieee.org/xpl/tocresult.jsp?isnumber=6065679

Salehi, A. (2010). *Low latency, high performance data stream processing: systems architecture algorithms and implementations*. Saarbrucken: VDM Verlag.

Schmarzo, B., (2013). *Big Data: Understanding How Data Powers Big Business*. John Wiley & Sons P&T.

Shvachko, K., Hairong, K., Radia, S., & Chansler, R. (2010). The Hadoop Distributed File System, *Mass Storage Systems and Technologies (MSST), IEEE 6th Symposium*, (pp.1-10).

Stonebraker, M. (2006). "One Size Fits All": An Idea Whose Time Has Come and Gone. In *Proceedings of the 21st International Conference on Data Engineering*, (pp. 2-11).

Sutter, J. D. (2010). *Texts, maps battle Haiti cholera outbreak.* Retrieved March 15, 2015 from http://www.cnn.com/2010/TECH/innovation/10/29/haiti.cholera.tech

Thusoo, A., Shao, Z., Anthony, S., Borthakur, D., Jain, N., Sen Sharma, J., . . . Liu, H. (2010). Data warehousing and analytics infrastructure at facebook, In *Proceedings of ACM SIGMOD International Conference on Management of Data*, (pp. 1013-1020). doi:10.1145/1807167.1807278

Westerman, D., Spence, P. R., & Heide Van Der, B. (2013). Social media as information source: Recency of updates and credibility of information. *Journal of Computer-Mediated Communication*, *1*(2), 1–14.

KEY TERMS AND DEFINITIONS

Big Data: High-volume, high-velocity and high-variety information assets that demand cost-effective, innovative forms of information processing for enhanced insight and decision making.

Big Data Technologies: Big Data technologies comprises of three major layers: Foundation Layer, Analytics Layer and Application Layer. Big Data Storage and Processing, and Reporting are handled in the Foundation layer, Analytics is handled in the Analytics Layer and the result of Analytics Layer is visualized in Application Layer.

Business Intelligence: An umbrella term that refers to a variety of software applications used to analyse an organization's raw data. BI as a discipline is made up of several related activities, including data mining, online analytical processing, querying and reporting.

Descriptive Analytics: Descriptive analytics depicts what has already happened and is the traditional analytics method.

Hadoop: Hadoop is a whole ecosystem of technologies designed for the storing, processing and analysing of data. The core Hadoop technologies work on the principle of breaking up and distributing data into parts and analysing those parts concurrently thus making it more efficient.

Predictive Analytics: Predictive analytics is the practice of extracting information from existing data sets in order to determine patterns and predict future outcomes and trends and make appropriate decisions.

Prescriptive Analytics: Prescriptive analytics is the practice of suggesting what should happen. Prescriptive analytics is about improving the outcome. It comprises of both descriptive and predictive analytics.

Compilation of References

Abadi, D. J., Carney, D., Cetintemel, U., Cherniack, M., Convey, C., & Lee, S. (2003). Aurora: A new model and architecture for data stream management. *The VLDB Journal*, *12*(2), 120–139. doi:10.1007/s00778-003-0095-z

Abidi, S. S. R., Hussini, S., Sriraj, W., Thienthong, S., & Finley, G. A. (2009). Knowledge sharing for pediatric pain management via a Web 2.0 framework. *Studies in Health Technology and Informatics*, *150*, 287–291. PMID:19745315

Acholonu, R. (2013). Social media and the social behaviour of Caritas University students. In D. Wilson (Ed.), *Communication and the new media in Nigeria: Social engagements, political development and public discourse* (pp. 133–151). Nigeria: Africa Council for Communication Education.

Adams, A., & Sasse, M. A. (1999). Users are not the enemy. *Communications of the ACM*, *42*(12), 40–46. doi:10.1145/322796.322806

Adduci, R., Blue, D., Chiarello, G., Chickering, J., Mavroyiannis, D., Mirchandani, S., . . . Schleier-Smith, J. (2011). *Big Data: Big Opportunities to Create Business Value, Report and recommendations based on discussion with the Leadership Council for Information Advantage*. Retrieved January 15, 2015, from http://www.emc.com/microsites/cio/articles/big-data-big-opportunities

Ahmad, M., Razak, A. H. A., Omar, M., Yasin, A., Romli, R., Mutalib, A. A., & Zahari, A. S. (2015). The Impact of Knowledge Management in Pair Programming on Program Quality. In *Pattern Analysis, Intelligent Security and the Internet of Things*. Springer.

Ahuja, G. (2000). Collaboration networks, structural holes, and innovation: A longitudinal study. *Administrative Science Quarterly*, *45*(3), 425–455. doi:10.2307/2667105

Akbar, H. (2003). Knowledge Levels and their Transformation: Towards the Integration of Knowledge Creation and Individual Learning. *Journal of Management Studies*, *40*(8), 1997–2021. doi:10.1046/j.1467-6486.2003.00409.x

Akerkar, R. (2014). *Big Data Computing*. Boca Raton, FL: CRC Press.

Akinbobola, A. O. (2015). Enhancing transfer of knowledge in physics through effective teaching strategies. *Information and Knowledge Management*, *5*(6), 85-92. Retrieved from http://iiste.org/Journals/index.php/IKM/article/view/23149/23661

Alavi, M., & Leidner, D. E. (1999). Knowledge Management Systems: Issues, Challenges, and Benefits. *Communications of the Association for Information Systems*, *1*(7), 1–37.

Alavi, M., & Leidner, D. E. (2001). Review: Knowledge management and knowledge management systems: Conceptual foundations and research issues. *Management Information Systems Quarterly*, *25*(1), 107–136. doi:10.2307/3250961

Albors, J., Ramos, J. C., & Hervas, J. L. (2008). New Learning Network Paradigms: Communities of Objectives, Crowdsourcing, Wikis and Open-source. *International Journal of Information Management*, *28*(3), 194–202. doi:10.1016/j.ijinfomgt.2007.09.006

Alexander, B. (2006). A new wave of Innovation for Teaching and Learning? *EDUCAUSE Review*, *41*(2), 32–44.

Alexander, B. (2006). Web 2.0: A new wave of innovation for teaching and learning? *EDUCAUSE Review*, *41*(2), 33–44.

Al-Hawamdeh, S. (2003). *Knowledge management*. Oxford, UK: Chandos Publishing. doi:10.1533/9781780631936

Allee, V. (2004). The future of knowledge. *The Learning Organization*, *11*(1), 94–95. doi:10.1108/09696470410515751

Amana, D., & Attah, C. (2014). Social media and security challenges: The relationship between security messaging, believability and social alarm. *International Journal of Media, Security and Development*, *1*(1), 22–30.

Amdocs. (2015). *About Amdocs*. Retrieved June 26, 2015, from: http://www.amdocs.com/about/pages/default.aspx

AMTA. (2009). *Asian Medical Tourism Association (AMTA) Growing Medical Tourism Industry in Asia*. Retrieved March 3, 2010, from http://www.1888pressrelease.com/asian-medical-tourism-association-amta

Anderson, P. (2007). What is Web 2.0? Ideas, technologies and implications for education. *JISC Technology & Standards Watch,* 1-64.

Anderson, C. (2012). *Makers: the new industrial revolution*. New York, NY: Crown Business.

Anderson, S., & Mohan, K. (2011). Social networking in knowledge management. *IT Professional*, *13*(4), 24–28. doi:10.1109/MITP.2011.68

Andreeva, T., & Ikhilchik, I. (2011). Application of the SECI Model of Knowledge Creation in Russian Cultural Context: Theoretical Analysis, Knowledge and Process Management. *Wiley Online Library*, *18*(1), 56–66.

Annual Status of Education Report. (2014). *Annual Status of Education Report (Rural) 2013: Provisional*. New Delhi: ASER Centre.

Antheunis, M. L., Tates, K., & Nieboer, T. E. (2013). Patients' and health professionals' use of social media in health care: Motives, barriers and expectations. *Patient Education and Counseling*, *92*(3), 426–431. doi:10.1016/j.pec.2013.06.020 PMID:23899831

Anthony, A. (2014). *Guest Post: SearchBlox Makes Sense Out of Multiple Data Sources*. Retrieved October 5, 2015, from https://channel9.msdn.com/Blogs/AzurePartner/Guest-Post-SearchBlox-Makes-Sense-Out-of-Multiple-Data-Sources

Aral, S., Brynjolfsson, E., & Van Alstyne, M. W. (2007). *Productivity Effects of Information Diffusion in Networks*. SSRN Electronic Journal. doi:10.2139/ssrn.987499

Aral, S., Dellarocas, C., & Godes, D. (2013). Social media and business transformation: A framework for research. *Information Systems Research*, *24*(1), 3–13. doi:10.1287/isre.1120.0470

Ardichvili, A., Page, V., & Wentling, T. (2003). Motivation and barriers to participation in virtual knowledge-sharing communities practice. *Journal of Knowledge Management*, *7*(1), 64–77. doi:10.1108/13673270310463626

Argyris, C. (1977). Double loop learning in organizations. *Harvard Business Review*, *55*(5), 115–125.

Ashley, P., & Vandenwauver, M. (2013). *Practical Intranet Security: Overview of the State of the Art and Available Technologies*. Springer Publishing Company, Incorporated.

Asur, S., & Huberman, B. A. (2010). Predicting the future with social media.*IEEE/WIC/ACM International Conference on Web Intelligence and Intelligent Agent Technology (WI-IAT)*.

Bacigalupe, G. (2011). Is there a role for social technologies for collaborative healthcare? *Families, Systems & Health*, *29*(1), 1–14. doi:10.1037/a0022093 PMID:21417520

Baker, P. (2015). *Data Divination Big Data Strategies*. Cengage Learning.

Bakker, M., Leenders, R. T. A., Gabbay, S. M., Kratzer, J., & Van Engelen, J. M. (2006). Is trust really social capital? Knowledge sharing in product development projects. *The Learning Organization*, *13*(6), 594–605. doi:10.1108/09696470610705479

Baloglu, S., & Pekcan, Y. A. (2006). The website design and internet site marketing practices of upscale and luxury hotels in Turkey. *Tourism Management*, *27*(1), 171–176. doi:10.1016/j.tourman.2004.07.003

Bandura, A. (1977). *Social learning theory*. Oxford, UK: Prentice-Hall.

Bandyopadhyay, S., Shaw, V., Banergee, A., & Nag, D. (2013). Social Knowledge Management: Use of Social Media for Disseminating Informal Wisdom of Elderly to the Youth. *International Journal of Knowledge. Innovation and Entrepreneurship*, *1*(1-2), 107–115.

Barbera, J. (1996). *The intranet: a new concept for corporate information handling*. Retrieved from http://cat.inist.fr/?aModele=afficheN&cpsidt=2726592

Barczyk, C. C., & Duncan, D. G. (2012). Social Networking Media as a Tool for Teaching International Business. *Journal of Teaching in International Business*, *23*(2), 98–122. doi:10.1080/08975930.2012.718703

Bardhan, A., Bandyopadhyay, S., & Mandal, K. S. (2014). *Redefining the role of elderly as facilitator to educate young generation through Information and Communication Technology*. Paper presented at International Conference on Ageing Well-Social and Managerial Challenges (ICAW), Kochi, Kerala, India. Retrieved from https://facultylive.iimcal.ac.in/sites/facultylive.iimcal.ac.in/files/2-Ageing-IIMC-Paper-final.pdf

Barney, J. (1986). Organizational culture: Can it be a source of sustained competitive advantage? *Academy of Management Review*, *11*(3), 656–665. doi:10.5465/AMR.1986.4306261

Barrons, G. (2012). Suleiman: Mubarak decided to step down #egypt #jan25 oh my God': examining the use of social media in the 2011 Egyptian revolution. *Contemporary Arab Affairs (London, England)*, *5*(1), 54–67.

Barrowman, R. A., Grubor, D., & Chandu, A. (2010). Dental Implant Tourism. *Australian Dental Journal*, *55*(4), 441–445. doi:10.1111/j.1834-7819.2010.01267.x PMID:21133945

Barsky, E., & Purdon, M. (2006). Introducing Web 2.0: Social networking and social bookmarking for health librarians. *Journal of the Canadian Health Libraries Association*, *27*(3), 65–67. doi:10.5596/c06-024

Bartol, K. M., & Locke, E. A. (2000). Incentives and motivation. In S. Rynes & B. Gerhardt (Eds.), *Compensation in organizations: Progress and prospects*. San Francisco: Lexington Press.

Bartol, K. M., & Srivastava, A. (2002). Encouraging knowledge sharing: The role of organizational reward system. *Journal of Leadership & Organizational Studies*, *9*(1), 64–76. doi:10.1177/107179190200900105

Barzilai-Nahon, K. (2005). Network Gatekeeping Theory. In K. E. Fisher, S. Erdelez, & L. McKechnie (Eds.), *Theories of information behavior* (pp. 247–254). American Society of Information Science and Technology.

Baskerville, R., & Dulipovici, A. (2006). The Theoretical Foundations of Knowledge management. *Knowledge Management Research & Practice*, *4*(2), 8M–105. doi:10.1057/palgrave.kmrp.8500090

Bassett, C. (2009). Elder Wisdom. *Second Journey.* Retrieved February 15, 2015, from http://www.secondjourney.org/itin/09_Fall/Bassett_09Fall.htm

Bastian, M., Hayes, M., Vaughan, W., Shah, S., Skomoroch, P., & Kim, H., … Lloyd, C. (2014). LinkedIn skills. In *Proceedings of the 8th ACM Conference on Recommender systems - RecSys '14* (pp. 1–8). New York: ACM Press. doi:10.1145/2645710.2645729

Beesley, L. (2003). The challenge of emotion management in cooperative tourism research settings. In CAUTHE 2003: Riding the Wave of Tourism and Hospitality Research (85-106). Lismore, N.S.W.: Southern Cross University.

Beesley, L. G., & Cooper, C. (2008). Defining knowledge management (KM) activities: Towards consensus. *Journal of Knowledge Management*, *12*(3), 48–62. doi:10.1108/13673270810875859

Bellmore, M. (2013, March 3). Working Together to get the job done. *New Haven Register*, p. B1.

Benbasat, I., Goldstein, D. K., & Mead, M. (1987). The case research strategy in studies of information systems. *Management Information Systems Quarterly*, *11*(3), 369–386. doi:10.2307/248684

Benckendorff, P. J., & Black, N. L. (2000). Destination marketing on the internet. A case study of Australian regional tourism authorities. *The Journal of Tourism Studies*, *11*(1), 11–21.

Benkler, Y., & Nissenbaum, H. (2006). Commons-based peer production and virtue. *Journal of Political Philosophy*, *14*(4), 394–419. doi:10.1111/j.1467-9760.2006.00235.x

Bennett, E. (n.d.). *Hospital Social Network Data & Charts.* Retrieved May 02, 2015 from http://ebennett.org/hsnl/data

Bennett, R., & Gabriel, H. (1999). Organisational factors & knowledge management within large marketing departments: An empirical study. *Journal of Knowledge Management*, *3*(3), 212–225. doi:10.1108/13673279910288707

Berger, P. L., & Luckmann, T. (1966). *The Social Construction of Reality: A Treatise in the Sociology of Knowledge.* London: Penguin Books.

Berners-Lee, T., Cailliau, R., Loutonen, A., Nielsen, H. F., & Secret, A. (1994). The world-wide web. *Communications of the ACM*, *37*(8), 76–82. doi:10.1145/179606.179671

Bernhardt. J. M., Mays D., & Kreuter, M. W. (2011). Dissemination 2.0: Closing the gap between knowledge and practice with new media and marketing. *Journal of Health Communication*, *16*(Sup1), 32-44.

Best, R. A., Jr. (2011). *Intelligence Information: Need-to-know vs. Need-to-share.* CRS Report for Congress R41848. Retrieved June 26, 2015, from: https://www.fas.org/sgp/crs/intel/R41848.pdf

Bharati, P., Zhang, W., & Chaudhury, A. (2015). *Better knowledge with social media? Exploring the roles of social capital and organizational knowledge management.* Management Science and Information Systems Faculty Publication Series *Paper*, *48*, 1–40.

Bhasin, R. (Frankfurt Airport Innovation and Knowledge Management Executive) (2015). Private communication.

Bhaskar, R. (1998). *The possibility of naturalism: A philosophical critique of the contemporary human sciences* (3rd ed.). London: Routledge.

Bhaskar, R. (2008). *A Realist Theory of Science* (2nd ed.). London: Verso.

Bhatt, G. D., Pankaj, P., & Rodger, J. A. (2014). Managing Knowledge in Shared Spaces. *Intelligent Information Management.*

Bhatt, G. D. (2001). Knowledge management in organizations: Examining the interaction between technologies, techniques, and people. *Journal of Knowledge Management*, *5*(1), 68–75. doi:10.1108/13673270110384419

Bhatt, G. D. (2002). Management strategies for individual knowledge and organizational knowledge. *Journal of Knowledge Management*, *6*(1), 31–39. doi:10.1108/13673270210417673

Bies, W., & Zacharia, L. (2007). Medical tourism: Outsourcing surgery. *Mathematical and Computer Modelling*, *46*(7-8), 1144–1159. doi:10.1016/j.mcm.2007.03.027

Biloslavo, R., & Zornada, M. (n.d.). *Development of a knowledge management framework within the systems context.* Retrieved August 15, 2015, from http://www2.warwick.ac.uk/fac/soc/wbs/conf/olkc/archive/oklc5/papers/h-3_biloslavo.pdf

Biocic, B., Tomic, D., & Ogrizovic, D. (2011). Economies of Cloud Computing, In *Proceedings of the 34th International Convention on Information and Communication technology, electronics and microelectronics (MIPRO'11)*, (pp.1438-1442).

Bloom, N., Garicano, L., Sadun, R., & Van Reenen, J. (2014). The distinct effects of information technology and communication technology on firm organization. *Management Science*, *60*(12), 2859–2885. doi:10.1287/mnsc.2014.2013

Bloomstein, M. (2012). *Content Strategy at Work: Real-world Stories to Strengthen Every Interactive Project*. Academic Press.

Bock, G. W., Zmud, R. W., Kim, Y. G., & Lee, J. N. (2005). Behavioral Intention Formation in Knowledge Sharing: Examining the Roles of Extrinsic Motivators, Social-Psychological Forces, and Organizational Climate. *Management Information Systems Quarterly*, *29*(1), 87–111.

Bode, L., & Dalrymple, K. E. (2014). Politics in 140 Characters or Less: Campaign Communication, Network Interaction, and Political Participation on Twitter. *Journal of Political Marketing*. doi:10.1080/15377857.2014.959686

Bodhanya, S. (2008). Knowledge Management: From Management Fad to Systemic Change. In E. Abou-Zeid (Ed.), *Knowledge Management and Business Strategies* (pp. 1–26). Hershey, PA: Information Science Reference. doi:10.4018/978-1-59904-486-6.ch001

Bodner, G. M. (1986). Constructivism: A Theory of Knowledge. *Journal of Chemical Education*, *63*(10), 873–878. doi:10.1021/cd063p873

Boff, E., Santos, E. R., & Vicari, R. M. (2006). *Social Agents to Improve Collaboration on an Educational Portal.* Academic Press.

Bolisani, E., Scarso, E., & Giuman, L. (2014). Wiki as a Knowledge Management System in a Small Project-Based Company: Benefits, Issues and Managerial Challenges. In *Proceedings of the 15th European Conference on Knowledge Management ECKM 2014*.

Bonk, C. J. (2009). *The World Is Open: How Web Technology Is Revolutionizing Education* (1st ed.). San Francisco, CA: JosseyBass, a Wiley Imprint.

Bonson, E., & Flores, F. (2011). Social media and corporate dialogue: The response of the global financial institutions. *Online Information Review*, *35*(1), 34–49. doi:10.1108/14684521111113579

Bookman, M. Z., & Bookman, K. R. (2007). *Medical Tourism in Developing Countries*. New York: Palgrave Macmillan. doi:10.1057/9780230605657

Borgatti, S. P., & Foster, P. C. (2003). The network paradigm in organizational research: A review and typology. *Journal of Management*, *29*(6), 991–1013. doi:10.1016/S0149-2063(03)00087-4

Bosslet, G. T., Torke, A. M., Hickman, S. E., Terry, C. L., & Helft, P. R. (2011). The patient-doctor relationship and online social networks: Results of a national survey. *Journal of General Internal Medicine*, *26*(10), 1168–1174. doi:10.1007/s11606-011-1761-2 PMID:21706268

Bouck, W. (2014). *The Information Economy: A Study of Five Industries*. Academic Press.

Bourdieu, P., & Wacquant, J. D. (1992). *An Invitation to Reflective Sociology*. Chicago: The University of Chicago Press.

Bowley, R. C. (2009). *A comparative case study: Examining the organizational use of social networking sites*. Hamilton: The University of Waikato.

Boyd, D. M., & Ellison, N. B. (2007). Social network sites: Definition, history, and scholarship. *Journal of Computer-Mediated Communication*, *13*(1), 210–230. doi:10.1111/j.1083-6101.2007.00393.x

Boyd, D., & Ellison, N. (2008). Social Network Sites: Definition, History, and Scholarship. *Journal of Computer-Mediated Communication*, 13.

Bradley, A. J., & McDonald, M. P. (2011a). Social Media versus Knowledge Management. *HBR Blog Network, Harvard Business Review*. Retrieved from http://blogs.hbr.org/cs/2011/10/social_media_versus_knowledge.html

Bradley, A. J., & McDonald, M. P. (2011b). *The Social Organization: How to Use Social Media to Tap the Collective Genius of Your Customers and Employees*. Harvard Business Review Press.

Bradley, A., & McDonald, M. (2011). *The Social Organization*. Boston: Harvard Business Review Press.

Brady, S. L., Mohaupt, T. H., & Kaufman, R. A. (2015). JOURNAL CLUB: A Comprehensive Risk Assessment Method for Pediatric Patients Undergoing Research Examinations Using Ionizing Radiation: How We Answered the Institutional Review Board. *American Journal of Roentgenology*, *204*(5), W510–8. doi:10.2214/AJR.14.13892 PMID:25905957

Bramwell, B., & Sharman, A. (1999). Collaboration in the local tourism policy making. *Annals of Tourism Research*, *26*(2), 392–415. doi:10.1016/S0160-7383(98)00105-4

Brauner, E., & Becker, A. (2006). Beyond knowledge sharing: The management of transactive knowledge systems. *Knowledge and Process Management*, *13*(1), 62–71. doi:10.1002/kpm.240

Briones, R. L., Kuch, B., Liu, B. F., & Jin, Y. (2011). Keeping up with the digital age: How the American Red Cross uses social media to build relationships. *Public Relations Review*, *37*(1), 37–43. doi:10.1016/j.pubrev.2010.12.006

Brodie, M., Hamel, E., & Altman, D. (2003). Health news and the American public,1996-2002. *Journal of Health Politics, Policy and Law*, *28*(5), 927–950. doi:10.1215/03616878-28-5-927 PMID:14604217

Brotman, B. A. (2010). Medical Tourism Private Hospitals: Focus India. *Journal of Health Care Finance*, *37*(1), 45–50. PMID:20973373

Brown, J. S., & Adler, R. P. (2008). Minds on fire: Open education, the Long Tail, and Learning 2.0. *EDUCAUSE Review*, *43*(1), 16–32.

Brownson, S. (2009). *A study of the integration of wikis and blogs into an online course on student interaction and satisfaction* (Doctoral dissertation). Retrieved from Dissertations & Theses: Full Text. (Publication No. AAT 3371718)

Bruges Communiqué. (2010). Review the strategic approach and priorities of the Copenhagen process for 2011-2020. The European Social Partners and the European Commission, Communiqué of the European Ministers for Vocational Education and Training, Bruges.

Bruni, L., Francalanci, C., & Giacomazzi, P. (2012). The Role of Multimedia Content in Determining the Virality of Social Media Information. *Information*, *3*(4), 278–289. doi:10.3390/info3030278

Bryman, A. (2008). *Social Research Methods* (3rd ed.). Oxford, UK: Oxford University Press.

Brzozowski, M. J. (2009). WaterCooler: Exploring an organization through enterprise social media. In *Proceedings of the ACM 2009 International Conference on Supporting Group Work* (pp. 219–228). New York: ACM Press. doi:10.1145/1531674.1531706

Brzozowski, M. J., Sandholm, T., & Hogg, T. (2009). Effects of feedback and peer pressure on contributions to enterprise social media. In *Proceedings of the ACM 2009 international conference on Supporting group work* (pp. 61-70). ACM. doi:10.1145/1531674.1531684

Buckman, R. H. (2004). *Building a Knowledge-Driven Organization*. McGraw-Hill. Retrieved from http://www.who.int/kms/resources/Building_a_knowledge_driven_organization_bookreview.pdf

Budnick, L. (1996). *Official Build a NetScape Intranet*. Ventana Communications Group, Incorporated.

Bughin, J., & Chui, M. (2010). The Rise of the Networked Enterprise: Web 2.0 Finds its Payday. *The McKinsey Quarterly*, *4*, 3–8.

Bukowitz, W. R., & Williams, R. L. (1999). *The Knowledge Management Field Book*. Financial Times Prentice Hall.

Bukowitz, W., & Williams, R. (2000). *The Knowledge management fieldbook*. London, UK: Prentice-Hall.

Burkhardt, A. (2010). Social media: A guide for college and university libraries. *College & Research Libraries News*, *71*(1), 10–24.

Burt, R. S. (1992). *Structural holes: The social structure of competition*. Cambridge, MA: Harvard University Press.

Busby, R., & Cronshaw, S. (2015). Political Branding: The Tea Party and Its Use of Participation Branding. *Journal of Political Marketing*, *14*(1-2), 96–110. doi:10.1080/15377857.2014.990850

Butler-Kisber, L. (2010). *Qualitative Inquiry: Thematic, Narrative and Arts- Informed Perspectives*. London: Sage Publications Ltd.

Butler, P., & Collins, N. (1994). Political Marketing: Structure and Process. *European Journal of Marketing*, *28*(1), 19–34. doi:10.1108/03090569410049154

Butler, P., & Collins, N. (1999). A Conceptual Framework for Political Marketing. In B. I. Newman (Ed.), *Handbook of Political Marketing* (pp. 55–72). Thousand Oaks, CA: Sage Publications.

Butler, P., & Harris, P. (2009). Considerations on the evolution of political marketing theory. *Marketing Theory*, *9*(2), 149–164. doi:10.1177/1470593109103022

Cabrera, A., Collins, W. C., & Salgado, J. F. (2006). Determinants of individual engagement in knowledge sharing. *International Journal of Human Resource Management*, *17*(2), 245–264. doi:10.1080/09585190500404614

Cameron, M. P., Barrett, P., & Stewardson, B. (2014). Can Social Media Predict Election Results? Evidence From New Zealand. *Journal of Political Marketing*, 1–17. doi:10.1080/15377857.2014.959690

Carver, C. S., & Scheier, M. F. (1982). Control theory: A useful conceptual framework for personality–social, clinical, and health psychology. *Psychological Bulletin*, *92*(1), 111–135. doi:10.1037/0033-2909.92.1.111 PMID:7134324

Castells, M. (2011). *The rise of the network society: The information age: Economy, society, and culture* (Vol. 1). New York: John Wiley & Sons.

Chalkiti, K., & Sigala, M. (2008). Information sharing and knowledge creation in online forum: The case of Greek Online Forum "Dialougoi". *Current Issues in Tourism*, *11*(5), 381–406. doi:10.1080/13683500802316006

Chamberlain, A., Schraefel, m. C., Poole, E., Munson, S., Danis, C., & Churchill, E. (2015). Moving Beyond e-Health and the Quantified Self. In *Proceedings of the 18th ACM Conference Companion on Computer Supported Cooperative Work & Social Computing - CSCW'15 Companion* (pp. 273–276). New York: ACM Press. doi:10.1145/2685553.2685555

Chang, L.-E., & Lin, S.-P. (2011). Newcomers' Socialization by Intranet System. In *2011 10th IEEE/ACIS International Conference on Computer and Information Science* (pp. 239–243). IEEE. doi:10.1109/ICIS.2011.45

Change Foundation. (2011). *Using social media to improve healthcare quality*. Retrieved, May 12, 2012, from https://www.changefoundation.ca/docs/socialmediatoolkit.pdf

Chan, I., & Chao, C. (2008). Knowledge management in small and medium-sized enterprises. *Communications of the ACM*, *51*(4), 83–88. doi:10.1145/1330311.1330328

Chan, R. C. H., Chu, S. K. W., Lee, C. W. Y., Chan, B. K. T., & Leung, C. K. (2013). Knowledge management using social media: A comparative study between blogs and Facebook.*Proceedings of the ASIS&T 2013 Annual Meeting*. doi:10.1002/meet.14505001069

Charnigo, L., & Barnett-Ellis, P. (2007). Checking Out Facebook.com: The Impact of a Digital Trend on Academic Libraries. *Information Technology & Libraries*, *26*(1), 23–34.

Chaves, M. A., & Cordoba, E. R. (2014). Deciphering event logs in SharePoint Server: A methodology based on process mining. In *2014 XL Latin American Computing Conference (CLEI)* (pp. 1–12). IEEE. doi:10.1109/CLEI.2014.6965174

Chen, C. J., & Huang, J. W. (2009). Strategic human resource practices and innovation performance—The mediating role of knowledge management capacity. *Journal of Business Research*, *62*(1), 104–114. doi:10.1016/j.jbusres.2007.11.016

Cheng, E. C. (2015). Knowledge Management for School Development. In Knowledge Management for School Education. Springer Singapore.

Chen, J., & Liu, Q. (2013). Information Markets, Product Markets and Vertical Merger. *Journal of Economics and Finance*, *37*(1), 33–61. doi:10.1007/s12197-010-9169-0

Chiu, C. M., Hsu, M. H., & Wang, E. T. (2006). Understanding knowledge sharing in virtual communities: An integration of social capital and social cognitive theories. *Decision Support Systems*, *42*(3), 1872–1888. doi:10.1016/j.dss.2006.04.001

Choi, S., Lehto, X. Y., & Morrison, A. M. (2007). Destination image representation on the web: Content analysis of Macau travel related websites. *Tourism Management*, *28*(1), 118–129. doi:10.1016/j.tourman.2006.03.002

Choo, C. (1998). *The Knowing Organization: How Organizations Use Information for Construct Meaning, Create Knowledge and Make Decision*. New York: Oxford Press.

Choo, C. W. (2006). *The knowing organization: How organizations use information to construct meaning, create knowledge, and make decisions* (2nd ed.). New York: Oxford University Press.

Chou, W. S., Hunt, Y. M., Burke, B. D., Moser, R. P., & Hesse, B. W. (2009). Social media use in the United States: Implications for health communications. *Journal of Medical Internet Research*, *11*(4), e48. doi:10.2196/jmir.1249 PMID:19945947

Chretien, K. C., Azar, J., & Kind, T. (2011). Physicians on Twitter. *Journal of the American Medical Association*, *305*(6), 566–568. doi:10.1001/jama.2011.68 PMID:21304081

Christenson, D. P., & Smidt, C. D. (2011). Riding the Waves of Money: Contribution Dynamics in the 2008 Presidential Nomination Campaign. *Journal of Political Marketing*, *10*(1-2), 1–2, 4–26. doi:10.1080/15377857.2011.540189

Chu, S.K.W. & Du, H. (2013). Social Networking Tools for Academic Libraries. *Journal of Librarianship & Information Science*, *45*(1), 64-75.

Chua, A. Y. K., & Banerjee, S. (2013). Customer knowledge management via social media: The case of Starbucks. *Journal of Knowledge Management*, *17*(2), 237–249. doi:10.1108/13673271311315196

Chugh, R. (2012). Social Networking for Business: Is it a Boon or Banes?. In Handbook of Research on Business Social Networking: Organizational, Managerial, and Technological Dimensions. IGI Global.

Chugh, R. (2012). Social networking for businesses: Is it a boon or bane? In M. M. Cruz-Cunha, G. D. Ptnik, N. Lopes, P. Goncalves, & E. Miranda (Eds.), Handbook of Research on Business Social Networking: Organizational, Managerial, and Technological Dimensions. Hershey, PA: IGI Global. Retrieved from http://www.researchgate.net/publication/275771610_Social_Networking_for_Businesses_Is_it_a_Boon_or_Bane

Chugh, R., Wibowo, S., & Grandhi, S. (2015). Mandating the transfer of tacit knowledge in Australian Universities. *Journal of Organizational Knowledge Management*. Retrieved from http://www.ibimapublishing.com/journals/JOKM/2015/297669/297669.pdf

Chugh, R. (2012). Knowledge sharing with enhanced learning and development opportunities.*IEEE International Conference on Information Retrieval and Knowledge Management*. doi:10.1109/InfRKM.2012.6205014

Chugh, R. (2012). Social networking for business: Is it a boob or bane? In Cruz-Cunha et al. (Eds.), *Handbook on Research on business Social networking: Organisational, managerial, and Technological dimensions*. Hershey, PA: IGI Global. doi:10.4018/978-1-61350-168-9.ch032

Chugh, R. (2013). Workplace dimensions: Tacit knowledge sharing in universities. *Journal of Advanced Management Science*, *1*(1), 24–28. doi:10.12720/joams.1.1.24-28

Chugh, R., Wibowo, S., & Grandi, S. (2015). Mandating the Transfer of Tacit Knowledge in Australian Universities. *Journal of Organizational Knowledge Management*, *2015*, 297669. doi:10.5171/2015.297669

Chu, M., & Nalani-Meulemans, Y. (2008). The Problems and Potential of MySpace and Facebook Usage in Academic Libraries. *Internet Reference Services Quarterly*, *13*(1), 69–85. doi:10.1300/J136v13n01_04

Churchill, D. (2007). Web 2.0 and possibilities for educational applications. *Educational Technology*, *47*(2), 24–29.

Chu, S. K. W., & Kennedy, D. (2011). Using online collaborative tools for groups to co-construct knowledge. *Online Information Review*, *35*(4), 581–597. doi:10.1108/14684521111161945

Clapper, J. (2012). *Information Sharing*. Speech in the Center for Strategic and International Studies (CSIS). Retrieved June 26, 2015, from: https://csis.org/files/attachments/120126_info_sharing_clapper_transcript.pdf

Clarke, T. (2001). The Knowledge Economy. *Journal of Education and Training*, *43*(5), 189–196. doi:10.1108/00400910110399184

Cline, R. J. W., & Haynes, K. M. (2011). Consumer health information seeking on the internet: The state of the art. *Health Education Research*, *16*(6), 671–692. doi:10.1093/her/16.6.671 PMID:11780707

Cogburn, D. L., & Espinoza-Vasquez, F. K. (2011). From Networked Nominee to Networked Nation: Examining the Impact of Web 2.0 and Social Media on Political Participation and Civic Engagement in the 2008 Obama Campaign. *Journal of Political Marketing*, *10*(1-2), 1–2, 189–213. doi:10.1080/15377857.2011.540224

Cohen, D. (2006). What's Your Return on Knowledge? *Harvard Business Review*, *84*(12), 28. PMID:16649692

Cohen, J. F., & Olsen, K. (2015). Knowledge Management Capabilities and Firm Performance: A Test of Universalistic, Contingency and Complementarity Perspectives. *Expert Systems with Applications*, *42*(3), 1178–1188. doi:10.1016/j.eswa.2014.09.002

Collins, N., & Butler, P. (1996). Positioning Political Parties: A Market Analysis. *The Harvard International Journal of Press/Politics*, *1*(2), 63–77. doi:10.1177/1081180X96001002006

Compeau, D., Higgins, C. A., & Huff, S. (1999). Social cognitive theory and individual reactions to computing technology: A longitudinal study. *Management Information Systems Quarterly*, *23*(2), 145–158. doi:10.2307/249749

ConnectingPeople. (2010). *Digital Learning Platforms, Research Series Paper No. 2, Education Policy and Research Division*. Research and Innovation Department of Education and Early Childhood Development Melbourne.

Connell, J. (2006). Medical Tourism: Sea, Sun, Sand and … Surgery. *Tourism Management*, *26*(6), 1093–1100. doi:10.1016/j.tourman.2005.11.005

Connell, J. (2013). Contemporary medical tourism: Conceptialisation, culture and commodification. *Tourism Management*, *34*, 1–13. doi:10.1016/j.tourman.2012.05.009

Connell, R. S. (2009). Academic Libraries, Facebook and MySpace, and Student Outreach: A Survey of Student Opinion. P*ortal. Libraries & the Academy*, *9*(1), 25–36. doi:10.1353/pla.0.0036

Cook, N. (2008). *Enterprise 2.0: How Social Software Will Change the Future of Work*. London: Gower Publishing, Ltd.

Cook, T. D., & Campbell, D. T. (1979). *Quasi-Experimental Design: Design and Analysis Issues for Field Settings*. Skokie, IL: Rand McNally.

Cordano, D. (2015). The conflict between Al-Shabaab and the Federal Government of Somalia. *Bradbury's Global Risk Partners*. Retrieved September October 10, 2015, from http://www.bradburys.co.uk/wp-content/uploads/2015/01/The-conflict-between-al-Shabaab-and-the-Federal-Government-of-Somalia.pdf

Cormany, D., & Baloglu, S. (2011). Medical travel facilitator websites: An exploratory study of web page contents and services offered to the prospective medical tourist. *Tourism Management*, *32*(4), 709–716. doi:10.1016/j.tourman.2010.02.008

Corneli, J., & Mikroyannidis, A. (2012). Crowdsourcing education on the Web: a role-based analysis of online learning communities. In A. Okada, T. Connolly, & P. Scott (Eds.), *Collaborative Learning 2.0: Open Educational Resources* (pp. 272–286). Hershey, PA: IGI Global. doi:10.4018/978-1-4666-0300-4.ch015

Counsell, J. (2012). Beyond Level 2 BIM, Web Portals and Collaboration Tools. In *2012 16th International Conference on Information Visualisation* (pp. 510–515). IEEE. doi:10.1109/IV.2012.88

Cress, U., & Kimmerle, J. (2008). A Systemic and Cognitive View on Collaborative Knowledge Building with Wikis. *International Journal of Computer-Supported Collaborative Learning*, *3*(2), 105–122. doi:10.1007/s11412-007-9035-z

Creswell, J. W. (2013). Qualitative Inquiry and Research Design: Choosing Among Five Approaches (3rd ed.). Sage Publications.

Creswell, J. W., & Plano Clark, V. L. (2007). *Designing and Conducting Mixed Methods Research*. Thousand Oaks, CA: Sage.

Creswell, J. W., & Tashakkori, A. (2007). Editorial: Differing Perspectives on Mixed Methods Research. *Journal of Mixed Methods Research*, *1*(4), 303–308. doi:10.1177/1558689807306132

Crooks, V. A., Kingsbury, P., Snyder, J., & Johnston, R. (2010). What is known about patients experience of medical tourism? A scoping review. *BMC Health Services Research*, *10*(1), 266. doi:10.1186/1472-6963-10-266 PMID:20825667

Crooks, V. A., Turner, L., Snyder, J., Johnston, R., & Kingsbury, P. (2011). Promoting medical tourism in India: Messages, images, and the marketing of international patient travel. *Social Science & Medicine*, *72*(5), 726–732. doi:10.1016/j.socscimed.2010.12.022 PMID:21310519

Crossler, R. E., Johnston, A. C., Lowry, P. B., Hu, Q., Warkentin, M., & Baskerville, R. (2013). Future directions for behavioral information security research. *Computers & Security*, *32*, 90–101. doi:10.1016/j.cose.2012.09.010

Cross, R., Borgatti, S. P., & Parker, A. (2002). Making invisible work visible: Using social network analysis to support strategic collaboration. *California Management Review*, *44*(2), 25–46. doi:10.2307/41166121

Croteau, A., & Dfouni, M. (2008). Knowledge Management Leaders' Top Issues. In E. Abou-Zeid (Ed.), *Knowledge Management and Business Strategies* (pp. 47–68). Hershey, PA: Information Science Reference. doi:10.4018/978-1-59904-486-6.ch003

Curca, M. (2013). The peace process will not be re-tweeted. *The Peace Journalist*, *1*(2), 10–11.

Curtin, G.G., Sommer, M.H., & Vis-Sommer, V. (2003) The World of E-Government. *Journal of Political Marketing,* *2*(3-4), 1-16. DOI: 10.1300/J199v02n03_01

Curtin, G. G., & Sommer, M. (2003). Is the Campaign Web Site Really "Dead"? *Journal of Political Marketing*, *2*(1), 107–111. doi:10.1300/J199v02n01_07

Curtin, G., McConnachie, R., Sommer, M., & Vis-Sommer, V. (2002). American E-Government at the Crossroads. *Journal of Political Marketing*, *1*(1), 149–191. doi:10.1300/J199v01n01_08

Cusumano, M. (2010). Cloud Computing and SaaS as New Computing Platforms. In Proceedings of Communications of the Association for Computing Machinery (ACM'10), (vol. 53, pp. 27-29). doi:10.1145/1721654.1721667

Dabbagh, N., & Kitsantas, A. (2012). Personal Learning Environments, social media, and self-regulated learning: A natural formula for connecting formal and informal learning. *The Internet and Higher Education*, *15*(1), 3–8. doi:10.1016/j.iheduc.2011.06.002

Dabbish, L., Stuart, C., Tsay, J., & Herbsleb, J. (2013). Leveraging Transparency. *IEEE Software*, *30*(1), 37–43. doi:10.1109/MS.2012.172

Daft, R. L., & Lengel, R. H. (1986). Organizational information requirements, media richness and structural design. *Management Science*, *32*(5), 554–571. doi:10.1287/mnsc.32.5.554

Dahlstom, E. (2012). *Study of Undregraduate students and Information Technology 2012 (Research Report).* Luiosville, CO: EDUCAUSE.

Dalkir, K. (2005). *Knowledge management in theory and practice*. Boston: Routledge.

Dalkir, K. (2011). *Knowledge Management in Theory and Practice*. Cambridge, UK: The MIT Press.

Danis, C., & Singer, D. (2008). A wiki instance in the enterprise. In *Proceedings of the ACM 2008 conference on Computer supported cooperative work - CSCW '08* (p. 495). New York: ACM Press. doi:10.1145/1460563.1460642

Darroch, J. (2005). Knowledge Management, Innovation and Firm Performance. *Journal of Knowledge Management*, *9*(3), 101–115. doi:10.1108/13673270510602809

Das, S. (2013). *Elements of knowledge management*. Retrieved September 15, 2015, from http://knowmgt.blogspot.com/2013/07/elements-of-knowledge-management.html

Das, S., Kim, H. J., Dabbish, L. A., & Hong, J. I. (2014, July). The effect of social influence on security sensitivity. In *Proc. SOUPS* (Vol. 14).

Data. (n.d.). In *Business Dictionary online*. Retrieved from http://www.businessdictionary.com/ definition/data.html

Davenport, T. H. (1994). Saving IT's Soul: Human Centred Information Management. *Harvard Business Review*, *72*(2), 119-131.

Davenport, T. H., & Prusak, L. (1998). *Working Knowledge: How Organizations Manage What They Know*. Boston: Harvard Business School Press.

Davenport, T., De Long, D., & Beers, M. (1998). Successful Knowledge Management Projects. *Sloan Management Review*.

Davies, A. (2013). Four key elements of successful knowledge management. *Ntegra, Newbury*. Retrieved September 10, 2015, from http://ntegra.com/blog/2013/01/16/four-elements-for-successful-knowledge-management/

Davila, T. M., Epstein, J., & Shelton, R. (2006). *Making Innovation Work: How to Manage It, Measure It, and Profit from It*. Upper Saddle River, NJ: Wharton School Publishing.

Davis, F. D. (1989). Perceived usefulness, perceived ease of use and user acceptance of information technology. *Management Information Systems Quarterly*, *13*(3), 319–339. doi:10.2307/249008

De Geus, A. P. (1988). Planning as learning. *Harvard Business Review*, *66*(2), 70–74.

Delmonicao, F. L. (2009). The implications of Istanbul Declaration on organ trafficking and transplant tourism. *Current Opinion in Organ Transplantation*, *14*(2), 116–119. doi:10.1097/MOT.0b013e32832917c9 PMID:19300258

Deloitte. (2010). *Social Networks in Health Care: communication, collaboration and insights*. Delight Centre for Health Solutions.

DeMatteis, P., & Brown, J. (2008). *Tabletop Exercises: Cost Effective*. Verifiable, Practical.

Demertzis, N., Diamantaki, K., Gazi, A., & Sartzetakis, N. (2005). Greek Political Marketing Online. *Journal of Political Marketing*, *4*(1), 51–74. doi:10.1300/J199v04n01_04

Den Hooff, V. B., & De Ridder, J. (2004). Knowledge sharing in context: The influence of organizational commitment, communication climate and CMC use on knowledge sharing. *Journal of Knowledge Management*, *8*(6), 117–130. doi:10.1108/13673270410567675

Deutsche Gesellschaft für Internationale Zusammenarbeit (GIZ Report). (2014). *The BoP Education Entrepreneurship Ecosystem in India*. Retrieved from http://responsiblebusinessindia.com/downloads/bop-education-entrepreneurship-ecosystem-india/

Dewett, T., & Jones, G. R. (2001). The Role of Information Technology in the Organization: A Review, Model, and Assessment. *Journal of Management*, *27*(3), 313–346. doi:10.1177/014920630102700306

DiGioia, P., & Dourish, P. (2005, July). Social navigation as a model for usable security. In *Proceedings of the 2005 symposium on Usable privacy and security* (pp. 101-108). ACM. doi:10.1145/1073001.1073011

Dignum, S., Kruschwitz, U., Fasli, M., Kim, Y., Song, D., Beresi, U. C., & de Roeck, A. (2010). Incorporating Seasonality into Search Suggestions Derived from Intranet Query Logs. In *2010 IEEE/WIC/ACM International Conference on Web Intelligence and Intelligent Agent Technology* (Vol. 1, pp. 425–430). IEEE. doi:10.1109/WI-IAT.2010.258

Dillon, A., & Gabbard, R. (1998). Hypermedia as an educational technology: A review of the quantitative research literature on learner comprehension, control, and style. *Review of Educational Research*, *68*(3), 322–349. doi:10.3102/00346543068003322

DiMicco, J. M., & Millen, D. R. (2007). Identity management: Multiple presentations of self in Facebook. In *Proceedings of the ACM 2007 International Conference on Supporting Group Work* (pp. 383–386.). New York: ACM Press. doi:10.1145/1316624.1316682

DiMicco, J., Millen, D. R., Geyer, W., Dugan, C., Brownholtz, B., & Muller, M. (2008). Motivations for social networking at work.*Proceedings of CSCW'08*.

Dlodlo, N., & Dhurup, M. (2013). Examining social media dimensions among a cohort of generation Y consumers in South Africa. *Mediterranean Journal of Social Sciences*, *4*(14), 329–338.

Dong, Y., Tang, J., Chawla, N. V., Lou, T., Yang, Y., & Wang, B. (2015). Inferring social status and rich club effects in enterprise communication networks. *PLoS ONE*, *10*(3), e0119446. doi:10.1371/journal.pone.0119446 PMID:25822343

Downes, S. (2005). *Elearning 2.0.* Retrieved from http://www.elearnmag.org/subpage.cfm?article=291&section=articles

Downes, S. (2005). An introduction to connective knowledge. In T. Hug (Ed.), *Media, Knowledge & Education - Exploring new Spaces, Relations and Dynamics in Digital Media Ecologies*. Innsbruck, Austria: Innsbruck University Press.

Dretske, F. (1981). *Knowledge and the Flow of Information*. Cambridge, MA: MIT Press.

Dreze, J., & Sen, A. (2013). *An Uncertain Glory – India and Its Contradictions*. Penguin.

Driscoll, M. (2005). *Psychology of learning for instruction*. Needham Heights, MA: Allyn & Bacon.

Dron, J. (2012). Self-paced and Social. In T. Bastiaens, & G. Marks (Eds.), *Proceedings of World Conference on E-Learning in Corporate, Government, Healthcare, and Higher Education 2012* (p. 962-976). Chesapeake, VA: AACE.

Dron, J., & Anderson, T. (2009). How the Crowd Can Teach. In S. Hatzipanagos & S. Wartburton (Eds.), *Handbook of Research on Social Software and Developing Community Ontologies* (pp. 1–17). Hershey, PA: Information Science Reference. doi:10.4018/978-1-60566-208-4.ch001

Drucker, P. (1988). The coming of the new organization. In *Harvard Business Review on Knowledge Management* (pp. 3–11). Boston, MA: Harvard Business School Press.

Drucker, P. (1989). *The new realities: in government and politics, in economics and business, in society and world view*. New York, NY: Harper & Row.

Drucker, P. (1993). *Post-capitalist Society*. Oxford, UK: Butterworth-Heinemann.

Duhon, B. (1998). It's All in our Heads. *Inform*, *12*(8), 8-13.

Duhon, B. (1998). It's all in our heads. *Inform (Silver Spring, Md.)*, *12*(8), 8–13.

Dumbrell, D., & Steele, R. (2014). Social Media Technologies for Achieving Knowledge Management Amongst Older Adult Communities. *Procedia: Social and Behavioral Sciences*, *147*, 229–236. doi:10.1016/j.sbspro.2014.07.165

Dundar, H., Beteille, T., Riboud, M., & Deolalikar, A. (2014). *Student Learning in South Asia: Challenges, Opportunities, and Policy Priorities*. Washington, DC: The World Bank. doi:10.1596/978-1-4648-0160-0

Durnu, V. I., & Uzochukwu, C. E. (2015). Social Media: An Effective Tool for Social Mobilization in Nigeria. *IOSR Journal of Humanities and Social Science*, *20* (4), 10-21. Retrieved from http://www.iosrjournals.org/iosr-jhss/papers/Vol20-issue4/Version-3/C020431021.pdf

Dürr, M., & Wiesner, K. (2011). *A Privacy-Preserving Social P2P Infrastructure for People-Centric Sensing*. doi:10.4230/OASIcs.KiVS.2011.176

Durr, M., Maier, M., & Dorfmeister, F. (2012). Vegas -- A Secure and Privacy-Preserving Peer-to-Peer Online Social Network. In *2012 International Conference on Privacy, Security, Risk and Trust and 2012 International Confernece on Social Computing* (pp. 868–874). IEEE. doi:10.1109/SocialCom-PASSAT.2012.42

Ebersbach, A., Glaser, M., Heigl, R., & Warta, A. (2008). *Wiki: web collaboration* (2nd ed.). Berlin: Springer.

Eboh, E. (2009). Developing Owa clan in the 21st Century: Opportunities & challenges. Enugu: El' Demak Publishers.

Edutech Wiki – affordances. (n.d.). Retrieved June 26, 2015, from: http://edutechwiki.unige.ch/en/Affordance

Edvinsson, L., & Malone, M. S. (1997). *Intellectual Capital*. London: Piatkus.

Efimova, L. (2004). Discovering the iceberg of knowledge work: a weblog case. In *Proceedings of 5th European Conference on Organizational Knowledge, Learning and Capabilities (OKLC)*. Innsbruck (Austria).

Egan, J. (1999). Political Marketing: Lessons from the Mainstream. *Journal of Marketing Management*, *15*(6), 495–503. doi:10.1362/026725799785045806

Eisenhardt, K. M. (1989). Building Theories from Case Study Research. *Academy of Management Review*, *14*(4), 532–550.

Ekeh, P. P. (1974). *Social exchange theory: The two traditions*. London, UK: Heinemann.

Empson, L. (2001). Introduction – Knowledge Management in Professional Service Firms. *Human Relations, Sage Publications.*, *54*(7), 811–817. doi:10.1177/0018726701547001

Engeström, J. (2005). *Why some social network services work and others don't*. Or: the case for object-centered sociality. Retrieved from http://www. zengestrom. com/blog/2005/04/why_some_social. html

Erickson, T., & Kellogg, W. A. (2000). Social translucence: An approach to designing systems that support social processes. *ACM Transactions on Computer-Human Interaction*, *7*(1), 59–83. doi:10.1145/344949.345004

Ertl, P., Selzer, P., & Mühlbacher, J. (2004). Web-based cheminformatics tools deployed via corporate Intranets. *Drug Discovery Today: BIOSILICO*, *2*(5), 201–207. doi:10.1016/S1741-8364(04)02413-8

Escalfoni, R., Braganholo, V., & Borges, M. R. S. (2011). A method for capturing innovation features using group storytelling. *Expert Systems with Applications*, *38*(2), 1148–1159. doi:10.1016/j.eswa.2010.05.008

Espíndola, R. (2002). Professionalised Campaigning in Latin America. *Journal of Political Marketing*, *1*(4), 65–81. doi:10.1300/J199v01n04_04

Esser, F., & Tenscher, J. (2005a). *The Professionalization Dilemma: Exploring a 'Strategic Approach' for Political Communication Experts*. Paper prepared for presentation to the Political Communication Division at the ICA conference.

Esser, F., & Tenscher, J. (2005b). *Measuring The Professionalization of Political Campaign*. Paper prepared for presentation to the Political Communication Division at the ICA Conference.

Eustis, J. M. (2011). Blogs and their place in the continuing education of catalogers. In E. R. Sanchez (Ed.), *Conversations with Cataloguers in the 21st Century* (pp. 219–225). Santa Barbara, CA: Libraries Unlimited.

Evans, M. M., & Ali, N. (2013). Bridging knowledge management life cycle theory and practice. In *Proceedings of 10th International Conference on Intellectual Capital, Knowledge Management and Organisational Learning (ICICKM '13)*. Washington, DC: George Washington University.

Evans, M. M., Dalkir, K., & Bidian, C. (2014). A Holistic View of the Knowledge Life Cycle: The Knowledge Management Cycle (KMC) Model. *Electronic Journal of Knowledge Management*, *12*(2), 85–97. Available online at http://www.ejkm.com/volume12/issue2

Express News Service. (2014). Retrieved July 2, 2015, from http://computer.financialexpress.com/news/hp-narayana-health-to-expand-cloud-enabled-ehealth-centres-in-india/1222/

Eyrich, N., Padman, M. L., & Sweetser, K. D. (2008). PR practitioners' use of social media tools and communication technology. *Public Relations Review*, *34*(4), 412–414. doi:10.1016/j.pubrev.2008.09.010

Eysenbach, G. (2008). Medicine 2.0. Social networking, collaboration, participation, apomediation, and openness. *Journal of Medical Internet Research*, *10*(3), e22. doi:10.2196/jmir.1030 PMID:18725354

Ezike, C. O. (2015). Adoption of social networking technology in teaching and learning process in Nigeria tertiary institutions. *International Journal of Science and Technology*, *1*, 79–93.

Falkner, M. (1997). *Using Lotus Notes as an Intranet*. New York, NY: John Wiley & Sons, Ltd.

Feldman, T. (1997). *An introduction to digital media*. London: Routledge. doi:10.4324/9780203398401

Feng, L. (2010). Research on the Construction of the Knowledge Service-oriented Learning Knowledge Portal System in Universities. *Information Studies: Theory & Application*, *1*, 29.

Fensel, D., van Harmelen, F., Horrocks, I., McGuinness, D. L., & Patel-Schneider, P. F. (2001). OIL: An ontology infrastructure for the Semantic Web. *IEEE Intelligent Systems*, *16*(2), 38–45. doi:10.1109/5254.920598

Ferdig, R. E. (2007). Editorial: Examining Social Software in Teacher Education. *Journal of Technology and Teacher Education*, *15*(1), 5–10.

Fernández-Luna, J., Huete, J., Rodriguez-Avila, H., & Rodriguez-Cano, J. (2014). Enhancing Collaborative Search Systems Engagement Through Gamification. In *Proceedings of the First International Workshop on Gamification for Information Retrieval SE - GamifIR '14* (pp. 42–45). New York: ACM. doi:doi:10.1145/2594776.2594785

Fink, S. (1986). *Crisis Management: Planning for the inevitable*. New York: American Management Association.

Firestone, J. M., & McElroy, M. W. (2003). The new knowledge management, special focus. *The new knowledge management.* Retrieved from http://www.kmci.org/media/New_Knowledge_Management.pdf

Fishbein, M., & Ajzen, I. (1975). Belief, attitude, intention and behavior: An introduction to theory and research. *Philosophy & Rhetoric*, *10*(2), 130–132.

Fisher, J., & Clayton, M. (2012). Who gives a Tweet: Assessing patients' interest in the use of social media for healthcare? *Worldviews on Evidence-Based Nursing*, 100-108.

Fishman, D. A. (1999). ValuJet Flight 592: Crisis Communication Theory Blended and Extended. *Communication Quarterly*, *47*(4), 345–375. doi:10.1080/01463379909385567

Fogg, B. (2002). Persuasive technology: Using computers to change what we think and do. *Ubiquity*, *2002*(December), 2. doi:10.1145/764008.763957

Foot, K., Schneider, S. M., Xenos, M., & Dougherty, M. (2009). Candidates' Web Practices in the 2002 U.S. House, Senate, and Gubernatorial Elections. *Journal of Political Marketing*, *8*(2), 147–167. doi:10.1080/15377850902813519

Ford, D. P., & Mason, R. M. (2013). A multi-level perspective of tensions between knowledge management and social media. *Journal of Organizational Computing and Electronic Commerce*, *23*(1-2), 7–33. doi:10.1080/10919392.2013.748604

Frand, J., & Hixon, C. (1999). *Personal knowledge management: who, what, why, where, when, and how*. Retrieved 15 September, 2015 from www.anderson.ucla.edu/faculty/jason.frand/researcher/ speeches/PKM.htm

Freberg, K. (2012). Intentions to comply with crisis messages communicated via social media. *Public Relations Review*, *38*(3), 416–421. doi:10.1016/j.pubrev.2012.01.008

Frechette, J. (2012). Learning beyond the classroom walls: Keeping students engaged in Class 2.0. *Journal of Media Literacy*. Retrieved on 3rd Sep 2015 from http://journalofmedialiteracy.org/index.php/current-issue/98-david-considines-ten-technology-tips-for-principals

Fuller, S. (2012). *Knowledge Management foundations*. Burlington, MA: Routledge.

Furnell, S. M., Jusoh, A., & Katsabas, D. (2006). The challenges of understanding and using security: A survey of end-users. *Computers & Security*, *25*(1), 27–35. doi:10.1016/j.cose.2005.12.004

Gaál, Z., Szabó, L., & Obermayer-Kovács, N. (2014). Personal knowledge sharing: Web 2.0 role through the lens of Generations. In *Proceedings of European Conference on Knowledge Management* (pp. 362-370). Santarem, School of Management and Technology Press.

Gahlinger, P. (2008). *The medical tourism travel guide*. North Branch, MN: Sunrise River Press.

Gao, F., Li, M., & Nakamori, Y. (2002). Systems thinking on knowledge and its management: Systems methodology for knowledge management. *Journal of Knowledge Management*, *6*(1), 7–17. doi:10.1108/13673270210417646

Garcia-Castañon, M., Rank, A. D., & Barreto, M. A. (2011). Plugged In or Tuned Out? Youth, Race, and Internet Usage in the 2008 Election. *Journal of Political Marketing*, *10*(1-2), 1–2, 115–138. doi:10.1080/15377857.2011.540209

Garcia-Perez, A., & Ayres, R. (2010). Wikifailure: The limitations of technology for knowledge sharing. *Electronic Journal of Knowledge Management*, *8*(1), 43–52. Available online at http://bit.ly/1I1js2O

Garvin, D. A. (2000). *Learning in Action: a Guide for Putting the Learning Organization to Work*. Harvard Business School Press. Retrieved from http://bit.ly/1WZubE7

Garvin, D. A., Edmondson, A. C., & Gino, F. (2008). Is yours a learning organization? *Harvard Business Review*, *86*(3), 109. PMID:18411968

Gaw, S., Felten, E. W., & Fernandez-Kelly, P. (2006, April). Secrecy, flagging, and paranoia: adoption criteria in encrypted email. In *Proceedings of the SIGCHI conference on human factors in computing systems* (pp. 591-600). ACM. doi:10.1145/1124772.1124862

Gears, D. A. (2012). Corporate wikis underground: An investigation of motivation and collaborative engagement. *Journal of Management and Marketing Research,* (9). Available online at: http://www.aabri.com/manuscripts/11894.pdf

Geisler, E., & Wickramasinghe, N. (2015). *Principles of Knowledge Management: Theory, Practice, and Cases*. Burlington, MA: Routledge.

Georgiadou, E., & Siakas, K. (2009b).*Collaborative projects: a bottom-up approach to European integratio*. International Technology, Education and Development Conference (INTED 2009), Valencia, Spain.

Gibbert, M., Ruigrok, W., & Wicki, B. (2008). Research Notes and Commentaries What Passes as a Rigorous Case Study. *Strategic Management Journal*, *29*(13), 1465–1474. doi:10.1002/smj.722

Gibson, R. K., & Rommele, A. (2001). Changing Campaign Communications: A Party-Centered Theory of Professionalized Campaigning. *The Harvard International Journal of Press/Politics*, *6*(4), 31–43. doi:10.1177/108118001129172323

Gibson, R. K., & Rommele, A. (2009). Measuring the Professionalization of Political Campaigning. *Party Politics*, *15*(3), 265–293. doi:10.1177/1354068809102245

Giddens, A. (1984). *The Constitution of Society: Outline of the Theory of Structuration*. Oxford, UK: Polity Press.

Glassman, M., & Kang, M. J. (2011). The logic of wikis: The possibilities of the Web 2.0 classroom. *Computer-Supported Collaborative Learning*, *6*(1), 93–112. doi:10.1007/s11412-011-9107-y

Golden, M. (2010). *Social Media: Strategies for Professionals and Their Firms*. Hoboken, NJ: John Wiley and Sons.

Gomez, J. B., Amado, J. B., & Montes, F. J. L. (2015). How do small firms learn to develop a social media competence? *International Journal of Information Management*, *35*(4), 443–458. doi:10.1016/j.ijinfomgt.2015.04.003

Gordon, S. (2010). *Facebook notches up 500 million members*. Retrieved July 27, 2010, from http://news.sky.com/sky-news/Home/Business/ Facebook-To-Hit-500-Million-Users-WorldwideJust-Six-Years-After-Mark-Zuckerberg-CreatedIt/Article/201007315668531

Gottschalk, P. (2007). *CIO and corporate strategic management: changing role of CIO to CEO*. Hershey, PA: Idea Group Publication. doi:10.4018/978-1-59904-423-1

Government of India (GOI). (2003). *Government of India (GOI) 2003 Health Sector in India*. New Delhi: Budget Papers.

Government of India, Planning Commission (GOI). (2013). Twelfth Five Year Plan 2012-17, Social Sectors (vol. 3). New Delhi: SAGE Publications.

Goy, A., Magro, D., Petrone, G., Picardi, C., & Segnan, M. (2015). Ontology-driven collaborative annotation in shared workspaces. *Future Generation Computer Systems*. doi:10.1016/j.future.2015.04.013

Grace, T. P. L. (2009). Wikis as a knowledge management tool. *Journal of Knowledge Management*, *13*(4), 64–74. doi:10.1108/13673270910971833

Graham, J. M., Faix, A., & Hartman, L. (2009). Crashing the Facebook party: One library's experiences in the students' domain. *Library Review*, *58*(3), 228–236. doi:10.1108/00242530910942072

Grail Research. (2011). *Consumers of Tomorrow Insights and Observations About Generation Z*. Retrieved January 09, 2013, from http://www.grailresearch.com/pdf/ContenPodsPdf/Consumers_of_Tomorrow_Insights_and_ Observations_About_Generation_Z.pdf

Granovetter, M. (1973). The strength of weak ties: A network theory revisited. *Sociological Theory*, *1*(1), 201–233.

Grant, R.M. (1996). Toward a knowledge-based theory of the firm. *Strategic Management Journal, 17*, 109-122.

Gray, P. H. (2001). The Impact of Knowledge Repositories on Power and Control in the Workplace. *Information Technology & People*, *14*(4), 368–384. doi:10.1108/09593840110411167

Griffis, H. M., Kilaru, A. S., Werner, R. M., Asch, D. A., Hershey, J. C., Hill, S., & Merchant, R. M. et al. (2014). Use of Social Media Across US Hospitals: Descriptive Analysis of Adoption and Utilization. *Journal of Medical Internet Research*, *16*(11), e264. doi:10.2196/jmir.3758

Grudin, J., & Poole, E. S. (2010). Wikis at work: success factors and challenges for sustainability of enterprise Wikis. In *Proceedings of the 6th international symposium on Wikis and open collaboration* (p. 5). ACM. doi:10.1145/1832772.1832780

Gruman, G. (2010). Tapping into the Power of Big Data: Making Sense of Big Data. In *Proceedings of Price Warehouse Coopers Technology Forecast*. Retrieved December 20, 2015, fromhttp://www.pwc.com/us/en/technology-forcast/2010/issue3/index.html

Guest, G. (2013). Describing Mixed Methods Research: An Alternative to Typologies. *Journal of Mixed Methods Research*, *7*(2), 141–151. doi:10.1177/1558689812461179

Gupta, A. (2009). The 24-Hour Knowledge Factory: Can It Replace the Graveyard Shift? *Computer*, *42*(1), 66–73. doi:10.1109/MC.2009.25

H1N1 Web and Social Media Metrics Cumulative Data Report April 22, 2009– December 31, 2009. (n.d.). Division of eHealth Marketing (DeHM) National Center for Health Marketing (NCHM) Centers for Disease Control and Prevention (CDC).

Halevy, A., Rajaraman, A., & Ordille, J. (2006). Data Integration: The teenage Years. In *Proceedings of the 32nd International Conference on Very Large DataBases (VLDB'06)*, (pp. 9-16). COEX.

Hall, H. (2001). Input-friendliness: Motivating Knowledge Sharing Across Intranets. *Journal of Information Science*, *27*(2), 139–146. doi:10.1177/016555150102700303

Hall, T. E., & Sinclair, B. (2011). The American Internet Voter. *Journal of Political Marketing*, *10*(1-2), 1–2, 58–79. doi:10.1080/15377857.2011.540194

Hall, W., Nousala, S., & Kilpatrick, B. (2009). One company – two outcomes Knowledge integration vs corporate disintegration in the absence. *VINE: The Journal of Information and Knowledge Management Systems*, *39*(3), 242–258. doi:10.1108/03055720911003996

Hanrahan, B., Quintana-Castillo, R., Stewart, M., & Perez-Quinones, M. A. (2010). *WikiAtoms: Contributions to Wikis as Atomic Units*. Available online at: https://www.parc.com/content/events/attachments/Hanrahan_revised_Group10.pdf

Hansen, M. T., Nohria, N., & Tierney, T. (1999). What's your strategy for managing knowledge? *The Knowledge Management Yearbook 2000–2001*.

Hansen, D., Shneiderman, B., & Smith, M. (2010). *Analyzing Social Media Networks with NodeXL: Insights from a Connected World*. San Francisco, CA: Morgan Kaufmann Publishers Inc.

Hansen, M. T. (1999). The search-transfer problem: The role of weak ties in sharing knowledge across organization subunits. *Administrative Science Quarterly*, *44*(1), 82–111. doi:10.2307/2667032

Hara, H., Matsutsuka, T., Kanaya, N., Ookubo, T., & Uehara, S. (1997). Model-Based Architecture for the Intranet. In *Proceedings of the 21st International Computer Software and Applications Conference SE - COMPSAC '97* (pp. 182–187). Washington, DC: IEEE Computer Society.

Harasim, L. (2012). *Instructional Design & Social Media Panel*. World Conference on Educational Media & Technology 2012.

Hardey, M. (1999). Doctor in the house: The internet as a source of lay health knowledge and the challenges to expertise. *Sociology of Health & Illness*, *2*(6), 820–835. doi:10.1111/1467-9566.00185

Harris, L., & Harrigan, P. (2015). Social Media in Politics: The Ultimate Voter Engagement Tool or Simply an Echo Chamber? *Journal of Political Marketing*, *14*(3), 251–283. doi:10.1080/15377857.2012.693059

Harris, P. (2000). *To Spin or not to Spin that is the Question: The Emergence of Modern Political Marketing*. Westburn Publishers Ltd.

Harris, P., & Andrew, L. (2010). "Mind the gap": The rise of political marketing and a perspective on its future agenda. *European Journal of Marketing*, *44*(3/4), 297–307. doi:10.1108/03090561011020435

Harrop, M. (1990).. . *Political Marketing. Parliamentary Affairs. Oxford University Press*, *1990*, 227–291.

Hartwig, M. (2008). *Introduction. In A Realist Theory of Science* (2nd ed.; pp. ix–xxiv). London: Verso.

Hassell, H. J. G. (2011). Looking Beyond the Voting Constituency: A Study of Campaign Donation Solicitations in the 2008 Presidential Primary and General Election. *Journal of Political Marketing*, *10*(1-2), 1–2, 27–42. doi:10.1080/15377857.2011.540192

Hattern, J. (2014). Many Say NSA News Changed Their Behavior. *The Hill*. Retrieved from http://thehill.com/policy/technology/202434-poll-nearly-half-say-nsa-news-affected-behaior

Hawamdeh, S., & Refai, H. (2008). Video Management and the Transfer of Knowledge through Audiovisual Material. In T. K. Srikantaiah & M. E. D. Koening (Eds.), *Knowledge Management in Practice* (pp. 223–238). Medford, NJ: Information Today Inc.

Hawn, C. (2009). Take two aspirins and tweet me in the morning: How Twitter, Facebook and other social media are reshaping healthcare. *Health Affairs*, *28*(2), 361–368. doi:10.1377/hlthaff.28.2.361 PMID:19275991

Hayek, F.A (1945). The use of knowledge in society. *The American Economic Review*, *35*(4), 519-530.

Heath, R. L., & Millar, D. P. (2004). A Rhetorical Approach to Crisis Communication: Management, Communication Processes, and Strategic Responses. In D. P. Millar & R. L. Heath (Eds.), *Responding to Crisis: A Rhetorical Approach to Crisis Communication* (pp. 1–17). Mahwah, NJ: Lawrence Erlbaum Associates.

Heisig, P. (2009). Harmonisation of knowledge management: Comparing 160 KM frameworks around the globe. *Journal of Knowledge Management*, *13*(Issue, 4), 4–31. doi:10.1108/13673270910971798

Hemsley, J., & Mason, R. M. (2013). Knowledge and knowledge management in the social media age. *Journal of Organizational Computing and Electronic Commerce*, *23*(1-2), 138–167. doi:10.1080/10919392.2013.748614

Hendriks, P. (1999). Why share knowledge? The influence of ICT on the motivation for knowledge sharing. *Knowledge and Process Management*, *6*(2), 91–100. doi:10.1002/(SICI)1099-1441(199906)6:2<91::AID-KPM54>3.0.CO;2-M

Hendrix, D., Chiarella, D., Hasman, L., Murphy, S., & Zafron, M. L. (2009). Use of Facebook in academic health sciences libraries. *Journal of the Medical Library Association: JMLA*, *97*(1), 44–47. doi:10.3163/1536-5050.97.1.008

Henneberg, S. C. M. (2002). Understanding Political Marketing. In N. J. O'Shaughnessy & S. C. M. Henneberg (Eds.), *The Idea of Political Marketing*. Westport, CT: Praeger.

Henneberg, S. C. M. (2004). The Views of an Avocatus Dei: Political Marketing and Its Critics. *Journal of Public Affairs*, *4*(3), 225–243. doi:10.1002/pa.187

Henneberg, S. C. M. (2008). An Epistemological Perspective on Research in Political Marketing. *Journal of Political Marketing*, *7*(2), 151–182. doi:10.1080/15377850802053158

Henneberg, S. C. M., & O'Shaughnessy, N. J. (2009). Political Relationship Marketing: Some macro/micro thoughts. *Journal of Marketing Management*, *25*(1-2), 5–29. doi:10.1362/026725709X410016

Henneberg, S. C. M., & Ormrod, R. P. (2013). The triadic interaction model of political marketing exchange. *Marketing Theory*, *13*(1), 87–103. doi:10.1177/1470593112467269

Henneberg, S. C. M., & O'Shaughnessy, N. J. (2007). Theory and Concept Development in Political Marketing. *Journal of Political Marketing*, *6*, 2–3, 5–31. doi:10.1300/J199v06n02_02

Henry, R. K., Molnar, A., & Henry, J. C. (2012). A survey of UD Dental Practices' use of Social Media. *The Journal of Contemporary Dental Practice*, *13*(2), 137–141. doi:10.5005/jp-journals-10024-1109 PMID:22665737

Henselewski, M., Smolnik, S., & Riempp, G. (2006). Evaluation of knowledge management technologies for the support of technology forecasting. In *System Sciences, 2006. HICSS'06. Proceedings of the 39th Annual Hawaii International Conference on System Sciences*. IEEE. Available online at: http://www.researchgate.net/publication/4216329_Evaluation_of_Knowledge_Management_Technologies_for_the_Support_of_Technology_Forecasting

Herath, T., & Rao, H. R. (2009). Protection motivation and deterrence: A framework for security policy compliance in organizations. *European Journal of Information Systems*, *18*(2), 106–125. doi:10.1057/ejis.2009.6

Herley, C., van Oorschot, P. C., & Patrick, A. S. (2009). Passwords: If we're so smart, why are we still using them? In Financial Cryptography and Data Security (pp. 230-237). Springer Berlin Heidelberg.

Herley, C. (2009, September). So long, and no thanks for the externalities: the rational rejection of security advice by users. In *Proceedings of the 2009 workshop on new security paradigms workshop* (pp. 133-144). ACM. doi:10.1145/1719030.1719050

Higgison, S. (2004). Personal knowledge management. *Inside Knowledge*, *7*(7). Retrieved 15 September, 2015 from http://www.kmmagazine.com/xq/asp/sid.7551F69D-2683-471C-A18C-C3365B30C312/articleid.DDDD6EE3-47C6-49CD-9070-F1B1547FD29F/qx/display.htm

Hinde, S. (2003). The law, cybercrime, risk assessment and cyber protection. *Computers & Security*, *22*(2), 90–95. doi:10.1016/S0167-4048(03)00203-7

Hislop, D. (2013). *Knowledge Management in Organizations: A Critical Introduction*. Oxford: Oxford University Press.

Holotescu, C., & Grosseck, G. (2010). Learning to microblog and microblogging to learn: a case study on learning scenarios in a microblogging context. In *Proceedings of 6th International Scientific Conference eLearning and Software for Education (eLSE)*. Bucharest (Romania).

Holtz-Bacha, C. (2002). Professionalization of Political Communication. *Journal of Political Marketing*, *1*(4), 23–37. doi:10.1300/J199v01n04_02

Holtzblatt, L. J., Damianos, L. E., & Weiss, D. (2010, April). Factors impeding Wiki use in the enterprise: a case study. In CHI'10 Extended Abstracts on Human Factors in Computing Systems (pp. 4661-4676). ACM. doi:10.1145/1753846.1754208

Hopkins, J. (2002). The community of cataloguers: Its role in the education of cataloguers. *Cataloging & Classification Quarterly*, *34*(3), 375–381. doi:10.1300/J104v34n03_09

Hopkins, L., Labonte, R., Runnels, V., & Packer, C. (2010). Medical tourism today: What is the state of existing knowledge? *Journal of Public Health Policy*, *31*(2), 185–198. doi:10.1057/jphp.2010.10 PMID:20535101

Horowitz, M. D., & Rosensweig, J. A. (2007). Medical Tourism-Health Care in the Global Economy. *Physician Executive*, *33*(6), 24–31. PMID:18092615

Horowitz, M. D., Rosensweig, J. A., & Jones, C. A. (2007). Medical tourism: Globalization of the healthcare marketplace. *Medscape General Medicine*, *9*(4), 33. PMID:18311383

Horwitch, M., & Armacost, R. (2002). Helping knowledge management be all it can be. *The Journal of Business Strategy*, *23*(3), 26–32. doi:10.1108/eb040247

Houses of Parliament (HoP) Parliamentary Office of Science and Technology. (2014). *Social Media and Big Data*. Retrieved March 16, 2015 from http://researchbriefings.files.parliament.uk/documents/POST-PN-460/POST-PN-460.pdf

Howard, R. (2015). An exploration of the motivation and impact of medical tourism. *Medical Markets and Media*. Retrieved March 20, 2015, from http://www.mmm-online.com/the-patient-abroad-an-exploration-of-the-motivations-and-impact-of-medical-tourism/article/404476/

Hsia, Z. L., Lin, M. N., Wu, J. H., & Tsai, H. T. (2006). A framework for designing nursing knowledge management systems. *Interdisciplinary Journal of Information, Knowledge, and Management*, *1*, 14–21.

Huber, G. P. (1991). Organizational learning: The contributing processes and the literatures. *Organization Science*, *2*(1), 88–115. doi:10.1287/orsc.2.1.88

Hughes, D. J., Rowe, M., Batey, M., & Lee, A. (2012). A tale of two sites: Twitter vs. Facebook and the personality predictors of social media usage. *Computers in Human Behavior*, *28*(2), 561–569. doi:10.1016/j.chb.2011.11.001

Huijster, H. (2008). Exploring the educational potential of social networking sites: The fine line between exploring opportunities and unwelcome imposition. *Studies in Learning, Evaluation, Innovation and Development*, *5*(2), 45–54.

Hussain, Z., Barber, K., & Hussain, N. (2009). An Intranet based system as an enabler in effective project management and implementation of quality standards: A case study. *Journal of Engineering and Technology Management*, *26*(3), 196–210. doi:10.1016/j.jengtecman.2009.06.003

Hustad, E., & Vikstøl, T. (2014). Implementing Intranet 2.0: A Study of Knowledge Requirements for External Consultants in Enterprise Systems. *Procedia Technology*, *16*, 694–703. doi:10.1016/j.protcy.2014.10.018

Huxtable, R. (2009). The Suicide tourist trap:compromise across boundaries. *Journal of Bioethical Inquiry*, *6*(3), 327–336. doi:10.1007/s11673-009-9170-5

Hwan, K. J., Youn-kyoung, J., & Do, N. S. (2009). Product Information Exchanges between CAD/PDM systems and the Collaboration Portal System using PLM Services. In *2009 WRI World Congress on Computer Science and Information Engineering* (pp. 718–721). IEEE. doi:10.1109/CSIE.2009.962

Hyde, K. (2006). Contemporary information search strategies of destination-naïve international vacationers. *Journal of Travel & Tourism*, *21*(2/3), 63–76.

IDC. (2015). *Smartphone Shipments Reach Second Highest Level for a Single Quarter as Worldwide Volumes Reach 355.2 Million in the Third Quarter*. Retrieved December 1, 2015, from http://www.idc.com/getdoc.jsp?containerId=prUS25988815

Ikenwe, I. J., & Igbinovia, M. O. (2015). Influence of knowledge sharing in reducing the spread of "HIV/ AIDS" among adolescents in rural areas in Delta State, Nigeria. *Kuwait Chapter of Arabian Journal of Business and Management Review*, *4*(12), 18-31. Retrieved from http://www.arabianjbmr.com/pdfs/KD_VOL_4_12/3.pdf

Indian Medical Tourism (IMT). (2009). *India ranks 2nd in medical tourism*. Retrieved August 15, 2009, from http://www.medicaltourism.org/consortium.jsp?sect=consortiumdetail&id=6

Iyer, S., & Sengupta, D. (2010, July 5). Top IT firms log on to social networking sites to hire middle & senior-level staff. *The Economic Times*.

Jackson, N. (2011). Perception or Reality: How MPs Believe the Internet Helps Them Win Votes. *Journal of Political Marketing*, *10*(3), 230–250. doi:10.1080/15377857.2011.588099

Jaeger, P. T., Schneiderman, B., Fleischmann, K. R., Preece, J., Qu, Y., & Wu, P. F. (2007). Community response grids: E-government, social networks, and effective emergency management. *Telecommunications Policy*, *31*(10-11), 592–604. doi:10.1016/j.telpol.2007.07.008

Jamali, M., & Abolhassani, H. (2006). Different Aspects of Social Network Analysis. In *Web Intelligence, 2006. WI 2006. IEEE/WIC/ACM International Conference on* (pp. 66–72). doi:10.1109/WI.2006.61

Jarrahi, M. H., & Sawyer, S. (2013). Social technologies, informal knowledge practices, and the enterprise. *Journal of Organizational Computing and Electronic Commerce*, *23*(1-2), 110–137. doi:10.1080/10919392.2013.748613

Johansen, H. P. M. (2005). Political Marketing. *Journal of Political Marketing*, *4*(4), 85–105. doi:10.1300/J199v04n04_05

Johnson, C., & Burclaff, N. (2013). Making Social Media Meaningful: Connecting Missions and Policies. In *Imagine, Innovate, Inspire* (pp. 399–405). Indianapolis, IN: American Library Association. Retrieved 1 Oct 2015, from http://www.ala.org/acrl/sites/ala.org.acrl/files/content/conferences/confsandpreconfs/2013/papers/JohnsonBurclaff_Making.pdf

Johnson, D. W. (2002a). The Electronic Information Candy Store. *Journal of Political Marketing*, *1*(4), 101–102. doi:10.1300/J199v01n04_07

Johnson, D. W. (2002b). Campaign Website. *Journal of Political Marketing*, *1*(1), 213–215. doi:10.1300/J199v01n01_11

Johnson, D. W. (2003a). Anthrax and Digital Mail. *Journal of Political Marketing*, *2*(1), 113–115. doi:10.1300/J199v02n01_08

Johnson, D. W. (2003b). The U.S. Congress Responds to Online Communication Needs. *Journal of Political Marketing*, *2*(3-4), 3–4, 235–254. doi:10.1300/J199v02n03_13

Johnson, D. W. (2004a). the 2004 U.S. Presidential Elections. *Journal of Political Marketing*, *3*(4), 111–113. doi:10.1300/J199v03n04_06

Johnson, D. W. (2004b). Rethinking Electronic Voting. *Journal of Political Marketing*, *3*(3), 107–109. doi:10.1300/J199v03n03_07

Johnston, A. C., & Warkentin, M. (2010). Fear appeals and information security behaviors: An empirical study. *Management Information Systems Quarterly*, *34*(3), 549–566.

Johnston, A. C., Warkentin, M., & Siponen, M. (2015). An enhanced fear appeal rhetorical framework: Leveraging threats to the human asset through sanctioning rhetoric. *Management Information Systems Quarterly*, *39*(1), 113–134.

Joinson, A. N. (2001). Self-disclosure in computer-mediated communication: The role of self-awareness and visual anonymity. *European Journal of Social Psychology*, *31*(2), 177–192. doi:10.1002/ejsp.36

Jue, A. L., Marr, J. A., & Kassotakis, M. E. (2010). *Social media at work: how networking tools propel organisational performance*. San Francisco, CA: Jossey-Bass.

Kagwanja, C. (2012, July-August). *Religious pockets of conflict – dealing with resurgence of radical Islamism and terrorism in Kenya. Horn of Africa Bulletin.*

Kah, J. A., Vogt, C., & MacKay, K. (2008). Online travel information search and purchasing by internet use experiences. *Information Technology & Tourism*, *10*(3), 227–243. doi:10.3727/109830508787157353

Kaila, P. (2008). OAuth and OpenID 2.0. *From End-to-End to Trust-to-Trust, 18.*

Kalyanam, R., Zhao, L., Song, C. X., Wong, Y. L., Lee, J., & Villoria, N. B. (2013). iData. In *Proceedings of the Conference on Extreme Science and Engineering Discovery Environment Gateway to Discovery - XSEDE '13* (p. 1). New York: ACM Press. doi:10.1145/2484762.2484813

Kaplan, A. M., & Haenlein, M. (2011). The early bird catches the news: Nine things you should know about microblogging. *Business Horizons*, *54*(2), 105–113. doi:10.1016/j.bushor.2010.09.004

Kaplan, A., & Haenlein, M. (2010). Users of the world, unite! The challenges and opportunities of social media. *Business Horizons*, *53*(1), 59–68. doi:10.1016/j.bushor.2009.09.003

Karabulut, A., et al. (2009). Student Level of Commitment and Engagement with Ning as a Learning Management System. In C. Maddux (Ed.), Research Highlights in Technology and Teacher Education (pp. 43-49). SITE.

Kara, T. (2013). *Sosyal media endüstrisi: insan, toplum ve ekonomi*. Istanbul: Beta Yayınları.

Kaske, F., Kügler, M., & Smolnik, S. (2012). Return on Investment in Social Media--Does the Hype Pay Off? Towards an Assessment of the Profitability of Social Media in Organizations. In *System Science (HICSS), 2012 45th Hawaii International Conference on System Sciences* (pp. 3898-3907). IEEE. Available online at: https://www.wiwi.uni-augsburg.de/en/bwl/paul/Downloads/Publications_Kaske/Kaske-Kuegler-Smolnik_2012.pdf

Kasten, J. (2008). Knowledge Strategy: The Linkage Between Business Strategy and Knowledge Management. In T. K. Srikantaiah & M. E. D. Koening (Eds.), *Knowledge Management in Practice* (pp. 115–124). Medford, NJ: Information Today Inc.

Katz, J. E., & Rice, R. E. (2002). *Social Consequences of Internet Use: Access, Involvement, and Interaction* (pp. 1–463). Cambridge, MA: MIT press.

Keckley, P. H. (2008). *Medical Tourism: consumers in search of value*. Washington, DC: Deloitte Center for Health Solutions.

Kerkhof, C., Ende, J. V. D., & Bogenrieder, I. (2003). Knowledge management in the professional organization: A model with application to CMG software testing. *Knowledge and Process Management*, *10*(2), 77–84. doi:10.1002/kpm.167

Khyzer, M. D., Asim, K. M., Zulfiqar, A., Zafar, A., Musarrat, M. N., Ishraf, A., & Naveed, A. et al. (2009). Interpersonal factors and tendencies to knowledge sharing among students: A case of Punjab University. *The Knowledge Economy*, *1*(1), 519–525.

Kiatpongsan, S., & Sipp, D. (2009). Monitoring and regulating offshore stem cell clinics. *Science*, *323*(5921), 1564–1565. doi:10.1126/science.1168451 PMID:19299604

Kickbusch, I. (2012). Learning for Well-being: A Policy Priority for Children and Youth in Europe. A process for change. *Learning for Well-being Consortium of Foundations in Europe: Universal Educational Foundations*.

Kietzmann, J. H., Hermkens, K., McCarthy, I. P., & Silvestre, B. S. (2011). Social media? Get serious! Understanding the functional building blocks of social media. *Business Horizons*, *54*(3), 241–251. doi:10.1016/j.bushor.2011.01.005

Kietzmann, J. H., Silvestre, B. S., McCarthy, I. P., & Pitt, L. F. (2012). Unpacking the social media phenomenon: Towards a research agenda. *Journal of Public Affairs*, *12*(2), 109–119. doi:10.1002/pa.1412

Kim, T. H., Lee, J. N., Chun, J. U., & Benbasat, I. (2014). Understanding the Effect of Knowledge Management Strategies on Knowledge Management Performance: A Contingency Perspective. *Information & Management*, *51*(4), 398–416. doi:10.1016/j.im.2014.03.001

Klein, P. D. (1971). A Proposed Definition of Propositional Knowledge. *The Journal of Philosophy*, *68*(16), 471–482. doi:10.2307/2024845

Klooster, M., Brinkkemper, S., Harmsen, F., & Wijers, G. (1997). Intranet facilitated knowledge management: A theory and tool for defining situational methods. In A. Olivé & J. Pastor (Eds.), *Advanced Information Systems Engineering SE - 22* (Vol. 1250, pp. 303–317). Springer Berlin Heidelberg; doi:10.1007/3-540-63107-0_22

Koenig, M. E. D. (2008). KM Moving into Stage IV? The Extra-Organizational Stage. In T. K. Srikantaiah & M. E. D. Koening (Eds.), *Knowledge Management in Practice* (pp. 9–16). Medford, NJ: Information Today Inc.

Kohli, C., Suri, R., & Kapoor, A. (2015). Will social media kill branding? *Business Horizons*, *58*(1), 35–44. doi:10.1016/j.bushor.2014.08.004

Korda, H., & Itani, Z. (2013). Harnessing social media for health pormotion and behaviour change. *Health Promotion Practice*, *14*(1), 15–23. doi:10.1177/1524839911405850 PMID:21558472

Kotler, P., & Kotler, N. (1999). Political Marketing: Generating Effective Candidate, Campaigns and Causes. In Handbook of Political Marketing. London: Sage Publication.

Kotler, P., & Armstrong, G. (2011). *Principles of Marketing* (14th ed.). Pearson Prentice Hall.

KPMG Academy. (2014).*Organizational Knowledge Sharing in Hungary 2013/2014. KPMG Academy – University of Pannonia Research Report*. Budapest: KPMG.

KPMG. (2012). *Human resources and social media*. KPMG International Research report. MCGraphics.

KPMG-BME Academy. (2006).*Knowledge Management in Hungary 2005/2006. KPMG-BME Academy – University of Pannonia Research Report*. Budapest: KBA Oktatási Kft.

Krackhardt, D. (1992). The strength of strong ties: The importance of philos in organizations. In Networks and organizations: Structure, form, and action (pp. 216-239). Cambridge, MA: Harvard Business School Press.

Krishna, A. (2002). *Active Social Capital: Tracing the Roots of Development and Democracy*. Columbia University Press.

Kugel, J., & Schostek, C. (2004). *Rewards for knowledge sharing*. Retrieved June 12, 2007, from http://www.gurteen.com/gurteen/gurteen.nsf/id/rewards-k-sharing

Kulkarni, U. R., Ravindran, S., & Freeze, R. (2007). A Knowledge Management Success Model: Theoretical Development and Empirical Validation. *Journal of Management Information Systems*, *23*(3), 309–347. doi:10.2753/MIS0742-1222230311

Kvale, S., & Brinkmann, S. (2009). Interviews: Learning the craft of qualitative research interviewing. *Sage (Atlanta, Ga.)*.

Kwahk, K. Y., & Ge, X. (2012). The effects of social media on e-commerce: A perspective of social impact theory.*45th Hawaii International Conference on System Sciences*. doi:10.1109/HICSS.2012.564

Laad, G., & Lewis, G. (2012). *Role of Social Media in Crisis Communication*. Retrieved June 12, 2013, from http://geraldlewis.com/publications/Role_of_Social_ Media_in_Crisis_ Communication_Jan_2012_Gitanjali_Laad.pdf

Lai, L. S. (2010). Social Commerce – E-Commerce in Social Media Context. *World Academy of Science. Engineering and Technology*, *4*, 12–27.

Lai, Y. L., Hsu, M. S., Lin, F. J., Chen, Y. M., & Lin, Y. H. (2014). The Effects of Industry Cluster Knowledge Management on Innovation Performance. *Journal of Business Research*, *67*(5), 734–739. doi:10.1016/j.jbusres.2013.11.036

Lamb, R. (2001). Tracing influence through intranets of compliance. In *Proceedings of the 34th Annual Hawaii International Conference on System Sciences* (p. 10). IEEE Comput. Soc. doi:10.1109/HICSS.2001.926354

Lamb, R. (2003). Intranet Boundaries as Guidelines for Systems Integration. *International Journal of Electronic Commerce*, *7*(4), 9–35. Retrieved from http://dl.acm.org/citation.cfm?id=1288207.1288210

Lang, J. C. (2004). Social context and social capital as enablers of knowledge integration. *Journal of Knowledge Management*, *8*(3), 89–105. doi:10.1108/13673270410541060

Lappas, G., Chatzopoulos, S., & Yannas, P. (2008). Parliamentary Candidates Running on the Web for the 2004 Greek National Elections. *Journal of Political Marketing*, *7*(3-4), 3–4, 256–277. doi:10.1080/15377850802008327

Laschewski, L. (2011). *Innovative E-learning in rural areas*. Retrieved from http://ssrn.com/abstract=1861912

Laszlo, K. C., & Laszlo, A. (2002). Evolving knowledge for development: The role of knowledge management in a changing world. *Journal of Knowledge Management*, *6*(4), 400–412. doi:10.1108/13673270210440893

Laszlo, K., & Laszlo, A. (2006). Fostering a sustainable learning society through knowledge based development. In *Proceedings of the 50th Annual Meeting of the ISSS*. Sonoma State University.

Lau, K. (2009). Three myths of enterprise wiki deployment. *Computerworld*, *28*(Jan). Retrieved from http://www.computerworld.com/article/2530642/networking/three-myths-of-enterprise-wiki-deployment.html

Lavie, D. (2006). The Competitive Advantage of Interconnected Firms: An Extension of the Resource-Based View. *Academy of Management Review*, *31*(3), 638–658. doi:10.5465/AMR.2006.21318922

Leavesley, J., & Hemus, J. (2013). *Braving the Social Media Crisis*. Retrieved June 12, 2013, from http://www.slideshare.net/Insignia_Communications/braving-the-social-media-crisis

Lee, J., Soutar, G., & Daly, T. (2007). Tourists' search for different types of information: A cross-national study. *Information Technology & Tourism*, *9*(3), 165–176. doi:10.3727/109830507782167006

Lees-Marshment, J. (2001a, September). The Marriage of Politics and Marketing. *Political Studies*, *49*(4), 692–713. doi:10.1111/1467-9248.00337

Lees-Marshment, J. (2001b). The product, sales and market-oriented party: How Labour learnt to market the product, not just the presentation. *European Journal of Marketing*, *35*(9/10), 1074–1084. doi:10.1108/EUM0000000005959

Lees-Marshment, J. (2001c). *Political Marketing and British Political Parties: The Party's Just Begun*. Manchester, UK: Manchester University Press.

Lees-Marshment, J. (2004). *The Political Marketing Revolution: Transforming the Government of the UK*. London: Routledge Publication.

Lees-Marshment, J. (2008). *Political Marketing and British Political Parties* (2nd ed.). Manchester, UK: Manchester University Press.

Lees-Marshment, J. (Ed.). (2012). *Routledge Hanbook of Political Marketing*. London: Routledge Taylor & Francis Group.

Lees-Marshment, J., & Lilleker, D. G. (Eds.). (2005). *Political Marketing: A Comparative Perspective*. Manchester, UK: Manchester University Press.

Lees-Marshment, J., Stromback, J., & Rudd, C. (Eds.). (2010). *Global Political Marketing*. London: Routlegde.

Lee, Y. (2011). Understanding anti-plagiarism software adoption: An extended protection motivation theory perspective. *Decision Support Systems*, *50*(2), 361–369. doi:10.1016/j.dss.2010.07.009

Lengel, R. H., & Daft, R. L. (1988). The selection of communication media as an executive skill. *The Academy of Management Executive*, *2*(3), 225–232. doi:10.5465/AME.1988.4277259

Lerman, K. (2007). Social Information Processing in News Aggregation. *IEEE Internet Computing*, *11*(6), 16–28. doi:10.1109/MIC.2007.136

Leroy, F., & Ramanantsoa, B. (1997). The cognitive and behavioral dimensions of organizational learning in a merger: An empirical study. *Journal of Management Studies*, *34*(6), 871–894. doi:10.1111/1467-6486.00076

Leskovec, J., Huttenlocher, D., & Kleinberg, J. (2010). Predicting positive and negative links in online social networks. In *Proceedings of the 19th international conference on World wide web - WWW '10* (p. 641). New York: ACM Press. doi:10.1145/1772690.1772756

Levin, D. Z., & Cross, R. (2004). The strength of weak ties you can trust: The mediating role of trust in effective knowledge transfer. *Management Science*, *50*(11), 1477–1490. doi:10.1287/mnsc.1030.0136

Levine, S. S., & Prietula, M. (2006). *Towards a Contingency Theory of Knowledge Exchange in Organizations*. Retrieved from http://papers.ssrn.com/abstract=2378060

Levy, M. (2009). WEB 2.0 implications on knowledge management. *Journal of Knowledge Management*, *13*(1), 120–134. doi:10.1108/13673270910931215

Levy, M. (2013). Stairways to heaven: Implementing social media in organizations. *Journal of Knowledge Management*, *17*(5), 741–754. doi:10.1108/JKM-02-2013-0051

Lewin, K. (1947). Group Decision and Social Change. *Readings in Social Psychology*, *3*, 197–211.

Li, C. & Bernoff, J. (2008). *Groundswell: Winning in a World Transformed by Social Technologies*. Academic Press.

Liang, H., & Xue, Y. (2009). Avoidance of information technology threats: A theoretical perspective. *Management Information Systems Quarterly*, 71–90.

Liang, H., & Xue, Y. (2010). Understanding security behaviors in personal computer usage: A threat avoidance perspective. *Journal of the Association for Information Systems*, *11*(7), 394–413.

Liang, T. P., & Turban, E. (2011). Introduction to the Special Issue - Social Commerce: A research framework for social commerce. *International Journal of Electronic Commerce*, *16*(2), 5–13. doi:10.2753/JEC1086-4415160201

Liebowitz, J. (2013). Big Data Business Analytics. Auerbach Publications. doi:10.1201/b14700

Liebowitz, J. (Ed.). (2011). *Beyond Knowledge Management*. Boca Raton, FL: Taylor & Francis Group/ CRC Press. doi:10.1201/b11511

Lievrouw, L. A., & Livingstone, S. (Eds.). (2002). *Handbook of New Media: Social Shaping and Consequences of ICTs*. Sage.

Lilleker, D. G. (2014). Interactivity and Branding, Public Political Communication as a Marketing Tool. *Journal of Political Marketing*. doi:10.1080/15377857.2014.990841

Lilleker, D. G., & Jackson, N. A. (2013). Reaching Inward Not Outward: Marketing via the Internet at the UK 2010 General Election. *Journal of Political Marketing*, *12*(2-3), 2–3, 244–261. doi:10.1080/15377857.2013.781475

Lilleker, D. G., Jackson, N. A., & Scullion, R. (2007). *The Marketing of Political Parties*. Manchester, UK: Manchester University Press.

Lilleker, D. G., & Negrine, R. (2002). Professionalization: Of What? Since When? By Whom? *The Harvard International Journal of Press/Politics*, *7*(4), 98–103. doi:10.1177/108118002236354

Ling, C. T. N. (2011). Culture and trust in fostering knowledge-sharing. *Electronic Journal of Knowledge Management*, *9*(4), 328–339.

Lin, H. F. (2007). Effects of Extrinsic and Intrinsic Motivation On Employee Knowledge Sharing Intentions. *Journal of Information Science*, *33*(2), 135–149. doi:10.1177/0165551506068174

Lin, H. F., & Lee, G. G. (2004). Perceptions of Senior Managers Toward Knowledge-sharing Behavior. *Management Decision*, *42*(1), 108–125. doi:10.1108/00251740410510181

Lipsitz, K., & Panagopoulos, C. (2011). Filled Coffers: Campaign Contributions and Contributors in the 2008 Elections. *Journal of Political Marketing*, *10*(1-2), 1–2, 43–57. doi:10.1080/15377857.2011.540193

Liu, Y., Zhou, J., & Guan, Q. (2015). Study on University-Industry Cooperation Platform Construction Based on Knowledge Management. *LISS*. Springer Berlin Heidelberg.

Lock, A., & Harris, P. (1996). Political marketing – *vive la différence! European Journal of Marketing, 30*(10/11), 14–24. doi:10.1108/03090569610149764

Lowendahl, B., Revang, Ø., & Fosstenløkken, S. M. (2001). Knowledge And Value Creation In Professional Service Firms: A Framework For Analysis. *Human Relations, Sage Publications., 54*(7), 911–931. doi:10.1177/0018726701547006

Lunde, A., Heggen, K., & Strand, R. (2013). Knowledge and Power: Exploring Unproductive Interplay Between Quantitative and Qualitative Researchers. *Journal of Mixed Methods Research, 7*(2), 197–210. doi:10.1177/1558689812471087

Lunenburg, F. (2011). Systems Thinking and the Learning Organization: The Path to School Improvement. *Schooling, 2*(1), 1–6.

Lunt, N., Hardey, M., & Mannion, R. (2010). Nip, Tuck and Click: Medical Tourism and the Emergence of Web-Based Health Information. *The Open Medical Informatics Journal,* (4), 1-11.

Lutz, J., Thonssen, B., & Witschel, H. F. (2013). Breaking free from your information prison: A recommender based on semantically enriched context descriptions. In *Proceedings of the First International Conference on Enterprise Systems: ES 2013* (pp. 1–9). IEEE. doi:10.1109/ES.2013.6690092

Macdonald, S., & Williams, C. (1994). The Survival of the Gatekeeper. *Research Policy, 23*(2), 123–132. doi:10.1016/0048-7333(94)90049-3

MacReady, N. (2007). Developing Countries Court Medical Tourists. *Lancet, 369*(9576), 1849–1850. doi:10.1016/S0140-6736(07)60833-2 PMID:17549816

Maddux, C., Sprague, D., Ferdig, R., & Albion, P. (2007). Editorial: Online Education: Issues and Research Questions. *Journal of Technology and Teacher Education, 15*(2), 157–166.

Maddux, J. E., & Rogers, R. W. (1983). Protection motivation and self-efficacy: A revised theory of fear appeals and attitude change. *Journal of Experimental Social Psychology, 19*(5), 469–479. doi:10.1016/0022-1031(83)90023-9

Maier, R., & Sametinger, J. (2004). Personal knowledge management in a peer-to-peer environment. In *Proceedings of the 5th European Conference on Knowledge Management*. Paris (France).

Majchrzak, A., Wagner, C., & Yates, D. (2012). *The Impact of Shaping on Knowledge Reuse for Organizational Improvement with Wikis*. Retrieved from http://papers.ssrn.com/abstract=2536091

Majchrzak, A., Wagner, C., & Yates, D. (2006). Corporate wiki users: results of a survey. In *Proceedings of the 2006 international symposium on Wikis* (pp. 99–104). ACM. doi:10.1145/1149453.1149472

Majchrzak, A., Wagner, C., & Yates, D. (2013). Knowledge Reuse for Organizational Improvement. *Management Information Systems Quarterly, 37*(2), 455–469.

Mancini, P. (1999). New Frontiers in Political Professionalism. *Political Communication, 16*(3), 231–245. doi:10.1080/105846099198604

Mangold, W. G., & Faulds, D. J. (2009). Social media: The new hybrid element of the promotion mix. *Business Horizons, 52*(4), 357–365. doi:10.1016/j.bushor.2009.03.002

Manmadhan, N., & Achuthan, K. (2014). Behavioural analysis for prevention of intranet information leakage. In *2014 International Conference on Advances in Computing, Communications and Informatics (ICACCI)* (pp. 1535–1537). IEEE. doi:10.1109/ICACCI.2014.6968644

Marasco, E., Mehjat, L., & Rosehart, W. (2015). Enhancing EDA education thruogh gamification. In *IEEE International Conference on Microelectronics Systems Education (MSE)* (pp. 25–27). Pittsburgh, PA: IEEE Press. doi:10.1109/MSE.2015.7160009

Marshall, C. C., & Shipman, F. M. (2015). Exploring the Ownership and Persistent Value of Facebook Content. In *Proceedings of the 18th ACM Conference on Computer Supported Cooperative Work & Social Computing - CSCW '15* (pp. 712–723). New York: ACM Press. doi:10.1145/2675133.2675203

Marshall, L. (1997). Facilitating Knowledge Management and Knowledge Sharing: New Opportunities for Information Professionals. *Online*, *21*(Sept/Oct), 92–98.

Martindale, T., & Dowdy, M. (2010). Personal learning environments, G. Veletsianos (Ed.), Emerging technologies in distance education. Athabasca University Press.

Marwick, D. (2001). Knowledge management technology. *IBM Systems Journal*, *40*(4), 814–830. doi:10.1147/sj.404.0814

Mason, A., & Wright, K. B. (2011). Framing Medical tourism: An Examination of appeal, rock, Convalescence, Accreditation, and Interactivity in Medical Tourism Web Sites. *Journal of Health Communication*, *16*(2), 163–177. doi:10.1080/10810730.2010.535105 PMID:21161812

Masrek, M. N., Rahim, H. A., Johare, R., & Rambli, Y. R. (2011). Intranet Supported Knowledge Sharing Behavior. *Journal of Organizational Knowledge Management*, *2011*, 1–11. doi:10.5171/2011.802263

Massingham, P. (2014). An evaluation of knowledge management tools: Part 1 – managing knowledge resources. *Journal of Knowledge Management*, *18*(6), 1075–1100. doi:10.1108/JKM-11-2013-0449

Masuku, C., & Moyo, P. (2014). An Assessment to the use of Facebook as a communication tool by Midlands State University students from 2012 to 2013. *Journal of Media and Communication Studies*, *6*(8), 130–143. doi:10.5897/JMCS2014.0391

Mata, F. J., & Quesada, A. (2014). Web 2.0, social networks and e-commerce as marketing tools. *Journal of Theoretical and Applied Electronic Commerce Research*, *9*(1), 56–69. doi:10.4067/S0718-18762014000100006

Matoo, A., & Rathindran, R. (2006). How Health Insurance Inhibits Trade in Health Care. *Health Affairs*, *25*(2), 358–368. doi:10.1377/hlthaff.25.2.358 PMID:16522578

Matthews, T., Whittaker, S., Moran, T., & Yuen, S. (2011). Collaboration personas. In *Proceedings of the 2011 annual conference on Human factors in computing systems - CHI '11* (p. 2247). New York: ACM Press. doi:10.1145/1978942.1979272

Ma, W. W., & Chan, A. (2014). Knowledge sharing and social media: Altruism, perceived online attachment motivation, and perceived online relationship commitment. *Computers in Human Behavior*, *39*, 51–58. doi:10.1016/j.chb.2014.06.015

Mayfield, A. (2008). What is social media? *iCrossing*. Retrieved 12 June, 2015 from http://www.icrossing.com/uk/sites/default/files_uk/insight_pdf_files/What%20is%20Social%20Media_iCrossing_ebook.pdf

McAdam, R., & Reid, R. (2000). A comparison of public and private sector perceptions and use of knowledge management. *Journal of European Industrial Training*, *24*(6), 317–329. doi:10.1108/03090590010346424

McAfee, A. (2006). *Enterprise 2.0*. Retrieved June 26, 2015, from: http://andrewmcafee.org/2006/05/enterprise_20_version_20/

McElfresh, L. K. (2010). Catalogers and social media: A whole lotta movin' and shakin' going on. *Technicalities*, *30*(4), 2–5.

McElroy, M. W. (2003). *The New Knowledge Management: Complexity, Learning and Sustainable Innovation*. Burlington, MA: KMCI Press/Butterworth-Heinemann.

McKinsey & Company. (2011). Big data: The next frontier for innovation, competition, and productivity. *McKinsey Global Institute*. doi:10.1080/01443610903114527

McLean, R., Richards, B. H., & Wardman, J. I. (2007). The effect of Web 2.0 on the future of medical practice and education: Darwikinian evoluation or folksonomic revolution? *The Medical Journal of Australia*, *187*(3), 174–177.

McLuhan, M. (1976). Inside on the Outside, or the Spaced-Out American. *Journal of Communication*, *26*(4), 46–53. doi:10.1111/j.1460-2466.1976.tb01935.x PMID:7577

Medhekar, A. (2014). Government Policy Initiatives for Developing Sustainable Medical Tourism Industry. *GSTF-Journal on Business Review, 3*(3), 95-105.

Medhekar, A., & Ali, M. M. (2012). A Cross-Border Trade in Healthcare services: Bangladesh to India. *The Business and Management Review, London*, *2*(1), 1–13.

Medhekar, A., & Newby, L. (2012). Information Search for Medical Treatment Abroad. *Journal of Applied Global Research*, *5*(3), 53–72.

Medhekar, A., Wong, H. Y., & Hall, J. (2014). Innovation in Medical Tourism Services Marketing: A case of India. In A. Goyal (Ed.), *Innovations in Services Marketing and Management: Strategies for Emerging Economies* (pp. 49–66). Penn, USA: IGI Global Publishing.

Meloche, J. A., Hasan, H. M., Willis, D., Pfaff, C., & Qi, Y. (2009). Co-creating corporate knowledge with a wiki. *International Journal of Knowledge Management*, *5*(2), 22–50. doi:10.4018/jkm.2009040103

Meyer, M. H., & Zack, M. H. (1999). The design and development of information products. *Sloan Management Review*, *37*.

Meyrowitz, J. (1985). *No sense of place: The impact of electronic media on social behaviour*. New York: Oxford University Press.

Millar, D. P. (2004). Exposing the Errors: An Examination of the Nature of Organizational Crises. In D. P. Millar & R. L. Heath (Eds.), *Responding to Crisis: A Rhetorical Approach to Crisis Communication* (pp. 9–31). Mahwah, NJ: Lawrence Erlbaum Associates.

Miller, K. (2015). *Organizational Communication* (7th ed.). Boston, MA: Wadsworth.

Miller, T. E., & Derse, A. R. (2002). Between strangers: The practice of medicine online. *Health Affairs*, *21*(4), 68–179. doi:10.1377/hlthaff.21.4.168 PMID:12117127

Miller, W. J. (2013). We Can't All Be Obama: The Use of New Media in Modern Political Campaigns. *Journal of Political Marketing*, *12*(4), 326–347. doi:10.1080/15377857.2013.837312

Milton, N., Shadbolt, N., Cottam, H., & Hammersley, M. (1999). Towards a knowledge technology for knowledge management. *International Journal of Human-Computer Studies*, *51*(3), 615–641. doi:10.1006/ijhc.1999.0278

Miron, E., & Ravid, G. (2015). Facebook Groups as an Academic Teaching Aid: Case Study and Recommendations for Educators. *Journal of Educational Technology & Society*, 18 (4), 371-384.

Mitchell, R., Boyle, B., Burgess, J., & McNeil, K. (2014). "You Can't Make a Good Wine Without a Few Beers": Gatekeepers and Knowledge Flow in Industrial Districts. *Journal of Business Research*, *67*(10), 2198–2206. doi:10.1016/j.jbusres.2014.01.007

Modebelu, M. N., & Duvie, A. N. (2015). Knowledge management creativity elements expected of academics in Nigerian universities. *American Journal of Educational Research*, *3*(3), 263–267. Retrieved from http://pubs.sciepub.com/education/3/3/2

Moloney, K. (2008). Is Political Marketing New Words or New Practice in UK Politics? *Journal of Political Marketing*, *6*(4), 51–65. doi:10.1300/J199v06n04_03

Moore, G. C., & Benbasat, I. (1991). Development of an instrument to measure the perceptions of adopting an information technology innovation. *Information Systems Research*, *2*(3), 192–222. doi:10.1287/isre.2.3.192

Mørch, A. I., Engen, B. K., & Åsand, H.-R. H. (2004). The workplace as a learning laboratory. In *Proceedings of the eighth conference on Participatory design Artful integration: interweaving media, materials and practices - PDC 04* (Vol. 1, p. 142). New York: ACM Press. doi:10.1145/1011870.1011888

Morschheuser, B., Henzi, C., & Alt, R. (2015). *Increasing Intranet Usage through Gamification -- Insights from an Experiment in the Banking Industry*. doi:10.1109/HICSS.2015.83

Moses, J. W., & Knutsen, T. L. (2012). *Ways of Knowing: Competing Methodologies in Social and Political Research* (2nd ed.). New York: Palgrave Macmillan.

Mueller, J. (2012). Knowledge sharing between project teams and its cultural antecedents. *Journal of Knowledge Management*, *16*(3), 435–447. doi:10.1108/13673271211238751

Munoz, C., & Towner, T. (2009). Opening Facebook: How to use Facebook in the college classroom. In *Society for Information Technology & Teacher Education International Conference* (No. 1, p. 2623-2627).

Murphy, G. D., & Salomone, S. (2013). Using social media to facilitate knowledge transfer in complex engineering environments: A primer for educators. *European Journal of Engineering Education*, *38*(1), 70–84. doi:10.1080/03043797.2012.742871

Murray, S., & Peyrefitte, J. (2007). Knowledge type and communication media choice in the knowledge transfer process. *Journal of Managerial Issues*, *19*(1), 111–133.

Nahapiet, J., & Ghoshal, S. (1998). Social capital, intellectual capital, and the organizational advantage. *Academy of Management Review*, *23*(2), 242–266.

Naisbitt, J. (1994). *Global paradox: the bigger the world economy, the more powerful its smallest players*. New York, NY: Avon Books.

Nambissan Geetha, B. (2014). *Poverty, Markets and Elementary Education in India.* Working Papers of the Max Weber Foundation's Transnational Research Group India. Retrieved from http://www.cprindia.org/sites/default/files/events/Geetha%20Nambissan%20paper.pdf

Nancy, M. D. (2000). *Common Knowledge: How Companies Thrive by Sharing What They Know*. Boston, MA: Harvard Business School Press.

Nassab, R., Hamnett, N., Nelson, K., Kaur, S., Greensell, B., Dhital, S., & Juma, A. (2010). Cosmetic Tourism: Public Opinion and Analysis of Information and Content Available on the internet. *Aesthetic Surgery Journal*, *30*(3), 465–469. doi:10.1177/1090820X10374104 PMID:20601579

National Archives and Records Administration White Paper. (2013). *A report on Best Practices for the Capture of Social Media Records*. Retrieved January 20, 2015 from http://www.archives.gov/records-mgmt/resources/socialmediacapture.pdf

National Archives and Records Administration. (2010). *A Report on Federal Web 2.0 Use and Record Value*. Retrieved September 14, 2015 from http://www.archives.gov/records-mgmt/resources/web2.0-use.pdf

Needham, C., & Smith, G. (2015). Introduction: Political Branding. *Journal of Political Marketing*, *14*(1-2), 1–6. doi:10.1080/15377857.2014.990828

Negrine, R. (2008). *The Transformation of Political Communication: Continuities and Changes in Media and Politics*. New York: Palgrave Macmillan.

Negrine, R., & Lilleker, D. G. (2002). The Professionalization of Political Communication: Continuities and Change in Media Practices. *European Journal of Communication*, *17*(3), 305–323. doi:10.1177/0267323102017003688

Negrine, R., Mancini, P., Holtz-Bacha, C., & Papathanossopoulos, S. (Eds.). (2007). *The Professionalization of Political Communication*. Bristol: Intellect.

Newman, B.I. (2012). The Role of Marketing in Politics: Ten Years Later. *Journal of Political Marketing, 11*. DOI: 10.1080/15377857.2012.642697

Newman, B. I. (1994). *The Marketing of the President: Political Marketing as Campaign Strategy*. Thousand Oaks, CA: Sage Publications.

Newman, B. I. (1999a).Preface. In *Handbook of Political Marketing*. Thousand Oaks, CA: Sage.

Newman, B. I. (1999b). *The Mass Marketing of Politics: Democracy in an Age of Manufactured Image*. London: Sage Publication.

Newman, B. I. (Ed.). (1999c). *Handbook of Political Marketing*. Thousand Oaks, CA: Sage.

Nielsen & NM Incite. (2011). *The Social Media Report: Spending Time, Money and Going Mobile*. Retrieved June 13, 2013, from http://blog.nielsen.com/nielsenwire/social/2012/

Nielsen, J. (2006). *The 90-9-1 Rule for Participation Inequality in Social Media and Online Communities*. Available online at: http://www.nngroup.com/articles/participation-inequality/

Nielsen, P., & Razmerita, L. (2014). Motivation and Knowledge Sharing through Social Media within Danish Organizations. In *Creating Value for All Through IT* (pp. 197–213). Springer Berlin Heidelberg. doi:10.1007/978-3-662-43459-8_13

Nonaka, I., Konno, N., Tokuoka, K., & Kawamura, T. (1992). Hypertext organization for accelerating organizational knowledge creation. *Diamond Harvard Business*, 12-22.

Nonaka, I. (1994). Dynamic Theory of Organisational Knowledge Creation. *Organization Science*, *5*(1), 14–37. doi:10.1287/orsc.5.1.14

Nonaka, I., & Kono, N. (1998). The Concept of "Ba': Building a Foundation for Knowledge Creation. *California Management Review*, *40*(3), 40–54. doi:10.2307/41165942

Nonaka, I., & Takeuchi, H. (1995). *The knowledge-creating company*. New York, NY: Oxford University Press.

Nonaka, I., & Takeuchi, H. (1995). *The Knowledge-creating Company*. New York: Oxford University Press.

Nonaka, I., & Takeuchi, H. (1995). *The knowledge-creating company: How Japanese companies create the dynamics of innovation*. Oxford University Press.

Nonaka, I., & Toyama, R. (2003). The knowledge-creating theory revisited: Knowledge creation as a synthesizing process. *Knowledge Management Research & Practice*, *1*(1), 2–10. doi:10.1057/palgrave.kmrp.8500001

Nonaka, I., Toyama, R., & Konno, N. (2000). SECI, Ba, and Leadership: A Unified Model of Dynamic Knowledge Creation. *Long Range Planning*, *33*(1), 5–34. doi:10.1016/S0024-6301(99)00115-6

Nonaka, I., & Von Krogh, G. (2009). Tacit Knowledge and Knowledge Conversion: Controversy and Advancement in Organizational Knowledge Creation Theory. *Organization Science*, *20*(3), 635–652. doi:10.1287/orsc.1080.0412

Norris, P. (2000). *The Virtuos Circle–Political Communication in Postindustrial Societies*. Cambridge, UK: Cambridge University Press. doi:10.1017/CBO9780511609343

Nunamaker, J. F., Applegate, L. M., & Konsynski, B. R. (1988). Computer-Aided Deliberation: Model Management and Group Decision Support. *Operations Research*, *36*(6), 826–848. doi:10.1287/opre.36.6.826

O' Schaughnessy, N. J., & Hanneberg, S. C. M. (2002). *The Idea of Political Marketing*. London: Praeger Series in Political Communication.

O'Cass, A. (2001a). Political Marketing: An Investigation of the Political Marketing Concept and Political Market Orientation in Australian Politics. *European Journal of Marketing*, *35*(9/10), 1003–1025. doi:10.1108/03090560110401938

O'Cass, A. (2001b). The Internal-External Marketing Orientation of a Political Party: Social Implications of Political Party Marketing Orientation. *Journal of Public Affairs*, *1*(2), 136–152. doi:10.1002/pa.59

O'Dell, C., & Hubert, C. (2011). *The New Edge in Knowledge: How Knowledge Management Is Changing the Way We Do Business*. John Wiley & Sons.

O'Leary, D. E. (1997). The Internet, intranets, and the AI renaissance. *Computer*, *30*(1), 71–78. doi:10.1109/2.562929

O'Leary, D. E. (1998). Enterprise knowledge management. *Computer*, *31*(3), 54–61. doi:10.1109/2.660190

O'Reilly, T. (2005). *Web 2.0: compact definition?* Retrieved 14 June, 2015 from http://radar.oreilly.com/2005/10/ web-20-compact-definition.html

O'Reilly, T. (2005). *What is Web 2.0? Design patterns and business models for the next generation of software*. Retrieved June 7, 2014, from http://www.oreilly.com/pub/a/web2/archive/what-is-web-20.html

O'Reilly, T., & Battelle, J. (2009). *Web Squared: Web 2.0 Five Years On*. Web 2.0 Summit Special report. Retrieved June 26, 2015, from: http://assets.en.oreilly.com/1/event/28/web2009 websquared-whitepaper.pdf

O'Shaughnessy, NJ. (2010) The marketing of political marketing. *European Journal of Marketing, 35*(9-10), 1047-1057.

Obermayer-Kovács, N., & Csepregi, A. (2007): Perspectives of Knowledge Management – Investigations at Hungarian Organizations. In *Proceedings of Business Scienes Symposium for Young Researchers, Feast of Hungarian Science 2007* (pp. 27-36). Budapest: Budapesti Műszaki Főiskola.

Obermayer-Kovács, N., & Komlósi, E. (2014). What emotional intelligent traits enable managers to Share knowledge for work-related quality of life? In *Proceedings of Makelearn 2014: Human Capital without Borders International Conference* (pp. 325-333). Portorož: International School for Social and Business Studies.

Obermayer-Kovács, N., Komlósi, E., Szenteleki, C., & Tóth, E. V. (2015). Exploring Emotional Intelligence Trait Enablers for Knowledge Sharing: An Empirical Study. *International Journal of Synergy and Research*, *4*(1), 7–23. doi:10.17951/ijsr.2015.4.1.7

Odabaşı, H. F., Mısırlı, Ö., Günüç, S., Timar, Z. Ş., Ersoy, M., Som, S., & Erol, O. et al. (2012). Eğitim için yeni bir ortam: Twitter. *Anadolu Journal of Educational Sciences International*, *2*(1), 89–103.

Odejobi, O. A. (2015). Self – knowledge and intellectualism: A perspective from Yoruba Cosmology. In Y. K. Salami, J. O. Famakinwa, & G. Fasiku (Eds.), *Nationalism and Economic Justice in Nigeria*. Ile – Ife: Obafemi Awolowo University Press.

Oduor, M., Alahäivälä, T., & Oinas-Kukkonen, H. (2014a). Persuasive software design patterns for social influence. *Personal and Ubiquitous Computing*, *18*(7), 1689–1704. doi:10.1007/s00779-014-0778-z

OECD. (1996). *The Knowledge-based Economy*. Paris: OECD.

Oinas-Kukkonen, H. (2012). A foundation for the study of behavior change support systems. *Personal and Ubiquitous Computing*, *17*(6), 1223–1235. doi:10.1007/s00779-012-0591-5

Oinas-Kukkonen, H., & Harjumaa, M. (2009). Persuasive Systems Design: Key Issues, Process Model, and System Features. *Journal of the AIS Electronic Library*, *24*(1). Retrieved from http://aisel.aisnet.org/cais/vol24/iss1/28

Okimoto, J. (2007). *Industry Trends: the evolution of knowledge management (KM 1.0 vs. KM 2.0)*. IBM Global Business Services. Retrieved June 26, 2015, from: http://www.slideshare.net/elsua/the-evolution-of-knowledge-management-km-10-vs-km-20

Okolie-Osemene, J. (2012). Social media and the question of cultural identity in Nigeria. *African Notes*: *Journal of the Institute of African Studies, 36*(3).

Oluikpe, P. (2012). Developing a corporate knowledge management strategy. *Journal of Knowledge Management*, *16*(6), 862–878. doi:10.1108/13673271211276164

Omrod, R. P. (2011). *Product-, Sales- and Market-Oriented Parties: Literature Review and Implications for Academics, Practitioners and Educators.* Working Paper Series in Management 2011/2 Institute for Economics and Management Aarhus University, Denmark.

Oorni, A. (2004). Consumer objectives and the amount of search in electronic travel and tourism markets. *Journal of Travel & Tourism Marketing*, *17*(2/3), 3–14. doi:10.1300/J073v17n02_01

Oosterlinck, A. (2004). *Knowledge management in post-secondary education: universities, OECD working paper*. Retrieved 4th Sep 2015, from www.oecd.org/dataoecd/46/21/2074921.pdf

Opdenakker, R. (2006). Advantages and Disadvantages of Four Interview Techniques in Qualitative Research. In *Forum Qualitative Sozialforschung/Forum: Qualitative*. *Social Research*, *7*(4).

Ormrod, R. P. (2009). *Understanding Political Market Orientation*. (Doctoral Thesis). Aarhus School of Business, University of Aarhus, Denmark.

Ormrod, R. P. (2012) *Defining Political Marketing*. Management Working Papers. Institut for Økonomi, Aarhus Universitet. 22 Oct 2012

Ormrod, R. P., & Henneberg, S. C. M. (2008). *Understanding Political Market Orientation*. Paper presented at International Conference on Political Marketing, Manchester, UK.

Ormrod, R.P., Henneberg, S.C.M., & O'Shaughnessy, N. J. (2013). *Political Marketing: Theory and Concepts*. London: Sage Publication.

Ormrod, R. P. (2005). A Conceptual Model of Political Market Orientation. *Journal of Nonprofit & Public Sector Marketing*, *14*(1/2), 47–65. doi:10.1300/J054v14n01_04

Ormrod, R. P. (2006). A Critique of the Lees-Marshment Market-Oriented Party Model. *Politics*, *26*(2), 110–118. doi:10.1111/j.1467-9256.2006.00257.x

Ormrod, R. P. (2007). Political Market Orientation and Its Commercial Cousin. *Journal of Political Marketing*, *6*(2-3), 2–3, 69–90. doi:10.1300/J199v06n02_05

Ormrod, R. P., & Henneberg, S. C. M. (2009). Different Facets of Market Orientation: A Comparative Analysis of Party Manifestos. *Journal of Political Marketing*, *8*(3), 190–208. doi:10.1080/15377850903044742

Ormrod, R. P., & Henneberg, S. C. M. (2010). Strategic Political Postures and Political Market Orientation: Toward an Integrated Concept of Political Marketing Strategy. *Journal of Political Marketing*, *9*(4), 294–313. doi:10.1080/15377857.2010.518106

Ormrod, R. P., & Henneberg, S. C. M. (2010, February). Understanding voter orientation in the context of political market orientation: Is the political customer king? *Journal of Marketing Management*, *26*(1–2), 108–130. doi:10.1080/02672570903574270

Ormrod, R. P., & Henneberg, S. C. M. (2011). Political Market Orientation and Strategic Party Postures in Danish Political Parties. *European Journal of Marketing*, *45*(6), 852–881. doi:10.1108/03090561111119949

Osazee-Odia, O. U. (2008). Assessing the Relevance of New Media Technology in Globalisation of Broadcasting. In E. M. Mojaye, O. O. Oyewo, R. M'Bayo, & I. A. Sobowale (Eds.), *Globalisaion and Development Communication in Africa*. Ibadan: Ibadan University Press.

Ozanne, L. K., & Ballantine, P. W. (2010). Sharing as a form of anti-consumption? An examination of toy library users. *Journal of Consumer Behaviour*, *9*(6), 485–498. doi:10.1002/cb.334

Palen, L., Hiltz, S. R., & Liu, S. (2007). Online forums supporting grassroots participation in emergency prepardness and response. *Communications of the ACM*, *50*(3), 54–58. doi:10.1145/1226736.1226766

Panagiotopoulos, P., Shan, L. C., Barnett, J., Regan, A., & McConnon, A. (2015). A framework of social media engagement: Case studies with food and consumer organizations in the UK and Ireland. *International Journal of Information Management*, *35*(4), 394–402. doi:10.1016/j.ijinfomgt.2015.02.006

Panagopoulos, C. (2011). Introduction: Money and Technology in the 2008 Elections. *Journal of Political Marketing*, *10*. DOI: 10.1080/15377857.2011.540188

Panahi, S., Watson, J., & Partridge, H. (2012). Social Media and Tacit Knowledge Sharing: Developing a Conceptual Model. In *Proceedings of World Academy of Science, Engineering and Technology, World Academy of Science, Engineering and Technology* (pp. 1095–1102). Paris, France: WASET.

Panahi, S., Watson, J., & Partridge, H. (2013). Towards tacit knowledge sharing over social web tools. *Journal of Knowledge Management*, *17*(3), 379–397. doi:10.1108/JKM-11-2012-0364

Pan, B., MacLaurin, T., & Crotts, J. C. (2007). Travel Blogs and the Implications for Destination Marketing. *Journal of Travel Research*, *46*(1), 35–45. doi:10.1177/0047287507302378

Parekh, R. A. (2009). Knowledge sharing: collaboration between universities and industrial organizations. In *Globalizing Academic Libraries: Vision 2020: Pre-conference Volume:The International Conference on Academic Libraries*. University of Delhi.

Parsons, M., & Rowling, M. (2015). Social Media and the Paradox of Fear: An Exploratory Study of Political Relationship Marketing Within South Wales. *Journal of Political Marketing*, 1–23. doi:10.1080/15377857.2015.1039746

Pasher, E., & Ronen, T. (2011). *The Complete Guide to Knowledge Management*. Hoboken, NJ: Wiley. doi:10.1002/9781118983782

Passy, F. (2003). Social movements and networks. In M. Diani & D. McAdam (Eds.), *Relational Approaches to Collective Action*. New York: Oxford University Press.

Patterson, I. (2007). Information sources used by older adults for decision making about tourist and travel destinations. *International Journal of Consumer Studies*, *31*(5), 528–533. doi:10.1111/j.1470-6431.2007.00609.x

Patton, M. Q. (2005). *Qualitative Research*. New York, NY: John Wiley & Sons, Ltd. doi:10.1002/0470013192.bsa514

Pavitt, C. (1999). The Third Way: Scientific Realism and Communication Theory. *Communication Theory*, *9*(2), 162–188. doi:10.1111/j.1468-2885.1999.tb00356.x

Peppler, K. A., & Solomou, M. (2011). Building creativity: Collaborative learning and creativity in social media environments. *On the Horizon.*, *19*(1), 13–23. doi:10.1108/10748121111107672

Pereira, H. G., Maria, M. D. F., & Mateus, I. (2014). Say yes to Facebook and get your customers involved! Relationships in a world of social networks. *Business Horizons*, *57*(6), 695–702. doi:10.1016/j.bushor.2014.07.001

Petrides, K. V. (2009). *Technical Manual for the Trait Emotional Intelligence Questionnaires (TEIQue)*. London: Psychometric Laboratory.

Petrides, L., & Nodine, T. (2003). *KM in Education: Defining the Landscape*. Half Moon Bay, CA: Institute for the Study of Knowledge Management in Education.

Pettenati, M. C., Cigognini, E., Mangione, J., & Guerin, E. (2007). Using social software for personal knowledge management in formal online learning. *Turkish Online Journal of Distance Education*, *8*(3), 52–65.

Pew Research Center. (2009). *The social life of health information.* Retrieved April 30, 2015, from http://www.pewinternet.org/Reports/2009/8-The-Social-Life-of-Health-Information/

PewResearch Center. (2014). *Social Networking Fact Sheet.* Pew Research Center, Internet, Science & Tech. Retrieved from http://www.pewinternet.org/fact-sheets/social-networking-fact-sheet/

Pfaff, C. C., & Hasan, H. (2006). Overcoming organisational resistance to using Wiki technology for Knowledge Management. In *Proceedings of the 6th international symposium on wikis and open collaboration* (p. 14). ACM.

Phosaard, S., & Wiriyapinit, M. (2011). Knowledge management via Facebook: Building a framework for knowledge management on a social network by aligning business, IT and knowledge management.*Proceedings of the World Congress on Engineering 2011.*

Pink, D. H. (2011). *Drive: The surprising truth about what motivates us*. Edinburgh, UK: Canongate Books Ltd. Retrieved from http://www.ted.com/talks/dan_pink_on_motivation

Plasser, F., & Plasser, G. (2002). *Global Political Campaigning: A Worldwide Analysis of Campaign Professionals and Their Practices*. Westport, CT: Praeger.

Pohs, W. (2001). Practical Knowledge Management: the Lotus Discovery System. IBM Press.

Polanyi, M. (1966). The Tacit Dimension. London: Routledge & Kegan Paul.

Polanyi, M. (1958). *Personal knowledge: towards a post-critical philosophy*. Chicago University of Chicago Press.

Polanyi, M. (1966). The Logic of Tacit Inference. *Philosophy (London, England)*, *41*(155), 1–18. doi:10.1017/S0031819100066110

Polányi, M. (1966). *The Tacit Dimension*. London: Routledge & Kegan Paul.

Policy Research Initiative. (2005). *Social Capital as a Public Policy Tool Project Report*. Ottawa: Policy Research Initiative.

Powell, W. W., & Snellman, K. (2004). The Knowledge Economy. *Annual Review of Sociology*, *30*(1), 199–220. doi:10.1146/annurev.soc.29.010202.100037

Power, D. J. (2014). *Using "Big Data" for analytics and decision support.* Retrieved from http://www.tandfonline.com/doi/abs/10.1080/12460125.2014.888848

Prahalad, C. K., & Hamel, G. (1990). The core competence of the corporation. *Harvard Business Review*, (May-June): 79–91.

Prange, C. (1999). Organizational learning – desperately seeking theory? In M. Easterby-Smith, L. Araujo, & J. Burgoyne (Eds.), *Organizational Learning and the Learning Organization*. London: Sage. doi:10.4135/9781446218297.n2

Price Water Cooper (PWC). (2014). *Deciding with data: How data-driven innovation is fuelling Australia's economic growth*. Retrieved October 20, 2015 from http://www.pwc.com.au/consulting/assets/publications/Data-drive-innovation-Sep14.pdf

Proenca, T., Moura, N. T., & Van Der Hoek, A. (2009). *On the use of emerging design as a basis for knowledge collaboration*. Retrieved from http://dl.acm.org/citation.cfm?id=1881958.1881972

Prpic, J., & Shukla, P. (2013). The theory of crowd capital. In *Proceedings of the 46th Annual Hawaii International Conference on Systems Sciences*. Washington, DC: IEEE Computer Society.

Prpić, J., Shukla, P. P., Kietzmann, J. H., & McCarthy, I. P. (2015). How to Work a Crowd: Developing Crowd Capital through Crowdsourcing. *Business Horizons*, *58*(1), 77–85. doi:10.1016/j.bushor.2014.09.005

Puerta, A., & Eisenstein, J. (1999). Towards a general computational framework for model-based interface development systems. *Knowledge-Based Systems*, *12*(8), 433–442. doi:10.1016/S0950-7051(99)00037-4

Putnam, R. D. (2000). *Bowling Alone: The Collapse and Revival of American Community*. New York: Touchstone. doi:10.1145/358916.361990

Rabaey, J. M. (2015). The Human Intranet--Where Swarms and Humans Meet. *IEEE Pervasive Computing / IEEE Computer Society [and] IEEE Communications Society*, *14*(1), 78–83. doi:10.1109/MPRV.2015.20

Rabelo, J. D. H., Oliveira, E. C. C. D., Santos, D. V. D., Braga, L. C. D. S., Souza, G. D. S., Steinmacher, I. F., & Conte, T. U. (2015). Knowledge Management and Organizational Culture in a Software Organization--A Case Study. *8th International Workshop on IEEE/ACM, Cooperative and Human Aspects of Software Engineering (CHASE).*

Rachel. (2008). *How Social Media Is Changing Communication + Organizations*. The Social Organization. Retrieved from http://www.thesocialorganization.com/2008/11/the-importance-of-social-networking-to-information-work.html

Rader, E., Wash, R., & Brooks, B. (2012, July). Stories as informal lessons about security. In *Proceedings of the Eighth Symposium on Usable Privacy and Security* (p. 6). ACM.

Rafaeli, S., & Ravid, G. (2003). Information sharing as enabler for the virtual team: An experimental approach to assessing the role of electronic mail in disintermediation. *Information Systems Journal*, *13*(2), 191–206. doi:10.1046/j.1365-2575.2003.00149.x

Ravid, G., Kalman, Y. M., & Rafaeli, S. (2008). Wikibooks in higher education: Empowerment through online distributed collaboration. *Computers in Human Behavior*, *24*(5), 1913–1928. doi:10.1016/j.chb.2008.02.010

Razmerita, L., & Kirchner, K. (2011). How wikis can be used to manage knowledge in SMEs: A case study. *Business Information Review*, *28*(3), 175–178. doi:10.1177/0266382111420354

Razmerita, L., Kirchner, K., & Nabeth, T. (2014). Social media in organisations: Leveraging personal and collective knowledge processes. *Journal of Organizational Computing and Electronic Commerce*, *24*(1), 74–93. doi:10.1080/10919392.2014.866504

Razmerita, L., Kirchner, K., & Sudzina, F. (2009). Personal knowledge management. *Online Information Review*, *33*(6), 1021–1039. doi:10.1108/14684520911010981

Read, B. (2006). To the Chagrin of Its Clientele, Facebook Expands Its Membership. *The Chronicle of Higher Education*, *53*(5), A35.

Reagans, R., & McEvily, B. (2003). Network structure and knowledge transfer: The effects of cohesion and range. *Administrative Science Quarterly*, *48*(2), 240–267. doi:10.2307/3556658

Redecker, C., Alla-Mutka, K., Bacigalupo, M., Ferrari, A., & Punie, Y. (2009). *Learning 2.0 The Impact of Web 2.0 Innovations on Education and Training in Europe*. JRC Scientific and Technical Report, Institute for prospective technological studies, European Commission. Retrieved from http://ftp.jrc.es/EURdoc/JRC55629.pdf

Redecker, C., Leis, M., Leendertse, M., Punie, Y., Gijsbers, G., Kirschner, P., . . . Hoogveld, B. (2011). The Future of Learning: Preparing for Change. JRC Scientific and Technical Reports, Institute for prospective technological studies, European Commission.

Redmiles, E., Malone, A., & Mazurek, M. L. 2015 How I Learned To Be Secure: Advice Sources and Personality Factors in Cybersecurity. *Symposium on Usable Privacy and Security* Poster 2015

Reeves, T. C., & Oh, E. J. (2007). Generation differences and educational technology research. In *Handbook of research on educational communications and technology* (pp. 295–303). Mahwah, NJ: Routledge.

Reichental, J. (2011). Knowledge management in the age of social media, The days of the single, authoritative voice are coming to an end. *Oreilly Radar*. Retrieved from http://radar.oreilly.com/2011/03/knowledge-management-social-media.html

Retna, K. S., & Tee Ng, P. (2011). Communities of practice: Dynamics and success factors. *Leadership and Organization Development Journal*, *32*(1), 41–59. doi:10.1108/01437731111099274

Richards, L. (2014). *Handling Qualitative Data: A Practical Guide*. London: Sage.

Richardson, W. (2009). *Blogs, Wikis, Podcasts, And Other Powerful Web Tools for Classrooms* (3rd ed.). Thousand Oaks, CA: Corwin Press.

Rifkin, J. (2011). *Third industrial revolution: how lateral power is transforming energy, the economy, and the world*. London: Palgrave Macmillan.

Rifkin, J. (2014). *The zero marginal cost society: the internet of things, the collaborative commons, and the eclipse of capitalism*. London: Palgrave Macmillan.

Ritchie, J., Lewis, J., Nicholls, C. M., & Ormston, R. (Eds.). (2013). *Qualitative Research Practice: A Guide for Social Science Students and Researchers*. London: Sage.

RNCOS. (2010). Booming Medical Tourism in India. Industry Report. New Delhi: RNCOS.

Roberts, D. (2014). *Move over Org Chart, make way for the Social Graph: Collaborative Decision Making for the Agile Enterprise*. Academic Press.

Rogers, R. W. (1975). A protection motivation theory of fear appeals and attitude change1. *The Journal of Psychology*, *91*(1), 93–114. doi:10.1080/00223980.1975.9915803

Roney, S. A., & Ozturan, M. (2006). A content analysis of the web sites of Turkish travel agencies. *Anatolia*, *17*(1), 43–54. doi:10.1080/13032917.2006.9687026

Ruggles, R. (Ed.). (1997). Knowledge Management Tools. Boston: Butterworth Heinemann.

Runnels, V., & Carrera, P. M. (2012). Why do patients engage in medical tourism? *Maturitas*, *73*(4), 300–304. doi:10.1016/j.maturitas.2012.08.011 PMID:23007007

Ruppel, C. P., & Harrington, S. J. (2001). Sharing knowledge through intranets: A study of organizational culture and intranet implementation. *Professional Communication. IEEE Transactions on*, *44*(1), 37–52.

Rutter, R. N., Hanretty, C., & Lettice, F. (2015). Political Brands: Can Parties Be Distinguished by Their Online Brand Personality? *Journal of Political Marketing*, 1–20. doi:10.1080/15377857.2015.1022631

Ryan, J. (2014). A Business Process Management Approach to Perioperative Supplies/Instrument Inventory and Workflow. In C. Lewis, B. Doster, & S. Daily (Eds.), *2014 47th Hawaii International Conference on System Sciences* (Vol. 0, pp. 2868–2877).

Ryu, S., Ho, S. H., & Han, I. (2003). Knowledge Sharing Behavior of Physicians in Hospitals. *Expert Systems with Applications*, *25*(1), 113–122. doi:10.1016/S0957-4174(03)00011-3

Sadegh, B. I. (2011). Relationship between Education and Social Capital. *International Journal of Humanities and Social Science*, *1*(12), 52–57.

Safko, L. (2010). *The social media bible: tactics, tools, and strategies for business success*. Wiley.

Şahin, K., & Turan, B. O. (2012). The impact of social networks on designing education. *Journal of Information Technology in Construction.*, *17*, 485–501.

Sakr, S., Liu, A., Batista, D. M., & Alomari, M. (2011). A survey of large scale data management approaches in cloud environments. In *Proceedings of IEEE Communications Society Surveys and Tutorials*. Retrieved February 14, 2015 from http://ieeexplore.ieee.org/xpl/tocresult.jsp?isnumber=6065679

Salehi, A. (2010). *Low latency, high performance data stream processing: systems architecture algorithms and implementations*. Saarbrucken: VDM Verlag.

Salomon, G., & Perkins, D. N. (1998). Individual and social aspects of learning. *Review of Research in Education*, 23.

Sandelowski, M., Voils, C. I., Leeman, J., & Crandell, J. L. (2012). Mapping the Mixed Methods–Mixed Research Synthesis Terrain. *Journal of Mixed Methods Research*, *6*(4), 317–331. doi:10.1177/1558689811427913 PMID:23066379

Savigny, H. & Temple, M. (2010). Political Marketing Models: The Curious Incident of the Dog that Doesn't Bark. *Political Studies, 58,* 1049–1064.

Savigny, H. (2004). *Political Marketing: A Critical Assessment-Caveat Emptor*. (Doctoral Thesis). The University of Birmingham.

Savigny, H. (2007). Ontology and Epistemology in Political Marketing. *Journal of Political Marketing*, *6*(2-3), 2–3, 33–47. doi:10.1300/J199v06n02_03

Savigny, H. (2008). *The Problem of Political Marketing*. New York: Continuum.

Sayer, A. (2000). *Realism and Social Science*. London: Sage. doi:10.4135/9781446218730

Scammell, M. (1999). Political Marketing: Lessons for Political Science. *Political Studies*, *67*(4), 718–739. doi:10.1111/1467-9248.00228

Schang, S. C., Li, E. Y., Wu, Y. L., & Hou, O. C. (2011). Understanding Web 2.0 service models: A knowledge-creating perspective. *Information & Management*, *48*(4-5), 178–184. doi:10.1016/j.im.2011.01.005

Schepers, P., & Van den Berg, P. T. (2007). Social factors of work-environment creativity. *Journal of Business and Psychology*, *21*(3), 407–428. doi:10.1007/s10869-006-9035-4

Schlegelmilch, B. B., & Chini, T. C. (2003). Knowledge transfer between marketing functions in Multinational companies: A conceptual model. *International Business Review*, *12*(2), 215–232. doi:10.1016/S0969-5931(02)00097-5

Schmarzo, B., (2013). *Big Data: Understanding How Data Powers Big Business*. John Wiley & Sons P&T.

Schmidt, M. B., & Arnett, K. P. (2005). Spyware: A little knowledge is a wonderful thing. *Communications of the ACM*, *48*(8), 67–70. doi:10.1145/1076211.1076242

Schneider, H. (2005). *Rapid ICT Change and Workplace Knowledge Obsolescence*. SSRN Electronic Journal, doi:10.2139/ssrn.870084

Schneider, M. C. (2014). Gender-Based Strategies on Candidate Websites. *Journal of Political Marketing*, *13*(4), 264–290. doi:10.1080/15377857.2014.958373

Schubmehl, D., & Vesset, D. (2014). *The Knowledge Quotient: Unlocking the Hidden Value of Information Using Search and Content Analytics*. IDC white paper. Retrieved, June 26, 2015, from: http://www.coveo.com/~/media/Files/WhitePapers/Coveo_IDC_Knowledge_Quotient_June2014.ashx

Schwartz, M., Shetret, L., & Millar, A. (2013). Rethinking international counterterrorism assistance to the greater Horn of Africa: Toward a regional risk reduction strategy. *Perspectives on Terrorism*, *7*(6), 100–112.

Seebach, C. (2012). Searching for answers - Knowledge exchange through social media in organizations.*45th Hawaii International Conference on System Sciences*. doi:10.1109/HICSS.2012.514

Seeger, M. W., Sellnow, T. L., & Ulmer, R. R. (2003). *Communication and Organizational Crisis*. Westport, CT: Praeger.

Seide, F., Thambiratnam, K., Lu, L., & Yu, R. (2009). Multimedia Retrieval Through Indexing Speech: An Enterprise Perspective. In *Proceedings of the Third Workshop on Searching Spontaneous Conversational Speech SE - SSCS '09* (pp. 1–2). New York: ACM. doi:10.1145/1631127.1631128

Selwyn, N. (2009). The Digital Native-myth and reality. *Aslib Journal of Information Management*, *61*(4), 364–379.

Semple, E. (2012). *Organizations Don't Tweet, People Do: A Manager's Guide to the Social Web*. Wiley.

Senge, P. M. (1990). The Fifth Discipline: The Art & Practice of The Learning Organization. New York: Doubleday

Senge, P. M. (2014). *The Fifth Discipline Fieldbook: Strategies and Tools for Building a Learning Organization*. London: Crown Business.

Sethi, M., Sachindran, N., & Raghavan, S. (2013). SASH: Enabling continuous incremental analytic workflows on Hadoop. In *2013 IEEE 29th International Conference on Data Engineering (ICDE)* (pp. 1219–1230). IEEE. doi:10.1109/ICDE.2013.6544911

Shachtman, N. (2009). *"Command Posts of the Future" Readied for Afghan Surge*. Wired.

Shah, S. A. M., Khan, I., & Amjad, S. (2013). The Role of Social Media in Developing an Effective Knowledge Management Process in Professional Service Firms. *Mediterranean Journal of Social Sciences*, *4*(14), 775–782.

Shapiro, C., & Varian, H. R. (1993). *Information rules: a strategic guide to the network economy*. Boston, MA: Harvard Business School Press.

Shaw, D. R. (2002). How the Bush and Gore Campaigns Conceptualized and Used the Internet in 2000. *Journal of Political Marketing*, *1*(1), 39–65. doi:10.1300/J199v01n01_04

Sherman, E., & Schiffman, L. G. (2002). Political Marketing Research in the 2000 U.S. Election. *Journal of Political Marketing*, *1*(2-3), 2–3, 53–68. doi:10.1300/J199v01n02_05

Short, J., Williams, E., & Christie, B. (1976). *The social psychology of telecommunications*. London: Wiley.

Shult, J., & Corey, J. J. (2006). *Beauty from afar: A medical tourist's guide to affordable and quality cosmetic care outside the U.S. Stewart* (1st ed.). New York: Tabori & Chang Publisher.

Shvachko, K., Hairong, K., Radia, S., & Chansler, R. (2010). The Hadoop Distributed File System, *Mass Storage Systems and Technologies (MSST), IEEE 6th Symposium*, (pp.1-10).

Siakas, K., & Georgiadou, E. (2006). Knowledge sharing: cultural dynamics. In *Proceedings of 7th European Conference of Knowledge Management (ECKM06)*. Public Academic Conferences Ltd.

Siemens, G. (2014). *Connectivism: A Learning Theory for the Digital Age.* Working Paper Series. Accessed at http://er.dut.ac.za/handle/123456789/69

Siemens, G. (2005). Connectivism: A learning theory for the digital age. *International Journal of Instructional Technology and Distance Learning*, *2*(1).

Sigala, M., Christou, E., & Gretzel, U. (2012). Social Media in Travel, Tourism and Hospitality: Theory, Practice and Cases. Ashgate Publications.

Sigala, M. (2010). Measuring customer value in online collaborative trip planning processes. *Marketing Intelligence & Planning*, *28*(4), 418–443. doi:10.1108/02634501011053559

Sigala, M., & Chalkiti, K. (2015). Knowledge management, social media and employee creativity. *International Journal of Hospitality Management*, *45*, 44–58. doi:10.1016/j.ijhm.2014.11.003

Sillence, E., Briggs, P. H., & Fyshwick, L. (2007). Going online for health advice: Change in usage and trust practices over the last five years. *Interacting with Computers*, *19*(3), 397–403. doi:10.1016/j.intcom.2006.10.002

Siu, E. (2015). 10 User Generated Content Campaigns That Actually Worked. *Hubsopt Blogs*. Retrieved from http://blog.hubspot.com/marketing/examples-of-user-generated-content

Skeels, M., & Grudin, J. (2009). When Social Networks Cross Boundaries: A Case Study of Workplace Use of Facebook and Linkedin. In *Proceedings of the ACM 2009 International Conference on Supporting Group Work SE - GROUP '09* (pp. 95–104). New York: ACM. doi:10.1145/1531674.1531689

Smith, M. A., Shneiderman, B., Milic-Frayling, N., Mendes Rodrigues, E., Barash, V., Dunne, C., … Gleave, E. (2009). Analyzing (social media) networks with NodeXL. In *Proceedings of the fourth international conference on Communities and technologies - C&T '09* (p. 255). New York: ACM Press. doi:10.1145/1556460.1556497

Smith, M. E. (2014). *Internationalization, partnership and research collaboration in tertiary education*. Convocation Lecture, University of Benin.

Smith, E., Behrmann, J., Martin, J., & Williams-Jones, B. (2010). Reproductive tourism in Argentina: Clinic accreditation and its implications for consumers, health professionals and policy makers. *Developing World Bioethics*, *10*(2), 59–69. doi:10.1111/j.1471-8847.2009.00256.x PMID:19508291

Smith, R. D., Chanda, R., & Tangcharoensathien, V. (2009). Trade in Health-related services. *Lancet*, *373*(9663), 593–601. doi:10.1016/S0140-6736(08)61778-X PMID:19167053

Somerville, M., Mirijamdotter, A., & Collins, L. (2006). Systems Thinking and Information Literacy: Elements of a Knowledge Enabling Workplace Environment. *HICSS, 7*.

Sommer, M., & Tavlin, B. (2003). Notes on the California E-Politics Campaign Trail. *Journal of Political Marketing*, *3*(1), 87–96. doi:10.1300/J199v03n01_05

Sousa, F., Aparicio, M., & Costa, C. J. (2010). Organizational wiki as a knowledge management tool. In *Proceedings of the 28th ACM International Conference on Design of Communication* (pp. 33-39). ACM. doi:10.1145/1878450.1878457

Speier, A. R. (2011). Brokers, consumers and the Internet: How North American consumers navigate their infertility journeys. *Reproductive Biomedicine Online*, *23*(5), 592–599. doi:10.1016/j.rbmo.2011.07.005 PMID:21955489

Spender, J. C. (1996). Making knowledge the basis of a dynamic theory of the firm. *Strategic Management Journal*, *17*(S2), 45–62. doi:10.1002/smj.4250171106

Sprague, R. W., & Carlson, E. D. (1982). *Building Effective Decision Support Systems*. Englewood Cliffs, NJ: Prentice Hall Inc.

Sridhar, S. (1998). Decision support using the Intranet. *Decision Support Systems*, *23*(1), 19–28. doi:10.1016/S0167-9236(98)00033-5

SSA Report. (2014). *Sarva Shiksha Abhiyan (SSA): A Critical Review of SSA*. Retrieved from https://socialissuesindia.files.wordpress.com/2014/03/ssa-report-2014.pdf

Stafford, C., & Mearns, M. A. (2010). *What happens when organisations embrace social networking? Knowledge sharing at a multinational business solutions corporation*. SA Journal of Information Management. doi:10.4102/sajim.v11i4.414

Standing, C., & Kiniti, S. (2011). How can organizations use wikis for innovation? *Technovation*, *31*(7), 287–295. doi:10.1016/j.technovation.2011.02.005

Stanton, J. M., Mastrangelo, P., Stam, K. R., & Jolton, J. (2004, January). Behavioral Information Security: Two End User Survey Studies of Motivation and Security Practices. In *10th Americas Conference on Information Systems, AMCIS 2004*.

Steinfield, C., DiMicco, J. M., Ellison, N. B., & Lampe, C. (2009). Bowling online: social networking and social capital within the organization. In *Proceedings of the Fourth International Conference on Communities and Technologies* (pp. 245–254). New York, NY: ACM Press. doi:10.1145/1556460.1556496

Steininger, K., Ruckel, D., Dannerer, E., & Roithmayr, F. (2010). Healthcare knowledge transfer through a Web 2.0 portal: An Austrian approach. *International Journal of Healthcare Technology and Management*, *11*(1/2), 13–30. doi:10.1504/IJHTM.2010.033272

Stephens, R. T. (2009).Empirical analysis of functional Web 2.0 environments. In *Web 2.0 - the Business Mode*. Springer.

Stewart, T. A. (1997). *Intellectual Capital: The New Wealth of Nations*. New York: Doubleday Dell Publishing Group. Inc.

Stieglitz, S., & Dang-Xuan, L. (2011). Adoption and Use of Corporate Wikis in German Small and Medium-sized Enterprises. In *AMCIS 2011 Proceedings – all submissions*. Paper 235. Available online at: http://bit.ly/1WZuDCc

Stonebraker, M. (2006). "One Size Fits All": An Idea Whose Time Has Come and Gone. In *Proceedings of the 21st International Conference on Data Engineering*, (pp. 2-11).

Street, R. L. Jr. (2003). Medicated consumer provided communication in cancer care: The empowering potential of new technologies. *Patient Education and Counseling*, *50*(1), 99–104. doi:10.1016/S0738-3991(03)00089-2 PMID:12767594

Stromback, J. (2009). Selective Professionalisation of Political Campaigning: A Test of the Party-Centred Theory of Professionalised Campaigning in the Context of the 2006 Swedish Election. *Political Studies*, *57*, 95–116.

Stromback, J. (2010). A Framework for Comparing Political Market-Orientation. In Global Political Marketing. London: Routledge Taylor & Francis Group.

Stromback, J. (2007). Political Marketing and Professionalized Campaigning'. *Journal of Political Marketing*, *6*(2), 49–67. doi:10.1300/J199v06n02_04

Stromer-Galley, J. (2000). On-line interaction and why candidates avoid it. *Journal of Communication*, *50*(4), 111–132. doi:10.1111/j.1460-2466.2000.tb02865.x

Surowiecki, J. (2005). *The wisdom of crowds*. Anchor books.

Surowiecki, J. (Ed.). (2005). *The Wisdom of the Crowds*. New York: Anchor Books.

Susanty, A. I., & Wood, P. C. (2011). The Motivation to Share Knowledge of the Employees in the Telecommunication Service Providers in Indonesia. *International Proceedings of Economics Development & Research*, *5*(2), 2–159.

Sutter, J. D. (2010). *Texts, maps battle Haiti cholera outbreak*. Retrieved March 15, 2015 from http://www.cnn.com/2010/TECH/innovation/10/29/haiti.cholera.tech

Sveiby, K. E. (1997). *The New Organizational Wealth: Managing and Measuring Knowledge Based Assets*. San Francisco: Berrett-Koehler Pub. Inc.

Sveiby, K. E. (2001). A Knowledge-based theory of the firm to guide in strategy formulation. *Journal of Intellectual Capital*, *2*(4), 344–358. doi:10.1108/14691930110409651

Swan, J., Newell, S., Scarbrough,, H., & Hislop, D. (1999). Knowledge management and innovation: Networks and networking. *Journal of Knowledge Management*, *3*(4), 262–275. doi:10.1108/13673279910304014

Szuprowicz, B. O. (1996). *Intranets and Groupware*. Charleston, SC: Computer Technology Research Corp.

Tanis, M. (2008). Health-related On-Line Forums: What's the Big Attraction? *Journal of Health Communication*, *13*(7), 698–714. doi:10.1080/10810730802415316 PMID:18958781

Tashakkori, A. (2009). Are we there yet? The State of the Mixed Methods Community. *Journal of Mixed Methods Research*, *3*(4), 287–291. doi:10.1177/1558689809346151

Tashakkori, A., & Creswell, J. W. (2007a). Editorial: Exploring the Nature of Research Questions in Mixed Methods Research. *Journal of Mixed Methods Research*, *1*(3), 207–211. doi:10.1177/1558689807302814

Tashakkori, A., & Creswell, J. W. (2007b). The new era of mixed methods. *Journal of Mixed Methods Research*, *1*(1), 3–7. doi:10.1177/2345678906293042

Tashakkori, A., & Teddlie, C. (Eds.). (2010). *Sage Handbook of Mixed Methods in Social & Behavioral Research*. London: Sage. doi:10.4135/9781506335193

Tavakolifard, M., & Almeroth, K. C. (2012). Social computing: An intersection of recommender systems, trust/reputation systems, and social networks. *IEEE Network*, *26*(4), 53–58. doi:10.1109/MNET.2012.6246753

Taylor & Francis. (2014). *Use of social media by the library: Current practices and future opportunities*. Retrieved 6th Sep 2015, from http://www.tandf.co.uk/journals/access/white-paper-social-media.pdf

Taylor, J., & Raden, N. (2007). *Smart Enough Systems: How to Deliver Competitive Advantage by Automating Hidden Decisions*. Prentice Hall PTR.

Tellis, W. M. (1997). Application of a Case Study Methodology. *Qualitative Report*, *3*(3), 1–19.

Temple, M. (2013). The Media and the Message. *Journal of Political Marketing, 12*(2-3), 2–3, 147–165. doi:10.1080/15377857.2013.781479

Tenscher, J. & Mykkänen, J. (2014). Two Levels of Campaigning: An Empirical Test of the Party-Centred Theory of Professionalisation. *Political Studies, 62*(S1), 20–41. DOI: 10.1111/1467-9248.12104

Tenscher, J. (2004, September). 'Bridging the Differences': Political Communication Experts in Germany. *German Politics, 13*(3), 516–540. doi:10.1080/0964400042000287482

Tenscher, J. (2013). First-and second-order campaigning. *European Journal of Communication, 28*, 241.

Tenscher, J., & Mykkänen, J. (2013). Transformations in second-order campaigning: A German-Finnish comparison of campaign professionalism in the 2004 and 2009 European parliamentary elections. *Central European Journal of Communication, 2*, 171–187.

Tenscher, J., Mykkänen, J., & Moring, T. (2012). Modes of Professional Campaigning: A Four-Country Comparison in the European Parliamentary Elections, 2009. *The International Journal of Press/Politics, 17*(2), 145–168. doi:10.1177/1940161211433839

Terragon Limited. (2013). *State of Digital Media Nigeria 2013*. Retrieved September 5, 2015, from http://twinpinenetwork.com/publications/Nigeria-%20State%20of%20Digital%20Media.pdf

Thackeray, R., Neiger, B. L., Hanson, C. L., & Mckenzie, J. F. (2008). Enhancing Promotional Strategies within Social Marketing Programs: Use of Web 2.0 Social Media. *Health Promotion Practice, 9*(4), 338-343.

Thackeray, R., Neiger, B. L., Smith, A. K., & Van Wagenen, S. B. (2012). Adoption and use of social media among public health departments. *BMC Public Health, 12*(1), 242. doi:10.1186/1471-2458-12-242 PMID:22449137

Thompson, R. L., Higgins, C. A., & Howell, J. M. (1991). Personal computing: Toward a conceptual model of utilization. *Management Information Systems Quarterly, 15*(1), 125–143. doi:10.2307/249443

Thusoo, A., Shao, Z., Anthony, S., Borthakur, D., Jain, N., Sen Sharma, J., . . . Liu, H. (2010). Data warehousing and analytics infrastructure at facebook, In *Proceedings of ACM SIGMOD International Conference on Management of Data*, (pp. 1013-1020). doi:10.1145/1807167.1807278

Tinker, T., & Fouse, D. (2013). *Expert Round Table on Social Media and Risk Communication. During Times of Crisis: Strategic Challenges and Opportunities*. Retrieved June 13, 2013, from http://www.boozallen.com/media/file/Risk_Communications_Times_of_Crisis.pdf

Tiwana, A. (2002). *The Knowledge Management Toolkit: Orchestrating IT, Strategy and Knowledge Platforms*. Englewood Cliffs, NJ: Prentice-Hall.

Toffler, A. (1980). *Third wave*. New York, NY: William Morrow & Co.,Inc.

Towner, T. L., & Dulio, D. A. (2011). The Web 2.0 Election: Does the Online Medium Matter? *Journal of Political Marketing, 10*(1-2), 1–2, 165–188. doi:10.1080/15377857.2011.540220

Towner, T. L., & Dulio, D. A. (2012). New Media and Political Marketing in the United States: 2012 and Beyond. *Journal of Political Marketing, 11*(1-2), 1–2, 95–119. doi:10.1080/15377857.2012.642748

Townley, C. T. (2001). Knowledge Management and Academic Libraries. *College & Research Libraries, 62*(Jan), 44–55. doi:10.5860/crl.62.1.44

Townsend, S. (2012). What Are You Working On? *eLearn, 2012*(1), 1. doi:10.1145/2090108.2090109

Trainer, E. H., & Redmiles, D. F. (2012). Foundations for the design of visualizations that support trust in distributed teams. In *Proceedings of the International Working Conference on Advanced Visual Interfaces - AVI '12* (p. 34). New York: ACM Press. doi:10.1145/2254556.2254566

Treem, J. W., & Leonardi, P. M. (2012). Social media use in organizations: Exploring the affordances of visibility, editability, persistence, and association. *Communication Yearbook*, *36*, 143–189.

Troshani, I., & Rao, S. (2005). Key elements in an effective knowledge management system: A case study approach. In *Proceedings of the Fifth International Conference on Electronic Business* (pp. 563-564). Retrieved August 5, 2015, from http://iceb.nccu.edu.tw/proceedings/2005/563-564.pdf

Tucker, T. G., & Winchester, W. W. (2009). Mobile learning for just-in-time applications. In *Proceedings of the 47th Annual Southeast Regional Conference on - ACM-SE 47* (p. 1). New York: ACM Press. doi:10.1145/1566445.1566469

Turbiville, G., Meservey, J., & Forest, J. (2014). *Countering the al-Shabaab insurgency in Somalia: Lessons for U.S. special operations forces.* Joint Special Operations University. Retrieved from http://jsou.socom.mil/JSOU%20Publications/al_Shabaab_Feb_2014%20PDF.pdf

Turkish Statistical Institute (TUIK). (2015). Retrieved from: http://www.turkstat.gov.tr/

Turner, L. (2008). Cross-border dental care: 'dental tourism' and patient mobility. *British Dental Journal, 553-554.* doi:10.1038/sj.bdj.2008.403 PMID:18500297

Turner, L. (2010). Medical tourism and the global market place in health services: US patients, international hospitals and the search for affordable healthcare. *International Journal of Health Services*, *40*(3), 443–467. doi:10.2190/HS.40.3.d PMID:20799670

Turoff, M., Van de Walle, B., & Hiltz, S. R. (2010). Emergency response information systems. In B. Van de Walle, M. Turoff, & S. R. Hiltz (Eds.), *Information systems for emergency management.* Armonk, NY: M.E. Sharpe.

Ulmer, R. R., Sellnow, T. L., & Seeger, M. W. (2007). *Effective Crisis Communication: Moving from Crisis to Opportunity.* Thousand Oaks, CA: Sage Publications.

Underwood, M. (2014). *A One-Person Firm Still Needs an Intranet.* Academic Press.

UNESCO. (2014). *Addressing Exclusion.* Retrieved from http://www.unesco.org/new/en/education/themes/strengthening-education-systems/inclusive-education/

UNESCO. (2015). *Asia-Pacific Statement on Education Beyond 2015.* UNESCO. Retrieved from http://www.unesco.org/new/en/education/themes/strengthening-education-systems/inclusiveeducation/single-view/news/inclusive_quality_lifelong_learning_for_all_asia_pacific

Urbach, N., & Müller, B. (2012). The updated DeLone and McLean model of information systems success. In *Information systems theory* (pp. 1–18). New York: Springer. doi:10.1007/978-1-4419-6108-2_1

Vacca, J. (1996). *Virtual Reality: Strategies for Intranet and World Wide Web Applications.* Charleston, SC: Computer Technology Research Corp.

Van de belt, T. H., Engelen, L. G., Berben, S. A., & Schoonhoven, L. (2012). Definition of health 2.0 and medicine 2.0: a systematic review. *Journal of Medical Internet Research, 12*, e18.

Vance, K., Howe, W., & Dellavale, R. P. (2009). Social internet sites as a source of public health information. *Dermatologic Clinics*, *27*(2), 133–136. doi:10.1016/j.det.2008.11.010 PMID:19254656

Venkatesh, V., & Davis, F. D. (2000). A theoretical extension of the technology acceptance model: Four longitudinal field studies. *Management Science*, *46*(2), 186–204. doi:10.1287/mnsc.46.2.186.11926

Venkatesh, V., Morris, M. G., Davis, G. B., & Davis, F. D. (2003). User acceptance of information technology: Toward a unified view. *Management Information Systems Quarterly*, *27*(3), 425–478.

Vesnic-Alujevic, L., & Bauwel, S. V. (2014). YouTube: A Political Advertising Tool? A Case Study of the Use of YouTube in the Campaign for the European Parliament Elections. *Journal of Political Marketing*, *13*(3), 195–212. doi:10.1080/15377857.2014.929886

Viaene, S. (2013). Data Scientists Aren't Domain Experts. *IT Professional*, *15*(6), 12–17. doi:10.1109/MITP.2013.93

Vicente, V., Sjöstrand, F., Sundström, B. W., Svensson, L., & Castren, M. (2013). Developing a decision support system for geriatric patients in prehospital care. *European Journal of Emergency Medicine : Official Journal of the European Society for Emergency Medicine*, *20*(4), 240–247. doi:10.1097/MEJ.0b013e328356452d PMID:22759990

Villamón, E., Piqueras, M., Meseguer, J., Blanquer, I., Berbegall, A. P., Tadeo, I., & Noguera, R. et al. (2013). NeuPAT: An intranet database supporting translational research in neuroblastic tumors. *Computers in Biology and Medicine*, *43*(3), 219–228. doi:10.1016/j.compbiomed.2012.11.011 PMID:23290604

Vis-Sommer, V. (2003). Surveying Government Web Sites. *Journal of Political Marketing*, *3*(1), 97–103. doi:10.1300/J199v03n01_06

Vlasov, M., & Panikarova, S. (2015). Knowledge creation in state-owned enterprises. *Mediterranean Journal of Social Sciences*, *6*(4), 475-480. Retrieved from http://www.mcser.org/journal/index.php/mjss/article/view/6954/6658

Von Krogh, G. (2012). How does social software change knowledge management? toward a strategic research agenda. *The Journal of Strategic Information Systems*, *21*(2), 154–164. doi:10.1016/j.jsis.2012.04.003

Vosgerau, J., Wertenbroch, K., & Carmon, Z. (2006). Indeterminacy and live television. *The Journal of Consumer Research*, *32*(4), 487–495. doi:10.1086/500478

Vrat, P. (2014). Systems Approach and Supply Chain Management. In *Materials Management* (pp. 357–378). New Delhi: Springer India.

Vuori, V. (2011). *Social Media Changing the Competitive Intelligence Process: Elicitation of Employees' Competitive Knowledge*. Academic Dissertation. Retrieved June 7, 2014, from http://dspace.cc.tut.fi/dpub/bitstream/handle/123456789/20724/vuori.pdf

Vuori, M. (2012). Exploring Uses of Social Media in a Global Corporation. *Journal of Systems and Information Technology*, *14*(2), 155–170. doi:10.1108/13287261211232171

Vuori, V., & Okkonen, J. (2012). Knowledge sharing motivational factors of using an intra-organizational social media platform. *Journal of Knowledge Management*, *16*(4), 592–603. doi:10.1108/13673271211246167

Wagner, C. (2006). Breaking the knowledge acquisition bottleneck through conversational knowledge management. *Information Resources Management Journal*, *19*(1), 14. doi:10.4018/irmj.2006010104

Waks, J. L. (2013). *Education 2.0: The Learning Web Revolution and the Transformation of the School*. Paradigm Publishers.

Wald, H. S., Dube, C. E., & Anthony, D. C. (2007). Untangling the web: The impact of internet use on healthcare and the physician-patient relationship. *Patient Education and Counseling*, *68*(3), 218–224. doi:10.1016/j.pec.2007.05.016 PMID:17920226

Walker, G. H., Stanton, N. A., Revell, K., Rafferty, L., Salmon, P. M., & Jenkins, D. P. (2009). Measuring Dimensions of Command and Control Using Social Network Analysis: Extending the NATO SAS-050 Model. *The International C2 Journal, 3*(2), 1–49.

Walker, J. W. (2002). Research, knowledge sharing and you. *Human Resource Planning., 25*(2), 10–13.

Wallsten, K. (2011). Many Sources, One Message: Political Blog Links to Online Videos During the 2008 Campaign. *Journal of Political Marketing, 10*(1-2), 1–2, 88–114. doi:10.1080/15377857.2011.540203

Wan, C. S. (2002). The web sites of international tourist hotels and tour wholesalers in Taiwan. *Tourism Management, 23*(2), 155–160. doi:10.1016/S0261-5177(01)00048-6

Wangpipatwong, S. (2009). Factors influencing knowledge sharing among university students. *17th International Conference on Computers in Education.* Asia-Pacific Society for Computers in Education.

Wang, S., & Noe, R. A. (2010). Knowledge sharing: A review and directions for future research. *Human Resource Management Review, 20*(2), 115–131. doi:10.1016/j.hrmr.2009.10.001

Ward, T. (2015). IBM's new intranet represents change in intranet design. *Intranet Blog.*

Warkentin, M., Shropshire, J., & Johnston, A. (2007). The IT security adoption conundrum: An initial step toward validation of applicable measures. *AMCIS 2007 Proceedings*, 276.

Warkentin, M., Johnston, A. C., & Shropshire, J. (2011). The influence of the informal social learning environment on information privacy policy compliance efficacy and intention. *European Journal of Information Systems, 20*(3), 267–284. doi:10.1057/ejis.2010.72

Wasko, M. M., & Faraj, S. (2000). "It is what one does": Why people participate and help others in electronic communities of practice. *The Journal of Strategic Information Systems, 9*(2), 155–173. doi:10.1016/S0963-8687(00)00045-7

Wasko, M. M., & Faraj, S. (2005). Why should I share? Examining social capital and knowledge contribution in electronic networks of practice. *Management Information Systems Quarterly, 29*(1), 35–57.

Waters, R. D., Burnett, E., Lamm, A., & Lucas, J. (2009). Engaging stakeholders through social networking: How nonprofit organizations are using Facebook. *Public Relations Review, 35*(2), 102–106. doi:10.1016/j.pubrev.2009.01.006

Weaven, S., Grace, D., Dant, R., & Brown, J. R. (2014). Value Creation through Knowledge Management in Franchising: A Multi-Level Conceptual Framework. *Journal of Services Marketing, 28*(2), 97–104. doi:10.1108/JSM-09-2013-0251

Weiermair, K., & Mathies, C. (2004). *The tourism and leisure industry: Shaping the future.* New York: Haworth Hospitality Press.

Weinberger, D. (2007). The real difference between the two 2.0s. *KM World, 16*(2). Retrieved 10 May, 2015, from www.kmworld.com/Articles/Column/David-Weinberger/The-real-difference-between-the-two-2.0s-19130.aspx

Weingarten, R. M. (2009). Four generations, one workplace: A gen x-y staff nurse's view of team building in the emergency department. *Journal of Emergency Nursing: JEN, 35*(1), 27–30. doi:10.1016/j.jen.2008.02.017 PMID:19203677

Wenger, E. (2000). Communities of practice and social learning systems. *Organization, 7*(2), 225–246. doi:10.1177/135050840072002

Wengraf, T. (2001). *Qualitative Research Interviewing: Biographic Narrative and Semi-Structured Methods.* London: Sage. doi:10.4135/9781849209717

Westerman, D., Spence, P. R., & Heide Van Der, B. (2013). Social media as information source: Recency of updates and credibility of information. *Journal of Computer-Mediated Communication*, *I*(2), 1–14.

Whitehouse, P., Reynolds, R., & Caperton, I. (2009). Globaloria Pilot Year One: New Directions for 21st Century Teacher Professional Development. In I. Gibson et al. (Eds.), *Proceedings of Society for Information Technology & Teacher Education International Conference 2009* (pp. 1590-1597). Chesapeake, VA: AACE.

Whitten, A., & Tygar, J. D. (1999, August). Why Johnny Can't Encrypt: A Usability Evaluation of PGP 5.0. In Usenix Security (Vol. 1999).

Wiewiora, A., Murphy, G., Trigunarsyah, B., & Brown, K. (2014). Interactions Between Organizational Culture, Trustworthiness, and Mechanisms for Inter-Project Knowledge Sharing. *Project Management Journal*, *45*(2), 48–65. doi:10.1002/pmj.21407

Wiig, K. (1993). *Knowledge management foundations*. Arlington, TX: Schema Press.

Wiig, K. M. (1993). *Knowledge Management Foundations: Thinking About Thinking - How People and Organizations Represent, Create and Use Knowledge*. Schema Press.

Wiig, K. M. (1994). *Knowledge Management Foundations: Thinking about Thinking - how People and Organizations Represent, Create, and Use Knowledge*. Schema Press, Limited.

Wiig, K. M. (1997). Knowledge Management: Where Did it Come From and Where Will it Go? *Expert Systems with Applications*, *13*(1), 1–14. doi:10.1016/S0957-4174(97)00018-3

Wikipedia. (n.d.a). *Forums*. Retrieved June 26, 2015, from: https://en.wikipedia.org/wiki/Internet_forum

Wikipedia. (n.d.b). *Wiki*. Retrieved 26 June 2015, from: https://en.wikipedia.org/wiki/Wiki

Wikipedia. (n.d.c). *Wiki platforms*. Retrieved June 26, 2015, from: https://en.wikipedia.org/wiki/Comparison_of_wiki_software

Wikipedia. (n.d.d). Wiki Portals. Retrieved June 26, 2015 from: https://en.wikipedia.org/wiki/Portal:Contents/Portals

William, C. B. (2012). Trends and Changes in Journal of Political Marketing Titles 2002–2011. *Journal of Political Marketing*, *11*, 1–2, 4–7. doi:10.1080/15377857.2012.642702

Williams, C. B., Aylesworth, A., & Chapman, K. J. (2002). The 2000 E-Campaign for U.S. Senate. *Journal of Political Marketing*, *1*(4), 39–63. doi:10.1300/J199v01n04_03

Williams, C. B., Gulati, G. J., & Foxman, E. R. (2009). What's In an Endorsement? An Analysis of Web-Based Marketing in the 2004 Presidential Campaign. *Journal of Political Marketing*, *8*(3), 173–189. doi:10.1080/15377850903048214

Wilson, C., Boe, B., Sala, A., Puttaswamy, K. P., & Zhao, B. Y. (2009, April). User interactions in social networks and their implications. In *Proceedings of the 4th ACM European conference on Computer systems* (pp. 205-218). ACM. doi:10.1145/1519065.1519089

Wolford, R. A., & Hughes, L. K. (2001). Using the hospital Intranet to meet competency standards for nurses. *Journal for Nurses in Staff Development : JNSD : Official Journal of the National Nursing Staff Development Organization*, *17*(4), 182–189. doi:10.1097/00124645-200107000-00004 PMID:12760000

Woodman, J. (2008). *Patients beyond borders: Everybody's guide to affordable, world class medical tourism*. Chapel Hill, NC: Healthy Travel Media.

Wright, K. (2005). Personal knowledge management: Supporting individual knowledge worker performance. *Knowledge Management Research and Practice*, *3*(3), 156–165. doi:10.1057/palgrave.kmrp.8500061

Wring, D. (1997). Reconciling Marketing with Political Science: Theories of Political Marketing. *Journal of Marketing Management*, *13*(7), 651–663. doi:10.1080/0267257X.1997.9964502

Wring, D. (2005). *The Politics of Marketing the Labour Party*. Hampshire, UK: Palgrave MacMillan.

Wu, Y. (2009). Influence of social context and affect on individuals' implementation of information security safeguards. *ICIS 2009 Proceedings*, 70.

Wu, H. W., & Dahmen, N. S. (2010). Web Sponsorship and Campaign Effects: Assessing the Difference Between Positive and Negative Web Sites. *Journal of Political Marketing*, *9*(4), 314–329. doi:10.1080/15377857.2010.522454

Wulf, V., Misaki, K., Atam, M., Randall, D., & Rohde, M. (2013). On the Ground. In Investigating Social Media use during the Tunisian Revolution. Social Networks During Major Transitions (Personal and Political). Academic Press.

Wynkoop, S. (1996). *Building an Intranet with BackOffice*. Indianapolis, IN: Que Corp.

Yaghi, K., Barakat, S., Alfawaer, Z. M., Shkokani, M., & Nassuora, A. (2011). Knowledge sharing degree among the undergraduate students: A case study at applied science private university. *International Journal of Academic Research*, *3*(1), 20–24.

Yang, C., & Chen, L. C. (2007). Can Organizational Knowledge Capabilities Affect Knowledge Sharing Behavior? *Journal of Information Science*, *33*(1), 95–109. doi:10.1177/0165551506068135

Yannas, P., & Lappas, G. (2005). Web Campaign in the 2002 Greek Municipal Elections. *Journal of Political Marketing*, *4*(1), 33–50. doi:10.1300/J199v04n01_03

Yasmeen, S., Alam, M. T., Mushtaq, M., & Bukhari, M. A. (2015). Comparative study of the availability and use of information technology in the subject of education in Public and Private Universities of Islamabad and Rawalpindi. *Sage Open*. Retrieved from: http://sgo.sagepub.com/content/spsgo/5/4/2158244015608228.full.pdf

Yates, D., & Paquette, S. (2011). Emergency knowledge management and social media technologies: A case study of the 2010 Haitian earthquake. *International Journal of Information Management*, *31*(1), 6–13. doi:10.1016/j.ijinfomgt.2010.10.001

Yeoh, E., Othman, K., & Ahmad, H. (2013). Word-of-mouth and virtual marketing as potent marketing tools. *Tourism Management*, *34*, 196–201. doi:10.1016/j.tourman.2012.04.010

Yeo, M. L., & Arazy, O. (2012). What makes corporate wikis work? Wiki affordances and their suitability for corporate knowledge work. In *Design Science Research in Information Systems. Advances in Theory and Practice* (pp. 174–190). Berlin: Springer. doi:10.1007/978-3-642-29863-9_14

Yesil, S., & Dereli, S. F. (2013). An empirical investigation of organisational justice, knowledge sharing and innovation capability. *SciVerse Science Direct.*, *75*, 199–208.

Yin, R. K. (2011). *Applications of Case Study Research*. London: Sage.

Yin, R. K. (2014). *Case Study Research: Design and Methods*. London: Sage.

Yoshida, T. (2015). Cultivation of Perception and Creativity by Repeating Soft Systems Approach. *58th Annual Meeting of the ISSS-United States*, *1*(1).

Yusof, A. N. M., & Ahmad, N. (2012). Quality and effectiveness of knowledge management transfer using of Mentor-mentee Program and on Job Training in work place. In *2012 International Conference on Innovation Management and Technology Research* (pp. 50–55). IEEE. doi:10.1109/ICIMTR.2012.6236359

Yu, T. K., Lu, L. C., & Liu, T. F. (2010). Exploring factors that influence knowledge sharing behavior via weblogs. *Computers in Human Behavior*, *26*(1), 32–41. doi:10.1016/j.chb.2009.08.002

Zack, M. H. (2012, Spring). Rethinking the knowledge based organization. *MIT Sloan Management Review*.

Zander, U., & Kogut, B. (1995). Knowledge and the speed of the transfer and imitation of organizational capabilities: An empirical test. *Organization Science*, *6*(1), 76–92. doi:10.1287/orsc.6.1.76

Zarella, D. (2010). *The social media marketing book*. O'Reilly Media Inc.

Zhang, Q., & Ma, S. (2008). Corporate Blogs and Communities of Practice. In T.K. Srikantaiah & M.E.D. Koening (Eds.), Knowledge Management in Practice (pp. 303-320). Medford, NJ: Information Today Inc.

Zhang, J., Qu, Y., Cody, J., & Wu, Y. (2010). A case study of micro-blogging in the enterprise. In *Proceedings of the 28th international conference on Human factors in computing systems - CHI '10* (p. 123). New York: ACM Press. doi:10.1145/1753326.1753346

Zhao, H., & Benyoucef, M. (2013). From e-commerce to social commerce: A close look at design features. *Electronic Commerce Research and Applications*, *12*(4), 246–259. doi:10.1016/j.elerap.2012.12.003

Zhao, Y., & Zhu, Q. (2014). Evaluation on Crowdsourcing Research: Current Status and Future Direction. *Information Systems Frontiers*, *16*(3), 417–434. doi:10.1007/s10796-012-9350-4

Zincir, O. (2014). *Yöneticilerin sosyal medya kullanım amaçları: bir kuramsal çerçeve önerisi*. (Unpublished master dissertation). Istanbul University, Istanbul, Turkey.

Zorzi, M., Gluhak, A., Lange, S., & Bassi, A. (2010). From today's INTRAnet of things to a future INTERnet of things: A wireless- and mobility-related view. *IEEE Wireless Communications*, *17*(6), 44–51. doi:10.1109/MWC.2010.5675777

About the Contributors

Ritesh Chugh is a senior lecturer in CQUniversity's School of Engineering and Technology. He teaches to both undergraduate and graduate students in the fields of Information Systems (IS) Management, Process Analysis and Design, and IS Project Management. Ritesh is an enthusiastic and committed educationalist who has been awarded several academic and teaching awards to recognise his teaching excellence, commitment to improved student outcomes and engagement in reflective learning and teaching activities. His work experience in the higher education sector has predominantly been in multi-cultural educational settings, which has provided him with both a domestic and global flair. Ritesh is also an active researcher and has published articles in international refereed journals and contributed to several book chapters. He has presented and published papers in many peer reviewed international conferences too. His publications demonstrate multi-disciplinary research interests. He has also been a peer reviewer, program committee member, session chair and program committee chair for multiple international refereed conferences thus providing a wide range of service diversity to the academic community. His range of research interests lie in the area of knowledge management, tacit knowledge ubiquity, information systems management and theory, project management, electronic commerce and developing varied teaching and learning practices on a formal note and philately and numismatics on a more casual note. Ritesh is a senior member of IEEE and the Australian Computer Society. He holds a membership of IEEE Computer Society and the IEEE Green ICT Community too.

* * *

Nyarwi Ahmad is Lecturer of Department of Communication Science, Faculty of Social and Political Sciences, University of Gadjah Mada (UGM), Yogyakarta, Indonesia and PhD Candidate at Politics & Media Research Group, Faculty of Media and Communication, Bournemouth University, UK. Previously, he was qualified from the Undergraduate program (BA Hons/By Research), Department of Communication Sciences, UGM, Yogyakarta, Indonesia (May, 2005), and the Graduate Program of Master of Management of Political Communication, the University of Indonesia, Jakarta (July 2008). He was former researcher associates of the Indonesian Circle Survey Group (Lingkaran Survei Indonesia Grup/LSI Grup-Jakarta) (2006-2008) and special advisers of the Indonesian Broadcasting Commission (Komisi Penyiaran Indonesia) (2007-2008) and consultants of public campaign program of the new Higher Education Regulation (the World Bank, Jakarta and the Directorate of the Higher Education, The Ministry of Education and Culture, Republic Indonesia) (2011-2012).

Shehla Amjad is a Professor in the Department of Management Sciences at COMSATS Institute of Information Technology. She did M.A from University of Sussex, UK, an M.A degree from University of Peshawar, Ph.D from University of Bradford, UK and Post Doc from University of Bradford, UK. She has earned a gold medal in M.A, COT scholarship for PhD degree and HEC funding for Post Doc. She is an active researcher who has published more than 40 papers in renowned journals and has participated in numerous research conferences. Her research interests include micro-econometric analysis, rural finance and business ethics. Mr. Shah and Dr. Amjad have jointly published three research papers and have earned a research project on "e-learning feasibility in Pakistan" by Higher Education Commission of Pakistan.

Somprakash Bandyopadhyay is a Professor of MIS Group and Project Director of Social Informatics Research Group at Indian Institute of Management Calcutta. He is a PhD in Computer Science from Jadavpur University and B.Tech in Electronics from Indian IIT, Kharagpur, India. He has around 25 years of experience in teaching, research and software development in several organizations of international repute, including PricewaterhouseCoopers, ATRI Japan, IIT Kharagpur, IIT Bombay, German Research Centre for Artificial Intelligence, Germany and TIFR Bombay. He is also one of the Board Members at Abheda Foundations, an NGO based in Kolkata.

Shrabastee Banerjee has done her MSc from Department of Economics of University of Warwick, UK and currently associated with Social Informatics Research Group at IIM Calcutta as Research Associate. Her research interests include economics of digitization and social aspects of social media. She is due to begin her PhD in Marketing at Boston University in September 2015.

Arina Bardhan is a PhD Scholar in Sociology from Jadavpur University, Kolkata. She has completed her Masters in Sociology from University of Hyderabad. Earlier she has worked with Cancer Foundation of India, an NGO based in Kolkata in a Research Project on Tobacco Control Project, India. She is one of the Board Members at Abheda Foundation, an NGO based in Kolkata.

Anikó Csepregi is an Assistant Professor at the Department of Management, University of Pannonia, Veszprém. She obtained her Ph.D. (The Knowledge Sharing and Competences of Middle Managers) at the Doctoral School of Management Sciences and Business Administration in 2011 at University of Pannonia, Hungary. Anikó has been teaching a variety of bachelor and master courses including Management, Competence and Incentive Management, Project Management, Project Planning and Controlling, Labor Connections Controlling Personnel Processes, Professional Socialization Training. Since 2006 she has worked as a researcher: research team member of "International Mapping of Knowledge Sharing Excellence" (2006-2009: focusing on Hungary, Serbia, and Bulgaria), "Middle Managers' Knowledge Sharing and Knowledge Sharing Competences" (2009-2013: Hungary), "Project Management in the XXI. Century" (2014-present: Hungary) research. She is a full member of IAKM (International Association for Knowledge Management). She has been an editorial board member of Management & Marketing and a reviewer of Knowledge Management Research and Practice and for several international management journals. She was also a conference committee member of international conferences: European Conference on Knowledge Management in 2012, 2013, 2014, and 2015, and International Conference on Knowledge Management in 2015. Her main fields of interest are organizational culture, knowledge, competence, and project management. She has published numerous papers and has presented her research results at national and international conferences.

Srimoyee Das has a Masters in Sociology from Jadavpur University, Kolkata. She has completed her Bachelor's from Presidency College. She was a fellow at Gandhi Fellowship (2011-2013 Mumbai batch) after which she worked with Muktangan engaged in evolving quality child-centered teacher education & school programs, and Antarang Foundation for empowering youth from vulnerable socio-economic backgrounds with employability skills, in Mumbai.

Priyadarshini Dey is a PhD Scholar in Sociology from Jadavpur University, Kolkata and has completed her Mphil in Sociology from the same university. She is also a guest faculty at Surendranath Law College, Kolkata. She has an experience of teaching in Calcutta International School as a senior faculty in sociology and has been a social activist since 2009 dealing with issues on safety of women and girl children. She is one of the Board Members at Abheda Foundation, an NGO based in Kolkata.

Zoltán Gaál is a praised expert in the field of the enterprise theory and practice, he is Professor Emeritus at the Department of Management of the University of Pannonia, Veszprém, Hungary. He is member of Science and Arts Habilitation Committee of Budapest Technical University, board member of Scientific Society of Management, member of Arts Habilitation Committee of University of Miskolc, elected member of Expert Committee of Management Science, Hungarian Academy of Sciences, elected Co-President of Union of Technical and Scientific Societies of Veszprém County, chairman of Corporate Cybernetics Task Force of the Veszprém Academic Committee of the Hungarian Academy of Sciences. He has published numerous articles and presented his work at national and international conferences. His main field of interest include strategy management, corporate culture, maintenance management.

Jatinder (Jeet) N. D. Gupta is currently the Associate Dean for Graduate and Sponsored Programs, Director of Integrated Enterprise Lab, Eminent Scholar of Management of Technology, and Professor of Information Systems in the College of Business Administration, and a Professor of Industrial and Systems Engineering and Engineering Management in the College of Engineering at The University of Alabama in Huntsville, Alabama. Dr. Gupta has published extensively in international journals including Operations Research, IIE Transactions, Journal of Management Information Systems, Electronic Commerce Research, Journal of Scheduling, and Mathematics of Operations Research. He serves on the editorial boards of several leading journals and is the co-author of a textbook on Operations Research. Recipient of the outstanding teaching, faculty, service and researcher awards, he edited several books including the Handbook of Research on Enterprise Systems, Handbook of Research on Information Assurance and Security, and Intelligent Decision-making Support Systems. Dr. Gupta's current research interests include Business Analytics, Social Media, Enterprise Resources Planning (including SAP), Information Security, Supply Chain and Logistics Management, Information and Decision Technologies, Scheduling, Planning and Control, Enterprise Integration, Corporate Governance, and Social Aspects of Corporate Activities. He earned his PhD in Industrial Engineering from Texas Tech University, M Tech in Industrial Engineering and Operations Research from the Indian Institute of Technology, Kharagpur, India and a B. E. in Mechanical Engineering from Delhi University, Delhi, India. Dr. Gupta has provided professional consulting services to various industrial and governmental organizations to enhance their productivity and competitive position. He has also provided consulting services to several private firms and government agencies including AMCOM. He held elected and appointed positions in several professional societies at the international, national and local levels including serving as President of the Production and Operations Management Society (POMS) and Vice-President of the Decision Sciences Institute (DSI).

Varun Jain is working at Star India which is India's largest and most influential entertainment company with weekly reach of more than 650 million viewers. He is a member of planning team for entertainment business of Star India Pvt Ltd. He holds a Bachelor in Commerce degree from Shri Ram College of Commerce (University of Delhi) and MBA from IIM Calcutta. Varun has a very rich and diverse corporate experience. He has performed propriety trading for Jaypee Capital, post that he worked for several enterprises deploying new technology solutions for corporates before he co-founded technology startup Media is you aimed at developing high tech media and communication tools for corporates and education firms.

Ashish Kumar Jha is a doctoral candidate at IIM Calcutta with specialization in Management Information Systems (MIS). He holds a Bachelor of technology in Electronics and Communication Engineering. His research interests are technology management, IT innovation management, IT strategy of firms and IT services strategy. He has presented papers at several conferences like Australasian Conference on Information Systems (ACIS), Asia Pacific System Dynamics Conference, and International Marketing Conference among others. He has also filed multiple patents in Indian, EU and US geographies on tools to manage IT services. Ashish has also reviewed for various journals and conferences like Information and Management, International Journal of Production Economics, Australasian Conference on Information Systems, European Conference on Information Systems, Academy of Management Annual Meeting 2015, InSITE 2015 among others.

Meena Jha has over 20 years of experience in teaching and research in software engineering. She is a faculty member at Central Queensland University, Sydney, Australia. Her research interests are Big Data, Enterprise Architecture, Legacy Modernisation, Enterprise Systems, and Software architecture to name a few. She holds a B Tech and M Tech from Birla Institute of Technology, Mesra, Ranchi, India and holds PhD from the University of New South Wales, Sydney, Australia. She is a member of the IEEE, and the IEEE Computer Society Australia.

Sanjay Jha has over 25 years of experience in systems engineering, systems information in mining industries, computer networking & security and computer aided design and manufacturing. He teaches at Central Queensland University, Sydney, Australia. His research interests are Big Data, Enterprise Architecture, Data Security, and Enterprise Systems to name a few. He holds a B Tech and MBA degree from Birla Institute of Technology, Mesra, Ranchi, India. He is a member of the IEEE, the IEEE Computer Society and Australian Computer Society (ACS) Australia.

Mahesh Joshi is a senior lecturer in Accounting at RMIT University, Australia. His research interests include Intellectual Capital, Knowledge management, IFRS and Accounting Regulation. Mahesh has published more than 30 refereed journal articles and has presented papers in various international conferences.

Kalyan Mandal is professor of Sociology, Public Policy and Management Group, Indian Institute of Management Calcutta. He is a PhD in Sociology from IIT Bombay. Before joining IIM Calcutta he was member of faculty, Tata Institute of Social Sciences, Mumbai and Gokhale Institute of Politics and Economics, Pune. During 2013 -14 he was Visiting Indian Council of Cultural Relations Chair Professor at Centre for Contemporary India Studies, Lund University, Sweden. He is President, SANCHAR (a voluntary organization working with poor people with disabilities and their families to improve their social and economic condition); Member, Governing Body of Child in Need Institute (CINI - a voluntary organization working to strengthen the capacity of deprived children and women to improve their health, nutrition, education and protection conditions); Founder Member of SAKAR (a voluntary organization working for the rehabilitation of mentally retarded persons).

Anita Medhekar has been teaching economics at under-graduate and post-graduate level for many years. She is a Senior Lecturer in Economics at the School of Business and Law, Central Queensland University, Rockhampton, Australia. Her teaching and research interests are in applied microeconomics and macroeconomics, business economics, developing countries' economies, Asia-Pacific economics, international trade and development, economics of e-commerce, medical tourism, banking and monetary systems, poverty and rural development, health economics, tourism economics, gender and development, public finance and public policy. She has to her credit publications as book chapters, journal articles and research papers presented at international conferences.

Munusamy Natarajan has a Ph. D. in Library & Information Science, MBA (HR) from Sikkim Manipal University. Dr M Natarajan, (Retired) as Senior Principal Scientist of National Institute of Science Communication And Information Resources (CSIR–NISCAIR(Ex-INSDOC)), New Delhi and worked in various divisions since his joining (Sep 1981) like: Document copy supply, Online Information Retrieval, CHEM/SDI service, Networking of CSIR Laboratories (SIRNET), MALIBNET, NUCCSI, Library automation, conducted various training programmes (since 1990) including UGC Refresher course for LIS professionals, HRD activity, given lectures, National Science Digital Library project and in Indian Science Abstracts. He was also Scientist-in-charge (Regional Director) of INSDOC Chennai (3 years) and INSDOC Bangalore (6 months) and managed the centres more efficiently with innovative ideas. He worked as a Faculty (Professor level) for the Associateship course in Information Science (AIS), a two year Masters degree course and Head of the Education & Training Division. He was a Full time Faculty since 2003 onwards upto 2012 and finally retired (on 30th June 2014) as Editor of Journal of Scientific and Industrial Research (JSIR), an internationally recognized Journal with impact factor. He is also a Research Guide (Six students currently) in the field of Library & Information Science for Five Universities in India viz. Nagpur University, Bharathiyar University, Coimbatore, Shri Jagdishprasad Jhabarmal Tiberwala University. Jhunjhunu, AMET University, Chennai and Singhania University, Pacheri Bari. He has published more than 180 papers in National and International Journals, conferences, seminars and conducted Tutorials and delivered keynote address, chairman of many technical sessions, and even worked as Rapporteur also, etc. He has visited many countries like Turkey, Nepal, UAE, Qatar, Ethiopia and South Africa. He has Edited Three Books (Conference volumes of i-KOAL series) and published recently ONE Book on "Knowledge Management: Challenges and Applications". He has guided more than 75 projects for Associateship in Information Science, MLIS, MPhil and PGDLAN courses. He was also Co-ordinator for the IGNOU (0722) Study centre for two years and continuing as Counsellor for IGNOU courses like MCA, BLIS, MLIS and PGDLAN. He is also in Editorial Board Member of Nine journals in India and outside and Reviewer for ELEVEN journals at National and International level. He is a Life Member of many professional organizations like AIS, IASLIC, ILA, MALA, RRC, SALIS, SIS & PRESIDENT of LIBRARY PROFESSIONALS ASSOCIATION (LPA), New Delhi.

Liam O'Brien has over 25 years' experience in research and development in software engineering. He is a Solution Architect at Geoscience Australia and prior to this he was Chief Software Architect at CSIRO and before that he was a Principal Researcher at NICTA's e-Government Initiative researching in SOAs, service migration, service integration, scoping of SOA and cost and effort estimation. He holds a BSc and PhD from the University of Limerick, Ireland. He is a member of the IEEE, the IEEE Computer Society and the Service Science Society Australia.

Nóra Obermayer is an Assistant Professor at the Department of Management, University of Pannonia, Veszprém. She obtained her Ph.D. (Conscious knowledge management in knowledge economy) in Economics and Management in 2008. She won the Best Young Researcher and Scientist Paper Award and received most prestigious Winner of Elsevier Scopus Young Researcher Awards in Engineering category. Nóra has been teaching a variety of management master courses including Strategic Human Resource Management, Globalization and Organizational Culture and Competence Management. She has gained international teaching experience as a participant in the Erasmus Teacher's Mobility Program. In 2013 she was a visiting lecturer at Fontys University of Applied Sciences in Eindhoven (The Netherlands) and had seminar focused on strategic human resource management and leadership. This year she is going to give lectures at the University of Lapland, Faculty of Social Science in Rovaniemi (Finland) in the field of Knowledge Management. Since 2004 she has worked as a researcher; as co-leader at "Knowledge Management in Hungary 2005/2006", „Organizational Knowledge Sharing in Hungary, 2013/2014", Knowledge sharing and emotional intelligence 2014/2015" national research and as recipient at international „Global Knowledge Survey 2012/2013" research. She is member of Hungarian Academy of Sciences (MTA), Section of Economics and Law (Committee on Economics – Knowledge Management) and the Program Committee of the European Conference on Knowledge Management. She has published numerous papers and presented at national and international conferences.

James Okolie-Osemene is a Lecturer in the Department of International Relations, Wellspring University Benin City, Nigeria, and a Research Fellow, IFRA-Nigeria. He holds Master of Arts degree in Peace and Conflict Studies from University of Ibadan and Bachelor of Arts degree in History and International Studies from Imo State University, Owerri. He is presently undertaking doctoral studies with focus on human rights violations. He is widely published in local and international peer reviewed scholarly journals and contributed chapters to several books. He is Associate Member of the Society for Peace Studies and Practice. His areas of research interest include international relations, peace education, human rights, violence research and post-conflict peacebuilding and development studies.

Adi Palmor is a systems analyst and IT projects manager at Rafael Advanced Systems. He specializes in IT solutions to organizational knowledge management issues.

Terri Toles Patkin is Professor of Communication at Eastern Connecticut State University, where she teaches courses in Interpersonal and Organizational Communication, Communication Law, and Persuasion. Her publications explore topics ranging from ancient cave art to internet memes. She holds the B.A. from Arcadia University and M.A. and Ph.D. from Cornell University.

Ravi Patnayakuni is an Associate Professor of Information Systems at the College of Business Administration at the University of Alabama in Huntsville. Prior to his current position, he has worked at

Temple University, Philadelphia and The University of Melbourne, Melbourne, Australia. His research focuses on how organizations adopt, implement and leverage information technology. Some of his more recent work focuses on supply chains and inter-organizational systems. His research has been published in MIS Quarterly, Journal of Management Information Systems, IEEE Transactions in Engineering and Management, Communications of the ACM among other Journals.

Gilad Ravid is a senior faculty member in Information Systems at the Department of Industrial Engineering and Management, Ben-Gurion University of the Negev, Israel. His Ph.D. work, with a thesis on "Information Sharing with CMC in Small Groups: Communication Groups and Tasks," is from Haifa University; his M.B.A. degree is from the Hebrew University; and his B.Sc. degree is in agricultural engineering is from the Technion. He was a postdoctoral fellow at the Annenberg Center for Communication, University of Southern California, Los Angeles. Dr. Ravid's main interests are focused on the relationship between social structure and human behavior, games and gamification, and computer-mediated communication systems. His work includes such research as information overload phenomena, social structure in web-based educational forums, wiki-based education and Wikipedia* as a social space, celebrity formation, the "social structure" of lightning synchronization, civil information needs and information sharing in groups, learning with games, and gamification solutions. He has published in top peer-reviewed journals including Information Systems Research, First Monday, and Information Systems Journal.

Syed Azfal Moshadi Shah is serving as an Assistant Professor in the Department of Management Sciences at COMSATS Institute of Information Technology, Pakistan since 2008. He also enjoys a diversified corporate sector work experience including Financial sector, Manufacturing sector and Non-governmental sector. He did M.Sc. in Management & HR from Birmingham City University, United Kingdom and an MBA from Quaid-e-Azam University, Islamabad, Pakistan. His PhD research area is "Consumer ethics and decision making". His major publications are in the field of social media, knowledge management, e-learning, performance measurement and cultural diversity in Pakistan.

Lajos Szabó was educated at the University of Pannonia (Master in Engineering Management) and ENI Scuola Superiore Enrico Mattei, Italy (Master in Energy and Environmental Economics). He received his Ph.D. in Engineering Management in 1997. He is a founder member of the Hungarian Project Management Association. He has published numerous articles and presented his work at national and international conferences. His main field of interest includes strategic, project and knowledge management. He has been the co-leader of the "Strategy research group" for 23 years. His research group has successful cooperation with research groups in Germany, Denmark, Netherland, USA and Romania. He was the Program Chair of the KMO 2010 (Knowledge Management in Organisation) Conference in Veszprém. He was guest researcher at the Technical University of Darmstadt, Germany from 1999 to 2000 and at Nazareth College, Rochester, USA in 2006. He was the Vice Dean (2007-2012) and the Dean (2012-2015) of the Faculty of Business and Economics.

Ariel Tikotsky is ClickSoftware's KM manager, and a Ph.D. candidate at the Bar-Ilan University in Israel. He held various positions in software development and KM in both start-up companies and global enterprises. Mr. Tikotsky's main KM foci are Enterprise 2.0 and embedded knowledge. He holds a B.Sc. in industrial engineering and an M.A (cum laude) in security studies, both from the Tel-Aviv University.

Mark Underwood is the President and CEO of Krypton Brothers LLC, a consultancy specializing in Big Data security, digital forensics, schema.org, rapid intranet exploitation, software quality and domain-specific frameworks. He is an advocate for patient-managed health information, including access to automated decision support systems like IBM Watson and to complex event processing resources. Founder or co-founder of five technology startups, he co-designed one of the earliest ambulatory care health information systems (IATROS). Underwood has served as lead engineer or principal investigator on artificial intelligence projects for DARPA and for Army and Air Force research laboratories. Most recently, he is working with standards organizations to foster information assurance and provenance transparency. Underwood is co-chair of the NIST Big Data Public Working Group's security and privacy subgroup, and co-chair of the 2015 Ontology Summit focused on the Internet of Things. In 2014, he served on the workshop committee for the IEEE Big Data Conference and moderated several panels. He is an ASQ Certified Software Quality Engineer and holds a US secret clearance.

Oya Zincir is full-time faculty as research and teaching assistant of Managament and Organization at the Business Administration Department of the Faculty of Political Sciences at Istanbul University, Turkey. She is studying on her PhD dissertation. Her major research interests and ongoing studies are about knowledge management, social media, open innovation and strategic management.

Index

I

K

L

M

N

O

P

R

S

T

U

V

W

Y

www.ingramcontent.com/pod-product-compliance
Ingram Content Group UK Ltd.
Pitfield, Milton Keynes, MK11 3LW, UK
UKHW050952290926
15470UKWH00005B/1773

9 781522 504955